THE HISTORY OF THE SOMERSET
LIGHT INFANTRY
(PRINCE ALBERT'S)
1914–1919

MILITARY HISTORIES BY THE SAME AUTHOR

THE HISTORY OF THE
SECOND DIVISION, 1914–1918
(2 Vols.).

THE WEST YORKSHIRE REGT.
IN THE WAR, 1914–1918.
(2 Vols.).

THE HISTORY OF THE 62ND
(W.R.) DIVISION, 1914–1919
(2 Vols.).

THE DIE-HARDS IN THE GREAT
WAR, 1914–1919
(2 Vols.).

THE EAST YORKSHIRE REGT.
IN THE GREAT WAR, 1914–1918
(1 Vol.—shortly).

THE KING'S REGT. (LIVERPOOL)
IN THE WAR, 1914–1919
(3 Vols.—shortly)

ETC. ETC.

H.R.H. THE DUKE OF YORK, K.G., K.T., G.C.M.G., G.C.V.O.
Colonel-in-Chief

THE HISTORY OF THE
SOMERSET LIGHT INFANTRY
(PRINCE ALBERT'S)
1914–1919

BY
EVERARD WYRALL

WITH A FOREWORD BY
H.R.H. THE DUKE OF YORK, K.G.

**WITH TWENTY-NINE PORTRAITS, SEVEN OTHER
ILLUSTRATIONS AND TWENTY-ONE MAPS**

METHUEN & CO. LTD.
36 ESSEX STREET W.C.
LONDON

First Published in 1927

FOREWORD

IT gives me much pleasure as Colonel-in-Chief of the Somerset Light Infantry (Prince Albert's), which, through its name, recalls its association with my great-grandfather the Prince Consort, to write a foreword to this volume of the History of the Regiment.

The object of such a book is not only to describe faithfully the part which the various battalions took in those momentous campaigns, including the marches and battles, the hardships and sufferings, but also to serve as a Memorial to those who fought and died for their country.

It seems to me that the esprit de corps of a Regiment rests mainly on its history. It is not unfair to say that official war histories are frequently as dry as dust to all but the professional student of War, and popular war histories are too often inaccurate. A Regimental History, however, should endeavour to avoid both these pitfalls, and should set forth in careful detail the collective and individual deeds of heroism that the Regiment has achieved. In my opinion the author, Mr. Everard Wyrall, has been eminently successful in this respect and his story will be an inspiration to all ranks of the Regiment present and to come.

A list of those who have won the Victoria Cross has always been kept, and the act of valour for which the cross was awarded is recorded. Many gallant acts, however, performed in the Great War have never been described in print, and I am glad to see that it has been found possible to mention some in this volume.

I consider that the most noticeable proof of regimental esprit de corps brought to light in the recent war is that, notwithstanding the fact that units were reduplicated over and over again, they all inherited, and fully acted up to, the traditions of the Regiment of which they formed part, a fact of which we all may feel proud.

Albert

THE SOMERSET LIGHT INFANTRY (PRINCE ALBERT'S). [13]

The Sphinx, superscribed " Egypt."   A Mural Crown, superscribed
" Jellalabad."

**" Gibraltar 1704–5," " Dettingen," " Martinique, 1809," " Ava,"
" Ghuznee, 1839," " Afghanistan, 1839," " Cabool, 1842," " Sevastopol,"
" South Africa, 1878–9," " Burma, 1885–87," " Relief of Ladysmith,"
" South Africa, 1899–1902," " Afghanistan, 1919."**

The Great War—16 *Battalions.*—" Le Cateau," " Retreat from Mons,"
" Marne, 1914, '18," " Aisne, 1914," " Armentières, 1914," **" Ypres, 1915,
'17, '18,"** " St. Julien," " Frezenberg," " Bellewaarde," " Hooge, 1915,"
" Loos," " Mount Sorrel," **" Somme, 1916, '18," " Albert, 1916, '18,"**
" Delville Wood," " Guillemont," " Flers-Courcelette," " Morval," " Le
Transloy," " Ancre, 1916, '18," **" Arras, 1917, '18,"** " Vimy, 1917," " Scarpe,
1917, '18," " Arleux," " Langemarck, 1917," " Menin Road," " Polygon
Wood," " Broodseinde," " Poelcappelle," " Passchendaele," **" Cambrai,
1917, '18,"** " St. Quentin," " Bapaume, 1918," " Rosières," " Avre," " Lys,"
" Hazebrouck," " Béthune," " Soissonnais-Ourcq," " Drocourt-Quéant,"
" Hindenburg Line," " Havrincourt," " Épéhy," " Canal du Nord,"
" Courtrai," " Selle," " Valenciennes," " Sambre," " France and Flanders,
1914–18." " Gaza," " El Mughar," " Nebi Samwil," " Jerusalem,"
" Megiddo," " Sharon," **" Palestine, 1917–18." " Tigris, 1916,"** " Sharqat,"
" Mesopotamia, 1916–18." " N.W. Frontier India, 1915."

AUTHOR'S PREFACE

THE Story of the Somerset Light Infantry in the Great War, as contained in the following pages, needs no further comment from me. Neither do I propose to lecture the reader on the subject of military history, as some historians in their prefaces seem to think necessary. This preface, therefore, is merely in the way of acknowledgment to those officers who have so ably assisted me by reading the manuscript before it was printed, and suggesting certain alterations based on a fuller knowledge of the operations since the War ended. I should like to point out, however, that where the official diaries and documents differed from the narratives in private diaries and comments made by those who were present during the actions described, the former, after due thought and consideration, have been accepted as the final verdict. Time plays tricks with the memory of man, and I have so often found that narratives written after the War have differed materially from the facts as recorded not only in Battalion, but also in Brigade and Divisional Headquarters Diaries. Personal narratives are invaluable, especially when written at the time: they give the necessary "atmosphere," but they cannot be regarded as the final verdict on matters of tactics and strategy, and they very often err in a correct appreciation of the situation.

H.R.H. The Duke of York, Colonel-in-Chief of the Somerset Light Infantry (Prince Albert's), has honoured this History by writing a Foreword, for which I am deeply grateful. The Regiment also has to thank its Colonel, Lieut.-General Sir Thomas D'O. Snow, K.C.B., K.C.M.G., for the interest he has taken in the initiation and preparation of this History, and Major-General Sir H. J. Everett, K.C.M.G., C.B., upon whom the task fell of not only reading the typescript, but of circulating it to all those officers of the various battalions who so willingly undertook to read it, and for the infinite trouble to which he has been in collecting additional narratives, maps and documents concerning the War, without which this History must have suffered. My best thanks are due to all these officers, also to the Committee, viz.: Brig.-Gen. H. C. Frith, C.B., Col. C. J. Troyte-Bullock, D.S.O., Lt.-Col. W. H. Maud, C.M.G., Major F. M. E. Kennedy, C.B., and the officers commanding the Home Battalion and Depôt.

I should like once more to acknowledge the kindly assistance and very real help afforded me at all times by Brigadier-General J. E. Edmonds, C.B., C.M.G., Director of the Historical Section (Military Branch) of the Committee of Imperial Defence and his Staff.

Finally, I venture to hope, for two reasons, that this History will be widely reviewed: first, because Somerset men are spread far and wide over the earth and will like to know that the story of their Regiment in the Great War has appeared: secondly, because of those who made the great sacrifice and gave their lives for England.   For the memories of those gallant souls, whom we all knew, there are no shrouds.   They have left us to fight the Shadows: *they* have gained the Realities.

Authors' Club
      S.W.1

EVERARD WYRALL

CONTENTS

LIST OF ILLUSTRATIONS

Photographers' names are given in italic

LIST OF MAPS

From drawings by John S. Fenton.

THE HISTORY OF THE SOMERSET
LIGHT INFANTRY
(PRINCE ALBERT'S)
1914–1919

LT.-GEN. SIR T. D'O. SNOW, K.C.B., K.C.M.G.
Colonel of the Regiment

THE HISTORY OF THE SOMERSET LIGHT INFANTRY

CHAPTER I

MOBILIZATION OF THE REGIMENT

IN 1914, when war was declared between the Nations of the Entente [1] and the Central Powers [2] and a state of war existed between Great Britain and Germany "as from 11 p.m. on the 4th August" the Somerset Light Infantry (Prince Albert's) numbered only five battalions. Two of these—the 1st and 2nd—were regular, one—the 3rd—formed the reserve, the remaining two—the 4th and 5th—were Territorial troops. The 1st Battalion (Lieut.-Colonel E. H. Swayne, commanding) was quartered at Colchester, where it formed part of the 11th Infantry Brigade (Brig.-General A. Hunter-Weston) of the 4th Division (Major-General T. D'O. Snow, commanding). The 2nd Battalion [3] (Lieut.-Colonel E. H. R. C. R. Platt, commanding) was in India, at Quetta. The 3rd Battalion (Lieut.-Colonel A. Llewellyn, commanding) and the depot troops were at Taunton (Major C. G. Rawling, commanding depot), soon to become a very busy centre. Of the two Territorial battalions, the 4th (Lieut.-Colonel W. C. Cox, commanding) had its headquarters at Bath, the 5th Battalion (Lieut-Colonel E. F. Cooke-Hurle, commanding) at Taunton. Both Territorial battalions formed part of the South-Western Infantry Brigade of the Wessex Division.

Not only the Regular but the Territorial battalions had seen war service, the battle honours of the former extending back over two centuries, whilst the Territorials had fought in the South African War of 1900–1901. Sturdy troops were these West Countrymen, who could be counted upon to give (as they did most gallantly give) a good account of themselves when face to face with the enemy.

The sequence of events after the German aggressions in Poland and France and the presentation of the ultimatum to Belgium was, as far as Great Britain was concerned, as follows :—All Territorial Troops were ordered to report to their H.Qs. and the Naval Reserves were called out on the 3rd August. At 4 p.m. on the 4th orders to mobilize were issued to the Army—Regular, Reserve, and Territorial troops.

On the 5th and 6th August the War Cabinet met to discuss the conduct

1914
4th August

1st, 2nd, 3rd, 4th
and 5th Battalions

5th August

[1] Great Britain, France, and Russia.
[2] The German and Austrian Empires.
[3] The 2nd Battalion was unfortunately one of the eight regular British battalions stationed in India throughout the whole course of the Great War, 1914–1918.

6th August

of the War.   Lord Kitchener became Secretary of State for War on the 6th. The main military question to be settled was the employment of the Expeditionary Force which consisted of six divisions of all arms and one cavalry division.[1]   Ultimately it was decided that this Force, less the 4th and 6th Divisions, should embark for the Continent.   The chances of a German landing on the East Coast of Britain had to be considered, and in order to meet this possibility the 18th Infantry Brigade of the 6th Division (then at Lichfield) was moved to Edinburgh and two brigades (10th and 12th) of the 4th Division to Cromer and York; the 11th Infantry Brigade was already at Colchester.

The destination of the Expeditionary Force was decided by the French, who reserved for it a place "on the left of the line of the French Armies, which it would thus prolong."[2]   Ultimately the B.E.F. concentrated between Maubeuge and Le Cateau.

It would have been difficult to select a period throughout the year when the British Army was more fit for military operations than the month of August 1914.   The strenuous days of the annual training were hardly over, the men were fit and in splendid fettle after weeks spent in the open under the summer sun.   The Army was never in better health, never more completely equipped (so far as the circumstances of that period demanded) and at no time in all its long and glorious career, more ready for war.

4th and 5th Battalions

More fortunate than the majority of Territorial battalions (for whom mobilization had fallen at an awkward moment—the 3rd August being a Bank Holiday), the 4th and 5th Somerset Light Infantry were already under canvas at Bulford when war was declared.

The first triumph for the British Government was the swift, but secret, embarkation at Southampton and disembarkation in France of the British Expeditionary Force.   It was with amazement that the British public learnt a few days later that the Force had left England and had landed on French soil, without loss or hindrance.   It was a remarkable feat.

1st Battalion

8th August

The 1st Bn. Somerset Light Infantry at 5 p.m. on 4th August had received orders to mobilize, the 5th being the first day of mobilization.   Reservists began to arrive with creditable punctuality, and by the 8th (at 6 p.m.) the Battalion stood ready mobilized for war, awaiting orders to move.   As already stated, the British Government had decided to despatch only four divisions (1st, 2nd, 3rd and 5th) with the Cavalry Division as a first Expeditionary Force.   Meanwhile the 4th Division had been ordered to concentrate, and in accordance with these instructions the 1st Somerset Light Infantry (with the 11th Infantry Brigade) left Colchester on 17th August for Harrow, where the division had already begun to collect.   The Battalion encamped on the playing fields of Harrow School.   The 10th and 12th Infantry Brigades also arrived from Cromer and York.   From the 18th to 20th inclusive the course of field training and route marching begun at Colchester was continued. On the 21st the 4th Division left Harrow for Southampton, the 1st Bn. Somerset

---

[1] 1st, 2nd, 3rd, 4th, 5th and 6th Divisions; the Cavalry Division.
[2] Marshal Joffre.

Light Infantry entraining at 7 p.m. and arriving at the port of embarkation at 1 a.m.   At 8.30 a.m., 22nd, the Battalion sailed from Southampton, reaching Havre at 7 p.m.   But the tide was unsuitable for disembarkation and it was midnight before the troops set foot on shore.   The extraordinary difference between the French and the British peoples at once became apparent.   Outwardly at least, Britain was calm and collected, but France was brimming over with excitement which her people took no pains to conceal.

As the troops stepped ashore at Havre, the crowds collected in the docks sent up cheer after cheer, whilst bloodthirsty shouts, such as "A bas Guillaume" and "Coupez la gorge," greeted the British soldier as he once more trod the historic soil of France, this time as an Ally and not as an enemy.   At about 2 a.m. on the 23rd, the 1st Somerset Light Infantry marched to the rest camp 6 miles from Havre : a painful march, uphill, in great heat.

"We had quite a triumphant procession," said an officer of the Battalion, "the inhabitants cheering and giving us flowers in exchange for the men's badges."   A breach of discipline which could not be countenanced.

Rest and numerous camp duties occupied the men during the day, but at 8 p.m., the Battalion entrained for an "unknown destination," the 4th Division having been ordered to join the B.E.F. already in the front line of battle. The Battle of Mons (23rd August) was being fought, whilst the 4th Division was completing disembarkation and moving up from Havre.

On the 24th August the 4th Division detrained at Le Cateau.   The journey from Havre had been none too comfortable, for the troops were packed in cattle trucks, and travelling all day in a scorching sun under such conditions would have damped the ardour of anyone but the British soldier.

The 1st Somersets detrained at 5 p.m.:

"We hoped to go into billets but were quickly disillusioned and ordered to march about 7 miles to the village of Briastre. . . .   Information is that we are now on the extreme left of British troops, with a German corps threatening our flank: none the less sleep well!' [1]

[1] Diary of the late Lt.-Col. W. Watson, 1st Somerset Light Infantry, killed whilst commanding the 2/5th King's Own Yorkshire Light Infantry 3.5.17.

CHAPTER II

LE CATEAU

THE first official despatch received by the War Office from Sir John French stated that

"The 4th Division commenced its detrainment at Le Cateau on Sunday the 23rd, and, by the morning of the 25th, eleven battalions and a brigade of artillery with Divisional Staff were available for service. I [Sir John] ordered General Snow to take up a position with his right south of Solesmes, his left resting on the Cambrai–Le Cateau road, south of La Chapelle."

1st Battalion
25th August

The 11th Infantry Brigade (with the 1st Somerset L.I.) billeted in Briastre and neighbourhood on the night of the 24th/25th August. "A" Company of the Battalion furnished two piquets, one on the road to Viesly and the other on the Solesmes road.

Very early in the morning of the 25th the 11th Infantry Brigade moved forward to the high ground south-east of Solesmes: the 10th Infantry Brigade taking up a position on the left of the 11th Infantry Brigade, near the farm of Fontaine-au-Tertre: the 12th Infantry Brigade remained at Viesly in reserve. The 4th Division was disposed in this manner in order to cover the retirement of the II Corps and the 19th Infantry Brigade from the Bavai–Bry–Jenlain line, to which Sir H. Smith-Dorrien had fallen back from Mons. The I Corps, on the right of the II Corps, occupied a line from Bavai eastwards to the outskirts of Maubeuge.[1]

The retention of Solesmes until the II Corps, the 19th Infantry Brigade and Cavalry had passed through was absolutely essential, for the town was the apex of roads running from the north-west, north and north-east, southwards, down which the troops of the II Corps, 19th Infantry Brigade and the Cavalry must pass in order to reach the new line which had been fixed approximately from (and including) Le Cateau, westwards along the Le Cateau–Cambrai road to Caudry: the I Corps was marching southwards, east of the Foret de Mormal and had been ordered to occupy the line Avesnes–Landrecies.

These moves had already begun when the 4th Division took up its position S. and S.W. of Solesmes, i.e. on the heights overlooking the village.

After the 1st Somerset L.I. had been disposed astride the Solesmes–Briastre road, two officers of the Battalion went forward to reconnoitre the former town. They found the streets barricaded and the civilians hastily collecting their household goods in small bundles, in perambulators, hand-

[1] The official story of the Battle of Mons, 23rd August 1914, and the beginning of the retreat from Mons, is now available.

carts, civilian carts and in every kind of vehicle up to six-horse farm wagons. 1st Battalion
25th August The roads southwards were already crowded with Belgians and French, anxiety and terror written large across their pale faces. "Les Allemands, les Allemands" was all many of them could utter.

North of Solesmes smoke and flame shot up from farms and villages and the dull boom of the guns, ever drawing nearer, warned the waiting 4th Division that it could not be long ere action was joined with the enemy.

About noon Solesmes became terribly congested. Masses of British transport and motors were jammed in the closely packed streets, confusion reigned and troops marching southwards were everywhere delayed. During the afternoon masses of cavalry could be seen manœuvring in the distance, the blue sky being plentifully dotted with little white balls—bursting shrapnel! The boom of the guns became ever more rapid and clear, and towards dusk a cavalry brigade with drawn swords passed through the 11th Infantry Brigade going southwards; they had had a hard day's work covering the retirement of the sorely pressed II Corps and 19th Infantry Brigade. The 5th Division of the II Corps had retired along the straight road from Bavai to Le Cateau; the 3rd Division through Bermeries, Le Quesnoy and Solesmes, the 19th Infantry Brigade,[1] west of Audregnies through Jenlain and Haussy and west of Solesmes to Le Cateau. A rearguard action just north of Solesmes between the 7th Infantry Brigade and the enemy did not seriously involve the 1st Somerset L.I., though C and D Companies of the Battalion opened sharp fire on a German cavalry patrol which had approached within a few hundred yards of the British position.

As dusk deepened to darkness, the horizon was red from the glare of burning villages, but the 4th Division stood fast immediately south of Solesmes whilst masses of transport and troops sorted themselves out as they retired southwards towards Caudry and Le Cateau.

During the early evening 4th Divisional Headquarters issued warning orders to its three infantry brigades to withdraw during the night to positions selected for them on the left of the 3rd Division—the 11th and 12th Brigades to hold the line Fontaine-au-Pire–Wambaix (respectively), the 10th Brigade to be in reserve at Haucourt.

The 12th Infantry Brigade moved off soon after 9 p.m. An hour later the 11th Infantry Brigade followed, the 1st Somerset L.I. marching in two parties; half Battalion Headquarters and C and D Companies accompanying the remainder of the 11th Infantry Brigade, whilst the remainder of Bn. H.Qs. with A and B Companies formed the rearguard under Colonel Swayne. The route followed was Viesly–Bethencourt–Beauvois–Fontaine-au-Pire. Rain was falling when the march began. Small detachments of troops who had fought at Mons, terribly worn and fatigued, were passed on the road and from these men something of what happened on 23rd August first became known to the Somerset L.I. and their comrades of the 11th Brigade.

About 2.30 a.m. (26th August) the rearguard of the 1st Somerset L.I., 26th August

[1] The Brigade during the day had been attached to the Cavalry Division.

under Colonel Swayne, reached Fontaine-au-Pire and found C and D Companies with the remainder of the 11th Brigade in the village.

The rearguard, under Colonel Swayne, was directed to prepare a position from which to cover the further retirement. After a reconnaissance the Colonel decided to take up a position about 800 yards N.W. of the village of Ligny, and marched the two companies off. But C and D Companies still remained with the Brigade, which for the time being had halted in Fontaine for a short rest. The 1st Rifle Brigade furnished the outposts which were placed at the northern end of Beauvois,[1] in a position to ward off attacks from the north and north-west, whilst C and D Companies of the 1st Somersets were posted in the southern end of the same village to hold off the enemy if he advanced from the north-east; also to ensure the safe passage of all wheeled transport to the east, and then southwards, the rain having made impassable the direct roads south from the halting place.

The two forward companies of the 1st Somersets had with them the machine-gun section and were commanded by Major Compton (2nd in Command of the Battalion). C Company was commanded by Major Thoyts, and D by Captain Yatman.

At 4.14 a.m., just as the 11th Brigade was about to move off from Fontaine in order to take up its allotted position on the left of the II Corps, rifle, machine-gun and shell fire were opened on the outposts west of the village of Beauvois, i.e. on the 1st Rifle Brigade. The two companies of Somersets, at the southern end of Beauvois, also came under shell fire, though up to this point they do not appear to have suffered any casualties.

Eventually the 1st Hants and the 1st East Lancashire of the 11th Brigade were safely withdrawn to the ridge (of which Carrieres[2] is the centre) about half a mile south-west of Fontaine. The 1st Hants then opened rifle and machine-gun fire on the enemy, under cover of which the Rifles and Somersets also moved off and retired to the ridge and Quarries south-west of Fontaine: all transport having previously been sent back.

At 5 a.m. on the morning of the 26th August (a day, let it be said, of great historical significance for the whole B.E.F.) the 1st Somerset Light Infantry was disposed in the following positions:—[3] C Company and half Bn. H.Qs. (Major Thoyts) holding the northern edge of the Quarries; D Company (less two platoons) under Captain Yatman, and the machine-gun section, holding the eastern edge of the Quarries; two platoons of D Company holding the road between Fontaine and the Quarries; A and B Companies (under Captain Jones-Mortimer and Major Prowse, respectively) and Col. Swayne with half Battalion Headquarters N.W. of Ligny village. At this hour the three other battalions of the 11th Infantry Brigade appear to have reached

---

[1] Beauvois and Fontaine-au-Pire might almost be described as one village; the former being much the larger place.

[2] The Quarries.

[3] The dispositions are taken from the Battalion Narrative of Operations of the 26th August, i.e. The Battle of Le Cateau (called in the Narrative "The Battle of Ligny").

the following positions—1st Rifle Brigade, on the right of the 1st Somerset Light Infantry; 1st Hants Regiment on the left (and astride the railway line), the 1st East Lancashire Regiment in reserve, in rear of the Brigade. The 12th Infantry Brigade on the left of the 11th Brigade was disposed from Longsart to Esnes facing north-west and west. The 10th Infantry Brigade had reached Haucourt about 4.30 a.m., wet, hungry and tired, where the men threw themselves down and slept, hoping that as reserve brigade of the 4th Division they might be allowed a little rest, not being in the front line. Away on the right of the 4th Division and immediately south of the Le Cateau–Cambrai road, the 3rd and 5th Divisions (in the order given) continued the British line eastwards to Le Cateau: the 19th Infantry Brigade was in reserve near Reumont. Of the I Corps, the 1st Division had passed an uncomfortable night in Dommierre–Marbaix and Le Grand Fayt, while the 2nd Division billeted in Noyelles, Maroilles and Landrecies, was not more fortunate, both the 6th Infantry Brigade and 4th (Guards) Brigade having been engaged with strong parties of the enemy who had crossed the Foret de Mormal. Thus, between the left of the I Corps (Landrecies) and the right of the II (Le Cateau) there was a considerable gap filled by the 3rd and parts of the 1st and 2nd Cavalry Brigades; the 5th Cavalry Brigade was at Taisnières, between the 1st and 2nd Divisions.

According to von Kluck (the commander of the First German Army) his corps on the night 25th/26th August were disposed in the following positions, whence he meant to continue his march:—

III Corps holding the extreme and south-eastern exits of the Foret de Mormal to Landrecies;

IV Corps from Landrecies to Solesmes;

II Corps on the right of the IV Corps;

IV Reserve Corps moving southwards from Valenciennes;

II Cavalry Corps on the right of the II Corps;

IX Corps on the left (and north) of the III Corps.

Part of VII, and the X Corps of von Bulow's Second German Army were marching in rear of the I British Corps.

One of the most interesting periods of the Le Cateau operations is the general situation at midnight 25th/26th August. Several hours earlier—at 7.30 p.m.—Sir John French had issued orders for the retreat to be continued some ten to fifteen miles south-west, the I Corps to billet in the Busigny area, the II Corps about Premont and Beaurevoir and the 4th Division at Le Catelet. In accordance with these orders, the I Corps Commander (Sir Douglas Haig) issued instructions to his divisions to set out for Busigny at 2 a.m. on the 26th. The II Corps Commander (Sir Horace Smith-Dorrien) had also (at 10.30 p.m.) ordered his divisional commanders to continue the retreat on the following day—the transport to start at 4 a.m. and the main bodies at 7 a.m.

But G.H.Q. orders to General Allenby, commanding the Cavalry Division, did not reach him until after 11 p.m., and shortly after receipt, the Colonel commanding 5th Dragoon Guards arrived and stated that in conjunction with the 4th Division, he had safely withdrawn from the high ground west of Viesly which overlooked Solesmes, and that the enemy was in possession of it. This was a serious matter, for it was only from the high ground overlooking Solesmes and the ridges abreast of it, that the cavalry could cover the retirement from the Le Cateau position. General Allenby's division was at this period much scattered and he had at his immediate disposal only the 4th Cavalry Brigade, much too weak a force with which to recapture the high ground. He therefore proceeded at once to General Smith-Dorrien's Headquarters at Bertry and explained the situation as it appeared to him. The enemy was close at hand and unless the II Corps and the 4th Division could set out before daylight, the Germans would be upon them and there would be only one thing to do— to stand and fight. At 2 a.m. on the 26th, General Smith-Dorrien sent for General H. I. M. Hamilton, commanding 3rd Division, and from him learnt that many units of the division were only just coming in and to get them formed up for the retreat would be almost impossible. This information, coupled with the fact that the Cavalry Division was too scattered to render useful service during the retreat, forced the II Corps Commander to the conclusion that he must stand his ground and strike hard at the enemy.

After reporting to Sir John French that owing to the exhaustion of the II Corps and in the face of the very superior forces before him and the number of hostile guns covering his position, he judged it impossible to continue his retirement at daybreak (as ordered), Sir Horace Smith-Dorrien set to work to make alternative dispositions and plans where possible for the inevitable battle. His message to Sir John French had brought the reply that every endeavour must be made to break off the engagement at the earliest possible moment and continue the retreat, as help was impossible, the I Corps being incapable of movement and the French Cavalry Corps too exhausted to intervene in any way.

Orders cancelling the retirement and instructing the troops to "stand fast" were then issued—some units actually receiving them when formed up ready to continue the retreat at 7 a.m.

At midnight orders from G.H.Q. had been received at 4th Divisional Headquarters in Haucourt to carry out the retirement to Le Catelet, but were not issued to Brigades as the troops were then on the march. About 5 a.m. on the 26th officers were sent out to locate the positions of the troops and orders were ready to be despatched as soon as the reports of these officers were received, should the situation permit retirement. But almost immediately after this a staff officer arrived from II Corps Headquarters with a request to the G.O.C. 4th Division to protect the left flank of the Corps as far as Haucourt as "it was going to fight in its present position." This General Snow agreed to do, and sent instructions to the 11th and 12th Infantry Brigades to take up the following positions: 11th Infantry Brigade from Le Coquelet Farm to railway about south of "O" in FONTAINE; 12th Infantry Brigade to carry on from left of 11th Brigade to Moulin d'Esnes just north-west of Esnes; 10th Brigade in reserve at Haucourt.

But action had already been joined with the enemy. At 5.30 a.m. heavy hostile artillery fire was opened on the Quarries position (south-west of Fontaine), which was very exposed and entirely unentrenched. Here C and D Companies of the 1st Somerset Light Infantry (under Major C. W. Compton) had taken whatever cover was possible, the surrounding country being very open. A glacis-like slope, which provided the only fair field of fire, led up to where the Companies were extended, but the enemy was too cautious to advance in this direction, his attention being turned to the flanks of the position.

By 6.30 a.m. masses of Germans [1] were advancing from the main Cambrai–Le Cateau road, west of Beauvois. They were supported by their artillery in action near the road. Their machine-gun detachments, which had worked their way round Fontaine and through the village, now opened very heavy flanking fire on the right of the 11th Infantry Brigade, and casualties amongst the 1st Somersets became severe. Major Compton was hit in the shoulder, Major Thoyts (commanding C Company) in the neck, Capt. Broderip and Lieut. J. Leacroft in the head, and Lieut. Philby in the leg; many other ranks had also become casualties.

A and B Companies, south of the railway, were then hurried up to reinforce C and D. They advanced in extended order, under heavy shell fire. As they reached the firing line German skirmishers were seen about 700 yards away advancing and taking cover behind the corn-stooks which dotted the fields. From Fontaine the enemy's machine guns now enfiladed the line, the rain of bullets clipping short the grass along the crest of the hill. But at the enemy's infantry there were fewer opportunities of firing, for having already had deadly proof of the British soldier's prowess with the rifle, his troops were careful to expose themselves as little as possible.

Shortly after 8 a.m. the Quarries became untenable. Both flanks of the position were exposed, the 7th Brigade (3rd Division) on the right, and the 12th Brigade on the left of the 11th Infantry Brigade having been forced back by heavy pressure and intense machine-gun and artillery fire. Measures were therefore taken to withdraw to the railway embankment which ran along the valley between Ligny and Fontaine. Just previous to the decision to retire, a German patrol waving a white flag evidently meant to invite the Somerset men to surrender, endeavoured to work round the right flank of the Battalion. "The men asked me what to do. 'Fire on the beggars, range 500 yards.' Germans drop hastily." [2]

So, leaving a single platoon behind under Lieut. Taylor, the Battalion in short rushes retired south of the railway, towards Ligny. But neither the platoon nor its commander escaped; Lieut. Taylor was wounded and fell into the hands of the enemy; the fate of the platoon can only be conjectured.

In Ligny the 1st Somersets reorganized and took up positions at the eastern end of the village. Casualties were collected and placed in the church.

[1] They were German Cavalry. A German Cavalry Division included all arms—Artillery and Jager Battalions, with M.G. Companies, as well as mounted troops.
[2] The late Lieut.-Col. W. Watson, S.L.I.

Unfortunately the Divisional Field Ambulances and other Divisional troops, excepting Artillery, had been held back by G.H.Q., and were at St. Quentin. The wounded could not be evacuated, though Capt. Holden, R.A.M.C., attached, managed to collect a few carts in which he placed some of the worst cases and despatched them southwards towards St. Quentin. For some inexplicable reason these carts were turned back to Ligny under the direction of a staff officer. All these wounded subsequently fell into the hands of the enemy.

The time was now about noon. Between 12 and 1 o'clock a message was received from 4th Divisional Headquarters stating that if Ligny could possibly be held until 4 p.m. the French were expected to make an attack on the German right and the situation would be saved.

Until about 3.45 p.m. the fighting was of a desultory nature, but just before 4 p.m. Ligny was heavily shelled and a storm of rifle fire broke out on the right of the 4th Division. Battalion after battalion of German infantry was launched against the village from the N.E., their skirmishers advancing with great dash and taking advantage of every scrap of cover, the standing corn and stooks affording them great opportunities. But none of their attacks could be pushed home, for the British artillery and the machine guns firing point-blank, took terrible toll of the enemy's troops. At 400 yards from the British line the German attack broke down. They were brave men those Germans, but the rifle and machine-gun fire of their opponents and the splendid devotion with which the Artillery (though outnumbered by four to one) served their guns snatched success from the enemy, just as they had done at Mons. Again and again the enemy tried to storm Ligny, but met by shrapnel and rapid rifle fire (at which the British soldier was an expert), the German attack melted away, and seeing persistence useless they gave up the attempt, leaving the 11th Infantry Brigade in undisputed possession of the village.

Well indeed had General Snow's Division performed its given task of protecting the left flank of the II Corps. For the success of the German plan of campaign depended largely upon the results of von Kluck's endeavours to envelop the left wing of the Allied line. At Mons the attempt had failed. Failure had also met the efforts of the commander of the First German Army, to press the British Expeditionary Force back upon the fortress of Maubeuge, and surround it. The third attempt on Le Cateau was likewise doomed, for with marvellous courage and tenacity the II Corps, covered on the left by General Snow's 4th Division, and assisted on the right by the 19th Infantry Brigade, fought the vastly superior forces of the enemy to a standstill, then broke off the battle in broad daylight and retired southwards. It was an altogether extraordinary military feat, reflecting the greatest credit and honour on General Smith-Dorrien and his devoted troops. On 26th August at Le Cateau there is no doubt whatsoever, that Smith-Dorrien's generalship saved the British Expeditionary Force from disaster.

It is, however, only possible to follow the fortunes of the 1st Somerset L.I. Throughout the day, the phlegm and endurance of the West Country-

ACTION OF LE CATEAU, 26TH AUG., 1914.

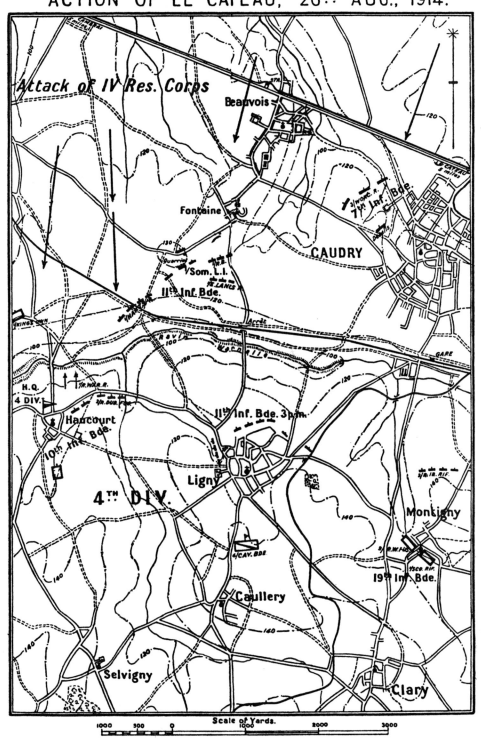

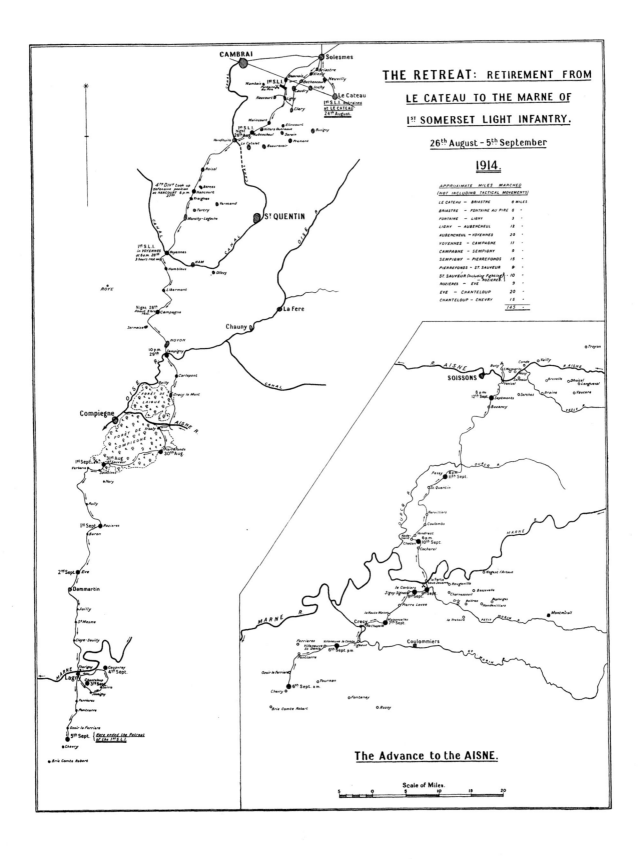

THE RETREAT: RETIREMENT FROM LE CATEAU TO THE MARNE OF 1ST SOMERSET LIGHT INFANTRY.

26th August – 5th September

1914.

APPROXIMATE MILES MARCHED
(NOT INCLUDING TACTICAL MOVEMENTS)

LE CATEAU – BRIASTRE	6 MILES
BRIASTRE – FONTAINE AU PIRE	6 "
FONTAINE – LIGNY	3 "
LIGNY – AUBENCHEUL	12 "
AUBENCHEUL – VOYENNES	20 "
VOYENNES – CAMPAGNE	11 "
CAMPAGNE – SEMPIGNY	9 "
SEMPIGNY – PIERREFONDS	15 "
PIERREFONDS – ST. SAUVEUR	9 "
ST. SAUVEUR (including Fighting) – ROZIERES	10 "
ROZIERES – EVE	9 "
EVE – CHANTELOUP	20 "
CHANTELOUP – CHEVRY	15 "
	145 "

The Advance to the AISNE.

Scale of Miles.

men had been most remarkable.[1] Thrust without food into the battle after 1st Battalion
marching all night, their discipline was splendid. In the sudden transition 26th August
from peace conditions to war with the greatest military power in the world,
they maintained the highest traditions of the Regiment.

Soon after 5 p.m., under personal orders from General Snow, G.O.C.,
4th Division, the 11th Infantry Brigade began to evacuate Ligny village and
retire on Malincourt—the next phase of the historic Retreat had begun.[2]

[1] For 5 hours one young officer of the 1st Somerset L.I. (Lieut. G. Rowarth Parr) held his position
under heavy artillery and machine-gun fire, losing three-quarters of his platoon.

[2] The casualties suffered by the 1st Battalion Somerset Light Infantry in the Battle of Le Cateau
were approximately 19 N.C.O.'s and men killed, 9 officers and 150 N.C.O.'s and men wounded,
100 N.C.O.'s and men missing.

CHAPTER III

THE RETREAT

IT has already been described how Sir Horace Smith-Dorrien, unaided on the right by the I Corps, and unassisted throughout the hardest fighting of the day by General Sordet's Cavalry Corps which had come up on the left rear of the B.E.F. (after retiring in the early morning returned about 3 p.m.), had broken off the Battle of Le Cateau and had begun the withdrawal of his troops in the very face of the enemy. Certain units, however, not having received orders to retire, still held the Germans at bay, wherever the latter attempted to advance. Towards the close of the action, along the front of the 4th Division, there was little rifle fire, but the volume of hostile artillery fire was on the increase, and on the left of the Division the enemy still persisted in his endeavours to turn the western flank of Esnes. But now (at about 4.30 p.m.) the boom of General Sordet's guns from the neighbourhood of Crevecœur fell on the ears of the worn British—assuring the latter that their left flank would be covered from the north-west during the retirement. In front of Ligny, the thwarted German infantry, after the repeated repulses to which they had been subjected, remained inactive.

Verbal orders given by General Snow to his infantry Brigadiers had been difficult to transmit to units in the front line. The 11th Brigade was apparently the only one of the three in any way collected, for the 10th and 12th Brigades had become somewhat intermixed during the day's fighting. The Somerset Light Infantry ultimately retired from Ligny in two parties—one under Lieut.-Colonel Swayne, who had with him the survivors of two companies, and the other under Major Prowse. Orders given to the 11th Infantry Brigade had been to retire on Vendhuille by way of Malincourt and Aubencheul, and with this intention Colonel Swayne set out first—the remainder of the Battalion remaining in Ligny, in touch with the enemy until a late hour.

No attempt was made by the Germans to follow up the retirement, though von Kluck's artillery shelled the British infantrymen as long as they were in sight and continued to bombard the evacuated positions until darkness fell.

After a march of about 12 miles, Colonel Swayne with 8 officers and about 150 men reached Aubencheul that night, and billeted. The half Battalion under Major Prowse had, however, taken the road to Clary, where it met with troops belonging to the 3rd Division and so pushed on to Elincourt. Outside the latter village the party fell in with the G.O.C. 11th Brigade, the Brigade Major and other units of the Brigade and subsequently spent the night at Serain.

Touch with the enemy had now been lost, and Sir Horace Smith-Dorrien had performed what had been thought the impossible.

At 2 a.m. on 27th Colonel Swayne's party left Aubencheul. The C.O.
had decided to march on St. Quentin. After marching south for some
3 miles the party was fired on by a sentry posted on the northern exits of
a village. The sentry was found to be British and the village Vendhuille, in
which 4th Division Headquarters[1] were resting. Colonel Swayne then joined
the Division.[2]

At 4 a.m. on the 27th the depleted Somersets left Vendhuille with
Divisional H.Qs. for Voyennes, via Roisel, Hancourt and Monchy
Lagache. Supplies were to be picked up en route. Hancourt was reached
at about 6 p.m., where a defensive position was taken up. But after a three
hours' rest the march was resumed in a southerly direction. Civilian carts
had been hired and men were given lifts in relays. "This" said the Battalion
diary, "proved an arduous march through Vraignes and Tertry to Voyennes,
which was reached at 6 a.m. on the 28th, after a march of 12 miles." From
Vendhuille to Voyennes is at least 20 miles!

" Here a party of about 4 officers and 300 other ranks under Major Prowse
rejoined Headquarters. The Battalion was allotted billets, but before they
could be occupied the order was given to move, as German Cavalry[3] were
pressing in pursuit. No supplies were obtainable, and the order was given
by Sir John French to burn kits and bury ammunition if necessary in order
that men might be carried in the wagons if they were not fit to march.
This was not however found to be necessary in the Battalion. The march
was resumed at about 10 a.m., and short halts were made at Hombleux
and Libermont.

"At the latter place (reached at 5 p.m.) bread and wine and apples were
purchased locally. At 7 p.m. the Battalion marched to Campagne and was
compelled to halt owing to a transport break-down ahead. About 5 hours'
sleep were obtained by the roadside and a day's supplies were issued by a
staff officer in a motor-car.

"29th. At 5 a.m. the march was resumed and no pursuit was apparent.
About 9 a halt was taken at Sermaize and breakfasts and dinners eaten. . . .
The Battalion marched at 8 p.m. and reached Sempigny at about 10 p.m.
Here a few hours' sleep were obtained in a field."

The Diary of the 11th Infantry Brigade at the close of the 29th August

---

[1] An officer of Colonel Swayne's party—the late Lieut.-Colonel Watson—stated in his private
diary that 4th Division Headquarters were met in Le Catelet.

[2] The records of the movements of the 1st Somerset Light Infantry and of the 11th Infantry
Brigade generally, are difficult to follow. The Brigade Diary states: "After the retirement from Ligny
the Brigade was split into two parties, the Brigade Headquarters and a portion of each battalion
of the Brigade retired via Caullery–Elincourt to Serain, arriving about 8 a.m. and billeting there.
The rest of the Brigade retired through Selvigny–Malincourt to Villers Outreaux where they
billeted."

[3] It was *not* the German Cavalry that hurried the 4th Division out of Voyennes as the former had
been shaken off and British Cavalry were between the Germans and troops of the 4th Division. The
latter had received orders from G.H.Q. to move towards Ham and cover the retirement of the 3rd
Division from the Somme.

records that the whole 4th Division bivouacked at night at Les Cloyes, "and here the two wings of the Brigade at length became united."

The 29th August had been a comparatively quiet day for the infantry of the B.E.F., only the cavalry being engaged with the enemy. There had been long periods of rest throughout the day and the men had time to indulge in a general "clean up" after the wear and tear of the past few days.

On the night of the 29th/30th August the B.E.F. occupied an approximate line from St. Gobain (I Corps) to Cuts and Carlepont (II Corps): the 4th Division lay just north of the latter place, the 10th Brigade forming the rearguard which remained north of the Oise. On the right front of the British Force was the Fifth French Army, and on the left front the newly formed Sixth French Army under General Maunoury. The march was resumed at

5 a.m. on the 30th, and an hour later Lieut. Montgomery and 300 N.C.O.'s and men of the 1st Somerset Light Infantry rejoined the Battalion. There are no records which relate the wanderings of this party after the Battle of Le Cateau. The 11th Brigade marched in Division via Carlepont–Bailly–Tracy le Mont–Trosly and Breuil to Pierre Fonds—a distance of 15 miles. Smallpox was reported in the village and in consequence the men spent a wretched night resting as best they could in the streets. Wine and bread were purchased for the men, who had had a very trying march in the heat of the day.

On 31st the 11th Brigade escorted the guns and the transport, while the 10th and 12th marched on a parallel grass road on the right—these being a flank guard. The march was westwards through the Forest of Compiègne which afforded welcome shade from the scorching sun. The Brigade was to have billeted in Saintimes (15 miles), but just as the units were moving into billets a report came in stating that a large German force were moving from Compiègne, and defence positions were taken up. Instead of billeting in Saintimes, the 1st Somerset Light Infantry was sent off to the high ground south of St. Sauveur, but as no attack was made during the night the men obtained a much-needed sleep. On this night a full day's rations were issued.

A brush with the enemy took place on the 1st September which the diary of the Somerset Light Infantry terms the "Battle of Verberie."[1]

"Sept. 1st. Saintimes. Marched at 7 a.m. with orders to occupy a rearguard position. The Hants and East Lancs were disposed on the high ground north of St. Sauveur and Vaucelles. The Somerset Light Infantry and Rifle Brigade on a ridge north of Saintimes and Verberie. The Somerset Light Infantry were disposed, D Company on right of the Hants, Battalion Headquarters, A, B and C Companies and Machine-Gun Section on the ridge north of Saintimes, holding La Hautber Farm. D Company were soon heavily

[1] The title is given, as it is of interest from a Regimental point of view, for during the War many engagements were known to Battalions by names other than those laid down in the Report of the Battles Nomenclature Committee. It is now known as the Affair of Nèry.

engaged.   The Hants and East Lancs suffered somewhat heavily and retired   1st Battalion
about 8.30.   The opposition consisted of cavalry and horse artillery.[1]   D   1st September
Company covered the Hants retirement, and themselves retired about 9 a.m.
on to the main position.   The Germans appeared to have suffered heavily
and did not press the pursuit, and about 10 a.m. the Battalion formed up in
artillery formation and moved across a wide open plain towards Rully.[2]   Here
the Battalion formed up and rested, and about 3 p.m. marched to Rosieres[3]
which was reached about 6 p.m.   Total distance marched about 10 miles.
The Battalion suffered 4 casualties."

This small action which took place after the Affair of Nèry in which "L"
Battery of the R.H.A. greatly distinguished itself, was the only occasion on
which the 1st Somerset Light Infantry was engaged during the final stage of
the Retreat.   Thereafter until the 5th September, on which date the Retreat   5th September
from Mons ended, and the British Expeditionary Force reached its halting
place south-south-east of Paris, the daily marches were those of tired and
exhausted men—cheerful to a wonderful degree, but nevertheless worn out
with marching and fighting.   Splendidly they had maintained the glorious
reputation of the British Army: their pluck and endurance had once again
demonstrated the extraordinary staying powers of the British soldier and his
cheery optimism under the most depressing circumstances.

In the history of the British Army, there had been up to the year 1914,
three famous retreats.   The first of these was Sir John Moore's retreat to
Corunna (1808–1809); the second, the retreat of Sir Arthur Wellesley to
Talavera (1809); and the third the retreat from Burgos to Ciudad Rodrigo
in 1812; all names which figure in the battle honours of the British Regiments.
The retreat from Mons will be no less famous in military history.

When night fell on the 5th September the British Expeditionary Force
occupied the following positions: I Corps in and west of Rozoy; the Cavalry
Division to its right rear in Mormant and the villages north of it; the II Corps
on the left of the I, in and east of Tournan, and the III Corps on the left of
the II, from Ozoir la Ferrière southwards to Brie Comte Robert touching the
defences of Paris.   The III Corps still consisted of the 4th Division and
19th Infantry Brigade.

The last stages of the Retreat (15 miles) had been covered by the 1st
Somerset Light Infantry between 1 a.m. and 12 noon on 5th.   Billets had
been allotted at Chevry, but the G.O.C. 11th Infantry Brigade (which had
acted as rearguard of the 4th Division) had halted the Somersets and East Lancs
at the Chateau la Mausadière, 2 miles short of Chevry, and in the cool shade
of the woods the two Battalions bivouacked.   A 2-hour breakfast halt at La
Ferrière had been made *en route* and here a French gentleman of a family well
known in England—Baron Rothschild—provided an excellent meal for the

---

[1] The Advanced Guard of the II Cav. Corps (First German Army) trying to get behind the
Fifth French Army.
[2] About 4 miles south-west of Nèry.
[3] In 1918 another Battalion of the Somerset Light Infantry (7th) fought at Rosières.

1st Battalion
5th September

officers. Bread, chocolate, cigarettes and matches were also purchased locally for the men.

All that night after it was announced that the Retreat was at an end there was great jubilation in the B.E.F. in spite of the tribulations troops had gone through. Von Kluck's march on Paris had failed, and he was now to be attacked.

COL. E. H. SWAYNE, O.B.E.

LT.-COL. C. W. COMPTON, C.B., C.M.G.

BRIG.-GEN. C. B. PROWSE, D.S.O.

LT.-COL. J. A. THICKNESSE

CAPT. BT.-MAJOR V. H. B. MAJENDIE, D.S.O.

COMMANDING OFFICERS OF THE 1ST BATTALION

CHAPTER IV

THE BATTLE OF THE MARNE: 6TH–9TH SEPTEMBER 1914

O N one page of his diary (dated 5th September 1914) the late 1st Battalion Lieutenant-Colonel W. Watson, 1st Somerset L.I., recorded:— "Good news at last. British Army is to turn and advance. . . . Our retreat is ended. . . . No disorganization nor lack of discipline made its appearance in the 4th Division. The men bore their hardships and fatigue of the long night-marches with dogged pluck, *maintaining the highest traditions of the old 13th.*"[1] And a Press correspondent (Frederick Coleman) who was with the B.E.F. from Mons to Ypres stated that: "We all closed our eyes in a different mood than on any night in the previous fortnight."

Yet, the next week was to demonstrate that an advance can be just as strenuous as a retreat.

It will be remembered that on the night of the 3rd September, the Somersets with the East Lancashires, bivouacked at the Chateau la Mausadière. During the day a party consisting of one officer and 90 other ranks, first reinforcements from England, joined the Battalion—a very welcome addition.

On the night of the 5th, the German outpost line along the front of the 5th September B.E.F. ran from Vaudoy to Mortcerf and Villers, the British outpost line running approximately in front of Rozoy and Fontenay (I Corps) Chatres and Tournan (II Corps), thence to Ozoir la Ferrière (III Corps), 4th Division and 19th Infantry Brigade.

On the right of the B.E.F. was Conneau's II Cavalry Corps and on the right of the latter, first the Fifth and then the Ninth French Armies. N.W. of the B.E.F. across Marne River the Sixth French Army was in process of forming up for an attack on the right flank of the First German Army.

The enemy appears to have considered that the Sixth French Army and the B.E.F. were practically put out of action. He was therefore marching against the left flank of the Fifth French Army.

With this intention von Kluck was advancing across the Marne and on the afternoon of 5th, four corps of his Army were across the Grand Morin with two cavalry divisions ahead of them, but with only a weak flank guard on his western flank, i.e. west of the Ourcq.

It was the moment for which General Joffre had waited.

After the rearguard actions of Nery, Crépy and Villers-Cotterets fought on 1st September, von Kluck still persisted in regarding the British Expeditionary Force as negligible. In his orders are to be found such expressions as: "If any British are met with they are to be driven back" (3rd Sept.): "Should the British be caught up anywhere they will be attacked" (on the 4th September).

---

[1] The 13th Foot: Somerset Light Infantry (Prince Albert's).

He had no idea, until his right flank was heavily attacked that "an immediate offensive of the whole French Army was imminent,"[1] or that the British Army had any offensive powers left whatsoever. He therefore continued his march towards the Seine.

General Joffre's instructions for the offensive reached British H.Qs. at Melun at 3 a.m. on the 5th September, but they did not reach Sir John French in time to cancel orders issued by the latter on the 4th for a further retirement to the line Rozoy–Ozoir la Ferrière. For the II Corps had started off before midnight and the I and III Corps long before daybreak: as already related, the 1st Somerset L.I., with the 11th Infantry Brigade of the 4th Division, had set out on the last stages of the retreat at 1 a.m. on the 5th. "Thus on the night of 5th September it" (the B.E.F.) "was 12 to 15 miles in rear of the positions in which the French Commander-in-Chief expected it to be."[2]

Sir John French's operation orders were issued at 5.15 p.m. on the 5th September. The British Army was to advance eastwards with a view to attacking the enemy. It was first to wheel to the east, pivoting on its right, until the line La Chapelle Iger (south-east of Rozoy)–Villeneuve le Comte–Bailly (5 miles south-west of Crecy) was reached. The line then occupied would bring the B.E.F. approximately parallel to the Grand Morin River, about 7 miles from it. The right of the Force was to be in position by 9 a.m. on 6th; the left, having further to march, by 10 a.m. The Cavalry was to cover the front and flanks and connect with the Fifth and Sixth French Armies, on the right and left respectively.

General Joffre's instructions for the B.E.F. were to attack N.E. from the front Changis (7 miles east of Meaux)–Coulommiers in the general direction of Montmiral. The Sixth French Army was advancing on Meaux and the line of the Ourcq.

The 11th Infantry Brigade was the rear Brigade of 4th Division. The 1st Somersets moved off at about 7 a.m. to Jossigny, a distance of nearly 8 miles. "We were" (records the Battalion Diary) "all in great hopes that this meant we should soon be rounding up defeated German Corps." Here a halt was called. On resuming, the Brigade marched on to Villeneuve le Comte, where the Somersets bivouacked in an apple orchard, A and B Companies finding the outposts. Thus, for the Battalion, passed uneventfully the first day of the Battle of the Marne.[3] At nightfall on the 6th only the Cavalry and the advanced guard of the I Corps appear to have been engaged with the enemy during the day.

No orders were issued for the next day's march, though all troops were warned to be ready to move at short notice. But Sir John French's Special

[1] von Kluck's "Marne."
[2] Official History (Military Operations) of the War.
[3] On the night of the 6th September the B.E.F. was disposed in the following positions:—
Cavalry Division—Jouy le Chatel: I Corps—Vaudoy–Touqin–Pezarches: 3rd and 5th Cavalry Brigades—Pezarches–Lumigny: II Corps, 3rd Division Lumigny northward to Faremoutiers: 5th Division—Montcerf northward to La Celle-sur-Morin: III Corps—Villers-sur-Morin southwards to Villeneuve le Comte and Villeneuve St. Denis. There were no German troops north of the Grand Morin River along the British front on the night of the 6th.

Order of the Day, in which the British Commander-in-Chief said: "I call upon *1st Battalion*
the British Army in France to now show the enemy its powers, and to push *6th September*
on vigorously to the attack beside the Sixth French Army," was circulated
to all units and read out to the men; and the cheers which greeted this Order
boded ill for von Kluck's troops!   Little the men cared that they were tired
and hungry and their clothes and boots worn and broken, they were advancing
now and the enemy was on the run.   For von Kluck had perceived the danger
in which he stood.   The Sixth French Army had, under General Joffre's
orders, fallen heavily upon the right flank of the First German Army along
the line of the Ourcq.

On the morning of the 7th, the Somerset Light Infantry, warned to *7th September*
march at 5 a.m., breakfasted at 4 o'clock.   No orders came, however, until
10.50 a.m.   Apparently, information concerning the successful attack of the
Sixth French Army or General Joffre's instructions to push on had not reached
Sir John French.   Thus it was about 11 a.m. before the infantry of the B.E.F.
were on the move.

Behind a Cavalry screen the Force moved forward, and very soon evidence
of the hurried departure of the enemy's covering forces was found.   The
11th Brigade (in Division) marching via Tigeaux–Crecy (where the Grand
Morin was crossed)–La Chapelle, reached Maisoncelles where comfortable
bivouacs were selected south of the village, but reports that German cavalry
with motor machine-guns were in the neighbourhood caused all units of the
Brigade to take up defensive positions round the village, the Hants and
Somersets covering the southern face.   The 12th Brigade (the advanced
guard of the 4th Division) was fired on from N.W. of the village, but the 11th
Brigade was not engaged and all units then bivouacked, C and D Companies
of the 1st Somersets being on outpost duty, H.Qs. and A and B Companies
settling down in a turnip field at about 7 p.m.   The day's march had
been 10 miles.   Most of the inhabitants of Maisoncelles had fled, but from
the few still remaining it was learned that the Germans had left the village
only 5 hours before the British arrived.   They had carried away or destroyed
all foodstuffs, and two officers of the Battalion searching for something to eat
found a small chateau in which, said Lieut.-Col. Watson: "Everything is just
as the owner left it; his hats, coats and sticks, etc., are in the hall.   Rooms
full of clothes, crockery and glass.   The emptiness has an eerie effect on us
both, and we are glad to get out into the open."

Throughout the day both the Fifth and Sixth French Armies on the right
and left of the B.E.F. had attacked the enemy and had gained ground.
Sir John French's orders for operations on the 8th stated that the advance
was to be continued against the line of the Marne, from Nogent l'Artaud to
La Ferte sous Jouarre, the Cavalry to push on in pursuit keeping touch with
the Fifth French Army on the right and the Sixth French Army on the left.

The B.E.F. was already north of the Grand Morin but between the latter
river and the Marne, the Petit Morin had to be crossed.   The Petit Morin
was only a stream running through a narrow valley, but the approaches were

difficult and favourable for defensive purposes. The river valley was bounded on either side by steep wooded sides, which could only be approached through close, intricate country studded with copses, villages, and hamlets, and only six bridges lay in the sector in front of the B.E.F. The Marne river runs through a similar valley, so that no easy task lay before Sir John French's troops.

On the 8th the enemy continued his retreat and all three Corps, greatly assisted by the vigorous action of the Cavalry, were engaged with strong hostile rear guards. In two columns the 4th Division continued its advance towards La Ferté sous Jouarre. The 11th Brigade marched via La Haute Maison–Pierre Levée–Signy Signets, the 1st Somerset Light Infantry billeting in the Chateau Venteuil (in Les Corbier) about 7 p.m. At Signy Signets (about 3 miles south of the Marne) the advanced guard of the III Corps (19th Infantry Brigade) was found held up by hostile artillery firing from N. of the Marne. The Brigade had been badly caught by shell fire whilst in column of route on the road. The 11th Brigade was therefore diverted from the road and moved across country to just south of the river of which the enemy still held the bridgeheads.

On all sides proofs of the hurried retreat of the enemy and of his demoralization were encountered; many houses in Pierre Levée had been sacked, also in Venteuil. Empty wine bottles and signs of drunken orgies, smashed furniture and wilful damage were found in almost every chateau, though in a private letter the late Lieut. G. R. Parr, 1st S.L.I., wrote, "On many houses was written 'Gute Leute-nicht plündern, aber schonen: Haben alles gegeben.'"

The whole of the 8th was practically spent in forcing the passage of the Petit Morin, and at nightfall the B.E.F. occupied the following positions: Cavalry Division—Replonges: I Corps—Basseville, Boitron, Handevillers: II Corps—Les Feucheres, Rougeville, Charnesseuil, Orly: III Corps—Grand Glairet, Venteuil Chayeau, Signy Signets: 3rd Cav. Bde.—Romeny: 5th Cav. Bde.—near Le Tretoire.

At dawn on the 9th the advance towards the Marne began. The 11th Infantry Brigade (after an officer's reconnaissance) moved by a steep track leading N.E. over the Petit Morin, at St. Martin. The order of march was Rifle Brigade, Somerset L.I., E. Lancs, Hants. The battalions had to move through thick woods down a steep slope, which took some time, but eventually the Rifle Brigade reached the high ground east of La Ferté which they held whilst the E. Lancs moved down to attack and clear the town. In descending the slope of the hill the E. Lancs were caught by machine-gun and rifle fire from La Ferté and lost their Colonel and about 40 men. German snipers were posted in houses and buildings guarding the broken bridges over the Marne and the latter for a while were unapproachable. At about 7 a.m. the Somersets had taken up a position of observation at Les Abymes and here the Battalion spent the whole day.

Shortly before noon the houses and buildings were bombarded by 4th Division howitzers, with the result that about 2.30 p.m. the enemy abandoned the approaches to the bridges. A little later the E. Lancs again advanced to clear the enemy from the houses and buildings covering the crossings. C Company of the 1st Somersets having been ordered forward towards the river, with the intention of establishing troops in a position from which it could assist the E. Lancs by fire, came suddenly under accurate rifle and machine-gun fire and sustained several casualties.[1]   The enemy, however, did not stay to meet the attack by the E. Lancashires but retired up the slope of the hill north of La Ferté, hurried on by the machine-gun section, and C Company of the Somersets who (the Battalion Diary records) "did some damage at long range."

When darkness fell on the 9th September only six battalions of the III Corps had crossed the Marne and of these three belonged to the 11th Infantry Brigade, i.e. Rifle Brigade, E. Lancs and Hants; the 1st Somersets still remained just south of La Ferte at Les Abymes and bivouacked for the night in the Chateau grounds.[2]   During the night the Battalion received second reinforcements—1 officer and 90 other ranks.

At 4 p.m. the Royal Engineers had begun work on the crossings over the Marne at La Ferte and when dawn broke on the following morning a pontoon and barrel bridge had been thrown across the river.

---

[1] 1 other rank killed and 3 wounded.

[2] On this date, 9th, The Battle of the Marne (6th–9th Sept.) properly ends.   The period given (7th–10th Sept.) in the Report of the Battles Nomenclature Committee cannot be sustained if the operations are carefully studied and compared with the official despatches.

CHAPTER V

THE PURSUIT TO THE AISNE

AT 5.15 a.m. on 10th the 1st Somersets left Les Abymes and reached La Ferté sous Jouarre, about 6 o'clock. Here a halt was called until the whole Division had crossed the river. The Battalion rested in a grindstone factory. In La Ferté bread, matches, chocolate and tobacco were obtained by purchase. At 1 p.m. the river was crossed, though A Company was left behind as bridge guard.

The 11th Brigade (the rear Brigade of the Division) then marched North via Porte-Ferée and Cocherel to Chaton and Rademont, where good billets were found. The Somersets and the Hants billeted in Chaton, reaching the village about 6 p.m. after a 10-mile march. The French inhabitants were delighted and did everything possible to make the men comfortable, though the Germans having been in the village for a week had used up all the supplies.

On this day (10th) General Snow (G.O.C., 4th Division) was unfortunately injured by a fall from his horse and Brigadier-General H. F. M. Wilson assumed command of the Division.

For five days now the 11th Brigade had been following in the tracks of the enemy, without having been engaged seriously, for the Brigade was always in rear of the Division. Barring the one small encounter at La Ferté, the Somerset L.I. had experienced none of the excitements which had fallen to other battalions. But none the less the hardship of the daily marches, the uncertain issue and often lack of food, the constant fatigue had to be borne, and how splendidly these discomforts *were* borne! It must be remembered that by this date the First German Army was in full retreat to the Aisne and that the German forces fronting the British Expeditionary Force were mostly Cavalry (backed by the 5th Division and Kraewel's Composite Bde.) left behind to cover the "helter-skelter" manner in which von Kluck's infantry divisions were hurrying back to the line of the river. And for infantry to follow the movements of cavalry is a very tiring operation.

At 4.15 a.m. on 11th September, the 1st Somerset L.I. and Hants, at short notice, marched out of Chaton and took the road to Vendrest to join the remainder of the 11th Brigade. The morning was cloudy and chilly and rain was obviously not far off. On the Somersets and Hants joining the remainder of the Brigade and Bde. H.Qs. on the road N.W. of Vendrest, the march was resumed via Coulombs and Hervillers to St. Quentin, where a two-hours' halt was called in order to allow the 5th Division (II Corps) to pass. At 3 p.m. the Brigade again moved forward on Passy where billets had been

allotted. Soon after leaving St. Quentin heavy rain began to fall and for
the next two or three hours the troops trudged along the road drenched to the
skin, and in the utmost discomfort. The 1st Battalion went into billets in
Passy at 6 p.m. The men were in barns, the officers in a billiard room
of the Chateau. Large fires were lighted and wet clothes dried. No
supplies were issued that night, the supply-wagons not turning up. "Peaceful
night," records the Battalion Diary, "Germans seem to have got clean away
and our visions of getting round them have vanished. The delay of the 7th
must have done the harm." Again, throughout the 11th, the 11th Infantry
Brigade was in rear of the 4th Division.

Without supplies, and as a consequence, very hungry, the 1st Somersets
left Passy (in Brigade) at 7.30 a.m. on 12th. Rain was still falling heavily,
but the troops plodded on, their cup of misery nearly full. Their morning's
breakfast, eaten at 2.15 a.m., had consisted of a quarter ration carried in the
cook's cart, issued to them at that early hour, as a preliminary order to move
at 3.30 a.m. had been received, but did not materialize until 7 a.m. Midday
came and the Battalion at Montrambœuf Farm, but there was nothing to
eat and so the men went hungry again. Suddenly there was a burst of excitement: orders from Divisional H.Qs. had been received by the Brigade to deploy
for action. The enemy was reported to be holding a ridge about 3 miles in
front. In artillery formation the Somersets awaited orders to advance to
the attack. But they waited in vain, for after standing for three hours in a
cold wind, the Battalion once more formed column of route and moved on:
"(The) men marched on with dogged pluck. Reached village of Septmonts
about 8 p.m." As best they could, drenched to the skin, cold and hungry,
but none the less in a cheery spirit the men sheltered in Septmonts: another
15 miles had been covered that day by the Battalion.

And here, for a few moments, it is interesting to review the events of the
11th and 12th September. On the former date the general pursuit of the
enemy had begun. The three British Corps had crossed the Ourcq practically
unopposed, the Cavalry reaching the line of the Aisne River. By the afternoon
of the 12th, however, the enemy's resistance had hardened: the Sixth French
Army, west of Soissons, the head of the III British Corps, south-east of that
place, and the II British Corps, south of Missy and Vailly, had encountered
considerable opposition and it was evident that the enemy intended disputing
the passage of the Aisne. At the close of the 12th the Germans, who had
been holding Mont de Paris, south of Soissons, had been driven back across
the river at the latter place, by the right of the Sixth French Army, which all
along the line had been meeting with strong opposition. The vigorous action
of Allenby's Cavalry in front of the B.E.F. was of great value in clearing the
line of advance of the three British Corps.

At nightfall on 12th the right of the British Line—I Corps—had reached
the neighbourhood of Vauxcere; the head of the 1st Division at Longueval
and that of the 2nd Division at Dhuizel. Of the II Corps, the head of the
3rd Division was at Brenelle and that of the 5th Division at Serches. Of the

1st Battalion
12th September

III Corps the 19th Infantry Brigade was at Buzancy, whilst the 4th Division was in the Septmonts area though actually still going forward.

"In this manner," said Sir John French, "the Battle of the Aisne commenced."

CHAPTER VI

THE BATTLE OF THE AISNE: 13TH–14TH SEPTEMBER 1914

IN pleasant anticipation of much-needed rest the 1st Somerset L.I. had 1st Battalion
12th September gone into billets in Septmonts at 8 p.m. on 12th, but the Battalion had barely settled down, when about 10 p.m. the men were ordered to turn out and form up ready to march off, for at 7 p.m. 11th Bde. H.Qs. had received orders that after halting to get food it was to push on and, if possible, seize the crossings over the Aisne at Venizel. While the Brigade halted in Septmonts two officers, accompanied by a local guide, went forward to reconnoitre the route. Having finished their reconnaissance these officers had received the following orders: the senior officer was to remain in observation on the bridge and, if possible, find out whether the enemy was holding the opposite bank, whilst the junior officer returned to guide the column. The very severe physical strain which the reconnaissance entailed was too much for the junior officer, who, on returning (the 11th Brigade Diary records) "was completely exhausted and incapable either of movement or of coherent speech." He had unfortunately dismissed the local guide and the column was thus forced to move forward by map direction.

So far as the 1st Somersets were concerned the "halt for food" was productive of nothing but disappointment—their diary says: "Men got nothing to eat. Ordered to move on at 10 p.m. to cross the Aisne by a bridge which had been partially destroyed by Germans and to endeavour to secure high ground north of the river. Started off in pouring rain with empty stomachs."

After a march of 7 miles the Battalion (in Brigade) reached Venizel about 13th September 1 a.m. Here the R.E. reconnoitring officers reported that one of the four charges laid by the Germans beneath the bridge had failed to explode and one girder remained across which it was possible to pass troops in single file. The Brigade again moved forward, the 1st Hants leading, followed by the 1st Rifle Brigade, 1st Somersets, and 1st E. Lancs in the order given. It was a tedious process but, covered by an advanced party of the Hants the crossing was safely accomplished, the Somersets getting across by 2 a.m. An hour later the whole Brigade was assembled north of the river.

In order to hold the crossing at Venizel effectively the Brigadier considered it necessary to seize the heights above Bucy-le-Long, which dominated the bridge and the flat ground between those heights and the river. The order was therefore given to fix bayonets and advance to the attack. The Hants were ordered to take the central spur on which La Montaigne Farm was situated; the Somerset L.I. the left spur N.W. of Bucy and the Rifle Brigade the right spur N. of St. Marguerite; the 1st E. Lancs were kept in reserve. The Brigade advanced to the attack.

"Thanks to the boldness of the movement," said General Hunter-Weston in his report, "it was completely successful and the heights were seized and entrenched without opposition, the enemy making no attempt to hold the trenches they had dug on the flat ground overlooking the bridge."

At Venizel, the Aisne runs in a flat valley from 2 to 3 miles wide, with steep hills on its northern bank. The slopes and crests are wooded, the tops or summits bare, but cultivated, rather similar to a monk's shaven crown with a ring of hair round the base of the skull.

The Battalion record is particularly interesting:—

"The summit, about 300 feet, was reached without opposition, but on moving across the plateau on top of the ridge German Cavalry were seen and at a range of about 800 yards, German infantry in trenches and also a tool cart. In fact the ridge appears to be strongly held. It seems incomprehensible that the passage across the bridge on the open plain between the river and village, or still more the narrow path through the woods up the hill should not have been held by the Germans, and it can only be assumed that they did not anticipate any British advance on such a wild night and after the long march the troops had already had. The total distance marched by the Battalion since 7 a.m. yesterday (12th) was about 25 miles, mostly in pouring rain with no food since 2.15 a.m. on the 12th, including two deployments for attack."

The Battalion was now established in a sunken lane overlooking the village of Crouay, with Soissons rather to the left rear. Throughout the day the warm sun enabled the men to dry their clothes and after a good meal, prepared from sheep, bread and vegetables requisitioned locally, and a sleep, officers and men alike recovered marvellously from the fatigues through which they had recently passed.

In spite of heavy hostile shelling throughout the day no casualties were suffered by the 1st Somerset L.I., indeed so far as the Battalion was concerned the Battle of the Aisne was quite a mild affair. There is one point, however, of considerable interest connected with the beginning of the Battle: the infantry of the 11th Brigade of the 4th Division were the first to cross the Aisne and establish positions north of the river. It is well to mention this, for the official despatches make no reference whatsoever to the very creditable advance carried out, under most trying conditions, by General Hunter-Weston's Brigade. There was very little fighting, it is true, but none the less that advance was of importance,[1] for the positions taken up on the night of the 13th/14th were held continuously until the B.E.F. left the Aisne for the Ypres–Béthune area.

And now began a period—about three weeks—of comparative peace and comfort. None of the hard fighting which took place on 14th and continued, in the neighbourhood of Missy, Vailly and Troyon, until the II and I Corps had obtained a firm footing north of the river, fell to the lot of the 11th

---

[1] Major C. B. Prowse, 1st S.L.I. and other officers of the 11th Brigade were especially mentioned by the Brigadier "For their initiative and for their brave and good leading of their units."

Infantry Brigade and the whole period from 14th September to 7th October might be dismissed in a few words were it not that from a Regimental standpoint it is interesting to look back upon that brief interval which witnessed the birth of trench warfare before that first terrible winter of 1914–1915, spent in water-logged and filthy trenches between Ypres and the La Bassée Canal.

CHAPTER VII

THE BEGINNING OF TRENCH WARFARE

1st Battalion

"WE remain in our trenches," said the late Lieut.-Colonel Watson, of the 1st Battn. Somerset L.I. "Life becomes regular and uniform. We are never attacked, and spend our time digging trenches and improving our dug-outs." That is a fair summary, though there is more to be said, for the dug-outs referred to in the above quotation were very different from the elaborate shelters constructed later: on the Aisne they were, comparatively, mere excavations in the ground, but a foot or two deep. There were, however, north of the Aisne, amongst the wooded heights, a number of natural shelter-caves, and in one of these the Battalion had its first Headquarters. On the 15th the Battalion Diary first mentions the German 8-in. howitzers, which had been transferred to the Aisne from before Maubeuge, where they had been in action during the investment of that place. The shells from these guns, termed Black Marias or Jack Johnsons, were, however, more terrifying than damaging. On bursting they threw up a huge black column of smoke and earth and created great holes in the ground, but they soon lost their terrors and on the troops digging themselves in more deeply the effects were largely mitigated.

15th September

On the 16th a French Battery came into action in front of B Company's trenches, and was soon located by German aeroplanes. Shortly afterwards the hostile guns opened heavy fire on the Battery and several shells fell in and about the trenches of the Somerset men. Unfortunately a number of officers and men of the Battalion were outside their trenches when the shelling began, and 2/Lieut. Read and four other ranks were killed, whilst Lieut. Newton and five other ranks were wounded. The German 8-in. guns continued their activity until the arrival of the 6-in. howitzers, which Sir John French had asked to be sent out from England: thereafter their activities became less marked. On the 20th September, third reinforcements for the Battalion (93 N.C.O.'s and men) arrived. They were section D men, seasoned soldiers. These were followed on the 24th by yet another draft.

24th September

In digging trenches and improving communications the Battalion passed its days and nights. The weather during the day was mostly warm and bright, but at night-time cold winds howled about the trenches and dug-outs. Several attacks on the enemy, mostly abortive, were made by the French on the left of the 11th Brigade, but in none of these were the Somerset L.I. involved. They were, however, visible from the Battalion trenches and the sight of them was the forerunner of many such visions in the time to come:—

"About 11 o'clock, suddenly tremendous artillery and rifle fire broke out in the French lines, and was promptly answered by the Germans. . . .

It was a clear bright night. Both combatants were sending up rockets. _{1st Battalion} Searchlights were throwing their sinister glare on the opposite hill sides. Soissons, in the valley below, was being shelled. This lasted about an hour, when everything became still and quiet."

One last picture of life on the Aisne:—

"The sight of dead and wounded in the heat of an action like that of 26th August has little or no effect on the spirits of the men; the excitement and nervous tension is too great. One solitary death from a stray bullet during our more or less quiet life here (on the Aisne) casts a gloom over us all. Private Sliny, C—'s servant, was hit while carrying tea from the cooking place to the officers. He was buried with military honours next day; his platoon paid their last tribute to this gallant man."

About 28th September the enemy's activities along the front of the _{28th September} B.E.F. seemed to have died down. The Second French Army, under de Castelnau, had come into action on the left of the Sixth French Army and the Germans had been forced to transfer troops to meet this new menace to their right flank. Again the French prolonged their left, bringing up a new Army—Tenth—and again the Germans prolonged their right. In this way the "race to the Belgian Coast" began.

The reasons which brought about the transfer of the British Expeditionary Force to the left flank of the Allied line are briefly as follows:—The abortive German attacks of the 26th, 27th and 28th September had been followed by a period of what might be described as inertia. The position was in fact that of "stalemate."

"Early in October," said Sir John French, "a study of the general situation strongly impressed me with the necessity of bringing the greatest possible force to bear in support of the northern flank of the Allies in order to effectively outflank the enemy and compel him to evacuate his positions. At the same time the position on the Aisne, as described in the concluding paragraph of my last despatch,[1] appeared to me to warrant the withdrawal of the British Forces from the positions that they held. The enemy had been weakened by continual abortive and futile attacks, whilst the fortification of the positions had been much improved."

There were also other reasons, foremost of which was, that the natural position of the British Army was on the left of the Allied line, where it could be reinforced quickly from England. The prevention of the fall of

---

[1] The concluding paragraph of the Despatch in question does not say very much:—"Similar attacks were reported during these three days (26th, 27th and 28th September) all along the line of the Allied front, and it is certain that the enemy then made one last great effort to establish an ascendancy. He was, however, unsuccessful everywhere, and is reported to have suffered heavy losses. The same futile attempts were made all along our front up to the evening of the 28th, when they died away, and have not since been renewed."

Antwerp and the retention of the Channel Ports were other reasons of importance.

The joint plan of action agreed upon between Generals French and Joffre was briefly as follows:—The II British Corps was to arrive on the line Aire–Béthune on 11th October, to connect with the right of the Tenth French Army (then about Béthune) and pivoting on its left attack in flank the enemy who were opposing the X French Corps in front: the Cavalry to move on the northern flank of the II Corps and support the attack of the latter, until the III Corps, which was to detrain at St. Omer from the Aisne, on the 12th, should come up. The Cavalry were then to clear the front and act on the northern flank of the III Corps until the arrival of the I Corps from the Aisne. The 3rd Cavalry Division and the 7th Division, then operating in support of the Belgian Army, and assisting in the withdrawal of the latter from Antwerp, were ordered to co-operate as soon as circumstances would allow.

"In the event of these movements so far overcoming the resistance of the enemy as to enable a forward movement to be made, all the Allied Forces (were) to march in an easterly direction. The road running from Béthune to Lille was to be the dividing line between the British and French Forces, the right of the British Army being directed on Lille."

For several days from the 1st October, trench life on the Aisne, so far as it concerned the 1st Somerset L.I., was enlivened by only one incident of any importance before the Battalion marched out of the trenches on the night of the 6th/7th October.

At about 10 p.m. on the night of the 1st an N.C.O. (Cpl. Windsor), in charge of an observation post held by H (late D) Company, saw a party of about 20 Germans approaching from the north-east. The post was about 550 yards in front of the main Battalion trenches, and approximately 1,000 yards from the enemy's position. Other Germans were advancing from rear of his post and one actually fell into the communication trench. This N.C.O. waited until the enemy were within 10 yards of his post and then opened rapid fire on them. Six Germans fell dead and others were wounded, but their comrades carried them away. About an hour later another party of 50 Germans returned and opened fire on the trench from a distance of about 50 yards. Corporal Windsor and his men replied vigorously, but without being able to see the effect of his fire. In these two little encounters no losses were sustained by the Somersets.

At 12 noon on the 5th the Battalion received orders to move. A and B Companies (then in reserve) at 6.45 p.m., and H.Qs. and C and H Companies when the trenches had been handed over to the French. These orders were

subsequently cancelled and the move took place on the 6th. A and B Companies marching off to Buzancy at 7 p.m. and H.Qs. and C and H Companies at about 1 a.m. on the 7th when the French had finished taking over the front-line trenches held by the latter Companies. By the early hours of the 7th October the whole Battalion was assembled in a large cave at Buzancy.

On the 7th the III Corps[1] moved on Compiegne, having been ordered 1st Battalion to entrain at and near that town for St. Omer.   After four days' marching in 7th October stages the 1st Somersets (in Brigade and Division) reached Vannette—a suburb of Compiegne—at 10.30 p.m. on 10th and at 2.30 a.m. on the 11th the men began to entrain.   At 6 a.m. the train left Compiègne *en route* for St. Omer.

[1] The III Corps at this period consisted of the 4th and 6th Divisions but on the move of the Corps from the Aisne, the 16th Infantry Brigade of the latter Division was left behind with I Corps, and the 19th Infantry Brigade was temporarily attached to the 6th Division.

CHAPTER VIII

OF THE RESERVE, THE TERRITORIAL AND SERVICE BATTALIONS

1st and 2nd Battalions

PRIDE of Regiment has always been one of the traditions of the British Army, and during those first strenuous weeks of the War, the thoughts of all ranks of the 2nd Somerset Light Infantry— in India when war was declared—were turned to their brethren of the 1st Battalion, upon whom had fallen the honour of being the first of the Regiment to join battle with the enemy. Nor were the eyes of those left behind in England less anxiously turned across the Channel waters where the grim struggle was going none too well for Great Britain, France, and Belgium.

With far less optimism, and greater foresight than many who failed to grasp the fact that the war was bound to last a considerable period, the then Secretary of State for War—Lord Kitchener—predicting a bitter struggle of long duration, set to work to mobilize and organize the man-power of the nation. Finding that men, munitions and money would be required in enormous numbers and quantities his famous call to arms was issued. Mobilization orders to the Territorials had been issued simultaneously with those to the Regular Army, on 4th August.

4th and 5th Battalions

Although for many units of the Territorial Army, mobilization came at an awkward period, some indeed being actually on the way to their annual camp, the 4th (Lieut.-Col. W. C. Cox) and 5th (Lieut.-Col. E. F. Cooke-Hurle) Territorial Battalions of the Somerset Light Infantry were not so affected. These two Battalions had gone into camp at Bulford, Salisbury Plain, on the 26th July; they formed part of the Wessex Division. They had scarcely begun their training when the war storm burst, orders to mobilize being received during the evening of the 4th. On the following day both Battalions proceeded to Plymouth, their preliminary War Station.

26th July

4th August

Meanwhile reservists had flocked to the Colours, responding splendidly to the call to arms. From the Depôt at Taunton (under the command of Major C. G. Rawling) men were despatched in parties to the 1st Battalion, then at Colchester, on 5th, 6th and 7th August.

3rd Battalion 8th August

On the 8th the 3rd (Reserve) Somerset Light Infantry (Lieut.-Col. A. Llewellyn) was mobilized, and, accompanied by the surplus Reservists, the Battalion proceeded to its War Station—Bull Point and the surrounding Forts at Devonport.

Immediately steps were taken to bring the Battalion to a state of "Readiness for Action," either at Home or abroad. But disappointment was at hand, for shortly after arriving in Devonport orders were received that the Battalion would not proceed overseas, but (in common with almost every

LT.-COL. T. F. RITCHIE,
D.S.O.
Commanded 6th Battalion

LT.-COL. R. D. TROLLOPE-
BELLEW, D.S.O., M.C.
Commanded 6th Battalion

BRIG.-GEN. C. G.
RAWLING,
C.M.G., C.I.E.,
D.S.O.
Commanded 6th
Battalion

COL. C. J. TROYTE-BULLOCK, D.S.O.
Commanded 7th Battalion

LT.-COL. R. PRESTON-WHYTE, D.S.O.
Commanded 7th Battalion

COMMANDING OFFICERS OF THE 6TH AND 7TH BATTALIONS

other Reserve Battalion) would remain at Home as a "Draft Finding Unit." 3rd Battalion
The first draft was despatched to the 1st Battalion in France on 26th August.

In the meantime, the arrival of the Special Reserve Battalions in Plymouth on 11th August, had released the 4th and 5th Territorial Battalions, which 4th and 5th Battalions returned to Salisbury Plain to carry on training.

On 21st August the Government issued orders for the raising of the First New Army of six Divisions, popularly known as "K.1," which resulted in the formation of the 6th (Service) Battalion Somerset Light Infantry. And 6th Battalion 21st August here it is permissible to quote from the diary of a Somerset man who, early recognizing his responsibilities, though a married man, "joined up," and, like so many more gallant men, eventually made the supreme sacrifice. His diary admirably reflects the feeling in England during that first tense period of the war:—

"On August 6th I signed fresh National Reserve papers, abandoning clause enabling me to resign at any time. This was two days after the declaration of war on Germany, and though I realized the gravity of the war more than many, I at first signed for Home Defence only, as I hardly expected that Great Britain would send a great Army to the Continent, besides the Expeditionary Force of 150,000 men [1] of the Regular Army. During the fortnight which followed it was brought home to me more and more that the young unmarried men had not yet realized their duty or the extent and thoroughness of the German preparations. Accordingly, upon the National Reserve being given an opportunity of joining the New Army of 100,000 for which Lord Kitchener had asked, I enlisted with other National Reservists at Yeovil, to the total number of 54 (45 of whom were married men) with the approval of my wife. . . . I was duly attested on 26th August and proceeded next day to Taunton and from there, on 1st September, to Tournay Barracks, North Camp, Aldershot. Here we were duly formed into a platoon of the 6th (Service) Battalion of the Somerset Light Infantry and went through a course of Army reservist training, culminating, after three months, with a course of musketry laid down in peace time for Territorials." [2]

Here, for the time being it is necessary to leave the 6th Battalion (now commanded by Lieut.-Col. G. C. Rawling, transferred from command of the Depôt at Taunton) and turn to the fortunes of the 7th (Service) Battalion, 7th Battalion also formed at Aldershot from the surplus N.C.O.'s and men of the former Battalion.

The 7th was formed on 13th September, Major C. J. Troyte-Bullock, 13th September of the 2nd Battalion, then home on leave from India, taking over command. On 21st September the Battalion, now 1,200 strong, marched from Aldershot to Woking, there joining the 61st Infantry Brigade of the 20th (Light) Division (Major-General H. R. Davies).

[1] The Expeditionary Force which sailed in August for France numbered not more than 100,000, all ranks.

[2] Diary of the late Corporal F. W. Loxton, 6th Somerset L.I.

On 11th September the Government again issued orders for the raising of another New Army—the Second—of six divisions, and two days later the formation of the Third New Army, of similar strength, was authorized.

8th Battalion
October

The 8th Battalion was raised in October and began training at Leighton Buzzard. The first C.O. was Lieut.-Col. H. C. Denny.

The training of the First New Army had necessitated the absorption of large numbers of Regular, Reserve and Territorial officers and N.C.O.'s, a heavy loss, especially to the Territorial Army, which had also been authorized to raise second-line units. Of the latter, the 2/4th Battalion Somerset Light Infantry was the first of the Regiment to come into being. Briefly, the history of the raising of this Battalion is as follows:—On 30th September Colonel H. F. Clutterbuck, late of the 4th Battalion, was asked to form a second-line Battalion, of some 240 men surplus to the requirements of the 1/4th Battalion, then under orders for India. This was done and the Battalion, early in October, went into billets in Bath.

2/5th Battalion
4th October

The 2/5th was also ordered to be raised in September 1914. Lieut.-Col. J. R. Paull was appointed to command the Battalion, on 4th October. The Battalion was first billeted in Taunton.

1/4th and 1/5th
Battalions
9th October

Early in October also (the 9th was the exact date) the 1/4th and 1/5th Battalions with the Wessex Division sailed for India. The circumstances under which these Territorials were sent overseas when, with every truth in the world, it may be said they most ardently wished to go to France, were given thus in the words of their own General Officer Commanding, i.e. Major-General C. G. Donald.[1]

"Towards the end of September I received a telegram saying that Lord Kitchener wanted to see me at the War Office next day. I went to the War Office and was taken into Lord Kitchener's room, and you can imagine that I got a little bit of a shock when he said: 'I want you to take your Division to India, will they go?' You must remember that at that time the Imperial obligation did not apply to the Territorials. I said, 'Well, sir, I do not think anybody has thought much about it, but I am perfectly certain that if you want them to go to India they will go there right enough.' He replied, 'Very well, go back to your Division now, get hold of them to-morrow morning on Salisbury Plain, use your personal influence and tell them from me that I want them to go to India and that by going to India they will be performing a great Imperial duty. I have to bring white troops back from India to Europe and I must replace them there by white troops from Home.'"

There was no doubt in General Donald's mind as to what his troops would say,[2] for the West Countryman is second to none in his love of Country and Empire. Other promises were made to them, to bring them back after six months and that they should share in all the honours just as if they had gone

[1] At the Royal United Services Institution on 11th October 1922.
[2] Of the 1/4th and 1/5th Somerset Light Infantry, the number of men who volunteered was actually several hundreds in excess of the requirements.

LT.-COL. L. C. HOWARD, D.S.O.
Commanded 8th Battalion

LT.-COL. J. W. SCOTT, D.S.O.
Commanded 8th Battalion

COL. W. ALAN GILLETT, T.D., D.L.
Commanded 11th Battalion

LT.-COL. C. J. DE B. SHERINGHAM, D.S.O., M.C.
Commanded 8th Battalion

COMMANDING OFFICERS OF THE 8TH AND 11TH BATTALIONS

to France, and although force of circumstances did not permit of these promises being carried out, right loyally and faithfully did the Somerset men, with their comrades of the Wessex Division, serve their Country and Empire during their long and tedious sojourn in India.

So, on 9th October, the 1/4th and 1/5th Battalions sailed from South-ampton to Gibraltar and from the latter place to India.

CHAPTER IX

THE BATTLE OF ARMENTIÈRES:
13TH OCTOBER–2ND NOVEMBER 1914

1st Battalion
11th October

AFTER a train journey lasting nearly fifteen hours, via Amiens, Boulogne and Calais, the 1st Somerset Light Infantry arrived at St. Omer at about 8.30 p.m. on the night of 11th October. The Battalion, however, did not begin to detrain until 11 p.m., for detraining accommodation was limited. Other units of the 4th Division and III Corps had to be cleared from the station—a lengthy process—and it was 1.30 a.m. on the morning of the 12th before the Somersets marched out of the station, *en route* for Blendecques, where at 3.15 a.m. the Battalion went into billets. Throughout the 12th the III Corps concentrated in, and about, Hazebrouck, the 11th Infantry Brigade of the 4th Division moving to Hondeghem in motor-buses, though the 1st Somersets did not reach the latter place until very early on the 13th and had to march again at 10 a.m.

The 11th Infantry Brigade was in reserve to the 10th and 12th Brigades which, on the 13th October, attacked Meteren, the III Corps having been ordered to advance to the line Armentières–Wytschaete, 6th Division on the right, 4th Division on the left. As the attack of the 10th and 12th Brigades progressed, the 11th Brigade moved forward.

In a cold rain, the 1st Battalion left Hondeghem, and after a slow march, with many long halts, the Battalion moving by Caestre eventually reached Flétre, where, in a turnip field, every one drenched to the skin by the heavy rain, the 11th Brigade waited in reserve until the capture of Meteren was reported. At dusk the 1st Somersets received orders to advance just east of Flétre and form an outpost line, but apparently only C and H Companies furnished the outpost, the remaining companies billeting in a farm. The two companies on outpost duty dug hard during the night and early on the morning of the 14th the whole Battalion set to work to improve the trenches. The work was, however, unnecessary, for Bailleul, reported on the previous day as being held by strong forces of the enemy, was found to be evacuated and, at 10 a.m. the town was entered by the III Corps. The 1st Somersets, therefore, were ordered forward with the remainder of the 11th Brigade and at 11 a.m. marched out of Flétre, through Meteren to Bailleul, where the Battalion went into billets in the Lunatic Asylum about 9 p.m. On the night of the 14th the III Corps occupied the line St. Jans Cappel–Bailleul.

15th October

On the morning of the 15th the III Corps received orders to make good the line of the Lys from Armentières to Sailly.

After a good night's rest—and the Battalion was much in need of it— the Somersets moved out of Bailleul at 12 noon to a point about a mile east of

the town, in support of the East Lancs.   All day long the men rested by the
roadside and at 4.30 p.m. marched off back towards Bailleul, but before they
could reach the town a message was received ordering the Battalion to move
immediately to the cross-roads, 400 yards north of Rabot on the Nieppe Road.
Having arrived at the cross-roads, fresh orders were issued about 6.30 p.m.
by the G.O.C., 11th Brigade; the Hants, supported by the E. Lancs, were
to attack and capture Nieppe; the 1st Somersets, supported by the Rifle
Brigade, were to endeavour to get across the bridge over the Lys at Erquinghem,
or, failing that, to dig in north of the bridge.   The latter column was under
the command of Major Prowse.

At 11 p.m. the 1st Somersets advanced, followed in the order given by
the Rifle Brigade, the Machine-Gun Section, 2 S.A.A. carts, 4 tool carts and
the 7th Coy., R.E.   But no opposition was encountered, a patrol of Somerset
men, under Lieutenant Bush, having found the bridge at Erquinghem intact,
but cleverly prepared for defence.   About 2.30 a.m. on the 16th, however,
a Brigade staff officer arrived and stated that orders had been received from
III Corps H.Qs. that the bridge was not to be crossed that night.   C and B
Companies of the Battalion therefore took up an outpost line Halte–Menegates,
whilst A and H Companies remained in support about the level crossing,
600 yards N.W. of the Halte.   During the evening of the 16th the line was
pushed forward to the line L'Hallobeau–Les 3 Tilleurs.   A and H Companies
relieving C and B Companies in the front line.

But although the III Corps was still engaged in driving the enemy back
on Lille, the next four days, from the Regimental point of view, were uneventful.
On 17th the Battalion rested in billets; on 18th the 11th Brigade, being still
in reserve, the Battalion marched forward through Nieppe to Armentières,
bivouacking for the night in the railway station.   On the following morning
the Somerset men moved out of the station to a linen factory on the river Lys.
About 1 p.m. on 20th the Battalion received orders to move at once to Pont
de Nieppe, where, on arriving, further orders came to hand to march to Ploegsteert (soon to be popularized as "Plugstreet") and report to Lieut.-Col.
Anley, temporarily commanding the 12th Brigade.   Here the Battalion (still
in reserve) billeted for the night, companies being much scattered, although
ordered to be prepared to move at 15 minutes' notice.   For at this period
the centre of the British line, i.e. the III and Cavalry Corps, were being heavily
pressed by the enemy in ever-increasing force.

The official despatches stated that

"On the 20th October advanced posts of the 12th Brigade of the 4th
Division, III Corps, were forced to retire, and at dusk it was evident that the
Germans were likely to make a determined attack.   This ended in the occupa-
tion of Le Gheer by the enemy."

The next paragraph in the despatch reported that

"As the position of the Cavalry at St. Yves was thus endangered, a counter-attack was decided upon and planned by General Hunter-Weston and Lieut.-Colonel Anley. This proved entirely successful, the Germans being driven back with great loss and the abandoned trenches re-occupied. Two hundred prisoners were taken and about forty of our prisoners released."

Now, the important point about the above is that no mention is made in the despatch of the 1st Somerset Light Infantry, though the Battalion, in a splendid counter-attack worthy of the highest traditions of the Regiment, recaptured from the Germans the village of Le Gheer, taking a large number of prisoners; indeed, as an officer of the Battalion said, "it was a brilliant day for the Regiment."

It will be remembered that on the night 20th/21st October the 1st Somersets, after reporting to the 12th Brigade, had billeted in Ploegsteert, and, although warned that they would probably have to march at 15 minutes' notice, no orders to move were received. At 4.30 a.m., however, the Battalion moved out of the village to Point 63, about 1 mile N. of Ploegsteert. Much rain had fallen during the night and the going was heavy, but having arrived at Point 63 the C.O. and Company Commanders set out to reconnoitre the ground towards Wulverghem. In their absence an order was received at 8 a.m. for the Battalion to move at once to the road junction near the Chateau. The senior officer then with the Battalion was the Adjutant, and the company commanders were all second-lieutenants. The Battalion had already moved off when it was met by General Hunter-Weston, who ordered the 1st Somersets to counter-attack Le Gheer, which had been occupied by the Germans at dawn, they having driven the Inniskilling Fusiliers out of the village. The loss of Le Gheer uncovered the flank of the line running about 200 yards E. of the Bois de Ploegsteert, occupied by the Cavalry, who were thus enfiladed. They were, however, hanging on with great gallantry, though losing heavily.

As General Hunter-Weston was issuing his orders, the C.O., the second-in-command and the company commanders of the 1st Somersets appeared. The Battalion now moved off through St. Yves to the N.E. corner of "Plug-street" Wood, where companies were drawn up for the attack. A Company (Capt. A. H. Yatman) supported by B (Capt. L. A. Jones-Mortimer) was to lead the advance through the eastern edge of the wood and attack the Le Gheer cross-roads and clear the village. C Company (Capt. F. S. Bradshaw) and H Company were kept in support. Bn. H.Qs. were in an estaminet, on the eastern edge of the wood.

By 10.50 a.m. A Company had reached the Le Gheer cross-roads, with B in support in the S.E. corner of the wood; a company of the East Lancs R. lined the southern exits. The attack was then launched. There are no details of the charge which followed, and the following extract from Lieut.-Colonel Watson's private diary gives the only information available. "I am told that the way A Company, followed by B Company, cleared the Saxons out of Le Gheer at the point of the bayonet, was a sight never to be forgotten." By 11.45 a.m. Captain Yatman's company was fighting its way through the village, whilst Captain Jones-Mortimer, with his company, had reached the cross-roads. As A forced its way through the village each house was surrounded whilst two men entered and made a thorough search of the premises. This method was carried out systematically, until by 12.55 p.m. Le Gheer had been cleared of the enemy and the southern and eastern edges held. A Company had captured 101 prisoners and had also released 2 officers and 40 men of the Inniskilling Fusiliers, taken by the Germans in the early morning.

This brilliant little affair, the first bayonet charge made by the 1st Bn. Somerset Light Infantry since its arrival in France, drew immediate and well-earned congratulations, first from the G.O.C., 11th Infantry Brigade (General Hunter-Weston), and later from the C.-in-C. himself. The former wrote:—

"Well done. I can always be sure that a task allotted to you will be well carried out aaa G.O.C., 2nd Cavalry Division, wishes me to express to you his appreciation of the way in which you have restored the dangerous situation on his right. Good old Somersets!"

As soon as the Somersets had captured the village and cut off the retreat of the Germans, some Inniskilling Fusiliers advanced from the west, and the East Lancs charged out of the wood to the south. The enemy was completely bewildered and ran about in all directions, during which more prisoners were captured.

It soon became evident, however, that the enemy was not going to take his defeat lying down. About 1.20 p.m. he launched a strong counter-attack from the south and south-east against Le Gheer, and Captain Yatman, after reporting that he might have to retire his company (A) to the edge of "Plugstreet" Wood, asked for reinforcements. All that could be sent to him were two platoons of C Company, for the Adjutant having asked Brigade H.Qs. for further assistance, was told that no more troops were available. With the two platoons, A Company held grimly to the line and repulsed all efforts to turn them out of the village.[1]

At 5.15 p.m. the Somersets were ordered to take over the line from Le Gheer to St. Yves, held by the 12th Infantry Brigade and 2nd Cavalry Brigade. The two brigades were relieved by C and H Companies of the Battalion at about 6.30 p.m., and A and B Companies moved into billets in St. Yves.

Casualties throughout the day, considering the nature of the fighting carried out by the Battalion, had been extraordinarily light; one officer (Lieut. Vincent) was wounded, seven other ranks were killed and nineteen wounded.

The operations in which the 1st Somersets were engaged formed part of the stubborn and heavy fighting against superior forces of the enemy, which the III Corps had to endure from 20th October to the early days of November. Two major operations—the Battle of Ypres, 1914, and the Battle of Armentières—were carried on simultaneously, the efforts of the enemy being turned

---

[1] Lce.-Cpl. J. S. Bowdidge was awarded the D.C.M. for skill and gallantry in house-to-house fighting at Le Gheer on 21st October.

especially to breaking through the British line about Ypres to Calais. Then both Wytschaete and Messines, south of Ypres, were also heavily attacked and the line held by the Somersets from Le Gheer to St. Yves on the night of 21st October was of vital importance, seeing that it was a portion of the British line from the western banks of the Lys, opposite Frélinghien to Messines, which had to be defended to the utmost extremity, for if it gave way there were possibilities of the enemy outflanking Armentières from the north.

The night of the 21st October passed quietly. Early on the 22nd A and B Companies of the Battalion moved to near the Chateau north of "Plug-street" Wood, Bn. H.Qs. moving to an estaminet in St. Yves. About 10 a.m. St. Yves was heavily shelled and almost immediately the estaminet became a mass of ruins. It was providential that when the shells burst on the building Bn. H.Qs. staff was outside and no one was hurt. H.Qs. then moved into a cellar of another house. During the afternoon the enemy again deluged St. Yves with shells, which arrived in quick succession, tearing gaps in the houses and flinging bricks and mortar in all directions. Officers and men of Bn. H.Qs. took shelter in bomb-proofs, constructed during the previous night, the former behind a wood stack. And it was not long before they had reason to congratulate themselves, for the house selected as new Bn. H.Qs. was utterly demolished, being hit by large shells shortly after a move had been made from the cellar to the wood stack. About 2 p.m. orders had been received for A and B Companies to take over the line from St. Yves to the river Douve, after dark, from the Hants R. The relief was duly carried out, all four companies of the Somersets being now in the front line from Le Gheer to the Douve. C Company, on the right of the line, was holding Le Gheer village, with H on the left of C. A and B followed in that order with the left of B on the river Douve. Bn. H.Qs. had found fresh billets in a house at the western exits of St. Yves.

All companies took advantage of the quiet night which followed to repair their trenches, while a bomb-proof was dug for Bn. H.Qs. near its present house. Another officer—2/Lieut. Glossop—was wounded on the 23rd, but otherwise the enemy's guns were almost inactive. Heavy firing broke out during the night 23rd/24th, but no hostile attack was made and all four companies remained in their positions. The 24th was a day of sniping, but little artillery fire. It was becoming increasingly dangerous to move about in the open during the day, for the enemy's snipers were cunningly concealed and seemed to be everywhere, and the Saxons were good shots. The West Countrymen, however, soon showed the Germans that sniping was a game at which two could play, and as a consequence the enemy became more respectful.

About 3 p.m. on the afternoon of the 25th the enemy's guns again pounded the British line and St. Yves came in for the usual attention. Houses were burned or blown to bits and ruin piled on ruin, but the Divisional guns soon replied and the men in the front-line trenches saw, with intense satisfaction, farms and houses and suspected machine-gun and snipers' posts "go up" and disappear in a dirty cloud of bricks and mortar and mud. There was even joy—unholy joy—as the mangled bodies of Germans were flung into the air, as so much refuse tossed on to a rubbish heap.   For war had become a ferocious and terrible business, shorn of its one-time chivalry; "to kill the enemy" was the intention of both sides.

All that night rain fell heavily and for the first time the Diary of the 1st Somersets records that the trenches were "absolute quagmires."   With mud and filth on all sides, little wonder the rifles became clogged, as the men standing over ankle-deep in water and wet to the skin beat off a German attack cursing the while because some of their rifles refused to work, the breech-blocks being choked with grit.   The 26th was a quiet day.   The 27th saw the arrival of further reinforcements of officers and men; they were very welcome.   On the 28th, after a week—the worst by far spent by the Battalion—relief came, the Hants R. taking over the trenches held by the Somersets, the latter moving back into reserve near the Chateau, north of "Plugstreet" Wood.   And here, it is interesting to note from the Battalion Diary the manner in which this first relief was carried out:—"Company commanders and platoon representatives of our companies met corresponding parties of Hants in rear of the line.   Platoon representatives took Hants representatives to their trenches and explained the situation, targets, etc.   The Hants representatives then brought up their platoons at short intervals and our platoons moved independently to company rendezvous and thence back to their new quarters." The relief took about 2½ hours.

A and B Companies now held the second line of trenches, east and west of the Messines–Ploegsteert road, north of Point 63; C and H Companies were in Ploegsteert Wood 300 yards S.W. of the Chateau.   Bn. H.Qs. were in an estaminet on the road also south of the Chateau.

The 29th was a quiet day, so quiet indeed that it aroused suspicion. About Messines, and north of that village, heavy fighting had been going on all day, though in the neighbourhood of "Plugstreet" all was quiet.   "The most peaceful day for a long time.   Fear it may be the calm before the storm," records the diary of the 1st Battalion.   And not without justification, for in the evening a heavy attack was launched by the enemy against Le Gheer, though it was beaten off by the East Lancs, who pluckily held their ground.

At 7 o'clock on the morning of 30th October the enemy's artillery opened a heavy bombardment of all the 11th Brigade trenches between the Warnave and Douve Rivers.   Throughout the day until 3 p.m. the German guns continued to pour shells on to the positions held by the devoted infantry— General Hunter-Weston's Brigade.   In the morning the Adjutant of the 1st Somersets was sent to Headquarters of the East Lancs, at Le Gheer, to make arrangements for the Battalion to take over the trenches of the latter at night, but owing to the heavy hostile bombardment, the probability of a general attack on, and the very dangerous approaches to, the village, the relief was cancelled.

About midday messages from the Hants R. at St. Yves were received at Battalion H.Qs. of the Somerset Light Infantry, stating that the Germans were massing in front of the trenches of the Hampshiremen. At 3.30 p.m. the latter reported the situation as critical, for the Germans had worked forward to within 300 yards, and already one platoon had been annihilated and its trenches destroyed by shell fire. Under the orders of the G.O.C., 11th Brigade, not more than half a company of the Somersets had been despatched to the cross-roads at "Plugstreet" in reserve to the right flank. These two platoons were, however, withdrawn by the G.O.C. on account of the critical situation at St. Yves.

A Company of the 1st Somersets had been detailed to furnish the reinforcements for C Company of the Hants, and 2/Lt. Braithwaite's platoon arrived in the trenches of the latter battalion just as the enemy broke through the line where the platoon of Hampshiremen had been wiped out. This trench was in a sunken road, across which the enemy was pouring in considerable strength. A barricade was hastily thrown up by the Somersets and from behind this 2/Lt. Braithwaite's men[1] inflicted great slaughter on the Germans. At 4.45 p.m. the enemy was still pouring into the trench and attacking the barricade, making frantic efforts to overwhelm the Somersets and Hampshiremen, who, firing steadily and with great precision, took heavy toll of the Germans. As the O.C. Hants R. still reported the situation as critical, the remainder of A Company of the 1st Somersets was sent up, at 5.15 p.m., to strengthen the line.

At 5.30 p.m., as the result of a message from G.O.C., 11th Brigade, Major Prowse (commanding 1st Somerset L.I.) visited the C.O. of the Hants and suggested a counter-attack by night. He then personally reconnoitred the ground over which the attack was to take place and found the Germans in possession of the trench previously held by the ill-fated platoon of Hampshiremen, and also holding some buildings in the neighbourhood. The C.O.'s of both Battalions then arranged that two companies of the 1st Somersets should surround the houses and trench and attack with the bayonet. C and H Companies were detailed as the attacking companies, whilst A and B Companies held a line behind the Hampshiremen, supporting the latter. The Divisional Cyclist Company, the Divisional Signallers and one company of R. Inniskilling Fusiliers were also sent up to Major Prowse, as supports, and were utilized to hold a third line.

At 12.30 a.m. on the 31st C and H Companies moved up to a spot about 400 yards in rear of the buildings to be attacked and Major Prowse personally took the officers forward and explained the scheme of operations. Then, split up into small parties, each given a definite locality, H Company moved forward to the attack. One by one the buildings were surrounded and searched, but no Germans were found in any of them. C Company immediately moved into the trench previously held by C Company of the Hants. Many German dead littered the ground and here and there the bodies of British soldiers were

---

[1] Both Lieut. Braithwaite and Sergt. C. Wilcox behaved in a very gallant manner on this occasion and undoubtedly saved the situation. The former was awarded the Military Cross and mentioned in despatches, and the latter the D.C.M. for his work on this occasion and on the 21st October.

found.   The trench, once held by the platoon of Hampshiremen, was full of dead bodies of the latter, only one survivor, seriously wounded, lay among them.   Neither company sustained any casualty and, at 4 a.m., on C Company occupying the trench, H, A and B Companies returned to quarters.

Although a bloodless victory, this little affair reflected great credit upon the Somerset Light Infantry, the episode being mentioned in Sir John French's despatches:—

"On the evening of the 30th the line of the 11th Infantry Brigade in the neighbourhood of St. Yves was broken.   A counter-attack carried out by Major Prowse with the Somerset Light Infantry restored the situation.   For his services on this occasion this officer was recommended for special award." [1]

The 31st October was the date upon which the Germans, in overwhelming numbers supported by a huge concentration of artillery, made particularly violent attempts, at Gheluvelt, to break a way through to Ypres, and as far south as Messines and the British trenches north and south of it, shells of all calibres deluged the thinly held line.   In spite, however, of the terrific gruelling to which it was subjected, the III Corps clung to its positions and drove off the enemy's infantry.

C Company of the 1st Somersets had a bad time and suffered heavily. The Battalion Diary gives few details, but a private diary thus describes more fully the events of that truly awful day:—

"We expected that we should get a good gruelling next day (31st) and we did.   The beauties of dawn have never appealed to me; on this particular occasion they were particularly unattractive.   Dead Saxons were lying close to the front of the trenches and some were actually on the road behind the support's dug-outs.   This particular section was considered the worst in the line.   It was situated on high ground, the possession of which would dominate the village of St. Yves and the Ploegsteert Wood and was, consequently, a particular objective of the enemy's heavy artillery, variety known as 'Jack Johnsons' and 'Coal-boxes.'   At the moment C Company occupied these trenches they possessed the following grave disadvantages from a defensive point of view.   Three platoons only could be accommodated in continuous line; one platoon on the left was isolated by 150 yards from the right of the next group of trenches, held by a company of the Hampshire Regiment. This isolated trench, capable of holding one platoon, had been captured the evening before C Company took it over (the circumstances have already been related).   No. 11 Platoon, under 2/Lieut. C. C. Ford, occupied this isolated trench at 5 a.m.   From 7.30 a.m. until dusk the whole line of trenches underwent a heavy shell fire. . . .   At about 8 p.m. the enemy's infantry advanced in skirmishing order, making short rushes on the most approved Aldershot pattern.   'Charles' (2/Lieut. Ford) sends for reinforcements.   An inspection of his trench shows that it is not feasible to place more men there.   He has

[1] Promoted to be Lieut.-Colonel.

already suffered considerable losses. Two sergeants—Sgt. Iliffe and Sgt. Chapman—had been badly wounded. Two machine guns and two sections are available in reserve. These are moved out and placed in a convenient ditch and so fill the gap between 'Charles' and the right of the Hampshire Regiment. This has the desired effect. Machine gun fires diagonally across front. Saxon attack withers away. H Company relieves C Company about 9 p.m., who retire to shelter in a corner of Ploegsteert Wood."

During the afternoon both Captains Jones-Mortimer and Smith had been wounded by a high-explosive shell, and Lieut. Bradshaw was left in command of A Company and 2/Lt. Chichester in charge of B. These two companies were now on the line, Bridge over Douve River–Chateau–Messines Road–St. Yves. B Company dug fire trenches during the night at the end of this line near St. Yves.[1]

In the early hours of 1st November the enemy attacked and broke into a trench about 600 yards N.E. of St. Yves, and 2 sections of B Company were lent to the O.C. Hants R. to recapture it. The counter-attack failed with heavy casualties. At daybreak, however, the Germans had evacuated the trench, which was reoccupied by the Hants R. During the night a platoon of A Company of the Somersets, under Lieut. Bush, had also been sent up to reinforce the left company of the Hants on the river Douve. Lieut. Bush was wounded.

On the 1st November, owing to the fall of Messines, a readjustment of the line, to take place during the night of 1st/2nd November, was decided upon.

Heavy shelling characterized the first day of November, the 1st Somersets sustaining many casualties. The trenches dug by B Company during the preceding night came in for special attention. About 12 noon Lieut. Chichester and one of his men were buried beneath the parapet of the trench and were dug out only just in time by the Battalion Medical Officer—Lieut. Waddy—who happened to be in the trenches attending to the wounded men. Unfortunately the man who was buried with Lieut. Chichester died from suffocation. During the afternoon H Company received a gruelling from the enemy's guns. Lieut. Montgomery was wounded, 4 other ranks were killed and 12 were wounded. The trench was held, but only with great difficulty.

At dusk arrangements made for readjusting the line began to materialize. A Company of the Lancashire Fusiliers dug front trenches just north of St. Yves, facing N.E. About 12 midnight these were completed and were occupied by A Company, 1st Somersets; H Company remained in its present position; C Company dug itself in around the farm some 500 yards N.W. of St. Yves, facing north-east. B Company of the Somersets was in reserve just west of St. Yves and Bn. H.Qs. remained at the estaminet, 300 yards south of the Chateau. The Hants R. held the line from St. Yves to Le Gheer, on the right of H Company, Somersets. The Inniskilling Fusiliers held from C Company's farm to the river Douve, west of the Ploegsteert–Messines Road.

[1] Lance-Cpl. F. Newberry was awarded the D.C.M. for gallantry during the 31st October.

The Lancashire Fusiliers remained in Brigade Reserve.

The new position held by the Somersets was no sinecure. It faced east, north-east and north, and was therefore, in fact, open to enfilade fire. This became apparent during the 2nd November, when both H and A Companies' trenches were heavily shelled by hostile heavy guns, one of the former and two of the latter companies' trenches being enfiladed from the east. Lieut. Bradshaw was wounded on this day, but although the Battalion Diary records that "Both this Battalion and the Hants suffered very heavily," no other details of casualties are given. At 6.30 p.m., however, the Hants and Somersets were relieved by the Worcesters and Lancashire Fusiliers respectively. The Somersets then (at about 9 p.m.) moved back to the wood on the southern slopes of Point 63.

Thus, so far as it concerned the 1st Somerset Light Infantry, ended the Battle of Armentières, the first major operation in which the Battalion took part since its transfer from the Aisne; and right worthily did it uphold the honour of the Regiment. No less than 6 officers (including Major Prowse, who was promoted to the rank of Lieut.-Colonel), five N.C.O.'s and two privates were mentioned in despatches for their distinguished conduct during the Battle.

CHAPTER X

TRENCH WARFARE

FROM 3rd November 1914 until the Battle of Ypres, 1915, which began on 22nd April, the 1st Somerset Light Infantry was not engaged in any action of importance. Yet the period which intervened between the two dates—nearly six months—was one of extreme discomfort; a period in which men grew old in a single night, so terrible were the conditions of life in the trenches, during that first winter of the War. For, as may be read elsewhere, the Allied plan to turn the German right wing and drive the enemy back through Belgium had failed; similarly the enemy was baulked in his intentions to turn the left flank of the Allies, whilst his final attempt (on 11th November) to smash a way through to Ypres broke down after his troops had been bloodily repulsed and great slaughter inflicted upon them.

In 1914 trench warfare was still in its infancy. The elaborate defence systems, which came into being as the War progressed, were literally non-existent during the first winter. The trenches, often dug of necessity in soft ground, were vastly different from the scientific constructions in which men lived and fought in later periods. Some of them were mere excavations in the ground, the earth thrown up to form the parapet, behind which men crouched and watched the enemy. Sandbags were scarce and men were often shot through the parapet, the bullet first penetrating the soft earth.

There were no trench-boards to walk upon, and dug-outs were primitive in construction. In front of the trenches the barbed-wire entanglements were of a simple character, not the formidable mazes of later years through which men had to force their way unless artillery fire had torn great gaps in them. Everything was of the most primitive description; there were no trench mortars, and hand and rifle grenades were only just being thought about. In the British Army high explosive was only used late in October for experimental purposes, whilst ordinary ammunition for the artillery was already running short. In fact all the disadvantages of having to begin an entirely new method of warfare (or some might say resuscitate old methods) were experienced by the Allies, though the Germans, having made careful preparations for the War and foreseeing the probability of trench warfare, had provided themselves with suitable howitzers of small and large calibre, as well as with hand grenades and rifle grenades for close trench fighting.

Since the 25th October, on which date the Battalion Diary recorded that the trenches were "absolute quagmires," conditions had grown steadily worse. On that date the water and mud were ankle-deep in the front lines; by the beginning of November the trenches, in places, were knee-deep in slime and filth. The stench from dead bodies, often partially buried in the spongy, 1st Battalion slimy ground, just as they had fallen, was awful. Unwashed, caked with mud, clothes sodden, but clinging to, and fighting with a wonderful tenacity for every inch of ground won, the British soldier, aching with rheumatism and the early symptoms of trench-feet, verminous and generally in a deplorable condition, held the line with a degree of stanchness, determination and cheerfulness of spirit, never surpassed in the whole glorious history of the Army.

As already stated, the 1st Somersets bivouacked in a wood on the southern slopes of Point 63 about 9 p.m. on the night of 2nd November. Heavy shelling on the morning of the 3rd cleared the Battalion out of its bivouacs and a move was made to about 300 yards south of the former position, where the remainder of the day and the night of the 3rd/4th were spent in quietude. The 4th was a typical raw November day and although 400 men of the Battalion were hard at work digging a second line of trenches and managed to keep themselves warm, the night was wretched in the extreme. It rained, and sleeping out of doors in a wet wood, the men, many of whom were racked with rheumatism, passed a miserable night. Again on the 5th the Somersets were heavily shelled, one man being killed and three wounded in A Company. A portion of the Divisional Artillery had come into action along the southern slopes of Point 63 and the enemy's artillery was obviously searching for the British guns.

On the 6th the Battalion again went into the front line, relieving the 6th November Lancashire Fusiliers in trenches N.W. of St. Yves. The night was foggy, which was fortunate, as the German front line was only a hundred yards away. A Company was on the right, C in the centre and B on the left, with H in reserve. After a heavy bombardment, which began at 5 a.m. on the 7th, the enemy (under cover of a thick mist) launched two battalions against the line from St. Yves southwards to Le Gheer and eventually broke through, occupying some trenches and a number of houses.[1] A counter-attack by the East Lancashires and Inniskilling Fusiliers failed. The Somerset men were not engaged, though A Company again suffered casualties—3 men killed and 5 wounded—from the enemy's shell fire, after which H Company relieved A. The enemy was now on the eastern edge of "Plugstreet" Wood. An officer and 50 men of the Royal Scots Fusiliers were then sent up to guard the exits from the N.E. corner of the Wood; they were disposed along the southern edge of St. Yves village.

The 10th was a bad day for B Company. The enemy's shell fire smashed the trenches of the Company, which lost 4 killed and 16 wounded. Amongst the killed was Sergeant Willcox, who had recently been mentioned in despatches. The Company was not, however, relieved, as the Germans had brought up a Bavarian Division to Warneton and a heavy attack was expected. A hundred men of the R.S. Fusiliers (all that was left of the gallant Battalion) were sent up to support the Somerset men, and were disposed behind the right trench

---

[1] In these operations Sergt. F. Harris specially distinguished himself by digging out four men who had been buried during the bombardment, by the explosion of a shell.

of the latter, in trenches running N. and S. on the N. of St. Yves. About 7 p.m. the Messines road below the Chateau was heavily shelled whilst supplies were being issued and the wounded evacuated, and two stretcher-bearers of the Somersets were killed.

From the Battalion Diary, it is evident that the 11th, the day on which the great Prussian Guard attack was taking place east of Ypres (the final German effort to break through to the coastal towns of Belgium and France), was a quiet day for the Battalion, a welcome change from the restless activity which had been going on almost without cessation since October. Indeed the records for the remainder of November and the first fortnight of December are mainly concerned with the terrible conditions prevailing in the trenches, inter-battalion reliefs, the brief periods spent in billets out of the front line and various other matters of small interest. It is necessary, however, to describe in somewhat close detail the life led by officers and men during those early months of trench warfare, before the line became stabilized.

The Lys River ran through country practically sea-level, therefore very low-lying. Numerous small tributaries branched in all directions from the main waterway, intersecting the country, and in many places forming boggy or marshy ground which in winter time became waterlogged. Quite half of the Bois de Plugsteert (the southern half) was on sea-level, but the northern portion was on slightly higher ground, rising gradually to Point 63, which had become a familiar spot in the sector held by the 1st Somersets. The line held by the Battalion, however, about St. Yves, lay between two small tributaries of the Lys, the Warnave on the south and the Douve on the north. Thus it was not to be wondered at that when the winter rains began the country-side generally became sodden and the digging of trenches and dug-outs, without the necessary means of draining them, became an almost hopeless task. Moreover, the ground in the neighbourhood of the trenches was pock-marked with gaping shell holes, into which water trickled, forming nauseous pools in which the mangled remains of friend and foe lay rotting, poisoning the air with sickening odours.

The terrible condition of the battlefield made attacks by both sides, at all times, difficult:—

"The deadly accuracy, range and quick-firing capabilities of the modern rifle and machine gun require that a fire-swept zone be crossed in the shortest possible space of time by attacking troops. But if men are detained under the enemy's fire by the difficulty of emerging from a water-logged trench, and by the necessity of passing over ground knee-deep in holding mud and slush, such attacks become practically prohibitive owing to the losses they entail."[1]

For hours on end men had to stand in trenches, often three feet deep in water, with a gale of wind blowing and in a driving rain, wet to the skin, shivering and shaking from cold and worn with fatigue. How they endured was

[1] Official despatches.

one of the marvels of the War. What was even more wonderful was the cheerfulness with which they "carried on" under such ghastly conditions.

The night of the 13th November was typical of the life the Somersets lived at that period. Rain had fallen hard all day when, at night, the Rifle Brigade arrived to relieve the Battalion. After standing and living in trenches thick in mud and deep in water, the Somerset men handed over to the Rifles and then began the move back to trenches in "Plugstreet" Wood. For hours on end this seemingly easy task went on. The rides through the Wood, the only possible way back to the support trenches, were *three feet deep in mud*, through which men floundered and struggled in the darkness to reach their destination.

It was 5.30 a.m. on the 14th before the relief was completed, and the support trenches were little better than those in the front line. Then came the question of getting up supplies. These had to be man-handled through the Wood, through the mud and slush and filth. The 15th was a day similar to the 13th, heavy rain falling. "Very wretched," records the Battalion Diary, "for men in the trenches, which are mostly half full of water."

The Battalion again took over the front-line trenches on the 16th (on the eastern edge of "Plugstreet" Wood), and that night it fell to the lot of B Company to man-handle the supplies up to the line, "from the house at 9th Milestone to our Headquarters, through heavy mud. This work occupied about 12 hours and was a great strain on the men." On the 18th hard frost set in. This was the day on which Captain Campbell, O.C. A Company, was wounded, handing over command to Lieutenant Whittock. But the latter also was wounded on the following day and Lieutenant Prideaux took command of A Company. Snow fell on the 19th, but with a hard frost to keep the mud down life became slightly more comfortable.

The 22nd November was a day of importance at that period, for H Company marched into Pont de Nieppe "to wash under Divisional arrangements," the other companies following in turn. "The scheme is," said the Battalion Diary, "that they move into billets at Pont de Nieppe one night, wash the next day and are provided with clean clothing. After washing they move to a clean set of billets at Armentières and return to supporting trenches the third day." The hot bath, followed by an opportunity of changing their verminous, muddy and often blood-stained clothing for a clean outfit, was hailed with delight by the men.[1]

---

[1] *Nov. 29th.* At 7.30 a.m. the company marched to a large linen factory, which had been rigged up as a washing place. The men marched into a big warehouse, where they took off their service dress (coats and trousers), tied them together with their identity disc and put them on a red barrow, which was then taken to the fumigator. They then were marched into the bleaching room, where there were 15 large vats of hot water ready. Here they took off all their clothes—which were boiled in disinfectant—were supplied with soap and towel and had a thoroughly good wash, ten men in a vat with as much hot water as they want. After they have dried themselves they are supplied with fresh underclothing, shirt, socks, pants, and a vest. When they have put on these they go into the warehouse again, when the service dress is brought in on white barrows, having been disinfected and ironed. A large number of women are employed, who iron the service dress and the disinfected

On the last day of November, a change was made in the period of time spent in the front-line trenches and in support, each company being six days in the former and three in the latter; it was a change much appreciated.

Apart from general conditions in the trenches, sniping was perhaps the most deadly of all the trying experiences through which the men passed.

In portions of the line the enemy's trenches were only 150 yards away and his snipers, with telescopic sights fixed to their rifles, waited and watched day and night for a chance shot at officers and men who unwarily exposed their heads or any part of their bodies above the parapets of the trenches. The utmost caution was necessary when moving about, a minute's forgetfulness to "keep down" and there was a sharp crack, followed generally by the thud of a falling body.   Trees, bushes, the tumbled ruins of houses and cottages, all provided cover for snipers.   Of course the Battalion's marksmen were as busily engaged in this deadly work as were the Germans and the latter very soon realized that the British soldier knew one thing at least, and that *perfectly*, the use of the rifle.   But many gallant officers and men fell to a sniper's bullet.

On 1st December another party of reinforcements arrived.   Wastage in killed and wounded and from sickness was considerable and constant arrivals to fill the gaps are recorded in the Battalion Diary.   It is recorded also that on the 2nd December, H.M. King George inspected H Company of the 1st Somersets at Nieppe.   For several weeks Territorial troops of the London Rifle Brigade had been attached to the Battalion.   The Londoners were keen fellows and gave their comrades of the Regular Army much assistance and the two Battalions soon became firm friends.

All the hard work put in on the trenches during November seems to have been of no avail in keeping down the water and mud, for conditions in the line were apparently worse during December.   Two extracts from the Battalion Diary will suffice to give an impression of life at that period.   The first is dated 6th December:—

"Quite a fine morning.   Bright sun.   Got cloudy in afternoon and by 5 p.m. was raining hard again.   Sent an urgent message this evening for a force pump for our right trench which is knee-deep in water, though the dug-outs are fairly dry.   This pump came during the night and was carried up with great labour.   Very dark night.   Coy. Q.M.S. Ricketts was killed after taking out rations to H Company in left trench to-night."

The second extract is dated 7th:—

"Trenches in a very bad state after last night's rain.   Continual pumping and bailing does not suffice to keep the water down.   The right platoon of left trench (H Company) has withdrawn to-day into Ploegsteert Wood, as their trench is knee-deep in water.   It will only be occupied at night in future.

underclothing (if it is worth it) and mend it ready to be issued out to somebody else.   The whole company of about 170 men were washed in about an hour and a quarter."   Extract from a letter by the late Lieut. G. R. Parr, 1st Somerset Light Infantry.

The gap caused by this trench not being held is filled in with barbed wire and 1st Battalion a barricade of sandbags is being erected across the road at N.E. corner of Wood. 7th December It rained hard all day to-day, driving in heavily from the S.W.   Wind rose to a gale in the evening.   Very wet night and very dark."

And to make matters worse, the pump broke down the following day, and when application was made for another, none were available!

CHAPTER XI

"THERE IS NO CHANGE IN THE SITUATION"

"It was one of those gallant and unrecorded feats of arms, performed with almost superhuman courage, and entailing the loss of many valuable lives, of which this war (where ground had to be gained from the enemy almost foot by foot) affords so many examples. But the heroism of the men who took part in it will never be forgotten by their comrades and the names of those who fell in it will be held in affectionate remembrance, honoured for all time by the Regiment to which they belonged."

From the Memoir of GEORGE ROWORTH PARR.

1st Battalion

THE phrase which forms the title of this chapter has been selected because it typifies the kind of official communiqué so often issued during the early months of the War, before the British Public had learnt to take the reports at their full value and understand that behind that cold sentence lay a world of suffering and agonizing horror; that even as the words were issued from G.H.Q., men were dying in the trenches from horrible wounds, or already lay dead, torn and mangled by shell fire or pierced through and through by rifle bullets; or, that in giving their brave lives for England, they had done so in deeds which deserved to be shouted from the hilltops, instead of being hidden behind the cryptic phrase—"There is no change in the situation."

10th December

On the 10th December there was disappointment in the Mess of the 1st Somerset Light Infantry. All officers who were to have gone on leave to England on the 11th, were suddenly summoned to Brigade H.Qs. and were there informed, under the strictest secrecy, that they could not go. No reason was given them; they were just told that their leave had been stopped.

Two days later the reason became known. At a C.O.'s Conference, held on 12th, the G.O.C. informed all Commanding Officers that a general advance of the Allies was contemplated; that the 1st Somersets and the Hants Regiments were to prepare to carry out an attack against the enemy who had penetrated the line east of "Plugstreet" Wood; that wire mattresses of rabbit-wire and straw, which would enable the men to cross the German wire, were to be constructed and that the British wire was also to be cut to allow the passage of the attacking troops through it.

Late that night A Company of the Somersets reconnoitred No Man's Land out in front of the trenches. The German trenches were found weakly held, but the ground over which the attack was to take place was broken and almost impassable. On all sides were gaping shell holes, full of water, and thick slimy mud which clung to and held the reconnoitring party as they floundered through it.

Unobserved and unmolested by rifle or machine-gun fire the party found it difficult enough to cross and re-cross No Man's Land—what would it be 1st Battalion like under a galling fire?

At another conference on 13th the Rifle Brigade (presumably in place of 13th December the Hants R.) was selected for the attack, and for the first time the Diary of the 1st Somersets mentions the objective—"The Birdcage"[1]—which was to be assaulted after the line Wytschaete-Messines had been taken. The advance planned by the Allies was undertaken for the purpose of preventing the Germans transferring forces from the Western Front to Russia, where all was not going well with the enemy.

After darkness had fallen on 13th another reconnaissance was made of the enemy's wire, which was found to be about 6 feet high and 6 feet thick and of considerable strength. Gaps in the wire in front of the Somersets' trenches were also prepared.

The next morning B Company set to work on the mattresses, making them out of rabbit-wire; they were then stuffed with straw. At 9 a.m. the attack on Wytschaete (north of the Battalion) opened and slight progress was made. All day long the guns of the 4th Division pounded the enemy's positions, but no attack was made by the 11th Infantry Brigade. Companies relieved companies during the night and B (now in the front line) sent out patrols, but no additional information was obtained. On the 15th the attack on Wytschaete came to a standstill. On the 16th rehearsals for the attack on the "Birdcage" took place, the supporting platoons of B Company erecting wire entanglements of German pattern, afterwards practising crossing them on the wire mattresses. "Four men," states the Battalion Diary, "crossed 5 feet 6 inch tripod obstacles with 16 strands of wire in 65 seconds on wire mattresses." The attack was again practised on the 17th and the C.O. personally reconnoitred the point of debouchment of the left attacking company, i.e. from the eastern edge of "Plugstreet" Wood.

By this time all ranks were in a state of feverish excitement but their ardour was suddenly chilled: "During the afternoon it became apparent from conversations with staff officers that an advance at once was not contemplated, and in the evening names of officers recommended to go on leave were called for."

It is not recorded whether the officers recommended for leave obtained it, but what is certain is that on the 18th at a conference held at 11th Brigade 18th December Headquarters definite orders were issued for the attack on the "Birdcage" to be carried out on the 19th. But the original intention of the attack—an advance—had meanwhile been modified and all the 4th Division was expected to do was (to use the words of III Corps Operation Orders) "attack some point in the enemy's line, the object being to occupy the enemy on the front of the Corps and prevent him moving his reserves to meet the French attack. The point selected for attack is the eastern end of Ploegsteert Wood between Le Gheer and St. Yves." In other words the "German Birdcage."

[1] The part known as the "Birdcage" was a portion of our (original) line into which the Germans had penetrated and established themselves.

1st Battalion

Another conference was held at Bn. H.Qs. (1st Somerset L.I.) later in the day—at 4 p.m.—when the C.O. described the attack and issued the necessary orders.[1]   B and C Companies were not to go into the trenches during the night of the 18th/19th,[2] but were to remain in billets.   Both of these Companies had been detailed to carry out the attack on the following day.   A Company of the Battalion then held the right and left trench: H Company remaining in reserve in the "Breastwork Line" in Hunter Avenue.   At this period B Company was commanded by Captain C. C. Maud; C Company by Lieutenant Ford; A Company by Captain F. S. Bradshaw, and H Company by Lieutenant R. L. Moore.

19th December

Dawn of the 19th December broke brightly, the Battalion Diary states that it was "a clear day."   About 9 a.m. the guns opened fire on the houses and trenches in the German "Birdcage," but only howitzers (4·5s and 6″) took part in this bombardment as the field guns were unable to clear the Wood. The machine guns blazed away at the German wire in order to cut gaps through which the infantry might pass when the attack began.   At 11 a.m. an officer observing for the 6th Siege Battery came to Battalion Headquarters and asked for an officer to point out exactly which were British and which were German trenches.   This seems somewhat incredible, but it should be remembered that the opposing trench systems in the early days of the War were often very close together, communications were bad and close co-operation between artillery and infantry had not attained anything approaching that degree of efficiency which existed later.   The Adjutant was therefore sent off to the observing station at St. Yves, where he pointed out a trench which was just about to be shelled as one occupied by the Hampshire Regiment.   Indeed, several shrapnel shells from the Divisional Artillery were even then bursting over the trenches.

By 1 p.m. the attacking Companies were in position: B lining the right trench, i.e. the eastern edge of Ploegsteert Wood, and C in rear of this trench: A Company then held the two trenches which formed the Battalion front: and H Company with Bn. H.Qs. were in the breastwork line.

The plan of attack adopted by B Company was as follows :—

"Two platoons commanded by 2/Lieuts. Dennys and Henson respectively, were to charge out of the wood at 2.30 p.m., pass over the German first-line trench in the 'Birdcage' and capture the second-line trench running north and south. . . .   The remaining two platoons, commanded by 2/Lieut. Orr, were to capture the German first-line trench in the 'Birdcage' "[3]

From 1.30 to 2.30 p.m. the guns shelled the German lines, but every shell burst short.   The shrapnel shells frequently burst over the breastwork

[1] Although the Battalion Diary states that—"A copy of orders for the attack is attached," they are missing from the Official Records.

[2] Sergt. B. Burge received the D.C.M. for gallant conduct during a reconnaissance of the enemy's trenches carried out on the night of 18th December 1914.

[3] Account by Lieutenant Dennys.

line held by the Somersets, while the howitzer shells seldom pitched east of
the Le Gheer–St. Yves road.

Meanwhile a mountain battery had been moved up to the eastern edge
of "Plugstreet" Wood and from 2 to 2.30 p.m., in co-operation with the
Divisional machine guns, endeavoured to tear gaps in the German wire and
demolish German House. Only the latter was destroyed, the machine-gun
fire (as it was eventually found) having no effect upon the hostile wire entanglements.

At 2.30 p.m. precisely, the two leading platoons of B Company, closely
followed by the remaining platoons, dashed forward from the edge of the wood,
towards the German front line, about 120 yards away. No one appears to have
recorded the strange (and in many ways inspiring) sight of those Somerset
men climbing over the parapets of the trenches, carrying, however it was
easiest, their mattresses of rabbit-wire and straw, staggering through the
mud and filth of No Man's Land, towards the enemy's lines; every other man
carrying wirecutters. No sooner had the platoons set foot in No Man's Land,
than at once sheets of flame leapt up from the German trenches and bullets
from machine guns and rifles met the advance of the gallant Somersets. Moreover the enemy's guns, which hitherto had done little in the way of retaliation,
joined in the action.

With splendid steadiness the men advanced, but the leading platoon had
gone forward only about 40 or 50 yards, when four 4·5 shells from the
Divisional Artillery fell amongst the men, inflicting considerable casualties.
The survivors, however, with great courage, still pressed forward and reached
the house marked "A," where a small gap was found in the wire. Captain
Maud, who had by now caught up the survivors of the two leading platoons,
with 2/Lieut. Dennys passed through this gap, and as they did so a German
ran out of the house and bolted back towards the enemy's second-line trench.
This man was about 15 yards from Captain Maud, who had a shot at him
with his revolver. The German, thereupon, turned round and fired his rifle
from the hip. Unfortunately the shot was well aimed and the bullet struck
Captain Maud in the stomach, that gallant officer dying about five minutes
later. Almost simultaneously 2/Lieut. Dennys was wounded in the arm and
again shortly afterwards in the hip; he was afterwards taken prisoner by the
enemy. Lieutenant S. B. Henson had been killed before reaching the German
wire. The only other person (officer or man) who got past the German first-
line trench was 2/Lieutenant R. C. Orr,[1] and he was shot through the head
and died immediately. The two supporting platoons of B Company had
already been absorbed into the first line when C Company was sent out (at
about 3.15 p.m.), but could get no farther than B Company's line, which was
then about half-way across No Man's Land and approximately in prolongation
of the Battalion's left trench. The terrible condition of the ground, pitted
with shell holes, covered with water and deep in heavy-clinging mud, made
the "going" extremely difficult. Of C Company, Lieut. G. R. Parr, in charge

---

[1] The official records give Lieutenant Orr's rank as Captain.

of his platoon, was well in front of his men when he was wounded in the leg by a machine-gun bullet. He fell, but immediately endeavoured to rise and carry on with the attack. He was, however, struck by another bullet and killed almost instantaneously.[1] Captain Bradshaw[2] next made a gallant attempt to go out and lead on B and C Companies, but he likewise was mortally wounded and died an hour later. At 4 p.m. C Company, under cover of darkness, had reached the Le Gheer–St. Yves Road. The position was, however, untenable, as it was enfiladed by houses on the right flank and the trench along the road was 3 feet deep in water.

On the right of the Somersets the Rifle Brigade had not succeeded in advancing to the road junction, their objective, and the left of the Rifles was only about 70 yards east of the Wood. About 5 p.m., therefore, two platoons (Nos. 14 and 16) of H Company of the Somersets which had been in support all day, were sent out to join up with the left of the Rifle Brigade. The survivors of B Company were then discovered holding one room of the house "A," the Germans being in possession of an adjoining room, each side taking "pot shots" at the other through holes in the wall.

The Battalion Diary gives the situation at 6 p.m. as follows:—

"Our left had gained about 80 yards of the road which was our objective and the line then followed about the line of the German wire until it joined the Rifle Brigade. The position which crossed the field was very wet and quite unsuitable for digging."

An order was received from Brigade Headquarters to entrench the ground gained preparatory to a further advance on the next day. But the Adjutant was sent back to point out the impossibility of digging in on such ground and eventually a withdrawal to the former trenches in Ploegsteert Wood was ordered.

The only tactical result of this very gallant attempt was that the enemy was driven out of the Wood, across which a line of breastworks was erected by the Sappers during the night 19th/20th, and held by one platoon of H Company.

"From the Battalion's point of view the effects of the action were of a sentimental nature—firstly, pride in the gallant behaviour of the attacking Companies who advanced without hesitation against an unshaken line of well-armed defenders, and secondly, grief at the loss of so many well-loved comrades who could ill be spared."[3]

Casualties had indeed been heavy! Five officers had been killed—Captains F. S. Bradshaw, C. C. Maud,[4] R. C. Orr and Lieutenants G. R. Parr

---

[1] Lieut. George Roworth Parr was son of Maj.-Gen. Sir Henry Hallam Parr, K.C.B., formerly Colonel of the Regiment.

[2] Captain Bradshaw was also son of a former officer of the Regiment.

[3] Colonel Swayne.

[4] During the "unofficial truce" which took place at Christmas-time the bodies of Captains Maud and Orr and Lieut. Henson were recovered. On handing over the body of Captain Maud a Saxon officer stated he was the bravest of the brave, or words to that effect.

The Attack on THE BIRDCAGE.
19ᵗʰ Dec. 1914.

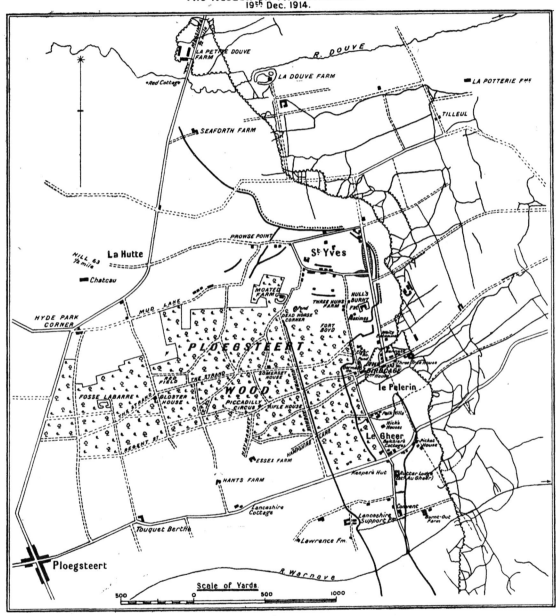

R. DOUVE

LA PETITE DOUVE FARM

LA DOUVE FARM

LA POTTERIE Fᵐᵉ

•Red Cottage

TILLEUL

SEAFORTH FARM

PROWSE POINT

St YVES

HILL 63 ½ mile

La Hutte

•Chateau

MOATED FARM

THREE HUNS FARM

HULL'S BURNT Fᵐ

HYDE PARK CORNER

MUD LANE

Pond DEAD HORSE CORNER

FORT BOYD

Maximes

PLOEGSTEERT

SOMERSET HOUSE

BIRDCAGE

Three Huts House

Three Huts House

RED FIELD

THE STRAND

WOOD

PICCADILLY CIRCUS

RIFLE HOUSE

le Pelerin

FOSSE LABARRE

THE STRAND

GLOSTER HOUSE

REGENT ST

HAMPSHIRE LANE

Falk Hills

Nick's Houses

Le Gheer

Belchier's Cottages

Picket House

ESSEX FARM

HANTS FARM

Keeper's Hut

Rutter Lodge (St Au Gheer)

Convent

Lancashire Cottage

Lancashire Support Fᵐ

Burnt-Out Farm

Touquet Berthe

Lawrence Fm.

Ploegsteert

R. Warnave

Scale of Yards.
500   0   500   1000

and S. B. Henson.   One officer, 2/Lieut. K. G. G. Dennys, was wounded   1st Battalion
and taken prisoner.   The losses in other ranks were 27 killed, 52 wounded   19th December
and 30 missing.

But it was, as the quotation at the head of this chapter states—a very gallant attempt.[1]

[1] It is interesting to note that the German Birdcage was never re-captured throughout the whole course of the War, and was only evacuated by the enemy in October 1918.

CHAPTER XII

20TH DECEMBER 1914–24TH APRIL 1915

1st Battalion

THE attack on the German Birdcage on 19th December was the last affair of any importance in which the 1st Somerset L.I. was involved until the Battles of Ypres 1915, which began with the Gas attack on the 22nd April. Many items of purely Regimental interest are, however, recorded in the Battalion Diaries during the interim period.

20th December

On 20th December, the morning following the attack on the Birdcage, Lieutenant R. L. Moore, who had gone out into No Man's Land for reconnoitring purposes, was killed. The officers of the Battalion were now reduced to 11, including the Medical Officer and the Quartermaster: the strength of the Battalion in other ranks is not recorded.

On 21st December, Major C. W. Compton, who had been wounded at Le Cateau, returned to the Battalion and took over command.

The Diary, kept by the 11th Inf. Bde. H.Q. for December 1914, contains some very interesting figures of approximate casualties incurred by all units of the Brigade from the time they landed in France in August to the end of the year. The figures concerning the 1st Somerset Light Infantry are illuminating. No less than 36 officers and 1,153 other ranks had become casualties, whilst of the original Battalion which landed on 22nd August, only 4 officers and 266 other ranks remained. The casualties amongst officers were as follows:—Killed, 8: Major F. G. Thoyts, Capts. C. C. Maud, F. S. Bradshaw, R. C. Orr; Lieuts. R. L. Moore, G. R. Parr; 2/Lieuts. A. B. Read, S. B. Henson. Wounded, 12: Major C. W. Compton, Capts. L. A. Jones-Mortimer, J. M. Smith, N. A. H. Campbell, G. E. Whittick; Lieuts. A. V. Newton, R. J. R. Leacroft, R. V. Montgomery, J. W. M. Vincent; 2/Lieuts. J. S. Bush, E. E. Glossop, R. A. A. Chichester. Wounded and Missing, 6: Capts. A. J. G. Hargreaves, J. G. M. Broderip; Lieuts. J. B. Taylor, O. G. B. Philby, J. C. W. Macbryan; 2/Lieut. K. G. G. Dennys. The Battalion M.O.—Captain C. W. Holden, R.A.M.C.—was also reported amongst the missing. Ten officers of the Regiment were in hospital, including Lieut.-Cols. E. H. Swayne and C. B. Prowse. Of the 1,153 "other ranks" casualties, 131 had been killed, 434 wounded, 58 wounded and missing, 80 missing and 450 sick in hospital.

The above figures are an eloquent tribute to the Regiment, showing how strenuous were the operations through which the 1st Battalion had passed.

1915
January
11th February

The month of January 1915 passed quietly, and it is not until 11th February that the Battalion Diary records the next officer casualty— 2/Lieut. G. M. Penn—who was killed by a sniper. On the 17th of the same month there is an entry in the Diary which states that the "Battalion is now up to strength." No figures are given. On the 19th Lieut.-Col. Prowse was

transferred to command a battalion of the Leinster Regiment in the 27th 1st Battalion
Division: "This leaves us," records the Diary, "with 1 Major, 1 Captain
(Adjutant) and 17 subaltern officers—some of the latter are very young and
inexperienced." Major Compton was gazetted on 1st March as Lieutenant-
Colonel and to command the 1st Bn. Somerset Light Infantry, *vice* Lieut.-
Colonel E. H. Swayne.

Two items of interest occur on 10th March. The first was a fire demon- 10th March
stration carried out along the Divisional front, with the idea of drawing attention
from the Neuve Chapelle front where the First British Army was launching
a heavy attack. But although the Somersets raked the enemy's positions with
machine-gun and rifle fire there was little hostile retaliation and no casualties
were suffered by the Battalion.

The second item of interest was a complete change in the organization
of the front line. Hitherto all four battalions of the 11th Infantry Brigade
had held the front line, but orders were received to reorganize the Brigade
sector into two sub-sectors, instead of **four** as hithertofore. The change meant
that for the first time one battalion would be in local reserve and one in Brigade
Reserve, with a fair opportunity of getting rested and properly "cleaned up."
As the Battalion Diary puts it: "New system will give a complete battalion
a rest in billets and opportunity for smartening up under its C.O., and also
gives Divisional Commander an intact battalion as his reserve."

On 17th the Battalion M.O.—Lieut. J. R. Waddy, R.A.M.C.—was
killed. The loss of this gallant officer was keenly felt by the Battalion. He
was a son of that hardy veteran of the Regiment, Lt.-Col. J. M. E. Waddy,
who formerly commanded the 2nd Battalion and who at an advanced age went
out to India as second-in-command of a Territorial Battalion.

In accordance with the new reorganization scheme the 1st Somerset L.I.
was relieved in the trenches during the evening of 18th March by the Rifle
Brigade, and moved into billets—A Company in Nieppe, B Company
in Hunterstown North, C Company to Hunterstown South and H Company
to Farm 1875; the relief was completed by 10 p.m.

Nothing of importance happened during the next three or four weeks and
on 11th April the 1st Somersets were relieved in the trenches and left the 11th April
St. Yves sector (without any regrets) for the last time. A few days later the
11th Brigade moved back to billets in the Noote Boom–Steenwerck area,
having been relieved (on the night 14th/15th) by a Brigade of the South
Midland Division. On the 15th the 1st Somerset L.I. was located in the area
Noote Boom–Steentje, billeted in many scattered farms within a radius of
about a mile. In this area a quiet week was spent in cleaning up, route-march-
ing and generally recuperating and refitting after the terrible time through
which the Battalion had passed during the winter months in the "Plugstreet"
sector. On the 22nd of the month the Battalion Diary states: "Names of
officers recommended for leave called for." Did they get their leave? Presumably not, for that very evening, at Ypres, (22nd April) the Germans launched
their great gas attack.

CHAPTER XIII

THE BATTLES OF YPRES, 1915

THE BATTLE OF ST. JULIEN: 24TH APRIL–4TH MAY, 1915

1st Battalion

DETAILS of the great German gas attack on the French on the 22nd April 1915 are available in the official despatches, but it was not until the Battle of Gravenstafel Ridge (22nd–23rd April) had been fought, and the Battle of St. Julien joined, that the 1st Somersets took part in the operations.

23rd April

At 11.30 a.m. on 23rd the 11th Inf. Bde. received instructions to "stand by ready to move at two hours' notice." Having packed everything in readiness to march off, the four Battalions of the Brigade awaited orders which, however, did not materialize until 9.30 a.m. on the 24th, when the Brigade was ordered to entrain at Bailleul for Vlamertinghe where it was to be in Corps Reserve under the orders of the G.O.C., V Corps (Sir Herbert Plumer).

The 1st Somersets (in Brigade) reached Poperinghe at 3.30 p.m. and, having detrained, marched off to Busseboom, towards Vlamertinghe. After some trouble Bn. Hqs. and A, B and C Companies were billeted, but H Company was unfortunate and had to bivouac; much rain fell during the night. At 6 a.m. the next morning the Brigade set out for Vlamertinghe where, arriving at 7.15 a.m., the 1st Somersets occupied "Huts B."

All day long the men waited in their billets for orders to go forward. Some slept, others watched the shells bursting in and about Ypres, from 2 to 3 miles away. To all, the roar of guns, the shrieking and moaning and the terrific explosions of the great howitzer shells which the enemy flung into Ypres, and deluged the British trenches in the Salient, were awesome in the extreme. The atmosphere was still sickly from the fumes of gas, and flames shot up into the air from burning villages and the ruined city of Ypres.

On the morning of 22nd April the line forming the Ypres Salient ran approximately from about midway between Steenstraate and Het Sas, almost directly eastwards to immediately west of Poelcappelle, then S.E. to W. of Wallemolen, a point where the Ypres–Roulers railway cut the Passchendaele–Broodseinde Road, just east of Broodseinde, then bending back in a south-westerly direction, west of Becelaere and Gheluvelt to Hill 60 (near Zwarteleen). The line from Steenstraate to just west of Poelcappelle was held by the French; from the French right W. of Poelcappelle the Canadian Division carried on the line towards the Passchendaele Road; 28th and 27th British divisions held the line south of the Canadians. These dispositions are important, for without them it is impossible to understand the *rôle* assigned to the 11th Infantry Brigade.

Under the terrible effects of the gas attack and the very heavy bombardment which accompanied it the French had given way completely on 22nd 1st Battalion and had retired to the banks of the Yser Canal. The left of the Canadian Division was now turned back and the 1st Can. Bde. with the 13th Inf. Bde. and the Composite Bde. of Battalions of the 27th Division under Colonel Geddes continued the line to the Canal.

On the 24th the 2nd and 3rd Canadian Brigades held their original line, 24th April but, attacked by gas, the 3rd retired through St. Julien, though the 2nd still held on, supported on the left by various detachments, especially by two battalions of the 28th Division under Colonel Wallace and two battalions of the Northumbrian (50th) Division under Colonel Bell.

On the morning of the 25th April the line was held by 85th Inf. Bde., 25th April two battalions of 2nd Canadian Bde., detachments of the 28th, 27th, and Northumbrian Division, the 10th Inf. Bde. (4th Div.), Geddes Bde. and the 13th Inf. Bde. (in that order from right to left). But by the evening the 2nd Canadian Bde. had retired and there appeared to be a gap between the left of the 85th Bde., near Gravenstafel, and Fortuin, S. of St. Julien.

This gap the 11th Inf. Bde. (4th Div.) was ordered to fill.

In the uncertain state of the situation Brig.-Gen. Hasler (Commanding the Brigade) decided to approach the gap from the two ends. Sending the 1st Hants to the 85th Bde. to the eastern end, he led the remaining three battalions to Fortuin, but being informed by a staff officer that the Gravenstafel Road was held by the enemy, he turned south-eastwards, intending to advance in a northerly direction later on. But light came all too soon and day-break found the battalions holding an exposed position on the Zonnebeke Ridge.

"It was believed," continues the Diary of the Somersets, "that there was a gap between Fortuin and Gravenstafel Ridge, though it was afterwards found that there were a few Canadians still left in their trenches east of the line allotted to the Brigade. These withdrew during the night."

"The 1st Somersets occupied and entrenched a line from Chapel in Fortuin to Hill 37, with Bn. Hqs. at a Farm in D. 13 c., central." [1]

Having reached their allotted positions the Battalion set to work to dig in as effectively as possible in the short time before dawn of the 26th broke, for with the coming of daylight it was certain they would be exposed to a merciless shelling. But as there was a scarcity of entrenching tools, and no Brigade tools were available, the 1st Somersets were only partly entrenched when morning arrived, and what trenches there were, were shallow and afforded little protection unless the troops laid down flat.

Dawn broke at about 3.30 a.m. and it was not long before the Somerset 26th April men and other battalions of the 11th Brigade were spotted by the enemy.

---

[1] Battalion Diary. The 11th Brigade Diary, however, gives the following dispositions of the 1st Somerset L.I.:—"The Rifle Bde. deployed and took up a position in the subsidiary line about Hill 37, D. 20a, with two companies of Somerset L.I. on their right. The Somerset L.I. (less two companies) and the L.R.B. dug in, in square D.19. The troops were in position half an hour before daylight (on 26th)."

Immediately the whole Brigade line was plastered with shell, which continued falling heavily throughout the day. "One battery absolutely enfiladed C Company's trench." The Germans "kept the supporting trenches under a rain of shrapnel, so that the supports did not dare show their heads above the parapet, and searched the high ground behind with high explosive to stop movements of reserves." [1]

All day long nothing could be done but lie close and make the best of a desperate situation. At night the line was partly reorganized, the Rifle Brigade taking over the trenches held by the two right Companies (A and B) of the Somersets who withdrew to some old dug-outs west of Bn. Hqs. H Company began entrenching a line connecting with East Yorkshire Territorials on the left, whilst C Company continued the line on H Company's right to within about 200 yards of the left of the Rifle Brigade. Only one attack (on A and B Companies) was made by the enemy, but it was a half-hearted attempt and melted away under the machine-gun and rifle fire. The Somersets had, however, suffered about 40 casualties during the day, three officers being wounded—Capt. Samuda and Lieuts. Pretyman and Knight.

Throughout the night 26th/27th until 3 a.m. all ranks were hard at work improving the defences, which presumably afforded better shelter for the men, for during the 27th, though the hostile shelling continued with great violence, only 18 N.C.O.'s and men were killed or wounded. The Bn. Medical Officer —Lieut. J. A. MacMahon—was badly wounded on this day.[2] Brigadier-General Hasler, commanding 11th Brigade, was killed by a shell and Lieut.-Colonel Compton (commanding 1st Somerset L.I.) took over temporary command of the Brigade.

For several days the enemy continued to shell the positions occupied by the Somersets and other battalions of the Brigade, and gradually he was pushing his line forward, so that soon it would be impossible for the Brigade to hold what was apparently an exposed position open to enfilade artillery, machine-gun and rifle fire. But for the present the British line was held with splendid tenacity.

On the 28th Col. Compton returned to the Battalion. During the day Bn. Hqs. were burnt to the ground and all the reserves of Véry lights, hand-grenades and S.A.A. were destroyed. On the 29th, to the great delight of the Somersets, Brevet Lieut.-Col. Prowse (late of the 1st Battalion) took over command of the 11th Inf. Bde. vice Brigadier-General Hasler. The line was again reorganized on this day, as each battalion in the Brigade had been ordered to absorb 2 companies of a Territorial battalion. The Somersets were allotted X and W Companies of the 4th Yorkshire R.

Less shelling, and fewer casualties characterized the 29th and 30th and at night on the latter date the Somersets' line north of the Fortuin Road ran, from left to right, A Company, X Company (4th Y.R.), H Company; south of the Fortuin Road, from left to right, were W Company (4th Y.R.) and C and B Companies of the Somersets.

[1] The late Captain G. A. Prideaux.   [2] Died of wounds 12th May 1915.

On 1st May the French, on the left of the 4th Division, made a counter-
attack to regain the ground lost by them on 22nd April.   The Somerset men
were warned that if the attack failed the 11th Brigade was to be withdrawn,
as the salient held by the Brigade was too difficult to maintain seeing that it
was under fire from "all four sides."   The move, however, did not take place
that night.

The next day (during the morning) the enemy's artillery appeared to
be registering the Battalion's trenches.   The early afternoon was quiet, but
about 5.30 p.m. a terrific bombardment swept the whole salient (front- and
second-line trenches).   Then from the German line there came a loud hissing
sound, and clouds of what appeared at first steam, but turned later to a dense
green mass of asphyxiating gas, floated across No Man's Land towards the
trenches of A Company of the Somersets, and of the L.R.B. and the 10th
Bde.   Of the Somersets A Company had about 35 casualties from gas poisoning and shelling, including 2/Lt. MacBryan.   Other companies lost 2/Lt.
E. E. Glossop (who died of wounds on 4th), Lieut. Ford and 15 N.C.O.'s
and men wounded.   Considering the intensity of the enemy's bombardment,
in which he used big howitzers and field guns, the losses were small.

Under cover of his guns and the gas clouds the enemy advanced his line
to within 200 yards of A Company of the Somersets, the L.R.B. and the 10th
Brigade; he had previously been about 800 yards away.

No substantial advance was made by the French in their counter-attack
and orders for the withdrawal to a new line which ran approximately just east
of Zwarteleen, Hooge and Wieltje, thence in a north-westerly direction just
east of Pilckem, Het Sas and Steenstraate, were issued to the gallant troops
who, from the 24th April, in the face of fierce bombardments, had held the
salient, shelled from all sides, with splendid tenacity.   The withdrawal was
ordered to take place during the night of 3rd May.

The morning broke fine and as soon as the British lines were distinguish-
able the enemy's artillery opened fire, fiercely bombarding the trenches of
the 11th Brigade, and in particular the Rifle Brigade and B and C Companies
of the 1st Somersets.   The Rifles suffered heavy casualties, but the losses of
the latter were fortunately light.

The enemy had been gradually working forward towards the line held
by the 11th Brigade and, at nightfall, he was within 70 yards of the left trenches
held by the Somersets.   The withdrawal which was to take place would therefore be an extremely difficult operation.   The retirement was to begin from
the right, the Hants first, followed in turn by the Rifle Brigade, 1st Somersets,
and London Rifle Brigade.   One Company (A) of the East Lancs R. had been
moved up to cover the withdrawal of the Somerset men which began about
midnight.   By extraordinary good luck the enemy was comparatively quiet, his
passive attitude combined with the unfavourable nature of the elements—a
strong east wind was blowing and rain falling—the whole of the 11th Brigade
got safely away to behind the second line which ran north and south just east
of Wieltje, held by troops of the 28th Division.

The late Captain G. A. Prideaux thus describes the withdrawal of the Somersets:—

"At about 12.15 a.m. the company on our right moved away in file, then we moved, leaving S.A.A. and tools behind and no covering party. We had to carry our own wounded as far as Wieltje, where they were put in motor ambulances. The Germans were sending up flares all the time and firing their howitzers and field guns at intervals. When we first got on to the road we were only 700 yards away from the German positions, and we thought they must hear us but, bar putting two 'Little Willies' at us on the road when we were trying to climb over two big trees which had fallen across the road, they never put a shell near us. I have never seen the men march so fast. They marched in the same way as they did in the retreat (they were very worn out) with lowered heads and stumbling gait. The road was in a worse state than when we came up before, more dead horses, men, and overturned carts. We marched via Wieltje–St. Jean–La Bryke–No. 2 Pontoon Bridge across the Yser Canal–Brielen–along main road to Elverdinghe to a line B.20.d– B.21.c. It rained most of the time. We arrived at 6 a.m., finding that we were to bivouac in a field as all the buildings were already occupied by French troops. . . . Here ended a very interesting, but the most unpleasant and trying time I have ever spent during the war. We were under a continuous and heavy shell fire from the front and both flanks, with hardly any of our artillery to help us. The Germans were in greatly superior numbers, which, with the gas, made the suspense very trying."

The 1st Somersets had marched 9 miles and the men were very tired. But at 9 p.m. the Battalion moved off still farther west, to a wood, the situation of which can best be described as just north of the Vlamertinghe–Poperinghe road. "Here," the Battalion Diary states, "there was no cover except the thin foliage, and a cold night was spent in the open."

The total casualties suffered by the 1st Battalion during the period 25th April–3rd May were 1 officer killed and 7 officers wounded and 212 other ranks killed, wounded and missing, but these casualties were small compared with the losses suffered by the Rifle Brigade (500), Hants (350) and L.R.B. (350). The Battalion Diary also adds, with pardonable pride: "Several G.Os.C. expressed their pleasure at the behaviour of the Brigade during these trying 9 days." Whilst Sir John French in his official despatch stated that: "I am of opinion that the retirement, carried out deliberately with scarcely any loss, and in the face of an enemy in position, reflects the greatest possible credit on Sir Herbert Plumer and those who so efficiently carried out his orders."

Thus ended the Battle of St. Julien.

The next operations, which figure in the Battle Honours of the Regiment, are the Battles of Frezenberg Ridge (8th–13th May) and Bellewaarde Ridge (24th–25th May).

THE BATTLE OF FREZENBERG RIDGE, 8TH–13TH MAY

In the first of these two Battles the 1st Somersets were on the extreme 1st Battalion left of the 11th Brigade front (and of the 4th Divisional front), having relieved the 2nd Essex (12th Brigade) on the night of the 9th/10th.

After the withdrawal on the 4th May the 11th Brigade had remained out of the line until 8th May, but during the morning of the latter date, the Brigade received orders to move to Vlamertinghe, where a move was to be made, east of the Canal, to relieve the 12th Brigade.   But the enemy had already launched a heavy attack against the line of the 4th Division, which ran approximately (from the right flank of the French) C.15.c.–C.15.d.–C.16.c.–C.16.d.— thence round the Farm in C.22.b.—thence in a south-easterly direction towards Verlorenhoek.   It was not, however, until the 9th that there was a lull in the battle, during which the 11th Brigade was put into the line, the 1st Somersets (as already stated) relieving the 2nd Essex R. on the extreme left of the Bde. front, i.e. C.15.c. and d.   In this position the Battalion passed the 10th quietly. On the 11th A and B Companies were worried by the enemy's trench mortars, hidden in farms opposite the Somerset men; the houses were shelled by the Divisional Artillery and the annoyance abated.   The 12th was likewise a quiet day, but on the 13th the enemy launched another big attack against the 13th May front held by the 11th Brigade and 1st Cavalry Division.[1]   The Battalion Diary thus describes the action:—

"It was fortunate that the wind was blowing from the south-west as it prevented the enemy using gas against us.   Briefly the salient features [of the attack] were as follows: Heavy bombardment of all our trenches with 8″ and 6″ howitzers and field guns started at 4 a.m. and continued, with a slight lull at midday, until 3 p.m.   The shelling of our trenches was not so accurate as was that of the battalions on our right [Hants, Rifle Brigade and East Lancs]. Very few shells actually burst in our trenches.   There were irresolute infantry attacks at 7 a.m., 9 a.m. and 10 a.m., which were easily repulsed.   Casualties were 2/Lieut. Doddington wounded, 3 N.C.Os. and men killed, 18 wounded. . . .   At the end of the day's fighting the line was intact."

The attack which took place on 13th was the final episode in the Battle of Frezenberg Ridge.

For several days after the battle the 1st Battalion Diary records little of outstanding interest.   By the middle of May 1915 the Ypres Salient had acquired that evil reputation which clung to it throughout the war.   By day and by night shells shrieked and howled through the air, bombing attacks went on, snipers were at work and trench-mortar bombs hurtled across No Man's Land, bursting with terrific force and churning up the already sore-troubled earth, or blowing parapets, traverses and dug-outs to bits.   Peace there was none.   Like an angry sea the ebb and flow of the war went on un-ceasingly, the hostile waves dashing themselves in vain against the Allied

---

[1] Presumably the 1st Cavalry Division was on the right of the 11th Brigade.

line, which stood firm as a rock, barring the way to the Channel ports. Both sides suffered heavy casualties. On either side of No Man's Land, sandbags and clods of earth and mud, and the bodies and limbs of men, flung into the air, was an almost hourly sight. Blazing farms and cottages and burning villages threw a lurid glare over the battlefield by night.

17th May On 17th B Company (occupying the left trench of the Battalion front) was heavily shelled by "Little Willies" and Lieutenant D. Kenworthy and 3 N.C.O.'s and men were killed, whilst a number were wounded. In the evening A Company (right trench) and H Company (in support) were very heavily shelled for four hours, though casualties are not recorded.

But that same night the Battalion was relieved, the first of the relieving troops arriving at 9.30 p.m. It was, however, about 1.30 a.m. before the whole Battalion was settled in wet and unpleasant bivouacs just N.E. of La Brique. At night on the 18th, after having spent a miserable day in the bivouacs, the Somerset men moved to the Canal Banks, Bn. Hqs. and H Company on the west side; A, B and C Companies remaining on the eastern bank in wretched and filthy dug-outs just vacated by other troops.

The Yser Canal, at the spot where the Somersets were bivouacking, was a long straight waterway, with high banks on either side, into which the troops had burrowed and made dug-outs as deep as possible, in order to provide shelter from the weather and the enemy's shell fire. Rows of tall, well-grown trees surmounted the banks. It was a picturesque place, though now the trees were somewhat shorn of leaves and branches, whilst on fine days the Canal banks resembled an Indian "Dhobi Ghat," so busy were the troops in washing and drying their clothes. On the night of the 20th the Battalion moved back to billets, about 2 miles N.E. of Poperinghe. Here, until the 24th, officers and men spent a restful period, cleaning up and resting.

THE BATTLE OF BELLEWAARDE RIDGE, 24TH–25TH MAY 1915

24th May Early on the morning of 24th May the troops were awakened by the sudden roar of guns, which seemed to come from the direction of Wieltje; the time was about 3 a.m. An hour later orders were received for the Somersets to move at once to Vlamertinghe Chateau. Without breakfast, but with their cookers and watercarts, Companies hurried off at 5.30 a.m. in the direction of Vlamertinghe. Blankets and officers' valises were packed and left behind to be brought along by the transport. About 7 a.m. the Battalion arrived at the Chateau and bivouacked in the surrounding woods.

At Vlamertinghe Chateau the Battalion learned that the enemy had made a very heavy gas and artillery attack on the 10th and 12th Infantry Brigades, and Shell Trap Farm[1] had been lost, together with a length of trenches each side of the buildings.

At 2 p.m. the 1st Somersets moved east to the Canal bank, followed by the Rifle Brigade, Hampshires and East Lancs. From the Canal bank the

[1] This is the same place as Mouse Trap Farm, as Shell Trap Farm is not shown on the map; being considered of ill-omen the name was changed by Corps orders.

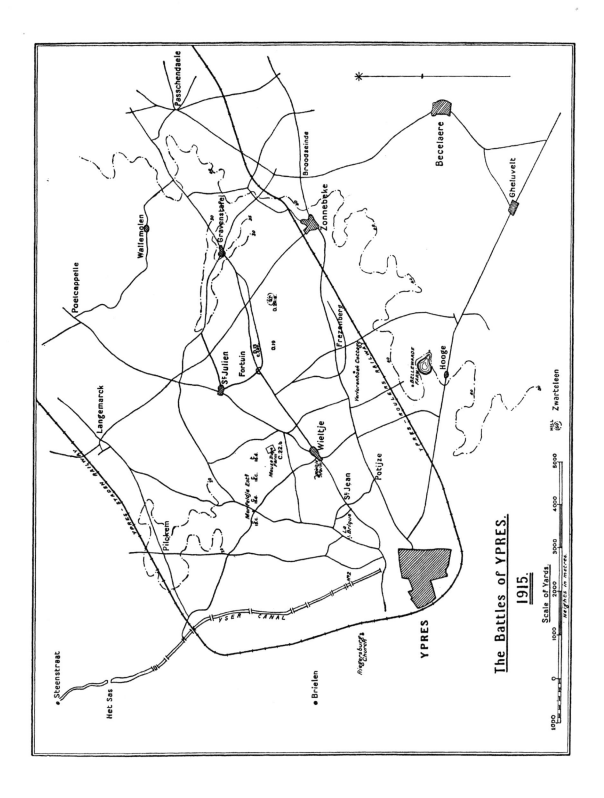

The Battles of YPRES.

1915.

Battalion moved to La Brique, arriving at 6.30 p.m.   A conference of Brigadiers   1st Battalion
followed, during which it was decided to withdraw the line slightly to cross   24th May
roads in C.15.c.–Farm in C.28.a., i.e., roughly, from the Morteldje Estaminet
to Wieltje Farm, which had been previously prepared as the Divisional second
line, thus (as the Battalion Diary states) "giving up to the enemy the salient
angle whose apex was Shell Trap (Mouse Trap) Farm."   The Somersets,
however, were ordered to withdraw to Reigersburg Chateau in H.6.b.[1] "where
we stayed the night."

For the 25th May the Battalion Diary records:—   25th May

"Remained in barns at Reigersburg Chateau. Hot day. Lost a few
men from stray shells.   The Chateau is surrounded by batteries, which are
continually being shelled.   Officers' mess established in the Chateau.   Cookers
brought up to-night and hidden under the trees and will do all the cooking
to-morrow [26th]."

The loss of Shell Trap Farm and the small length of trench on either side
of the buildings was the only gain by the enemy in the Battle of Bellewaarde
Ridge, which the official despatches describe as a "most determined attack."

This attack concluded the series of operations officially known as the
Battles of Ypres, 1915.

[1] On the Ypres–Brielen road, and about half-way between those two places.

CHAPTER XIV

THE 6TH AND 7TH (SERVICE) BATTALIONS ARRIVE IN FRANCE

6th Battalion

THE Battles of Ypres were drawing to a close when the 6th (Service) Battalion of the Regiment landed in France. Since the raising of the Battalion in August 1914, the 6th had spent the first three months in hard training at Aldershot. A move was then made to Witley Camp, Godalming, the Battalion returning to Aldershot again in February 1915, where brigade and divisional training was continued until the middle of April. The 6th Battalion, Somerset L.I.[1] was now in the 43rd Infantry Brigade[2] of the 14th (Light) Division, brigaded with the 6th Duke of Cornwall's L.I., 6th K.O.Y.L.I., and 10th Durham L.I. A month later (about the middle of May) spare kit had been sent home and all ranks awaited

21st May

embarkation orders. A few days later they came, and on 21st May the Battalion crossed the Channel in a S.E. & C.R. mail boat and, on reaching Boulogne, disembarked. The night was spent in the rest camp on the hills overlooking the town.

On 23rd May (a Whit-Sunday) the Battalion (in brigade and division) moved to Cassel, detrained, and marched 8 miles to Buysseheure and there billeted. "This march," said an N.C.O. of the Battalion, "was by far the most trying we had had yet, as we carried full marching order with blankets strapped on behind . . . every one was nearly done."

The Battalion remained in billets in Buysseheure until the 27th May, when a move was made to Nordpeene. On the 28th the 6th Somersets marched via Cassel and Bailleul to Eecke, billeting in the latter place until the morning of the 30th, when the Battalion (in brigade) set out (via Bailleul) on the march to Scherpenberg. The Battalion Diary records that: "This march was a trying one on account of the high N.E. wind and the traffic round Bailleul. No man fell out."

For over a week the 6th Somersets remained at Scherpenberg, supplying working parties for the digging of trenches for a secondary position S.W. of

11th June

Ypres. On the 11th June battalions of the 43rd Brigade were ordered to be allotted to troops of the 46th Division for instructional purposes in the front-line trenches. The Battalion Diary thus describes the first tour in the front line:—

"Saturday, June 12th. The Battalion left Scherpenberg at 7.15 a.m.

[1] Strength of Battalion: 31 officers, 1 M.O., 961 other ranks, 6 attached. Lt.-Col. C. G. Rawling was in command.
[2] Brigadier-General G. Cockburn.

and reached billets about the vicinity of S. 22, sheet 28, S.W. on the Bailleul— 6th Battalion
Neuve Eglise Road by 10 a.m.   That evening Battalion Hqrs., 2 companies and 12th June
half the Machine-gun Section went for a tour of duty in the trenches, being
attached to the 5th N. Stafford R., the remainder of the Battalion remaining in
billets, the trenches being situated almost 2,000 yards N.E. of Wulverghem.

"Sunday, June 13th.   The trench life was very quiet.   A little shelling
early in the morning and desultory rifle fire during the day."

Battalion H.Q. returned to billets on 14th.   On 15th the remaining
two companies relieved the other companies in the front line, the whole Battalion
coming out on Saturday, June 19th.

"Throughout the whole week the men of the Battalion had been under
fire, both artillery and infantry, and their behaviour has been excellent.   No
complaints at all.   The Battalion who were our instructors were full of praise
of the bearing and behaviour of the 'Kitcheners,' whom they saw for the
first time." [1]

On 20th the 6th Somersets received orders to join up with the remainder
of the 43rd Brigade at Poperinghe.   Setting out at 9.45 p.m., the Battalion
marched all night via Locre and reached billets, about 1½ miles from Poperinghe, at 2.35 on the 21st.   The 43rd Brigade was then billeted in depth
along the Poperinghe–Watou Road.

On 22nd orders were received by the 43rd Brigade to move up to the 22nd June
trenches and relieve the 42nd Brigade (on the night 24th/25th June) in the
line east of Ypres.   The Durhams were to take over the right sub-sector and
the Somersets the left.   The latter arrived just west of Vlamertinghe at 4 p.m.
and there had tea.   At 8.30 p.m. the march was continued, though progress
was evidently slow, as the Battalion did not reach Ypres until 9.15 p.m.

"We passed through Ypres, and the memory of this scene of desolation
has made the greatest impression on me of anything in the war up to the present.
Whole streets of shattered houses, especially around the Cathedral and Cloth
Hall, but the builders of the two latter knew their work so well that the outer
walls of both mostly remain standing.   The Cathedral tower bids defiance to
the Huns and the façade of the Cloth Hall is sufficiently intact to show what
its original beauty must have been.   Modern buildings, however, are smashed
to atoms." [2]

Whilst waiting in Ypres to go forward, hostile shells fell frequently, and
when at last the Battalion got on the move, the relief took a long while to
complete, so that it was 2.30 a.m. on 25th before the Somerset men were
settled in.   One casualty from shell fire and one from rifle fire were suffered
by the Battalion.

The trenches taken over were situated in a dangerous position.   They had

[1] Battalion Diary, 6th Somerset L.I.
[2] The late Cpl. F. W. Loxton, 6th Bn. Somerset L.I.

6th Battalion

been captured from the enemy only a few days previously and occupied the most easterly point of the British position in Belgium, in front of Hooge. The line generally was in a very bad state and under incessant shell fire from the north, east and south.

The following phrases culled from the Battalion Diary during this tour sum up the happenings of the five days spent in the line:—

"The Battalion worked very hard in improvement of trenches. The behaviour of all ranks was excellent. . . . Enemy very busy sapping and wiring, but shows no inclination to attack. . . . Heavy shell fire from 11 a.m. to 2 p.m. [28th]. High explosive poured upon us."

Relief came during the night 29th/30th June, when the 8th Rifle Brigade and 7th K.R.R. took over the line held by the 6th Somersets, and the latter marched back to billets in A.17.d.3.10 (near Vlamertinghe). The total casualties suffered by the Battalion during the five days were 43—six officers being wounded (Capts. A. R. S. Sale Hill, Wilmer and Bellew, and Lieuts. Caillard, Roberts and Hopewell), 6 other ranks killed and 31 wounded.

30th June

From 30th June to 18th July the 6th Somersets remained in billets, supplying large working parties day and night. Only two casualties (gun-shot wounds) were incurred during this period. At 6 p.m. on the 18th, however, the Battalion marched out of billets through Ypres and reached the Menin Gate at 9 p.m. Here guides from the 5th K.S.L.I. met the Somerset men and conducted the Battalion to the front-line trenches, which were only reached after one and three-quarter hours' hard walking. The new line was the left sub-sector of the 43rd Brigade front, described in the Diaries as "D.10.11 and 12, S.11.12a.12b.12c.F.12." This tour lasted until 22nd and was of a very strenuous nature. The enemy's guns were particularly active and on the very first day the casualties of the Battalion were heavy—4 other ranks killed and 29 wounded. Work on the defences, wherever hostile shell fire was less heavy, proceeded night and day and all ranks were not sorry when the 10th Durham Light Infantry filed into the trenches on the night of 22nd/23rd and took over the line from the Somerset men, who proceeded

26th July

to the Ramparts—Ypres. Here, until 26th, the Battalion remained, supplying large parties of from 600–700 men for carrying R.E. stores and ammunition up to the front-line trenches. On the 26th the Battalion moved back to bivouacs in "H.5.d.3.7." for the remainder of the month of July.

Whilst the 6th Somersets were waiting in Ypres to go forward to the trenches east of that place, the 7th Battalion landed in France.

7th Battalion

The 7th Somerset Light Infantry, commanded by Lieut.-Colonel C. J. Troyte-Bullock, on reaching Woking on 21st September 1914, was brigaded with the 7th Duke of Cornwall's Light Infantry, 7th K.O.Y.L.I. and 12th Durham Light Infantry; the four battalions formed the 61st Infantry Brigade of the 20th (Light) Division of Kitchener's Second Army ("K.2").

Several months were passed in training and equipping, and on 22nd February 1915, the 61st Brigade marched from the Woking area to Witley

Camp, Godalming, where the Division was concentrating.   A month later   7th Battalion
(21st March) the Division moved to Salisbury Plain.

The 20th Division was inspected by H.M. the King on 24th June, and   24th June
all ranks felt that the time was close at hand for a move to France.   However,
another month was spent on Salisbury Plain, the Battalion finally entraining at
Amesbury for Southampton and, embarking at the latter port, sailed for France
on 24th July.   At 11 p.m. the 7th Somersets disembarked at Boulogne and
marched to the Rest Camp above the town, where it stayed until the following
afternoon, when it proceeded by train to Wizernes.   Here the Somerset men   25th July
billeted, the remainder of the Brigade occupying billets in the neighbouring
villages.

On 28th July the 61st Brigade marched to Hazebrouck—a 15-mile
march in very hot weather.   The 7th Somersets were billeted in the New
Hospital.   The march was continued on 29th to Noote Boom and Le Rossignol,
near Steenwerck.   In this place the Battalion settled down for several days'
training.

CHAPTER XV

HOOGE

"H.5.d.3.7," to which place the 6th Somersets had marched on relief from the Ramparts, Ypres, on 26th July, was a hop field about half-way between Vlamertinghe and Poperinghe, and here the Battalion set to work to make itself as comfortable in bivouacs as the circumstances and summer weather would allow; all ranks were anticipating a week's rest at least. But at 4.30 a.m. on 30th a telegram was received at Battalion Headquarters from the Brigade: "Stand to arms: Germans attacking 41st Brigade." The 41st Brigade was then occupying trenches at Hooge.

Very early in the morning the front-line trenches of the Brigade were suddenly flooded by liquid fire, which belched from jets in the German lines opposite. This new device momentarily caused surprise and confusion, and the victims of this dastardly attack fell back from the front-line trenches which were then occupied by the enemy.

At 5.15 a.m. the 6th Somersets stood ready to move off at a moment's notice, but after waiting until 7.30 a.m. the men were given orders to fall out. But at 6.35 p.m. that night, the Battalion received orders to march to dug-outs at H.7. *En route* to H.7, however, the Battalion was given further orders—to occupy the Ramparts, Ypres. Very tired, the Somerset men reached their destination at about 10.15 p.m., relieving two companies of the Shropshires and Rifle Brigade.

Meanwhile, during the afternoon, the 41st Brigade had counter-attacked, but only succeeded in regaining a portion of the lost trenches, the enemy holding on to the most advanced trench.

At 3.10 a.m. on 31st A and B Companies were ordered to proceed at once to G.H.Q. line, where they stayed until 5 p.m. and were then ordered to reinforce the Durhams in the firing line in Zouave Wood. At 8.49 p.m. Bn. Hqs. and C and D Companies were ordered to relieve A and B Companies, but on the former moving forward they were held up at the Lille Gate (Ypres) by violent hostile artillery fire. "We moved off," said Lieut. A. H. Foley, "but before we had got clear of the town the bombardment recommenced with such violence that it was impossible to go any farther. We waited crouching along under a garden wall opposite the ruins of a church, while around us raged a perfect tornado. Branches of trees were strewn about and pieces of brick and masonry hurtled into the roadway, but luckily our hiding-place was not directly subjected to shelling, so that we escaped serious damage." Until 10.30 p.m. Bn. Hqs. and C and D Companies were thus held up, but on the bombardment quietening down, a move was made towards the G.H.Q. line, which was reached about 12.50 a.m.

DISCHARGE FROM TRENCH FLAME PROJECTOR

All day long on 1st August Bn. Hqs. and C and D Companies were
"standing to," but at night on receipt of orders they moved off to reinforce
A and B Companies [1] in Zouave Wood.   By midnight A, B and C Companies
of the 6th Somersets occupied the firing line in the Wood, with D Company
in reserve in dug-outs known as Half-way House.

At daybreak, a veritable tornado of shells again swept Zouave Wood,
and work on the trenches, repairing parapets, etc., that had been blown in,
was difficult.   When night fell one other rank had been killed and 37 wounded.
For four days British and German shells hurtled and shrieked through the
air—the artillery of both sides engaging in desperate duels.   Casualties on
2nd August were: 2 officers wounded, 6 other ranks killed, 16 wounded and
1 missing; on 3rd: 1 other rank killed and 7 wounded; on 4th: 3 other
ranks killed and 16 wounded; on 5th: 16 other ranks wounded.

A private diary thus briefly describes the scene on the night of 3rd August
when D Company moved up from reserve and relieved A Company in the
front line:—

"Moved up to firing line to-night relieving A Company; worst part of
front in the hollow of 'U' facing trench captured by Germans, the space
between it and us being open ground covered with long grass, and our position
being on edge of Sanctuary Wood,[2] beautifully marked off by German artillery.
The whole hollow of the 'U' was covered with dead bodies of K.R.Rs. and
R.Bs., killed in original retreat and subsequent counter-attacks on retreat,
and the stench was awful and outlook appalling.   The captured trench was on
rising ground and also beautifully ranged by our artillery, who were dropping
in shells all day.   It is doubtful whether the Germans occupy the trench at
all.   If they do, or did, then their losses must have been frightful, as our fire
from 9·2 and other guns was terrible, practically every shell dropping in trench
or parapet.   We saw several bodies on parapet in German uniform, a sign
that their losses had been heavy, otherwise they would have been recovered
and buried." [3]

On 5th August the 6th Somersets were relieved by troops of the 6th
Division, and marched back to dug-outs west of Ypres.   But death followed
the Battalion even out of the trenches, for as another diarist records: "On our
way out we lost Tinknell, a Bridgwater man, who was hit in the stomach by
a stray bullet and died very soon afterwards."

[1] Capt. P. E. Bradney, commanding B Company, was killed on 31st July.
[2] Zouave Wood was immediately W. of Sanctuary Wood.
[3] The late Corporal F. W. Loxton, 6th Somerset L.I.

CHAPTER XVI

THE BATTLE OF LOOS:
25TH SEPTEMBER–8TH OCTOBER 1915

I

THE MAIN OPERATIONS

8th Battalion

FROM a Regimental point of view there are two aspects of the Battle of Loos—the main attack in which the 8th Somersets took part, and the subsidiary operations in which the 6th and 7th Battalions were involved.

The official despatches may be searched in vain for the intentions of the Allied Commanders which resulted in the Battle of Loos. But briefly they were as follows: to break the enemy's front; prevent him re-establishing his line; to defeat decisively his divided forces.

The operations were designed on a larger scale than had hitherto been attempted. Throughout the summer of 1915 the Allies had been preparing for the battle and ammunition had been conserved so that the guns (of which just over one thousand had been detailed for the operations) might not go short. East and west of Rheims four French Armies were to attack the enemy, whilst north and south of Arras the First British and Tenth French Armies were to launch a combined attack; the Second British Army and the Indian Corps were to carry out subsidiary attacks north of the La Bassée Canal and in the neighbourhood of Ypres, and the Third British Army, between Monchy and the Somme. The I and IV Corps were to make the main attack along the British front, from Loos to Givenchy, just north of the La Bassée Canal; the XI Corps (Guards, 21st and 24th Divisions) was in reserve. Such, briefly, were the intentions of the Commanders and the forces to be engaged.

But this story concerns only the fortunes of the 21st Division (one of the reserve divisions of the XI Corps) which, when the battle opened on the 25th September, stood ready north-west of Beuvry, awaiting orders to go forward to the front line.

Scarce fourteen days had elapsed since the Division had arrived in France (7th–11th September), quite inexperienced and totally lacking in knowledge of the enemy's methods which trench warfare had given other units; it may be said that as a whole the Division had never fired a shot at the enemy, neither had it been fired upon. These details should be borne in mind.

10th September

The 8th Somerset Light Infantry (Lieut.-Col. H. C. Denny) of the 63rd Brigade had landed at Havre (in Brigade) on the 10th September. This Battalion, a unit of "K.3" (raised in October 1914), had spent about ten months in strenuous training at Leighton Buzzard, Halton and Witley, and

74

embarked at Southampton (about 1,100 strong) on 9th September. After landing at Havre and spending 24 hours in the Rest Camp, the 8th Somersets proceeded by train to Watten, marching from the latter place to Bayenghem where, until 8 p.m. on the 19th, the Battalion carried out the usual preparations for moving up to the front line. The subsequent movements of the Battalion, until it went into action on the night of the 25th, are interesting, for they throw some light on the condition of both officers and men when they were called upon to take part in the battle. The Battalion Diary states that:—

"We left Bayenghem about 8 p.m. 19th September, arriving Wardrecques on 20th September; Bourecq, on the 21st September; Ferfay (where we stayed two days) on the 22nd September and bivouacked near Nœux les Mines on the 24th September. On the morning of the 25th September we marched to Vermelles and deployed to go into action about 7 p.m."

And the 63rd Brigade Diary records that when just south of Houchin at 11.30 a.m. on 25th:—

"Divisional operation orders received to march to area L.15–L.16 (S.W. of Noyelles les Vermelles). Area reached at 2.30 p.m. At 4 p.m. Brigade started to march via Philosophe (Fosse No. 3 de Béthune), and at 8 p.m. reached Fosse No. 7 on Loos Road with a view to subsequent advance to the line of the Hulluch–Lens Road by night, thence to continue advance against German trenches in direction of Annay."

From Bayenghem to Fosse No. 7 was a distance of approximately 60 miles, covered by the Battalion between the 19th and 25th September, of which two days were spent in Ferfay. No mean performance considering the weight of the kit and equipment carried by each man on bad roads.

The official despatches should be studied for a brief account of the sanguinary struggle which began with the abortive gas attack early on the morning of the 25h September, and continued throughout the day until night, when the reserve divisions, which should have been available much earlier, were flung into the line to continue the battle. So far as the 8th Battalion Somerset Light Infantry is concerned, only one detailed account is available, written by Major L. C. Howard who, in command of B and C Companies of the Battalion, handled his men so ably as to win from the G.O.C., 63rd Brigade, well-deserved commendation: "I consider that this officer's behaviour is worthy of all praise and shows what influence over the *morale* of the men one single strong mind can bring to bear." Of the doings of Bn. H.Qs. and A and D Companies, under the command of Lieut.-Col. Denny, there are few details.

The Battalion Diary describes the action:—

"B and C Companies went to the Hulluch–Lens Road; held the Road for the night of the 25th and on the morning of the 26th were counter-attacked by the enemy and ordered to retire by the Brigade Major at 1 p.m. 26th September. They retired to first-line trenches and held them until 8 a.m. 27th September, when they marched to bivouac near Vermelles and joined A and D Companies there. A and D Companies participated in an attack on Hill 70 on the night 25th/26th September, and retired about 12 (noon) on 26th, when they went into support line, old German trenches, and were joined on the morning of the 27th by B and C Companies."

Thus the Battalion's account.

Major Howard's report is so interesting that it is given *in extenso*:—

"At 7 p.m. on the 25th September 1915 I received verbal orders to take B and C Companies, 8th [S] Battalion, Somerset Light Infantry as a firing line, and go due east to make good the Hulluch–Lens road at H.25a. The 8th [S] Bn. Lincoln Regiment was on my left. I started about 7.30 p.m., and about 9.45 p.m. I stopped for twenty minutes to make all my men fill their water-bottles and haversacks with water and provisions of which there was a good supply in our vacated first-line trenches. I also sent back a messenger to ask Col. Denny, who was bringing A and D Companies along as my supports, to put out connecting files between the supports and me. The messenger brought back word that the Adjutant did not think connecting files necessary. I then resumed the advance, keeping close touch with the Lincolns on my left and arrived at my objective, the Hulluch–Lens road—H.25.8.7, at about 3.30 a.m., having searched the wood H.25 on my way. During the advance we were under machine-gun fire from the direction of H.25 but had only two casualties.

"I then received orders from Brigadier-General Nickalls to take up a position with one company facing east along the Hulluch–Lens road, H.25.a.8.7. to H.25, and place the other company, as brigade reserve, in the chalk pits at H.25.a.7.7. I placed B Company, under Capt. Nichols, along the Hulluch–Lens road, but finding the company too weak to hold so much line I asked for and obtained permission from Brigadier-General Nickalls to place another platoon there. This gave me 5 platoons along the Hulluch–Lens road, from H.25.a.8.7. to H.25, and three platoons in the chalk pits.

"[A and D Companies, who had started out as my supports, had gone astray and never found their way back to me.] I made all hands spend the remainder of the night vigorously digging themselves in. From dawn onwards we were persistently sniped at but could not find the snipers. At 8.20 a.m. I received orders for an advance on Annay and at 8.45 a.m., whilst reading and explaining these orders to my officers, I was called for by the Brigade Major who informed me that we were being counter-attacked on our right and asked me to place my three reserve platoons in position along the edge of the wood, H.25.a., facing S.E. This I did, finding them good natural cover and an old deserted shallow trench. A continuous heavy rifle fire was then opened upon us, but I only had about three casualties as my men were well under cover. At about 9.20 a.m. Capt. Rose [the Staff Captain] came

to me in an exhausted [winded] condition and asked me to send a messenger
to the York and Lancaster Regiment who were on my right in front of wood
H.25.a., and tell them to send a company back to the trenches they had vacated
along the Hulluch–Lens road, H.19.c.   Nobody volunteered to go so I went
myself and, finding no officer in capable control, I ordered about one hundred
men back to their trenches and saw them safely in position there, H.19.c.
The Brigade Major asked me if I could spare a platoon to go there also.   I
sent Lieut. Marsh and his platoon there and spread out my men to take the
place he had vacated.   During this time a heavy rifle and machine-gun fire
was turned on us, accompanied by a very heavy and accurate shell fire.   However, we were well entrenched and our casualties were remarkably few."

At about 10.15 a.m. some troops on Major Howard's left retired.

"I could see a few men were still left in the trenches.   The Germans
now began to show their hand, coming out in the open from wood H.25 and 26
and attacking along my left front in a half-hearted manner.   The York and
Lancs on my right had already retired owing to the intensity of the enemy
shell fire, so I drew in my right flank and made a redoubt of the chalk pits.
The enemy then concentrated their fire on my position but without great
effect—their shells going over our heads and bursting at the bottom of the
chalk pit.   Their snipers were deadly though, and 2/Lt. Hopkins was killed
and Lt. Fitzmaurice wounded about this time.   A few minutes later 2/Lt.
Baker was killed.   Earlier in the morning at the suggestion of the Brigade
Major I had called for ten volunteers to bring ammunition.   These men now
returned with 2,000 rounds, saying it was all they could get.   A few of my
men whose officers had been killed had retreated whilst I was otherwise engaged.
However, we were all in good spirits and blazed away at the Germans who
were coming into full view all the time now.   Capt. Stromquist of the 8th
Lincolns, who had joined me earlier saying he could not find his company,
was killed at about 11 a.m.

"Things began to get warm now and we all took rifles and shot carefully
along the wood wherever the enemy debouched, at ranges varying from 400 to
800 yards.   Ammunition ran low so we stripped the dead of theirs and got
enough to keep going, and at 11.40 a.m., to our great joy, we saw reinforcements [the attacking brigade] coming over the brow of the slope behind us.

"We shot freely now and held the Germans to their ground.   Capt.
Nicholls was killed and Lieut. Robinson wounded.   At 12.30 p.m. reinforcements [the attacking brigade] reached our line, the Buffs joining me at the
chalk pits and bringing a very much-needed machine gun with them, which was
very capably and pluckily handled by the machine-gun officer.   About 1 p.m.
the attacking brigade retired, and at 1.15 p.m. Major Macdonald [the Brigade
Major] ordered me to retire because the attacking brigade, in its retirement,
had left both my flanks clear, and because I had no ammunition left.   I effected
a retirement with very little loss, gathered together the men of the different
regiments and manned the English front-line trenches, relieving Capt. Wilson

of the Highland Light Infantry. I remained there until 8 a.m. 27th September, when I marched to bivouac.

"Whilst at the chalk pits neither I nor any of my men saw or smelt any sign of gas.

"I cannot speak too highly of the two young dead officers of mine—2/Lieutenants Baker and Hopkins. Their coolness and bravery was a great example to their men. Capt. Huntingdon and 2/Lieut. Warden also rendered me good assistance, and the following N.C.O.'s and men stuck it well: C.S.M. Biss, Sergts. Kelly and Tyler, L/Cpls. Robinson and Kennedy, Privates Lambley, Carr, Green, Ockleford, Davis, Hooper, Jeffries and Johnson [brought in wounded under heavy fire] and Feltham."

Of what happened to Colonel Denny's two companies (A and D) there is no detailed account, and only the following brief reference to them occurs in the Brigadier's report of the operations:—

"Half a battalion of the Somerset L.I. under Colonel Denny and with the machine guns had failed to keep touch during the night advance, and in consequence had lost their way and were not seen again until 7 p.m., after the withdrawal had been effected. It appears that this half-battalion took part in the attack against Hill 70, but its absence from the Brigade [63rd], especially the machine guns, was a serious loss." [1]

Amongst several "comments" added by the Brigade Major to the Brigadier's report, there is one vital statement: "The absence of information of what was happening elsewhere was nothing short of disastrous, as no one knew what anyone else was doing." In other words, co-operation, the very essence of success in war, was almost entirely lacking.

Back in the old German trenches to which the Somersets had retired, the roll was called, and it was then learned how heavy were the losses of the Battalion. Three officers had been killed,[2] seven wounded, and five were

[1] The following notes regarding A and D Companies have been supplied by an officer of the 8th Somersets:—

A and D Companies were in support of B and C but were ordered forward, owing to an anticipated attack by the Germans. The majority of A Company intermingled and became subordinated to the 9th (Scottish) Division, who had made the initial attack. A portion of A Company were searching cellars and dug-outs in Loos, one Section of No. 4 Platoon entirely disappeared whilst so engaged, Captain R. Milne and the other Officers of A Company were all casualties. The total of A Company after the action was 26 O.R.

D Company was mainly round the Slag heaps. Lieut. H. B. Hatt, who remained with the remnants of this Company, was awarded the M.C.

Colonel Denny and the Adjutant were forward with the Battalion, also the M.O. (Lt. A. S. Cohen) who did wonderful work, before he was badly wounded, and later died. The Transport, including the Machine-gun Section, were left at Vermelles, and on the afternoon of the 26th an attempt was made to get the guns and ammunition to the line. The German Artillery spotted them when on rising ground and with their sighting shot put two limbers out of action, and owing to the heavy fire the transport were ordered back. The guns were later recovered from the limbers that had been disabled.

[2] Second-Lieuts. S. W. Baker, L. Hopkins, R. H. Basker.

reported "wounded and missing."[1]   In other ranks the Battalion had lost 8th Battalion 26 killed, 156 wounded, 3 gassed and 86 missing.

The Battalion remained in bivouac near Vermelles until the evening of 28th, when the whole Brigade marched to the Estree Blanche–Linghem–Rely area, where two more days were spent.   On 1st October the Brigade marched 1st October to Steenbecque and on the following day to Borre to reorganize and refit.

II

THE SUBSIDIARY ACTIONS

Neither in the main nor the subsidiary actions were the 1st Somersets 1st Battalion engaged, for on the first day of the operations (25th Sept.) the Battalion was billeted in Mesnil—a quiet village from 2 to 3 miles N. of Albert—the 4th Division having in July moved down to the Somme area to join the Third Army.   The 6th and 7th Battalions were, however, both involved in 6th and 7th the subsidiary actions, the former in the second attack on Bellewaarde, whilst Battalions the latter carried out fire demonstrations in accordance with orders issued to all units holding front-line trenches in those areas from which infantry or fire attacks were to be made for the purpose of attracting the enemy's attention from the main operations between Loos and Givenchy.

The section of trenches held by the 7th Somersets on 25th September 7th Battalion lay east of La Cordonnerie Farm, the 61st Brigade of the 20th Division then holding a sub-sector east and south-east of Petillon; the Brigade therefore was between the areas of the Actions of Pietre, and of Bois Grenier.[2]

The 7th Battalion from the end of July to the 10th August had remained 10th August in billets at Le Rossignol, "carrying on our training," said Lieut.-Colonel Troyte-Bullock, "and listening to the guns in the distance and wondering when our turn would come to make their close acquaintance."

It was to come soon enough!

On 10th August the Battalion moved to Armentières to be attached to the 27th Division for instruction in trench warfare.   A and B Companies went into the trenches that night and were relieved on the following night by C and D Companies.

The opposing trenches were not very wide apart, and on the first night the Somerset men were considerably surprised and indignant to hear a voice from the German trenches call out: "Hullo!   You Somerset cuckoos."

In these trenches the Battalion suffered its first casualty, Private C. Stephens of A Company being shot by a sniper whilst on sentry-go.

On the 17th the Battalion returned to its old billeting area W. of Steen- werck and remained there until 28th August, when the 61st Brigade moved 28th August to Estaires.   Work on the defences S.W. of the town kept the Battalion

---

[1] Major W. H. Nichols died on 13th October 1915, whilst Lieut. A. S. Cohen (R.A.M.C.), the Battalion M.O. and 2/Lieuts. E. C. Robinson and F. J. Ealand were subsequently found to be amongst the "killed."

[2] Only the right of the 20th Division was involved in the former action.

busy for several days, but on the 5th September the 61st Brigade relieved a brigade of the 8th Division in the front line, from south of Petillon to W. of La Boutillerie, the 7th Somersets being in support in farms and posts in the Rue du Quesne.

On 12th September the Battalion relieved the 12th Bn. King's R. in the trenches east of Cordonnerie Farm—A and B Companies in the front line, C in support and D in reserve.   The dangers of active trench warfare became almost immediately terribly apparent, for early on the following morning (at about 5.20 a.m.) the ground beneath the section of trench held by B Company suddenly shook, there was a deafening roar and sand bags and earth, equipment and men shot up into the air—the enemy had exploded two mines under the Somerset men.   The Germans then opened heavy shell and machine-gun fire on the craters formed by the explosion.   Twenty men of B Company were buried in the debris, but with fine courage and tenacity the Company not only set to work to dig them out, but also to consolidate themselves.   Five men were killed and twelve wounded by the explosion, and two men killed and five wounded by shell and machine-gun fire.   Second-Lieut. Mitchell showed great courage and coolness in dealing with a very difficult situation.[1]   Both on the 14th and 15th the enemy continued to shell the trenches of the Battalion and hurl trench-mortar bombs into the mine-craters.   About 9 p.m. on the 16th, whilst D Company was relieving B Company, Captain F. M. Y. Nepean and his orderly were killed by a trench-mortar bomb.   On the 19th September the 7th Somersets were relieved and returned to the old billets in Rue du Quesne.

Preparations for the subsidiary operations of the Battle of Loos had already begun on 21st September, when on the night of 24th the Battalion with the 7th K.O.Y.L.I. moved back into the front line with orders to "go over the top in the event of the Huns showing any inclination to run away." The Somerset men took over the left sub-sector, with the now-familiar Convent wall on their left (where the 25th Brigade (8th Division) held the line) and the K.O.Y.L.I. on their right.

Fortunately the Battalion was not called upon to "go over," for the enemy was very far from being in the mood to run away.   He was, indeed, particularly active and alive to all that was going on in front of and around him.   On the right of the 61st Brigade the 60th Brigade, attacking opposite Fromelles, suffered very heavy casualties and the 25th Brigade on the left, after having driven the enemy out of his front-line trenches, was forced to retire to its original jumping-off line, having lost heavily.   So far as the 7th Somersets were concerned, the following account sums up the action in which the Battalion took part :—

"Most of our artillery having gone south to help the real battle, we were

---

[1] Major Preston-Whyte, commanding B Company, received written congratulations from the Divisional Commander, and Lieut. Mitchell was awarded the Military Cross—the first honour won by the 7th Battalion.

practically without artillery support. Our 18-pdrs. opened the ball at 4.20 a.m. _{7th Battalion} with what some wag on the Staff was pleased to call a 'bombardment.' The enemy replied with heavy stuff, mostly 5·9, on our support line, but their shooting was poor and did us no harm. It was a misty, drizzling morning and visibility was bad. We assisted with bursts of rapid rifle fire and Lewis guns, and the Hun machine guns were busy all along the line . . . the Rifle Brigade alone had 300 casualties. . . . We were devoutly thankful that we had not also been put into the soup."

The Battalion remained in its position of assembly until 11 p.m. on the 26th when it returned to billets in the Rue du Quesne.

THE SECOND ATTACK ON BELLEWAARDE, 25TH–26TH SEPTEMBER 1915

More costly to the Regiment, and of a very different nature, were the subsidiary operations in which the 6th Somersets took part on 25th and 26th 6th Battalion September, although the Battalion made no attack on the enemy.

After the strenuous days from 1st to the 6th August, the 6th Battalion 6th August remained in Camp W. of Vlamertinghe until 10th, when orders were received to take over the front line at Railway Wood from the 5th Shropshire L.I. The night was very quiet and the relief was completed by 12.35 a.m. (11th), no casualties being incurred. The Somerset men found the trenches in a terrible condition, the parapets had been blown down, the communication trenches blocked and machine-gun emplacements destroyed. During the afternoon the enemy's artillery was very active and 5 other ranks were killed and 12 wounded. At night the Battalion worked hard in repairing old, and digging new, trenches, but it was a seemingly hopeless task, for on the following day the enemy's artillery again blew the parapet in and subjected the whole line to a heavy bombardment. On 12th 1 other rank was killed and 16 wounded. These heavy hostile bombardments and similar retaliation by British and French artillery were typical of the restless activity prevailing in the Ypres Salient, where peace was practically unknown. Relief came on 16th, and the Battalion was not sorry to quit the front line after a very uncomfortable tour. For a fortnight the Battalion was out of the front line, but on 1st September left camp between 4.30 and 5.30 p.m. and relieved the 6th 1st September D.C.L.I., whose guides were to meet the Battalion at the Menin Gate. Just west of Ypres the enemy suddenly opened a heavy bombardment with "whizbangs," and the Battalion had 16 other ranks wounded Eventually the relief was completed at 1.30 a.m. on 2nd. The trenches were again found in a wretched condition, wet weather combined with the enemy's activity having damaged the defences very badly. Three other ranks killed and thirty-three wounded were the losses during this tour which ended on 7th. Several days (from 15th to 20th September) were spent in the G.H.Q. line south of the Ypres–Menin road, followed by three days in camp at "H.1.5.a," and it was at the latter place that orders for the Second Attack on Bellewaarde reached the Battalion.

The information contained in orders was that the 14th Division would capture the Bellewaarde Farm position on 25th September. The 42nd Brigade was detailed for the operation, and the 6th Somerset L.I. was attached to the Brigade with orders to place 3 companies in reserve in G.H.Q. line and one company in A.1, H.22, R.2, 3, 4, 6. A.1 and H.22 were front-line trenches; R.2, 3, 4, 6, were redoubts.[1]

A Company of the Somersets, under Captain H. L. Skrine, was ordered to move up to the front line during the night of 23rd September, whilst Bn. Hqs. and B, C and D Companies were to arrive in the G.H.Q. line the following night. Both moves apparently took place, the Battalion Diary on 24th recording that at 7.15 p.m.:—

"Battalion (less A Company) marched off and at 8 p.m. entrained at siding for transport to Ypres, detraining at back of Asylum. Night quiet, clear, but moon obscured by clouds. Not much rifle fire and no shell fire. Roads wet from the rain that fell persistently earlier in the day. By 11 p.m. Battalion (less A Company) was secure in G.H.Q. line."

At 3.50 a.m. on the 25th the guns opened an intense bombardment of the enemy's line extending from Railway Wood to Sanctuary Wood, and at 4.19 a.m. a mine was exploded beneath a German post at 0.4 One minute later the guns lifted and the three front-line battalions of the 42nd Brigade— 5th Shropshire L.I., 5th Oxford and Bucks L.I. and 9th Rifle Brigade— assaulted the German first- and second-line trenches. The Battalion Diary 6th Somersets states that at "4.22 a.m. guns again lifted" and at "4.23 a.m. guns established barrage of fire." Thereafter there is no entry until 7.15 a.m., when a message was received at Bn. H.Qs. in G.H.Q. line that one company of the 6th Somersets was to "stand by" ready to reinforce firing line. Five minutes later a runner was despatched to No. 4 Company (Capt. F. Bramwell) to get ready and the second-in-command, Major T. Ritchie, was ordered to take command of the forward companies. Almost directly this message had reached Capt. Bramwell a further message was received to "send up 3 companies." The message read as follows:—

"Move 3 companies up at once Railway Wood aaa Situation is that troops after capturing German line have been forced back and (enemy) are attacking our original trenches and your Battalion will hold the original lines and the original line of 'H Sector.'"

Major Ritchie with No. 4 Company at once went forward to reinforce the front line, followed by Colonel Rawling, commanding 6th Som. L.I., and his Adjutant who led the two remaining companies to Railway Wood via E. Lane. This advance was made under shell fire, but casualties were slight. It should be noted that it was now broad daylight.

On arrival at Railway Wood (9.45 a.m.) the situation was found to be critical, and the following message was sent back to 42nd Brigade Hqs.:—

[1] Maps being unavailable, further descriptions of these trenches and redoubts are impossible.

"Oxfords and Shropshires retired to original British trenches aaa R.B. about 6th Battalion 100 strong only aaa Have reinforced H.21, H.20 and H.19 aaa Oxfords asking 25th September for assistance.   I will therefore hold H.18, H.17, H.16 aaa Shropshires too weak to counter-attack shall support them lightly aaa Our front-line trenches obliterated.   I shall follow first order, hold the trenches and not attack."

In a dug-out close by Colonel Rawling found the C.O.'s of the 9th K.R.R. and 9th R.B., together with various officers of both Battalions, discussing the situation.   Both Battalions had apparently established themselves in the German line, but being too weak to hold it, were driven out again.   They had suffered so heavily that a counter-attack was out of the question.

The next phrase in the Battalion Diary is one pregnant with meaning: "The Battalion held on all day in trenches H.19–A.1, and at dusk the 9th K.R.R. and 9th R.B. were withdrawn."   The dearest thing of a soldier's heart is "Pride of Regiment," and it was because of the proud traditions of the Regiment that those Somerset men, with fierce tenacity and splendid courage, "held on all day" in the face of a terrible bombardment.   Only those who fought in France and Flanders know what lay behind that grim phrase.   About 5 p.m. the enemy's artillery fire gradually became less and by 7 p.m. had almost died down.   The 6th Somersets at that hour held A.1, A.22 and the redoubts A.21, A.2, A.12 and H.20.

The night was quiet, and under cover of the friendly darkness the men set to work to repair the trenches and parapets, recover the dead and bring in the wounded.   When the roll was called it was found that Capt. H. L. Skrine and 2/Lieuts. J. N. Purkiss and C. E. C. Talbot had been killed and Lieut. S. Birrell wounded.   In other ranks the Battalion had lost 11 killed, 38 wounded and 3 missing.[1]

The morning of the 26th was sunny, and quietude reigned where the day 26th September before the din of battle had been awesome and horrible.   The whole day was devoted to reorganizing and strengthening the defences, upon which all ranks worked hard.   At intervals the sharp crack of a sniper's rifle rang out, but otherwise both forces were too much occupied with the repair of defences to think about the opposing side.   Six killed and eight wounded were the casualties suffered by the Battalion on this day.

The 27th was uneventful except for one small incident (all too rare) which produced a certain amount of mutual respect between the Somerset men and the Germans.

It had not been possible to bring in all the wounded from No Man's Land, and one poor fellow lay out in that dread space moaning in a most heart-rending fashion.   About 5.30 p.m. the Germans, after attempting (in vain) to bring the poor fellow in, allowed two men of No. 3 Company to go out and carry him back to the Battalion's trenches, this operation, records the Diary, "being concluded with mutual cheers from both sides."

[1] C.S.M. T. Peppin was awarded the M.C. for gallantry during the 25th and 26th September. When all officers of his Company had become casualties he took command for two days.

At 11 p.m. on 28th, in the midst of heavy rain, the 6th Somersets were relieved by the 7th R. Brigade and returned to Camp. But before the Battalion left the trenches the G.O.C., 14th Division and B.-G.C., 43rd Brigade, visited the lines. The former expressed himself very satisfied indeed at the work done by the Battalion when in the trenches, and further said that he was charged by the Corps Commander (General Pulteney) to express the latter's thanks to the Battalion for their behaviour and gallant conduct. The G.O.C., 42nd Brigade (to which the Somersets were attached), also sent the following letter to the C.O.:—

"Dear Colonel Rawling, I have to thank you and your fine regiment for the great assistance you gave me on the 25th. It was not an easy thing to reinforce, in broad daylight, as you did, and the movement was exceedingly well and quickly carried out. You arrived at a critical time and your dispositions were exactly what was required. The company of your Regiment which formed the garrison of the trenches rendered valuable assistance and I much regret to hear of the losses they sustained."

And Colonel Rawling, in his Battalion Diary, pays tribute to the stretcher-bearers—those brave fellows who at all times carried out their dangerous duties with a noble disregard of their own safety:—

"The outstanding part was the conduct of the stretcher-bearers, who worked magnificently, especially on the morning of the 25th."

On the last day of September the 6th Battalion moved to Camp L.4 and Brielen House. The total casualties suffered by the 6th Somersets during the month were: officers, 3 killed, 4 wounded; other ranks, 26 killed, 107 wounded.

CHAPTER XVII

IN THE LINE: INCIDENTS AND ITEMS OF INTEREST

AFTER the Battle of Loos and the subsidiary operations connected therewith to the close of the year 1915, no one of the four Battalions of the Somerset Light Infantry then in France and Flanders was involved in attacks of tactical importance on or by the enemy. Nevertheless, there happened many incidents and items of interest which cannot be omitted from the history of the Regiment.

1st BATTALION

The 1st Somersets encountered nothing but the rigours of trench warfare—always dangerous and full of discomfort—from the close of the Battles of Ypres (26th May) until the Battalion assisted the Rifle Brigade in a small attack which took place on 6th July; the Somerset men digging communication 6th July trenches to the trenches captured by the Rifles. After satisfactorily completing its task the Battalion went back to bivouacs in Elverdinghe Chateau grounds, having (though not known then) served its last tour in front-line trenches in the Ypres Salient.[1] This operation, though of a minor character, cost the Battalion one officer (2/Lt. H. V. Webber) and 27 N.C.O.'s and men killed; three officers and 102 N.C.O.'s and men wounded, and 5 N.C.O.'s and men missing.

On the 9th July the 11th Bde. (in Division) moved to the Houtkerque–Watou Area, the 1st Somersets marching to billets near the former place, a distance of 14 miles, over pavée roads, a tiresome march. Sir Herbert Plumer, C.-in-C., Second Army, inspected the 11th Bde., and after the inspection thanked the Brigade for its good work during the Battle of Ypres and particularly the successful attack which terminated its stay in the Ypres Salient. He then informed the Brigade that the 4th Division was to leave the Second Army "for another destination." On 21st July preparations were made for the move, 21st July and at 3 p.m. on 22nd the Battalion (in Brigade) marched out of billets to Gudewaersvelde, from which place the move southwards was begun on 23rd. Doullens was reached at 4.30 p.m. the same day, where the 1st Somersets detrained and marched to bivouacs at Freschvillers. Heavy rain had made the

[1] On 28th May Colonel Compton assumed temporary command of 85th Inf. Bde. (28th Div.), handing over command of 1st Somersets to Major Hume-Kelly, 3rd N. Staffs. R. On 30th May Bt.-Major Watson took command of the Battalion from Major Hume-Kelly, the latter becoming 2nd-in-command. Colonel Compton rejoined the Battalion on 17th June, but left again on 27th to take command of the 14th Bde., Captain G. Fleming assuming temporary command of the 1st Somersets. Several officers of the Battalion were wounded, and 2/Lt. T. E. Williams was killed by a sniper on 1st July. Yet another C.O. arrived on 2nd July—Major (Bt. Lt.-Col.) Crosthwaite, D.L.I.—to take temporary command of the Battalion.

1st Battalion

bivouacs wet, but tents and tarpaulins having been issued, the men got under cover and the Battalion Diary records that: "Sir T. D'O. Snow and Capt. Allfrey (our new Corps Commander and his A.D.C.), both of the Regiment, came to see us in bivouac. We are in the VII Corps of the Third Army."

29th July

On 29th July the Battalion marched to Englebelmer and billeted, and on the following day the C.O., Adjutant and Company and Platoon Commanders reconnoitred the defences and billets in Mesnil, which the Battalion had been ordered to take over from the French.

"The village is in a state of defence, and there is a second line of trenches on the ridge immediately north of the village. The defences are not completed and the work is not very thorough; and a great deal is still to be done. The billets are dirty." [1]

For several days work on the defences in and about Mesnil occupied the Somerset men, but at 8.30 p.m. on 5th August, moving off by companies, the Battalion marched off to relieve the Rifle Brigade in the left sub-sector, the relief being completed by 11.30 p.m. A, B and C Companies went into the front line, leaving H Company in the support dug-outs.

The quietude of the sector to which the Somersets had been transported was almost unbelievable after the noisy unrest of the Ypres Salient.

"Since we have been here," reads the Battalion record, "the enemy's guns have been more active, but there is practically no sniping. All observations can leisurely be made from above the parapet without disturbance. But it seems incredible that this state of things can last for any length of time."

14th August

With the exception of the arrival of Major J. A. Thicknesse, Somerset L.I., on 14th August, to take over command of the Battalion, and greetings from General Snow on 26th (the first anniversary of Le Cateau), the month passed without incident. Indeed, there is little to record for the remainder of the year, but strenuous work in the front-line trenches, patrol work,[2] periodical rests out of the line, and the gradual change of the heat of summer to the biting cold winds, rain, frosts and snow of winter.

31st December

6TH BATTALION

4th October

Whilst billeted at Brielen Houses the 6th Somersets received orders on 4th October to occupy trenches at St. Eloi, and the Battalion left camp at 5 p.m., relieving the 7th Yorkshire R. The relief was completed by midnight. But after a quiet tour the Battalion was relieved on 14th and moved to a rest camp at Poperinghe. A week later the 14th Division was placed in Corps Reserve, the 43rd Brigade to remain in its present billets. At the end of October the

---

[1] The Battalion at this period was temporarily commanded by Capt. G. Fleming, Col. Compton having been evacuated sick to Hospital.

[2] Lieut. H. G. A. Fellowes, 11th K.E.O. Lancers (Probyn's Horse) attached 1st Bn. S.L.I. and Corpl. E. A. E. Cox displayed most conspicuous gallantry during one of these patrols, on the night of the 7th October. The former was awarded the M.C. and the latter the D.C.M.

Diary records: "Spirits of the men splendid.   With incessant rain, plenty of
fatigues and no change of clothes and no chance yet of getting warm they can
still stand for hours playing and watching football matches."

The first three weeks of November were passed under the most wretched
conditions, but on 23rd the Battalion marched from the Seminaire–L.4–
Machine Gun Farm–Brielen Area to the front-line trenches just north-east of
St. Jean, relieving the 10th Durham L.I.   Two days in and two days out of
the front line was the rule at this period, but between the miserable conditions
of the billets and the filthy state of the trenches there was little choice.   On
the 14th December the 43rd was relieved by 71st Brigade, the Somersets
marching to a camp, described in the Diary as "G.5.d."   On 16th the Battalion
moved to "our old Rest Camp 'A,'"[1] occupied six weeks previously.   Here
the Somerset men stayed until the close of the year without any incident with
the exception of a rumour that the 14th Division was going out to Egypt,
which rumour was subsequently dispelled by the receipt of orders for the
Division to relieve the 49th Division in the Ypres Salient next to the French.

7TH BATTALION

From the 26th September (when the Battalion was withdrawn from its
assembly positions and returned to billets in Rue du Quesne) until the 31st
December 1915, the 7th Somersets settled down to a period of trench warfare,
unrelieved by hostile attacks: neither was the Battalion engaged in more
active operations than sniping, patrolling No Man's Land, and the usual
round of life in the trenches, broken by occasional "rests" behind the front
line.   On the whole, the sector held by the 20th Division was particularly
quiet, and casualties were small—one per day being the average suffered by
the 7th Somersets when in the line.

Nevertheless, insignificant as the number was, the loss of brave and gallant
officers and men was an ever-present source of sorrow.   On the night of
4th/5th October Sergeant Langley (A/C.S.M. A Company) was wounded
by a machine-gun bullet and died in the Casualty Clearing Station at Merville
on 8th.   The loss of this gallant N.C.O. was keenly felt by the Battalion
and especially by A Company.   Another fine N.C.O.—an old Somerset L.I.
man—C.S.M. Harris of D Company, was shot dead in his billet by a man
who had run "amok" on 19th October.   Before the end of that month two
officers lost their lives out in No Man's Land, the first being 2/Lieut. J. V. S.
Melhuish, who was killed on 27th October whilst reconnoitring the enemy's
wire.   "In him," said Lieut.-Col. C. J. Troyte-Bullock, "the Battalion lost a
most promising young officer, who was quite fearless and loved his work.
He was continually out on patrol and would never allow any other officer to
take his place."   The other officer was 2/Lieut. H. L. W. Armstrong, killed
by a bullet whilst visiting a listening post in No Man's Land on the night of
the 28th/29th October.   November was uneventful.

On 4th December the 61st Brigade went into Divisional Reserve in Bac

[1] The co-ordinations are given as F.27.a.5.8.

7th Battalion

St. Maur for ten days, returning again to the line on 14th. But by the time Xmas came round the Battalion was again in billets in Fleurbaix. On Xmas Eve the enemy shelled the village, and one Company—C—had to take to the fields for an hour or more until the Germans ceased their unfriendly attentions. However, the records state that "our Xmas dinner was a great success." The Battalion returned to the line on Boxing Day. With the

31st December

exception of a futile gas attack on the night of 8th January 1916, no further incidents are recorded, and by the 10th January the Battalion was once more billeted in Fleurbaix.

8TH BATTALION: THE ATTACK FROM THE MUSHROOM

15th October

At Borre, to which place the 8th Somersets had been withdrawn after the Battle of Loos, the Battalion spent thirteen days (2nd–15th October) in refitting. A draft of 248 N.C.O.'s and men sent out by the 3rd Battalion arrived on 6th—a very valuable addition to the Battalion which had lost heavily during the Battle. "They were a very good lot of men," said the Battalion Diary, "and had many old soldiers among them." Again, on the 9th, a further draft of 100 N.C.O.'s and men and 12 officers, this time from the 9th Battalion, arrived. The Battalion moved to Strazeele on 15th, to La Creche on 24th, and to Armentières on 25th October. At the latter place the Battalion held a trench line under the guidance and instructions of the 50th Division. From the 3rd to the 10th November the Battalion carried out trench work under the C.R.E., 50th Division. C Company was unfortunate on 10th November, a shell striking that Company's billets, causing 16 casualties. On the following day the Somersets took over trenches 70, 71, 72 and 73 ("on our own"), which had been held previously by the 50th Division, and held them until 14th November when the Battalion was relieved by the 10th Y. and L.R.

9th/10th December

Until the night of 9th/10th December (when the Battalion was relieved by the 10th York and Lanc. R. and returned to billets in Armentières) the Somerset men were in and out of the front-line trenches. On this occasion the relief was for eight days in order to allow full arrangements to be made for a "cutting-out" enterprise on the German front-line trenches. This small operation was so successful that it deserves full notice.

The enterprise had the following objects—to kill as many Germans as possible, take prisoners for identification purposes, to destroy a mineshaft if found and to ascertain whether arrangements for installing gas had been made. Previous reconnaissances had shown that the enemy's sentries were not always on the alert, and therefore it was decided that the attack should be made from Trench 70 (The Mushroom) in order that the distance to be traversed should be as short as possible; the operation would be in the nature of a surprise.

"It was decided," said the Battalion report of the enterprise, "that the importance of maintaining the fighting spirit of the men was paramount and to make the strength of the attacking party as large as possible in consonance with the object to be attained.   The strength was limited to 120 men selected from volunteers."

Officers and men were to blacken their faces and hands and were to have a countersign.   Each man was to "go as lightly as possible," no haversacks, packs, gum boots or water bottles to be carried, neither were caps to be worn, but each man's gas helmet was to be rolled up to fit round the forehead.   All bayonets were to be darkened and watches synchronized.   Gloves were to be worn by the wire-cutters, mats to be thrown over the enemy's wire, and ladders carried.

On the night of 12th/13th December, a patrol under 2/Lt. Hall went out for the purpose of ascertaining whether the enemy's listening post was held, to test the wire-cutters on the German wire, to discover whether there was any sunken wire in the ditch in front of the enemy's trenches and to examine the condition of No Man's Land.   It was a hazardous undertaking, but was splendidly carried out.   The listening post was empty and showed no signs of having been recently occupied; a large piece of the German wire was cut off and brought in, but it was impossible to discover whether any wire existed in the ditch.   No Man's Land was found in good condition, the long grass was beaten flat, there were no pools of water, no trip wires and very few tin cans.   It may seem superfluous to record the presence of "few tin cans," but the sharp sound of a tin being kicked was usually sufficient to arouse the enemy and bring a hail of bullets from his trenches.

On 15th December (the day before the operation) a very complete artillery bombardment was carried out and the hostile wire entanglement opposite the point of attack was well cut in several places, sufficiently to allow the passage of troops.   Lt.-Colonel L. C. Howard (O.C. 8th Somerset L.I.) spent the day with the "F.O.O.," and watched the bombardment of the enemy's machine-gun emplacements and the wire-cutting operations, the effects of which were carefully noted.

The attacking party was under the command of Capt. R. H. Huntingdon, and consisted finally of 6 officers and 117 N.C.O.'s and men, subdivided as follows:—5 scouts (with wire-cutters) under C.S.M. Smith; 4 wire-cutters, 16 roller-mat men and 4 bridging-ladder men under 2/Lt. Withers; 5 squads of bombers under 2/Lts. Wright and Vernon; an R.E. party with explosives; 16 bayonet men under 2/Lt. Morgan to search dug-outs and with orders to kill all Germans offering resistance; 10 men under Lieut. Hatt to keep up communications and take charge of all prisoners; 4 men to carry steps and act as orderlies to O.C. Party; 3 signallers.

These parties were to act thus:

"The wire-cutters, roller-mat men and bridging-ladder men under 2/Lt. Withers, on arrival at the enemy's trenches would proceed to search all dug-outs *to left of breach*, following 2/Lt. Wright and his bombers.   They will bayonet all enemy offering resistance.   The 16 bayonet men, under 2/Lt. Morgan, will follow 2/Lt. Vernon and his bombers *to right of breach*, searching all dug-outs. The wire-cutters should pay attention to all barbed wire only. . . . All men must be prepared to hear the enemy speak in English and must not be taken unawares by this ruse. All men who have white faces must be bayoneted."

15th December On the morning of 15th at 5 a.m. the party, back in its billeting area, practised the attack for the last time. Officers and men then rested for the remainder of the day, moving forward at night to The Mushroom, from which the attack was to take place.

16th December At 12.15 a.m. a patrol under 2/Lt. Wallis was sent out to see if the enemy's listening post was occupied and to see if the enemy were on the alert. After spending about twenty minutes in No Man's Land the patrol returned and reported the listening post still unoccupied, and from the sounds of shouting and talking coming from the enemy's trenches it was evident he was all unconscious of the impending attack.

By 2.15 a.m. the concentration of the attacking party was complete, and the order was given for the bridging ladders and mats to be taken over the parapet. This was done, the men following them and laying down behind the knife rests in the correct order of advance. At 3 a.m. the knife rests were removed noiselessly and the signal given for the advance. Slowly and quietly the men, led by their officers, crept towards the enemy's trenches. The officer leading the advance carried a roll of broad white tape, the end of which was left behind (in Bay 13). Unrolling the tape as he advanced, he left behind him a white path from his own trenches to that point in the German wire through which a path had been cut. He then passed the tape through the German wire and secured it. The advance across No Man's Land was perilous, for on the flanks of the positions to be attacked Véry lights burst in the air. The men, however, were very steady and remained motionless whenever a light went up.

The first party to reach the enemy's wire was that under 2/Lt. Withers. Putting down their mats over the broken knife rests, the whole assaulting party then crossed the wire and ditch by the mats without the slightest noise. Officers and men then extended along the German parapet, crawling up to the top of it. Taking a careful look over 2/Lt. Withers saw three Germans talking together in the trench. He shot one and then jumped into the trench followed closely by his party. The other two men tried to run away, but were bayoneted. The enemy was completely surprised, and the assaulting troops were into the trenches before any alarm was given; indeed, it was about 3.16 a.m. when 2/Lt. Withers jumped into the German trench and the last man of the party was in by 3.20 a.m., just as the guns opened fire on the enemy's flanking and support trenches. This artillery fire was supplemented by trench-mortar fire and rifle grenades on the flank of the position assaulted. The majority of the garrison of the trench were in their deep dug-outs and were all put out of action. Of the few men encountered in the trenches some showed fight. Three Germans tried to rush Sergeant Coxon, but he shot two with his revolver and took the third man prisoner.   An officer who would not surrender had to be shot.   Lieut. Shepherd, R.E., who had been ordered to search for and blow up a supposed mineshaft could not find it, he therefore exploded his charge inside a steel machine-gun emplacement; the gun being too heavy to bring away was abandoned.   At the end of 20 minutes the attacking party heard a whistle, it was the signal for the return.   Bringing seven German prisoners with them, and carrying such trophies as gas masks, oxygen apparatus, grenades, Véry lights and other items, the men filed regularly out of the trenches and, following the white tape line, reached The Mushroom in safety, though the latter was by now under heavy hostile shell fire.   Not a man of the attacking party had been killed or wounded, but 48 dead Germans had been left behind in the enemy's trench.

The success of the undertaking was not only due to the splendid co-operation of all arms (also the Royal Artillery and Royal Engineers), but to the enthusiasm shown by the C.O. of the 8th Somersets:

"From the moment that he was told that the enterprise was to be entrusted to his Battalion he worked with the greatest energy to ensure its success.   He impressed all ranks with his enthusiasm and confidence, and the success of the operation owes much to his example both before the day and on the night of the enterprise when he organized the advance from, and the retirement to, The Mushroom, the latter under heavy shell fire, with much skill and with complete indifference to personal danger." [1]

For about an hour and a half after the return The Mushroom was heavily shelled by the enemy and three other ranks were killed and four wounded.   A little later the attacking party marched off to billets, "and," records the Battalion Diary, "had a day's sleep."   They deserved it.

The success of this well-organized and splendidly carried-out enterprise aroused the somewhat apathetic Saxons (who held the sector opposite The Mushroom) to instant action, and when on the evening of the 17th the Battalion again returned to the trenches, relieving the 10th Y. and L.R., it was obvious that this particular tour would be of a lively nature.

At 6.55 a m. on 19th there was a sudden roar and a cloud of earth and debris shot up into the air, whilst 40 yards in front of the right portion of The Mushroom the Germans had exploded a mine.   Two large craters were formed by the explosion, each about 30 feet deep and 30 feet in diameter. Immediately the enemy made an attempt to occupy these craters, but the Somersets drove him back to his trenches by means of bombs and rifle grenades. Again and again the enemy attempted to occupy the craters, but on each occasion he was compelled to beat a hurried retreat.   That night, after their gallant C.O. had made a personal examination of the crater, the Somerset men

[1] London "Gazette" in which Lieut.-Col. L. C. Howard was awarded the D.S.O. for his gallantry on this occasion.   Capt. R. H. Huntingdon was also awarded the D.S.O., 2/Lieut. F. D. Withers the M.C. and Sergeant J. W. Coxon, Corpl. A. L. Fenwick and Pte. A. F. Jefferies the D.C.M. for their conspicuous conduct in the raid.

set to work and, after pushing out a sap to the craters, dug a new trench in front of them. The enemy had gained nothing by his experiment; indeed, as Colonel Howard wrote in his report: "The enemy by exploding his mine has very kindly given us another 40 yards of territory."

But whilst work on the craters was proceeding further desperate efforts were made by the enemy to occupy the craters. Showers of bombs (machine thrown) were hurled on the Somerset men and work was difficult. Then, under cover of a barrage of bombs and shell fire, two determined attempts were made by the enemy to occupy the western edge of the craters. An S.O.S. was sent up and the guns replying with splendid promptitude drove the Germans off. The latter then tried creeping round on both sides of the craters, but were descried by the listening posts. At last, however, under cover of particularly violent bombing, the enemy succeeded in occupying the craters, but his success was short lived, for the Somerset men quickly ejected him and once more held this position. Both sides had lost heavily (moans and cries were continuous from behind the German wire), though the Battalion report of this affair states "not in numbers but in the quality of my men." Of No. 1 Section of Bombers nearly all were killed or wounded.[1] One N.C.O. and a private are specially mentioned as most worthily upholding the traditions of the Regiment. Of Sergeant J. Black the C.O. said: "He continued to give direction after his leg was shot off and told me how to fire rifle grenades, etc.; although suffering intensely, he cheered the men."[2] And of Private Jefferies the Battalion Diary records "that Private Jefferies, a bomber, protecting a working party in the mine crater, drove off a German patrol: he was killed before he could return."

On the 21st the Battalion was relieved and returned to billets.

The final tour of the 8th Somersets in the trenches before the year ended was marked by the loss of the Battalion's gallant C.O. On the night of 23rd/24th December D Company relieved a company of the 10th Y. and L.R. in The Mushroom, Lieut.-Col. Howard accompanying them. The latter then went out to reconnoitre between the two craters, and whilst there was unfortunately shot. His body was carried in that night and buried next day. On 28th the Battalion was again relieved and returned to billets in Armentières.

[1] The only figures given in the Diary or reports are: 1 officer and "about 13 other ranks wounded."
[2] Sergt. J. Black was awarded the D.C.M. for his conspicuous gallantry.

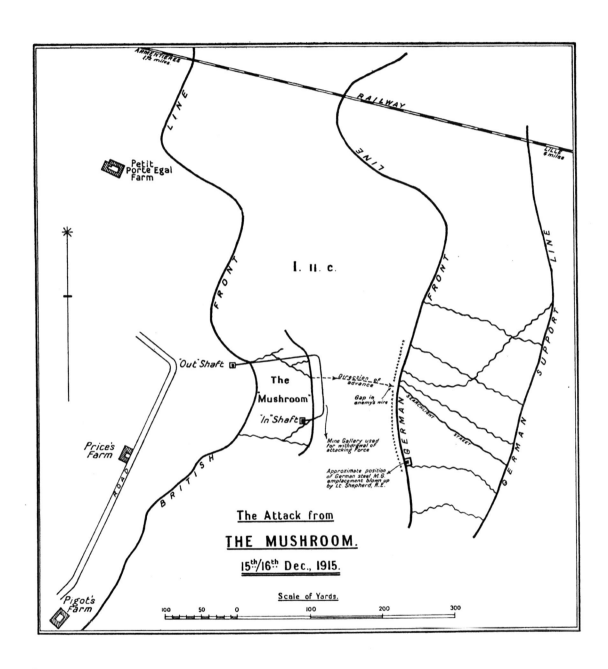

The Attack from

THE MUSHROOM.

15th/16th Dec., 1915.

Scale of Yards.

CHAPTER XVIII

OF THE TERRITORIAL BATTALIONS

THE 4TH (OR 1/4TH) BATTALION

O N 9th November the 1/4th Somerset Light Infantry, in company 1/4th Battalion
with other units forming the Wessex Division, arrived at Bombay
and disembarked on 11th—the first Territorial Troops to set foot
in the great Indian Dependency, where previously only Regular
Forces of the British Army had been sent.

Immediately on disembarkation Bn. H.Qs. and four companies entrained
for Madras, two and a half companies for Wellington and two small detachments for Malapuram and Calicut. Madras gave the Somerset men a wonderful reception and their first Christmas in India was one to be remembered.
On 12th January 1915 the 1/4th Somersets were relieved by the 2/4th Devons 12th January
(fresh out from England) and proceeded to Jullundur, where the Battalion
underwent the "Kitchener Test" and came out of it with flying colours.

The "Kitchener Test"[1] was thus described by Major-General Nigel
Woodyat (who was Inspector of Infantry in India at the time the 1/4th Somersets
carried out their test):—

"It meant three very strenuous days and all this time the Battalion, having
been provided with the necessary supplies and transport, had to fend for itself,
protect itself and undertake aggressive action when the situation required it.
Other troops were utilized in opposition and the General Officer concerned,
with his training staff, was present at the time and allotted marks for each
performance as it was completed. Brigadiers were given a free hand to modify
the original conditions of this test as regards the Territorials, especially as
the training season was far advanced, with the hot weather approaching. Personally, I cut down the total period to about thirty-six to forty hours, and
generally began before dawn with a fifteen-mile march in field service order,
each man carrying 100 rounds of ball ammunition. This was followed immediately by an attack with ball on a position prepared by another unit. On
the completion of the attack the commanding officer was told to select a bivouac
camp, arrange its protection and await orders. He was then (as soon as he
was in position) attacked by other troops, and shortly afterwards received
instructions for a small night operation, and so on."[2]

Seditious riots at Lahore robbed the 1/4th Somersets of leave in the hills,
and so the hot season had to be passed on the plains. The Battalion had to

---

[1] Inaugurated by Lord Kitchener when Commander-in-Chief in India.
[2] "The Territorials (Infantry) in India." A lecture at the Royal United Services Institution on
11th October 1922.

send a detachment of men to Amritsar, the hotbed of sedition, and although two demonstrations in force were made in the district, the 1/4th were not involved in any bloodshed.   A draft of 50 men, under Lieut. G. W. R. Bishop, was despatched to Mesopotamia during the summer, followed later by another draft of 25 men.   These two drafts [1] saw a lot of fighting in the Battle of Ctesiphon, and the majority were unfortunately shut up in Kut with General Townshend and afterwards became prisoners in the hands of the Turks.

20th August   On 20th August 1915 the 1/4th Somersets received orders to move to Peshawar, trouble with the Mohmads having broken out.   The Battalion was now within 100 miles of Jellalabad, the scene of the greatest achievement in the glorious history of the Somerset Light Infantry.   During the operations in the Mohmad country the 1/4th Somersets were moved up across the frontier to Adeza to hold a strong position, but there are no records extant showing what action was taken by the Battalion.

1916   Early in January 1916 the Somerset men marched to Nowshera, a two-stages march along the grand trunk road, where the Battalion became part of the permanent Frontier Force.   Special training in mountain warfare was now carried out and it became a popular rumour that the Battalion was doomed to remain in India throughout the whole period of the war.   This rumour was dissipated, however, on 4th February [2] when orders were received to mobilize for service with Indian Expeditionary Force "D" (as the Mesopotamian Expeditionary Force was then known).

The Battalion on 4th February numbered 27 officers and 705 other ranks, but on 11th, when mobilization was reported complete, the strength (owing to "sick" and "infirm") had been reduced to 25 officers and 597 other ranks. On the 16th and 18th February the Battalion entrained at Nowshera for Karachi, embarking in half-battalions at the latter port for Mesopotamia, and on the
23rd February   21st and 23rd reached and landed at Basra.

2/4TH BATTALION [3]

By the end of October 1914 the 2/4th Somerset Light Infantry (Lieut.-Col. H. F. Clutterbuck) were 1,000 strong, being the first second-line Territorial Battalion in the West to reach strength.   It was at that period located at Prior Park, where everything possible had been done to make all ranks comfortable.

On 12th December the second-line Wessex Division sailed for India, the 2/4th Somersets leaving Bath in the early hours of a foggy morning—800 strong.   They went out to India with the 2/4th Wilts aboard H.M.T. "Saturnia" and, on arrival at Bombay early in January, proceeded at once to Bangalore.   From the latter station two detachments of the 2/4th were sent

---

[1] Only Lieut. Bishop and 4 men survived of these drafts.   Many died in captivity and the rest were killed in action.

[2] The War Diary of the 1/4th Somersets begins on this date and is headed: "4.30 p.m.   February 4th, Nowshera."

[3] There was a 3/4th Battalion, but it did not go overseas, though reinforcements were sent abroad to other Battalions of the Regiment.

off, one to relieve a party of the 1/4th at Malapuram and the other on a similar 2/4th Battalion
errand to Calicut.   At Malapuram the Somerset men were twice called upon
to send out a mobile column to quell risings by Moplahs, though the latter
were actually taken by native police.

In August 1915 the 2/4th were suddenly mobilized and moved to Madras, August
where all sorts of rumours were afloat.   Finally, the Battalion sailed for the
Andaman Islands upon which a German raid was expected.

After several months spent in the Islands amidst somewhat novel surround- 1916
January
ings, the Battalion, early in January 1916, embarked and sailed for Calcutta,
proceeding to Dinapore where detachments were sent off to Barrackpore and
Dum Dum.

THE 5TH (OR 1/5TH BATTALION

On 9th October 1914 the 1/5th Somerset Light Infantry left Salisbury
Plain for Southampton *en route* to India.

The Battalion embarked on H.M.T. "Alnwick Castle," and together
with eight other transports, escorted by two cruisers, proceeded on their way.

On 10th November the Battalion disembarked at Bombay and proceeded
forthwith to Jubbulpore; one Company (C) to Nagpore.   The Battalion remained at Jubbulpore until 5th December, when it proceeded to Ambala.
At Ambala strenuous training was carried out, terminating in the ordeal known
as "Kitchener's Test," which took place in March 1915.   On 13th May 13th May
1915 a draft of one officer (Lt. E. S. Goodland) and 29 other ranks were
despatched to reinforce the 2nd Dorset Regiment in Mesopotamia and formed
part of the ill-fated garrison of Kut.   The latter half of the hot weather was
spent at Dagshai in the Simla Hills doing Musketry and Company Training.
A further draft of 15 other ranks were sent to the 2nd Dorsets on 13th August
1915.

The Battalion marched out of Dagshai on 2nd November 1915, and after 2nd November
a month under canvas at Chandigarh reached Ambala again on 3rd December.
Strenuous training culminated in the second "Kitchener's Test" (24th February
1916).   On 31st March the Battalion moved to Meerut.   On 5th May a 1916
31st March
large draft of 9 officers and 449 other ranks arrived from England.   During
the ensuing hot weather the Battalion was divided, Headquarters and two
companies going to Chakrata, while two companies under the command of
Major E. B. Kite remained at Meerut.   The following months were mainly
occupied training the draft; even in the hills little was done beyond this owing
to the exceptionally wet season.

On 20th October, Captain R. E. Gifford, Lieut. Hennesey, and 150 20th October
other ranks were despatched to Mesopotamia to reinforce the 1/4th Bn. Somerset
Light Infantry.

On 22nd October the Battalion was reunited at Meerut.

A month under canvas (15th Nov. to 15th Dec.) at Tughlakabad, given 15th December
up almost entirely to Brigade Training, practically ended the sojourn at Meerut.
In January 1917 the 16th Indian Division was concentrated at Burhan, 1917
January

1917
1/5th Battalion

between Attock and Rawal Pindi in the N.W. Frontier Province with a definite Military or at any rate Political purpose.   The 1/5th Somersets were posted to the 43rd Infantry Brigade.   On 6th March the Battalion was hurried back into standing camp from manœuvres and on 26th March entrained for Poona *en route* to Bombay and service overseas.

26th April

The 30th March to 25th April was spent at Poona awaiting news of transports.   On the evening of the 25th Poona was left behind and on the 26th H.M.T. "Chakdara" with 17 officers and 838 other ranks of the 1/5th Somerset Light Infantry on board sailed out of Bombay Harbour; 11 officers proceeded by another boat.

During the stay of 2½ years in India the Battalion suffered a continuous drain of officers and men.   Reinforcements for units in Mesopotamia and for specialist services of every kind, took away nearly one-half of the original personnel; out of the 28 officers and 838 other ranks who proceeded to Egypt from Bombay, only 15 officers and 441 other ranks were originals.

2/5TH BATTALION [1]

2/5th Battalion

Of the 2/5th Somerset Light Infantry there are few written records. But, apparently, the Battalion was raised in September 1914 and, under the command of Lieut.-Col. J. R. Paull, sailed for Burma on 12th December,

1915
January

arriving in January 1915.   The Headquarters of the Battalion were at Meiktila, with detachments at Rangoon, Shwebo, Bhamo and Thayetmye.

These detachments were chiefly employed in garrison duties, though on one occasion Major W. H. Speke's Company was ordered to make a demonstration in force against the border tribes along the Chinese frontier.   This entailed a march lasting three weeks and was the only eventful incident in the history of the 2/5th Battalion in Burma.

[1] There was also a 3/5th Battalion, which was, however, for Home Service only.

LT.-COL. W. C. COX
Commanded 1/4th Battalion

LT.-COL. E. H. OPENSHAW, T.D.
Commanded 1/4th Battalion

COL. H. F. CLUTTERBUCK, V.D.
Commanded 2/4th Battalion

LT.-COL. E. B. POWELL, D.S.O., RIFLE BRIGADE
Commanded 2/4th Battalion

COMMANDING OFFICERS OF THE 1/4TH AND 2/4TH BATTALIONS

CHAPTER XIX

THE FIRST CAMPAIGN FOR BAGHDAD

THE SECOND ATTEMPT TO RELIEVE KUT, 7TH–10TH MARCH 1916

THE Battle of Ctesiphon in November 1915 and the subsequent retirement of General Townshend's force to Kut on 3rd December, followed by the investment of that place by the Turks, completed by 7th December, had all taken place when the 1/4th Somersets 1/4th Battalion (Lieut.-Col. W. C. Cox) landed at Basra towards the end of February 1916.

In the first attempt to relieve Kut (4th–23rd January), the Action of Shaikh Sa'ad (6th–8th January) ended in the Turks retiring up-stream followed by General Aylmer's force. In the Action of the Wadi (13th–14th January) the enemy was again driven out of his positions and retired five miles farther west, entrenching himself across a defile bounded on the north by a marsh and on the south by the Tigris, but General Aylmer's attack on Hanna on 21st January, owing to strong Turkish counter-attacks with overwhelming forces, was unsuccessful—the first attempt to relieve Kut had failed. Throughout the remainder of January and February preparations were made for resuming the offensive, and at the end of the latter month the situation was given briefly in the official despatches as follows:—

"On the left bank (of the Tigris) the enemy, having been reinforced, still held the Hannah position in force; farther in rear were other defensive lines at Falahiyah, Sannaiyat, Nakhailat and along the northern part of the Es Sinn position. All except the last named had been constructed since the Battle of Hannah on 21st January. They were all protected on both flanks by the Tigris and the Suwaikieh Marsh respectively. On the right bank the Es Sinn position constituted the Turkish main line of defence, with an advanced position near Beit Aiessa. The right flank of the Es Sinn position rested on the Dujailah Redoubt, which lay some 5 miles south of the river, and 14 miles south-west of the British lines on the right bank."

After the heavy fighting of 21st January G.H.Q. had received a report (dated 25th Jan.) from General Townshend to the effect that he could hold 25th January out for another 84 days.[1] On receipt of this information it was decided to attack the right flank of the Turkish position, i.e. the Dujailah Redoubt, as the first step towards the relief of Kut, for the flood season would arrive about the middle of March and if the Turks broke the banks so that the Tigris flooded the country, offensive operations would be impracticable.

By route-march and river steamer reinforcements were pushed up from the base at Basra, and amongst those to arrive were the 1/4th Somerset L.I.

---

[1] Kut held out for 94 days from the date of General Townshend's report. The surrender took place on 29th April 1916.

For several days after their arrival the Somerset men remained camped amidst pleasant surroundings at Basra. The Battalion now formed part of the 37th (Indian) Infantry Brigade (3rd Indian Division).

At midnight on 24th/25th February orders were received for the 1/4th Somersets to proceed up-country by river instead of by route-march, as pre- viously ordered, and at 11.30 a.m. on 27th February B and D Companies embarked on Launch P11 and Barges 67 and 72 and Bn. H.Qs. and A and C Companies on Launch P12 and Barges 68 and R.F.C. The two former Companies got well away, but A and C Companies were delayed as Barge R.F.C. ran aground, which caused a delay of some 30 hours. But eventually Bn. H.Qs. with A and C Companies were able to resume the journey and early on the morning of the 1st March Ezra's Tomb was passed, and Amara reached at dawn on the 2nd, where the launches and barges were tied up for a few hours. The journey was continued at 11 a.m., Shaik Sa'ad being reached at 6 p.m. on the 3rd. At 6.15 p.m. on the 4th March the delayed Companies and Bn.H.Qs. arrived at Orah and disembarked, marching to a camp previously prepared by B and D Companies who had arrived on 3rd.

Until the evening of 6th March the 1/4th Battalion remained at Orah, but at 7 p.m. on that date marched out to bivouac in the Senna position, arriving there at 2 a.m. on the 7th.

On the afternoon of the 7th March General Aylmer assembled his sub-ordinate commanders and gave them final verbal instructions, laying particular stress on the point that the attack was to be a surprise and that the first important phase of the operation was the capture of the Dujailah Redoubt. Two columns —A and B—were to attack the Redoubt, B making a turning movement from the south, whilst A operated from due east. The 37th Brigade appears to have furnished Column C whose rôle was not to attack the Redoubt, but support the attacks of A and B by rifle and machine-gun fire; the Brigade was ordered under no circumstances to advance closer than 500 yards from the enemy. The maps and records are, unfortunately, quite inadequate, and it is impossible to define more closely the action by the Brigade, though all accounts state that the 1/4th Somersets acquitted themselves splendidly.

The Turkish forces on the left bank of the river were to be "contained," A and B Columns marching to rendezvous at the Ruined Hut under cover of the dark hours of 7th/8th March.

The 1/4th Somersets left their bivouacs in the Senna position at 6 p.m. on 7th and marched to the rendezvous area, reaching that neighbourhood— the Ruined Hut—at 8.30 p.m. The Battalion had to be in position east of the Dujailah Redoubt from which to cover the attack of B Column at 6.15 a.m. on the following morning (8th March).

The assembly at the rendezvous and the night march across country absolutely unknown and previously untrodden by British was a truly remarkable performance, and should live long in the annals of the 1/4th Battalion Somerset Light Infantry.

Thousands of men were assembled from different points of the compass and moved off in a south-westerly direction in orderly columns without the slightest confusion, though it was impossible to see the nature of the country over which they must pass, owing to the darkness.   It was a night march without precedent.   A point had been selected at which the three columns were to bifurcate and take a new direction, Columns A and B making for a depression south by south-east of the Dujailah Redoubt and Column C for a point facing the Turkish position between the Dujailah and Sinn Abtar Redoubts.   The 1/4th Somersets were the leading Battalion of C Column and moved off from the rendezvous in line of companies in fours, A Company leading.

After the bifurcation and marching off of the two Columns A and B, the Somersets were in the van of the latter.   Almost noiselessly the Columns cautiously moved to their allotted positions, crossing here a sandhill and there a nullah, striking the Dujailah depression accurately, where in front of them beyond the Turkish lines and the Redoubt, the flash of General Townshend's guns in Kut could be seen.   So surprised were the enemy that the British flank guards passed among the Arab tents without a shot being fired, though the camp fires still burned.   The twenty-mile march had been so splendidly carried out that just before dawn, when the men arrived at their destination, it barely seemed possible that they had marched that distance.

From the sandhills in front of Dujailah, the Redoubt could be seen grim and clearly about 3,000 yards away.   The guns were not long in getting to work and were soon firing on the Redoubt and the Arab encampments close to it; the Arabs in the latter fled hurriedly.   Opposite the Somersets the Turkish trenches were practically empty and could easily have been occupied, but it was just as well they were not for they were mined.   It will be remembered that the only orders issued to the 37th Brigade were to maintain a covering fire during the attack.

The area for a distance of 800 yards from the Redoubt was strongly fortified with skilfully hidden trenches concealed amongst the brushwood with which the ground was covered.

Having occupied the position allotted to the Battalion, i.e. 1,400 yards from the Redoubt, the 1/4th Somersets waited for the attack to begin; the Brigades on both flanks of the Somersets were heavily engaged and the latter kept up a steady covering fire.   Shrapnel fire was directed on the Battalion and a number of casualties were suffered, but the principal loss was caused by Turkish snipers whose activities were a constant source of annoyance and danger; these pests were, moreover, gradually working round the left flank of the Somerset men.   Two platoons, one each from C and D Companies, were sent out to drive the snipers back and were successful in so doing.   These two platoons, however, became heavily engaged with a hostile advanced post cleverly hidden in the bracken.   Rifle and machine-gun fire from this post swept the ranks of the platoons and Captain Baker was killed, whilst Major Graves-Knyfton and Lieuts. H. R. Tanner and E. O. Milne were wounded. The ground having been cleared of snipers, the platoons were withdrawn.

The Battalion continued its covering fire on the Redoubt as the attacking

Brigades advanced, the Somersets also moving forward slowly.   The first attack appears to have been unsuccessful and a second was launched during the late afternoon.   One Brigade (that on the right) passed to the attack almost through the Somersets and on troops of the force penetrating the enemy's front-line trenches two companies of the 1/4th were ordered forward in support.

Companies at once moved forward, A and B, C and D, with Bn.H.Qs. remaining in Brigade Reserve.   By this time the left Brigade had already occupied the enemy's front line and was pushing through to the second line when suddenly there were two violent explosions, and the Turkish trenches on the right which had been occupied by the right Brigade "went up"; they had been mined by the enemy.   The Turks now began a heavy bombing offensive and, being in superior numbers, the Brigade had to retire to its original line.   A and B Companies of the Somersets were ordered to retire and it was during this retirement, carried out slowly and with great steadiness, that the Battalion sustained severe casualties.   Captain E. Lewis had already fallen as he was gallantly leading his men to the attack.   A little later 2/Lieut. Lillington was also killed, while Capt. and Adjutant Sir Charles Miles and Lieut. W. Lewis were wounded.   In other ranks the Battalion lost, during the day's fighting, 9 killed, 50 wounded and 4 missing.

On reaching their old line, A and B Companies reorganized, whilst the attacking troops of the other Brigades, on withdrawal, were similarly engaged.

When darkness had set in the whole force was withdrawn a considerable distance from the Dujailah Redoubt to the sandhills.   The following day, after it had been ascertained that it was impossible for the force to maintain its positions, owing principally to lack of water, a further withdrawal was ordered to Orah.   The 1/4th Somersets formed part of the rear-guard, the general retirement beginning in the early afternoon.

At first the Turks, who had evidently been badly shaken and in some doubt as to whether to exploit another attack, were slow in following up the withdrawal, but as soon as they realized that the British troops were retiring, the rear-guard was heavily shelled with shrapnel.   The 1/4th suffered few casualties, but the Battalion on the right of the Somersets lost heavily, and it became necessary for the latter to dig in and hold a position until the former had collected and withdrawn its wounded.   Bodies of Turks followed up the withdrawal of the force close to Orah, which was reached about midnight on 10th, but no serious attack was made.

On 11th the 1/4th marched out to the Senna position as reserve to a force then engaged in driving back the enemy's advanced troops.   As this operation was successful the Somerset men were not called upon and returned to Orah. One more trip up to the Senna position on 13th March, during which the Battalion remained in its trenches until 21st, and then moved back again into Brigade Camp on west side of The Mall, and a move to Thorny Nala on 29th (when the 37th Brigade relieved the 9th Brigade) closed the month of March.

Thus ended the Second Attempt to relieve Kut—a gallant though unsuccessful effort.

Early in April the operations for the relief of Kut were continued, though 1/4th Battalion the situation of the besieged troops was desperate.   Heavy rain fell on 1st and for several days the trenches were in a very bad state.   On the 2nd Mills 2nd April grenades were first issued to the 1/4th Somersets.   The Battalion was still at Thorny Nala, engaged in digging a communication trench forward.   On the afternoon of 3rd a picquet of the Somerset men, stationed at the farther end of the communication trench about 400 yards out to keep down the activities of snipers, was approached by a Turkish patrol; a rifle duel ensued, the picquet finally driving the enemy off.

On 5th April the Third Attempt to relieve Kut began and the Hanna position on the left bank of the Tigris was assaulted and captured from the enemy by the 13th Division; the 8th Infantry Brigade, on the right bank of the river, also advanced against Abu Roman and took it without difficulty. The 1/4th Somersets were not, however, actively engaged in these operations, though in consequence of orders received on 4th to be prepared to move at 20 minutes' notice from 6 a.m. on 5th, the Battalion moved forward at 11.30 a.m. on the latter date and took up a new line about 1,500 yards "beyond the enemy's trenches" with three Companies (B, C and D), keeping A Company in reserve. The three forward Companies dug themselves in, with the 36th Sikhs on the left.   On 6th the Battalion again advanced, D Company being sent forward about 1,000 yards west (to about 1,500 yards east of Beit Aieesa) in order to form a picquet line with 36th Sikhs on the left and Manchester Regiment on the right.   Two more Companies (B and C) and two machine guns were moved up later to reinforce D Company, whilst the reserve Company—A— was ordered to the original line occupied by B, C and D Companies.

On this day (6th) the First Attack on the Sannaiyat position took place, but beyond the advance already stated the Somersets were not involved. Neither was the Battalion engaged in the Second Attack on Sannaiyat on 9th April, all Companies holding to the positions taken up on 5th.   On the 11th the Battalion was again warned to be prepared to move forward, but a torrential rain fell and the movement was postponed 24 hours.

Early on the morning of 12th patrols were sent out and reported the 12th April ground unsuitable for movement, but at 3.30 p.m. orders were received to establish a picquet line east of the Boil and the Twin Pimples.   At 3.40 p.m. one double company (C) was sent forward to carry out this duty, B Company supporting the movement.   C Company (Capt. R. Moger) advanced under artillery and long-range rifle fire, having in places to wade through water waist-deep.   B Company, advancing on the left of C, was delayed by a sheet of water about 200 yards across, with two banks about 4 feet to 4 feet 6 inches in height, and, in crossing, was subjected to rifle fire.   The advance, however, was continued and eventually C Company reached a position 200 yards from the Twin Pimples,[1] where it was held up.[2]   At 6 p.m. a platoon from B Company

[1] The Battalion Diary calls them the "Twin Boils," but the official maps name them the "Twin Pimples"; it is presumed the two are identical.

[2] The Battalion Diary is here very obscure, no mention being made of any fighting with the enemy.

was sent forward and found that the 36th Sikhs, on the left, were held up about 500 yards in rear of C Company. The 59th Rifles, on the right, were also delayed and did not come upon the right of the 1/4th Somersets until after dusk.

A platoon of the supporting Company (B) moved off to the right and cleared some Turkish snipers and a hostile machine gun from a nullah; the platoon then occupied a Turkish trench 200 yards to the right of C Company, where it was ordered to remain.

Darkness had now fallen and the Battalion stretcher-bearers had great difficulty in getting the wounded back over the flooded stretches and nullahs. The O.C., C Company (Captain R. Moger) and 2/Lieut. F. W. Baines were wounded within two or three minutes of each other and the command of the Company now devolved upon Company Sergeant-Major Davis. The officer commanding the support company (B) sent forward another 20 men to reinforce C, also instructing C.S.M. Davis to "carry on." [1]

The 36th Sikhs, on the left of C Company, had lost heavily and joined up with the left of the 1/4th Somersets about 11 p.m. The 59th Rifles, on the right, had been ordered to withdraw to a drier place more suitable for holding and sent word to C Company asking the latter to conform. The Sikhs, however, urged the Somerset men to delay this movement until they had been able to complete arrangements to evacuate their extensive casualties. The whole line (59th Rifles, 1/4th Somersets and 36th Sikhs) retired at 3.30 a.m. on 13th a distance of about 800 yards, being then some 1,200–1,500 yards east of the Twin Pimples. The two Companies—C and D—reinforced by a third Company, now dug themselves in, the fourth Company remaining in reserve 800 yards in rear.

The casualties sustained by the Battalion on this occasion were 2 officers wounded, 6 N.C.O.'s and men killed, 25 wounded and 1 missing.

On 15th the 37th Brigade was again ordered to establish a picquet line in conjunction with the 8th Brigade, and the 1/4th Somersets took up a line from a point about 400 yards from the right of the Twin Pimples, thence extending some 250 yards, joining up with 8th Brigade troops on the right. But during the night of the 16th the Somerset men were relieved and moved back 1,000 yards, where all Companies bivouacked.

On 17th April the Action of Beit Aieesa took place, the attacking Brigades being the 7th and 9th, the 37th Brigade acting in Divisional Reserve, moving forward in support of the operations. The 37th Brigade was formed up: 1/4th Somersets on the right, 1/2nd Gurkhas on the left, as the front line; 36th Sikhs for the second line; all were facing N.W.

The 1/4th had moved off at 6.10 a.m. and by about 7.10 a.m. had got into position. For the next half-hour the Battalion came under very heavy artillery fire and the troops were not sorry when orders were received to push on for another mile. This advance was also made under shell fire but it was less destructive and, although the going was difficult across flooded areas and nullahs, a line about a mile from the battle front was occupied.

[1] Subsequently awarded the D.C.M. for his work.

By midday the 7th and 9th Brigades had successfully carried the first line of the Beit Aieesa position and bombing parties of British troops were busy driving the Turks still farther back.   At 4 p.m. the 37th Brigade was ordered to move for the night towards the left flank beyond the Twin Pimples in order to hold it against counter-attacks.   The 1/4th Somersets occupied some trenches behind two companies of the Manchester Regiment, but were not long in position before fresh orders came to hand to move off a little farther to the left.   About 10 p.m. this order was changed and eventually the 1/4th occupied trenches recently held by the 1/2nd Gurkhas, who had been moved off to the right.

These trenches formed a triangular strong point on the extreme left flank.   A heavy counter-attack was expected at this point, and close behind, the British guns would have been in danger if any withdrawal had been forced, as they could only be moved with great difficulty, being surrounded by flooded ground.   The Battalion was ordered to hold on at all costs, as they were entirely unsupported.   The counter-attack by a fresh Turkish division was however directed against the strongest point of the line, well to the Battalion's right, and after all-night fighting was repulsed with very heavy Turkish losses. Had it proved successful the Battalion would have become completely isolated.

Here, so far as the Battalion Diary is concerned, end the operations of 17th April.   Nothing, however, is recorded of the manner in which Lieut.-Col. W. C. Cox (commanding 1/4th Somersets) and Lieutenant W. E. Phillips were wounded.   The C.O. was apparently shot in the arm about midday, whilst Lieutenant Phillips received his wound early in the morning.   Three other ranks were killed during the day and 20 were wounded.   The 18th April was uneventful.   On 20th the Battalion was ordered to proceed to Twin Canals protecting the left flank of the British front on the right bank of the Tigris.   The Battalion reached its destination at 11.30 a.m., relieving troops of the 35th Brigade.

The next day—21st—witnessed the welcome arrival of reinforcements numbering 2 officers and 211 other ranks.   Thereafter to the end of April [1] there is little to record—though mild excitement prevailed on 27th when five brigades of Turkish infantry were reported marching from west to east north of the trenches of Twin Canals, but although preparations to meet an attack were made, none materialized.

The last entry in the Battalion Diary for April is as follows: "April 29th. General Townshend, owing to total exhaustion of food supplies, compelled to surrender Kut-el-Amarah."   Here the Diary ends.

After the failure of the Third Attempt to relieve Kut, vigorous operations ceased, for the summer was close at hand during which little fighting could be done.   On 2nd May the 37th Brigade was relieved and marched to Shaikh Sa'ad and, reaching a position about 4 miles from that place at 6 p.m., bivouacked for the night.   On 5th May the 1/4th Somersets left the 37th Brigade and joined the 41st Brigade, embarking on the same day on board

[1] The Third Attack on Sannaiyat on 22nd April is not mentioned in the Battalion Diary.

1/4th Battalion   "P 2" with orders to return to Basra.   The strength of the Battalion on leaving Sheikh Sa'ad was 14 officers and 590 N.C.O.'s and men.

In easy stages the Somerset men proceeded down river, arriving at Basra about 11 p.m. on 8th May.   Next morning the troops disembarked and marched to Makina Masus Camp, where tents were pitched.   Parades and drill now kept the men busy.   On 15th Lieut.-Colonel Cox returned to the Battalion.   Throughout May and June drafts of officers and men arrived to swell the depleted ranks.   Most of the officers were sent out from England by the 3/4th Battalion Somerset Light Infantry, but a draft of 2 officers and 17th June   198 N.C.O.'s and men, who rejoined for duty on 17th June, came from the 2/4th Battalion in India.   During June inoculation of the Battalion against cholera and enteric fever was carried out and by the end of the month practically every officer and man had been inoculated.

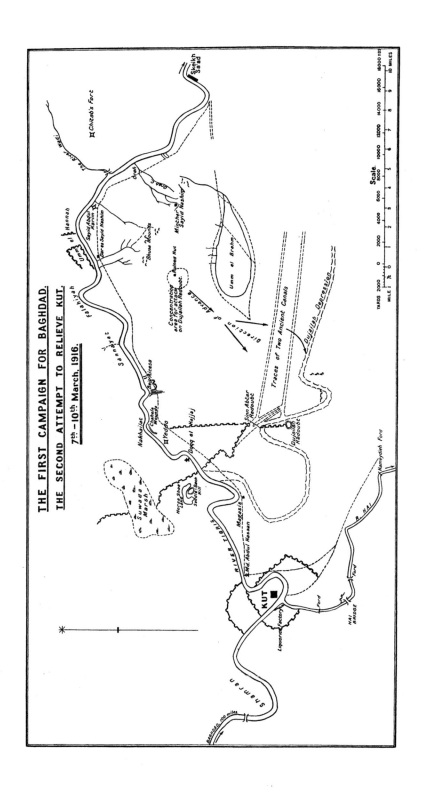

THE FIRST CAMPAIGN FOR BAGHDAD.

THE SECOND ATTEMPT TO RELIEVE KUT.

7th – 10th March, 1916.

CHAPTER XX

FRANCE AND FLANDERS AGAIN

FROM the heat and the flies and the sand the story of the Somerset Light Infantry in the War now turns from Mesopotamia back to France and Flanders, where the 1st, 6th, 7th and 8th Battalions of the Regiment had passed through the usual period of torment inseparable from winter in the trenches.

On the 1st January 1916 the 1st Battalion was on the Somme in a comparatively quiet sector; the 6th Battalion was in Camp "A" near Poperinghe, the 7th Battalion at Fleurbaix and the 8th Battalion in Armentières. In the Diary of the 1st Battalion there is nothing which needs recording until the beginning of the Somme Battles, 1916, in July. The Diaries of the 6th, 7th and 8th Somerset Light Infantry, however, contain several items of Regimental interest, especially as both Battalions were engaged in minor operations before they too were moved south to the Somme area to experience worse things than they had ever suffered in the noisy Ypres Salient.

6TH BATTALION

The rumour that the 14th Division was to be relieved in the line and leave the Ypres Salient for "an unknown destination" farther south was dissipated for the time being on the 4th January 1916, when the 6th Somersets marched out of camp at 3.15 p.m. with orders to entrain at Poperinghe at 4.30 p.m., the Battalion having received orders to relieve the D.C.L.I. during the night 4th/5th in the front line.

Detraining at the Asylum, the 6th Somersets marched out along the railway line, nearly the whole way to Essex Farm, where the Battalion was to relieve the Cornwalls in the left sub-sector of the 43rd Brigade (14th Division) front. The relief completed, the Somerset men found themselves in possession of a line which consisted of isolated posts "which even the Company Commanders in the front line," so the Diary states, "can't patrol by daylight. The trenches are simply full of water or falling to pieces." Nothing of outstanding interest happened during this tour in the trenches and it is mentioned merely to show the conditions in the line at that period; pitiable indeed is the reading contained in the Battalion Diary: "The front line is in an almost impossible condition and no troops can remain there more than 48 hours without much sickness." Relief came on the 9th, however, and the Battalion moved back again to a Camp near Poperinghe.

An entry in the Battalion Diary, dated 10th January, is too good to be omitted:—

"Gum boots, thigh, were handed in and checked ready to be sent to K.O.Y.L.I. 'Gum boots, thigh,' is a nightmare to some people, as Brigade wire about once a week, generally reads—'How many gum boots had you on charge two months ago?' and such-like conundrums."

On 18th February the 6th Somersets received orders to move to Ledringhem on 19th—a distance of about 13 miles—which place was reached at 5.30 p.m. The whole Division had by this time been relieved and had received orders to move south, to an "unknown destination."[1]

An advanced party of Somersets left Cassels on the morning of 20th, followed by the Brigade on 22nd February.

The "unknown destination" was just south of Arras—Longeau being the detraining station of the 43rd Brigade, which place was reached during the evening of the 22nd. Vignacourt had been allotted the Brigade as its billeting area, and on reaching Longeau, the 6th Battalion set out to march the distance —14 miles—led by their band. The men marched well and only one man fell out. Two days later a move was made to Beauval, followed by yet another move on 25th to Humbercourt. At the latter place orders were received on 27th which stated that the 14th Division would take over trenches from the 32nd French Division at Agny and Achicourt between the nights 28th/29th February and 2nd/3rd March. In accordance with these orders the 43rd Brigade marched on 28th to positions of readiness from which to move up and take over the front line from the Frenchmen; Brigade H.Qs. and the K.O.Y.L.I. were at Dainville, 6th Somersets and Brigade Machine Gun Company at Bernaville, and the Durhams and D.C.L.I. at Simencourt.

At 6 p.m. on 29th the 6th Battalion moved off to the trenches, which were about 6 miles away. The following extract from the Battalion Diary is given in order to show what a quiet sector of the line was like early in the year 1916: "French occupied the line which runs mainly north and south in front of Achicourt–Agny, just south of Arras. The line is easily the best we have as yet been in. Communications and front line properly revetted with brush-wood and all trenches boarded. Trenches about 8 feet deep in chalk and quite dry. Dug-outs on the average 8 feet below trenches, therefore at least 10 feet of earth on top of each dug-out. Dug-outs dry and well constructed. The place is extremely quiet. Achicourt, about half a mile from front line, has still a population of about 150 civilians. Hardly a house has been damaged and the shell fire is absolutely infinitesimal as compared with the Salient, the French casualties being about 8 *in the last five months.* The wire is good in front, but a little more barbed wire is required. Companies are all in the front line, the D.C.L.I. being in support. Our total length of line is about half a mile, A Company on the right of the line next to the 55th Division, which also relieved the French a few days ago. After A Company comes B, C and D Companies. On the left of our Battalion are the K.O.Y.L.I.

[1] Two D.C.M.'s were earned by the Battalion for conspicuous gallantry during the tour in the Salient—one by Pte. R. G. K. Baker, the other by Pte. J. Miller.

RUINS OF CLOTH HALL AND CATHEDRAL, YPRES, APRIL, 1916

The line is so quiet that cookers are brought up to Agny, put in houses there 6th Battalion and the food will be brought up in the dixies, it will of course have to be heated on arrival. This can easily be done by the Primus stoves which come in very handy. Water is fetched from Agny. S.A.A., grenades, Véry lights, had to be brought up for the relief. These were distributed later. No trench stores were signed for as the French were unable to bring them out, we thought it was better to get them for nothing than sign and let the British Government pay." The relief was completed at 10.30 p.m.

In this quiet sector March passed practically without incident. Casualties were very few, but Captain G. B. S. Walrond was shot in the head and killed on 19th whilst looking over the parapet.

April and May were not more exciting than March, though the diaries show a gradual increase in activity on both sides. Shelling gets more frequent, snipers claim more victims and the German 150-lb. trench mortars—called by the 6th Somersets "Crashing Christophers"—are beginning to make trench life uncomfortable. Then, on 4th June, a portion of the trench is reported 4th June as being "completely flattened out"—things are warming up!

On 12th June Lieut.-Col. C. G. Rawling (commanding the 6th Battalion) was appointed Brigadier-General and in the evening left the Battalion to take over command of the 62nd Infantry Brigade. Major Ritchie was left in command of the Battalion.

About the middle of June (on 18th) the 6th Somersets were relieved by the 1/4 North Lancs R. and moved from the Agny sector to Dainville where, on 20th, the Battalion moved forward into the Blagny district I Sector, and relieved the 1/Devons of the 5th Division. B, C and D Companies went into the front-line trenches, whilst A was in reserve; the left of the Battalion rested on the River Scarpe, whilst on the right the Somerset men had the 42nd Brigade. The front line ran through the village of Blagny.

One single entry in the Battalion Diary, and that on the last day of the month—30th June—is the only mention made of the beginning of the Somme 30th June Battles: "Bombardment still continues with intensity down south."

7TH BATTALION

From Fleurbaix, where the 7th Somersets went into billets on 10th January, 10th January the Battalion moved (in Brigade) via Vieux Berquin to Steenbecque, which place was reached on 12th. The 7th Battalion then set to work to refit and train and had just begun to settle down when the 20th Division was informed that it was to move into the Second Army area, which eventually meant the Ypres Salient.

The 61st Brigade marched out of Steenbecque on 23rd January to the Arneke area, the 7th Somersets billeting at Waermers Cappel. On 3rd February the Brigade marched to Wormhout, a clean town with good billets in farms round about. Whilst at Wormhout 8 officers and 13 N.C.O.'s were sent up to the Canal Bank N. of Ypres to spend 24 hours in the sector which the Battalion was to hold eventually, but it was not until 23rd February that

the 61st Brigade relieved the 60th Brigade in the front line.   The Somersets
relieved the 6th Bn. Oxford and Bucks L.I., B and D Companies going into the
front line which extended from D.22—a series of shell-hole posts S. of Lancashire Farm—to No. 17 "Grouse Butt."   C Company was in support posts and
on the Canal Bank; A, the reserve company, was also on the Canal Bank.   The
first four days in the front line in the Salient cost the Battalion 3 killed and
16 wounded.   The trenches were water-logged and there were no dug-outs
of any description for officers or men.   Only Company H.Qs. had a certain
amount of shelter from the weather, the rest had to "stick it," sitting on the
fire-steps up to their knees in water when they were resting.   Tours in the
front line lasted four days, followed by four days in support.   The 61st Brigade
was relieved by 60th on 14th March, but went back again to the front line
on 22nd, the Somersets relieving the 6/Oxford and Bucks L.I. in support
on the Canal Bank.   The Battalion had one more tour in the front line before
the close of March.   The first few days of April promised better weather
and the ground began to dry up.   As a consequence trenches were improved
and a new trench was dug to take the place of the shell-hole post known as
"D.22."   This trench was finished on 10th April, but whilst superintending
the work Major Preston-Whyte was wounded in the shoulder.

On 11th April the enemy attacked.   He began at 1 p.m. by shelling the
Canal Bank violently, and at 5 p.m. opened fire on the front-line trenches, and
the 7th D.C.L.I. holding Sector E.28 to D.22 of the 61st Brigade front had a
bad time of it.   Simultaneously with the latter bombardment the enemy put
over a heavy barrage of 5·9s on the right flank of D.23 and along the support
line Lancashire Farm–Nile–Skipton Post.   It was by now obvious that a
night attack would follow.   Bn.HQs. of the 7th Somersets, with C and D
and half of B Companies, "stood to" on the Canal Bank and A Company with
the remaining half of B, then at Pellissier Farm, were ordered to join
the Battalion as quickly as possible.   Apparently the Germans attacked about
7 p.m., for the Battalion Diary states that the S.O.S. from the front line went
up at 7.15 p.m.   The violent hostile bombardment had cut the telephone
wires and as darkness had fallen it was quite impossible to see what was going
on in the front line.   In spite of the heavy shell fire, however, all bridges
over the Canal were intact, and as soon as the S.O.S. went up the
Battalion moved over the Canal to the eastern bank.   At 7.30 p.m. a message
from the 7th D.C.L.I. reached Colonel Troyte-Bullock asking for S.A.A. to
be sent up to their left company.   2/Lieut. R. L. Tawney [1] of D Company,
7th Somersets, was ordered to take his platoon and carry up as many boxes
of ammunition as they could.   This officer divided his platoon into two parties,
taking one himself and his platoon Sergeant (Sergt. Bristowe) the other.   These
two parties passed through the enemy's barrage and delivered all the ammunition,
having suffered only 4 casualties on the way up.   They then gave a hand in
repelling the Germans who were trying to break through a gap between the
battalions at E.28.   At 8 p.m. the Cornwalls asked for another platoon to

[1] 2/Lieut. Tawney was awarded the M.C. for his gallantry on this occasion.

7th Battalion

14th March

11th April

reinforce their left and 2/Lieut. Andrews of D Company (7th Somersets) was 7th Battalion
sent up with his platoon. He succeeded in passing through the barrage and 11th April
reported to the Cornwalls without suffering a single casualty.

Excepting the two messages received by the Somersets asking for assistance no news had been received as to what was happening in the front line and the Brigadier asked the C.O. to send an officer forward to find out what was going on. Another officer of D Company was selected—Lieut. Cartwright. This officer started out on his journey and had reached the neighbourhood of Lancashire Farm when suddenly there was a loud explosion and the next thing he knew was that he had been blown into a very unsavoury pond. Scrambling out he found he was unhurt and again went forward in the direction of the front line, from which he eventually returned unhurt. He reported that the enemy had attacked the left flank and front, and a party of some fifty Germans had also attacked the left post (E.28) but had been driven back with loss. The frontal attack was caught beautifully by the barrage which fell on the Germans as they came over their own parapets; of this attack only about 50 or 60 succeeded in reaching the wire in front of the Cornwalls and they were dealt with in an extremely satisfactory manner. The front-line trenches, however, especially Skipton Post and Skipton Road, were badly knocked about and the Cornwalls had lost between 50 and 60 men. By 10 p.m. the situation was again normal and the 60th Brigade relieved the 61st.

The 20th Division was now going out of the line for a rest and each Brigade was to have 10 days in Calais in turn.

The 7th Somersets (in Brigade) marched to the troop siding at Hopoutre, west of Poperinghe, on 16th and entrained for Calais. The stay at Calais was disappointing and the troops were not sorry when, on 26th April, the 61st Brigade marched to Zutkerque—12 miles—continuing the march on the following day to Merckeghem—15 miles.

Gradually moving back to the Salient the 7th Somersets went back into the front line on 19th May, relieving the 2nd Coldstream Guards astride the 19th May Ypres–Zonnebeke road. The relief was completed by 12.30 a.m. and, although no casualties had been suffered, the enemy's artillery shelled the trenches during the night and breached the parapet where it crossed the road, keeping the breach under fire until dawn so that it could not be repaired. Throughout the 20th this shelling continued, the wire in front of the trenches receiving special attention, a sure sign of an impending attack.

At 12.45 a.m. on the 21st the Germans launched their attack, advancing in three parties, one on each flank and one in the centre. The centre party bumped into the Somersets' listening post, enabling the latter to give the alarm. The right attack reached the parapet and threw bombs into the trenches of the Somerset men, which caused most of the casualties, but was eventually driven back with bomb and bayonet, whilst the Lewis guns got to work as the enemy retired to his own line. The left attack came within range of the Battalion bombers and had a warm reception; this party was also driven off with loss. The centre attack failed owing to rifle and Lewis-gun fire, for two platoons of the Support Company happened to be in the trench at work repairing the parapet, when the attack was made, and these, putting aside their tools for the time being, formed a very useful reinforcement to the garrison of the front trench which, owing to the extent of front allotted to the Brigade, was normally very thinly held.

When the attack was over the corpses of three dead Germans hung on the wire in front of the Somersets' trenches. The casualties suffered by the 7th Battalion in this affair were 2/Lieut. P. E. O. Addis, who had lost a foot, the other being badly injured, 2/Lieut. Willcox also severely wounded; one other rank was killed and 22 other ranks wounded.[1]

On the night of 23rd/24th May the Battalion was relieved and returned by train to "B" huts at Brandhoek. On the 26th the Battalion was moved to billets in the Rue Boscehepe, Poperinghe, all four Companies being billeted in a large factory.

For several days (from the 2nd June) during this period the Battalion was continually "standing to," for the enemy had attacked the Canadian Corps, north of the Menin Road, and had succeeded in capturing Maple Copse, Mount Sorrel and Observatory Ridge, whilst German patrols were reported to have reached Zillebeke. In a counter-attack the Canadians had recovered the lost ground as far east as the foot of Mount Sorrel and the Ridge, which both remained in the enemy's hands.

MOUNT SORREL

Sir Douglas Haig stated in his despatches that the German attack on Mount Sorrel on 2nd June was one of two attempts to interfere with his final preparations for the Somme Battles of 1916; the other was an attack against the British line south and south-east of Souchez, on the Vimy Ridge.

The recovery of the ground captured from the Canadians was essential, as the southern part of the lost position commanded the British trenches. The final counter-attack took place on the 13th June, the lost position being recaptured. But before that date the 7th Somersets had again moved back into the front line and the Battalion was in the forward trenches when the Canadians made their attack.

On the night of the 8th June the 61st Brigade relieved the 60th Brigade, and the C.O. of the 7th Somersets said: "It was a great relief to us to get away from the continual 'standing to' business in Poperinghe."

The line of trenches taken over by the Somerset men lay between Railway Wood and "Y" Wood (west of Bellewaarde Lake) just north of the Menin Road. Railway Wood was the site of a small copse standing on a slight eminence on the southern side of the Ypres–Menin Railway. From this position the British trenches overlooked the enemy's line on either flank. Immediately opposite the "wood" the German front line bulged outwardly, forming a salient, and at this point the opposing trenches were only about 40 yards apart.

---

[1] In this affair Pte. D. H. Dare earned the D.C.M. for conspicuous gallantry and determination.

The 29th Canadian Infantry were on the right of the Somersets and the 7th Battalion 7th K.O.Y.L.I. on the left.   Battalion Headquarters of the Somersets were in Railway Embankment, about 500 yards from Hell Fire Corner.   Two Companies held the front line, one Company was in support trenches about 70 yards in rear, and one Company in reserve trenches about 300 yards behind the support line.   The relief passed off quietly and without casualties.

With the exception of intermittent shelling the 9th and 10th were quiet days, and it became apparent that a determined attempt was to be made to turn the Germans out of the captured trenches when, during the night of 10th, gas cylinders were installed in the front-line trenches of the 61st Brigade.

Throughout the 11th and 12th, during the hours of darkness, the work of installing the gas cylinders proceeded, the enemy being particularly quiet, and when "Zero" hour (12.45 a.m. on 13th) for the attack arrived all was ready and a favourable wind blowing.   The 20th Division had been ordered to assist the Canadian attack by gas discharge followed by raids, two of which were to be made by the 7th Somersets under cover of smoke clouds.

At 12.45 a.m. the bombardment of the enemy's trenches began.   This 13th June was followed by a gas discharge at 1.30 a.m., which continued for 15 minutes.

The night was pitch dark and a heavy rain was falling, though a strong south-westerly wind was blowing "almost perfect" (records the 61st Brigade Diary) towards the enemy's trenches.   Heavy rain, which fell during the 12th, had turned No Man's Land into a swamp with the result that one of the raids (that on the left) planned to take place from Railway Wood had to be abandoned.   The right raid, however, to be carried out by C Company of the Somersets, was ordered to take place.   The raiding party consisted of 30 N.C.O.'s and men and was commanded by Lieutenant J. C. N. Peard.

After the gas had been turned off and the cloud was sufficiently clear of the British trenches, the left raiding party went forward, screened by a smoke cloud.   But the wet and sodden ground out in No Man's Land still reeked of gas, which clung about the damp earth and shell holes, so that the raiding party had to don gas helmets.   The trench mortars were supposed to have cut the wire in front of the trenches to be raided, but when Lieut. Peard and his men reached the entanglements they were found intact.   The raiders at once began cutting the wire themselves, although hostile machine guns had already opened fire.   Presently, however, one of the party was hit and cried out as he fell.   Immediately, a machine gun about 20 yards away opened fire on the raiders.   Lieut. Peard was hit twice and Sergeant Dillon and eight men wounded, whilst three men were killed outright.   The signal to retire was then given and, less the three men killed, the whole party, wounded and unwounded, returned to the trenches; the killed had to be left out in No Man's Land.[1]

A Company of the 7th Somersets, holding the support trenches, had suffered during the raid from the enemy's bombardment; Capt. S. W. Brown, Sergt.-Bugler Gale and nine men were wounded and four men were killed.

[1] For conspicuous gallantry on this occasion Pte. G. Jenkins was awarded the D.C.M.

7th Battalion

The Canadians were successful and gained all their objectives.

On the night of 13th the Somersets were relieved and moved back to Ypres. On the 16th two officers of the Battalion, Lieut. E. G. E. Wright and the M.O.—Capt. S. Parker, R.A.M.C.—were walking down a street in Ypres when they were both killed by a shell.

30th June

During the remainder of June there is little to record, and on the last day of the month the 7th Battalion was in trenches in the Potijze sector, due for relief on the night of 1st July.

8TH BATTALION

1st January

From Armentières on the night of 1st January the 8th Somersets moved up again into the front-line trenches, in which two quiet days were passed, the Battalion being relieved on night of 5th. That afternoon, however, the Somersets had lost a valuable officer, Captain B. S. Marsh, who was killed by a sniper about 3 p.m., at the junction of trenches 69 and 70.[1]

January, February and the better part of March were uneventful days for the Battalion, but on the 20th of the latter month, the 17th Division relieved the 21st Division in the Armentières sector, the latter marching to the Strazeele area where the Division was reviewed by General Plumer (Commanding Second Army) and General Ferguson (G.O.C., II Corps); the 8th Somersets were congratulated by these two Generals on their smart turn-out.

1st April

Early on the morning of 1st April the Battalion (in Brigade) left the Strazeele area and, entraining at Godewaersvelde, reached Longeau, near Amiens, at 3 p.m. Here the Somersets detrained and marched to Allonville whence, after a few days, the Battalion moved to Ville (on 7th) and Meaulte (on 9th). Thus the 8th Battalion had also arrived in the Somme area, for Meaulte is south-west of Fricourt village where desperate fighting took place on 1st July and thereafter.

On the afternoon of 14th April the 8th Somersets went into the trenches, taking over a portion of the front line from the 1st East Yorkshires, about a mile north-west of Fricourt. A Battalion of the Middlesex Regiment was on the right of the Somerset men and Irish Rifles on the left.

The Somme area was a quiet part of the line in those days and when the Battalion was relieved on 23rd only four casualties had been suffered. From Buire, where the Battalion had been billeted, the Somersets marched back to the trenches on 12th May, taking over the left sub-sector from the

13th/14th May

10th K.O.Y.L.I. On the night of 13th/14th May the Battalion carried out a small "cutting out" expedition. This affair, though entirely insignificant, is recorded, because it furnishes yet another instance of a young officer sacrificing his life in attempting to rescue one of his comrades whom he conceived to be in danger.

The "cutting out" party consisted of 70 officers, N.C.O.'s and men. Captain Jollivet was in charge of the main party, whilst 2/Lieut. Withers was

[1] Lt.-Col. J. W. Scott assumed command of the 8th Battalion at this period.

in charge of a small advanced party whose duty it was to lay an explosive charge in the barbed wire in front of the German trenches.

After some delay the charge was fired and the main party rushed forward. The outer wire had been destroyed, but at the foot of the German parapet there was a quantity of uncut wire and some "knife rests." A yard southwards, 2/Lieut. Roger Vernon and the leading men tried to force their way through the wire, but were unsuccessful. Both sides were now engaged in bombing duels and presently the order to retire was given. But Captain Jollivet, who had become entangled in the enemy's wire, was a minute or two behind the remainder of the party. His absence was discovered and 2/Lieut. Vernon went out again to look for him. What happened it is impossible to say. The young subaltern's body was found close to the German wire, but some distance off the original line of advance, where it is supposed he was shot down and died. Captain Jollivet reached the trenches safely, though wounded. One N.C.O., Sergt. Fenwick, who went out to look for 2/Lieut. Vernon was also killed.

The remainder of May passed without incident though the last entry in the Diary records that: "The Battalion was mentioned among other units in Sir Douglas Haig's first despatch, dated 19th May 1916, for specially good work while in the trenches in carrying out or repelling local attacks and raids."

On the 2nd June the Battalion marched from Neuville to Ville, where it was billeted for ten days, returning on 11th to the trenches. On 15th it was again relieved and held the intermediary line for five days, marching on the 20th to Neuville, thence to Ville.

The preliminary bombardment of the enemy's position began on 24th June whilst the Battalion was at Ville, and still continued when, on the following day, the Somerset men marched to the trenches and took over the assembly trenches, Marischal Street and Stonehaven Street.

CHAPTER XXI

THE BATTLES OF THE SOMME, 1916

EVEN from a Regimental point of view no story of the Somme Battles of 1916 would be complete without a brief outline of the situation when the Allied offensive opened, the general scheme of operations, preparations for the Battles, and some description of the terrain of the battlefields-to-be. For unless these various points of interest are touched upon, be it ever so lightly, it is impossible to appraise the value of the desperate and hard fighting in which Battalions of any Regiment were involved.

That an offensive Allied Campaign during the Summer had been decided upon several months earlier, was apparent from the gradual movements of British Divisions southwards to the Somme area in the Spring of 1916. Large numbers of troops of the New Armies had arrived in France and Flanders between January and July, the strength of the British Armies increasing during that period from 450,000 to 660,000. But thousands of these troops had to complete their training, and the longer the attack could be deferred the more efficient they would become. On the other hand, the Germans, who had attacked Verdun with large forces in February, and were continuing to press their attacks, and the precarious position of the Italians in the Trentino, where on 14th May the Austrians had launched a heavy offensive, might precipitate the Somme operations before preparations had been completed to relieve the pressure on the hard-pressed French and Italians.

Towards the end of May, in view of the general situation in the various theatres of war, Sir Douglas Haig agreed with General Joffre that the combined French and British offensives should not be postponed beyond the end of June; for neither the French nor British Forces were deemed strong enough to undertake the offensive unaided.

The objects of the Somme Battles of 1916 were to relieve the German pressure on Verdun, to assist the Italians and Russians by preventing the transfer of troops from the Western Front, and to wear down the forces opposing Sir Douglas Haig's and General Joffre's troops.

Preparations for the offensive were very elaborate and of a strenuous nature. Huge stocks of ammunition and stores were collected; many miles of railways and trench tramways were laid; roads improved and others made; causeways built over neighbouring valleys; thousands of dug-outs in which to shelter troops, for use as dressing stations, as magazines for the storage of ammunition, food, water and engineering materials, had to be constructed, and scores of miles of deep communication trenches, trenches for telephone wire, assembly and assault trenches, and numerous gun emplacements and observation posts, had to be dug.

All this labour had to be done by the troops in addition to trench warfare 1st and 8th Battalions and the maintenance of existing defences, and to their eternal glory let it be said that the very heavy strain upon them was borne with wonderful cheerfulness.

The enemy's position was of a formidable character, (as reference to a trench map of the period will prove) situated on high undulating ground, rising in places to more than 500 feet above sea-level, forming a watershed between the Somme and the rivers of south-western Belgium. On the southern face of this watershed the ground falls in a series of long irregular spurs and deep depressions to the valley of the Somme. The enemy's first system of defence was well down the forward slope of this face, his trenches starting from the Somme near Curlu, thence running first northwards for 3,000 yards, then westwards for 7,000 yards to near Fricourt, where it turned nearly due north, forming a great salient angle in the enemy's line. Some 10,000 yards N. of Fricourt the enemy's trenches crossed the Ancre, running northwards, west of Beaumont Hamel and east of Hebuterne, thence round the Gommecourt Salient. At an average distance of from 3,000 to 5,000 yards behind his first system, the enemy had a second system of trenches, on the whole 20,000 yards of front between the Somme and the Ancre. Both of these systems consisted of several lines of deep trenches, well provided with bomb-proof shelters and communication trenches. Formidable wire entanglements, many of them in two belts forty yards broad, built of iron stakes interlaced with barbed wire often almost as thick as a man's finger, protected the front trenches of each system. Between these systems of defence the numerous woods and villages had been turned into veritable fortresses. The deep cellars in the villages, the pits and quarries, provided cover for machine guns and trench mortars. Many of these cellars had been supplemented by elaborate dug-outs, sometimes in two stories, connected up by passages often as much as thirty-five feet below ground-level. The salients in the enemy's line were made into self-contained forts, from which he could bring an enfilade fire across his front: mine-fields protected these forts. Strong redoubts and concrete machine-gun emplacements were constructed in positions from which he could sweep his own trenches should they be taken.

Between the Somme and the Ancre the British trenches ran parallel with, and close to, those of the enemy, but below them. Observation on the German front system and on the various defences sited on the slopes above the British trenches, was good and direct, but in many places the second system could not be observed except from the air. North of the Ancre command of the opposing trenches was practically on level terms. So much for the general description of the battlefields-to-be. Two places, however, are of special interest to the Somerset Light Infantry, i.e. the German Quadrilateral, north of Beaumont Hamel, and the hostile trench system just north of Fricourt Village; in these two parts of the line the 1st and 8th Battalions of the Regiment came into action on the 1st July.

As already stated, the early days of 1916 were uneventful so far as the

1st Somersets were concerned.   But as the weather became finer it was possible to note the increasing demands upon the Battalion for working parties, and the words "fatigues as before" are continually appearing in the diaries.   So

hard were the men worked that on 8th June the Battalion Diary records: "Usual fatigues.   The men are evidently feeling the strain of these all-night fatigues as the sick parades are becoming very large."   Zero day had been fixed for the 29th June, and from the records it is possible to tell the approach of active operations.   On 14th June the Battalion was out of the front line at Beauval and one entry states: "At 2.30 p.m. all officers and N.C.O.'s visited some miniature models of the trenches which will concern us.   At 6 p.m. the Brigadier lectured to all officers and N.C.O.'s on the forthcoming attack."   The Battalion returned to Bertrancourt on 15th when the usual working parties had to be supplied; from 17th to 20th June (inclusive) "absolutely every available man was taken for day and night fatigues."

The 1st Somersets moved to Mailly Maillet on the afternoon of 22nd and two days later the preliminary bombardment of the enemy's trenches, from the Somme northwards along the whole position to be attacked, opened. A huge number of guns had been brought into action for this purpose and the noise was deafening.   With something akin to awe the troops watched thousands of shells burst upon the enemy's trenches, throwing up clouds of dust and bricks and timber; it seemed as if nothing could possibly emerge alive from that terrible inferno.   Day after day the bombardment continued with a relentless fury, while at over forty places along the front line gas was discharged over the German line.   Raids were made to find out the state of the enemy's wire and trenches; Allied aeroplanes destroyed his balloons, thus depriving him for the time being of this form of observation.   On 28th June Zero day was postponed until 1st July.   By the 28th the enemy's front line appeared to be in an appalling condition—battered and broken.   Beaumont Hamel had disappeared.   The hostile wire entanglements were torn and thrown into wild confusion, the very earth seemed to have been disembowelled, for wooden planks and sand-bags and all the impedimenta usually contained in trenches and dug-outs were flung about in horrible confusion; dead bodies of Germans littered the ground.   On the night of 29th June a final reconnaissance of the enemy's wire was made by the 1st Somersets, but the reconnoitring officer (2/Lt. Winstanley) was unable to get near the Quadrilateral.

When morning of the 30th dawned the 1st Battalion was in Mailly Maillet, under orders to move up to the assembly trenches during the night 30th June/1st July.

Meanwhile, the 8th Somersets who, on the night of 27th, moved up to the assembly trenches, Marischal Street and Stonehaven Street, had taken over a new front line which had been tunnelled out and only just opened at the top.

THE BATTLE OF ALBERT: 1st–14th JULY 1916

All along the line on the night 30th June/1st July troops were moving up to their assembly positions, trench ladders were being placed in position and the wire removed from the front of trenches from which assaults were to be made. Zero hour for the general attack was 7.30 a.m. on 1st July, preceded by a final hour of intense bombardment. But long before that time everything was ready.

8th Battalion 30th June/1st July

The 21st Division (to which the 50th Infantry Brigade of the 17th Division was attached) was to attack due east, just north of Fricourt, whilst the 7th Division (on the right of the former) was attacking Mametz with the idea of joining hands with the 21st Division east of Fricourt Village.

The first objective allotted to the 21st Division was Fricourt Farm–Trench Junction X.28.c.8.7. (just east of Fricourt Farm)–Crucifix Trench–Birch Tree Wood. The second objective was X.29.b.5.6. (joining with 7th Division)–X.23.c.6.6.—Quadrangle Trench to Trench Junction X.22.b.6.6.

The 63rd Brigade was to carry out the right attack and the 64th Brigade the left attack.

The whole of the 50th Brigade (on the right of the 63rd Brigade) was first to cover the right flank of the 63rd Brigade and then assault and clear Fricourt Village and Wood and ensure contact between the 7th and 21st Divisions.

Of the latter Brigade the 4th Middlesex (the right attacking Battalion) was to seize and consolidate Fricourt Farm—X.28.c.8.7.—the bend of trench at X.28.a.5.0. inclusive, with Advanced Posts in Railway Alley and Copse, up to the railway line about X.28.b.1.3. inclusive; the 8th Somerset L.I. (the left attacking Battalion) was to seize and consolidate from bend of trench at X.28.a.5.0. (exclusive)—Crucifix Trench to X.27.b.7.4. with Advanced Posts from X.28.b.1.3. exclusive to S. end of Shelter Wood (exclusive).

To the 10th York and Lancaster R., on the right, and 8th Lincoln R., on the left, the capture of the second objective had been allotted.

The line of trenches held by the Somersets appears to have been due east of Becourt Village and Wood. The Battalion had been ordered to attack in the following formation: B Company on the right and C on the left, in four lines of platoons at two paces interval, about 100 yards between lines. These two Companies were to be supported by A Company in two lines of half-companies. D Company was to follow in rear in artillery formation, i.e. lines of platoons in file, carrying S.A.A., bombs, picks and shovels, trench stores, etc.

Ever since the 24th June, when the preliminary bombardment of the German trenches and rear positions across No Man's Land had begun, the troops had watched the gradual demolition of the enemy's front line with lively satisfaction. At night-time those who were in support or reserve spent many hours in gazing awe-stricken at the flash of guns, the screaming and moaning of the different kind of shells as they passed overhead, to burst with a roar and sickening detonation in the enemy's lines. Burning dug-outs, farms, woods and houses lighted the skies with a dull angry glare, clouds of earth and debris shot up into the air, and it was the general impression that nothing could survive that terrible holocaust.

Dawn broke on the 1st July on thousands of men all ready in position to go forward at Zero hour. There were the trench ladders placed ready to assist the attackers into No Man's Land, the Company Officers and Platoon Commanders with their men, ready to lead them forward. Behind were the troops waiting to support the attack, and behind these again, the carrying parties with ammunition, bombs, tools, etc.

At 6.25 a.m. there was an ear-splitting roar as the final hour of intense bombardment opened. The official despatches speak of this final hour as "exceptionally violent." Never, indeed, during the previous period of the War had ammunition been expended with such prodigality.

Almost immediately the enemy replied and his guns poured an accurate, but not very heavy, storm of shells on to the British front-line and close support trenches, causing a good many casualties amongst the assembled troops. Five minutes before Zero hour the 4th Middlesex, on the right of the 8th Somersets, attempted to leave their trenches and crawl towards the German lines. But they were observed and a storm of machine-gun and rifle bullets from the right compelled them to return to their trenches, after having suffered heavy losses.

Simultaneously the 8th Somersets (Lieut.-Col. J. W. Scott, commanding) left their trenches and crept forward and, although machine-gun and rifle fire from their immediate front and both flanks met their advance, the Somerset men, or rather the survivors, lay down in No Man's Land waiting for Zero hour and the barrage to lift off the enemy's front line. Of those tragic five minutes the Battalion Diary records nothing, but in the 63rd Brigade Diary are the following words:—

"This (the machine-gun and rifle fire) caused heavy casualties, the C.O. and Adjutant and, as far as can be ascertained, all the remaining officers except Lieuts. Hall, Kellett and Ackerman becoming casualties."

It is therefore obvious in what a plight the Battalion was, ere ever the final order to assault the enemy's trenches was given, and from which point the Battalion Diary begins its story:—

"Directly the artillery barrage lifted our men advanced in quick time. They were met by very heavy machine-gun fire and, although officers and men were being hit and falling everywhere, *the advance went straight on*, and was reported by a Brigade-Major who witnessed it to have been magnificent." [1]

[1] After heavy officer casualties had been incurred, the command devolved largely upon N.C.O.'s, one of whom, Sergt. H. Cornwell, was awarded the D.C.M. for taking charge of and leading his Company.

EXPLOSION OF A MINE BEFORE AN ASSAULT

By the time the leading platoons had reached the German side of No
Man's Land they had lost 50 per cent of their effectives, and then were momentarily held up in front of the devastated hostile trenches by a machine gun.
But the Battalion bombers got to work quickly and as the survivors of the leading
platoons were now joined by the successive supporting lines, the machine
gun was silenced and the attackers swept on and over the German front line.
In the latter only a few of the enemy's machine gunners were found alive and
these were bayoneted or shot down as they tried to escape.   Heavy fire again
met the Somerset men as they advanced on the German Support Line, and
men fell fast.   But again the bombers got to work and some stiff fighting took
place before Ball Lane and Arrow Lane were cleared.   Down the German
communication trenches the men worked their way, bombing dug-outs as
they went, then on to where the trenches had been battered out of all recognition, all that remained being a mass of shell craters.   A Stokes mortar lent
the Somersets timely assistance, but the officer and team were unfortunately
knocked out: next a Lewis-gun team belonging to the Battalion was brought
up and, under cover of fire from the gun, a further advance was begun.   The
Lewis gunners, who were commanded by 2/Lieut. Kellett, worked their way
from crater to crater until they got into Lozenge Alley, "which," the records
state, "had not been straffed by our artillery."   Lozenge Alley was then
consolidated, fire-steps having to be dug as it was only a communication trench.
A heavy hostile shrapnel barrage prevented further advance.

In Lozenge Alley 2/Lieut. Kellett's party joined up with 2/Lieut. Hall[1]
and his men, the combined parties totalling about 100.   With fine tenacity
these hundred men and their officers clung to the position they had won,
repulsing during the night a heavy bombing attack from the direction of
Fricourt.   At midnight the position of the 63rd Brigade was as follows:
4th Middlesex held Empress Trench from Ball Lane and Empress Support;
8th Somerset L.I. in west end of Lozenge Wood, Sunken Road and Lozenge
Alley; 10th Y. and L. in Dart Lane; 8th Lincoln R. from Dart Alley to Lozenge
Wood.

Meanwhile, north of the Ancre and of Beaumont Hamel the 1st Somerset
Light Infantry, with other troops of the 4th Division, had attacked the German
Quadrilateral.

The 1st Battalion (Lieut.-Col. J. A. Thicknesse) had marched out of
Mailly Maillet at 10 p.m. on the previous night to take up positions in the
assembly trenches.   The Brigade, with the exception of the Bde.T.M.Bs.,
Bde. M.G. Coy. and Bde. carriers, marched to the assembly trenches in
two columns—the Somersets being included in the right column—which
moved forward in the following order: 2 Coys. E. Lancs, Somerset L.I.,
Hampshire Regt.   From the starting points all Battalions marched across
country; casualties were very small during the "move up."[2]

---

[1] Awarded the M.C. for conspicuous gallantry on this occasion.
[2] No details exist in the official diaries of the place of assembly of the Battalion, but the 4th
Divisional front ran apparently from north of Beaumont Hamel to just south of the Serre Road.

The 11th Brigade had been ordered to attack with three battalions in the front line and three in support; the 10th and 12th Brigades were to continue the attack through the 11th.   Of the latter, the East Lancs R., Rifle Brigade and 8th Warwicks (in the order given from right to left) formed the front line; the Hampshires, Somerset L.I. and 6th Warwicks (also from right to left) were in close support.   Battalions were to advance on a frontage of one company.

The three first Battalions had been ordered to assault, capture and consolidate the line Q.5.c.8.9.–K.35.c.6.2.–K.36.a.0.5., upon which the three supporting Battalions were to advance through the leading Battalions and in the same way assault, capture and consolidate the final objective of the Brigade—the line Q.6.c.5.3. (inclusive)–Q.6.a.3.9.–K.36.a.8.2. inclusive.

At 7.20 a.m. there was a roar as a huge mine under Hawthorn Redoubt, south of Beaumont Hamel, exploded.   This mine was stated to have been the largest fired during the War: it was 80 feet below the surface and contained 20¼ tons of explosive.

Ten minutes later the advance began: "The 11th Brigade advanced in magnificent style," records the Diary of the 1st Somersets: the latter in four lines as follows: 1st line, 2 platoons of A Company on right, 2 of B on left: 2nd line, 2 platoons of A Coy. on right, 2 of B on left; 3rd line, 2 platoons of C Coy. on right, 2 of H on left: 4th line, 2 platoons of C Coy. on right, 2 of H on left.

At the outset the advance was carried out in excellent style and an officer of the 1st Battalion said: "The sight was magnificent, line after line of men advancing at a slow trot towards the German line with hundreds of shells, ours for the most part, bursting behind the German line."   With but little loss the attacking lines on the left and centre advanced to the first objective. On the right flank, however, heavy machine-gun fire swept the ranks of the East Lancashires and Hampshires, and these two Battalions were unable to get beyond the enemy's wire.   The Somerset men, owing to the ridge which they should have crossed being swept by machine-gun fire, had to ease off to the left, and the Battalion found itself in the German trenches in the neighbourhood of the Quadrilateral.   The Warwicks gained their objective but were unable to hold on.

From this point onwards all is confusion.   The Battalion Diary states that "it is impossible to get a detailed account of the fighting that ensued, but the situation after the first hour or two was that men of various battalions in the Division were holding part of the Quadrilateral and were engaged in a fierce grenade fight.   Our men were for some time severely handicapped by shortage of grenades, but these were afterwards sent up."   Desperate fighting, indeed, went on in the German first and second lines throughout the day.   Unfortunately some of the German front-line trenches which had been captured were not properly cleared of their defenders, who hid themselves in their deep dug-outs until the British troops had passed on towards the second line.   The crafty Germans then came out of their first-line dug-

outs and, mounting their machine guns and using their rifles, shot down
the advancing British troops from behind; hundreds of men were lost in
this way.   Heavy casualties were also suffered by all battalions from enfilade
machine-gun and rifle fire from both flanks.   For the 29th Division, on the
right, had failed to take Beaumont Hamel, while the 31st Division, on the
left, who had to form a defensive flank through Serre, had similarly failed to
reach and hold its objectives.   Thus the 11th Brigade of the 4th Division
was out in a salient with both flanks "in the air."

Only two officers (Capt. Harington and Lieut. Greatham) now remained
with the Somerset men, who with other troops were holding a part of the
Quadrilateral.   But about 1.30 p.m. both these officers, having been wounded,
went back to have their wounds dressed and the command of men of
the Battalion in the Quadrilateral devolved upon C.S.M. Chappell.

On the first day of the Somme Battles 1916 the casualties amongst officers
were truly terrible, and all up and down the line platoons, companies and even
battalions (as with the Somerset L.I.), were temporarily commanded by N.C.O.'s.
And how well these splendid fellows "carried on!"   Under a galling fire
R.S.M. Paul crossed No Man's Land leading the Brigade carriers.   Another
gallant N.C.O. and a private (Sergeant Imber and Pte. Hodges), in the face
of rifle and machine-gun fire, signalled message after message from the German
trenches back to the old British line, asking for grenades and the assistance
of the guns.

About 4.30 p.m. Major Majendie arrived with reinforcement officers
and took command of the Battalion which had been collected together in
assembly trenches by R.S.M. Paul.[1]

After dark troops of the 11th Brigade, holding portions of the German
trenches, were relieved by Royal Irish Fusiliers and withdrew to the old British
line and, at 10 p.m., the Brigade was ordered to return to Mailly Maillet as
Divisional Reserve; the 10th and 12th Brigades to hold the front line.

This sums up very briefly the operations of the 1st Somerset L.I. on the
first day of the Somme Battles.

Back in Mailly Maillet the 1st Battalion "called the roll"; it was a mournful task for death had laid a heavy hand upon the Somerset men.   The C.O.
and Adjutant (Lieut.-Col. J. A. Thicknesse and Capt. C. C. Ford) "were both
killed before our trenches were passed," records the Diary.   Fourteen other
officers were also killed;[2] one was missing and nine were wounded, one of
whom died of his wounds on 6th July.[3]   While, to the deep regret of all
Somerset men, Brigadier-General C. B. Prowse (late of the 1st Battalion
Somerset Light Infantry and G.O.C. 11th Inf. Bde.) was wounded and died

[1] It is assumed that a portion of the Battalion, under C.S.M. Chappell, was still in the Quadrilateral.
[2] Capts. R. J. R. Leacroft and G. H. Neville, Lieuts. E. C. MacBryan and V. A. Braithwaite,
2/Lieuts. G. P. C. Fair, J. A. Hellard, J. A. Johnson, A. V. C. Leche, R. E. Dunn, W. H. Treasore,
F. A. Pearse, G. S. Winstanley, H. E. Whitgreaves and T. M. Doddington.
[3] 2/Lieut. H. L. Colville.

of his wounds later in the day.[1]   Thus no less than 26 officers of the 1st Battalion had become casualties whilst, in other ranks, the losses were 438 killed, wounded and missing.   In what a plight was the Battalion for, though they had died gloriously or had fallen wounded in gallant fighting, nothing could recompense the survivors for the loss of their heroic comrades.[2]

The story now turns to the 8th Battalion, still holding their somewhat precarious position in the German lines north of Fricourt.   The night of 1st/2nd July (as already stated) was an anxious time for the small party of 100 men and officers (representing the 8th Battalion).   They had bloodily repulsed one attack coming from the direction of Fricourt, but when dawn

broke on the 2nd July the enemy had made no further attempt to turn the Somerset men out of their hard-won position.   About 8 a.m. Captain Campbell arrived with a party of reinforcements, carrying rations, having previously found Lieut. Ackerman and about 30 men in Brandy Trench and given them rations.   At 11 a.m. the whereabouts of Major R. H. Huntingdon and his party of reinforcements (which included two subalterns) was located and they were guided to Lozenge Alley.

Throughout the morning the Battalion awaited an expected counter-attack from Fricourt, but none came.   Orders were also received to be prepared for an attack from "either direction," which apparently meant from east and north as well as from the south.   "We arranged the trench accordingly," records the Diary, "and remained in the same position all day and throughout the night of the 2nd."

During the night three more subalterns arrived and the condition of the Battalion at this period may be gathered from the fact that all four Companies were commanded by Second-Lieutenants, i.e. A Coy. by 2/Lieut. F. G. Adlam, B Coy. by 2/Lieut. S. Baker, C Coy. by 2/Lieut. Kellett and D Coy. by 2/Lieut. G. A. Ham.

During the morning of the 3rd July three officers went out on a reconnaissance with a view to occupying Crucifix Trench in support of an attack to be launched by other troops from that position on the line Shelter Wood– Bottom Wood.   But apparently the attack did not take place as the Battalion Diary records that "The Battalion was not ordered to take up this position."

About 2 p.m. a message was received from 63rd Brigade to send a senior officer to Brigade Headquarters.   Capt. Campbell was sent and was given instructions to reconnoitre Patch Alley and, if it was unoccupied, move the 8th Somersets up there, as aeroplanes had reported enemy columns marching in a S.W. direction towards Round Wood, and a counter-attack was expected. This move was completed by 5 p.m., and in this position the Battalion remained

---

[1] "At about 9.45 a.m. the General decided to move his Headquarters into the German line, thinking that it had been cleared of all Germans.   Just as he was getting out of our front-line trench near Bret Street he was shot in the back by a machine gun in the Ridge Redoubt and died in the afternoon."—The late Capt. G. A. Prideaux, 1st Somerset L.I.

[2] Capt. A. J. Harington received a bar to his M.C., 2/Lieut. B. J. Corballis the M.C., and R.S.M. E. Paul and C.S.M. P. E. E. Chappell the D.C.M. for their conspicuous gallantry on 1st July.

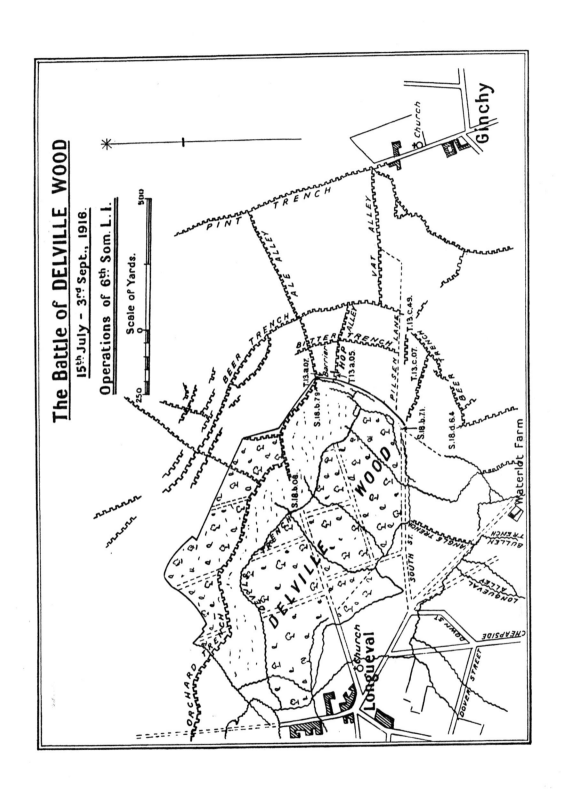

The Battle of DELVILLE WOOD

15th July – 3rd Sept., 1916.

Operations of 6th Som. L.I.

Scale of Yards.

until the early hours of 4th, when it was relieved by a company of 12th Man- 8th Battalion
chester Regt. The 8th Somersets then moved back via Happy Valley and 4th July
Meaulte to Dernancourt, arriving at the latter village about 10 a.m.

Scarcely less terrible than those sustained by the 1st Somersets were the
losses of the 8th Battalion. Ten officers had been killed or had died of their
wounds during the first day of the Battle.[1] One officer was missing and
seven wounded, including the C.O.—Lieut.-Col. J. W. Scott—a total of 18.
In other ranks the losses were 425 killed, wounded and missing.

So far as the 8th Battalion was concerned, it did not again take part in
the Battle of Albert, having moved from Dernancourt via Vaux Bertangles,
Talmas and Halloy, from which place trenches east of Hannescamps were
reconnoitred by officers of the Battalion on 10th July. The Battalion took
over these trenches from the 47th Division on 11th, was relieved on 14th 14th July
and marched back to Humbercamps.[2]

The 1st Somersets, however, had one more tour in the line before the 1st Battalion
Battle of Albert ended on 14th July. From Mailly Maillet the Battalion
marched at 6 p.m., on 4th July, to hutments at Bertrancourt, and it was during
the brief stay of the Battalion in the latter village that the Corps Commander
visited the Somerset men and congratulated them on their courage and determination on the first day of the Battle.

On 9th July the C.O. (Major V. H. B. Majendie), Adjutant and Company 9th July
Commanders reconnoitred the line east of Mailly, and on the 10th the Battalion
took over front-line trenches on the left of the Divisional front, relieving
the 2nd Essex R. B and H Companies went into the front line, with A and
C in support. Patrol work occupied the Battalion during the nights of the
tour, the chief characteristics of which were the heavy artillery bombardments
by both sides. Casualties were few, but the gallant Medical Officer of the
Battalion—Capt. J. H. Dyke-Acland, R.A.M.C.—was shot on the night of
the 12th. He was killed whilst gallantly discharging his duty, looking for
wounded out in No Man's Land.

On the 15th the 1st Somersets were relieved by the 1st Rifle Brigade 15th July
and moved back, A and C Companies into support in Ellis Square, View
Trench and the Sucrerie, and B and H Companies to Mailly in reserve.

THE BATTLE OF DELVILLE WOOD: 15TH JULY–3RD SEPTEMBER

Few places during the Battles of the Somme, 1916, changed hands
more frequently, each time during bloody fighting, than Delville Wood—or
the "Devil's Wood" as it was popularly called. When first attacked, in the
middle of July, the Wood was thick with leafy trees and dense undergrowth,
but as the Battle progressed branches were torn away by shell fire, the ground
was churned up to a state of unutterable confusion, until at last only gaunt

[1] Capts. W. G. Warden and A. B. Hatt, 2/Lieuts. H. Dalrymple, W. Scott, W. G. Leathly,
J. V. Young, F. D. Withers, J. E. Lewis, J. R. T. Chalmers and W. H. Baker.
[2] Owing to severe casualties, the 63rd Bde. (including 8th Somersets) was transferred to the 37th
Division.

stumps, shorn of their one-time beauty, bare of leaves and branches, marked a once-beautiful spot. The ground, littered with broken branches and tangled masses of bushes, pock-marked with shell holes, which both sides had turned as far as possible into posts and machine-gun nests, intersected here and there by trenches, and what had been roads through the Wood, was a truly terrible place over which to fight.

Such was the condition of Delville Wood in August 1916, when the 6th Somersets of the 43rd Brigade (14th Division) moved up into the line; the Wood was then held partly by British and partly by the Germans.

On the 1st July the 6th Somersets were holding front-line trenches in the Blagny area, east of Arras—a quiet sector. This quietude was more noticeable during the early days of the Somme Battles, for on 2nd the Battalion Diary records: "It is possible that the Germans have taken away most of their guns and men from here as everything is extraordinarily quiet. A few shells were sent into Arras. The opposing trenches in this part of the line had been pushed forward until they were within a few yards of one another. The Somerset men had one sap which was only five yards from a German sap, while the trenches were only fifteen yards apart. This fact is recorded in the following extract taken from the Diary of 6th July:—

"The Germans had also been doing some work on their sap which is only five yards from ours. They are making a cutting out to-night. However, if they start again we will bomb them as the distance is only 15 yards. When a bomb is thrown over the Germans get very annoyed and reply with about 60 into our sap."

This closeness of the trenches was responsible for the death of a gallant officer and a most efficient Company Commander of the 6th Somersets. Just after midnight on the 10th July—at 12.40 a.m.—Capt. S. E. Birrell and Pte. Hoyle went out on patrol and were surprised by a standing German patrol. A bombing contest ensued and rifle shots were fired. Capt. Birrell fell wounded and Hoyle went back for assistance, but while he was gone the Germans ran out and captured the wounded officer: "How badly he was hit it is impossible to say, but when hit he collapsed immediately." The wound was mortal, for he was reported "died of wounds" on 11th July—a great loss to his Battalion.

The remainder of the tour in the trenches, which ended on the night of 22nd/23rd July, passed without incident of an unusual character and, at 3 a.m. on 23rd, the Somerset men arrived in billets in Agnez-les-Duisans. On the 28th at 10 a.m. the Battalion set out from Agnez to march to Warluzel— a distance of 11 miles, for the 21st Division had come north from the Somme area and had relieved the 14th Division, which had received orders to move south into the battle area. With full packs and all the impedimenta of troops on service, the Battalion (in Brigade) left Warluzel and, although the heat was excessive, but few men had fallen out when billets were reached. The 29th was spent in resting and cleaning up, but at 9 a.m. on 30th the 43rd Brigade again set out and, marching through the heat of the day, the 6th

Somersets arrived at Villars l'Hopital at 3.30 p.m. and there billeted. The
31st was another "rest day." On the 1st August Prouville was the destination,
and here the Battalion went into billets until the 6th. Route-marches occupied
these few days, for the Brigade had been warned that "the men must be as
fit as possible in four days as we shall probably be in the 'show' at Albert
shortly." At 3.15 p.m. the 6th Battalion marched to Candas and there
entrained for Mericourt, where, after many stoppages and wayside halts,
detraining took place and the troops were "marched 5 miles where we
camped on the top of a hill overlooking Albert, about 5 or 6 miles from the
firing line. Guns all around us. The amazing thing is that so many men,
horses and ammunition were so near the firing line, absolutely in the open."
On the 8th August the Battalion Diary records: "How long we shall be here
(the Battalion was still in camp) before going into the line is unknown." It
was not very long. For on the following morning at 5 a.m. Colonel Ritchie
(commanding 6th Somersets) and his four Company Commanders went up
to Delville Wood to have a look round. They came back with the information
that "the trenches hardly exist."

At 6 a.m. on 12th the 6th Somersets left camp for the front line and, *en*
route, tools were distributed, and bombs, rifle-grenades and water were issued,
together with two days' rations. As the Battalion moved forward the men
were astonished at the number of troops encountered: "There were masses
of troops and guns in the open just behind the lines."

At 4 p.m. the Battalion began the relief of the Lancashire Fusiliers in
the front-line trenches in Delville Wood, and for the next five hours the tiresome
and dangerous business of taking over the trenches proceeded. At length, about
9 p.m., the relief was complete and the Somerset men began to settle down for
the night. They found themselves in trenches which were fairly continuous,
but the position of the German line was not definitely known, though it was
evident that the enemy was not far away within the borders of the Wood.

Whenever officers and men got into fresh trenches they involuntarily
compared them with those last held. Blagny had been quiet and comparatively
clean and wholesome, but this new line was surely the most noisome spot it
was possible to be in. The stench from the decaying dead was awful, gas
fumes hung about the shell holes and clung to the undergrowth, weird and
ghostly in the semi-darkness were the gaunt long arms of the torn and blasted
trees, or all that remained of them. The uncertainty of the whereabouts of
the German trenches kept the nerves of both officers and men at high tension;
at any time a crowd of grey-clad, shouting figures might rise up as if from
the earth and, under cover of a shower of bombs, try to rush the position.
How different it all was from Blagny!

About 1 a.m. on the 13th patrols crept out with the object of discovering
something of the enemy's position. In wandering about the Wood they
bumped into two separate German patrols, one an officers' patrol, of which
the Somerset men killed three, wounded two and captured one; of the other
patrol three were captured and one killed.

By midday on 13th the 6th Somersets reported Lieut. F. H. Fuge killed, Lieut. Malet wounded and 6 other ranks casualties from shell-fire.   From one of the captured prisoners it was learned that a Battalion relief had taken place and some of the German officers and their men had passed over their own front line by mistake and were surprised by the Somerset patrols.   Throughout the night of 13th/14th shell fire was intermittent and, with every truth, the Battalion Diary records: "It is always much heavier during the night than day."   Another officer wounded, 4 other ranks killed and 6 wounded were the casualties received on the 14th, and at night-time patrols again went out into the Wood on the task of trying to find out the dispositions of the enemy. During the night a futile attack was made by the enemy on a sap held by the Somersets: it was easily repulsed.   At 6 o'clock the next morning the 6th Somersets were relieved by the D.C.L.I. and returned to the support trenches just in front of Montauban Alley.   But although in support the Somerset men had not yet finished with Delville Wood, for both on the nights of 15th and 16th the Battalion supplied a working party of 250 which was sent up to the Wood to dig all the night.

On the 16th Divisional orders had been received at 43rd Bde. H.Qs. stating that on 18th the Brigade was to attack the German line along the N.E. edge of Delville Wood and trenches to the east of the Wood.   The order as issued to the 6th Somersets is not available for, as the Battalion Diary states: "Owing to the close proximity of the enemy and the likelihood of a counter-attack all operation orders had to be destroyed."   But from the Brigade Diary the following points are gleaned: A simultaneous attack was to be made on the 18th August by three Corps, i.e. XIII and XV and III Corps. Two Brigades (43rd on the right and 41st on the left) were to carry out the attack of the 14th Division.   The objectives allotted to the former Brigade were S.18.d.6.4–the angle formed by the German trenches at S.18.d.6.5.–T.13.c.4.9.–Beer Trench to junction with Ale Alley–Ale Alley to T.13.a.0.7. –S.18.b.7.9, and thence back to the Divisional front-line about S.18.b.0.8. The 41st Brigade was to attack the line S.11.d.8.6.–Orchard Trench–Wood Lane to S.11.a.3.2.   The 17th Brigade of the 24th Division was attacking on the right of the 43rd Brigade and the 33rd Division on the left of the 41st Brigade.

The 6th Somerset L.I. (on the right) and the 6th D.C.L.I. (on the left) were to carry out the attack of the 43rd Brigade; the objectives allotted to these two Battalions were as follows:—

"The 6th Somerset L.I. will attack that portion of the enemy trenches between Hop Alley and S.18.d.6.4, and will consolidate themselves along the line from the junction of Hop Alley and Beer Trench inclusive to S.18.d.6.4, and also along Hop Alley to point T.13.a.0.5.   The 6th D.C.L.I. will attack that portion of the enemy's trenches between T.13.a.0.5–T.13.a.0.7–S.18.b.7.9, and thence draw back the line to our present front line about S.18.b.0.8." [1]

[1] 43rd Infantry Brigade Operation Order No. 54.

Other interesting points in the attack to be made by the Somerset men were: (1) For three-quarters of an hour after Zero the Divisional Artillery was to bombard that portion of Beer and Bitter trenches which lay north of Hop Alley, also Ale Alley west of its junction with Bitter Trench. The barrage was then to lift and the 6th Somersets were to bomb northwards from Hop Alley up Bitter Trench and Beer Trench, whilst the 6th D.C.L.I. were to bomb up Ale Alley as far as the junction of Ale Alley and Beer Trench; (2) When the objectives allotted to the Battalions had been reached the O.C. 6th Somersets was to see that a communication trench was dug from a point about T.13.c.0.7 back to the original Brigade front line about S.18.b.7.1. A preliminary bombardment was to take place from 8 a.m. until 8 p.m. on 17th and open again at 6 a.m., and continue until 2.50 p.m. on 18th August, the day of attack.

The assembly positions of the three Companies of the 6th Battalion, who were to make the attack, are given approximately, as they could not be ascertained accurately from the Diary. A Company, on the right, was to attack the southern portion of Beer Trench to the junction of the latter with Pilsen Lane. To D Company had been allotted that portion of Beer Trench northwards from Pilsen Lane to the junction with Hop Alley. C Company was to attack Hop Alley. B Company was held in reserve in order to construct a communication trench from Beer Trench back to the original Brigade front line, when Beer Trench had been captured.

The attack on Hop Alley by C Company was a particularly desperate operation, as it necessitated the Company moving out in single file of platoons and then turning to the left and waiting till the barrage lifted. This movement would only be possible if the bombers rushed the junction of Beer Trench and Hop Alley and immediately established a post in order to keep down hostile enfilade machine-gun fire from Hop Alley, which would not only prevent the capture of the latter trench, but in all probability hold up the remainder of the attack.

On the morning of 18th, at 3 a.m., all four Companies of the 6th Somersets moved up from Montauban to their assembly positions in the S.E. corner of Delville Wood, the two flank assaulting Companies (A and C) occupying the forward trench and the centre assaulting Company (D) the rear trench. B, the Reserve Company, was in rear of D Company.

The 6th D.C.L.I. were on the left of the Somersets, who were in position by 6 a.m. At that hour the preliminary bombardment opened with guns of all calibre pouring shell on to Beer Trench and Hop Alley. With the exception of two "intense bombardments" with enemy guns firing rapid at 8.45 a.m. and 12.10 p.m. the guns continued during the morning to shell the enemy's trenches, but so difficult was observation for the gunners that some of the "heavies" fired short and 15 casualties were suffered by the Somersets "from our own guns."

No reply was made by the enemy to the bombardment which, at 2.45 p.m. (Zero hour), again became intense. At 2.35 p.m. the two flank assaulting

Companies, A and C, had "closed up outwards" and the centre Company, D, came in between them.   It was not possible to get all three Companies in the front line earlier as the Northern end was very close to Hop Alley, then being heavily shelled.

At Zero hour the attacking troops advanced, and once in No Man's Land found themselves right under the barrage from 20 to 25 yards from the German trenches.   Here the men halted waiting for the barrage to lift—a matter of five minutes.   At 2.50 p.m. the screen of fire moved on and almost immediately the Somerset men were in the German trenches, bayoneting or shooting down all those who refused to surrender.

A Company came up against two hostile machine guns mounted in a salient in the German line, though only one was in action.   This was rushed and the gun team bombed.   The Battalion narrative records that "two good N.C.O.'s were killed doing this."   A German was seen trying to get the second machine gun into action, the remainder of the gun team having bolted; he was dealt with.   There was little further resistance along the front of this Company, for the enemy had been taken by surprise, and although his "S.O.S." rockets had been fired soon after the attack began, most of the captured Germans were found without equipment.   Their resistance was futile in the extreme; the terrific bombardment to which they had been subjected had done its work and had spread demoralization amongst the enemy's troops, whose one idea was to surrender.   Some of them, in their mad desire to get away from their horrible trenches, literally ran over to the British lines, others bolted back towards Ginchy.   Most of the latter were shot down.   A party of from 30 to 40 made off towards Waterlot Farm, where they circled about in the open like a herd of deer, with their hands above their heads until they were eventually taken prisoner.   A Company, having reached its objective, began consolidating the position immediately, being helped by a party of the King's Regiment.

The centre Company (D) was able to follow close on the barrage, over Bitter Trench to Beer Trench.   Only ten Germans were found in the former and these were either killed or forced to surrender.   In Beer Trench some 30 Germans suffered a similar fate.   Two German officers, one of whom said in English, "You English are too villainous for words," refused to surrender and were shot.   Other Germans were seen crawling from shell hole to shell hole back towards Ginchy.   A portion of the trench lying between the junction of Vat Alley with Beer Trench and the junction of the latter with Hop Alley, had been completely obliterated by shell fire, so that it was difficult to tell when the objective had been reached.   As a consequence one platoon of the Somersets rushed on towards Ginchy, but returned and joined up with the remainder of the Company and consolidation was proceeded with, a more useful post for bombers and Lewis guns being established some sixty yards up Vat Alley.

The left flank Company (C), whose task it was to capture Hop Alley, had the stiffest job.   The bombers found little difficulty in rushing and establishing a post at the junction of the Alley with Beer Trench.   But at the western end of the Alley, where it joined up with Delville Wood, the Germans had two machine guns in a sap, and they also put down a heavy trench-mortar barrage in front of the second wave of the Somerset men. A young subaltern (2/Lieut. W. E. Berridge, who was mortally wounded and died on 20th August) was the first to reach the enemy's trench in which some 90 Germans were killed and a few prisoners taken. In this part of the line the enemy's troops were found ready, wearing their equipment.

The whole of Hop Alley having passed into the hands of the Somerset men, the latter then began to bomb northwards up Beer Trench to the junction of the latter with Ale Alley. But the Battalion on the left of C Company had been unable to work up Ale Valley and join hands as arranged. The Somersets were therefore forced to retire, but a barricade was established in Beer Trench some 30 yards N. of Hop Alley.

Of B Company which, as soon as the attacking Company had gone forward, began to dig like mad the new communication trench ordered between Beer Trench and the old British line, the C.O. (Colonel Ritchie) reported: "This Company worked very hard. They dug new C.T. under a heavy fire and did it quickly and well. Also carried wire, stakes, etc., to the front line. Sent back 82 prisoners under escort. Carried bombs and sand-bags. Put up artillery boards. Sent 20 men to fill gap on our left. Sent 20 men to make and hold a strong point in gap between right Companies. Sent 30 men to support C Company in Hop Alley." And then, when night had fallen, the remainder of this gallant Company carried bombs, S.A.A., water, etc., to the front line.

The inevitable German counter-attack came about 6 p.m. In extended order the enemy advanced from Pint Trench, but rifle fire and Lewis-gun fire met their advance and the attack melted away. At 6.30 p.m. they again attempted to advance, this time in small batches, but were again repulsed. This last attack cost the enemy about 200 casualties.

All along the line snipers were very active, and the Somerset snipers, lying some 25 yards out in front of their new trenches, had difficulty in coping with the enemy's marksmen, who were everywhere.

At 8 p.m. the Germans were again observed from Hop Alley massing for an attack, but Lewis and Vickers guns took them in flank, and with the guns which opened fire about 8.30 p.m. the threatened attack was broken up.[1]

The night of the 18th/19th August was a terrible trial to the 6th Battalion, for by the time darkness had fallen the enemy's artillery had got the range of the newly won trenches and had put down a very heavy bombardment from guns of all calibre on the Somerset men, who worked strenuously in consolidating their position, but all the same casualties were heavy. Throughout the 19th this heavy shelling continued, though the British guns retaliated with marked effect.

About 4.30 p.m. the Cornwalls, on the left of the Somersets, asked the

[1] Capt. G. P. Manson was awarded the M.C., and Sergts. T. Bartlett and W. G. Bryant the D.C.M., for gallantry during this attack.

latter if they could get a message through to the guns to shell the Germans who were massing for a counter-attack. By this time most of the Somerset runners had been killed or wounded, and the only means of getting a message back to the guns was by signalling to an aeroplane. So the Somerset men stretched their aeroplane letter "O" out on the ground in the hope of attracting the attention of one of the many "planes then up." This signal indicated that a barrage was wanted immediately on the enemy's lines. By good fortune an aeroplane picked up the signal and, hastening off back to the guns, gave the information, with the result that about three minutes later a rain of shells began to fall on the hostile trenches and the threatened attack did not materialize.

A little later (at 5 p.m.) officers of the 9th Rifle Brigade came to look round the trenches of the 6th Somersets and made arrangements for taking them over. Hostile shelling, however, prevented the relief taking place until almost midnight, but this was all to the advantage of the Somerset men, who had no casualties in coming out of the line. The relief was completed at 4.15 a.m., the Battalion being billeted in Fricourt. "The men," stated the Battalion Diary, "on arrival in rest billets, were absolutely beat; the authorities had wisely kept them until the last possible moment and then taken them out."

Thus ended another phase of the Battle of Delville Wood, a phase which cost the Regiment: Capt. E. D. Pain, Lieut. B. M. Denton and 2/Lieuts. W. E. Berridge, Davy and A. S. Pullen killed, and seven other officers wounded. In other ranks 48 had been killed and 220 wounded and missing. On the 22nd the 43rd Brigade was paraded and the Brigadier complimented the 6th Somersets especially on the fine behaviour of the Battalion in Delville Wood.

Less than two months had passed since the beginning of the Somme Battles, but already the battlefield had been sprinkled freely with the blood of the gallant West Countrymen, and if blood be the price of victory the men of Somerset had already spilt it freely.

THE BATTLE OF GUILLEMONT: 3RD–6TH SEPTEMBER

Some 1,500 yards south-east of the "Devil's Wood" there lay a ruined shell-blasted village, which again and again had been captured and lost; this was Guillemont. West of the village was Trônes Wood (place of horrible memories to all who fought on the Somme in 1916), while along the northern outskirts ran the railway, the Station being included in the German line. Between Guillemont and Trônes Wood there was a road, south of which lay Arrow Head Copse. A quarry on the western outskirts of the village, a cemetery on the eastern exits along the road which led to Leuze Wood were other places which figured in a more or less degree in the story of the Battle of Guillemont.

The enemy's positions in and about the village were of a very powerful nature. On the surface his trenches were deep and well made, whilst below ground the place was literally honeycombed with deep dug-outs, huge cellars, and subterranean passages in which whole battalions could be accommodated. The forward trenches ran in a semicircle, south, west and north-west of Guillemont, those on the southern flank dominated the whole of the ground south _{7th Battalion} of the village.

The first attack on Guillemont had taken place on 30th July. The village was captured, troops passing through to the other side, but as the flanks were held up the positions had to be abandoned. On 8th August the village was again captured and abandoned for similar reasons. On 16th August another attempt met with only partial success, the troops establishing themselves in the outskirts of the village and occupying the Railway Station, beating off a violent counter-attack on the latter place on 23rd, and on the 24th further progress was made north and east of the "Devil's Wood," which had an important effect on the subsequent capture of the village. Little wonder that the official despatches refer to these operations as "The Problem of Guillemont."

The next and final assault on the village formed part of a general attack which took place at 12 noon on the 3rd September, on a front extending from the extreme right (just south of Trônes Wood) to the enemy trenches on the right bank of the Ancre, north of Hamel. Preparations for the attack were carried out during the 1st and 2nd September, and the 20th Division with an attached Brigade of 16th Division, having been detailed to storm Guillemont, was busily engaged in making the necessary movement and in working out the final details for the assault.

The 20th Division had left the troubled Ypres Salient about the middle of July and, moving by stages southwards, reached the Somme area towards the end of the month, the 7th Somersets marching into Mailly Maillet at noon on 27th where, with other units of the 61st Inf. Bde., they were billeted. 27th July That same afternoon all Company Commanders were ordered to reconnoitre the trenches in front of Auchonvillers and, on the evening of the 28th, the Battalion filed into the first sector held by it in the Somme area, relieving the 13th Battalion R.W. Fusiliers. "We were quite thankful," said Colonel Troyte-Bullock, the C.O., "to have landed somewhere where we knew we should be stationary for at least four days."

Strange indeed that the 7th Somersets should have come to this part of the Somme battlefield, for the very trenches they now held were those from which the 1st Battalion of the Regiment had made its attack on Serre on the 1st July. And on 28th, when the 7th Somersets took over the line, the trenches and the surrounding country were still full of half-buried corpses, amongst which were the remains of many men who had belonged to the 1st Battalion; these were reverently laid to rest by their newly arrived comrades.

On 16th August the 20th Division was relieved by the Guards Division 16th August and marched southwards with orders to go into the line east of Albert. By the 21st of the month the 61st Brigade had reached Camp in Happy Valley, relieving the 8th Brigade of the 3rd Division. On the following day the Brigade took over trenches opposite Guillemont from the 17th Brigade (24th Division), but it was not until 25th August that the 7th Somersets went into 25th August the front line, relieving the 7th D.C.L.I. on that date.

The Battalion was disposed as follows: D Company in the front line,

A Company in support and B and C in reserve. Bn. H.Qs. were in a dug-out between the support and reserve line. The relief was barely completed ere the enemy began a heavy bombardment of the front line, which lasted an hour and a half, killing two privates and wounding thirteen others. On 26th A and C Companies were ordered to take over part of the front line on the right of the Battalion, opposite Guillemont Quarries. In moving up the communication trench to carry out this relief Capt. E. B. Hatt was killed by a shell and four men were wounded. On the 27th in broad daylight and in full view of the enemy, these Companies had to be withdrawn owing to an impending bombardment of the Quarries by the "Heavies," the Somerset men being too close to the "targets" for the guns to fire with safety. The withdrawal, a very difficult operation, was, however, carried out with such success that not a casualty was sustained. That night the Battalion moved back to Carnoy Craters, though the relief took place under horrible conditions. Rain fell in torrents (rain had fallen "on and off" since 24th) and the trenches were knee-deep in mud and full of half-buried corpses.

On 29th Colonel Troyte-Bullock, Major Lyon and the four Company Commanders returned to the line and reconnoitred the ground between Bernafay Wood and the trenches south of Arrow Head Copse—the line of advance to be taken by the 7th Somersets in the forthcoming operations.

In the original orders the assault was to be carried out by the 60th and 61st Brigades, the 59th Brigade being in reserve. But the experiences of the past few days had robbed the 20th Division of its freshness on going into the line and, owing to the number of casualties and sick men in four of the attacking Battalions, two Composite Brigades were formed and the 7th Somersets were attached as a reserve Battalion to the 59th Brigade under Brigadier-General Cameron Shute.

On the 31st August Bn. H.Qs., with A and C Companies, moved up to the Briqueterie, south of Bernafay, in support of the 59th Brigade who held the front line. C and D Companies remained at Carnoy Craters. At dusk the enemy opened a heavy bombardment, using "tear" shell, and the two Companies of Somerset men suffered about 20 casualties. On the night of 1st September a similar bombardment took place and Major Preston-Whyte and Capt. Blanckensee were both badly gassed and had to be evacuated to hospital.

At 12 midnight 2nd/3rd September, Bn. H.Qs., with A and B Companies marched back to the Carnoy Craters in order to prepare for the operations on 3rd. At 8.30 a.m. on the latter date the Battalion, as a whole, having breakfasted at 7.30 a,m., left Carnoy Craters to take up its assembly positions on the western edge of Trônes Wood.

The morning was bright and pleasant, and the men were in the best of spirits as they moved forward. As the Battalion reached the eastern edge of Montauban village, hostile shells fell on the road and the Companies were therefore sent off by different routes across country to their assembly positions, which were reached without casualties.

Zero hour for the attack was 10.30 a.m., and the 7th Somersets were ordered to move from their assembly positions at 12 noon.

The 20th Division had been ordered to capture Guillemont, clear it, and establish itself on the Wedge Wood–Ginchy Road from T.26.a.1.7. on the right to T.20.a.1.5. on the left, where touch with the 5th and 7th Divisions, respectively, was to be obtained. The 59th Brigade was to attack on the right and the 60th Brigade on the left. The objectives of the 59th Brigade (to which it will be remembered the 7th Somersets were attached for this operation) were: 1st Objective—German trenches in Sunken Road from T.25.a.3.3. to T.25.a.2.7. inclusive (the second sunken road east from Arrow Head Copse), thence north to Mount Street; 2nd Objective—Trench junction T.25.b.1.4. inclusive, thence South Street as far as Mount Street; 3rd Objective—Wedge Wood–Ginchy Road from T.26.a.1.7. to cross-roads T.20.c.1.4. inclusive, touch being established with 5th Division on the right and 60th Infantry Brigade on the left.

The 3rd Objective was allotted to the 7th Somersets who, at Zero plus 2 hours, were to go forward from the line of the 2nd Objective, on the latter being captured.

The Battalion Diary records the subsequent action in the following brief words:—

"Advanced in support at 12 noon. Companies in lines of two platoons in file. Men advanced steadily through German barrage. 59th Brigade, having taken 2nd Objective, two Companies Somerset L.I. pushed on and, advancing close under an artillery barrage, took 3rd Objective. The enemy garrison, 46 men and 1 officer, having retired to two dug-outs, surrendered on our arrival. Other units of 59th Brigade arrived and trenches consolidated. At 8 p.m. two Companies ordered to dig in support line E. of Guillemont. At 8 p.m. B Company sent to reinforce 47th Brigade on N. side of Guillemont–Combles Road. Casualties, 1 officer killed, 9 wounded (including C.O.), 140 other ranks killed and wounded."

But fortunately it is possible to supplement this all too brief account, from a private narrative written by the C.O., Col. Troyte-Bullock.

After the attack had begun at 10.30 a.m. the Somerset men fully expected the enemy would put down a very heavy bombardment on Trônes Wood and Bernafay Wood and that, as the Battalion was then assembled between the two, heavy casualties would be suffered. But for some extraordinary reason, excepting for an odd shell or two, the German guns did not worry the Battalion at all. At 12 noon, therefore, the 7th Somersets began the advance under good conditions. The Battalion moved in four lines of Companies in artillery formation, A Company leading, followed by D, then Bn. H.Qs., B and C Companies. After crossing the Montauban–Guillemont road a hostile 5·9 barrage fell right across the front of the Battalion, but the platoons, in single file, never wavered for an instant, but went steadily through it as if they were on Salisbury Plain. About 40 casualties were sustained in going through this barrage.

In the old British front line, where the Somerset men came in touch with the 6th Oxford and Bucks L.I., information was gained that the attack was progressing well though casualties were very heavy. The German guns had, however, got the range of the trenches in which the Somersets halted and shrapnel with marvellous precision was bursting over the West Countrymen. The Battalion, therefore, pushed on down the slope of the hill and got into touch with the left of the 5th Division from whom it was learnt that the right Brigade of the latter was held up by an enemy strong point in Falfemont Farm, situated on the forward slopes of a spur which ran westwards from the high ground above Combles. At this time A and D Companies were in line, each on a two-platoon frontage. Bn. H.Qs. were about 200 yards in rear, followed by B and C Companies in similar formation in echelon. The German shells were soon going well overhead and there was very little hostile rifle or machine-gun fire.

The 10th Rifle Brigade and the 11th K.R. Rifles of the 59th Brigade, having taken the 2nd Objective, the 7th Somersets were now ordered to capture the 3rd, and final, objective, i.e. the Sunken Road running southwards down the valley from Guillemont cemetery.

The attack on the final objective was organized on a two-company frontage, A and D leading, followed immediately by Bn. H.Qs. with C and B Companies in close support. There was only just time to make all arrangements for the attack before the Divisional barrage fell on the line of the objective.

Advancing close on the heels of the barrage the two leading Companies very quickly reached the enemy's trenches, but found them almost deserted for, in order to escape the barrage the Germans had retired to their dug-outs. One Company (A) had lost its Commander in the advance—Capt. G. Shufflebotham—who was hit in the head by shrapnel and killed. From their dug-outs to which they had retired, 1 German officer and 46 other ranks, unwounded, emerged and surrendered to the Somerset men; these were sent back under escort. A and D Companies now began to consolidate the captured position, while B and C Companies were ordered to dig a support line with the right flank thrown back, as the Battalion was now under hostile machine-gun fire from the Falfemont Farm ridge, on the right rear. In the distance the German machine gunners could be seen running from their dug-outs and shell holes to man their gun positions, but the Somersets' snipers, firing at a range of about 800 yards, and a section of the 61st Brigade Machine Gun Company, attached to the Battalion, came into action and the enemy's activities were considerably curtailed.

Meanwhile the situation in Guillemont was still somewhat obscure. As the Somerset men were advancing from Arrow Head Copse, patrols were sent out to obtain touch with the 60th Brigade. But beyond ascertaining that the village, or rather the heap of ruins representing the village, was clear of the enemy no definite information of what was happening on the left of the 7th Somersets was obtainable. On the right the 5th Division had been completely held up so that the right flank of the Somersets turned sharply back almost at right angles.

About 7.45 p.m. instructions from Brigade H.Qs. were received at Bn. 7th Battalion H.Qs. ordering the Battalion to make a further advance on Leuze Wood, 3rd September directly east of the Somerset men. Brigade Headquarters were apparently under the impression that the Wood was clear of the enemy. From the volume of fire coming from the Falfemont Spur and certain knowledge that the Wood was strongly held by the enemy, it was obvious that Bde. H.Qs. were not in possession of the true facts. Colonel Troyte-Bullock therefore held a consultation with the C.O., 6th Oxford and Bucks L.I., and they decided to send a situation report back to the Brigade, though getting ready to carry out the order.

"The Companies," said the C.O., 7th Somersets, "were now all well dug in and full of beans," but as he was going round to give the Company Commanders their orders for the attack he was hit in the leg by a machine-gun bullet. The wound was dressed and for a little while Colonel Troyte-Bullock "carried on." 2/Lieut. Hill of D Company, who had been sent out on patrol with orders to find out whether Leuze Wood was held, got right into the Wood, finding it unoccupied on the edge, but strongly held farther in. Just as he returned with his report orders arrived from the Brigade cancelling the attack.

At 8 p.m. a call for help came from troops of the 47th Inf. Bde. (on the right of the Somersets) north of the Guillemont–Combles road, and B Company, under Capt. B. E. F. Mitchell, was sent out to their assistance. By this time darkness had fallen and the exact position of the troops whom they were ordered to assist being unknown to the Somerset men, it was no easy task to find their way across slippery, muddy country, pitted with shell holes and craters.

On reaching the Cemetery, B Company came under heavy rifle and machine-gun fire. Captain Mitchell and Lieut. Knight were both wounded, also two N.C.O.'s (Sergts. Tozer and Wiltshire). Though hit in the thigh and bleeding profusely Capt. Mitchell gallantly struggled on. From the increase in volume of the enemy's machine-gun fire it was apparent that the Germans were counter-attacking, and changing direction half-left Capt. Mitchell got his men under cover in a depression, closed his Company up and sent out scouts to try and obtain touch with the 47th Brigade. By rare good fortune a straggler from the latter was met with, who was able to direct the Somerset men to where his Battalion was situated. Capt. Mitchell was now so weak from loss of blood that he could go no farther and handed over command of the Company to 2/Lieut. J. Jenne. Under this young officer, who had but recently joined the Battalion, the Company marched off in the direction indicated by the straggler and presently came upon an Irish Battalion which had suffered very heavy casualties and been forced to retire. B Company of the Somersets reached the trenches from which the Irishmen were retiring just in time to beat off an enemy counter-attack. The Somerset men then consolidated the position and held it until they were relieved at midnight, when they rejoined their Battalion.

In his own narrative of the action Colonel Troyte-Bullock very rightly adds: "If B Company had not done their job in the way they did the left flank of the 20th Division would have been turned and most of the ground gained would have been lost."[1]

During the night of the 3rd/4th September Capt. W. S. Whall assumed temporary command of the Battalion, as the C.O. was evacuated to hospital.

The 4th September was a quiet day, which enabled the 7th Somersets to improve their trenches. At 8 p.m. two and a half Companies were sent forward to dig and hold a trench extending from the S.W. corner of Leuze Wood to the Guillemont–Combles Road. In a perfect deluge of rain, and under fire of 5·9's, the work was carried out and the trench held without the loss of a single casualty.

At 8 a.m. on the 5th, the 7th and 8th Inniskilling Fusiliers arrived to relieve the 7th Somersets and, although hostile snipers were active during the relief, no casualties were suffered, and very tired, but in good spirits, the Battalion reached Carnoy Craters about 10 a.m. On this day Major Lyon took over command of the 7th Somersets from Capt. Whall.

The Battle of Guillemont had cost the 7th Somersets, all ranks, 11 killed and 155 wounded. By Companies the casualties were: A Company—Capt. G. M. Shufflebotham (Coy. Commander) and 6 men killed, 2/Lieut. H. E. Makins wounded; B Company—Capt. B. E. F. Mitchell (Coy. Commander), Lieut. A. Knight and 11 other ranks wounded; C Company—3 other ranks killed, Lieut. E. C. Cartwright, 2/Lieut. W. W. Chard, 2/Lieut. W. B. Giles, Sergt. J. Winzar, Sergt. T. Williams and 37 other ranks wounded; D Company —1 other rank killed, Lieut. A. A. Andrews wounded, 34 other ranks wounded.

But "The Problem of Guillemont" had been solved, and no more was it a thorn in the side of the British, in whose possession it remained until the great German offensive of 1918.

THE BATTLE OF FLERS–COURCELETTE, 15TH–22ND SEPTEMBER

Of the operations of 16th September, in which the 7th Somersets were engaged, Col. Troyte-Bullock said it was "a platoon and section commander's battle," and when the records are examined it will be seen that this description is in every way accurate.[2]

In the capture of Ginchy (9th September), which followed close on the final taking of Guillemont, the 7th Somersets had no part, being then resting
and refitting in Maricourt. But on 12th the Battalion moved from Maricourt to the Sandpits, Meaulte, thence to Citadel on 14th and to Talus Boise on 15th, where the Somersets were formed up and awaited orders. At midday these orders came to hand and the Battalion (in Brigade) moved forward to the neighbourhood of Waterlot Farm in the old British front line north of Guillemont. The 61st Inf. Bde. was now attached to the Guards Division

---

[1] Lt.-Col. C. J. Troyte-Bullock was awarded the D.S.O., Capt. W. E. Whall, Lieut. E. C. Cartwright, and 2/Lieut. J. H. R. Hill, the M.C., and Sergt. J. Shortman the D.C.M., for conspicuous gallantry on this occasion.

[2] Lieut.-Col. R. P. Preston-Whyte was in command of the 7th Battalion S.L.I. from 17th September 1916 to 5th November 1916.

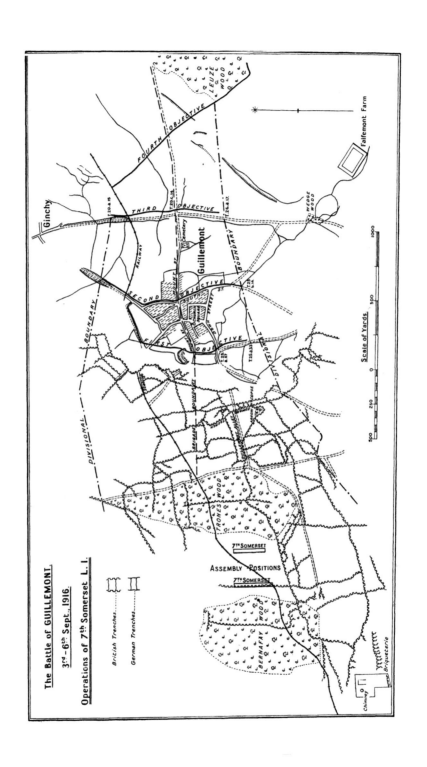

and the Brigade Diary contains the following entry which throws useful light 7th Battalion
15th September
upon the general situation:—

"15th Sept. 5.8 p.m.   Divisional (20th) wire received stating situation
still uncertain, but believed Guards had entered Les Bœufs.[1]   6th Division
(on the right of Guards Division) still held up, presumably on 1st objective.
61st Inf. Bde. to be placed at disposal of Guards Division, with proviso that
it is to be used on south flank towards Morval.   Intention later to interpose
20th Division between Guards and 6th Divisions."

The general plan of the combined Allied attack, which had begun at
6.20 a.m. on 15th September, was

"to pivot on the high ground south of the River Ancre and north of the
Albert–Bapaume Road, while the Fourth Army directed its whole effort to
the rearmost of the enemy's original systems of defence between Morval and
Le Sars."

On the right of the Fourth Army Sir Douglas Haig had arranged with
the French

"to continue the line of advance in close co-operation . . . from the Somme
to the slopes above Combles, but directing their main efforts northwards
against the villages of Rancourt and Fregicourt, so as to complete the isolation
of Combles and open the way for their attack on Sailly-Saillisel."

In this attack—the first action in which tanks were used—two of the
enemy's main defence systems had been broken into and the British line had
been pushed forward on a front of over 6 miles to an average depth of a mile.
Three large villages—Flers, Martinpuich and Courcelette—had been captured
and the line had been pushed forward to within assaulting distance of Les
Bœufs; Combles, and a strong point—The Quadrilateral—north of it, had,
however, defied capture.

At 9.45 p.m. on 15th orders were received by the Guards Division stating
that the attack of the XIV and XV Corps would be continued at 9.25 a.m.
on 16th, and this Division, with 61st Inf. Bde. on the right and 3rd Guards
Brigade on the left, would assault Les Bœufs.   At midnight, 15/16th, therefore,
the 7th Somersets (in Brigade) moved up through Ginchy to within 600 yards
of the German position protecting Les Bœufs.

Here the Battalion dug in preparatory for the attack at 9.25 a.m. on 16th. 16th September

A series of casualties on the morning of 16th resulted in the Battalion
at the hour of attack being under the command of a second-lieutenant.   Captain
W. E. Whall was hit by a bullet in the chin at an early hour.   Before the
attack began Major Lyon (temporarily in command of the 7th Somersets)
was mortally wounded whilst trying to get in touch with troops on his left.
He had already sent out two runners, but both of them had become casualties.
He then very gallantly went out himself with the result that he was mortally

---

[1] This was incorrect.

7th Battalion
16th September

wounded and died later at Corbie.   The acting Adjutant—Lieutenant F. C. Humphries—was also wounded, and when Zero hour arrived the senior officer was 2/Lieut. Jenne, who commanded the Battalion throughout that day of brilliant fighting.

In this attack the objective of the 7th Somersets was the German front-line trench, which the Battalion was to capture and hold until a new line was dug just west of it, to the north of the Ginchy–Les Bœufs road.

All the honours of war fell that day to the 7th Battalion. The attack, splendidly carried out, began at 9.35 a.m. (Zero plus 10 minutes); the German front line on a front of 150 yards was captured and held while the new line was dug just west of it, and about fifty prisoners were captured.   Having used up all their bombs, as well as a large quantity captured from the enemy, the bombers were unable to cover the Battalion, which then fell back to the new trench which had been dug and held it until relieved on the night of 16th/17th September by the Shropshire Light Infantry.   That is the story contained in the official Diary.   Bald indeed; bare of all those little details and thrilling episodes which make military history live.   Yet none the less did they happen.   Two incidents occurred which alone should live for all time in the history of the 7th Somersets.   With bayonet and bomb the Battalion had cleared the Germans out of their front-line trench, two bombers of B Company—L/Cpl. Hill and Pte. Barrow—single-handed, bombing the enemy out of 150 yards of his trench, using German bombs.   Brilliant as was this bombing affair, it was outshone by the extraordinary gallantry of Private Hill (also of B Company, and a Lewis gunner).   With another man of his section, Hill pushed forward with the gun to a new position some 60 yards in front of the Battalion's most advanced posts.   For no less than 36 hours Hill held on to his post, at one time, with his comrade taking a prominent part in breaking up a hostile counter-attack, by bringing heavy enfilade fire on the attackers. He fought on and on until at last, his comrade being killed and his ammunition exhausted, he picked up his gun and empty magazines and retired to where he imagined the Battalion to be, only to find that it had been relieved 12 hours previously.   Eventually he rejoined the Battalion at Talus Boise.

Ten officers and about 162 other ranks were the casualties suffered by the Battalion on 16th September.[1]   Major E. L. Lyon died of his wounds at Corbie.

Not again throughout the remainder of the month were the 7th Somersets involved in any attack on or by the enemy.

But to return to the 16th September.

On the left of the Guards Division (to which the 61st Brigade was attached) the 14th Division had been ordered to attack the enemy's trench system in front of Gueudecourt, with the village as the final objective.

6th Battalion
16th September

The front of attack allotted to the 6th Somersets was Gird Trench and Gird Support.   These trenches lay N.E. of Flers, which had been captured on the previous day, i.e. the 15th September.

[1] 2/Lieuts. T. G. Jenne and W. L. Batterley were awarded the M.C., and Pte. W. Saunders the D.C.M., for conspicuous gallantry in action on 16th September.

After the Battle of Delville Wood, the 6th Somersets had spent several days in billets in Fricourt. On the 26th August, however, the Battalion moved forward again to reserve trenches 300 yards in front of Bernafay Wood. On 27th one company was sent up to reinforce the Durhams, who occupied a trench on the right of Delville Wood. The casualties this day were 2/Lieut. J. A. Munden and 3 other ranks killed, and 3 other ranks wounded.

The 28th and 29th were days of great discomfort. Rain fell heavily and the working parties supplied by the Battalion carried on their duties under wretched conditions. Relief, however, came on 30th, the 6th Somersets returning first to temporary billets in Fricourt and then to a rest camp. On 31st the Battalion entrained at Mericourt for Selincourt, 20 miles west of Amiens where, until the 12th September, all ranks enjoyed a complete rest. At 6 a.m. on the latter date the Somerset men marched out of Selincourt to a station 4 miles away, whence they travelled by train to Mericourt, and at night bivouacked just south of Albert. On the 14th the Battalion began to move up towards the front line, encamping that night at "F.13.c." On the following morning bombs, flares and small arms ammunition were issued and at 7.30 a.m. the Battalion moved off, arriving at Pommiers Redoubt at 9.30. Orders arrived at 11.15 a.m. to occupy the check line in front of Bernafay Wood. Somewhat sarcastically the Battalion Diary states that at 2 p.m. the 6th Somersets marched off "to occupy trenches which did not exist between Delville Wood and the Switch trench." Here, as no tools had arrived, the men began to dig themselves in, using their entrenching tools. Later the Transport officer arrived with the tools, having brought them up under heavy shell fire.

At 11 p.m. orders were received that the 43rd Brigade was to relieve the 42nd Brigade in the front line, the 6th Somersets taking over trenches which had been newly captured by the 9th K.R.R., known as "A–A" and "B–B" trenches.

As no rations had arrived the Somerset men had to go into the trenches without them—not a pleasant prospect:—

"No rations had arrived" (recorded the Battalion Diary at 1.30 a.m. on 16th), "so we moved to the front line and relieved the 42nd Brigade which had attacked in the morning (of 15th) and had suffered heavy losses. The line was very vague but we managed to get relief over just before daybreak. Rations only arrived for two companies, the other companies ate their iron rations. The worst difficulty was water, which was very scarce."

On the previous evening Lieut.-Col. T. F. Ritchie (commanding 6th Somersets) had been told that he was to attack the enemy next morning, but it was 4.30 a.m. on 16th before final orders arrived—the attack was to take place at 9.25 a.m.

After relieving the Rifles, the 6th Somersets were thus disposed: B Company held the right of "A–A" Trench, C Company the left of the same trench, A Company was in "B–B" Trench, and D Company in support in Gun Alley.

The attack was to be made in two waves by the Companies in the front line, the first objective being Gird Trench. Each Company was to have one bombing squad and 6 men in Gird Trench and then follow the barrage to, and capture, Gird Support.

No time was given the Battalion for a reconnaissance of the ground over which the attack was to take place and, in consequence (this is important) the existence of a partially dug trench, called "X–X" Trench, was unknown. Between "A–A" and "X–X" Trenches there was a slight ridge and thus the latter could not be observed.

Owing to the peculiar "lay" of Gird Trench, Companies on leaving "A–A" and "B–B" Trenches, had received orders to "right incline."

At Zero (9.25 a.m.) the attack began, the Somerset men following close on the heels of the barrage. The three attacking Companies—B, C and A—went forward in fine style, but the right of B, instead of reaching Gird Trench, occupied the right of "X–X" Trench under the impression that they had captured the former. The other Companies occupied the remainder of "X–X" Trench from the left of B Company to the Sunken Road. Six Germans were captured and many were seen running away, several being shot down. Until the evening Colonel Ritchie was under the impression that his men had actually captured Gird Trench, but on finding out that he really held "X–X" another attempt to advance was made. C Company pushed forward and dug in on a line some fifty yards from Gird Trench; A Company dug in about 1,000 yards N. of "X–X" Trench with its left on the road. B Company remained in the positions won earlier in the day, whilst D Company, which had been ordered up to assist two companies of the K.O.Y.L.I., who were in close support of the Somerset, was unable to advance farther than "X–X" Trench.

At 6.20 p.m. orders were received for the remainder of the Battalion and the two companies of the K.O.Y.L.I. to attack Gird Trench at 6.55 p.m., but it was impossible to get instructions out to the companies in time and the K.O.Y.L.I., being already formed up, went forward at Zero hour with a proportion of the Somersets who had received orders. The barrage was, however, quite inadequate (it is described in the Diary as "very feeble") and heavy machine-gun fire met the advance with the result that the attack broke down with heavy losses.[1]

When darkness had fallen parties were sent out to try and collect the various small detachments of men known to be in front of Gird Trench. With great difficulty "X–X" Trench was consolidated and the remnants of the Somersets, with one company of K.O.Y.L.I., held on until relieved, just before daybreak on 17th, by the 13th Northumberland Fusiliers. At 8 a.m. the Battalion—all that remained of it—reached Pommiers Redoubt and there rested until 5 p.m., when it marched back to the Camp in F.14.c. (Fricourt Camp) where the night of 17th/18th was spent.

The casualties of the 6th Battalion in this affair were truly terrible. Every

[1] C.S.M. W. Giles, who led his Company after all officers had become casualties, received the D.C.M. for his conspicuous gallantry on 16th September.

officer who went over the parapet (and there were 17) had become a casualty. 6th Battalion
Three had been killed, 12 wounded and 2 were missing.[1] In other ranks the
Battalion had lost 41 killed, 203 wounded and 143 missing. The ridge
between "A–A" and "X–X" Trenches was a veritable death trap, and here
the Somerset men, as they advanced, were shot down in dozens by German
machine gunners firing from the north and east.

On the 18th September the 6th Somersets moved to billets in Ribemont, 18th September
where the remainder of the month was spent.

The Battle of Flers–Courcellette ended on 22nd September, and the
results are thus given in the official despatches:—

"The result of the fighting of the 15th September and following days
was again more considerable than any which had attended our arms in the
course of a single operation since the commencement of the offensive. In
the course of one day's fighting we had broken through two of the enemy's
main defence systems and had advanced on a front of over 6 miles to an
average depth of a mile."

Three large villages, powerfully defended, had been captured. The
enemy appears to have had warning of the intended use of tanks, but all the
same they struck terror into the German troops; they certainly gladdened the
heart of the British soldier, who saw with delight and amazement German
trenches and strong points crushed out of existence.

THE BATTLE OF MORVAL, 25TH–28TH SEPTEMBER

In this action the 7th Somersets were in Brigade Reserve. The Somerset 7th Battalion
men, on 22nd September, had moved into billets in Meaulte, where a very
welcome draft of North and West Somerset Yeomanry—a splendid lot of
N.C.O.'s and men—joined the Battalion. On 25th another move forward
to the Citadel was made, the 61st Brigade having again taken over the front
line, though the 7th Somersets were in reserve. The next day the Battalion
(still in reserve) was moved up to the Quadrilateral, part of the old German
trench system between Ginchy and Les Bœufs, and remained there until 28th.
Twenty-two men had been wounded by shell fire during the three days' tour
in the line. Returning to Carnoy Craters on 28th, the Battalion, on 29th, 29th September
once more moved up to the trenches (south of Gueudecourt) where, during
that day and on 30th, two other ranks were killed and one officer and 20 other
ranks were wounded.

THE BATTLE OF THE LE TRANSLOY RIDGES: 1ST–18TH OCTOBER [2]

The capture of the villages of Morval, Les Bœufs and Gueudecourt had
given Sir Douglas Haig possession of high ground of considerable strategic

---

[1] No names are given in the Diaries.

[2] Here, again, the decisions of the Battle Honours Committee are of an arbitrary nature. No
recognition is made of the operations of 29th September, on which date the 20th Division alone
captured some 2,000 yards of the enemy's trenches east of Gueudecourt and gained a footing on the
crest of the long spur which screened the defences of Le Transloy.

value. But between these villages and the Sailly-Saillisel–Le Transloy–Beaulencourt line there yet remained one ridge, the capture of which was expected to yield important results; this high ground was known as the Le Transloy Ridges. A strong system of trenches covered the villages of Le Transloy and Beaulencourt and the town of Bapaume yet, although the enemy was digging hard, he had not been able to create any formidable defence behind this line, but in view of his efforts to construct these new systems of defence it was desirable to lose no time in dealing with the situation.

On 1st October the 61st Brigade, which had taken over the front-line trenches S.E. of Gueudecourt, was ordered, in view of future operations, to push forward strong patrols under an artillery barrage and dig in and consolidate whatever position was obtained. The objects of this manœuvre were to secure a good jumping-off place from which to attack Rainbow Trench and the Brown Line, or Cloudy Trench; to observe where the enemy's artillery barrage was placed and might be expected in future operations. The 7th Somerset L.I., on the right, and the 7th D.C.L.I., on the left, were to carry out these orders. So far as the 7th Somersets were concerned, this operation was of a difficult nature, for it meant that the Battalion would have to cross the valley which separated the opposing trenches and dig in on the dead ground right under the enemy's nose.

The advance began at 3.15 p.m. under heavy artillery fire and, despite the difficult nature of the operation, was completely successful. The two Battalions gained, and dug in on, a line varying from 200 yards on the right to 50 yards on the left, in front of their old line, and despite counter-attacks, held the new position. The Brigade Diary states that "casualties were not heavy," but the 7th Somersets lost at least one gallant young officer and several brave men killed, who could ill be spared, besides many others wounded.

The young officer—Lieut. D. A. W. S. Steele—who had only just joined the Battalion, was leading the advance when, unfortunately, he went too far and got into the German trench. He was last seen standing on the enemy's parapet firing his revolver, until he was shot down. On the loss of Lieut. Steele, command of the leading line fell upon an N.C.O.—L/Cpl. Tucker—who greatly distinguished himself. Observing some of his men on the left falling back, he at once went to them, rallied them and led them back to the objective. As the men were digging in on the new line the enemy made several attempts to counter-attack, but on each occasion the men of the West Country "downed tools," picked up their rifles and, firing steadily, beat off the attack. Battalion H.Qs. had remained in the old front line from which the C.O. had a fine view of the operations, but the Germans also had a similar view of Battalion H.Qs. and every five minutes for the next twenty-four hours the enemy fired 5·9 shells at H.Qs.

Four other ranks were killed besides Lieut. Steele, and 36 were wounded. On the 2nd consolidation of the new trenches proceeded, and until 11 a.m. on the 3rd October the 7th Somersets held on to their new positions, handing them over to the 7th K.O.Y.L.I. and taking the place of the latter in support 7th Battalion in Gird Trench.   Casualties on the 2nd and 3rd October were 8 other ranks killed and 3 wounded.

The next day the K.O.Y.L.I. came back to Gird Trench and the 7th Somersets marched back to Carnoy, where the Battalion rested until the 6th, 6th October when the 61st Brigade concentrated near Montauban and then moved back to the trenches S.E. of Gueudecourt.

The 20th (Light) Division, in conjunction with the 56th Division on the right and the 12th Division on the left, had been ordered to push forward a sufficient distance to obtain a suitable line for the preparation and carrying out of future operations on a large scale.   To the 61st Brigade the following objectives had been allotted: the capture and consolidation of Rainbow Trench and the capture and consolidation of Cloudy Trench and the occupation of the ridge in such a manner as to give the fullest observation of Le Transloy. The 7th K.O.Y.L.I., on the right, and the 12th King's R. on the left, were to make the initial attack and these two Battalions were to be supported by the 7th Somersets—two companies behind the K.O.Y.L.I. and two behind the King's.   The 7th D.C.L.I. were in Brigade Reserve in Needle Trench. The dispositions of the K.O.Y.L.I. and King's are given in the Brigade Narrative of the operations, 29th September–9th October, as: 7th K.O.Y.L.I. from N.27.d.8.7. to N.27.b.3.0; 12th King's R. from N.27.b.3.0. to about N.26.a.8.2.   The Somerset men occupied Rose and Leek Trenches behind these two Battalions.

Zero day for the attack was 7th October, and the hour 1.45 p.m. 7th October

Taking advantage of the delay occasioned by the inclement weather during the first few days of October, which had interfered with the general attack planned by Sir Douglas Haig, the enemy had wired his position and had dug himself in still more securely.   But during the morning of the 7th the British artillery pounded the hostile wire and trenches with shrapnel and flung the heavy entanglements about, cutting great gaps, through which attacking troops could advance.

At 1.45 p.m. standing barrages were placed on Rainbow and Cloudy Trenches and the infantry immediately got out of their trenches, following the creeping barrage at Zero plus 2 towards the first objective.   Observers from the "O.P." reported the advance as an inspiriting sight, for the men went forward steadily "as though on Salisbury Plain."   As the K.O.Y.L.I. and King's advanced the 7th Somersets moved up and occupied the trenches vacated by the former Battalions.   The Somerset men had received orders that if the attack on the first objective was successful they were to go forward again at Zero plus 20 and assist in the consolidation of Rainbow Trench.

The latter trench was taken quite easily.

"At 1.51 p.m.," records the Brigade Narrative, "the enemy was reported to have come forward from their trench in large numbers, holding up their hands and, shortly afterwards, the extraordinary spectacle, in one portion of the line was seen, of the two lines (our own and the enemy) meeting, a moment's hesitation, succeeded by our advance and a large return of a number of the enemy under escort as prisoners."

On the left and on top of the ridge there was a clash of bayonets, followed by a rapid retreat of all of the enemy who could get away. The attacking troops then pushed on to Cloudy Trench. Meanwhile, the 7th Somersets had carried out their orders to the letter. A and D Companies were sent forward to support the two attacking Battalions; C Company was moved up to support the right of the line and gain touch with the 12th R.B. of the 60th Brigade which, after losing three officers and 40 other ranks, it succeeded in doing. Two platoons of A Company had been ordered to take up a position on the left of the line which, owing to the attacking troops on the left of the King's R. being held up, was in the air. By this time there was only one officer left in A Company, so the two platoons were placed under the command of Sergt. W. E. Parker, who led his men well, reaching the objective and driving off a strong counter-attack. The remaining platoons of A Company and the whole of D Company then held and consolidated Rainbow Trench. B Company was posted in a trench to the left rear of Rainbow Trench, forming a defensive flank on the left, as the Somerset men were out of touch with the neighbouring troops on that flank who had not succeeded in reaching their objective. Only one counter-attack was made by the enemy and this was dealt with adequately by Sergt. Parker and his two platoons. After that, the enemy contented himself with violently shelling and machine-gunning the

Somerset men. Until the night of the 8th October the 7th Somersets held on to the positions gained, and then handed over to troops of the 6th Division which had come up to relieve the 20th Division.

Casualties suffered by the 7th Battalion during the 7th and 8th October were: Captain E. C. Cartwright and 2/Lieuts. P. J. Doherty, A. C. Parsons, A. L. Watts, W. S. Knight, G. Ross and W. L. Batterley wounded; C.S.M. J. H. Sears and 9 other ranks were killed, and 3 N.C.O.'s and 87 other ranks wounded.

On relief the Battalion went into billets at Meaulte on 9th October; 400 rank and file joined at Meaulte a fine batch of reinforcements, as a considerable number of them were Somerset Yeomanry.

The attack of 7th October was the last action of the Somme Battles of 1916 in which the 7th Somersets were engaged. Meanwhile, the fight for the Le Transloy Ridges continued, and on the last day of the Battle the 1st Somersets became involved in the operations.

Several months had passed since the 1st Battalion was withdrawn from the front line after its terrible losses during the Battle of Albert (1st–13th July). Eight weeks of that period had been spent amidst the discomforts and the horrors of the Ypres Salient, whither the 4th Division had moved towards the end of July. The 1st Somersets entraining at Doullens on 22nd and, travelling via

Hazebrouck to Esquelbecq, detrained and marched off to Wormhoudt, which ~1st Battalion~ had been allotted to the 11th Brigade as its billeting area. "It is nearly a year ago," said an officer of the Battalion, "since we left the Ypres district, hoping that we should never see it again." How many hundreds of thousands of gallant fellows wished the same thing, numbers of them finding at last a silent resting place amidst the Flanders poppies!

The 4th Division relieved the Guards Division on 25th, 26th and 27th July, the 1st Somersets taking over front-line trenches from the Scots Guards on the latter date. But the tour, which ended on 31st, was uneventful and the Battalion moved back into support on the Canal Bank. At the close of the second tour, however, just as the Battalion was being relieved by the 1st ~1st August~ Rifle Brigade on 8th August, the enemy (about 10.30 p.m.) made a violent gas attack, accompanied by heavy shelling. Dense clouds of the noxious fumes floated over the trenches and, although the Somerset men had only three casualties from shell fire, 12 officers and 161 other ranks became casualties from gas poisoning. Of these, six officers (2/Lieuts. R. P. Thompson, V. F. de Ritter, R. C. Róseveare, D. E. Sully, H. J. Griffiths and D. A. le Peton) and 27 other ranks died from the effects of gas. H Company, closest to the enemy, lost most heavily—5 officers and 72 other ranks. The gas, a mixture of chlorine, phosgene and prussic acid gas, was very insidious and clung to the ground and the men's clothes, so that if a man slept in his equipment he invariably developed gas poisoning and had to be evacuated to hospital. On 11th the Battalion moved back from the Canal Bank to Elverdinghe, whence motor-buses conveyed the men to "J" Camp, until the 21st, when the 1st Somersets relieved the 49th Canadian Regiment in the front line. But the tour was bare of excitement and, indeed, the remainder of the period spent in the Salient witnessed only the usual amount of shelling and sniping and the discomforts which were always more or less present. Three or four days in, and in the neighbourhood of, Dunkirk (from about 12th to 15th September) created a little mild excitement and change from the dirty trenches of the front line, but it was soon over and, having moved on 15th to Bollezeele, the ~15th September~ Battalion received welcome orders to entrain on 16th for a "new area south." On the following day the 1st Somersets (in Brigade and Division) once more left the Ypres area and, entraining at Esquelbecq, reached Longeau at 1.30 p.m., marching thence to billets at Cardonette. From the latter place a move was made on 25th September to Corbie, where training and practising the attack, bayonet fighting, etc., occupied the Battalion until 7th October, when the 11th Brigade moved to Meaulte and on the 8th to Citadel Camp. But only a few hours were spent in the latter place, for on 9th the Brigade set out for ~9th October~ bivouacs near Montauban. In mud and slush the troops, often knee-deep, moved by cross-country tracks to the Briqueterie, S.E. of Montauban, where the 11th Brigade relieved the 169th Brigade. In this abominable place several days were spent, the troops training in the morning and doing salvage work for the remainder of the day. Both the 10th and 12th Brigades of the 4th Division were engaged with the enemy during the period, but it was not until 17th that the 1st Somersets relieved the 1st Rifle Brigade in the support trenches, the 11th Brigade having taken over the front-line sector. "A very wet and dirty night, all ranks wet through," records the Battalion Diary.

The operations in which the 1st Somersets became involved on 18th October were the continuation of a series of attacks (whenever the inclement weather allowed) against the Le Transloy Ridges in co-operation with the French who were attacking Sailly-Saillisel. "My right flank" (on 17th October, the 4th Division), said Sir Douglas Haig in his official despatches, "continued to assist the operations of our Allies against Saillisel, and attacks were made to this end whenever a slight improvement in the weather made the co-operation of artillery and infantry at all possible."

The objectives of the 11th Brigade were Frosty, Hazy, Dewdrop and Rainy Trenches, together with the Northern and Southern Gun Pits and a strong point. The 12th Brigade had been ordered to assist the attack on Dewdrop by a bombing attack from the flank. The attack by the 11th Brigade was to be made by the 1st Rifle Brigade and the 1st East Lancashire R., but the 1st Somersets were apparently in reserve. Zero hour for the British attack was 3.40 a.m. on 18th, the French launching their attack on Saillisel at 11.40 a.m.

Apart from the Diary of the Somersets (which is given in full) there is no information of what actually happened on the Battalion front: "Attack on enemy trenches in conjunction with French at 3.40 a.m. Owing to incessant rain men found it very difficult to get out of trenches. Attacking troops subjected to heavy machine-gun fire. Attack on Gun Pits failed. Right of Rifle Brigade got on, but was eventually driven back. French attacked at 11.40 a.m. A Company detailed to support right company Rifle Brigade[1] and keep touch with the French. Two platoons of B Company sent to support right company of Rifle Brigade and take over and improve Frosty Trench which had been captured and retained. Frosty Trench consolidated by B Company, communication trenches dug to Warwick Avenue. Casualties —2/Lieut. D. I. Backlake killed, Lieut. F. M. Turner wounded. Other ranks—killed 1, wounded 10, missing 3."

The French attack on Saillisel apparently failed, though another attack on 19th was successful, the Frenchmen retaining the village, or rather the tumbled mass of bricks and mortar, all that was left of the village. On this day the Somerset men were hard at work improving the trenches which were narrow and shallow, as well as knee-deep in filthy mud. The discomfort was terrible. Rain continued to fall and though chilled and wet through, all ranks continued to make the best of a bad job, the Battalion Diary stating they "were fairly cheerful." But they were suffering badly. Indeed, no pen can adequately picture all those poor fellows went through in their gallant efforts to maintain their position, and it is with relief that one reads the next

[1] The late Capt. G. A. Prideaux, 1st Somerset L.I., in his diary states that H Company, 1st Somersets, was "in reserve under the orders of the O.C., 1st Rifle Brigade."

entry in the Battalion Diary, dated 19th October: "A brighter day for which
all were very thankful." But in the early morning the trenches were very
heavily shelled, and C Company lost 6 other ranks killed and 4 wounded.
The German guns had also located Bn. H.Qs. and from 3 p.m. till 7 p.m.
Colonel Majendie (commanding 1st Somersets) and his staff had a very uncomfortable time, though only one other rank was killed and four wounded.
The Germans then attempted to retake Frosty Trench but were beaten off
with loss. On the right of the Somersets the French made a small attack
which was successful and communication was established between the Somerset
men and their Allies.

That night the ground was covered by a hard frost and the men who
all day long (and for two or three days) had been wet through began to develop
trench feet. On the following morning (21st) a subaltern was evacuated to
hospital suffering from trench feet and exhaustion—he was the first in the
Battalion—and was very soon followed by others. At night the 1st Somersets
(less H Company) were relieved by the 1st East Lancashire R. and marched
to Guillemont, where, arriving about 2 a.m. on 22nd, the Battalion spent the
remainder of the night in trenches and shell holes. As soon as daylight appeared
the Battalion was inspected by the M.O. who promptly ordered two more
officers and 66 other ranks off to hospital, suffering from trench feet and exhaustion, while three officers and 80 other ranks were sent back to the transport
lines for rest and attention. Late in the day the S.M.O. arrived and not
only upheld the decision of the Battalion M.O. but added more to the number
already evacuated. The Battalion now numbered only about 300 rifles and
was ordered to remain in the trenches as Brigade Reserve.

On 23rd October the 4th Division, in conjunction with the 8th Division
on the left and the French on the right, made another attack on the enemy's
trenches at 2.30 in the afternoon. Though the attacking troops were subjected to very heavy and continual machine-gun fire, the Southern Gun Pits
were captured and a line was formed about 200 yards in front of them; the
attack on the right was a failure. H Company of the 1st Somersets was sent
forward at 5.30 p.m. to carry bombs and small arms ammunition to the Gun
Pits, having to move with great caution as the position was very uncertain.
Second-Lieutenant Holdernes, with 20 men and a Lewis gun, was sent forward
to report on the situation on the right, which was somewhat obscure. This
officer made a very successful reconnaissance and his report was later confirmed
in every particular. Throughout the day the remainder of the 1st Somersets
were used for digging and carrying parties—very unpleasant work, as rain again
fell heavily and all ranks were wet through.

The 11th Brigade was relieved by the 19th Brigade on the 24th October
and marched back to Trones Wood, where poor shelters were obtained for
the night. Utterly exhausted the Brigade moved on the 25th to Mansell
Camp, Carnoy, and there rested—not before it was time. Mansell Camp
in winter was not a delectable spot, and yet to the worn-out Somerset men it
must have seemed a Haven of Rest, for the Battalion Diary concludes with

1st Battalion

these words: "All ranks who had *had no sleep for 8 nights* enjoyed the luxury of tents."

Thus ended the operations of the 1st Somersets in the Somme Battles of 1916. The remainder of October the Battalion spent in refitting, "cleaning up" and preparing for a period of training, for on the 30th the 4th Division moved to the neighbourhood of Abbeville, the Somerset men being billeted in Citerne.

30th October

BATTLE OF THE ANCRE, 1916: 13TH–18TH NOVEMBER

" On the 9th November the long-continued bad weather took a turn for the better, and there-after remained dry and cold, with frosty nights and misty mornings for some days. Final prepara-tions were therefore pushed on for the attack on the Ancre, though as the ground was still very bad in places, it was necessary to limit the operations to what it would be reasonably possible to consolidate and hold under the existing conditions."—*Official Despatches.*

8th Battalion

For four months the enemy had been improving and adding to his defences along the banks and north of the River Ancre. St. Pierre Divion, Beaucourt-sur-Ancre and Beaumont Hamel (or all that remained of them) had been turned into veritable fortresses and it was evident from the number of guns which had been brought up to this section of the battle front, as well as the arrival of a fresh division, that the enemy intended holding this part of the line permanently.

The British front line on the left of the Somme battlefields at this period crossed the Bapaume–Achiet road about 1,000 yards N.W. of Martinpuich, thence skirting the northern exits of the ruined village of Courcelette and running almost due westwards to Thiepval which, after many bloody contests, had passed into British hands at the end of September. From Thiepval the line crossed the Ancre about half-way between St. Pierre Divion and Hamel, running west of Beaumont Hamel and thence almost due north to the Gommecourt Salient.

The preliminary bombardment began on the morning of 11th November and continued with bursts of great intensity until Zero hour (5.45 a.m.) on the 13th November, when it developed into a very effective artillery barrage under cover of which the infantry went forward to the attack.[1] Dense fog covered the whole of the battlefield, baffling the artillery observers of the opposing forces, but nevertheless screening the attacking troops from the enemy's "O.Ps." By 7.20 a.m. all objectives east of St. Pierre Divion (in-cluding the latter) had been captured, and from the enemy's trenches on the northern slopes of the Thiepval Ridge many prisoners were taken; indeed, by 9 a.m. the number of prisoners captured was actually greater than the attacking force. North of the Ancre the 63rd Division reached its objectives north and north-west of Beaucourt, the 51st Division carried Beaumont Hamel and the 2nd Division captured half a mile of the enemy's first-line system,

[1] From right to left the British Divisions engaged in the initial attack were 19th and 39th (east of the Ancre), 63rd, 51st, 2nd, 3rd and 31st (north of the Ancre).

north of the latter village.   But north of the 2nd Division the attack had to 8th Battalion
be abandoned owing to the appalling condition of the ground.   On the 14th
the attack was continued and resulted in the gain of the whole of Beaucourt
and a line extending thence N.W. along the Beaucourt road across the southern
end of the Beaumont Hamel spur.   But by now the gallant Divisions which
had made the initial attack had suffered heavy casualties, were much exhausted
and the reserves were put into the line.   At 11.30 p.m. on 14th November
the 63rd (Naval) Division, which had captured Beaucourt, was ordered to be
relieved by the 37th Division (less 112th Brigade Group attached to 2nd
Division), the relief to be completed by 12 noon on 15th.   The remaining
two Brigades of the 37th Division—the 63rd Brigade on the right and the
111th on the left—were to take over the front line north-west of Beaucourt,
having on their right the 19th Division and on their left the 51st (Highland)
Division.

The 63rd Infantry Brigade, which contained the 8th Somerset Light
Infantry, had been permanently transferred from the 21st to the 37th Division
on 8th July, after the first terrible week of the Somme Battles.   The 37th
Division having been transferred to the IV Corps on 14th July, moved
north to west of the Vimy Ridge, the 8th Somersets taking over front-line
trenches from London troops of the 47th Division in the Berthonval I sector
on 31st of the month.

For the first few days of August it is evident, from the Battalion and
Brigade Diaries, that the new sector which the Somerset men had taken over
was in a quiet part of the line, and it is not until the 6th of the month that 6th August
the first casualty, that of an officer, is recorded.   At 11 p.m. on that date
2/Lieut. H. Emms took a party of eight men out into No Man's Land; it
was his first patrol.   For two hours the party remained out without encountering any of the enemy and the signal to return was then given.   The last man
was coming in over the parapet when suddenly a German Véry light burst
in the air, revealing the man getting into his trench.   Immediately, a rifle
grenade or aerial torpedo was fired from the hostile trenches which landed
in the trench held by the Somerset men, killing 2/Lieut. Emms instantly
and wounding two other ranks.   The 8th Somersets were relieved by the
4th Middlesex on the night 6th/7th August and moved back to support
trenches.   On 12th/13th August the 9th Division took over the sector from
the 37th Division, the latter moving back into reserve, the 63rd Brigade marching independently by units to the Chateau de la Haie area; the Somersets
were billeted in Gouy Servins.   Over a month was spent out of the line and
it was not until 18th September that the Somerset men, having moved (in 18th September
Brigade) back to the front line, took over trenches in "Souchez I" from the
Drake Battalion of the 63rd Division.   But the enemy was too busily occupied
in the Somme area to attack or provoke attack in other sectors of the line,
and throughout the remainder of September and October the 8th Somerset
had a comparatively quiet time.

Towards the end of October the 37th Division began to move south again to the Somme, the Somerset men reaching Beauval on 30th, where the Battalion billeted with other units of the 63rd Brigade.

At Beauval the 8th Somersets remained until the 12th November. Hard training, prior to operations in the line, was carried out daily and when orders came to move forward to the battle area the Battalion was in fine fettle and had a strength of 32 officers and 778 other ranks. From Beauval the 63rd Brigade moved to Lealvillers and Acheux Wood for two days' final training. At 10 a.m. on 14th the 8th Somersets marched from Lealvillers to Hedauville, halting at the latter place about 2 p.m., and resuming the march at 5.30 p.m. for Englebelmer, where the 63rd Brigade was to assemble before taking over the front line which a Brigade field message stated "extends from the Ancre to trench running from Q.12.b.6.6. to R.7.a.7.9.[1] exclusive." The York and Lancaster R. was to hold the right of the line and the Leicesters the left. The Somersets were to be in support in Beaucourt Trench, which ran from the western outskirts of Beaucourt in a north-westerly direction along the southern side of the Beaucourt–Beaumont Hamel road. The relief of the 189th Brigade began at midnight (14th) when the units of the 63rd Brigade moved forward to take over the front line.

From the official diaries it is impossible to obtain details of that extremely difficult move on a pitch-black night. The area over which the troops had to move (as every one knows whose unhappy lot it was to be in this sector of the line in November 1916) was in an appalling condition. Mud and water, gaping shell holes and craters, the remains of obliterated roads and trenches, wrecked dug-outs, and everywhere the silent putrefying bodies of the unburied dead, all the grim horrors of the battlefield, in fact, made such reliefs nerve-racking experiences. The term "front-line trenches" was often misleading, the so-called line consisting in many places of shell-hole posts terribly difficult to locate at night and almost isolated by day. Strong and elaborate as the German trenches were when the attack began, the terrific gruelling to which they had been subjected by the British guns had wrecked and blown and blasted them almost beyond recognition.

The Somerset men appear to have reached, very early on the 14th, a high bank near Station Road, west of Beaucourt, where they dug in. On the 15th they furnished working parties and assisted in making Engine Trench into a good communication trench. On the 16th the whole Battalion was employed as carrying parties for the York and Lancaster Regt. as well as working on Engine Trench and searching German dug-outs, from which much material (including three German Stokes mortars) was gathered and sent back. Intermittent shell fire throughout the day inflicted a few casualties. Late at night (about 10.20 p.m.) instructions were received at Bn. H.Qs. for the Somersets to occupy Ancre Trench with one company and push out patrols to the junction of Ancre and Puisieux Trenches. C Company was detailed for this duty and, moving out east of Beaucourt, took up a position holding

[1] This trench (running from E. to W.) lay between two roads, i.e. Artillery Lane and Beaucourt Road, N.W. of Beaucourt.

Ancre Trench and Bois d'Hollande facing Puisieux Trench. In the early
hours of the 17th a German bombing party made an attack on the Somerset
men, but it was beaten back and the hostile bombers retired discomfited,
The three remaining companies were again employed as carrying parties.
carrying out their duties under shell fire. During the afternoon an unlucky
shell fell in the midst of one of these working parties, which had 15 casualties
from the burst.

At 9 p.m. orders were received for operations on the following day—
18th November. Briefly they were as follows: The II and IV Corps
were to make simultaneous attacks south and north of the Ancre respectively;
the V Corps was to drive the enemy off the spur south of Ten Tree Alley
and to establish a line on the spur west of Bois d'Hollande; the 32nd Division,
which had taken over the line on the left of the 37th Division, was to make
the main attack and capture Frankfurt Trench, pushing its left northwards
towards Ten Tree Alley; the 37th Division was simultaneously to occupy
and consolidate a line from the River Ancre at R.8.b.0.4 (the crossing S.E.
of Bois d'Hollande) through Bois d'Hollande, thence eastwards to the Puisieux
Road about R.8.d.6.1 (the junction of the two sunken roads running north
from Beaucourt) to junction of Muck Trench and Leave Avenue and to assist
the attack of 32nd Division by machine-gun and trench-mortar fire on Frankfurt
Trench, directed from Beaucourt Trench.

The 63rd Brigade orders to Lieut.-Col. J. W. Scott (commanding 8th
Somersets) stated that his Battalion would, during the night 17th/18th
November, "establish strong points in River and Puisieux Trenches and
reconnoitre Baillescourt Farm aaa They will endeavour to assist 56th Brigade
S. of River in the capture of Grandcourt in the morning aaa Posts will be
established as soon as possible aaa Zero hour will be at 6.10 a.m. aaa It is of
the utmost importance that the work of patrols and the establishment of the
line of posts should be forwarded to the Brigade at the earliest possible
moment."

At 1 a.m. on 18th the Somersets moved off by companies through
Beaucourt and completed a line of posts from Bois d'Hollande in a westerly
direction across the open to Puisieux Road. A Company was on the right
from Ancre Trench to Bois d'Hollande, B Company came next in the centre,
and C on the left. D Company, about Ancre Trench, had orders to reconnoitre
Puisieux Trench and establish strong points in that Trench and in (Puisieux)
River Trench if possible. Two Stokes mortars and two machine guns were
attached to D Company to assist in the attack on Puisieux Trench. In the
worst weather imaginable the Battalion set out on their unenviable and difficult
task. Snow was falling, the ground was heavy with filthy, clinging mud
and the going was terrible. As the patrols neared Puisieux Trench German
patrols were discovered out in front of their line and the Somersets, unable
to get near the Trench, took shelter in shell holes.

Coming generations will read of those gallant fellows taking "shelter
in shell holes" without a tremor, knowing nothing of the remembrance of

agony conjured up in the minds of those who went through the Great War in France and Flanders: of the dull misery of plodding through seas of viscous mud, weighted down by equipment, pack, rifle and bayonet, ammunition, bombs and rations, clothes soaked through, covered from head to foot in slime, stumbling, slipping, ever expecting death, some even longing for it as a happy release from such untold misery: of the brain atrophied almost by suffering, of the constant expectation of attack and the tremendous nerve tension when moving against a concealed enemy.

Towards dawn the guns began to boom and the air was thick with shells shrieking and howling as they passed overhead to burst with a roar on the enemy's positions. At 6.10 a.m. the II Corps attacked north of the Ancre. A thin mist somewhat obscured the view, but the Somersets from their shell holes could just make out the form of the advancing troops.

The next entry in the Battalion Diary is timed 9.20 a.m.: "Received orders to be prepared to attack Puisieux and Puisieux River Trench from S. end to its junction with Miraumont Alley supported by 4th Middlesex." The order to move was to be sent later.

Owing to the difficulty of crossing very heavy ground swept by continuous shell, machine-gun and rifle fire, it was impossible to get the orders for attack circulated until about 10.40 a.m. and the attack was due to take place at 11 a.m. But Colonel Scott was able to see the Os.C., C and D Companies, to whom he gave the following instructions: half of C and the whole of D Company were to attack Puisieux Trench, S. of the Miraumont road, and the remaining half of C was to co-operate north of the road. At 11 a.m. the 4th Middlesex began to arrive and the Somerset men launched their attack.

Scarcely had the Somersets left their shell-hole positions when they came under very heavy rifle fire from Puisieux Trench and the river banks which were alive with enemy riflemen. On all sides officers and men began to fall and soon casualties became heavy. About 11.20 a.m. Colonel Scott went forward to reconnoitre. He found that C and D Companies were advancing very slowly from shell hole to shell hole, but he also discovered that the attacking companies of his Battalion were under quite a heavy fire from the British guns. He therefore stopped the attack and hurried back to stop the guns firing on his men. In this he was apparently successful for a little later, holding a consultation with the O.C., 4th Middlesex, with a view to a fresh attack later under a new barrage, he ordered patrols to push on if possible.

About 12 noon bombing parties of C Company entered Puisieux Trench south of the Miraumont road and captured 20 Germans in a dug-out. D Company followed quickly and together the two Companies set to work to consolidate the trench. At one time bombs ran out, but fortunately a fresh supply was soon brought up: without bombs it would have been impossible to hold on. A company of Middlesex, followed later by another company of the same Battalion, moved up to support the Somersets, and a covering barrage on Puisieux Trench north of the road was asked for. Meanwhile

A and B Companies, of the Somersets, in accordance with the orders to attack, _{8th Battalion} had been withdrawn from the line occupied.[1] _{18th November}

By about midday the attack apparently ended, for at 1 p.m. the forward companies of Somerset men could see that the attempt to take Grandcourt had failed and men were observed dribbling back along the railway south of Ancre Trench.   The results, so far as the Somersets were concerned, are thus given in the Battalion Diary: "Puisieux Trench was held but no further advance was made."

At 2.30 p.m. the Battalion Bombing Officer (2/Lieut. C. B. Tubbs) was sent up to take command of A Company and explain the situation to B Company,[2] the latter being still under heavy sniping fire.   An hour later orders were sent out to the same officer to reoccupy the line of posts held in the early morning.   The latter movement was carried out at dusk.

At 7 p.m. the 4th Middlesex began the relief of the Somersets in Puisieux and Ancre Trenches, while two companies of the York and Lancaster R. took over the line of posts.[3]

By 11 p.m. all companies of the Somersets had been relieved and were located in support trenches and the Quarry just east of Beaucourt.

The day's fighting had cost the Battalion many valuable lives.   Four officers (three of whom were company commanders) had been killed—Captains A. H. Hall and L. Fitzmaurice, Lieut. F. H. T. Joscelyne and 2/Lieut. B. T. Chippendall—five officers were wounded and in other ranks the Battalion had lost over one hundred.

Throughout the 19th November, shelled all day, the Battalion remained _{19th November} in support, and on 20th moved back into the old German second line, from which position, both on 21st and 22nd, cleaning and working parties were sent out for work on the battlefield.   After "standing to" in reserve to the 111th Brigade on 23rd the Somersets marched back to Englebelmer on 24th, glad indeed to be out of the line for a period of training and reorganization. About the middle of December the 37th Division moved north, and on the 22nd the Diary of the 8th Somersets records that the Battalion "left L'Eclme for the Brigade area east of Paradis and went into billets."   The Brigade area was Vieille Chapelle.

* * * * *

The Battles of the Somme 1916 were over so far as the Somerset Light _{1st, 6th, 7th and} Infantry was concerned.   Every Battalion of the Regiment at that period _{8th Battalions} in France and Flanders (1st, 6th, 7th and 8th) had been engaged in the operations.   They had fought splendidly, their courage was praised again and again and most worthily had they upheld the fine traditions of the Regiment.

---

[1] It is impossible to tell from the Diaries whether A and B Companies made a flank attack, or what was the position occupied by them.

[2] See above footnote.

[3] Lce./Sergt. W. Hedley was awarded the D.C.M. for conspicuous gallantry on the night of 17/18th November, and for their gallantry on 18th November 2/Lieuts. F. H. Baker and C. B. Tubbs were awarded the M.C. and C.S.M. W. Henman the D.C.M.

Their devotion to duty, their tenacity often in the face of appalling loss and difficulty, their suffering and agony amidst all the horrors of the Somme battle-fields will for ever remain a monument to those who made the supreme sacrifice as well as to the more fortunate who came through unscathed, though some there be who will for ever bear upon their bodies the visible signs of those hitherto unparalleled battles.

To the Regimental officer and his men only one thing matters—to do their duty faithfully; the Staff and the higher commands are concerned chiefly with planning the operations and upon them falls praise or blame according to the results. The Regimental historian, therefore, cannot concern himself with discussions on higher tactics, his duty consisting only of faith-fully recording the doings of Battalions. But, briefly, it may be said of the Somme Battles of 1916 that the heroic dead did not die in vain, neither did the gallant living receive their lifelong wounds to no purpose, for the Allied scheme of operations resulted in the achievement of the British and French Commanders-in-Chief's plans, though at terrible cost. In paragraph 38 of his despatch, dated 23rd December 1916, Sir Douglas Haig stated:—

"The three main objects with which we had commenced our offensive of July had already been achieved at the date when this account closes, in spite of the fact that the heavy, continuous rains had prevented full advantage being taken of the favourable situations created by our advance, at a time when we had good grounds for hoping to achieve yet more important successes. Verdun had been relieved, the main German forces had been held to the Western front and the enemy's strength had been very considerably worn down. Any one of these three results is in itself sufficient to justify the Somme Battles. The attainment of all three of them affords ample compensation for the splendid efforts of our troops and for the sacrifices made by ourselves and our Allies. They have brought us a long step forward towards the final victory of the Allied cause."

For the first three days of the Somme Battles the British casualties were 60,600 other ranks and 1,910 officers,[1] scarce a month hence and they totalled 116,000 other ranks and 4,428 officers,[2] and by the end of November 1916 over a quarter of a million, including 11,000 odd officers; nevertheless, there is no greater proof that the operations were successful than in the German retirement to the Hindenburg Line early in 1917, an operation which Ludendorff admitted was forced upon the German Army by the appalling losses it had suffered on the Somme in 1916.

The story of the close of the year 1916, after the various Battalions of the Somerset Light Infantry had been involved in the Somme operations for the last time, is one of indescribable misery and suffering, upon which it is needless to dwell at length.

Throughout the whole of November and until the 7th December the

[1] Casualties of Fourth Army and VIII and X Corps only.
[2] Casualties of Fourth Army only.

1st Battalion remained at Citerne, but on the latter date marched, at 5 a.m., 1st Battalion to Oisemont Station, entraining at the latter place for Morlancourt, the Somerset 7th December men reaching their destination at 6 p.m. The following day a move was made to Camp III, north of Bray, and on the 9th the Battalion marched to Camps 16 and 107 near Bromfray, a dirty place, indeed some idea of the condition of the Camp may be gathered from the diary of the late Capt. G. A. Prideaux (1st S.L.I.) in which he stated: "General Lambton (G.O.C.) came to lunch and afterwards walked round, or rather *waded round*, the Camp. The mud in many places is nearly knee-deep." This entry is followed by another on 12th December, when orders having arrived to take over front-line trenches, the latter were reconnoitred:—

"Rain, snow, howling wind and bitterly cold. The General, Bell and I started at 7 a.m. to go to 10th Brigade H.Qs. to reconnoitre the line preparatory to taking over on 15th inst. The conditions beggar description: the trenches are flooded and have all fallen in: there is no cover either in front, support or reserve lines, and men are being evacuated sick with frost-bite and exhaustion by the hundred. *To-day four men were dug out of the mud who had been unable to move for three days.* Battalions were about 250 strong. The conditions were so bad that we were unable to see the actual trenches."

On the 15th, the 11th Brigade relieved the 10th Brigade in the right sub-sector of the line, which lay between Rancourt and Saillisel. The 1st Somerset Light Infantry, having moved by buses to Maurepas, relieved the 1st R. Warwick R. The Battalion Diary of the 1st Somersets thus describes the relief:—

"Conditions up to and in trenches fearful. Very dark. Several men found in morning stuck in mud and had to be dug out, *some men only got out by leaving their thigh boots behind.* Conditions in front line almost impossible."

This picture of life on the Somme at the close of 1916 will give coming generations some idea of what anguish those gallant fellows passed through while "maintaining the line." The enemy was in no better circumstances. In one part of the line the front posts of the opposing forces were no more than 10 yards apart and the Germans made attempts (which were firmly discouraged) to fraternize. Probably they thought that their miseries were bad enough without adding to them mutilation or death from bullet or shell. But such is war.

Yet, terrible as were the lives the men of the West Country were living, the Battalion Diary records: "conditions telling on officers and men *who continue to be very cheery.*" Gallant souls! who can read of such magnificent spirit with a stiff lip? The end of the year found the 1st Battalion back in Camp 12 31st December where "cleaning up" and refitting took place.

In Arras, whither the Battalion had moved on 27th September, the 6th

6th Battalion

Somersets remained for a few days only and, on 3rd October, relieved the 6th K.O.Y.L.I. in the H.1. (Achicourt) sector. But the tour in the front line was comparatively quiet and the end of October found the Battalion billeted in Penin, whence on 8th November the Somersets moved to Houvin Houvineul, and on 15th December to Sombrin. "This," records the Battalion Diary, "being the end of a most enjoyable six weeks' rest, the first proper one since our arrival in France." On 18th December, having moved via Wanquetin and Arras, the Battalion relieved the Norfolks in H.1. sector, Achicourt, occupying the same trenches held in October. The 6th Somersets were relieved on 24th December and marched back to Arras, the companies being finally billeted in Arras, Achicourt, and Ronville. They remained here until the end of the year.

18th December

31st December

7th Battalion

From Meaulte, where the 7th Somersets had billeted on 9th October, a move was made to Corbie on 15th, and on the 19th to Allonville. On 20th the Battalion marched to Vaux where training was carried out until 1st November, on which date a further move to Reincourt took place. But on 14th the move back to the front began, the Battalion marching to Warlus, on the 18th to Bettincourt and on 25th (in heavy rain) to Belloy-sur-Somme, where it remained until 28th. Several more moves took place and finally, on 12th December, the 7th Somersets relieved the 10th K.R. Rifles in the trenches between Les Bœufs and Morval. In this part of the line similar conditions prevailed to those through which the 1st Battalion was passing, and in his private diary Colonel Troyte-Bullock (commanding 7th Somersets) has the following amusing items:—

12th December

"The man who had sunk in up to his armpits had to be handed over as 'Trench Stores.' Sergeant Dawson, who was always a keen patroller, went out into No Man's Land as soon as the relief was completed to have a look at the wire. He got some way into No Man's Land when he became hopelessly bogged and unable to move. He was found by a party of 5 Bosche who proceeded to pull him out. He, of course, expected to be taken off to the Hun lines, but not a bit of it. They informed him that they were his prisoners and demanded to be taken across to our trenches. Sergeant Dawson had hopelessly lost his way and said so, but they said it was quite all right as they knew the way and conducted him back to our advanced Bn. H.Qs. On the way they picked up another of our men, also bogged, and took him along with them. Major Preston-Whyte (temporarily in command of the Battalion) was somewhat surprised when the sentry shouted down to say that there were five Huns coming down the stairs!"

Relief on the 14th December, another tour in the line from 18th to 20th and finally billets in Meaulte on 22nd (where a cold, muddy but merry Christmas was spent) carries the story of the 7th Battalion to New Year's Day 1917.

31st December

8th Battalion

The 8th Somersets were also fortunate in being out of the line (billeted east of Paradis, the 63rd Bde. area) on Christmas Day. The last entry for

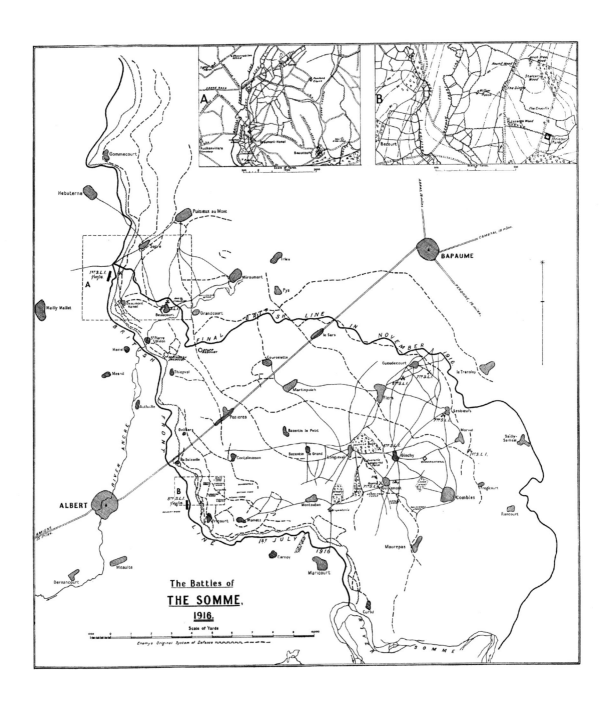

The Battles of
THE SOMME,
1916.

Scale of Yards

Enemy's Original System of Defence

1916 in the Battalion Diary is worthy of note: "The Divisional Commander has much pleasure in recording that the Corps Commander has on more than one occasion expressed his satisfaction at the smartness of the Divisional Guard when turned out to him and has particularly noticed guard of the 8th Somerset L.I."

8th Battalion
31st December

CHAPTER XXII

THE BRITISH ADVANCE [1] AND GERMAN RETREAT [2] TO THE HINDENBURG LINE, 1917

"The decision to retreat was not reached without a painful struggle. It implied a confession of weakness bound to raise the morale of the enemy and lower our own. But as it was necessary for military reasons we had no choice: it had to be carried out."—LUDENDORFF.

IN the above trenchant sentence lies one of the results (and justification) of the Somme Battles of 1916. And the Chief of the German General Staff also said:—

"Our first object was to avoid a battle, our second to effect the salvage of all our raw material of war and technical and other equipment that was not actually built into the position, and finally the destruction of all high roads, villages, towns and wells, so as to prevent the enemy establishing himself in force in the near future in front of our new position."

The diabolical intentions of the enemy were carried out with a degree of brutality which the Germans described as "a success," but their endeavours to hoodwink Sir Douglas Haig were unsuccessful and the new British line, thanks chiefly to the superb work of the Sappers and Pioneers, was established in front of the Hindenburg Line with marvellous rapidity: indeed Ludendorff's troops were hardly settled in their new quarters ere heavy attacks were made upon them and they were hard put to it to maintain their position.

1st, 6th, 7th and 8th Battalions

But to return to the beginning of the year. On the 1st January 1917 four Battalions of the Somerset Light Infantry were in France, i.e. 1st Battalion (Lieut.-Colonel V. H. B. Majendie) located in Camp 12, the 6th Battalion (Major F. D. Bellew) in H.1 Sector, Arras area, the 7th Battalion (Lieut.-Colonel C. J. Troyte-Bullock) billeted in Meaulte and the 8th Battalion (Lieut.-Colonel J. W. Scott) at Paradis, near Vieille Chapelle.

1st Battalion

15th January

Hard training and the improvement of camp, relieved by football matches and concerts in the evening, occupied the 1st Somersets until the middle of January, but on the 15th a move up towards the front line was begun, the Battalion moving to Camp 18, Suzanne. On the following day the Somersets relieved a Battalion of the 77th French Regiment in the left sub-sector, Bouchavesnes. Although the march up to the front line was long and trying, snow falling heavily during the latter part of the relief, the relief was carried out quickly, the enemy's attitude being described as "very quiet." On arrival, however, A Company having developed mumps, had to be sent back to Camp

[1] 11th January–13th March 1917.
[2] 14th March–5th April 1917.

158

13.   Comparative quietude reigned in the front line until 19th when the German guns and machine guns became more active.   During a burst of shell fire about noon the Brigade Major—Capt. G. A. Prideaux, 1st Somerset Light Infantry—was killed whilst visiting the front line.   The loss of this gallant young officer, who had seen all his military service with the Somerset Light Infantry since he was gazetted to the Battalion in 1911, was keenly felt by the Regiment.   On 20th January the Battalion was relieved and moved back to support trenches at Junction Wood.   Alternate tours in the front line amidst truly appalling conditions, and days in support and reserve, during which attempts were made by all ranks to cleanse themselves from mud and filth, brings the story of the 1st Somersets to the 22nd February, when the Battalion marched to Hem Wood, returned to Camp 117 and on the following day marched again to billets in Sailly Laurette.   On 28th the 4th Division received orders to be ready to move to the Third Army area.   Leaving Sailly Laurette on 4th March the Somersets, marching via Allonville, Talmas, Gazaincourt, reached Nœux on 7th, where several days were spent in training and cleaning up.   Eventually, on 21st March the Battalion reached Dieval, north-west of Arras, where training for the offensive which was to begin on 9th April was carried out until the time came to move forward to the trenches. This move was begun on 7th April, which as every Somerset man knows is "Jellalabad Day": it was a good omen for the Battalion.

Extracts from entries in the Diary of the 6th Somersets for 1st and 2nd January 1917 give an excellent idea of the kind of life passed by that Battalion when the New Year dawned:—

"1st: Raid on our left put off owing probably to the condition of the trenches and wire not being cut.   A dug-out was 'crumpled' in, one of our men was killed and 7 of the 20th Lancashire Fusiliers (Bantams) who were working close by got into this dug-out and are missing.   Endeavours are being made to get them out. . . .   2nd: Trenches are in a frightful condition, mud in some places being up to the men's thighs and in many places up to their knees.   The trenches are collapsing all round due to no revetment.   It looks extremely like as if no work was done on them during the summer. Day quiet."

For several weeks this kind of life, relieved every now and then by a "rest" in some back area, went on until the middle of March, when the Battalion began to follow up the retreating Germans.

On 14th March the 6th Somersets relieved the 6th K.O.Y.L.I. in H.2 Sector, Nos. 2 and 4 Companies going into the front-line trenches while Nos. 1 and 3 Companies were in support in Ronville and the White Chateau.

The German retreat had been timed to begin on 16th March, though Ludendorff admits that in certain parts of the line he was forced to retire before that date.   Under the rubric of "Alberich" he had begun the work of demolition—that devastation of a wide area of France which will for ever remain a monument of German brutality—on 9th February, so that when the

Somersets took over H.2 Sector on the night of 14th March, the work of destruction had been in progress a month and the enemy had made final preparations for that retrograde movement which, with a strange lack of humour, he described as "a success." The German signal for the retirement to begin was the burning of red lights, not of the kind which suddenly illuminated the dark sky and then went out, but a continuous glare.

On the morning of the 17th there was a strange stillness across No Man's Land. This continued throughout the day—not a single gun or rifle shot breaking that extraordinary quietude. When darkness fell the sky was illuminated by flares, whilst loud explosions and sudden bursts of flame behind the German front lines indicated unusual happenings. About 8.45 a.m. on 18th a British aeroplane was forced to descend just behind the British front line and twenty men of the Somersets ran out to assist the pilot. For at least a quarter of an hour they were not fired on, and then only a few rifle shots came from the direction of Beaurains and the Brickstacks, both some distance behind the German front line. At 9 a.m. the C.O. of the 6th Battalion received a report that two miles farther south the enemy could be seen vacating his front-line trenches in a retrograde movement. Two divisions on the right of the 14th Division were sending out patrols.

The Battalion on the right of the Somerset men next reported (at 10.15 a.m.) that their right and centre companies had entered Beaurains but their left company was held up. The Brigade H.Qs. was informed and the C.O. of the Somersets was ordered to send out patrols across No Man's Land. At 11.15 a.m. an officers' patrol crossed over the German front line and got through a gap in front of the Brickstacks, sending back almost immediately the report: "Enemy front line completely destroyed and unoccupied." In the distance against the skyline, the summit of Telegraph Hill, the Germans could be seen disappearing over the farther side: the Retreat was in progress. B and D Companies of the Somersets were then advanced, their objectives being (i) the German front line, (ii) Kreiger Stellung, (iii) The Tilloy–Beaurains Road; these positions were to be consolidated. By 11.40 a.m. the first objective had been reached; at 12.30 p.m. Kreiger Stellung had been entered and the Somerset men were working north: by 2 p.m. the Tilloy–Beaurains Road had been reached and patrols were pushing down Prussen Weg towards the Beaurains–Neuville Vitasse Road. But then came a check. From Tilloy the enemy began to shell the advancing troops and the positions he had evacuated, and at 2.30 p.m. it was reported that: "Definitely established that enemy are holding Tilloy–The Harp–Neuville Vitasse line." The Harp was a strong system of defences situated about 1,200 yards behind Telegraph Hill. At 4 p.m. A and C Companies of the Somersets were moved up to the old German front line, the 6th D.C.L.I. occupying the old British front-line system and Ronville. At 5.25 p.m. the two forward Companies (B and D) were ordered to occupy and consolidate a line just east of the Beaurains–Tilloy Road, but were instructed not to advance beyond that line, though patrols were to be pushed out.

The night of the 18th/19th March was noisy. The enemy persisted in 6th Battalion
barraging the new British front line, the village of Beaurains and the Beaurains–
Ronville Road, but casualties were small. During the night much work
was done on the trenches and when dawn of the 19th broke the new line had 19th March
been made secure. The enemy could be seen in large numbers walking
about in the open behind the Harp and in Tilloy and Neuville Vitasse, while
from the latter place a battalion, in fours, with officers mounted, was seen
marching out in an easterly direction, an inviting target for the gunners, but
unfortunately the guns had not registered. At 7 p.m. that night the 6th
Somersets were relieved and moved back to their original billets.

From the 20th March to the 5th April (the German Retreat to the Hindenburg Line finishing on the latter date) the 6th Battalion made no further move
forward. The line occupied on the 18th March remained stationary, for
the enemy's retirement in this portion of the line was but a mile in extent.
Consolidation of the trenches and the digging of new communication trenches
while in the front line, and the furnishing of working parties, occupied the
Battalion during this period. Hostile shelling was frequent but not very
effective, for there are few records of casualties suffered by the Somersets.
One officer, however, was killed on the 24th March—2/Lieut. R. N. Straight.
On the 3rd April (the first day of artillery preparations for the Battles of Arras,
1917) three Companies were moved to the Caves at Ronville near Arras and
one Company up to the old British front line, where they remained during
the 4th and 5th. 5th April

On 1st January the 7th Somersets (in Brigade) marched from Meaulte 7th Battalion
to Combles, where the Battalion halted until the following night, when it 1st January
relieved the 1st Irish Guards in front-line trenches situated on the far side
of the ruins of the village: a large chalk-pit with some good dug-outs sheltered
Battalion H.Qs.

The circumstances under which the Somerset men returned to the detest-
able mud of the Somme are as follows: whilst at Meaulte the Corps Commander
(Lord Cavan) visited Brigade H.Qs., on 27th December, and, during a talk
with the assembled officers, told them that the XIV Corps had been specially
selected to hold the Sailly-Saillisel sector of the line which was the most important position now on that part of the Somme Battlefield, and on the holding
of which depended the safety of the British defences in that area. It is not
recorded what the officers said to one another after Lord Cavan had departed,
but it is not difficult to imagine how they viewed the prospects of a further
period amidst the mud and filth of the Somme trenches.

At that period, with the idea of giving the men a longer spell out of the
trenches, the 20th Division was organized into two Groups of six battalions
each, Colonel Troyte-Bullock being in temporary command of the 61st Brigade
Group.

The first fortnight of the New Year was uneventful, though the enemy's
guns were unpleasantly active: Combles, which was full of "Heavies," the
roads and the duck-board tracks from the village to the front line, the ruined

Chateau, a large mound all that remained of Sailly–Saillisel Church, and some cellars occupied by a Battalion H.Qs., were regularly and heavily shelled, but the German machine gunners and snipers were moderately quiet.   On 13th January, however, 2/Lieut. W. E. S. Ellis was killed by a sniper—the only officer casualty during the month.

Quite the worst tour in the line began on 8th February, when the 7th Battalion relieved the 8th Hampshires in trenches between Morval and Sailly–Saillisel.   Of the abominable conditions in this part of the line it is perhaps sufficient to say that the communication trenches were only usable *when the ice bore*.   The rest may be imagined.   And yet amidst so much wretchedness and discomfort the Somerset men held the line with fine fortitude and gallantry.   Two instances will suffice to show the spirit which animated all ranks, they are given *in extenso* from the official reports.[1]

"In the front line Morval Sector on 1.3.17 the posts were being heavily shelled by the enemy and casualties were occurring in them.   The line back to Company H.Qs. in Vaux was broken during the firing and communication with Battalion H.Qs. cut.   2/Lieut. A. E. Brown left the front line and crossed over the open to the signal office in Vaux, a distance of about 500 yards, to report what had occurred.   He was constantly fired on by the enemy while doing so, with rifle and machine gun.   He sent through his report and then returned to the front line over the open and again came under the enemy's fire.   On reaching the front line he went to No. 9 Post and reorganized the Post personally, superintending the removal of the wounded to a safer position in No. 12 Post.   He then returned to No. 9 Post and remained with the men there to see that everything was put right and to cheer them up after their experience." [2]

Some idea of what had been happening is contained in the next report:—

"At about 3.30 p.m., 1.3.17, 2/Lieut. Buckland and No 11 Platoon were the garrison of No. 2 Post, Morval Sector, U.2.c.1.1., when a direct hit was obtained by hostile artillery on the extreme left of the Post, blowing in a shelter in which Mr. Buckland was sitting, and next to which two men were standing. Sergt. Towler immediately went to the spot and found the two men quite dead.   Thinking he heard Mr. Buckland call he immediately began digging, Corporal Robinson coming to his aid.   But, owing to the fact that the parapet had also been blown away he found himself exposed to heavy machine-gun and rifle fire and they had to lie down and dig in that position.   While digging they were twice buried themselves by earth thrown up by the shells dropping near them, nevertheless at the end of about three-quarters of an hour they succeeded in getting the body of Mr. Buckland out and on examination found that death must have been instantaneous.   Sergt. S. J. W. Towler was in-

---

[1] From the standpoint of history no paraphrase can ever equal in historical value the actual story contained in the official records, and therefore no apology is needed for giving the reports verbatim.
[2] Awarded the M.C. for his conspicuous gallantry on this occasion.

defatigable in restoring the moral of his men, which was badly shaken by the _{7th Battalion} heavy shell fire, and he took it in turns with Corporal Robinson in acting as sentry and patrolling the post, his platoon being badly reduced by the two casualties and three sick men. Before dawn on the morning of the 4th Sergt. Towler's own shelter was blown down and he himself thrown some yards up the trench. He remained unconscious for 3 or 4 hours but on regaining consciousness continued to control and command his post and on relief brought his men safely back to Combles." [1]

The next fortnight (from 4th to 18th March) was spent by the 7th Somer- 18th March sets in the following places: 5th and 6th in Carnoy, 7th and 8th in Guillemont, 9th, 10th and 11th in the line Morval Sector, 12th in Guillemont and from 13th to 18th in Carnoy. At 11 a.m. on the latter date, however, the Somerset men marched out of Carnoy for No. 3 Camp, Guillemont, where dinners were taken, the march being continued at 3 p.m., the Battalion finally relieving the 10th K.R.R.C. in the Le Transloy line. For several days there was little doing, the Battalion Diary using the words "very quiet" frequently. But in this part of the line also the Germans had begun their retirement to the Hindenburg Line, and the British outpost line was gradually pushed forward so that on 28th the Somersets moved to Bus; Metz, Neuville and Bertincourt had already been occupied by British troops and the Germans were holding the western edge of Havrincourt Wood when, on 1st April the Somerset men were relieved and marched back to Le Transloy, three men being killed by shell fire during the relief. On the 5th April (the date on 5th April which the German Retreat officially ends) the 7th Somersets again moved forward, taking over trenches on the east side of the Canal du Nord about 2 miles S.E. of Lechelle, where for the time being it is necessary to leave the Battalion and turn to the Battle of Arras, the first of the Allied Offensives of 1917.[2]

[1] Sergt. Towler was awarded the D.C.M.
[2] The 8th Somersets did not arrive in the Arras area until 10th March and then they spent the remainder of the month out of the front line in training for the coming offensive of 9th April.

CHAPTER XXIII

THE BATTLES OF ARRAS, 1917

THE FIRST BATTLE OF THE SCARPE: 9TH–14TH APRIL

1st, 6th, 7th and 8th Battalions

FROM a Regimental point of view it is interesting to note that all four Battalions of the Somerset Light Infantry, i.e. 1st, 6th, 7th and 8th, then in France took part in the first of the Allied Offensives of 1917, the 1st, 6th and 8th in the Battles of Arras and the 7th in the Flanking Operations near Bullecourt.

It is impossible, and indeed undesirable, in a Regimental History to discuss in detail the general plan[1] of campaign unanimously agreed upon by the military representatives of all the Allied Powers at a conference held at French G.H.Q. in November 1916.[2] But briefly it may be said that the plan adopted by Sir Douglas Haig for the Armies under his command was as follows: "In the spring, as soon as all the Allied Armies were ready to commence operations, my first efforts were to be directed against the enemy's troops occupying the salient between the Scarpe and the Ancre into which they had been pressed as a result of the Somme Battles. It was my intention to attack both shoulders of the salient simultaneously." Subsequent developments in the early weeks of the year, the collapse of the Russian Armies, the German submarine campaign, a change in the command of the French Armies (General Nivelle succeeding Marshal Joffre), and the German Retreat to the Hindenburg Line, necessitated certain changes in Sir Douglas Haig's plan, but in the main he was able to carry out his original plan. The principal alteration was in the action of the Fifth Army on the Ancre, which, instead of attacking side by side with the Third Army, had to follow up the retreating enemy and establish itself firmly in front of the Hindenburg Line.

Preparations for the offensive began early in the year. They were very extensive, resembling in detail the preparatory measures adopted in the Somme Battles of 1916, though as a result of the great experience gained in the latter, improvements and additions were made in the new scheme. The troops who were to take part in the initial attack on 9th April were carefully trained over model trench systems which closely resembled the powerful German defences along the front of attack.

Along the British front the new German lines of defence (part of the Hindenburg Line) ran in a general north-westerly direction from St. Quentin

---

[1] "This plan comprised a series of offensives on all fronts, so timed as to assist each other by depriving the enemy of the power of weakening any one of his fronts in order to reinforce another."— *Despatches.*

[2] The "Introductory" passage of Sir Douglas Haig's despatch dated 25th December 1917 should be read in conjunction with this Chapter on the Arras offensive.

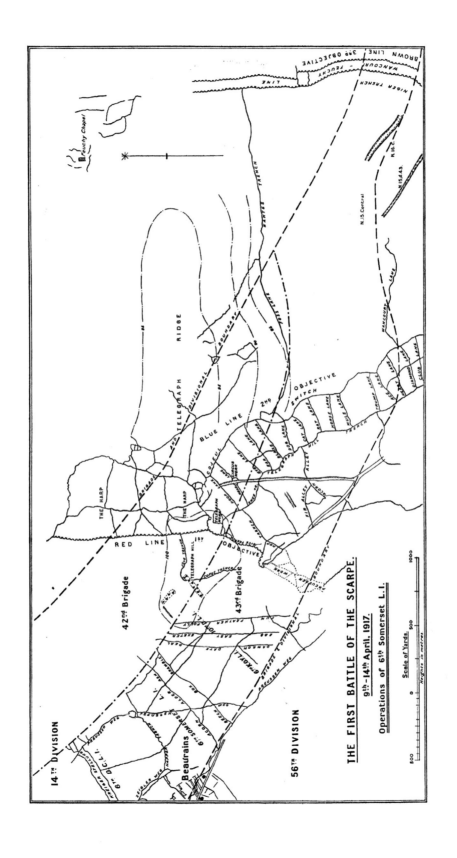

THE FIRST BATTLE OF THE SCARPE.
9th–14th April, 1917.
Operations of 6th Somerset L.I.

1st, 6th and 8th Battalions

to the village of Thilloy-lez-Mofflaines, immediately south of Arras. From the latter point the German original trench system ran northwards across the valley of the Scarpe River to Vimy Ridge which, rising to a height of some 475 feet, dominated a wide view to the south-east, east and north. The Vimy Ridge was of great strategic value to the enemy.

The Third and First British Armies (from right to left) were to attack from just north of the village of Croisilles, S.E. of Arras to just north of Givenchy-en-Gohelle, a distance of nearly 15 miles. The southern portion of the enemy's defences included about 4 or 5 miles of the now powerfully defended Hindenburg Line. From the Scarpe at Fampoux to Lievin, the German defences comprised three trench systems, forming a highly organized defensive belt of some 2 to 5 miles in length. From 3 to 6 miles farther east a new line of resistance, known as the Drocourt–Queant Line forming a northern extension of the Hindenburg Line, linked up with the former at Queant. It will thus be seen that the task before the Third and First Armies was extremely difficult and likely to be costly. For three weeks prior to Zero day the whole area to be attacked was subjected to very heavy artillery bombardment, the "Heavies" searching the enemy's back areas and communications. Prisoners captured subsequently testified to the terrible losses inflicted by this bombardment and the enormous damage done by the British guns to the German defences.

On Zero day (April 9th, 5.30 a.m.) the Divisions in line from right to left were as follows: 21st (just south of Henin), 30th (S.E. of Mercatel), 56th (west of Neuville Vitasse), 14th (east of Beaurains and west of Telegraph Hill), 3rd and 12th Divisions (south and north respectively of the Cambrai–Arras road) and the 15th (east of Arras and between the Douai railway and the Scarpe).[1] From the left flank of the 15th Division the line was carried in a slightly north-westerly direction by the 9th, 34th, 51st, 1st (Canadian), 2nd (Canadian) 13th Brigade, 5th Division, 3rd (Canadian) and 4th (Canadian) Divisions to west and to the western slopes of Hill 145, one of the dominating features of the Vimy Ridge; the 37th Division was in Arras with orders to pass through the 12th and 15th Divisions, while the 4th Division (just north of Arras) was to go through the 9th Division.

From these Divisions it is possible to locate immediately the approximate positions of the Somerset Light Infantry on the first day of the operations: the 6th Battalion was with the 14th Division, the 8th Battalion with the 37th and the Senior Battalion (1st) of the Regiment was with the 4th Division: the 7th Battalion with the 20th Division does not enter the story until later.

Of the three Battalions of Somerset Light Infantry which took part in the main operations only one—the 6th—was in the front line during the first stages of the Battle, the 8th and 1st Battalions leap-frogging the forward Divisions after the latter had made their initial attack.

[1] It is of Regimental interest to note that the first four Divisions, i.e. 21st, 30th, 56th and 14th, forming the VII Corps, were commanded by Lieut.-General Sir T. D'O. Snow, now Colonel of the Somerset Light Infantry.

On the 7th April Colonel Bellew (commanding 6th Somerset L.I.) issued operation orders to his Battalion. The 14th Division, with the 56th Division on its right and the 3rd Division on the left, was to capture and consolidate the enemy's position as far as the Wancourt Line. After securing the latter other troops were to pass through and secure the line Heninel–Guemappe–Monchy-le-Preux. Of the 14th Division the 43rd Brigade was to attack on the right and the 42nd on the left, the assault by the former Brigade being carried out by the 6th K.O.Y.L.I. on the right and the 10th D.L.I. on the left: the 6th Somersets were to leap-frog the K.O.Y.L.I. and Durhams, the remaining Battalion of the Brigade—the 6th D.C.L.I.—being in reserve. One company of the Somersets was attached to the K.O.Y.L.I. for "mopping-up" duties, a company of the D.C.L.I. acting similarly for the Durhams.

There were three objective lines, Red (1st), Blue (2nd) and Brown (3rd). The Red Line was Nice Trench and the trench line forming part of the Preussen Redoubt: the Blue Line was the eastern trench line of the Cojeul Switch: the Brown Line was the trench east of Niger Trench, part of the Wancourt–Feuchy Line.

The 3rd objective (Brown Line) was allotted to the 6th Somerset Light Infantry who were to pass through the 6th K.O.Y.L.I. and 10th D.L.I. on the Blue Line.

The ground over which the 43rd Brigade was to advance was difficult, it was hilly and much broken up by a formidable trench system which ran north and south between the Red and Blue Lines. The Harp, a powerful German defence area, lay north of Nice Trench, the left of the latter joining with Telegraph Redoubt, a strongly fortified position on the southern extremity of the Harp. Only a portion of the latter, however, lay in the 14th Divisional area of attack and that portion was allotted to the 42nd Brigade. Nevertheless the German trenches were so placed that if the flanking units of the 14th Division failed to get on the latter would be open to much enfilade fire.

Zero hour was to be at 5.30 a.m., at which hour the 3rd Division, on the left of the 14th, was to attack the German system of trenches on its front. Zero hour for the 14th Division was, however, 7.34 a.m., when the leading units of the 43rd and 42nd Brigades were to advance from their assembly trenches and creep as close to the artillery barrage as possible, ready to attack as the barrage lifted off the first objective. Such, briefly, were the principal points set out in Operation Orders.

On the night 8th/9th April the 6th Somersets moved up to the assembly trenches allotted to the Battalion, i.e. "A" and "B" Trenches (Acorn, Alder, Ash, and Beech and Box) about 1,000 yards W. of Telegraph Hill and Napper Trench. All companies were in position by 12.25 a.m. on 9th: the total strength of the Battalion was then 20 officers and 560 other ranks.

For three weeks prior to the day of attack the guns had pounded the enemy's position—the field guns his wire entanglements and the "Heavies" his back areas and communications. Captured Germans stated that the storm

of shell poured on to their trenches was terrifying, especially on the days immediately preceding the attack when the general bombardment began. Gas
discharges and raids along the whole front to be attacked kept the enemy in
a state of paralysed expectancy. The final period of intense bombardment,
before the barrage fell at Zero, was truly appalling and when later captured
Germans began to be passed back to the prisoners' cage, they were in many
instances stunned and dazed by the terrifying experiences through which
they had passed, deeming it a miracle that they were still alive.

At 5.30 a.m. on 9th the general attack was launched under cover of a
most effective artillery barrage. Closely following on the heels of the barrage
the British infantry swarmed over the German trenches so that within forty
minutes of the opening of the battle practically the whole of the enemy's
front-line system had been captured.

On the left of the 14th Division the 3rd Division had reached the Harp
and was still engaged in securing their stronghold when, at 7.34 a.m., the
6th K.O.Y.L.I. and the 10th D.L.I. left their lines and attacked the Red
Line (1st objective). Keeping well up to the barrage, these two Battalions,
as the barrage lifted, rushed on the German trenches. By 7.55 a.m. the whole
of the German front line allotted to the 43rd Brigade had been captured and
ten minutes later German prisoners were being passed back. The advance
was then begun to the Blue Line (2nd objective).

At 8.46 a.m. the Somersets received orders to move into "E" and "D"
Lines (Ebb, East, Exeter, and Damson, Date and Deal). From this position
two more platoons were sent up at 9.25 a.m. (in addition to the company
already there) to help "mop up" Prussian Work and Nice Trench. The
work of clearing the captured positions was not difficult for (as the Brigade
Diary reports) "the enemy was chiefly in his dug-outs waiting to surrender."
As the K.O.Y.L.I. and Durhams advanced to the Blue Line, however, touch
was lost with troops on the right belonging to the 56th Division and there
was a gap of several hundred yards between the right of the 43rd Brigade
and the London Division.[1] Progress to the Blue Line was therefore slow,
as machine-gun and rifle fire, in enfilade, caught the attacking Battalions as
they pressed on to the Cojeul Switch. But apparently the latter had been
captured and was being consolidated when the 6th Somersets arrived to pass
through and attack the final objective.

On the 6th Somersets reaching the Blue Line hardly any check was
necessary and B, C and D Companies (in the order given) with A Company
rejoining and coming on behind, crept out to the barrage line. Companies
had by now shaken out into artillery formation. At 12.30 p.m. the barrage
lifted and in lines of skirmishers the Somerset men advanced. At this period
no troops either of the 56th Division or 42nd Brigade were visible on either
flank, which were thus in the air. From high ground on the left of the Somersets rifle and machine-gun fire swept the line of advance and Colonel Bellew
found it necessary to detach two platoons to deal with the enemy at this point.

[1] Four tanks which should have taken part in the attack were "bogged" in the Blue Line.

These platoons captured one machine gun and 30 Germans. The two leading Companies of the Somersets, however, pushed on towards the Brown Line. About 1.10 p.m. a platoon of the Rifle Brigade appeared on the left of the Battalion, relieving the two platoons on the high ground and establishing the fact that the left of the Somersets was supported by troops of the 42nd Brigade. But on the right the Somerset men were still unsupported and at 1.20 p.m. came under heavy enfilade machine-gun fire from the right flank and rear. This heavy fire was responsible for the serious casualties suffered by the leading Company, which was now forced to seek shelter in a newly dug German trench about 600 yards from the objective: here the Somersets set to work to consolidate their position.

It was nearly 2 p.m. when some Royal Scots belonging to the 3rd Division appeared on the northern flank of the 6th Battalion, the leading waves of the former Battalion losing direction and getting mixed up with the 3rd and 4th waves of the Somersets. These troops, however, formed a defensive flank on the left. Similarly a company of the London Scottish (56th Division) advanced up the valley in right rear of the Somersets and, mixing with the 5th wave of the latter, formed a defensive flank on the right. These London troops were, however, withdrawn shortly afterwards, the 56th Division holding the Cord and Heart Trench.

At 4 p.m. the 6th D.C.L.I. were moved up to support the Somersets and form a defensive flank on the right.

The reports contained in the diaries of the 6th Somersets and 43rd Brigade, of the fighting throughout the daylight hours of the 9th April are quite colourless and bare of details of an interesting nature, though the Battalion advanced about a mile and captured 110 prisoners.

At 6.15 p.m. a warning order was received at Battalion Headquarters that a fresh attack on the Brown Line (the Wancourt Line) would take place at 6.30 p.m. The barrage was to fall at 6.24 p.m. and creep forward at 6.34 p.m., lifting off the Brown Line at 7 p.m., and the second Brown Line trench five minutes later.

With such short notice it was impossible to organize a fresh attack efficiently, for it was 6.55 p.m. before the O.C. the two front Companies of the Somersets received his orders. Colonel Bellew, however, ordered his reserve (about one Company) to push up at once and attack, the three other Companies to advance with their right on Wancourt Tower. At this period the right flank of the Somersets was still in the air, and the chances of attacking successfully were very small. Two companies of the D.C.L.I., supported by another company of the same Battalion, were also ordered to advance with their left on Wancourt Tower and attack on the right flank of the Somerset men. The remaining company of Cornwalls was ordered to push up to the cross-roads, about 1,000 yards west of Niger Trench. Neither the Somersets nor the Cornwalls received their orders in time to allow the attacking companies to follow close on the heels of the barrage, which was too far in advance when the attack was finally launched. The Somerset men had high

ground on their right and the flanking division was some 1,200 yards in rear.
The result was that, although the attack went forward gallantly, it was quickly
brought to a standstill by very heavy machine-gun fire. "Our men were
killed by German machine guns firing into their backs." Only the left
Company made any appreciable advance.

At 9.40 p.m. the 6th Somersets were ordered to consolidate their positions
and dig a support line for part of the garrison.[1]   The 6th D.C.L.I. held the
right of the line and formed a defensive flank.

Meanwhile, the 3rd and 12th Divisions, astride and south and north of
the Arras–Cambrai road, respectively, and the 15th Division from between
the railway and the Scarpe, had made fine progress, and at 7.30 a.m. the advance
was resumed against the second objective.

By about 2 p.m. the 15th Division, south of the Scarpe, after a grim
and bloody struggle, had carried the Railway Triangle and, continuing its
advance, stormed Feuchy Village, making a breach in the German third line
and capturing many of the enemy's field guns.   At this stage of the operations
the 37th Division, advancing from Arras, made an attempt to widen the breach
and advance beyond it in the direction of Monchy-le-Preux.

North of the Scarpe the 9th Division, having stormed St. Laurent Blagny,
swept on and captured Athies, but here, in accordance with the general scheme
of attack, the Division halted in order to allow the 4th Division to pass through,
with orders to take Fampoux Village and the Hyderabad Redoubt.

Of the 37th Division, the 112th Infantry Brigade had been ordered to
support the 3rd or 12th Divisions (according to the situation), the 63rd Infantry
Brigade the 12th Division, and the 111th Infantry Brigade the 12th or 15th
Divisions.

The 63rd Brigade Group left the neighbourhood of Porte Baudimont
about 9.30 a.m., marching through Arras to its assembly trenches which were
reached at 11.30 a.m.   For four hours the Brigade waited in their positions
and then, at 3.35 p.m., pushed on to Battery Valley, all units being assembled
in the neighbourhood of Broken Hill by 6 p.m.   But the position of the
111th Infantry Brigade, which had advanced ahead of the 63rd Brigade, had
not been ascertained, and it was not until 7.30 p.m. that the former was located
in the road running north from Feuchy Chapel and west of the Brown Line.

At 7.35 p.m. (at sunset) the 8th Somerset Light Infantry (Lieut.-Col.
J. W. Scott) and the 8th Lincolns, with one section of the 63rd Brigade M.G.
Company, were ordered to advance and occupy Orange Hill, which lay about
500 yards east of the Brown Line, the latter being the German trench system
running due south from Feuchy.   Two Companies of the Somersets then
advanced and dug themselves in on the crest of Orange Hill, their right flank

---

[1] No casualties are given in the Diary of the 6th Somersets, but on the 13th April, after the
Battalion had been withdrawn from the front line, there is the following entry: "During the operations
Capt. J. N. Black (one of our original officers) was killed, also Capt. Cherry, 2/Lieuts. A. L. Spring-
field, A. P. Abecasis. Wounded, 2/Lieuts. Hensley, Webster, Couldrey, Battie, Butler. Other
ranks killed, 14; missing, 12; wounded, 102."

turned back to the Brown Line joining up with a battalion of H.L.I. belonging to the 15th Division, and their left prolonged by the 8th Lincolns. One Company of Somerset men on the western slopes of Orange Hill supported the two Companies on the crest and the fourth Company was in reserve in the Brown Line with a post pushed forward some distance southwards in touch with the enemy. At 10.15 p.m. Colonel Scott sent word back to Brigade Headquarters that he had not gained touch with the 111th Infantry Brigade and that there appeared to be a very large gap on his right. Later, however, an officer patrol reported that the 111th Brigade was on the road running north from Feuchy Chapel. The only other item of interest throughout the night of 9th/10th was that a platoon of Somerset men was pushed out towards the head of Lone Copse Valley, east of Orange Hill. The action of the 8th Somersets, however, in occupying Orange Hill, had important results, adding materially to the subsequent successful attack on Monchy-le-Preux.

On 8th April the 11th Brigade Group of the 4th Division had moved from Hermaville to the Marœuil area. An entry on the previous day in the Diary of the 1st Somerset Light Infantry is of interest to the Regiment:—

"7th. Jellalabad Day. The Battalion marched to Hermaville. Concert for all ranks in the Officers' Hut from 5.30 p.m. to 8 p.m. Concert to all N.C.O.'s of the Battalion with the officers from 9 p.m. to 11 p.m. Speech by the Commanding Officer [1] on Jellalabad Day. 1st Move in the offensive to-day, good omen for the Battalion."

On the Battalion reaching Marœuil on the 8th, preparations were made for the offensive on 9th and again the Diary is interesting: "Every one in most cheerful mood."

The objective allotted to the XVII Corps (of which the 4th Division formed part) was the German third trench system from the River Scarpe, east of Athies, through Le Point du Jour–Maison de la Cote–Commandant's House; this was the Brown Line which the 9th, 34th and 51st Divisions (XVII Corps), in the order given from right to left, was to capture. The Brown Line having been secured, the 4th Division was to pass through the captured position and attack the northern portion of the Vimy Ridge, the fourth German system of trenches west of Fampoux (the Green Line) [2] and the latter village. In this attack the 12th Infantry Brigade was to be on the right and the 11th Infantry Brigade on the left: the 10th Brigade was in reserve.

The first objective allotted to the 11th Brigade was the German trench system between points H.10.d.9.0. and H.11.b.5.2. (there is no other way of describing it), the 12th Brigade making a simultaneous attack immediately south of the 11th Brigade. The second objectives were the Hyderabad Redoubt (11th Bde.) and Fampoux (12th Bde.). The first objective was to be assaulted by the 1st Somersets on the right and the 1st Hampshires on the

---

[1] Lieut.-Col. V. H. B. Majendie.
[2] Given in co-ordinates the Green Line was as follows: H.18.d.3.1–H.12.a.2.0–H.4.c.2.0.

left. The Hyderabad Redoubt was to be captured by two companies of the 1st Rifle Brigade passing through the Somerset men when the latter had reached their objective.

Of the 1st Somersets, A, C and H Companies were to attack the enemy, while B Company was to be employed as a carrying company. The Battalion was to advance in four waves in artillery formation of platoons in diamond formation, C and H Companies in the front two waves and A Company forming the rear two waves: H Company, on the right, to direct the line of advance.

Such, briefly, were the orders issued to the 4th Division and by Colonel Majendie to his Battalion. Battalion Orders contained many more details, all of a more or less interesting nature. But perhaps the most interesting (apart from the actual orders for the attack) are the detailed instructions as to dress and equipment of officers and men taking part in the assault. In the hard school of experience the British and French Armies had learnt much since 1914, and the difference between the dress and equipment of a British soldier in the first years of the war and in 1917, was the outcome of many bloody struggles with the Germans, who entered upon hostilities very much better prepared than were the Allies.

The first paragraph in the "Instructions re dress, equipment, etc.," issued before the opening of the Battles of Arras, 1917, orders that: "All officers taking part in the attack and all officers with the carrying party will be dressed exactly as the men. Sticks will not be carried." With the Germans it had been the practice when attacked to pick out the officers and shoot them down first of all, officers being distinguished by their dress which differed somewhat from that of the British private or N.C.O. As far back as 1914 officers' swords had been discarded and sticks were mostly carried in their place.

The second paragraph of these "Instructions" deals with the "Fighting Dress": the haversack was not to be worn, in place of it the pack was to be carried, containing "cap comforter, cardigan, fork, iron ration, unconsumed portions of the day's rations, mess tin and waterproof sheet." Steel helmets had replaced the old field-service cap in the early months of 1916.[1] Webbing equipment was worn, but the carrying capacity of the bandolier had been largely increased. Rifle sections were to go into the Battle area carrying 170 rounds of small arm ammunition per man. Bombing sections and Rifle Grenade sections were to carry 100 rounds per man. Lewis-gun sections, signallers, runners and the men of "B" Company (detailed, it will be remembered, as a carrying company) 50 rounds each. In addition to the S.A.A., every man, with the exception of the "mopping-up" sections, was to carry two No. 5 grenades; the "mopping-up" sections were to carry two "P" bombs instead. The two No. 5 grenades were to be carried in a S.A.A. bandolier slung over the left shoulder and fastened tightly under the right armpit; they were to be used only in cases of emergency and when the objectives had been captured

[1] A limited number, for experimental purposes, was issued during the latter part of 1915, but the first general issue was just before the Somme Offensive of 1916.

were to be collected and Company dumps formed. Each man was to carry two aeroplane flares in the breast pockets of his jacket; he was also to carry three sand-bags in his pack, placed on top of the other articles, so as to be ready to hand. Water-bottles were to be filled and "used most sparingly as no water may be available for a considerable time." Box respirators were to be carried in the "alert" position, but P.H. helmets were to be left behind.

The next paragraph deals with "Specialist Sections"—Lewis Guns, Bombing and Rifle Grenade Sections. Of the Lewis gunners every man, with the exception of No. 1, was to carry four magazines. Every man of the Bombing Sections was to carry a bucket containing eight No. 5 grenades. Of the Rifle Grenade Sections of C and H Companies each man was to carry a bucket containing eight No. 23 grenades, the cartridges being carried in the coat pocket. Of A Company every man of the Rifle Grenade Section was to carry a bucket, "half of the men will carry buckets each containing eight No. 23 grenades and half buckets each containing ten No. 20 grenades."

Each Company was to carry two 1-inch Véry Light Pistols, in addition to the one per Lewis gun sections. Company commanders were to arrange the distribution of a certain number of illuminating and S.O.S. cartridges amongst officers and N.C.O.'s. The 1½-inch Pistols (S.O.S. and illuminating) were to be brought up by B Company (the carrying company) on the first journey. Wire cutters were also to be issued under Company arrangements.

It will thus be seen that the British soldier in 1917 had a heavy load to carry as he advanced across No Man's Land to the attack, often over soft and slippery ground, inches (and sometimes feet) deep in viscous, stinking mud, and through water-logged shell holes.

Of considerable interest, also, is that part of the "Preliminary Operation Orders" which deal with "Personnel that will not accompany the Battalion in its attack." Amongst the officers of the 1st Somersets who were not to go into action were second-in-command (Major Waddy), Capt. Mordaunt, two company commanders (Capts. Marshall and Codner) and two seconds-in-command of companies (2/Lieuts. Frith and Banfield). Only 20 officers of the Battalion were to accompany the Battalion in the attack, the surplus remaining behind. In other ranks the regimenal sergeant-major, two company sergeant-majors (of A and B Companies), seven signallers, the buglers, the gas instructor, bombing instructor, two Lewis-gun instructors, instructor in dug-outs, and two pioneers of Bn. H.Qs. From each Company one sergeant, one corporal, one lance-corporal and from each platoon one rifle bomber, one scout or sniper and two Lewis gunners.

The equipment and organization of a Battalion taking part in an attack was therefore by no means an easy matter and it had taken a long while to evolve a system under which a unit in 1917 went into battle.

Throughout the night of 8th/9th April the 11th Infantry Brigade was at Marœuil, awaiting orders to move forward to the positions of assembly, a field just S.W. of St. Catherine (one of the northern suburbs of Arras).

From the first entry in the Diary of the 1st Somersets on 9th April, it is

very evident that it was written at the time: "5 a.m. Tremendous bombard- 1st Battalion
ment now on. Zero hour 5.30 a.m." At 6.5 a.m. the Battalion (in Brigade) 9th April
marched off to its assembly positions and there awaited orders to attack. A
heavy rain was falling and although the weather cleared later the early hours
of the morning were dismal in the extreme. At the assembly area breakfast
was issued, which somewhat broke up the tedium of a long wait until information regarding the attacks of other divisions were received. Some doubt
existed as to the rôle the 4th Division would be called upon to play. Alternative orders had been received: if the attacks by other divisions were not
successful or only partially successful, the 4th Division was to be prepared
to reinforce any part of the line held up and unable to advance: if, on the
other hand, all went well the 4th was to carry out the attack on the enemy's
fourth system of trenches. Before 10 a.m., however, welcome news came to
hand that the initial attack had been completely successful, and at 10 o'clock
the 1st Somersets left the assembly area and moved in column of route to the
Blue Line (the railway) in H.7.d. A few stray shells fell as the Battalion
advanced, but no casualties were suffered and it was not found necessary to
deploy. The Battalion formed up in the railway cutting and behind the
embankment, in touch on the right with the 2nd Essex Regiment and on the
left with the 1st Hampshires. The 11th Brigade was timed to reach the
area in rear of the Blue Line at Zero plus 6.40. The Battalion objective in
the attack was that portion of the fourth German system of trenches which
lay between points H.10.d.0.7. and H.11.c.1.9.,[1] and then push out patrols
to clear the Sunken Road in H.11.c. and assist in the capture of the Hyderabad
Redoubt by covering fire.

At Zero plus 7.40 the 11th Brigade was timed to pass the Blue Line in
its advance to positions of assembly in the third German system (the Brown
Line). Marching on compass bearing the Somersets reached the assembly
positions well in advance of the time-table and there awaited final orders to
attack. These came to hand shortly before 3 p.m.

At Zero plus 9.40, i.e. 3.10 p.m., the Battalion advanced to the assault
in artillery formation. It was not possible to follow closer behind the barrage
than 100 yards as shells were falling short owing to the extreme range from
which the guns were firing. The hostile barrage through which the Battalion
had to pass was fairly heavy and some casualties were suffered, but the men
went forward splendidly and extended below the crest of the hill in H.9 and
10 exactly as had been practised. Machine-gun and rifle fire met the Battalion
on approaching the wire in front of the fourth German system and it was seen
that the thick entanglements had not been cut by the artillery. For a moment
(and only a moment) there was hesitation, then several German tracks through
the wire were found and along these the men rushed towards the enemy's
trenches. Others, anxious not to be behindhand, climbed the wire, whilst
their comrades halted and shot down any Germans who showed themselves
above the parapets of their trenches. The cool manner in which some of

[1] Map, Sheet 51–B. N.W.

the Somerset men thus covered the advance of their comrades through the wire was too much for the nerve-shattered Germans, the majority of whom put up their hands and surrendered. A few showed fight, but they were shot down immediately. Those who surrendered were so anxious to get away from their trenches that they were merely pushed out through gaps in the wire and ran westwards through the ranks of the Battalion advancing in rear of the Somersets (Rifle Brigade), their hands still in the air. No escorts were necessary and, as the Diary of the 1st Somersets (rather proudly) records, "no man showed any desire to go back as such." The Battalion's objective having been captured, patrols from C Company were then pushed out to the Sunken Road, where several Germans with a machine gun showed some resistance. They were quickly killed or taken prisoner, three German officers were also taken from dug-outs. The patrols were subsequently relieved by the Rifle Brigade, the latter Battalion passing through the Somersets to capture the Hyderabad Redoubt. Meanwhile, the Somerset men set to work to consolidate their new line, Companies were reorganized and a system of defence instituted.

It was not long before the German guns were turned on to the trenches they had lost and a considerable amount of heavy shelling had to be endured by the 1st Battalion, but about 6.30 p.m. the line was thinned out, Bn. H.Qs. and two Companies withdrawing to Effie Trench. At midnight, however, orders were received to move one of these Companies forward again to the captured fourth German system and to garrison Hymen, Humid and Husack trenches with two Companies. As the latter trench was found already occupied by troops of the 12th Brigade the two Companies were placed one in Hymen and the other in Humid.

The attack on the whole had been generally successful: on the left all objectives had been gained and the Vimy Ridge (with the exception of a portion of Hill 145) captured. Just north of the Scarpe the 12th Brigade had at first met with severe opposition in Fampoux, but later in the day the village was taken. South of the river stiff resistance was encountered around Monchy-le-Preux and the point of the wedge driven into the German position was not as deep as had been hoped; a complete break-through was therefore not achieved.

Considering the degree of success attained by the 1st Somersets, casualties throughout the 9th April had been slight: Capt. H. J. Tanner and 2/Lieut. A. M. Hill were killed and in other ranks the Battalion had lost 50 killed and wounded.

Thus ended the first day of the Battle, which the official despatches summarize in the following words:—

"At the end of the day, therefore, our troops were established deeply in the enemy's positions on the whole front of attack. We had gained a firm footing in the enemy's third line on both banks of the Scarpe, and had made an important breach in the enemy's last completed line of defence."

Throughout the night of 9th/10th snow fell and it was bitterly cold, 1st Battalion
conditions were therefore very bad and difficult for the troops in the front 9th/10th April
line, some of whom were engaged in making good the captured positions,
whilst others still continued their attacks on the enemy.

Soon after midnight (at 12.50 a.m.) 9th/10th a warning was issued by
43rd Brigade H.Qs. (14th Division) to all Battalions that the Brigade would
attack the Brown Line again during the morning and that the 6th K.O.Y.L.I.
and 10th D.L.I. would be engaged.

At 8 a.m. Brigade H.Qs. ordered the formation of a Composite Battalion, 6th Battalion
made up of the 6th Somerset L.I. and the 6th D.C.L.I., under the command 10th April
of Lieut.-Colonel Bellew (of the former Battalion), and at 9.20 a.m. orders for
an attack to take place at 12 noon were sent to all units. The 6th K.O.Y.L.I.,
on the right, and the 10th D.L.I., on the left, were to assemble in a position
from which they could deploy and reach N.15 central (about 1,000 yards
W. of Niger Trench) in 30 minutes on receipt of orders for the barrage. The
Composite Battalion was to co-operate by fire. Zero was subsequently altered
to 12.25 p.m., at which hour the K.O.Y.L.I. and the Durhams advanced close
behind the barrage. On the left the 10th D.L.I. and 3rd Division appeared
to carry out their assault up to time, but on the right no troops of the 56th
Division could be seen advancing on the right of the 6th K.O.Y.L.I. The
result was that the latter soon came under heavy machine-gun fire from the
south and the leading waves edged along to the left. This caused the Durhams
to lose direction, but finally both Battalions entered the Brown Line, though
somewhat intermingled, and occupied it as far south as N.16.c. The entanglements in front of the trenches were new and undamaged on most of the front,
but a gap was found near the right of the Durhams and through this the troops
entered. There was no opposition from the Germans in the trenches, but
machine-gun fire in enfilade and reverse from the south (i.e. just north of the
Cemetery, W. of Wancourt).

On receiving reports that the Brown Line had not been occupied south
of N.16.2. Brigade H.Qs. ordered the Composite Battalion to push on and
secure the line to the southern divisional boundary. Two composite companies
of the 6th D.C.L.I. went forward to carry out this order: they had to cut the
wire in front of the trench but succeeded in doing so and, without difficulty,
took possession of the remaining portion of the Brown Line.

Meanwhile two platoons of the 6th Somerset L.I. attacked a German
strong point at N.15.d.4.3. in the Sunken Road west of the Brown Line.
It was soon obvious that this point was responsible for the reverse fire which
had caught the K.O.Y.L.I., for over 100 Germans were driven from the road,
the Somerset men capturing two new trench mortars and a bomb store. The
43rd Infantry Brigade had now captured all its objectives and the Brown
Line was handed over to the 41st Brigade at 4 p.m.

Half an hour later the 43rd Brigade received orders to march back to
the Caves at Ronville. The 6th Somersets were settled in by 9 p.m.

An order to move forward again in artillery formation was received at

6th Battalion

5 a.m. on the 11th, but this was cancelled and, at 8 p.m., the Battalion marched back to Montenescourt, a distance of 10 miles, the 43rd Brigade having been ordered to the Agnez-les-Duisans area. On 12th the Brigade moved to Manin, the Somersets being billeted in Beaufort. Finally, at 7.30 a.m. on

14th April

14th April, the 43rd Brigade marched to Warluzel, where the Battalions billeted, the Diary of the Somersets recording that "men's billets were quite comfortable and not very cramped. The day was fine for once."

Thus, so far as the 6th Battalion of the Regiment was concerned, ended the First Battle of the Scarpe.

In the meantime, on the morning of the 10th April, both the 8th and 1st

1st and 8th Battalions

Somersets (of the 37th and 4th Divisions respectively) and other troops with whom they were brigaded had continued their attacks on the enemy.

Throughout the night of the 9th/10th the 37th Divisions had "made considerable progress through the gap in the enemy's defences east of Feuchy and had occupied the northern slopes of Orange Hill, south-east of the village."[1] This quotation from the official despatches refers to the 8th Somerset Light Infantry and 8th Lincolns, who had occupied the Hill after dark on the 9th.

8th Battalion

About midnight the Adjutant of the 8th Somersets was told by the G.O.C., 63rd Brigade, by telephone, that the Lincolns were to push down to the Sunken Road, and to send forward one platoon of the Somersets to the head of Lone Copse Valley. But whether this was done (and with what result) it is impossible to say, the Battalion Diary being very incomplete and, what there is of it, difficult to understand.

10th April

When dawn of the 10th broke considerable movement was observed in the enemy's lines and large parties of Germans, busily engaged in "digging-in," were seen north of Monchy. About 10 a.m. two Companies of the Somersets were sent forward to make good Lone Copse Valley. As the leading Company neared the Copse enclosures the C.O. (who had been watching the advance of the two Companies), with the rest of the Battalion, followed in the wake of the two forward Companies.

At noon the positions of all four Companies of the 8th Battalion appear to have been as follows: one Company north of the enclosures about half a mile N.W. of Monchy, one Company about a quarter of a mile north of the first Company, and the remaining two Companies in Lone Copse Alley.[2]

About half a mile east of the two right Companies was a small network of German trenches, and against these and the crest of the hill, one Company of the Somersets was ordered to advance. But little progress could be made, for no sooner did the advance begin than heavy rifle and machine-gun fire from the enclosures and the small network of trenches brought the attack to a standstill: even supported by the 8th Lincolns, who had come up in rear of the Somersets, no progress could be made.

[1] Official despatches.
[2] The Battalion Diary gives the positions in co-ordinates thus: "One company about H.36.c.34, one company about H.36.a.7.4, two companies in valley."

Between 12 noon and 1 p.m. the 111th Brigade was seen advancing 8th Battalion
towards Monchy-le-Preux, and two Companies of Somersets were ordered to 10th April
attack the enclosures again. These Companies, though caught by enfilade
fire in Lone Copse Valley, advanced gallantly but were stopped at the hedges
by a murderous machine-gun fire and had to take whatever cover offered
itself. The attack of the 111th Brigade had also been brought to a standstill,
the Brigade finally occupying a position in right rear of the Somersets. These
positions were still held at 7.20 p.m. At 7.30 p.m. (under orders received
at 4.55 p.m.) the Somersets, Lincolns and 4th Middlesex made another attempt,
all three Battalions advancing, but they were stopped almost immediately.
From Monchy, from the small network of trenches north of the village, and
from the left flank, heavy machine-gun fire swept the ranks of the advancing
troops, and finally the Battalions consolidated along Lone Copse Valley.[1]

At 5 o'clock next morning, however, the 111th Brigade and troops of 11th April
the 15th Division (one battalion of which passed through the line of the
Somersets) attacked and captured the trenches and swept on eastwards.
Monchy was apparently taken in this attack, for at 10.30 a.m. a message was
received from 37th Divisional Headquarters stating that the 15th Division
held the line Keeling Copse–Pelves, and orders were then issued to the 63rd
Brigade to move to the high ground half a mile east of Monchy and Bois des
Aubepines. The information concerning the position of the 15th Division
was apparently incorrect, for about 11 a.m. as the 10th York and Lancaster
Regiment moved forward over the ridge north of Monchy heavy enfilade
machine-gun fire from the direction of Roeux and from the N.E. was encountered
and the Battalion was held up in the small network of trenches. The Middlesex
and Lincolns were then moved into Monchy, but the Somersets remained in
Lone Copse Valley and held this position until relieved, at 4 a.m. on 12th 12th April
April, when the Battalion marched back to the Feuchy Chapel Road.

There is an interesting note at the close of the Report of the Operations
by the Brigadier-General commanding the 63rd Brigade. He said: "The
action of the 8th Somersets in their advance from Orange Hill to Lone Copse
Valley was executed with great skill and with a minimum of losses considering
the heavy fire." But the operations had cost the Battalion two officers wounded
(2/Lieuts. J. H. B. Gegg and H. C. Frost), 26 other ranks killed and 70
wounded and missing. On the night of the 12th April the Battalion reached
billets in Arras.

North of the Scarpe the 4th Division had similarly gone through hard
fighting on the 10th April and subsequent days to the close of the first phase
of the operations.

The 1st Somersets had spent the night of 9th/10th April somewhat 1st Battalion
dispersed, for Battalion Headquarters and one Company were in Effie Trench, 9th/10th April
one Company in the Fourth German System, and one Company in each of
Hymen and Humid Trenches. Rain and sleet fell in abundance and every one

---

[1] For conspicuous gallantry and devotion to duty on 10th April 2/Lieut. J. H. B. Gegg was
awarded the M.C. and Pte. F. Dolling the D.C.M.

was miserably cold, though all were very much elated owing to the successes gained throughout the day.

During the morning of 10th the 1st Battalion concentrated in the Hydera-bad Redoubt, and about midday orders were received that cavalry would pass through the 11th Brigade and that the Somersets were to send out patrols after them and secure the line of the Gavrelle–Chemical Works Road from the Inn southwards, to a point [1] about half-way between the Inn and the Arras Railway, which point was the dividing line between the right of the 11th Brigade and the left of the 12th Brigade. A and C Companies were detailed to send out two patrols, each a platoon in strength, with Lewis guns, to make good the line; the remainder of these two Companies to be held in readiness to move forward in support of the leading patrols. H Company, though ordered to support A and C Companies (should such support be necessary), was not to move without instructions from Battalion Headquarters.

The sending out of these patrols was more difficult than may appear: the Hyderabad Redoubt was strongly wired on all sides and very few gaps existed, none on the eastern side. It was therefore necessary for the patrols to emerge from the Redoubt by the road which ran through it—those of A Company from the north and of C Company from the south; they were then to turn eastwards.

During the afternoon the C.O. of the Somersets was informed that the cavalry were not going through, but his Battalion was to act as ordered, the patrols advancing at 6.30 p.m. Artillery support was promised. In the event of serious opposition being met with, the C.O. was not to press home the attack unless he thought there was a chance of success.

At 6.30 p.m., promptly, the leading platoon left the Redoubt as ordered. But no artillery support was forthcoming and the patrols had hardly turned eastwards before very heavy machine-gun fire was opened on them, with the result that, with the exception of two or three men, the leading platoons were wiped out. After such a disastrous beginning it was clear that there was little chance of success and the C.O. ordered the attack to cease. The night of the 10th/11th passed without incident.

On the morning of 11th orders were received that the 4th Division would advance and secure the line Plouvain–Greenland Hill, the Order of Battle of the Division being, from right to left, 12th, 10th and 11th Infantry Brigades. There were two objectives: First, the Roeux–Gavrelle Road, with the formation of a defensive flank from the Inn to the Hyderabad Redoubt; Second, Plouvian–Greenland Hill and the formation of a defensive flank from the latter to the Inn.

The 1st Somerset Light Infantry formed the extreme left of the attack and was allotted the task of securing the road from the Inn to the cross-roads in I.7.a., both inclusive, and of forming a defensive flank from the Redoubt to I.7.a.2.8., inclusive. H and A Companies were to carry out the attack, H leading with A in support, each Company advancing in two waves on a two-

[1] Viz.: I.7.C.7.o.

platoon frontage. C Company formed the reserve and was located in the Redoubt. The defensive flank was to be formed from right to left, by H, A and C Companies.

The assembly position allotted to the Battalion—the only one available—was the Hyderabad Redoubt, which owing to its size and shape was inadequate. The right platoons of Companies were, therefore, ordered to emerge from the communication trench running out from the eastern apex of the Redoubt, and the left platoon through a gap in the wire on the northern side. The operation was not going to be easy.

The Redoubt was already overcrowded when, shortly before Zero, two battalions of the 10th Infantry Brigade, who had moved up too far to their left, poured into it and threw the whole arrangements into confusion. The jam in the Redoubt prevented the platoons of Somerset men advancing as arranged, the leading platoons not getting clear of the wire until Zero plus five minutes, and in those days five minutes lost was all the difference between success and failure.

Those lost five minutes gave the enemy an opportunity of massing and, no sooner had the leading platoon of Somersets cleared the wire, than a murderous machine-gun and rifle fire was opened on them and progress was impossible. The right platoon jumped at once into a trench running out of the apex of the Redoubt and worked down to within 200 yards of the advanced German line, but no further ground could be made good as the trench was blown in by shell fire and the gap swept by machine-gun fire. This platoon, however, gallantly maintained itself on the ground won for the remainder of the day.

The attack of the 4th Division, as a whole, practically gained no ground and must be written down as a failure. During the night a line of posts was established east and north of the Redoubt and touch with the Seaforths, on the right, and the Hampshires was maintained. Owing to the splendid way in which the men dug, a fairly strong line of posts had been made by daylight. On 12th April the 9th Division failed in a similar attack and throughout the day the Redoubt was subjected to heavy artillery fire, inflicting on the Somersets a number of casualties.

About 4 a.m. on 13th A Company of the Cameronians arrived at the Redoubt and stated they had been ordered to dig a line of posts from the right of the Somersets to Hubble Trench. The Somerset men lent the Scotsmen every assistance, trying to get them into position and dug in before daylight. This was, however, impossible, and when dawn broke they had to be accommodated in the communication trench and in the right post held by the Somersets. At daylight three more companies of the Cameronians arrived and these also had to be put under cover at once. One company was taken into the Redoubt, the other two companies were sent back to the Sunken Road. On this day also the Redoubt was shelled heavily.

On the 14th the weather, which had been vile since the Battle began on 9th, improved a little. Again the Redoubt was a target for the enemy's shell fire, but, at midnight, the 1st Hampshires arrived to relieve the tired and worn-out Somerset men, who moved back into Brigade Reserve, holding the Brown Line.

The First Battle of the Scarpe was over and splendid progress had been made all up and down the line of attack, but casualties were heavy. The 1st Somerset lost 7 officers killed (Captains H. J. Tanner and S. V. Wasbrough, 2/Lieuts. A. M. Hill, E. M. Gardner, S. H. Card, E. R. Fry and N. E. Herapath), 4 officers wounded (Lieut. C. J. O. Daubeney, 2/Lieuts. D. W. Gardner, F. C. Barlow and C. A. B. Elliott [1]). In other ranks the Battalion had lost 23 killed and 104 wounded. Of his officers and men the C.O. (Lieut.-Col. V. H. B. Majendie) said:—

"All ranks behaved splendidly through a very trying operation. Every one suffered very much from the bad weather and loss of sleep, hot food, etc., but the men were very cheery and ready to carry out anything asked of them. At one period seven officers collapsed through their exhaustion, only three being fit to carry on, i.e. the C.O., Adjutant and Lewis Gun Officer."

Captures by the Battalion were about 300 prisoners, 5 machine guns, one cooker and innumerable other stores.[2]

THE SECOND BATTLE OF THE SCARPE, 1917: 23RD–24TH APRIL

On the 16th April the French launched their offensive on the Aisne and shortly after that date the weather began to improve. Under these changed conditions preparations for the next phase of the Arras operations progressed rapidly and plans for the next attack were made. Originally the Second Battle was to begin on 21st April, but high winds and indifferent visibility forced postponement until 23rd. On that date, at 4.45 a.m., another attack on a front of about 9 miles from Croisilles to Gavrelle was launched. By 10 a.m. the remainder of the high ground west of Cherisy had been captured by the 30th and 50th Divisions, and the 15th Division had pushed through Guemappe. East of Monchy-le-Preux the 29th Division gained the western slopes of Infantry Hill: north of the Scarpe the 51st Division had heavy fighting on the western outskirts of Roeux Wood and the Chemical Works. On the left of the 51st Division the 37th had reached the buildings west of Roeux Station and gained the line of its objectives on the western slopes of Greenland Hill, south of the railway. On the left of the main attack the 63rd Division had taken Gavrelle.

But it is with the 37th Division and its hard struggle against Roeux Wood and the Chemical Works that this chapter deals.

After the 8th Somersets (63rd Infantry Brigade, 37th Division) had been withdrawn from the line on the night of 12th the Battalion billeted in

---

[1] Died of wounds, 12.4.17.

[2] For conspicuous gallantry and devotion to duty throughout the operations Lt.-Col. V. H. B. Majendie was awarded the D.S.O., Capt. R. A. A. Chichester and 2/Lieuts. L. A. Osborne and F. C. Barlow the M.C., and Sergt. H. W. P. James the D.C.M.

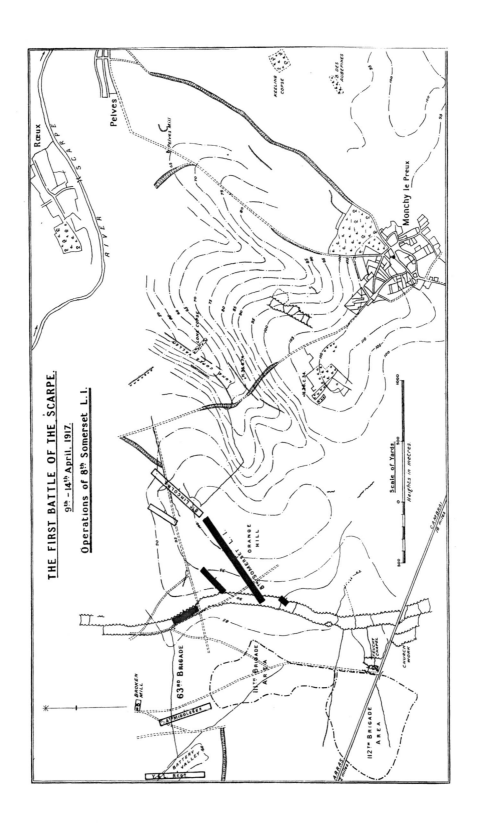

THE FIRST BATTLE OF THE SCARPE.
9th – 14th April, 1917.

Operations of 8th Somerset L.I.

Arras, moving the next day to Duisans, in which place billets were occupied 8th Battalion
for one night.　On the 13th the Battalion moved to Agnez-les-Duisans, on
the 15th to Beaufort, whence, on 19th, the Somerset men marched to billets 19th April
in Montenescourt.　From the latter village the Battalion moved forward to
Arras in order to take part in the forthcoming operations.

The 63rd Infantry Brigade (37th Division) took over the line held by the
10th Infantry Brigade (4th Division) on the night of the 20th April, the relief
being completed at 4.20 a.m. on 21st.　On 22nd (the night before the Battle) 22nd April
the 63rd Brigade was disposed in the following positions: the 4th Middlesex
held a line of posts east and north of the Hyderabad Redoubt, joining up on
the left with the 10th York and Lancs R., who carried the line northwards to
the right flank of the 63rd Division S.W. of Gavrelle, west of Hood Trench: the
8th Lincolns were in support in Heron, Lucid and Haggard Trenches, the 8th
Somersets in reserve south of Point du Jour, in Laurel, Cam and Effie Trenches.

The task allotted to the 37th Division was the capture of the Roeux–
Gavrelle Road along the Divisional front: the 51st Division was attacking on
the right and the 63rd Division on the left of the 37th.

During the night of 22nd/23rd the 63rd Brigade moved up to its assembly
positions for the attack, which was timed to begin at 4.45 a.m. the following
morning.　At 11.15 p.m. all four Companies of the 8th Somersets moved
forward independently to Halo and Hoary Trenches, in which positions the
Battalion was to support the 4th Middlesex.　The 8th Lincolns similarly
were formed up in Hudson and Hazard Trenches where they were to support
the 10th York and Lancs R.　The two forward Battalions of the 63rd Brigade
held a line facing N.E. immediately east and north of the Hyderabad Redoubt,
i.e. 4th Middlesex on the right and 10th York and Lancs on the left.　At
3 a.m. on 23rd the 8th Somersets apparently moved forward again in close 23rd April
support of the 4th Middlesex, for the Battalion Diary gives the position as
"in front of Hyderabad Works (Redoubt) in H.12 a. and c." [1]

At 4.45 a.m. the barrage came down and the attacking battalions moved
forward to the assault.　On the right the 4th Middlesex met with considerable
opposition from all directions, but gallantly pushed on in rear of the barrage
to the road, south of the cross-roads about 1,200 yards east of the Hyderabad
Redoubt.　The Middlesex men were, however, unable to get farther forward
than a line about 200 yards east of the road, for heavy enfilade machine-gun
fire from the right flank was sweeping the advance.　Heavy frontal and enfilade
machine-gun fire also met the advance of the 10th York and Lancs R., and
during the delay the barrage moved away from the Battalion, causing the 8th
Lincolns to pass through at an earlier stage than had been anticipated, but
the Lincoln men pressed on to Chili Trench and occupied a portion of it, the
northern portion being held by a party of some 50 or 60 Germans.　The latter
were, however, outflanked and captured.

Meanwhile, the main body of the 8th Somersets, following closely behind

[1] The dispositions given in the Battalion Diary do not agree with those given in the 63rd Brigade
"Narrative of Operations."

the Middlesex men, had also reached the road south of the cross-roads. But the Battalion had suffered heavily, and only two officers (Captain Saunders and 2/Lieut. Owen) remained. Colonel Scott, his Adjutant, Battalion H.Qs. and the remainder of the Battalion were at the western end of the cross-roads. At this period the whole front was swept by heavy machine-gun fire and a terrific hostile shrapnel barrage. First the Adjutant fell wounded and then the C.O. (Lieut.-Col. J. W. Scott) was killed whilst gallantly leading his men.[1] The hostile barrage was followed by a violent counter-attack, the enemy pouring down the western slopes of Greenland Hill in artillery formation towards the line of the 63rd Brigade. But the attack was broken by rifle and machine-gun fire. Collecting all Somerset men he could find, Capt. Saunders dug in in Clasp Trench (running along the road south of the cross-roads) and hung on in this position until he was relieved. The 4th Middlesex were about 300 yards in front of the Somersets. The afternoon of the 23rd was spent by the latter in the consolidation of Clasp Trench. The Battalion was relieved

on the night of 24th April without incident and returned to Heron Trench about 200 strong in "other ranks," with Captain M. K. F. Saunders and 2/Lieut. Owen.

The general results of the attack of the 37th Division in the Second Battle of the Scarpe were as follows: the Division had reached the buildings west of Roeux Station and had gained the line of its objectives on the western slopes of Greenland Hill, north of the railway. Gavrelle was captured by the 63rd (Naval) Division and held, despite five violent counter-attacks on the 23rd and three on the 24th, all of which were completely broken.

THE BATTLE OF ARLEUX, 28TH–29TH APRIL

From the standpoint of military history the subsequent operations at Arras, after the Second Battle of the Scarpe, are of considerable importance. They were undertaken with the sole object of assisting the French who were attacking the long plateau, north of the Aisne River, traversed by the Chemin des Dames. They were continued until the results of the French offensive declared themselves. The first of these Battles (there were two) was the Battle of Arleux, fought on 28th and 29th April, the 8th Somersets of the 37th Division again taking part in the operations, though the only Battalion of the Regiment to do so.

The front of attack was about 8 miles, from north of Monchy-le-Preux, though demonstrations were continued southwards to the Arras–Cambrai Road, and northwards to the Souchez River, to give the impression of an attack on a much larger scale.

The attack of the XVII Corps was to be carried out by the 34th Division

---

[1] Second-Lieutenant L. H. Vaughan was also killed on 23rd April 1917, and the following officers are given amongst the wounded: Capt. C. W. G. Wright, Capt. S. Baker (died of wounds 28/5/17), Lieut. R. G. W. Husbands, Lieut. F. G. Hinton, 2/Lieuts. F. J. Clark, E. J. Rowland, W. C. Whiting, E. A. Matthews, R. W. Bullivant (died of wounds 1/5/17) and P. F. M. Hooper.

on the right and the 37th Division on the left.   The First Army was to capture   8th Battalion
the line Oppy–Arleux-en-Gohelle.   All three Brigades of the 37th Division
were to attack the enemy, the 112th Brigade on the right, the 63rd in the
centre and the 111th on the left.   The objectives of the 37th Division were
Wish and Whip Trenches (running along the Plouvain–Gavrelle Road), thence
a north and south line from the latter trench southwards to the right Divisional
boundary.

Of the 63rd Brigade the 8th Somersets were to attack on the right and
the 8th Lincolns on the left, the 4th Middlesex supporting the Somersets
and the 10th Y. and L. the Lincolns.   The forming-up line of the Somersets
was Cuba Trench from the left of the 112th Brigade to the Brickstack.[1]

Zero hour was 4.25 a.m. on 28th April.

During the night of 27th/28th the 8th Battalion, under the command
of Captain M. K. F. Saunders,[2] moved forward from Heron Trench and
assembled in Cuba Trench; the Battalion was in position by 3 a.m. on 28th,
two platoons in front and two in rear,[3] as each attacking Battalion had been
ordered to advance on a two-platoon frontage.

It was so dark when Zero hour arrived that it was impossible to see more   28th April
than twenty yards ahead, British and Germans being indistinguishable.   Compass bearings had been taken and given to officers and N.C.O.'s, but even so,
when the attack went forward, there was loss of direction.   A few minutes
after Zero a very heavy hostile barrage fell on the line of the road and the
smoke, combined with the darkness, caused considerable confusion, with the
result that the Somersets swung off to the left and Cuthbert Trench (directly
east of Cuba Trench) was only partially attacked, the full weight of the attack
passing on to Whip Trench, which lay some 500 yards east of Cuthbert.
In the latter, however, 2/Lieut. F. R. Cooksley was left behind with thirteen
men to mop up and consolidate the trench.

No opposition was encountered in Whip and Wish Trenches, and the
Battalions pushed on across Why and Weak Trenches (about 1,000 yards
east of Whip and Wish) in a north-easterly direction towards Railway Copse.
They had now got far beyond the Black Line, their objective, and returning
wounded stated that had there been a few more troops the village of Fresnes
could have been taken easily.   But all Battalions were pitifully weak and,
being unsupported, the inevitable retirement had to be made.   A few troops
had remained behind in the northern portion of Cuthbert Trench and in
Whip Trench, and the consolidation of the latter was at once put in hand by
a mixed party of Somersets, Bedfords, and men of other Battalions.   Other
troops soon began to work back from in front of Railway Copse, but as the
morning advanced the position of these men became precarious, for they
were a mark for the enemy's machine gunners and riflemen.   Many of them

[1] In co-ordinate the position of the Brickstack is given as I.7.a.6.9.
[2] For his conspicuous gallantry on this occasion Capt. M. K. F. Saunders was awarded the M.C.
[3] During the time the 63rd Brigade was in Divisional Reserve each Battalion, being then only
of an average strength of 220, was reorganized on a four-platoon basis.

8th Battalion
28th April

had to take shelter until the night of 28th/29th, but some men succeeded in rejoining their Battalions.   If only it had been possible to signal the situation back to Brigade Headquarters something might have been done to consolidate a line much farther east than Whip Trench, but the telephone wires had all been cut by the intense fire of the enemy's guns, runners became casualties, and visual signalling was impossible.[1]

About 11 p.m. the 112th Brigade (on the right of the 63rd Brigade) fell back to its jumping-off position in Cuba Trench.   Thus 2/Lieut. Cooksley was left isolated with a party of about 50 Somerset men in Cuthbert Trench and all efforts to relieve him failed, until the night of 29th/30th, when he got in touch with the Seaforths of the 9th Division (which, in the meantime, had relieved the 37th Division).[2]

Neither the Battalion Diary of the 8th Somersets nor the 63rd Brigade Diary are illuminating on the operations of the 28th–29th April, but reading between the lines it appears that the attack, from the 37th Divisional point of view, was a failure.

29th April

By 4 a.m. on 29th the 63rd Brigade had been withdrawn to the neighbourhood of Point du Jour and, embussing at Point Rond Arras, moved back to the Lignereuil area, the Somersets being billeted in Beaufort.   The 8th Battalion apparently lost two officers killed (2/Lieuts. C. G. B. Gordon and G. F. Gibbs) and four officers (Capt. M. K. F. Saunders and 2/Lieuts. A. C. Owen, R. W. Heal and E. H. Morgan) wounded.   Other ranks' casualties are given for the operations on 23rd *and* 28th as 17 killed, 180 wounded and 99 missing.   The losses in officers (18) had been very heavy.[3]

The Official Despatches give the results of the Battle of Arleux as follows:—

"The village of Arleux-en-Gohelle was captured by Canadian troops (1st Canadian Division) after bitter hand-to-hand fighting and English troops (2nd Division) made further progress in the neighbourhood of Oppy, on Greenland Hill (37th Division), and between Monchy-le-Preux and the Scarpe (12th Division)."

THE THIRD BATTLE OF THE SCARPE, 1917: 3RD–4TH MAY

1st Battalion

The last of the Battles of Arras, 1917, which opened on 3rd May, was of a similar nature to the operations of 28th and 29th April.   The French had planned a heavy attack on the Chemin des Dames to take place on 5th and, in order to distract the attention of the enemy and hold his troops east of Arras, Sir Douglas Haig considerably extended his active front.   While the Third and First Armies attacked from Fontaine-lez-Croisilles to Fresnoy the Fifth Army was to launch a second attack upon the Hindenburg Line in the neighbourhood of Bullecourt [4]—a total front of over 16 miles.

[1] Lieut. J. H. M. Hardyman was awarded the M.C. for his gallantry and devotion to duty.
[2] 2/Lieut. F. R. Cooksley was awarded the M.C. for his gallantry.
[3] Lieut.-Col. H. K. Umfreville, West Yorkshire Regt., succeeded Lieut.-Col. Scott in command of the 8th Somersets on 30th April.
[4] The Battle of Bullecourt, 3rd–17th May 1917

Zero hour was timed for 3.45 a.m. on 3rd May.

In these final operations the 1st Battalion Somerset Light Infantry (4th *1st and 6th Battalions*
Division) and the 6th Battalion (14th Division) were engaged. Neither of
these Battalions had been engaged with the enemy after the close of the First
Battle of the Scarpe on 14th April. The 14th Division having relieved the
4th Division on 20th April, the 1st Somersets moved out of the line and did
not go in again until 2nd May. On 30th April the 4th Division relieved
the 34th Division in the line east of Arras. The 11th Brigade being in reserve,
the Somersets remained that night in Arras and throughout the 1st May.
But on the 2nd May, having been attached to the 10th Infantry Brigade for
the operations of 3rd, its special duty being to capture the village of Roeux,
the Battalion moved from Arras to the assembly positions allotted to it in the
Ravine N.W. of Athies.

The 6th Somersets, after the operations which closed on 14th April, *6th Battalion*
had similarly spent a period of rest and training out of the line, and it was
not until the early morning of 27th that the Battalion marched back again to *27th April*
Telegraph Hill, relieving the 8th Durham Light Infantry in the Hart trench
system. In the Third Battle of the Scarpe the 43rd Brigade (of which the
6th Battalion formed part) remained in Divisional Reserve and the Somerset
men, though they were in the area of the Battle and were subjected to heavy
shell fire, were not called upon to attack the enemy. The Battalion, throughout *3rd May*
the operations, was west of Wancourt, in shelters, with two Companies occupying Niger Trench. R.S.M. Buss, a gallant Warrant Officer, was killed here
by shell fire.

On the 1st Battalion, however, fell the brunt of an attack which, though *1st Battalion*
gallantly made, was unsuccessful and was the cause of the loss of many brave
fellows.

The 4th Division, on the right, and the 9th Division, on the left of the
XVII Corps, were to attack a line from the northern bank of the River Scarpe
to an east-to-west line 1,000 yards south of the Gavrelle–Fresnes Road. The
villages of Roeux and Plouvain were amongst the objectives allotted to the 4th
Division. Of the latter the 10th Brigade, on the right, and the 12th Brigade,
on the left, were to attack the enemy, the 11th Brigade was ordered to remain
in support, though the 1st Somersets were attached to the 10th Brigade for
the purpose of clearing Roeux Cemetery and village, and the 1st Rifle Brigade
to the 12th Brigade.

The right flank of the 10th Brigade rested approximately on the southern
edge of Mount Pleasant Wood, the Somersets, therefore, were assembled
from the Wood to the River west of Roeux Woods. The Battalion was to
attack on a two-company front, B Company on the right and A (or "Light")
Company on the left: C Company, less the sections detailed as "moppers up,"
was to form the third wave, and to H Company the duties of "carrying" were
allotted. The first objective was the road running north to south through
Roeux, from the Church to the River. As soon as this objective had been
gained A Company (in two waves) was to advance through the village with

its centre on the road: B Company (also in two waves) was to follow on, 1,000 yards in rear of A, and act as "moppers up." In view of the result of the operations it is unnecessary to go into details of the remaining objectives.

The 1st Somersets moved from the Ravine N.W. of Athies at 8 p.m. on 2nd May to take up positions in the front line north of the River Scarpe and west of Roeux Woods. On leaving Athies the Battalion crossed the River to the southern side and, moving forward along the railway, crossed the River again to the northern bank about 1,000 yards west of Roeux Woods. Some shelling was encountered, but no casualties were suffered, and by midnight the Battalion was in position: its attacking strength was then 9 officers and 217 other ranks.

It was very dark and dull when, at 3.15 a.m.—Zero hour—the attack, under an artillery barrage, was launched. The assaulting troops went forward perfectly to time, but were immediately met by intense fire from the German machine guns of which Roeux Woods appeared to shelter a large number. The Wood had apparently been missed by the barrage, probably its close proximity to the British front line induced the gunners to avoid the risk of short shooting. The trench mortars of the 10th Brigade which were supposed to mortar the Wood before the attack began were ineffective. The Somerset men, however, got into the Wood and, although touch was lost owing to the darkness and confusion, the left of the attack succeeded in reaching the western outskirts of Roeux village, but were unable to remain there for they were too few in numbers and the enemy's machine-gun and rifle fire was very heavy. The right of the attack had been held up in the Wood. Eventually both the right and left of the attack dribbled back to their original trenches, having gained nothing but the honour of reaching Roeux, though unable to hold it. Back in their original trenches the survivors of the Battalion reorganized and counted their losses. Captain C. C. Codner and 2/Lieut. R. H. D. Bailey were killed, the latter at first being reported missing: 2/Lieut. W. E. Marler was wounded and died on 5th May. Other wounded officers were 2/Lieuts. R. J. Middleton, E. R. Foley, H. G. S. Backhouse, F. H. Davies and E. H. C. Frith. In other ranks the Battalion had lost 132 killed, wounded and missing. Captain E. W. Marshall was also reported wounded and missing, but came in during the night of 4th, having laid out all day in a shell hole within a few yards of the enemy.[1]

Throughout the 4th May the Battalion remained in the same positions. During the afternoon it was decided to push strong patrols out into the Wood with the object of finding the position and testing the strength of the enemy and, if possible, gain ground. The patrol consisted of 2/Lieut. W. J. Drake, 50 men and two Lewis guns. Touch was established with the enemy, who was found in strength, and posts were established. At night a line of posts was established from the Scarpe to other posts north of the Wood. Thus the excellent work of the patrol had provided a line parallel with the enemy, which

[1] For conspicuous gallantry and devotion to duty in taking command of his Company when his officers had become casualties, C.S.M. T. J. Johnson was awarded the M.C.

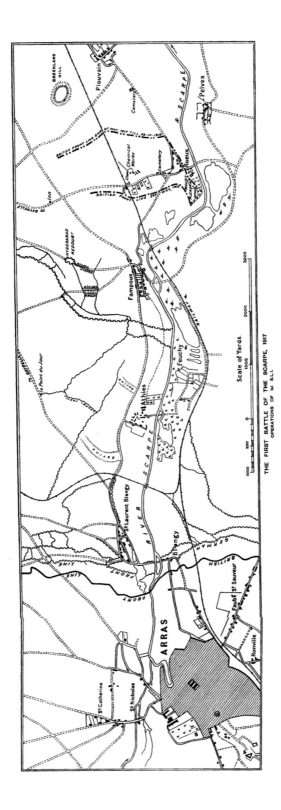

THE FIRST BATTLE OF THE SCARPE, 1917
OPERATIONS OF 1st S.L.I.

would greatly facilitate the next attack.   But the 1st Somersets were not called upon again, for late the same night the Battalion was relieved by troops of the 10th Brigade and marched back to the old fourth German system of trenches north of Fampoux, where it (or all that remained of the Battalion) came once more under its own Brigade.   It was 2 a.m. on the 5th before the Somerset men reached this position.

The Battles of Arras, 1917, were over—the official despatches thus sum up the results:—

"On the British front alone in less than one month's fighting we had captured over 19,500 prisoners, including over 400 officers, and had also taken 257 guns, including 98 heavy guns, with 464 machine guns, 227 trench mortars and immense quantities of other war material.   Our line had been advanced to a greatest depth exceeding 5 miles on a front of over 20 miles, representing a gain of some 60 square miles of trenching.   A great improvement had been effected in the general situation of our troops on the front attacked, and the capture of the Vimy Ridge had removed a constant menace to the security of our line."

But, gallant and splendid as were the attacks of the assaulting troops, the cost had been great.   The Somerset Light Infantry had lost heavily in officers and other ranks and, though they had inflicted equal losses on the enemy, it was poor comfort for the loss of so many valuable lives.

CHAPTER XXIV

THE FORMATION OF THE 12TH BATTALION SOMERSET LIGHT INFANTRY AND THE SECOND BATTLE OF GAZA

12th Battalion

THE Spring of 1917 not only witnessed Allied offensives on the Western Front but in other theatres of the War also. In the Balkans early in March the Allies launched an offensive to free Monastir; almost simultaneously Baghdad was occupied by British Forces, while towards the end of the month the British offensive into Palestine began, the First Battle of Gaza taking place on the 26th and 27th March. In these operations, however, the Somerset Light Infantry were not engaged, and it was not until the Second Battle of Gaza (17th–19th April 1917) that a Battalion of the Regiment—the 12th—took part in the British offensive which had as its object the freeing of Palestine from Turkish domination.

January

The 12th Battalion Somerset Light Infantry was originally the 1/1st West Somerset Yeomanry. The metamorphosis took place early in January 1917, when the 74th (Yeomanry) Division was formed. In December 1916, the West Somerset Yeomanry had moved to Moascar Camp, Ismailia, on the banks of the Suez Canal. Here, from the arrival of quantities of infantry drill books and infantry instructions and the joining up of a number of officers from England, who talked of nothing but platoons (instead of troops) and bugles (not trumpets), it was evident to the Yeomen that a change was imminent in the organization and functions of their beloved Regiment. But to their credit let it be said that they met the change philosophically and cheerfully, entering into their altered conditions with right good will.

"Infantry drill now became an obsession: squad, platoon, company and battalion drill, in succession caused many searchings of heart and of the drill book, while the Colonel's ready adoption of the new order of things caused less adaptable folk to marvel at his versatility." [1]

In the reshuffling and reorganization in which the Regiment was now engaged the Yeomanry personnel of N.C.O.'s and men became extinct and emerged with new regimental numbers as members of the Somerset Light Infantry. The Yeomanry officers remained so to the end, being "attached" to the 12th Battalion Somerset Light Infantry. From a three-squadron regiment the Yeomen became a four-company battalion. Lieut.-Col. F. N. Q. Shuldham was the C.O. and the four Companies were commanded as follows: H.Qs. and A Company—Captain A. T. L. Richardson; B Company—Captain C. P. Hayward; C Company—Captain T. A. Rattray; and D Company— Captain E. F. S. Rodd. Major Poole was Second-in-Command.

[1] "A Record of the West Somerset Yeomanry, 1914–1919," by Capt. R. C. Boyle, M.C.

The 12th Somerset Light Infantry were brigaded with the 16th (Devon 12th Battalion Yeomanry) Battalion, Devonshire Regiment, 14th (Ayr and Lanark Yeomanry) Battalion, Royal Scots Fusiliers, and 14th (Fife and Forfar Yeomanry) Battalion, Royal Highlanders.   The Brigade was the 229th (74th Division), the remaining Brigades being the 230th and 231st.

The official date of the reorganization was 7th January 1917, and three 7th January days later the Battalion marched to El Ferdan on the Suez Canal and

"at that blighted spot worked hard and unceasingly during the whole of January and February at infantry drill and tactics, night marches and outposts, varied with musketry, bombing and football, with opportunities for which our camp was well supplied." [1]

From the sandy discomforts of El Ferdan the 12th Somersets moved early in March to Kantara, *en route* for El Arish, where the 74th Division was concentrating.   The Battalion was fortunate in being railed up to the latter place, arriving on 8th March, thus avoiding the long and weary desert marches to which the troops who had fought their way across the Sinai Peninsula had been subjected.

On 21st March the 74th Division began its forward march and successively 21st March the Somersets bivouacked at El Burj, Sheikh Zowaid and Rafa.   Whilst the Battalion was in bivouacs at Sheikh Zowaid (26th March) the First Battle of Gaza began and ended on 27th, the official despatches giving the results in the following words:—

"primary and secondary objects were completely attained, but that the failure to attain the third object—the capture of Gaza—owing to the delay caused by fog on the 26th, and the waterless nature of the country round Gaza, prevented a most successful operation from being a complete disaster to the enemy." [2]

In consequence of that Battle, however, the divisions in reserve were immediately ordered forward and, on the 29th of the month, the 12th Somersets arrived at Khan Yunus (the traditional birthplace of Delilah) and took over the outpost line from the 8th Scottish Rifles of the 52nd Division.   Three Companies were placed out in the line and one in support with Battalion Headquarters.

It would appear that the term "outpost line" was something of a misnomer, but it was not so, for the line of advance ran parallel with, and close to, the seashore, and the Somersets were therefore on L. of C. protecting the railhead and the right flank of the Battalion, stretching out into open country, was to a certain extent exposed to the enemy.   The outpost line ran roughly around the entrances to Khan Yunus, its main direction facing east, with Battalion Headquarters in the village of Beni Sela.   The line was an extraordinary

[1] "A Record of the West Somerset Yeomanry, 1914–1919," by Capt. R. C. Boyle, M.C.

[2] The result of the First Battle of Gaza was that about 1½ miles of country in front of the town were permanently occupied.

length and a company commander's nightly round took a considerable time to complete.

On the 6th April the Battalion was again on the move, marching to Deir el Belah.   The 12th Somersets, after passing through the Brigades and Battalions of the 54th Division resting after their efforts of 26th/27th March, were now in immediate support of the front line of the Army.

The next attempt to capture Gaza had been fixed to begin on 17th April, but before that date much work had to be done.   It was necessary for the next advance that two divisions should be able to water in the Wadi Ghuzze where the prospects of obtaining water by well-sinking were small.   Tanks therefore had to be set up in the Wadi and arrangements made to pump rail-borne water from Deir el Belah over the In Seirat Ridge to fill them.   In front of the outpost line was the hill of Um Jerrar (the Gerar of the Bible), bored with many a well and cistern, and these cisterns were being filled at night by endless streams of camels loaded with their burdens of two full water fanatis apiece. Nightly protection for these wells and for the camel convoys filling them was the work of the support battalions of the 229th Brigade, and the outposts covering them were furnished by the 12th Somersets in turn with other units of the Brigade.

Sufficient water having been collected the operations began.

Although the 74th Division was in general reserve during the Second Battle of Gaza and the 12th Somersets were not, therefore, engaged with the enemy, the part played by the Battalion (though small) is of interest to the Regiment.

In the general plan of operations three infantry divisions and two cavalry divisions were to advance in two stages.   The first stage was to be the occupation of the Sheikh Abbas–Mansura Ridge, south of Gaza, and its preparation as a strong point from which any flank attack could be easily repelled.   A short period of development was then to elapse during which the water supply and communications could be improved, heavy artillery and tanks brought up and supplies advanced so that the final stage—an advance on Gaza after a heavy bombardment—should be accomplished rapidly.   The British dispositions were as follows: The 54th Division, on the right, and 52nd Division, on the left, were to seize and occupy the line Sheikh Abbas–Mansura–Kurd Hill; the 53rd Division to remain in position just north of the Wadi Ghuzze between the sea and the Gaza–Khan Yunus road, but to reconnoitre strongly northward along the coast; the 74th Division to remain in general reserve in the neighbourhood of In Seirat.   Of the Desert Column (two mounted divisions and the Imperial Camel Corps) one division was to be disposed about Shellal with the object of immobilizing enemy forces at Hereira, while the remainder of the Column protected the right flank of the 54th Division. Against these forces the Turks disposed at least five infantry divisions and a cavalry division, in a chain of detachments, along the 16 miles between Sheria and Gaza, with strong trenches at El Atawineh.   South-east and south-west of Gaza the enemy's defences were of a formidable nature.

The right of the enemy's line between Gaza and the sea ran in an arc of a circle west and south-west of the town. This section consisted of a double line of trenches and redoubts, strongly held by infantry and machine guns well placed and concealed in impenetrable cactus hedges, built of high mud banks enclosing orchards and gardens on the outskirts of the town. The enemy's machine guns were manned by Germans who were specialists in this work.

At dawn on the 17th April the advance began and by 7 a.m. the Sheikh Abbas–Mansura–Kurd Hill positions were taken with little opposition and practically no casualties. At nightfall on 19th the position, approximately, was that the 53rd Division held the Samson Ridge–Sheikh Ajlin line, the 52nd Division on its right facing north towards Outpost Hill and Ali Muntar; the 54th Division carried the line south-eastwards and southwards round the Sheikh Abbas Ridge to El Meshrefe, whence the mounted troops continued the line southwards to the Wadi Ghuzze.

All day long the 74th Division remained in General Reserve. The 12th Somersets moved up to In Seirat on 8th and occupied this position until 18th with parties sent out to guard the water cisterns at Um Jerrar, awaiting orders to join in the operations. But none came that day. Indeed, it was not until 7.45 a.m. on 19th that the Battalion advanced again. At that hour the Somerset men moved off from their bivouacs at In Seirat and crossed the Wadi Ghuzze at 8.30 a.m. At 11 a.m. they halted and took up a position of readiness on the southern slopes of a Wadi about 800 yards S.E. of Tel el Ahmar in rear of the 54th Division. At 7.30 p.m. A, B and C Companies again advanced and occupied a position on the Mansura Ridge, D Company providing picquets at the head of the Happy Valley. The Battalion's first casualties in Palestine occurred this day. During the first halt on the battlefield a few minor wounds from shell fire were suffered and at night one man was killed. Colonel Shuldham was slightly wounded in the hand but remained at duty.

On the morning of the 20th April—as the Turks were reported to be concentrating for a counter-attack on the right flank—the 12th Somersets moved off at 7.30, via Tel el Ahmar, and crossed the Wadi Nahhabir. This counter-attack, however, never developed, and, as it was evident that the Second Battle of Gaza was over, consolidation of the ground gained was begun. On 22nd, at 5.30 p.m., the Battalion moved to El Mendur, where B and C Companies began work on the new trenches and A and D Companies occupied the outpost line.

With the close of the operations on the night of the 19th April the first offensive in the Invasion of Palestine ended. For some months it was not possible to launch the second offensive (27th October), by which time the Battles of Ypres, 1917, had begun on the Western Front.

CHAPTER XXV

THE BATTLES OF YPRES, 1917

THE object of an operation, or of a particular group of operations, must always be the first consideration of a student of military history. Even from a regimental point of view the actions of one battalion, or a number of battalions of that regiment, cannot be intelligently appreciated unless a general idea of the Army Commander's intentions, briefly outlined, prefaces the actual record of the battle or battles. Therefore, before describing those battles of the Battles of Ypres, 1917, in which the Somerset Light Infantry took part, it is helpful to consider for a moment Sir Douglas Haig's intentions before the operations began. Two paragraphs in the official despatches [1] supply the key to the plans adopted by the British Commander-in-Chief and French General Headquarters.

In describing his scheme of operations for launching the Arras Offensive of 1917, Sir Douglas Haig said:—

"With the force at my disposal, even combined with what the French proposed to undertake in co-operation,[2] I did not consider that any great strategical results were likely to be gained by following up a success on the front about Arras and to the south of it, beyond the capture of the objectives aimed at. . . . It was therefore my intention to transfer my main offensive to another part of my front after these objectives had been secured."

And, again:—

"It was further agreed that if this combined offensive did not produce the full results hoped for within a reasonable time the main efforts of the British Armies should then be transferred to Flanders as I had originally intended."

But neither the British offensive at Arras nor the French attack on the Chemin des Dames in May had produced "the decisive action which it had been hoped might follow," and Sir Douglas Haig turned his attention to the northern plan of attack. An essential preliminary was the capture of the Messines–Wytschaete Ridge, which, "owing to the observation from it over our positions farther north in the Ypres Salient," was absolutely necessary.

The attack began on 7th June and continued until the 14th, by which time Wytschaete had been captured and with it the whole of the ground north

---

[1] It cannot be too urgently insisted that the reading of the official despatches, side by side with regimental histories, is the only method of appreciating the value of the fighting of any particular battalion or battalions.

[2] The French were to attack on the Aisne.

AERIAL VIEW OF YPRES, OCTOBER, 1917

and south, from east of Hill 60 to just north of Battle Wood, which had for so long enabled the enemy to overlook the British trenches.

The preliminary operations ended, final preparations for the main offensive north and east of Ypres were hurried on, as the first attack was to be launched on 31st July. The front of attack in the first battle (Battle of Pilkem Ridge, 31st July–2nd August) extended from the Lys River opposite Deulemont northwards to beyond Steenstraat, a distance of just over 15 miles. The main blow, however, was to be delivered by the Fifth Army on a front of about 7½ miles from the Zillebeke–Zandvoorde road to Boesinghe, inclusive. The Second Army was to advance only a short distance, its orders being to cover the right flank of the Fifth Army, but to increase the area threatened by attack with the object of forcing the enemy to distribute his artillery fire. The First French Army was to advance on the left of the Fifth British Army.

But it is only with the attack by the Second Army, of which the 37th Division then formed part, that this narrative is concerned, one Battalion (8th) of the Somerset Light Infantry being engaged in the operations.[1]

It will be remembered that after the Battle of Arleux (28th–29th April) 8th Battalion the 8th Somersets, after withdrawal from the front line, reached Beaufort on 30th April and billeted in the village, the 63rd Brigade (37th Division) having been allotted the Lignereuil area. The 37th Division was now out of the line for a month's "rest," though all units were training hard during that period. At the end of May the 63rd Brigade moved back into the line for two or three days though only in support, relieving the 111th Brigade in and around Tilloy from 28th to 31st of the month. On the latter date the Brigade marched back to billets in Arras. On the 1st June the Brigade was again on the move to 1st June the Manin–Beaufort area where training was again begun. The 8th Somersets were billeted in Manin, but only for a few days, for on the 6th, 7th and 8th the Battalion moved to Hericourt, Bergueneuse and Fruges respectively, carrying out training in the latter place until 21st. On the 22nd the Somersets (in Brigade) began to move north to the Scherpenberg area, arriving on 25th June. Two days later the 37th Division was ordered to relieve the 36th (Ulster) Division in the sector extending from the Blauwepoortbeek to Rose Farm inclusive: the 63rd Infantry Brigade was to relieve the 109th Brigade in the front line from about Joye Farm to Rose Wood. The 8th Somersets left Scherpenberg on the night of 29th and relieved a battalion of the York 29th June and Lancs Regiment in the right support line of the left sub-sector, i.e. Joye Farm to Rose Wood. Until the last day of July the month was uneventful, the Battalion doing several tours in the front-line trenches, during which a number of casualties were suffered. The enemy's shell fire was at times very heavy. On 12th Lieut.-Colonel M. C. C. Miers [2] (the C.O., 8th Somerset

---

[1] Again it is necessary to point out the arbitrary decision of the Battles Nomenclature Committee. The boundary of the whole of the Battles of Ypres, 1917, is given as from the Comines–Ypres Canal to Bixschoote, therefore as the Second Army operated south of the Canal it is excluded, though its operations were successful and of the utmost tactical importance.

[2] Lieut.-Col. Miers took over command of the Battalion from Lieut.-Col. H. K. Umfreville on 10th July.

Light Infantry), Major J. G. Underwood and 2/Lieut. H. A. de F. Ford were wounded, while on 17th 2/Lieut. H. B. Smith and eight other ranks were killed, and 2/Lieuts. C. D. Hagon, G. Durston and A. J. Crease and

17th July

sixteen other ranks were wounded. It was on the night of July 17th that a working party consisting of about 60 was practically wiped out close to Battalion Headquarters, one officer and eight other ranks being killed and 50 wounded. On 13th Major H. S. C. Richardson arrived and assumed command of the Battalion *vice* Lieut.-Colonel Miers.

Preparations for the coming offensives occupied the troops whenever it was possible to detach them from trench warfare, and on the night of 30th July the 8th Somersets were in the front line, having relieved the 10th Royal Fusiliers on the previous night. Battalion Headquarters were at Lumm Farm.

THE BATTLE OF PILKEM, 31ST JULY–2ND AUGUST 1917

8th Battalion

It has already been stated that the rôle of the Second Army was to follow the right flank of the Fifth Army (apparently the 24th Division just west of Shrewsbury Forest) and increase the area threatened by the attack so as to compel the enemy to disperse his artillery fire over a wider front, and IX Corps orders (to which the 37th Division belonged) stated that, in conjunction with corps on the right and left, it was desired to create the impression that a serious attempt was being made to capture the Warneton-Zandvoorde line. But the objectives allotted to the 19th and 37th Divisions (IX Corps) were only from 1,000 to 1,500 yards in depth, running from the head of the road running south-west (and also 500 yards) from Hollebeke, thence to July Farm and from the latter to where the trenches cut the Blauwepoortbeek, about 500 yards east of Delporte Farm.

The attack of the IX Corps was to be in two phases: (*a*) at Zero hour north of July Farm by the 19th Division to which two Battalions (4th Middlesex and 8th Lincolns) of the 63rd Infantry Brigade (37th Division) were attached; (*b*) south of July Farm by the 63rd Infantry Brigade at Zero plus four hours, the 4th Middlesex and 8th Lincolns having again come under the orders of this Brigade at Zero plus three hours. In the second phase (*b*) of the operations the attack by the 63rd Brigade was to be made by the 10th York and Lancs Regiment and 8th Somerset Light Infantry. Such, briefly, were the orders so far as they affected the Somerset men. Zero hour was to be 3.50 a.m. on 31st July.

The defences at this period between Hollebeke and Warneton were still far from complete. The enemy's main line, along the Divisional front, from Cinema Road ran roughly through Head Farm, Bow Farm, Eel, Trout and Pill Farms (the latter forming a strong salient), thence through Trio Farm back to the banks of the Comines–Ypres Canal just west of Kortewilde. But out in front of this line he had strong protective detachments occupying the many farms which lay between the opposing lines of trenches. Of these, Beek, Wam, July, May, June, Rifle, Bab, Bee and Wasp Farms were (from the Divisional point of view) the most important. The British front line was very irregular, running directly south (though much broken) from a point about 700 yards west of Hollebeke. Some idea of the nature of the line may be gathered from the fact that when, between 10 and 11 p.m., on the night of 30th July the 8th Somersets moved forward in readiness for the operations on 31st, the Battalion occupied the "Shell Hole Line" between Grass Farm on the right and the Wambeek Stream on the left. Three Companies—A, C and D—occupied this line, C Company in shell holes on the right and D Company, with A Company in immediate support, just in advance of the "Shell Hole Line" on the left: B Company had gone out as a covering party prior to the move forward of A, C and D Companies.

Scant details are given of the attack by the Second Army in conjunction with the main operations by the Fifth Army which began at 3.50 a.m. on the morning of 31st July. But while the latter was advancing and overrunning the enemy's front and second-line defences, the 41st Division of the former had captured Hollebeke, and south of the latter village the 19th and 37th Divisions were advancing their line to a depth of from 200 to 800 yards, every part of which had been bloodily contested.

At 3.50 a.m. the 4th Middlesex (63rd Brigade, 37th Division), prolonging the right of the 19th Division, advanced under an artillery barrage to the line of its objective, July Farm–Rifle Farm, while a company of the 8th Lincolns also advanced and formed a defensive flank with its left on July Farm and its right thrown back to the British line about 100 yards north of the Wambeek. The Lincolns were thus in touch with the left flank of the 8th Somersets who, lying close in their shell holes, were awaiting Zero hour for the second phase of the attack.

Into what happened to the gallant Middlesex men who had gained their objectives—the line July Farm–Rifle Farm—it is impossible to go. Neither is it possible to more than mention the grim hand-to-hand struggle which took place between a party of Middlesex men and the enemy in front of Bab Farm and which, from all accounts, was of a desperate and bloody nature, the Brigade narrative stating that: "This party fought it out where they were until they were all either killed or wounded."

Before Zero hour (7.50 a.m.) for the second phase of the attack arrived the enemy's barrage had fallen on the front-line and support trenches occupied by the Somersets. A few casualties occurred, 2/Lieut. H. R. Kirk being severely wounded and dying soon afterwards. At 5 a.m. Lt.-Colonel Richardson (commanding 8th Somersets), whose H.Qs. were in a dug-out on a road just west of Anzac Farm, was informed by a liaison officer that Rifle Farm had been captured. From July Farm the line now ran northwards through Rifle Farm, but south of the former, and bent sharply back to the "Shell Hole Line," the Lincolns forming the defensive flank. On the left of the Lincolns the Somerset men were awaiting the order to advance, i.e. the second phase of the attack.

At 7.50 a.m. D Company of the Somersets, with C Company on the right and two companies of Lincolns on the left, advanced to clear Beek Wood and to establish a new line from the Wambeek just south of Wam Farm to a post which the 10th York and Lancaster Regiment (on the right of C Company, Somersets) had been ordered to establish near Grass Farm. For some while no information reached Battalion Headquarters of the results of the attack, until at 9 a.m. Captain Hunt,[1] who had been shot in the left arm, returned and reported to Colonel Richardson that the western outskirts of Beek Farm and the enclosures about the Farm had been reached, his Company (A) being then engaged in digging-in. Apparently A Company, in support of D Company, had moved up into the front line during the attack. At 10 a.m. a progress report from Captain H. G. Baker (O.C., D Company) reached Battalion Headquarters stating that two platoons of D had gone forward to clear Beek Wood, the remainder of the Company digging-in on the left of A Company, in touch with the Lincolns; all officers of A Company had become casualties, Captain Hunt and 2/Lieuts. Kirk and Adam being wounded, and that A Company was not in touch with C Company on the right, but the latter could be seen digging-in on the other side of a small ridge. Meanwhile, Rifle Farm, which had been captured in the first advance, had been recaptured by the enemy, and as this exposed the left of the Lincolns at July Farm, that Battalion withdrew its left to June Farm. At 1.5 p.m. a Somersets' runner from Captain Baker brought back a report that the remainder of the two platoons of D, which had gone forward to clear Beek Wood, had returned, that posts had been established at the N.W. and S.W. corners of the enclosures at the Farm and that 2/Lieut. Blake had been killed. The next report, which came to hand at 3 p.m., stated that Captain Baker had been wounded and that C Company was digging-in, in touch with the 10th York and Lancaster Regt. on the right. Finally, another progress report reached Battalion Headquarters about 5.40 p.m., also from Captain Baker, which stated that platoons sent forward had returned and two posts had been established north and south of Beek Farm; he had many casualties, but at that hour it was impossible to bring in the wounded.

Throughout the day the artillery and machine-gun fire of the opposing sides had been very heavy and snipers were also extremely active. The enemy's advanced detachments were well entrenched and in several places were able to enfilade the British positions, but his troops on many occasions provided fine targets for the divisional artillery and the machine gunners and a heavy toll was taken: on both sides the casualties were very heavy.[2]

A threatened counter-attack about 8 p.m. was reported by the Heavy Artillery observers, who saw the enemy was massing, but the guns opened quickly and the threatened attack did not materialize.

Throughout the night the captured positions were consolidated, companies reorganized and posts were established. B Company of the Somersets moved up from the old Shell Hole Line and filled the gap between A and

---

[1] Capt. H. J. Hunt was awarded the M.C. for conspicuous gallantry on this occasion.

[2] 2/Lieut. H. K. Pople was awarded the M.C., and Sergt. F. Wells and L/Cpl. G. W. A. Hobbs the D.C.M., for conspicuous gallantry on 31st July 1917.

C Companies, and C Company of the 10th York and Lancaster Regt. was moved into the old Shell Hole Line, in support of the Somerset Light Infantry; a company of Royal Fusiliers was also placed in reserve to the Somersets, under the O.C. of the latter Battalion.

The line gained by the 63rd Brigade on 31st July varied in depth from a few yards to 400 yards.

The 1st August passed quietly, no counter-attacks being made by the enemy, and during the night of 1st/2nd August the 8th Somersets were relieved by the 13th Royal Fusiliers and marched back (independently of other units of the 63rd Brigade who had also been relieved) to the reserve line east of Kemmel. Here one night was spent, and on the following morning the Battalion continued its journey to Dramoutre.

Before the 63rd Brigade was relieved a message, dated 31st July, had been received from the Divisional Commander: "The Divisional Commander congratulates you heartily on your magnificent fight to-day." And on the 3rd August Sir Douglas Haig wired to the G.O.C., Second Army:—

"My warmest congratulations to you personally and to Commanders, Staffs and Troops under your command for the complete success of the Second Army operations yesterday. Such a satisfactory opening to the Battle is full of promise for further and still greater successes."

And of the northern attack (the attack by the Fifth Army) Sir Douglas said in his despatches: "At the end of the day (31st July) therefore, our troops on the Fifth Army front had carried the German first system of defence south of Westhoek. Except at Westhoek itself, where they were established on the outskirts of the village, they had already gained the whole of the crest of the ridge and had denied the enemy observation over the Ypres plain. Farther north they had captured the enemy's second line also as far as St. Julien. North of that village they had passed beyond the German second line and held the line of the Steenbeek to our junction with the French" (just north of the Ypres–Staden railway).

Small as were the operations of the Second Army, compared with those of the Fifth Army, they were, nevertheless, completely successful. Many brave and gallant soldiers had given their lives and many more were wounded in order that the Battle north of the Ypres–Comines Canal might yield the results anticipated. The 8th Somersets had lost heavily. On 31st 2/Lieuts. H. R. Kirk and F. W. R. Blake were killed, and Captains H. J. Hunt and H. G. Baker, Lieut. S. Donne and 2/Lieut. R. Wadams were wounded. In other ranks the Battalion lost 37 killed, 90 wounded, 6 wounded and missing, and 14 missing. On 1st August 2/Lieut. W. R. Worsley was killed.

THE BATTLE OF LANGEMARCK, 16TH–18TH AUGUST 1917

The operations of 31st July/3rd August had shaken the enemy badly. Along the whole front of the attack the Germans had lost ground to a depth of from two to four kilometres, and what was even more serious for the enemy,

7th Battalion

he had sustained considerable losses in prisoners and stores, and a heavy expenditure of reserves. Of the Battle of Langemarck, which opened on 16th August, General Ludendorff said: "We sustained another great blow." That the Battle was postponed until the 16th of the month was due entirely to the bad weather, for during the fighting of 31st July rain fell and continued all through the night and thereafter for four days. The low-lying, clayey soil, torn by shells and sodden with rain, turned to a succession of vast muddy pools. The valleys of the choked and overflowing streams were speedily transformed into long stretches of bog, impassable except by a few well-defined tracks which became marks for the enemy's artillery. To leave these tracks was to risk death by drowning. In these conditions operations of any magnitude became impossible. Thus again the weather intervened on the side of the enemy, for, as in the Arras Battle, this unavoidable delay in the development of the offensive was of the greatest service to the Germans, enabling them to bring up their reserves, improve their defences and generally prepare for the next attack. It was not until the 16th August that the attack took place. It was in this Battle that the enemy's "pill boxes" (strong points built of reinforced concrete many feet thick) first came into prominence.

The second of the Battles of Ypres, which had been planned for the 16th August, was to begin at 4.45 a.m., the front of attack, east and north of Ypres, extending from the north-west corner of Inverness Copse to the junction of the French and British Armies south of St. Janshoek. The French, on the left of the Fifth British Army, were to clear up the remainder of the Bixschoote Peninsula. From right to left it is impossible to give the British Divisions engaged in the Battle, but the left of the assault was carried out by the 29th and 20th Divisions,[1] by the former on Wijdendrift and by the latter on Langemarck itself. The 20th Division had been in reserve during the Battle of Pilkem, in the Houtkerque–Proven area, having moved up to the Ypres Salient about the middle of July.

For nearly seven months the 20th Division had been fighting and digging continuously in the Somme area. In the German retreat of March it had followed up the enemy from Sailly-Saillisel to the Hindenburg Line opposite Havrincourt Wood, a distance of about 10 miles, side-stepping to the left to the Lagnicourt–Noreuil sector, where a great deal of work had been carried out on the defences, the Division harassing the enemy meanwhile. As the Divisional Commander (Major-General Matheson) said: "The spirit which had been shown in all these operations, rewarded as they have been by no sensational victory or startling success, is beyond all praise." The 7th Battalion of the Somerset Light Infantry, as part of the 61st Brigade, 20th Division, had taken its full share of the fighting and hardships through which the Division had passed.

5th April

On the 5th April the 7th Battalion had moved up from Le Transloy into trenches about 2 miles S.E. of Lechelle. On the 7th the Somersets moved

---

[1] With the Guards and 38th (Welsh) Divisions, the 29th and 20th Divisions formed the XIV Corps, Fifth Army.

to Metz, relieving the 12th King's Regiment in the front line. Two days   7th Battalion
later the Battalion took part in an attack on Havrincourt Wood, driving the
enemy from the southern part of it and establishing an outpost line 300 yards
inside the Wood. In this attack the Somersets lost only one man killed and
seven wounded. The attack was made at 4 p.m. without artillery support,
as the Divisional guns were still struggling in the mud on the other side of
Le Transloy. The surprise of the enemy was complete, as he was having his
tea when the first wave of the Somersets arrived. The German picquets put
up a fight but were soon driven back and by 7 p.m. the new outpost line was
established and the men were enjoying an excellent meal which the Germans
had, therefore, left behind them.

No counter-attack followed this small, but successful, exploit, and, on
14th April, the outpost line was again pushed forward another 500 yards   14th April
without opposition. Yet another advance took place on the night of 27th,
the line was pushed forward 1,000 yards from the Wood in full view of Havrincourt Village, which was part of the Hindenburg Main Line Defences. The
posts were sited and dug during the night and, contrary to expectation, the
enemy, excepting a few bursts of machine-gun fire, remained quiet.

May was a quiet month. The 61st Brigade was relieved on 19th by a
brigade of the 42nd Division and marched back to billets in Ruyaulcourt.
The next day the Battalion marched to Beaulencourt and on the 21st
to Beugnatre, relieving a battalion of Australian infantry. On the 28th the
7th Somersets moved forward, relieving the 11th Battalion, 60th Rifles, in
the support line S.E. of Lagnicourt. At this period Lagnicourt was a very
peaceful part of the line, No Man's Land being about 1,000 yards wide. On
the previous day, while reconnoitring the way up to the trenches, Lieut. J.
Scott was wounded. On 1st June 2/Lieut. A. D. Kinsey was wounded and
on the 5th Captain C. D. Holt and one other rank became casualties (wounded)   1st June
from shell fire. From the support trenches the Somersets moved into the
front line on 6th June, relieving the 12th King's Regt. On the 7th seven
other ranks were killed, four by shell fire and three by snipers. The snipers'
bullets came from an advanced enemy post alongside the road to Pronville
and a raid was organized to deal with it. Patrols went out to reconnoitre
the post on the nights of 8th, 9th and 10th, and on the latter occasion 2/Lieut.
Fry and his orderly tumbled into a German patrol and were captured.

The raid was carried out on the night 12th/13th by a platoon of A Com-   12th/13th June
pany, under the command of 2/Lieut. C. J. Lewin.[1] A box barrage of 18-pdrs.
was first placed on the enemy post and at 12 midnight the raiding party rushed
the post with the bayonet, killing 18 Germans and capturing one man alive.
Others were seen to run back from the post, but they were caught in the barrage
and must have suffered further casualties. The captured German provided
a much-needed identification and the raiding party was congratulated by the
Corps Commander on its fine work. On 26th June 2/Lieut. W. L. Betteley

[1] For conspicuous gallantry during this raid 2/Lieut. Lewin was awarded the M.C. and L/Cpl.
A. J. H. Gibbs the D.C.M.

(7th Somerset Light Infantry and Brigade Intelligence Officer) was killed whilst reconnoitring out in No Man's Land—"A gallant officer much regretted by all ranks."

On 1st July the 61st Brigade entrained at Achiet-le-Grand for Candas, the 7th Somersets marching thence to billets in Atheux. In the latter place training and organization were carried out until 19th of the month when, the 20th Division having been ordered up to the Ypres Salient, a move north began. On 20th the Somerset men detrained at Godewaersvelde and marched to Haandeket, a collection of a few farms between Watou and Rousbrugge–Haringhe. There was, however, no accommodation for the troops, who went into bivouacs.

On 1st August, the Battles of Ypres having begun on the previous day, the 7th Somersets moved to Paddock Wood—a canvas camp on the Houtkerque–Proven road and about a mile from the latter village. The 20th Division was once more in the XIV Corps, under Lord Cavan, the other Divisions of the Corps being the Guards, 38th and 29th. In the first of the Battles (The Battle of Pilkem Ridge, 31st July–2nd August) the 20th Division was in reserve and the Somersets, therefore, were not engaged with the enemy. The Battalion remained in camp near Proven until 4th August, when it moved up to another camp near Dawson's Corner, a well-known spot on the Elverdinghe–Braelen road, as the 20th Division had been ordered to relieve the 38th Division on the night of the 5th.

During the daylight hours of 5th August the 7th Somersets moved up to the Pilkem Ridge and took cover in some old German trenches. The latter had been considerably knocked about by the British artillery before the battle and in their wrecked condition did not offer much protection. The Ridge was under shell fire, for the enemy kept the positions which had been wrested from him under a vicious storm of shell. During the afternoon Captain and Adjutant F. S. Mills, who had just stepped out of a trench to visit a company in another trench, was killed by a shell: seven N.C.O.'s and men were also killed or wounded.

As soon as darkness had fallen the relief of the 38th Division began. The front line was a series of posts in shell holes running from the railway to the Langemarck road, along the main bank of the Steenbeek. This stream, which was to become terribly familiar to the Somerset men, needs further description. Normally it was a small winding stream from 14 to 17 feet wide, and of an average depth of 7 feet. When the Battalion first made its acquaintance, however, it had been shelled so heavily that the banks were much knocked about; the bed of the stream was also full of great shell holes so that it had become a serious obstacle and the only means of crossing it was by the practically destroyed bridge of the Boesinghe–Standen railway or a bridge, also practically destroyed, on the Pilkem–Langemarck road.

About 500 yards in rear of the shell-holed front line was the support line, also a series of shell holes; the reserve line was still another 500 yards farther back, where an old trench sheltered the reserve company and a concrete "Pill

Box" with its door facing the wrong way, known as Periscope House, Battalion Headquarters.

Rain fell heavily during the night and the shell holes became slimy pits. The men dug hard trying to improve their position, but as the whole country was liquid mud little work of a satisfactory nature could be done. Daylight dawned on the 6th miserable and wet. Throughout the day rain continued to fall from the leaden skies. With devilish persistence the enemy's guns shelled the outpost lines and the advanced positions of the British artillery. For the first time the Somerset men experienced mustard gas, and five men were sent back suffering from gas poisoning. One N.C.O. and one private were killed and fifteen other ranks wounded. Periscope House was taken over by 61st Bde. Adv. H.Qs., and Bn. H.Qs. moved to Stray Farm—a more secure spot but a loathsome place. The farm had been used by the Germans as a soup kitchen for troops going to and from the front line: it had a large cellar in which were bunks. The latter were an advantage, for the floor was covered by black slime and water to a depth of about a foot, which stank horribly whenever stirred up, and baling and pumping made no impression on it.

The 7th saw no change in the conditions, but casualties were heavier. At about 4 p.m. the enemy put down a barrage on the line Vulcan–Iron Cross–Stray Farm. The Signal Officer—2/Lieut. W. B. Paul—was wounded; 12 other ranks were killed, 20 wounded and 2 were missing.

Relief came that night, the Rifles marching in and taking over the position held by the 7th Somersets who moved back to Roussel Camp; the 61st Brigade had been taken out of the line to fatten up (as Colonel Troyte-Bullock said in his diary) for the next battle, and the 59th Brigade (which relieved the 61st) had received orders to push the line of outposts on to the eastern banks of the Steenbeek, sufficiently far forward to cover the troops assembling on that side for the attack. In Roussel Camp the Somersets remained until the 14th August, getting ready for the Battle of Langemarck, due to begin on 16th.

On the 14th, after dinner, the 7th Somersets marched to Solferino Farm and halted. Here the remainder of the day was spent, Companies drawing tools, bombs, etc., after which tea was issued. Later, just as the men were putting on their equipment and getting ready to move up to the front line, the enemy's artillery opened fire on an 8-inch howitzer battery in action near the farm. A hostile shell fell and exploded right in the middle of a platoon of B Company, killing seven men and wounding twenty, indeed the platoon was almost wiped out. The strength of the attacking troops of the Battalion, all ranks, was only about 470, so that the loss of 27 men before the operations began was a serious matter.

The Battalion moved off as soon as possible after this unfortunate incident and it was dark when the line held by the 59th Brigade, west of Steenbeek, was reached. The Brigade had had a terrible time in the outpost line and had only succeeded in pushing a few posts just across the stream. Hostile machine-gun fire from a very strong pill box, Au Bon Gite, had continually swept the positions held by the Brigade, whose losses had been heavy. All attempts to capture this strong point, and all endeavours by the Divisional Artillery to destroy it, had proved fruitless. Orders to the 61st Brigade definitely stated that the posts of the 59th Brigade across the Steenbeek were not to be relieved until the 61st were assembled for the attack on the eastern bank. By dawn on 15th the 61st was assembled and the remnants of the 59th moved back to reserve positions.

The 15th was uneventful. The early morning mist enabled all officers to reconnoitre the crossing places for their companies by daylight. These consisted of two somewhat rickety bridges which the Sappers had placed across the stream. The Diary of the 7th Somersets for 15th August reads: "Battalion in front line in front of Langemarck, waiting to attack."

The strength of the Battalion was about 470 all ranks.

The order of battle of the 61st Brigade was: First Line—7th Somerset Light Infantry on the right, 7th K.O.Y.L.I. on the left. Second Line—12th King's (Liverpool) Regiment on the right and 7th D.C.L.I.[1] on the left. The 60th Brigade was to attack on the right of the 61st and the 88th Brigade (29th Division) on the left. Three objectives were given to the 61st Brigade: (i) The Blue Line, which ran along the western outskirts of Langemarck from the Station to the Cemetery; this objective was to be captured by the two leading companies of each first-line battalion. (ii) The Green Line, about 500 yards from the Blue Line and through the extreme eastern edge of the village; this objective was to be captured by the second-wave companies, who were to pass through the first wave as soon as the latter had captured the Blue Line. (iii) The Red Line, the first line of German trenches about 600 yards in front of the Green Line; this was to be captured by the two second-line battalions. The troops were to advance under three distinct barrages. The first was a creeping barrage, moving at the rate of 100 yards per five minutes, the infantry following close behind; the second, a standing barrage moving in front of the creeping barrage to engage definite objects and catch the enemy as he retired; the third, a back barrage, to search an area of from 300 to 1,200 yards in front of the advancing infantry and keep down the enemy's machine-gun fire. A machine-gun barrage of 48 guns, firing on selected areas, was also to cover the advance of the troops. In addition, low-flying aeroplanes were to pass over the enemy's lines firing machine guns to keep the Germans down in their shell holes.

It was expected that Au Bon Gite, a strong enemy post which lay on the right boundary of the 61st Brigade, between the jumping-off line and the first objective, would cause trouble.

The night of 15th/16th August was spent in making final preparations. The attacking troops had to be in position on the Steenbeek an hour before Zero, which had been fixed for 4.45 a.m.

Of the 7th Somersets, A Company, on the right, and D Company, on

[1] The 7th D.C.L.I. was commanded by Lt.-Col. H. G. R. Burges-Short, detached from 2nd Bn. Somerset Light Infantry.

7th Battalion

the left, were to form the first wave. In darkness these two Companies set out to take over the outpost line from the 11th Rifle Brigade. They had to cross the flooded stream, whose banks were boggy and slippery with slimy mud. The garrisons of the posts on the eastern bank had only been able to push forward about seventy-five yards from the bank and in that limited space the leading Battalions had to form up for the attack. A few yards away on the right flank there was an enemy machine-gun nest very much on the alert. The position of the enemy on the immediate front of the Battalion was doubtful, and beyond the fact that he was holding a line of shell-hole posts about 125 yards in advance of the British post, his exact positions had not been located.

B Company, on the right, and C Company, on the left, formed the second wave of the 7th Somerset Light Infantry. Soon after midnight the enemy began shelling the Langemarck–Pilkem road on either side of the Steenbeek and for half an hour plastered that area with 5·9 shells. But by 3.30 a.m. 16th August all Companies were assembled, though A, in getting into position on the eastern banks of the Steenbeek, had apparently been observed by the enemy, who opened fire with rifles and a 7·7 gun, causing about six casualties. Before reaching the Steenbeek Captain Ledsham, O.C., A Company, was severely wounded by a shell, and command of the Company was taken over by 2/Lieut. Lewin.

Immediately on reaching their allotted positions all Companies dug themselves in, and while this work was in progress the enemy frequently sent up Véry lights from Au Bon Gite and shell holes about fifty yards in front of A and D Companies; a certain amount of desultory hostile machine-gun and rifle fire swept the eastern banks of the Steenbeek, but casualties were few.

At 4.45 a.m. the creeping barrage fell with great precision on the enemy's shell-hole posts, and all along the line the advance began. A and D Companies of the Somersets moved forward immediately, but almost at once A was checked by flanking machine-gun fire from Au Bon Gite and the two remaining officers of the Company became casualties—2/Lieut. A. T. Kinsey being killed and 2/Lieut. Lewin wounded. The loss of these two officers caused A to lose direction and move across to the left flank. Captain Foley, commanding B Company (the right second-wave Company), had also been wounded and command of that Company was taken over by 2/Lieut. Goode. The latter, realizing that A had lost direction, pushed on with B and eventually took the first objective. Au Bon Gite was captured by B Company. After it had fallen the attacking troops pushed on with very little opposition from the front until a line of trenches west of the village was reached. Here the ground, which all along had been in a deplorable condition, became even worse. Men were continually stuck fast in the mud and had to pull each other out, the while, under a galling machine-gun fire from a line of concrete emplacements (pill boxes) near Reitres Farm: here the advance was checked.

The check lasted fourteen to fifteen minutes and during that time casualties were heavy. Eventually, largely through the gallantry of a private and an N.C.O. of the 7th K.O.Y.L.I. (the emplacements being in the area of that Battalion) the pill boxes were captured and the line of the first objective was reached by D Company and about two sections of A Company, the remainder of A having completely lost touch. Though wounded in the face and right leg, 2/Lieut. Hill, commanding D Company, remained in command until he was satisfied that his men were in good positions and had started to dig themselves in on the Blue Line. Then, having handed over command to his senior N.C.O., he returned to Battalion Headquarters, which by this time were established in shell holes about 500 yards due south of Langemarck Church, and reported his position to Colonel Troyte-Bullock.

At Zero plus 50 minutes (5.35 a.m.) B and C Companies left the Blue Line and followed the barrage right through the village, the Langemarck–Poelcapelle road being the inter-company boundary, the road and houses inclusive to C Company. Heavy machine-gun fire, again from concrete buildings at the N.W. end of the village, met the advance of these two Companies, who were also worried by hostile snipers from the right flank. Snipers from both Companies, however, were told off to deal with the enemy and, having reduced their activities to nil, B and C organized an attack on the front of the concrete buildings. Both Companies sent forward parties of bombers, under cover of Lewis-gun fire, and very soon the enemy's offensive was broken down, one German officer and 30 men surrendering. The next stronghold was dealt with in a similar manner, bombing parties working forward from shell hole to shell hole, finally bombing the enemy out of his stronghold. Forty more prisoners and four machine guns were captured here. This last operation effectively cleared the village and no further opposition was met with. The consolidation of the Green Line (second objective) was begun at once.

The enemy now opened heavy shell fire on the ground south of the southern enclosure of the village and the C.O. decided to move his Battalion Headquarters to a concreted building about 200 yards on the left of the Somersets' position. On reaching this place, however, he found the ground in such a boggy state that it was impossible to get forward from it, so Battalion Headquarters were moved to another building on the N.W. side of the Langemarck–Pilkem road, 450 yards east of the bridges over the Steenbeek. Colonel Troyte-Bullock then went forward to the first objective and got in touch with D Company, but not with A. He found the men consolidating their position amongst ruined houses and battered tree trunks. He then went to the southernmost cross-roads of the village, where stood a large concreted building, apparently the old cemetery chapel. From the top of this building he could get a good view as far as the crest of the ridge beyond the second objective.

At 7 a.m. (Zero plus 2 hours 55 minutes) the 12th King's crossed the line of the second objective on the way to the final objective, keeping close on the heels of the barrage. Away on the right of B Company of the 7th Somersets was a farm—Alouette Farm—and just as the King's passed through the second objective about seventy Germans left the farm buildings and began to run back, crossing the right flank of the Somerset men. The Lewis guns quickly got to work and at least 75 per cent. of the Germans were shot 7th Battalion down. 16th August

The time was now about 7.15 a.m. and the Somersets had reached all objectives allotted to the Battalion, touch being maintained on both flanks. The southern portion of Langemarck was under heavy shell fire, the enemy plastering the ruined houses and ground about the tumbled trenches with trench-mortar bombs and 5.9 shells. But the village was fortunately clear of troops, with the exception of those on the Blue Line, who had, however, provided themselves with a fair amount of cover.

Owing to heavy machine-gun fire the 12th King's had not been able to reach the Red Line, but had taken up positions about 200 yards from it, where they dug in. About 2 p.m. the King's sent back a message to the 7th Somersets asking for assistance, as they were losing heavily. The C.O. of the latter Battalion thereupon ordered Captain Jenks, O.C., C Company, to take his Company forward to reinforce the King's. This left the line of the second objective weak, so that D Company and a portion of A had to be sent up from the first objective to reinforce the second objective. During the night 16th/17th August the whole Battalion was concentrated on the line of the second objective and beyond it. The night passed quietly, but the men were forced to take shelter mostly in shell holes, for the R.E. parties, detailed for the construction of strong points, had arrived during the morning, but were unable to dig at all owing to heavy shell fire.

At sunset on 16th a Battalion of the Welch Regiment of the 38th Division had arrived at Colonel Troyte-Bullock's Headquarters. This Battalion rendered the Somerset men the greatest assistance during the night, one company moving to the southern end of the village, another to the N.W. of 7th Somersets' Battalion Headquarters and two companies to the north-west of Au Bon Gite. The Welshmen carried up water and ammunition for the Somersets and their help was greatly appreciated.

Excepting for intermittent shell fire round the southern portion of Lange- 17th August marck and on the eastern bank of the Steenbeek, the night was without incident. When dawn broke, however, the Germans were seen on the right front of the 61st Brigade, massing for a counter-attack. The S.O.S. was promptly sent up, and the guns opened fire with such good effect that the enemy's troops were dispersed.

During the morning nothing happened but the usual artillery duels and the strengthening of the defences on the first and second objectives. But at 2 p.m. the C.O., 7th Somersets, received an order to organize an attack on the Red Line in conjunction with the 60th Brigade on the left of the 61st. After a conference with the C.O. of the 12th King's and 7th D.C.L.I., it was agreed that the King's and the D.C.L.I. should attack the Red Line, the Somersets supporting the former and the K.O.Y.L.I. the latter. Zero hour was fixed at 7 p.m. Preparations for the attack were then put in progress. At 6.30 p.m. the C.O., 7th Somersets, established his Advanced Battalion Headquarters in a concreted house on the north-east outskirts of the village.

The artillery barrage fell at 6.30 p.m. and was replied to immediately, the enemy's guns shelling the northern end of Langemarck. Heavy hostile machine-gun fire swept the right flank of the line of advance and from the left the enemy's riflemen poured a stream of bullets on to the ground over which the attacking troops would have to move. At 7 p.m. the attack began, C and D Companies of the Somersets occupying the line held by the King's as soon as the latter had advanced, C Company of the 15th Welch Regiment holding the Green Line. But little could be seen of the attack, and it was not until about 7.30 p.m. that a report reached Colonel Troyte-Bullock of the progress of the King's. At that hour a message from the C.O. of the latter Battalion stated that he could see a few small groups of his men on the line of the objective, but his casualties were heavy. He suggested that the Somersets should reinforce him. Two Companies of the latter—B and D—were at once ordered to push forward and join up with the King's on the Red Line. The two Companies found the King's men held up by very boggy and impassable ground, the battalion on their right being in a similar predicament. On sending back a report of the situation they were ordered to dig in where they were.

About 8 p.m. the C.O., Somersets, returned to his old Battalion Headquarters and there consulted with the C.O. of the 15th Welch Regiment, who agreed to take over the situation as it was then and carry on with the relief. By 1 a.m. on the 18th the relief was completed and the 7th Somersets marched back to camp near the Brielen–Elverdinghe road. After dinners the Battalion marched to Elverdinghe, where it entrained for Proven, returning to its old camp in Paddock Wood.

Later in the day Lord Cavan came to Paddock Wood and congratulated the 7th Somersets on the part they had taken in the capture of Langemarck. He said that he expected it would have taken the best part of a week for the Division to get across the Steenbeek and establish itself on the farther side, but it had done it in much less time. He also said that he was going to send the 20th Division out of the line for a month's rest and to reorganize: welcome news indeed.

Again, however, the 7th Battalion had paid dearly for its triumph; success was always at the sacrifice of brave and gallant lives. Second-Lieuts. A. D. Kinsey, C. B. Crisp, H. R. Russell and M. B. Checkland, Sergeants T. Avery and A. G. Burgess, Corporals W. Brigg and H. Dyer, as well as 33 other ranks had been killed. Captains H. A. Foley, R. Ledshaw and J. H. R. Hill, 2/Lieuts. C. J. Lewin, L. A. Phelps, J. H. C. Liddon, J. H. Ross, G. R. Colsey and J. H. Goode and 139 other ranks were wounded and 18 other ranks were missing. These losses were heavy, but the Battalion had the satisfaction of knowing that along the whole front of the battle, from the N.W. corner of Inverness Copse to the line of junction with the French south of St. Janshoek, the 20th and 29th Divisions had captured their objectives, Langemarck and Wijdendrift respectively: success had not been so marked on other parts of the battle front, as in other sectors of the line heavy German

counter-attacks had succeeded in forcing the attackers back to their original 6th Battalion
trenches.[1]

THE ATTACK ON INVERNESS COPSE BY THE 14TH DIVISION,
22ND AUGUST 1917

Between the Battle of Langemarck, 16th to 18th August, and the Battle
of the Menin Road Ridge, 20th and 25th September, minor operations of
considerable local importance took place on 19th, 22nd and 27th August.
These small operations, carried out east and north-east of Ypres, were designed
to reduce certain of the more important of the enemy's strong points. In
combination with one of these attacks (on 22nd August) the 14th Division
attacked astride the Menin Road in the direction of Inverness Copse: an
attack in which the 6th Somerset Light Infantry took part.

On the last occasion (4th May) the 6th Battalion of the Regiment was 4th May
referred to, it had just moved up from the Wancourt area to the front line in
the Wancourt left sector, having relieved the 5th K.S.L.I. in the forward
trenches. The 4th May witnessed the close of the Battle of Arras, 1917.
Thereafter, for the 6th Somersets, there set in a period of trench warfare lasting
some four months, during which patrol work and the maintenance of the
defences when in the front line, and training when out of it, occupied the
Battalion from morning till night and at times throughout most of the hours
of darkness, and kept it free from the possibility of becoming stale. Indeed,
on 13th May, the Battalion Diary records: "A quiet night. Rain fell during
the day, increasing enormously the discomfort. Men working all night are
beginning to feel the strain of the prolonged tour." On 14th the Battalion
was relieved and on the 15th marched to a rest camp, described as "M.10.d," [2]
where only twelve tents and two Nissen huts were provided for all four companies. Many men were crowded out, and of these unfortunates the Diary
records: "The remainder of the Battalion living in self-made bivouacs. Rain
fell slightly during the night." Nine days were spent in this camp, during
which those men in bivouacs were made more comfortable. On 25th the
Battalion marched back again to the Cojeul Switch, the support area south-east
of Telegraph Hill. But even here, though all ranks were in more comfortable
quarters, the weather was wretched. On the 30th a violent thunderstorm
broke over the area, completely flooding dug-outs and bivouacs, and the last
day of May was spent in recovering from the effects of the storm and in building new quarters. June was uneventful, most of the month and the first nine
days of July being spent at Bus les Artois. On the 10th July the Battalion 10th July
marched to Gezhincourt, on 12th to Doullens, entraining at the latter place
for Bailleul. Arrived at the latter town, the 6th Somersets (in Brigade) marched
to Mont Noir, where accommodation for the Battalion was found in tents.

---

[1] For conspicuous gallantry and devotion to duty during the operations on 16th August 2/Lieuts.
L. A. Joscelyne and J. H. Goode were awarded the M.C., 2/Lieut. J. H. R. Hill, M.C., a bar to
his M.C., and Sergts. T. Jenner, C. L. King and L./Sergt. F. W. F. Howse the D.C.M.
   [2] It was apparently in the Beaurains area.

Here the Somerset men remained until the end of July and the 5th August. On the 6th, however, a move was made to Caestre, where several more days of training were put in. At last, on 17th, the Battalion reached Dickesbusch Huts and it was at this camp that the scheme of the forthcoming attack by the 14th Division was first made known and described.

At 4 a.m. on 19th August the C.O. and all Company Commanders went forward to reconnoitre the front-line trenches in the Inverness Copse Sector, as the 43rd Infantry Brigade had been ordered to relieve the 41st Brigade on the night 20th/21st August. The 6th Somersets were to take over the right sub-sector and the 6th D.C.L.I. the left. The front line, at this period, crossed the Menin road in a north-to-south direction, about half-way between Clapham Junction and the western edge of Inverness Copse, the latter being held by the enemy. The support trenches were in Crab Crawl, the reserve positions were at Zillebeke Bund and Railway Dugouts.

The 6th Somersets (Major F. D. Bellew temporarily commanding)[1] had been detailed to relieve the 7th Rifle Brigade in the right front-line sector, which lay just east of Stirling Castle and south of the Menin Road. Two companies of the Battalion were to take over the front line, i.e. No. 1 on the right, No. 4 on the left; No. 2 and No. 3 were in support. Major Bellew had his Headquarters at the junction of Jam Avenue and Jam Reserve Trench, near Stirling Castle.

On the night of 20th/21st the Battalion moved up into the front line as ordered, the relief being completed without incident and without loss.

The orders to the 43rd Brigade stated that the line to be captured on 22nd August ran from Herenthage Chateau (inclusive) to the southern edge of Glencorse Wood; Fitzclarence Farm and the "L" shaped farm along the road north of the former farm were to be included in the objective. A defensive flank was to be formed from Herenthage Chateau back to the front line with its western extremity roughly on the bend of the road, running directly south from Clapham Junction and immediately south-east of Stirling Castle. North of the 43rd the 42nd Brigade was to attack and establish posts in Glencorse Wood, in order to cover the operations of the 43rd Brigade. The guns of the II Corps were to support the attack, and machine-gun barrages were also to be placed on the flanks of the attack and east of the objective. Four tanks were to follow the infantry attack on Inverness Copse for the purpose of dealing with strong points.

For several days the weather had been fine and warm with a drying wind and as a consequence the battle area was in better condition than in previous operations which had taken place during August.

Zero hour for the attack was 7 a.m. on 22nd, and at 7.5 a.m., when the artillery barrage lifted, the two Battalions of the 43rd Brigade—6th Somersets on the right and 6th D.C.L.I. on the left—"went over the top." Of the Somersets No. 1 Company was on the right, No. 4 on the left, No. 2 in immediate support, and No. 3 formed the last wave.

[1] The C.O., Lt.-Col. T. F. Ritchie, was at Etaples during the operations.

With the exception of a portion of No. 4 Company the leading waves _{6th Battalion} reached the edge of Inverness Copse with only slight casualties. A strong _{22nd August} point at the north-west corner of the Copse had held up a portion of No. 4 Company.   No. 2 Company, detailed for mopping up, also suffered casualties from another enemy strong point about 200 yards west of Fitzclarence Farm; but the point was successfully dealt with, though the defenders fought gallantly enough, the post being in flames, from bombs, when captured.   At 8.1 a.m. a message was sent back to the Brigade that the post had been taken.

Meanwhile Nos. 1 and 4 Companies had pushed on, followed by the remainder of No. 2 and No. 3 Companies.   Small numbers of No. 4 reached the objective but without officers.   No. 1 had heavy fighting round Herenthage Chateau before it was captured and the O.C. Company (Captain Brooke) was killed among the ruins.   Some sixty prisoners were taken here and sent back.   In all 130 Germans were sent back from the western edge of the Copse.

About 8.30 a.m. Nos. 1, 2 and 4 Companies sent back word to Battalion Headquarters that they had been severely depleted in numbers.   The C.O. therefore pushed No. 3 Company up to the eastern edge of Inverness Copse and asked for support from the Brigade and 10th Durham Light Infantry. The O.C., No. 3 Company (Captain G. C. Lance), on reaching the eastern edge of the Copse, reported that he had picked up very few detachments of Nos. 1, 2 and 4 and these were without officers—all being casualties.   Two platoons of the 10th D.L.I. now began to move up, but the C.O., 6th Somersets, deemed them insufficient and suggested a whole company would be safer.   A series of messages showing the desperate position in the front line now reached the C.O. from the O.C., No. 3 Company.   These messages are admirably set out in the Battalion narrative of operations and give a clear view of the straits the gallant Somerset men were put to: the messages are given in full as they would lose force if paraphrased.

"9.30 a.m.   Arrived at eastern edge of Copse with few oddments, about 70 men in all.   We were being surrounded so had been forced to withdraw. Both flanks in air.   We must have reinforcements."   This was followed by a pigeon message: "9.55 a.m.   Have arrived.   Strength 2 platoons east edge of Copse.   Am being surrounded so we must fall back.   No further supports have arrived."   The next message is timed 10.5 a.m.   "Pushed back from east edge of Copse.   More reinforcements required.   Lees (10th D.L.I.) unable to give me any more.   Am still holding largest part of Copse." A message which followed this gives the dispositions of the Somerset men:—

"My line now runs from J.14.c.8.5. (northern edge of Copse) to Tank Trap (on the Menin road running through the Copse) to J.14.c.7.3. (a point on the road which runs north-west from the Chateau to the Menin road and about 300 yards from the ruined buildings).   Still cannot find Cornwalls (6th D.C.L.I. who attacked on the left of the 6th Somersets).   Germans are congregating at strong point about J.14.c.9.4. (on the Menin road and about 150 yards east of the Somersets).   Two platoons of Durham Light Infantry have come up on our left.   We have 90 men in all."

At 11.15 a.m. another message from O.C., No. 3 Company, was sent back: "We hold strong point at J.14.c.9.5. Several enemy machine-guns in front of us and Copse is strongly held. *We will hold on at all costs.*" The precarious position of these brave fellows can be better appreciated from these two last messages, which give the co-ordinates of the opposing strong positions: they were but fifty yards apart.

About 1 p.m. a hostile party of about one hundred Germans marched up the Menin road and turned south, just where the Chateau road joined up with the former. Several small parties of the enemy, each of about twenty men, were also seen moving up north and south. Next, a whole battalion of Germans was observed advancing over the ridge east of Inverness Copse. In response to our S.O.S. the guns opened fire and these hostile advances were checked. But again, about 2 p.m., the enemy was seen massing in the valley of the Basse-villebeek and some minutes later he was reported "advancing towards us north of Menin road, 400 yards in front of our line." Machine-gun, Lewis-gun and artillery fire again checked this advance and dispersed the enemy. At evening the line held by the 6th Somersets appears to have been from a point about 250 yards in and from the western edge of Inverness Copse, back along Jasper Avenue to the bend in the road running directly south from Clapham Junction and just south-east of Stirling Castle. During the night the 6th Somersets and one company of the D.L.I., who had been holding the front line throughout the whole day, were relieved by the K.O.Y.L.I. and other companies of the Durhams, and moved back to the western edges of Inverness Copse in support. The Somerset men were greatly exhausted. In addition to the attack early in the morning of 22nd, they had had to beat off three counter-attacks pressed with vigour. It is impossible to give the numbers of the Battalion at this period, but they must have been small, and it was but a remnant which held the western edges of the Copse.[1]

No hostile movement developed on the 23rd, but it is apparent that the enemy's shell fire was very heavy over the whole area. On the night 23rd/24th the shelling was so fierce that the narrative states: "The hostile shelling on the night 23rd/24th was the heaviest ever encountered by this Battalion and was continuous." But if casualties were heavy, those of the enemy must have been heavier. When the third counter-attack was delivered at 8.30 p.m., by the enemy on 22nd, no less than ten boxes of S.A.A. had been poured into his ranks, and the artillery had completed his discomfiture.

Although the Battalion Narrative does not mention it, the 6th Somersets were engaged with the enemy on 24th. Throughout the night 23/24th the enemy concentrated the fire of his heavy batteries upon the Clapham Junction—Inverness Copse Sector. This bombardment intensified after midnight, and at dawn on the 24th the enemy launched his fourth counter-

[1] Major F. D. Bellew was awarded the D.S.O. for conspicuous gallantry and fine leadership throughout the operations. Captain G. C. Lance and 2/Lieut. R. G. C. Drake were awarded the M.C., and Sergts. A. T. Trott and S. G. Rawlings and Cpl. S. E. Gay the D.C.M., for their gallant conduct.

attack.   This attack was delivered by a fresh German Division led by "Sturm"
troops.   The two leading waves were lightly equipped, the four succeeding
waves carried full arms, tools and equipment.   The forward posts, now held
by Coys. of the K.O.Y.L.I., fell back upon the supports, which consisted of
the survivors of the 6th Somersets (under Capt. Lance) and 10th Durham L.I.
(under Capt. Jerrard).   These two officers and their troops put up such a
determined resistance that the hostile waves were broken in succession.   "Sturm
Truppen" infiltrated round the north of the Copse and actually crossed the
Menin road, west of the Copse.   Here fortunately they bumped into Battn.
Hd. Qrs. 6th Somersets, now situated in Jasper Avenue 70 yards west of the
wood, and were repulsed.   Capt. Manson, the Adjutant, fell at the junction
of the Menin road and the Copse, though not till the enemy had been driven
back, and his comrades in the wood made safe from being surrounded.   As
a result of these operations the C.O. was able to report that though heavily
attacked he was still holding the N.W. end of the Copse.   The 6th Battalion
was by this time reduced to three officers (Capt. Lance and Lieut. Denman
in the Copse and the C.O. at Battn. Hd. Qrs.).   At 10 a.m. the C.O., after
reporting that his Adjutant had been killed, asked that command of the right
sector should be taken over by the O.C., 10th D.L.I.   This was eventually
done.

At 12.20 the enemy counter-attacked in force all along the whole line
and every gun in the neighbourhood opened on his troops as they advanced.
But no supports or reserves were left and at 12.45 the O.C., 10th D.L.I.,
informed the Brigade that his men were retiring from Inverness Copse and
forming posts along the western edges.   Driven out of their position also the
Brigade, nevertheless, managed to hold the western edge of the Copse and
when relieved, on the night 24th/25th August, held the line Jasper Avenue
—western edge of Inverness Copse to Menin road to a point where Jargon
Drive cut the sunken road north of the Menin road.

The Brigade moved back to Dominion Camp, Busseboom, on 25th,
where the usual cleaning-up process was carried out and reorganization begun.
The losses had been very heavy.   The total casualties suffered by the 43rd
Brigade were 59 officers and 1,345 other ranks.   Of these the 6th Somersets
had 6 officers killed,[1] 9 wounded and 2 missing.   In other ranks the Battalion
lost 44 killed, 213 wounded and 74 missing.

On 29th the 6th Battalion marched to new billets in the Le Roukloshille
area, where training was begun.   On 31st the Battalion was paraded and the
G.O.C., Division, addressed the Somerset men, congratulating them on their
gallant conduct during the recent severe fighting.

No other battalion of the Somerset Light Infantry was engaged in the
minor operations which took place towards the end of August.

[1] No names are given in the Battalion Diary or 43rd Brigade H.Q.'s Diary, but "Officers died in
the Great War" records the following officers killed during the operations: 2/Lieut. W. Hornsby
(21/8/17), 2/Lieut. C. R. Selwyn (22/8/17), 2/Lieut. H. E. Dudley (23/8/17), Capt. G. P.
Manson (24/8/17).

THE BATTLE OF THE MENIN ROAD RIDGE, 20TH–25TH SEPTEMBER 1917

7th Battalion   The front selected for this battle extended from the Ypres–Comines Canal, north of Hollebeke, to the Ypres–Staden Railway, north of Langemarck, a distance of about 8 miles.   The 20th Division still held the line in the Langemarck sector, astride the Ypres–Staden Railway, though the 61st Brigade was out of the front line when, on 20th September, the battle began.

27th August   After the hard fighting of mid-August the 7th Somersets remained at Proven until the 27th of that month, when the Battalion marched to Herzeele and went into billets in farms in the neighbourhood of the town.   Here the Somerset men remained until the 2nd September, when they returned to the Proven area.   On the 8th a move forward to the Canal bank brought the Battalion nearer the front line, and on the night of 10th/11th it relieved the 14th Welch Regiment in the shell-hole positions north-east of Langemarck. This line was practically the same as when the Battalion handed it over after capturing it during the Battle of Langemarck, though the left of the position on the railway had been slightly advanced.   The relief was not carried out without loss to the Somersets, for on the way up the Battalion bumped into a 5·9 barrage which the enemy had put down,[1] the Acting Adjutant—2/Lieut. R. A. Malpas—being wounded, one other rank killed and eleven wounded. Major R. P. Preston-Whyte was in temporary command of the Battalion and Battalion Headquarters were established in the same old pill box, now christened the "Pig and Whistle."

Daylight on the 11th revealed the fact that the enemy's aircraft was particularly active.   A hostile plane, reconnoitring over the Somersets' line, spotted one of the Battalion's front-line posts and it was not long before that particular spot became an inferno with shells bursting all round it.   Casualties for the 11th were five other ranks killed and fifteen wounded.   During the night of 11th/12th the enemy was located holding a line of shell-hole posts about 200 yards in front of the Somersets.   The difficulty of digging in soft ground had compelled both sides to make use of shell holes for the front and support lines.   Fortified with sand-bags and whatever material could be collected they afforded good shelter and were, moreover, difficult for aeroplanes to locate.   On the afternoon of 12th the enemy's guns turned their attention to the "Pig and Whistle" and obtained three direct hits on it, killing a signaller who was on duty at the entrance and wounding two other men.   Total casualties for the day were four other ranks killed and four wounded.

13th September   On the night of 13th the 7th Somersets moved back into Brigade Reserve on the west side of the Steenbeek, returning to the front line on the night 14th/15th.   Three days later, after a heavy bombardment along the whole of the XIV Corps front, the enemy attacked the Guards Division (on the left of the Somersets) and the 12th King's (on the left of the Battalion).   The attack failed; three other ranks killed and nine wounded were the casualties suffered by the 7th Battalion on 16th September.   On the night of 18th/19th the 61st Brigade was relieved by the 59th and 60th Brigades as the latter were to carry

[1] For conspicuous gallantry on this night Corpl. G. C. Gane was awarded the D.C.M.

out the attack on Eagle Trench on the 20th September as part of the general 7th Battalion
operations.   The Somerset men moved back to Redan Camp in the Elverdinghe 20th September
area whence, on the nights of 20th and 21st, most of the Battalion was employed
in carrying ammunition and stores up to the troops in the front line.

The night of 22nd September was made hideous by a hostile air raid
on Redan Camp, in which the Battalion Intelligence Officer (2/Lieut. S. H.
Rich) was wounded, seven other ranks killed and twenty-four wounded.

At dawn on 23rd the 59th and 60th Brigades attacked and captured
Eagle Trench.   This particular trench is referred to in the official despatches
in the following terms: "North-east of Langemarck stubborn fighting took
place for the possession of the short length of trench which, as already recounted,
had resisted our attacks on the 16th August.   It was not till the morning of
20th September that the position was finally captured by us (20th Division)."
The 7th Somersets took no part in this attack, but during the night of 23rd/24th
relieved the 10th and 11th Battalions, Rifle Brigade, in the first line which
had been established just beyond the captured trench.   The following morning,
under cover of mist, the Battalion patrols found and brought in several wounded
men of the 59th and 60th Brigades; also several wounded Germans who
belonged to a Storm Troops unit, which had been sent up to retake Eagle
Trench.

During the night of 25th the 7th Somersets pushed their outpost line
forward about 200 yards without opposition and dug themselves in.   On
this night the Battle of the Menin Road Ridge ended, as a result of which,
Sir Douglas Haig said, "the whole of the high ground crossed by the Menin
Road, for which such desperate fighting had taken place during our previous
attack, passed into our hands."

THE BATTLE OF POLYGON WOOD, 26TH SEPTEMBER–3RD OCTOBER 1917

Although the area of this Battle is officially the same as for the preceding 7th Battalion
operations—the Battle of the Menin Road Ridge—it is evident that the action
was more local than general, for the 20th Division did not, apparently, attack
the enemy.   The 61st Brigade of the Division still held the line east of Langemarck when, at dawn on 26th September, the assault was launched farther
south.   The Divisional artillery shelled the German positions in front of the
61st Brigade, to which the enemy replied vigorously, one N.C.O. and six other
ranks of the Somersets being killed and seventeen wounded.   The Battalion
was relieved that night (26/27th) and (less one company) moved back to reserve
trenches between Langemarck and the Steenbeek, with Battalion Headquarters
at Au Bon Gite; the Company left behind remained in the support trenches
with orders to assist the 12th King's if necessary.   The night of 27th/28th
was spent by the Battalion in carrying water and rations up to the front line.
On the 28th the enemy's artillery shelled the Battalion area heavily—one other 28th September
rank was killed and eleven were wounded.

On the night of 28th/29th the 20th Division was relieved by the 4th
Division.   The 7th Somersets were relieved by the 1st King's Own.   The

1st Somersets of the 4th Division relieved the 7th D.C.L.I., 20th Division, and thus two Battalions of the Regiment met.   On the 29th the 7th Battalion was located in Patiala Camp, Proven.

So far as the Battles of Ypres, 1917, were concerned, the 20th Division had finished with them and in a few days' time was *en route*, south, for Bapaume. Before leaving the Ypres area, however, the Divisional Commander received a complimentary letter from the Army Commander which said: "The Army Commander is sorry to lose such a fine fighting Division."

The total casualties suffered by the 7th Somersets during the operations in the Ypres area were 5 officers killed and 14 wounded; in other ranks the losses were 102 killed and 335 wounded.[1]

As the 37th Division had relieved the 39th Division in the line just west of Gheluvelt, between the nights of 27th September and 1st October, the 8th Somersets came within the official area of the Battle of Polygon Wood, but in the Battalion Diary and, indeed, in the Diary of the 63rd Brigade, there are no references to any action with the enemy before the 4th October, the day on which the Battle of Broodseinde was fought.

THE BATTLE OF BROODSEINDE, 4TH OCTOBER 1917

Two Battalions of the Regiment, the 1st and 8th (of the 4th and 37th Divisions respectively) were engaged in this Battle, which, lasting officially only one day, was nevertheless an exceedingly bitter struggle, General Ludendorff stating that the German losses were enormous.

The Battle of Broodseinde was the first of the Battles of Ypres, 1917, in which the 1st Somerset Light Infantry (Lieut.-Col. V. H. B. Majendie) took part.   After the costly attack on Roeux during the Third Battle of the Scarpe (3rd–4th May) the Battalion was in Brigade Reserve on 5th, relieving the 1st Rifle Brigade in the left sub-sector of the Chemical Works on 7th. On 8th May 2/Lieut. S. E. Massie, who had taken a party out to cover Pioneers at work on Clarke Trench, was first reported missing and afterwards as killed.   During the operations between the 11th and 13th May, which resulted eventually in the capture of Roeux, the Battalion, owing to its weakness in numbers, was organized into two companies only and was

in Brigade Reserve.   On the night of 11th May, after the attack had been launched, the Battalion carried stores and ammunition to four forward dumps and then moved into Cawdor Trench.   At midnight it relieved two companies of the East Lancashires, who were occupying the new line just south of the railway, the latter troops side-stepping to the south.   Another attack, on 12th May, was equally successful, little opposition being met with.   The German guns were very active but fortunately the casualties of the 1st Somersets were small, one officer—2/Lieut. Pratt—and twelve other ranks being wounded. Relief came that night, though the relieving troops were not settled in until 3 a.m. on 13th.   The Battalion breakfasted near a railway embankment

[1] From figures given by Lieut.-Col. C. J. Troyte-Bullock.

west of Athies, and then marched into billets in Arras. On the 14th the 1st Battalion Somersets moved to Gouy en Ternois, arriving in billets about 2 p.m.

For nearly a month the Battalion remained out of the line at Gouy training and reorganizing after the hard gruelling it had gone through during the Battles of Arras. This period of rest and welcome change from incessant fighting in the front line came to an end on 11th June when the 1st Somersets moved by buses back to Arras, arriving at about 3 p.m. and billeting there for the remainder of the day. On the 12th the Battalion marched out of Arras 12th June to a railway embankment east of the town. Here a halt was made until 8.45 p.m., at which hour the Somerset men moved off to take over a portion of the front line south of the River Scarpe, south of Roeux, with the left of the Battalion on the River and the right in touch with the 3rd Division.

Work was begun immediately on the trenches which were in a bad condition. Active patrolling was carried out to determine exactly the enemy's position, and posts on the tow-path south-west of Roeux were pushed forward some 300 yards. An aggressive attitude was evidently adopted, for the Battalion Diary repeatedly mentions the constant harassing of the enemy by snipers, grenadiers and Lewis gunners without drawing anything but feeble retaliation. A few trench-mortar shells were fired by the enemy and one of them mortally wounded Captain C. J. O. Daubeny, who died on 16th of his wounds. On the night of 19th/20th the Battalion was relieved by the Rifles and moved back to the railway embankment east of Arras. For the remainder of June and the whole of July, August and the early part of September, there is little of outstanding interest in the Battalion Diary to record. Both British and Germans in the line south of Vimy were glad of a period of comparative quietude after the heavy fighting of the spring; both sides had lost heavily and much reorganization and training were necessary before anything like a big attack could be launched. On the 19th September, however, the 1st Somersets (in Brigade and Division) moved north to the Poperinghe area, the Battalion arriving in a camp at Houtpertre, about a mile south-west of Poperinghe, at 4 a.m. on 20th. In this camp training was carried out until the morning of 28th, when the 1st Battalion moved by train to Cariboo Camp near Elverdinghe. Final preparations now began for the operations which were to be carried out on 4th October, i.e. the Battle of Broodseinde.

As already stated in a previous chapter, the 1st Somersets met the 7th 3rd/4th October Battalion when moving forward to take up its assembly position on the night 3rd/4th October, the 4th Division having been ordered to relieve the 20th Division in the Langemarck sector.

The 1st Battalion was in its assembly position by 11 p.m. with the loss of only one man. This position was in three lines: the first consisting of the leading platoons of A and B Companies with the mopping-up platoons of C and H in the first line of posts running approximately from just in front of Louis Farm to U.24.c.9.3.

The 4th Division was to attack with two Brigades in the front line and one in reserve. The 11th Brigade, on the right, and the 10th Brigade, on the left, the 12th in reserve. The 11th Brigade was to attack with two battalions in the front line, one in support and one in reserve; the 1st Somerset Light Infantry was to be the right assaulting Battalion, the Hants Regiment the left, the East Lancashires in support and the Rifle Brigade in reserve.

The Somersets were to attack on a two-company front, A on the right, B on the left, with H Company in rear of A and C in rear of B. The leading Companies were to go right through to the final objective.

The German defences in front of the Battalion sector consisted first of Kangaroo Trench with a pill box in its immediate rear, next a road running west of Ferdan House and Lemnos House (both of which were in the Battalion area) beyond which was another short length of trench; the road formed the first objective. The Green Line (the final objective) was east of the two houses and ran through Tragique Farm, also in the area to be captured by the Somerset men.

The orders for mopping up during the attack are interesting: Os.C., H and C Companies, were each to detail one platoon as moppers. The platoon of H was to follow closely behind the leading two platoons of A Company, dropping one section to clear Kangaroo Trench and neighbourhood: the remaining sections were to capture, clear, and hold a concrete dug-out and pill box east of Kangaroo Trench. The platoon of C Company was to follow close in rear of the leading two platoons of B Company, similarly dropping one section to clear Kangaroo Trench and neighbourhood, the remainder capturing, clearing and holding the Strong Point and neighbourhood on the Poelcapelle Road, north-east of the pill box allotted to the section of the platoon of H Company. These two Companies, H and C, were also to detail four sections for the following purpose: H—two sections to follow immediately in rear of the right rear platoon of A and two to follow immediately in rear of the left rear platoon of A Company; C Company—four sections were to carry out a similar duty for B Company. These were mopping-up sections whose functions were to mop up the various dug-outs and strong points captured by the platoons they were to follow. The task allotted to the right rear platoon of A Company was to capture Ferdan House, the left rear platoon of the same Company was to capture the concrete dug-out on the line of the first objective. B Company's right rear platoon was detailed to capture the Strong Point 47, west of Kangaroo Pond, while the left rear platoon was to take Lemnos House. After these two rear platoons of A and B Companies had captured the points allotted to them they were to hand them over to their mopping sections and push on with the leading troops.

It will thus be seen that the Support Companies of the Battalion had to find a considerable number of men for mopping-up duties, which left only a small number available for the capture of the final objective. But subsequent events justified the somewhat involved method of attack.

Zero hour was to be 6 a.m. 4th October.

The night of 3rd/4th passed quietly, though one man was killed by

machine-gun fire. At about 5.30 a.m. on 4th the German guns became active
and many shells fell just behind the rear section of the Battalion. In order
to avoid casualties the Battalion moved forward about thirty yards before Zero.

At 6 a.m. the British barrage fell and the advance began. The men
had been impressed with the necessity of keeping close on the heels of the
barrage and so eager were they to carry out these instructions and thus minimize
casualties, that there was a tendency to keep too close and the result was that
several men were wounded. Hostile machine-gun fire met the advance of
the Battalion, but the Somersets do not appear to have suffered very much
from the hostile barrage. The intense darkness made direction difficult to
keep and there was a noticeable tendency to ease off to the right.

Kangaroo Trench was found occupied by the Germans, but they gave
little trouble; the British barrage had accounted for a good many and the
remainder were only too glad to give themselves up. The attack swept on
and no serious opposition was met with until the line of the track running south
from Lemnos House was reached. On the road, which was the line of the
first objective, were several piles of stones and these were held by the Germans,
in force. Heavy fire was opened on them and after several had been killed
opposition broke down and the Somerset men again advanced. The right of
the Battalion, together with some men of the 11th Division (on the right of
the 1st Somersets), then attacked a concrete house on the Poelcapelle Road,
south of Ferdan House. A German machine gun was firing from the roof
of this house and another from the side of it. A Lewis gun was then brought
into action and, under cover of its fire, the attackers worked round a flank
and got in rear of the house. Several Germans were killed before the remainder
(about sixteen of the enemy) and the two machine guns were captured.

On the left another German machine gun at Lemnos House held up the
attack for a while, but eventually by means of rifle fire and rifle grenades the
gun was knocked out and the house taken.

At this period heavy machine-gun fire was coming from Ferdan House,
but the British barrage had halted. The line of the first objective had been
captured and reorganization now took place, direction was checked and Lewis
guns and rifles cleaned.

Presently the barrage moved on again and the attack was renewed towards
the Green Line, the right of the Battalion being directed on Ferdan House.
Heavy machine-gun fire was still coming from the latter as the Somerset men
moved forward but, aided by the Lewis guns and the fire of a Stokes mortar
belonging to the 11th Division, the house was attacked. The East Lancashires
worked round the right flank, the Somersets round the left and the house was
rushed and captured. Two German officers and thirty other ranks, several
of whom were wounded, were taken, together with two machine guns and
two trench mortars. Ferdan House having been captured, the advance was
continued to the Green Line, but by now the enemy's resistance was feeble
and although some casualties were suffered from machine-gun fire from the
direction of 19 Metre Hill, the line was reached, when the Battalion was

reorganized and distributed in depth.   Touch was maintained on both flanks. The advanced line of posts ran from Tragique Farm south-eastwards along the Green Line to the right Battalion boundary.

The attack had gone splendidly, but the 1st Somersets had suffered severely. The equivalent of four platoons only could be collected, with about thirty men of the East Lancashire Regiment under one officer.   Of the Somersets' officers there were only five remaining and of these Captain Greetham, who had been ill during the two days preceding the attack, had to be sent back in the afternoon.

About 2 p.m. a German counter-attack developed on the left of the Somersets where a battalion of Seaforths held the line.   The latter had to fall back, and in consequence the left of the 11th Brigade had to conform; but rifle, Lewis gun and the fire from captured machine guns was opened on the enemy and the whole line was shortly afterwards re-established.   At about 5.40 p.m. another counter-attack was launched by the enemy on the left of the Somersets and again the line was forced back.   Finally, the Somerset men had to fall back as the line of the Battalion was "continuously shelled by our guns." The new line was established from about 50 to 100 yards in front of Lemnos and Ferdan Houses.

The concluding paragraph in the Battalion Diary of 1st Somersets for 4th October is of special interest to those in England who were responsible for the training of drafts for the Regiment:—

"A satisfactory feature of the day was the way in which the last draft of 200 behaved.   Though, for the most part only nineteen years of age, and never having been under fire before, they showed the greatest keenness and determination and behaved excellently."

Of individual acts of gallantry it has only been possible to obtain particulars concerning the bravery of an N.C.O.   This was Lance-Corporal W. V. Watkins [1] of C Company.   A portion of the line was held up by machine-gun fire from a pill box, but Watkins, though already wounded in the arm, went forward alone to attack it.   Advancing under heavy fire he worked round a flank, attacked the pill box single-handed and captured the machine gun and its crew, thus enabling the line to advance.   Other gallant acts were seen but are unrecorded in the Diary of the Battalion.

On the 5th after a stormy day the 1st Somersets were relieved and marched back into Divisional Reserve, being located in Candle Trench.

Nine officers and 284 other ranks were the casualties of the 1st Battalion in the Battle of Broodseinde, the former including 2/Lieut. A. R. Barnes, who, first reported wounded and missing, was afterwards numbered amongst the dead.   Captains D. C. H. Edwards and C. A. S. Hawker, Lieuts. S. V. Butcher and P. J. Sylvester, and 2/Lieuts. E. G. Haskins, C. E. Matthews, J. W. Harper and L. M. Mogg were wounded.

Meanwhile at the southern extremity of the line which attacked the

[1] He was awarded the D.C.M.

enemy on the morning of the 4th October, i.e. south of the Menin Road, the 37th Division had slightly advanced its front, gaining the limited objectives allotted to it with the exception of two strong points. 8th Battalion 4th October

The 37th Division had taken over the front line on the night 27th/28th September, the 63rd Brigade relieving the 118th Brigade from about J.26.d.7.9. to J.21.c.2.1. The maps which accompany the Brigade Narrative of Operations of 4th October are almost devoid of place names and it is almost impossible to fix the front line of the Brigade. Indeed, the Brigade Narrative states that:—

"It was understood from the outgoing unit that the general line held was the line of the road running north and south through Jute Cotts.[1] This was subsequently found to be not the case, the general line running about 150 yards west of the road and in places even more. Owing to the previous heavy shelling of the area the road was no longer a landmark, which would easily account for the mistake made by the outgoing Brigade and for the subsequent difficulty experienced by the Brigade in determining its exact position, no movement being possible by day."

The 63rd Brigade held the right of the Divisional Front and the 111th Brigade the left, the 112th Brigade being in reserve. The 63rd Brigade was to attack with the 8th Somersets (Lt.-Col. H. S. C. Richardson, commanding) on the right and the 8th Lincolns on the left. One company of the 10th Y. and L. Regiment and two companies of the 4th Middlesex were to be at the disposal of the Somersets and Lincolns respectively. Two Companies of the 8th Somerset and three of the 8th Lincolns were to make the initial attack, the remaining companies of each Battalion being distributed in depth in the front line, immediate support, and support lines.

There were two objectives, the Red and the Blue Lines. In front of the Somersets, the Red Line, was the line of the road running north and south along the Battalion front; this road continued north in front of the Lincolns until some houses were reached, then bent back eastwards. The Blue Line appears to have been those portions of Jager and Joist Trenches in front of both Battalions and beyond the Red Line.

As soon as it was known that offensive operations were to be undertaken posts were pushed out, and reconnaissance showed that the road line was the German outpost line with strong points beyond.

During the period up to 4th October preparations were carried out under very arduous conditions. The ground was difficult to work on, shell holes were everywhere and the absence of landmarks made the locating of places almost impossible. Moreover, communication with the front line was only possible by night: by day even individual runners were shot at from the moment they left Headquarters of Battalions in the line. Across the Basseville Brook the country was exceptionally difficult and it was only the excellence of the weather and the night being lit by a brilliant moon that movement was at all possible.

[1] Not named on any map.

Both the 8th Somersets and 8th Lincolns reached their assembly positions without incident, though according to his usual custom the enemy put down a heavy barrage and this fell about an hour before Zero, causing some casualties. The troops detailed for the assault were necessarily somewhat crowded, for it was impossible to reinforce attacking troops by day and the reserves had therefore to be east of the Basseville Brook before daylight and in assembly trenches: the latter were limited owing to the hurried preparations for the attack and the wet nature of the ground.

The original intention was to have only one objective, but owing to the lie of the ground and the forward German posts being on the high ground just east of the road through Jute Cotts, it was impossible to reconnoitre Berry Cotts and the trench north and south of it, neither could they be observed from the British front line or forward posts. It was, therefore, decided to gain the high ground first.

By 5 a.m. the attacking troops were ready in position and at 5.30 a.m. the forward posts were withdrawn in order to allow the barrage to fall on the line of the first objective.

At Zero hour (6 a.m.) the British barrage came down, but at once it was noticed that the curtain of fire appeared very thin. The leading waves went forward gallantly. As the right of the Somersets lay already far enough forward, only the centre and left of the Battalion advanced. As these troops went forward they found that the barrage was falling mostly beyond the first objective, so there was no opportunity of getting close up behind it. The enemy was holding a series of posts north and south of a strong point on the right front of the Battalion. This line was just east of the high ground which was the objective of the Somersets and was practically on the same level.

Immediately the attacking companies appeared on the crest-line they came under very heavy rifle and machine-gun fire. By means of sectional rushes, however, they reached their objective and attempted to consolidate their position, but only under intense machine-gun fire from the hostile post on the right front of the Battalion, and the fire of three more machine guns in Jager Trench about 450 yards away on the right flank. These latter guns were known and it had been anticipated that the barrage would have put them out of action, but such was not the case.

Immediately companies reached their objective they were not only subjected to violent machine-gun fire (as already stated) but also to heavy bombing counter-attacks. The German bombers advanced carrying no equipment and each threw two stick bombs simultaneously. The right company of the Somersets was fully employed in trying to keep down the hostile machine-gun fire from the three enemy guns in Jager Trench and was therefore unable to go to the assistance of the two companies on the left. These two companies tried hard to overcome the machine-guns on the right front of the Battalion, but were almost annihilated in trying to do so. Their losses caused a large gap between the left of the Somersets and the right of the Lincolns. Major

Hardyman therefore moved a Lewis-gun team forward to fill the gap, at the same time reinforcing the objective line.

Another attack (most gallantly led by 2/Lieut. N. H. Crees) on the strong point proved unsuccessful.

On the left of the Somersets the 8th Lincolns had similarly advanced and had then to withdraw. This withdrawal was seen by Major Hardyman, and he, appreciating the fact that it was absolutely necessary to retain sufficient men to hold the original line at all costs, sent these men back and planned a second attack upon the strong point on his front. This attack consisted of one officer (2/Lieut. H. J. Smith), two Lewis-gun teams and twenty men, the objective line and the right flank of the Battalion being reinforced simultaneously by the reserve company. The attack was launched but, though gallantly led by 2/Lieut. Smith (who was shot down and killed before the attack had gone far) none of the party was able to reach the strong point.

On the right flank a strong post was dug in advance of the posts previously held by the right company: this was successfully held against repeated bombing attacks. In the centre and on the left 2/Lieut. Pickard (8th Somersets), who had been sent up with reinforcements, withdrew the only three remaining men who were unwounded. This young officer, though twice wounded, and his three comrades, had been repeatedly called upon by the enemy to surrender but refused. At this stage the Brigade Narrative says: "The situation on the whole front was therefore the same as we originally started from."[1]

When darkness had fallen 2/Lieut. Crees (who had made the first attack on the strong point) returned to the original front line: he and three men had laid out all day in shell holes close to the strong point and twice as he fired his rifle at the enemy his bayonet had been broken by the explosion of bombs thrown at him. During the night units were reformed and reorganized and attempts were made to push out posts along the front of the Brigade.

On the 5th the 63rd Brigade was relieved, the 8th Somersets enbussing at Buss Corner for Fermoy Farm, where the Battalion arrived at 6 a.m. on the morning of 6th October.

The casualties suffered by the 8th Battalion on 4th October were three officers killed—Captain F. C. Humphreys, 2/Lieut. H. J. Smith and 2/Lieut. H. J. Friend; three officers wounded—Captain F. G. Hinton, 2/Lieuts. W. H. Pickard and E. N. Eskell; 27 other ranks were killed, 74 wounded and 12 were missing.

Speaking generally of the Battle of Broodseinde the official despatches stated:—

"The success of this operation marked a definite step in the development of our advance. Our line had now been established along the main ridge for 9,000 yards from our starting point near Mount Sorrel. From the farthest point reached the well-marked Gravenstafel Spur offered a defensible feature along which our line could be bent back from the ridge."

[1] For conspicuous gallantry during the operations on 4th October two N.C.O.'s, Sergts. E. Dyer and W. Davis, were awarded the D.C.M.

8th Battalion

The 63rd Brigade moved back into the line on 10th October, relieving the 112th Brigade, and the following story of a raid upon the 8th Somersets (no mention of which appears in the Battalion Diary) is given here in order that the continuity of the story of that Battalion's tour in the same sector may not be interrupted. Moreover, the story is in a way a sequel to the attack of 4th October.

The 8th Somerset Light Infantry had apparently taken over their old line of trenches on the 63rd Brigade front, which included "No. 4 Post." The latter was in advance of the general line of the remainder of the posts and was not more than thirty yards from the main German post, which was higher than "No. 4," but hidden from it by the bank of a cutting. "No. 4" had never conformed to the alignment of the other posts but was the remains of the peaceful penetration tactics carried out prior to the attack of 4th October. The position of this post prevented sudden attack on the front line and, moreover, kept the enemy from coming forward at night to the British side of the ridge. It was strongly held by bombers and riflemen—15 all told—in charge of a sergeant. Its orders in the event of attack were to hold out at all costs until supported from the front line. As will be seen, these orders, owing to the suddenness of the attack, the darkness, ground mist and wet ground, were impracticable.

14th October

At 10.45 p.m. on 14th the enemy attacked "No. 4 Post" and, sweeping past it, approached the front line of the Battalion. The Post had been visited shortly before by the O.C., Company, and the garrison was therefore on the alert. Even so the enemy was able, owing to the darkness and ground mist, to approach swiftly across the 20 yards intervening between the two posts and, after throwing a regular shower of stick bombs into the post, push forward under cover of the confusion caused by the explosions. The darkness and smoke and the broken nature of the ground outside "No. 4" made it almost impossible for the gallant garrison to see the Germans approaching and very quickly the post was surrounded. The enemy's troops numbered about fifty, they were armed with bombs and revolvers and carried no greatcoats or equipment. Inside the post all was confusion. The thick mud clogged the feet of the garrison and made quick movement impossible: some had been wounded by the bombs, others killed, yet the remainder held their ground, gallantly fighting to the last. When all had been put out of action the Germans jumped into the post and with their revolvers killed all the wounded but one, who, feigning death, afterwards crawled back to the front line and gave details of the attack.

The attack on the front line was driven back by Lewis-gun and rifle fire and by fire from the neighbouring posts, but "No. 4" was held by the enemy.

An immediate counter-attack was not made as the O.C., Company, had been ordered by Battalion Headquarters to withdraw all posts at dawn owing to a proposed heavy bombardment of all enemy forward positions by the "Heavies" on the 15th. Neither was a counter-attack ordered by the O.C., 8th Somersets, not only because of the pending bombardment, but because of the difficult nature of the ground and the fact that his men had been in the line for five days and were almost worn out.

The enemy did not continue to hold "No. 4 Post," but returned to his own line.   The formation of a new post was, however, begun which had a better field of fire.

On the following afternoon (15th) the troops in the front line had the satisfaction of watching the havoc created by the "Heavies" amongst the enemy's forward positions.   The great shells blew posts and emplacements to pieces, and trench traverses, debris, and the bodies of mangled Germans shot up into the air to the delight of the Somerset men, who had suffered at the hands of the enemy.   It is admitted that all war is horrible, but it is necessary.   The killing of the wounded in "No. 4 Post" was the work of savage brutes, not soldiers.

On the night of 15th the 63rd Brigade was withdrawn from the line as the 37th Division had been relieved by the 39th Division.

The Battle of Broodseinde is of special interest to the Somerset Light Infantry, for it was in this action that the Victoria Cross was awarded [1] to Private Thomas Henry Sage (of Tiverton), of the 8th Battalion, under the following circumstances:—

For most conspicuous bravery during an attack on an enemy strong post on October 4th 1917, at Tower Hamlets Spur, east of Ypres.

He was in a shell hole with eight other men, one of whom was shot while in the act of throwing a bomb.   The live bomb fell into the shell hole, and Private Sage, with great courage and presence of mind, immediately threw himself on it, thereby undoubtedly saving the lives of several of his comrades, though he himself sustained very severe wounds.

THE BATTLE OF POELCAPELLE, 9TH OCTOBER 1917

Four days of bad weather followed the Battle of Broodseinde, but in spite of the terrible state of the ground the next combined British and French attack took place on the morning of the 9th October, Zero hour being 5.20 a.m. On the British front the attack was renewed from a point east of Zonnebeke to the right flank of the French, north-west of Langemarck (a distance of about six miles), the French troops attacking from the left of the British to a point opposite Draaibank.   The attack was successful, villages, farm-houses, and woods being captured along the whole front.

The 4th Division continued its progress along the Ypres–Staden railway and secured a line well to the east of the Poelcapelle–Houthulst road.   Again stiff fighting took place for the possession of certain enemy strong points and a hostile counter-attack was repulsed.   The 1st Somersets, however, were not engaged in the operations, the Battalion being still in Divisional Reserve at Leipzig Farm.   At Zero hour on the 9th they "stood to" ready to move if necessary, but were not called upon and remained in camp all day.

[1] London *Gazette*, dated 18th December 1917.

As already described, the 8th Somersets (of the 37th Division) were at Fermoy Farm on the 9th October and did not move back again into the trenches until the following night when the Battalion relieved the 6th Bedfordshire Regiment in the right sub-sector (Bassevillebeek) of the Divisional front line.

THE FIRST BATTLE OF PASSCHENDAELE, 12TH OCTOBER 1917

The Battalion Diary of the 8th Somersets contains no entries between 10th and 15th October, and it is therefore assumed that the Battalion took no part in this battle.[1] The Battalion, however, was apparently still in the front-line trenches.

The 1st Somersets moved from Leipzig Farm to Proven on 12th, though the 4th Division again attacked the enemy: "Farther north on both sides of the Ypres–Staden railway English County Divisions (4th and 17th Divisions) and the Guards gained their objectives in spite of all difficulties."

About the middle of October the 4th Division was relieved, and on the 18th the 1st Somersets (in Brigade) entrained at Pezelhoek and arrived once more in the Arras area, reaching Marœuil at 12 midnight.

THE SECOND BATTLE OF PASSCHENDAELE, 26TH OCTOBER–10TH NOVEMBER 1917

The 8th Somersets were at work making and repairing roads 1,500 yards east of Ypres during part of the time the Battle was in progress. On 15th October the 37th Division was relieved by the 39th Division and the Somersets, embussing at Spoil Bank, moved back to Frontier Camp (M.13.b.8.9). The Battalion left this Camp on the morning of the 21st and marched to Moolenaeker via Berthen, Schaexken and Meteren. On 29th, plus one company of 8th Lincolns, the Battalion embussed from Moolenaeker for a Camp (1.3.b.) 1,500 yards east of Ypres, and from this place working parties were sent out for road-making and repairing. The Second Battle of Passchendaele was then in progress. On 6th November the Battalion had completed its tour as working parties in the area east of Ypres and, having been relieved by a battalion of the Rifle Brigade, proceeded in motor-lorries to the Merris area. On the 9th another move was made by the Battalion to Locre, via Bailleul. On the following morning the 8th Somersets again set out, this time for Moated Grange Camp, a three-hours' journey. And here, for the moment, it is necessary to leave the Battalion, for the Battles of Ypres, 1917, so far as they concerned the Somerset Light Infantry, were over, and preparations were being made for a continuation of the British offensive farther south at Cambrai.

[1] The Report of the Battles Nomenclature Committee gives the area of all the Battles in the Battles of Ypres, 1917, as between the Comines–Ypres Canal and Bixschoote. Sir Douglas Haig gives the area of the battle on 12th as between the Ypres–Roulers railway and Houthulst Forest and on both sides of the Ypres–Staden railway.

1st Battalion
9th October

8th Battalion
15th October

1st Battalion

18th October

8th Battalion

6th November

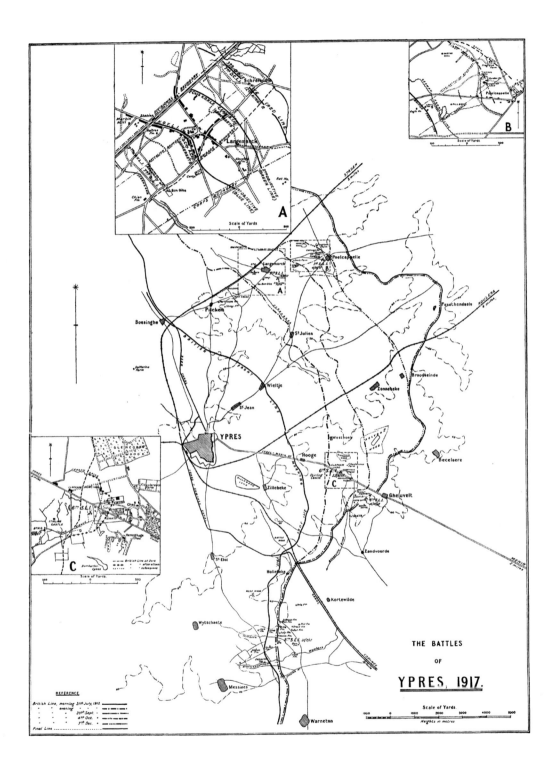

THE BATTLES

OF

YPRES, 1917.

CHAPTER XXVI

THE BATTLE OF CAMBRAI, 1917: 20TH NOVEMBER–3RD DECEMBER

I. THE TANK ATTACK, 20TH–21ST NOVEMBER

MILITARY tacticians and strategists have always regarded the surprise attack as one of the greatest tests of soldierly skill, and it must be admitted that the Battle of Cambrai, 1917, was a totally unexpected blow for the Germans, who little expected an attack in a sector which had been regarded by them as a particularly quiet part of the line, least likely to be attacked. The enemy's surprise is best illustrated in the words of the Chief of the German General Staff—General Ludendorff—who said: "We were expecting a continuance of the attack in Flanders and on the French front when, on the 20th November, we were surprised by a fresh blow at Cambrai."

In November 1917, the circumstances which, after the Battle of Broodseinde on 4th October, had almost compelled Sir Douglas Haig to continue the Battles of Ypres, though the conditions under which the troops fought were appalling, still held good: the essential thing was to keep the enemy from regaining the initiative. Russia had collapsed, and German reinforcements were arriving in large numbers from what had been the eastern theatre of the War: Italy had had a severe set-back: America was not yet in a position to give any assistance on land: the French Army was weakened both by losses and internal troubles. Under these circumstances it was impossible to accept the risk of the enemy regaining the initiative, and a continuance of the offensive was therefore necessary.

The Battles of Ypres, 1917, came to an end on 10th November, and ten days later the great tank attack, the first phase of the Battle of Cambrai, 1917, was launched.

The repeated attacks in Flanders and the operations of the Allies on other parts of the front had forced the enemy to concentrate large forces in the area of the threatened parts of his line, with the consequent weakening of other sectors, and of these weakened sectors the Cambrai front had been selected as the most suitable for the surprise operation in contemplation. In this area the ground was particularly suitable for the employment of tanks, which were to play an important part in the enterprise.

Sir Douglas Haig's intentions are thus set out in the official despatches:—

"If, after breaking through the German defensive system on this front, we could secure Bourlon to the North and establish a good flank position to the East in the direction of Cambrai, we should be well placed to exploit the situation locally between Bourlon and the Sensee River and to the North-West.

The capture of Cambrai itself was subsidiary to this operation, the object of our advance towards that town being primarily to cover our flank and puzzle the enemy regarding our intentions."

To General Sir Julian Byng, to whom the execution of the plans in connection with the Cambrai operations had been entrusted, belonged the honour of initiating what was probably the principal element in the early success of the Battle, viz. the dependence on tanks to smash a way for the infantry through the enemy's formidable wire entanglements, instead of relying upon the usual artillery preparation: and it will be seen how great was the measure of success brought about by this new idea. For hitherto the opposing forces, regarding artillery preparation as heralding an attack, prepared accordingly.

The front selected for the initial attack extended for a distance of about six miles, from east of Gonnelieu to the Canal du Nord opposite Hermies. On this front six divisions of infantry, with some 420 tanks, were to attack the Hindenburg Main and Support Lines and pass through in the direction of Cambrai. These six Divisions, from right to left, were: 12th about Gonnelieu, 20th between Villers Plouich and La Vacquerie, 6th just north of Beaucamp, 51st at Trescault, 62nd in the northern end of Havrincourt Wood. The 36th Division was on the left of the 62nd. The 29th Division was at Guyencourt ready to go through to Masnières.

No easy task lay in front of the 20th Division, for the enemy held almost the whole of Welsh Ridge across which ran three powerful lines of German trenches, sited on high ground and commanding the lower slopes up which the British troops must advance. But at this period the Division was full of fight.

When, on 1st October, the 20th Division moved south from the Proven area to Sorel-le-Grand, exhausted by the heavy fighting it had gone through in the Ypres Salient, the troops were told they were being sent to a quiet part of the line to recuperate. Apparently it was that kind of recuperation which took place before the Somme Battles of 1916, when divisions behind the front line were trained and amused and had such a good time generally that one of the officers said: "They are fattening us up for the slaughter." There was no doubt, however, about the Cambrai front at this period (early October 1917) being a quiet sector. Colonel Troyte-Bullock of the 7th Somersets said: "It proved to be for the time being a really pleasant spot."

The 7th Somerset Light Infantry, after entraining at Proven on 1st October, reached Bapaume on the following day, marching thence to Lechelle and spending the night in a camp. On 3rd the Battalion moved to Ytres, on 4th to Haut Allaine near Peronne, where the 61st Brigade was concentrated in canvas camps: the 20th Division now formed part of the III Corps. Until the 8th October the Somerset men remained near Peronne, but on that date moved to Heudecourt and were accommodated in huts amongst the ruins of the village. The strength of the 7th Battalion was now 20 officers and 560 other ranks.

On the night of 9th/10th October the 20th Division relieved the 40th 7th Battalion 9th/10th October Division in the front line, Villers Guislain–Gonnelieu–Villers Plouich, the 7th Somersets relieving the 20th Middlesex in the Villers Guislain sector: this was the pleasant spot. For here No Man's Land was from 1,000 to 1,200 yards wide. The opposing trenches were divided by a deep and wide valley through which ran the Canal de l'Escaut. The country was not unlike the Downs of the South of England, covered with long grass or stubble in which partridges abounded. The birds afforded the men quite a lot of amusement and many ("sitters," of course) were shot and sent back to Battalion Headquarters for the C.O.'s dinner: there were others also who dined off partridge besides the Colonel! Battalion Headquarters were in Elephant shelters built along the side of the sunken road running from Villers Guislain to Honnecourt. Honnecourt was in the dead ground which lay between the British and German trenches.

In this quiet little place time passed without incident. Only an occasional shell hurtled through the air and exploded in Villers Guislain—nothing more. The wide expanse of No Man's Land made active patrolling necessary, but although four patrols went out each night, not once did they come into contact with hostile parties. Similarly snipers, concealed in the long grass, lay out all day in front of the trenches frequently without firing a single shot. The weather generally was fine and warm and altogether life in this sector was so pleasant that the Battalion wags began to wonder whether the Higher Commands would forget the 20th Division and leave it in its present sector for the duration of the War.[1]

But already there were certain signs that before long there would be something doing. Road-making, which suddenly became urgent, and the building of light railways, pointed surely in the direction of offensive operations in the near future. The formation of dumps began and soon there was no longer any doubt.

On 15th October the 7th Somersets were relieved by the 12th King's and moved back to Vaucelette Farm, where in the neighbourhood was a collection of huts and dug-outs. The Battalion was now in Brigade Reserve and vigorous training in musketry, with Lewis guns, and bombing, became the order of the day. The Battalion went back into the front line on 21st, but came out again on 29th, being relieved on the night 29th/30th by troops of the 55th Division which was taking over Villers Guislain from the 20th Division. The Somerset men then moved back to Sorel-le-Grand into a hut camp, where snug and comfortable quarters were obtained until 5th November. The latter date, however, saw a change in the conditions in the front line. The Battalion had moved back into the trenches on the night 5th/6th, relieving the 7th D.C.L.I. in the Gonnelieu sector. This sector was 5th/6th November by no means a health resort. The enemy's trenches were much closer and the Germans in them were not, apparently, as peace-loving as those who manned the hostile trenches opposite Villers Guislain, for they were especially

---

[1] The Battalion casualties during October were three other ranks wounded.

7th Battalion

active with large trench mortars. The Battalion Diary, however, describes the trenches as being good, all parts of the line easily accessible by daylight, all trenches (fire and communication) duck-boarded, and Battalion and Company Headquarters in deep dug-outs.

10th November

Early on the morning of 10th November the Battalion was relieved by the 12th King's and moved back into support positions, i.e. Cemetery Road, Villers Guislain. Only a few hours were spent in this spot, for at night the 7th Somersets were relieved in support by the 7th K.O.Y.L.I. and marched to Fins, entraining at the latter place under sealed orders at 4 a.m. on 11th November.

By this period preparations for the Cambrai offensive had made good headway. Large numbers of tanks had been collected and gradually every Battalion was withdrawn from the line and given twenty-four hours' training with the steel monsters. The sealed orders under which the Somersets had left Fins soon became known when the Battalion arrived at Bray-sur-Somme where the tanks were collected.

Bray was reached about 7.20 a.m. on 11th November and, after all ranks had had a clean up and breakfasts had been eaten, the remaining hours of daylight were spent in drilling with the tanks and in manœuvring with them. The morning and afternoon of 12th were similarly spent, but at 6 p.m. the Battalion again entrained at Bray station and about 10.30 p.m. reached Fins and marched to Sorel-le-Grand, billeting in the old huts previously occupied. This little trip to Bray had removed the last vestige of doubt as to what was to happen to the Battalion. "No one had any doubt now," said the C.O., "as to what was in store for them, and training became more intense than ever." On the 13th November a draft of thirty other ranks arrived which helped to swell the somewhat depleted ranks of the 7th Somersets. Until the night of 18th/19th November the Battalion remained at Sorel-le-Grand training and preparing generally for the coming offensive.

18th/19th November

Preparations for the Battle of Cambrai were indeed a triumph in Staff work. In spite of the constant movement of troops, the concentration of tanks, the digging of gun emplacements, the massing of artillery, the building of dumps, erection of camouflage screens and a hundred and one other things necessary to the successful launching of a great offensive, not a suspicion reached the enemy of what was going on behind the British front lines. No large attack had ever been made without artillery preparation and certainly the guns had not taken part in operations without previous registration. But in the preparatory stages of the Battle of Cambrai no registration of guns was allowed and (as already stated) no artillery preparation was to precede the launching of the tank and infantry attack. At Zero hour a barrage was to fall and behind it the tanks and infantry were to advance immediately. For once weather conditions favoured the Battle and for several days, during which final preparations were made, a thick mist hung over the battlefield-to-be, preventing the enemy's aeroplanes from obtaining any information of what was going on behind the front line.

The general attack of the 20th Division was to be north-east across the Hindenburg Main and Support Lines: the left Divisional boundary was the Villers Plouich–Marcoing railway, the right boundary a line approximately 2,500 yards to the south-east.   The first objective of the Division followed the general line of a track from Banteaux to Ribecourt, between the road from La Vacquerie to Bonavis and the railway.   On the right La Vacquerie formed a particularly strong point in the enemy's line of defence and this village and the trenches north-west of it formed the initial objective allotted to the 61st Infantry Brigade.   The second and final objective included the whole of the Welsh Ridge from a point in the sunken road nearly 3,000 yards north-east of La Vacquerie to the railway about 1,200 yards south-west of the railway junction at Marcoing.   It is, however, with the village that this chapter is chiefly concerned, for the 7th Somersets had been ordered to capture La Vacquerie Support and Strong Point.

The 61st Brigade was to attack on the right, the 66th Brigade on the left and the 59th Brigade form the Divisional Reserve.   The attack was to be in three waves, each wave to be accompanied by a wave of tanks.

Of the 61st Brigade, the first wave consisting of 7th Somersets on the right and the 7th D.C.L.I. on the left (less two companies), accompanied by nine tanks, was to capture La Vacquerie and the system of trenches north-west of it.   The Somersets, accompanied by nine tanks and assisted by four machine guns, were to capture the objectives already named, the 7th D.C.L.I. capturing Corner Work and a portion of the sunken road north-west of the village. The second wave was to consist of the 12th King's (less two companies) on the right and two companies D.C.L.I. on the left, each accompanied by six tanks: the objective of the second wave was the Blue Line.   The third wave, formed of two companies 12th King's on the right and 7th K.O.Y.L.I. on the left, each accompanied by three tanks, was to capture the Brown Line on the Brigade front.   Each wave was to consolidate the positions captured by it.

On the night of 18th/19th a patrol of 60th Brigade lost a man wounded, who had fallen into the hands of the enemy and speculation, (and fears) were rife lest, in an unguarded moment, the Germans might worm information concerning the attack from their prisoner.   But the 19th passed quietly without any undue activity on the part of the enemy.   As soon as darkness had fallen the Battalions holding the front line set to work to fill in part of the trenches so as to allow the tanks to get across without difficulty.

All Companies of the 7th Somersets (Lieut.-Colonel Troyte-Bullock) began moving into their assembly positions at 4.30 a.m., about 500 yards behind the front line.   The order of attack was to be C Company on the right, B Company in the centre, and D on the left, each Company finding its own support: to each of these three Companies three tanks had been allotted.   Bn. H.Qs. and A Company were in reserve.   The distance between the British and German lines was about 1,200 yards.

The tanks were originally ordered to form up in front of the front line, but on the night of 19th/20th there was a brilliant moon, and it was not considered safe for them to carry out the original intention; they therefore formed up about 200 yards in rear. This meant that the front-line companies had to move out of their trenches in order to form up in rear of their allotted tanks so as to avoid confusion when the advance began.

As Zero hour (6.20 a.m.) drew near intense excitement reigned along the whole line, and at 6.10 a.m., when the tanks began to move up slowly so as to go over punctually at Zero, it seemed impossible that the enemy should not hear them and put down a heavy barrage. But apparently he had no suspicion that he was about to be heavily attacked.

At 6.20 a.m. the tanks, followed by the infantry, entered No Man's Land, and at that moment there was a terrific crash from the hundreds of British guns massed behind the front line. A swarm of British aeroplanes, flying low, also swept over the enemy's lines. It was an inspiring moment.

At once it was evident that the enemy had had no warning of the attack, for all the response he made was a weak barrage, wild and scattered, mostly of 4·2 H.E. placed on the front-line trenches, which did little harm.

Before the attack, when the Battalion's objective had been explained to the men, they were told the 7th Somersets had been specially selected for the task of capturing La Vacquerie as it was the key position, and on its capture rested the success of the right flank of the attack.

Dawn was breaking at Zero hour, and by the time the second line of the attack cleared the Battalion front line, La Vacquerie could be seen wreathed in smoke from shell bursts, a pleasing spectacle to attacking troops. The advance went splendidly, like clockwork. From the right flank there was a certain amount of machine-gun fire and very shortly after the advance began C Company lost its Commander—Captain J. C. N. Peard—who fell wounded. By 6.40 a.m. the first-line Companies were well in La Vacquerie and Battalion Headquarters and the Reserve Company (A) were established in a sunken road at the southern edge of the village. By 7.30 a.m., the Battalion Diary states that, meeting with little resistance, the whole of the village defences had been captured and were being consolidated. An hour later the three Companies, C, B and D, reported that they were in the trenches on the northern edge of the village which had been cleared of the enemy. Battalion Headquarters and A Company again moved forward into some trenches on the north-east side of La Vacquerie, as the sunken road was now under heavy machine-gun fire from the south.

Up to this period casualties had been very small: 2/Lieut. E. J. Rice and four other ranks had been killed, and one officer (already given) and twenty other ranks wounded. These small casualties were due to the actions of the tanks, which had a paralysing effect on the enemy. These ungainly monsters literally fell on and crushed out of existence hostile machine-gun nests and strong points, and the terrified Germans either fled or gave themselves up immediately. They crossed trenches without trouble, while the wire-cutting tanks swept or cleared a way through the formidable wire entangle-

ments with the greatest ease. Their success all along the line was extraordinary.

All Companies of the Somersets were hard at work consolidating their positions and in between times trying to get breakfast, when about 11 a.m. the Brigade Commander (Brigadier-General Banbury) arrived. He ordered work to be stopped and the men rested, for the Battalion was to move forward again at 2.30 p.m. to Les Rue Vertes, a suburb of Masnières on the south side of the canal, which had fallen into the hands of the 59th Brigade. The latter Brigade had advanced along the right flank of the 20th Division, passing through the left of the 12th Division who were engaged in forming a defensive flank along the high ground between the Villers Guislain–Bantouzelle road and Lateau Wood. The 29th Division had also pushed forward across the canal and were in Masnières. Thus the Hindenburg Line had been broken and the Germans in it either dead, captured, or in full flight.

About 1 p.m. the infantrymen in La Vacquerie had a wonderful sight: the Cavalry Corps could be seen moving up across the downs towards Masnières, for the Cavalry had received orders to push through as far as possible, even to Cambrai if it could be reached. But unfortunately the canal bridge at Masnières broke down under one of the tanks attached to the 29th Division: the tank remained sitting on top of the ruins, effectively blocking the crossing and checking the advance of the Cavalry. Some units did succeed in getting across and within a mile of Cambrai, then had to retire through lack of support. Thus the splendid advance of the tanks and infantry was robbed of complete victory. The 29th Division was held up by a strong system of trenches running through Rumilly to Wambaix and could not get on. And, although a battalion of the 59th Brigade with orders to capture Crevecœur, succeeded in getting a footing in the village, it was driven back across the canal by a strong hostile counter-attack.

At 2.30 p.m. the 7th Somersets moved off from La Vacquerie, having received orders to advance to Les Rue Vertes. On arrival at the latter place the Battalion was to report to the G.O.C., 88th Brigade (29th Division), in Masnières. Rain was now beginning to fall and the road to Les Rue Vertes (an unmetalled track running through a deep valley) was a sea of mud, hopelessly blocked with broken-down tanks and guns. The Battalion had, therefore, to make a wide detour over the high ground on the north-west side of the road, and it was 6 p.m. and just getting dark before Les Rue Vertes was reached. The C.O. had, however, gone on ahead and when Companies arrived had selected an old trench line just outside the village. On reporting to the 88th Brigade the Battalion was ordered to remain in this position for the night. In the midst of a drizzling rain, and dog-tired after considerable work on the trenches they occupied, the Somerset men settled down to a very uncomfortable night.

In spite of their cheerless surroundings they were in the best of spirits: the Battalion had done well, had gained all its objectives and had suffered comparatively few casualties—five killed and thirty-five wounded, all ranks.

Of the general attack on the 20th November the official despatches said:—

"At the end of the first day of the attack . . . three German systems of defence had been broken through to a depth of some 4½ miles on a wide front, and over 5,000 prisoners had already been brought in. But for the wrecking of the bridge at Masnières and the check at Flesquières, still greater results might have been attained."

The night of 20th/21st November was comparatively quiet, the enemy firing only a few shells into La Vacquerie. At dawn on 21st the rain had ceased and the day broke fine and bright. About 11 a.m. orders were received from the 88th Brigade for the 7th Somersets to move across the canal to the eastern end of Masnières in anticipation of an enemy counter-attack on the 29th Division. The Staff Officer who brought these orders assured Colonel Troyte-Bullock that his Battalion, by going direct across country instead of through Les Rue Vertes which was under hostile shell fire, could get across the canal by a temporary footbridge.

At noon the Somersets moved off, C Company under Lieut. Spark, going via Les Rue Vertes with orders to take up positions covering the bridges across the canal between Les Rue Vertes and Masnières. Battalion Headquarters and the three remaining Companies, with a section of the 61st Machine-Gun Company, moved across the open ground between the main road and the canal in lines of platoons extended. The C.O. and his orderly had fortunately gone on ahead: they found the footbridge without difficulty, but also found that there was a wide belt of swampy ground all along the southern side of the canal, with only a narrow, but fairly firm, track across it. The Companies were thus enabled to cross without delay. Across the canal they got under cover of the houses and garden walls immediately opposite. During this advance a certain amount of machine-gun fire was encountered, but only one casualty was incurred—one man killed. Battalion Headquarters were established in two small houses on the canal bank and Companies were accommodated in cellars. As the expected counter-attack did not materialize the Battalion was therefore given permission to stand down and take over the guarding and searching of some subterranean passages discovered in the centre of the village. The remainder of the 21st passed without incident, but the G.O.C., 88th Brigade, sent back the following message to the G.O.C., 61st Infantry Brigade:—

"I wish to tell you how much I appreciate the excellent work done by the 7th Somerset L.I. in Masnières in clearing the houses of snipers and exploring the many underground passages. The place is quite quiet now with a Somerset on guard at each hole."

Thus, so far as the Somerset Light Infantry were concerned, ended the first phase—The Tank Attack—of the Battle of Cambrai, 1917.

BRITISH TANK COVERING AN INFANTRY ADVANCE WITH SMOKE SCREEN

II. THE GERMAN COUNTER-ATTACKS: 30TH NOVEMBER–3RD DECEMBER   7th Battalion

"From our old front line east of Gonnelieu the right flank of our new positions lay along the eastern slopes of the Bonavis Ridge, passing east of Lateau Wood and striking the Masnières–Beaurevoir line north of the Canal de l'Escaut at a point about half-way between Crèvecour and Masnières. From this point our line ran roughly N.W. past (and including) Masnières, Noyelles and Cantaing to Fontaine, also inclusive. Thence it bent back to the south for a short distance, making a sharp salient round the latter village, and ran in a generally western direction along the southern edge of Bourlon Wood, and across the southern face of the spur to the west of the Wood, to the Canal du Nord, south-east of the village of Moeuvres. From Moeuvres the line linked up once more with our old front at a point about midway between Boursies and Pronville."—*Official Despatches.*

The above quotation gives the British line after the first phase of the Battle of Cambrai, i.e. the Tank Attack on 20th and 21st November. Between the 23rd and 28th November Bourlon Wood was attacked and captured, but the 7th Somersets were not actually engaged during these operations. During the evening of 23rd the 88th Brigade (to which the Battalion was 23rd November still attached) was relieved by the 87th Brigade and, as the C.O. facetiously said: "The Battalion was handed over as trench stores" to the incoming Brigade. At 7 p.m. the enemy put down a very heavy bombardment on Masnières and the line of the Canal. Every one stood to in anticipation of a strong counter-attack which the enemy was expected to make, but no infantry attack developed. Casualties on this day were three other ranks killed and four wounded. On the 24th the 7th Somersets occupied the same position, supplying large working parties to work on the trenches of the 87th Brigade. The next evening, however, at dusk, the Battalion rejoined the 61st Brigade and went into Brigade Reserve in the rear system of the Hindenburg Line. The 26th was a quiet day—ominously quiet—for no one imagined that the enemy would take the beating he had received sitting down. Snow fell during the day, and the men were hard at work putting up shelters.

On 28th the 7th Somersets relieved the 7th K.O.Y.L.I. in the front line, the relief being completed by 9 p.m.: the Battalion occupied the left sub-sector of the 61st Brigade front. The main line of the 20th Division at this period ran from Lateau Wood (held by the 12th Division) in a south-easterly direction along the Spur, thence northwards to the Canal. The 59th Brigade held the right sub-sector and the 61st Brigade the left. The trenches taken over by the Somerset men consisted of a system of posts dug on the top of the Spur. On the night of 29th the outpost line was pushed forward some 200 yards and the men dug themselves in. There was a reserve line in a deep ravine which ran roughly parallel with the main Gouzeaucourt–Masnières road.

On the 28th, when the Battalion went into the front line, Colonel Troyte-Bullock (in common with all C.O.'s) had been ordered back to the Detail Camp for a short rest and Major R. P. Preston-Whyte took command of the Battalion. But the Brigadier of the 59th Brigade was ill and, on reaching the transport lines at Fins about 1 a.m. on 29th, Colonel Troyte-Bullock 29th November was ordered to take temporary command of the 59th Brigade.

Nothing of importance happened during the 29th though every one was

7th Battalion watchful. The enemy had been heavily reinforced, though, as yet, he had made no heavy counter-attack. The position of the 61st Brigade was no sinecure; the ridge upon which the Brigade (and indeed the 20th Division) line was extended was dominated by higher ground on the enemy's side of the Canal and was open to hostile artillery fire from the south-west, east and north-west—not a pleasing prospect. Moreover, in front of the line held by the Somerset men, and on their side of the Canal, there was a small house held by the enemy with machine guns, which were particularly active.

30th November The night of 29th/30th was quiet, and when dawn broke on the 30th the ground was heavy with mist. About 7 a.m. a very heavy trench-mortar barrage, from the other side of the Canal, fell suddenly on the front-line posts. Fortunately, owing to the foresight of Major Preston-Whyte, these posts had been evacuated during the night, the intention being to reoccupy them by day. The posts were practically wiped out and, had they been occupied, heavy casualties must have been incurred.

Immediately behind the trench-mortar barrage the enemy's infantry could be seen advancing in great strength. It was indeed a sight which almost made men gasp. Line after line, in massed formation, the Germans advanced to the attack, providing splendid targets for Lewis guns, machine guns and rifles. By sheer weight of numbers they intended recapturing the line which had been wrested from them. Swarms of low-flying aeroplanes, the observers using machine guns, crossed from the enemy's side and flew up and down above the British trenches at an altitude of from fifty to one hundred feet. Above the Somerset men, at least forty-five hostile machines were counted—a wonderful sight.

The German counter-attack was not general along the whole front, but directed at the southern and northern portions of the salient: on the south between Vendhuille and the Canal at Masnières and on the north between Fontaine and Moeuvres. It was another of those German attempts to "pinch off" salients. During the War both the Allies and the enemy made many such attacks and they were invariably costly in the extreme. In this instance the German losses were terrible. The heaviest attacks were on the northern portion of the salient, where at one time eleven waves of German infantry advanced successively to the attack—the enemy's casualties here were enormous.

With rifle and Lewis-gun fire the 7th Somersets did great execution as the Germans advanced from the Canal towards the front-line posts: seldom had the Battalion been offered such splendid targets, but now they took full advantage of their good luck and shot the Germans down by scores. But presently ammunition began to run short and to every one's dismay it was discovered that a Battalion on the right of the Somersets had given way in the face of sheer numbers: also that the enemy was working round the right flank and rear of the Battalion. Orders were then given to withdraw to the reserve line in the ravine running roughly parallel with the main Gouzeaucourt–Masnières road. Here a short stand was made, but the enemy again worked round the right flank and a further withdrawal was made to the Hindenburg

Line, then being held by the 7th K.O.Y.L.I. and 61st Brigade Headquarters. Here the enemy was held and though, throughout the day, he made brave efforts to force the line back farther, all his attempts were fruitless and time after time he was bloodily repulsed.

But the 7th Somersets had been practically wiped out. The only officers who survived were Lieuts. Spark and McMurtrie with the remnants of their Companies, acting C.S.M. J. Bulson, Sergt. Peaty and about sixty other ranks.

C.S.M. Bulson had put up a splendid fight, covering the withdrawal of the remnants of his Company with Lewis-gun fire: he was afterwards awarded the D.C.M. Captain L. Wild (commanding C Company) and Lieut. R. L. Tawney (commanding D Company) were both killed fighting, revolvers in hand, to the very last. Capt. Andrews (A Company) fell at the head of his men as he was leading them forward to make a local counter-attack with the bayonet: he was captured by the enemy. The Battalion Signal Officer—Lieut. Paul—who had taken a hand in the fighting, was severely wounded; rifle in hand, he also was taken prisoner. Early in the morning Major Preston-Whyte, who with Battalion Headquarters was making a stand, was also wounded, as well as Captain Jenks, the acting second-in-command: both were got away. The Battalion's Nonconformist Padre—Reverend Hines, the Battalion M.O.—Captain Pickup, R.A.M.C., and the Bombing Officer—2/Lieut. Stoker, all with Battalion Headquarters, were wounded. Besides Captain Wild and Lieut. Tawney, 2/Lieuts. Pearcey and Caulfield were killed: 2/Lieut. Cox was wounded and died of his wounds on 8th December. In other ranks the 7th Somersets lost 158 wounded and 174 missing. The total casualties suffered by the Battalion on the 30th November 1917 were 12 officers and 332 other ranks.

Throughout the 1st December the attack continued, the 61st Brigade holding the rear element of the Hindenburg Line on the eastern side of the La Vacquerie–Les Rue Vertes sunken road, against repeated attempts by the enemy to break through. He also made desperate efforts to reoccupy La Vacquerie, gallantly held by a battalion of the 60th Rifles, who were commanded by an old Somerset officer, Lieut.-Colonel G. Moore. But these efforts broke down before the splendid defence put up by the British troops. During the night of 1st/2nd December the 61st Brigade was relieved by a portion of the 61st Division sent up to relieve the 20th Division, and the 7th Somersets marched back to Sorel-le-Grand and went into camp at the transport lines there. The Battalion, on coming out of the front line, numbered two officers—Captain D. S. Spark and Lieut. G. D. J. McMurtrie—and about ninety other ranks: Captain P. E. E. Chappell was now in temporary command of the Battalion.

By the close of 3rd December the German attacks had died down, and although Havrincourt, Flèsquieres and Ribecourt and considerable territory on both sides of these villages remained in the hands of the British, Villers-Guislain and Gonnelieu, with a wide stretch of ground south of the former village, had been lost.

7th Battalion
3rd December

Thus the Cambrai Battle of 1917, begun with such fine prospects of success, had turned the scale but little in favour of the Allies, though the enemy had suffered enormous losses in men and material, and it was fortunate for him that he was able to draw reinforcements from the East.

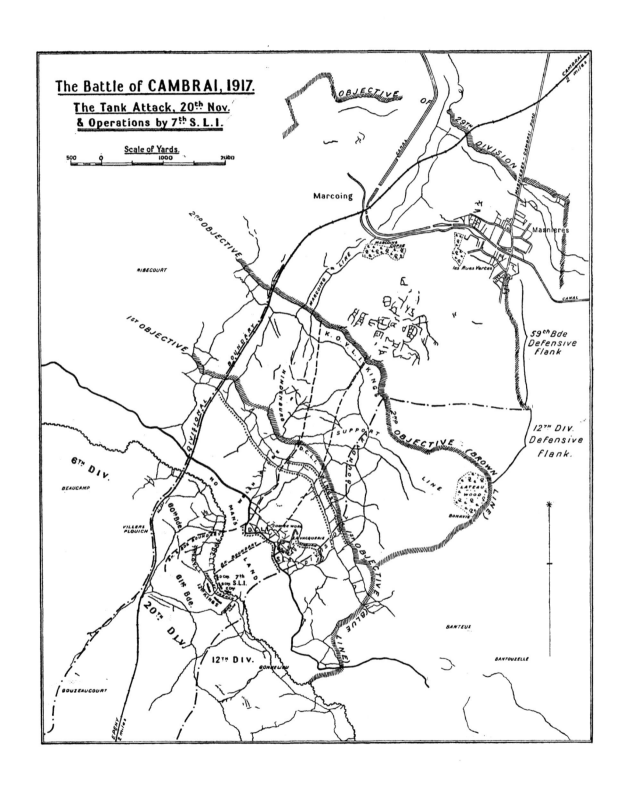

The Battle of CAMBRAI, 1917.

The Tank Attack, 20th Nov. & Operations by 7th S.L.I.

Scale of Yards.

CHAPTER XXVII

THE INVASION OF PALESTINE

THIRD BATTLE OF GAZA, 27TH OCTOBER–7TH NOVEMBER 1917

BETWEEN the close of the second unsuccessful attempt (17th–19th   12th Battalion
April) to capture Gaza and the Third Battle which began on 27th
October of the same year, no action of importance took place in
Palestine. During the summer months operations were impossible
and it was necessary to wait for the autumn or winter before further offensive
action could be undertaken against the line Beersheba–Gaza. General Sir
E. H. H. Allenby had taken over command of the Egyptian Expeditionary
Force in June and after a thorough reconnaissance of the enemy's positions
he reported the situation of the latter to the War Office with proposals for
attacking the Turks.

About the middle of July 1917 the Turkish Army held a line extending
from the sea at Gaza, thence roughly along the Gaza–Beersheba road to Beersheba. Gaza occupied a naturally strong position, but it had been rendered
additionally strong by the construction of powerful trenches heavily wired,
so that the town was in reality a modern fortress capable of affording a pro-
tracted defence. Between Gaza and Beersheba the enemy's line consisted
chiefly of several strong localities, i.e. the Sihan group of works, the Atawineh
Group, the Baha Group, the Abu–Hareira–Arab-el-Teeaha trench system,
and, finally, the works covering Beersheba. The distance between the Hareira
Group and the Beersheba defences was about four and a half miles, though
the other groups were closer and averaged from 1,500 to 2,000 yards apart.
The distance from Gaza to Beersheba was about thirty miles, but the enemy's
communications were good and he could quickly reinforce any threatened
portions of his line.

The British force held a line of about twenty-two miles, extending from
the sea in front of Gaza to Gamli. An insufficient water supply made it impossible, without extensive preparations, to approach within striking distance
of the enemy, excepting in the small sector near the sea coast opposite Gaza.

The main blow of the British attack was to be made against the left flank
of the Turkish main position: this was the line Hareira–Sheria. A necessary
preliminary operation to the attack was the capture of Beersheba in order to
secure the water supplies in that place, also to give room for the deployment
of the attacking force on the high ground north and north-west of Beersheba,
from which direction the attack on the Hareira–Sheria line was to be made.
To deceive the Turks as to the real objective of the attack, Gaza was to be
bombarded for several days up to Zero hour, and other means taken to impress
the enemy that his right flank on the sea was the object of the attack. The

12th Battalion Navy was to co-operate by bombarding Gaza and the enemy's railway stations and depôts north of the town.

The chief difficulties to be overcome were those connected with the water supply and transport. So far as water was concerned, the troops would be operating a considerable distance from their original water base, and the transport trouble was aggravated by the steep banks of many of the wadis which intersected the area of operations, so that the routes for wheeled transport were very limited. Railway lines had also to be laid and the troops carefully trained and instructed in the parts they were to take.

The enemy's forces on the Palestine front were increased between the months of July and October, and it was evident from these reinforcements and the construction of certain railway extensions behind his front line that he was determined to make every effort to maintain his position on the Gaza–Beersheba line.

The date of the attack on Beersheba, the opening stage of the operations, was fixed for the 31st October. Work on the extra railway communications from Shellal towards Karm, and the development of the water supply at Esani, Khalasa and Asluj, proceeded as rapidly as possible: Khalasa and Asluj were to be the starting points from which the Mounted Force, detailed to make the wide flanking movement on Beersheba from the east and north-east, would make its attack.

On the morning of 27th October the Turks made a strong reconnaissance in force towards Karm from the direction of Kouwukah, cavalry, infantry and artillery being employed. They attacked a line of outposts near El Girheir held by some Yeomanry who were protecting the troops at work on railway construction. A small post was rushed and cut up after inflicting heavy losses on the enemy, but on the arrival of the 53rd (Welsh) Division the Turks withdrew. The bombardment of the Gaza defences began on this date, and on 30th the warships of the Royal Navy, assisted by a French battleship, co-operated.

On the night 30th/31st October the XX Corps moved forward to positions of deployment. By dawn on Zero day these troops were in position ready for the attack. Simultaneously the Desert Mounted Corps (less the Yeomanry Mounted Division) moved up to positions about Khasim Zanna ready to co-operate with the XX Corps in the attack on Beersheba. The Desert Corps was to attack the town from the east.

In the plan of attack on Beersheba the 60th and 74th Divisions were to seize the enemy's works between the Khalasa road and the Wadi Saba, the defences north of the wadi being rushed by the Imperial Camel Corps and two battalions of the 53rd Division. The Anzac Mounted Division, the Australian Mounted Division and the 7th Mounted Brigade were to attack the Beersheba defences from the north-east, east and south-east.

Such, briefly, was the plan of attack.

At this period the XX Corps comprised the 10th Division (newly arrived from Salonica), the 53rd, 60th (also recently arrived from Salonica) and the

74th, the latter containing the 12th (West Somerset Yeomanry) Battalion of 12th Battalion the Somerset Light Infantry.

After the Second Battle of Gaza (17th–19th April 1917) the 12th Somersets (229th Infantry Brigade, 74th Division) moved on the 22nd April to El 22nd April Mendur, to dig a new line to complete the Army defences from the Wadi Ghuzze at Tel el Jemmi to the Abbas Apex, whence to the sea the Gaza divisions had already "dug in." Work on the new line was strenuous and when, on the 6th May, the Battalion was relieved and moved back to Sharta Wadi a completed fire trench, wired all along its length, was handed over to the incoming battalion: moreover, a support line and communication trenches were well under way, when the relief of the Somerset Yeomen took place. In Sharta Wadi the Battalion was now in General Reserve to the section of outpost line occupied by the 229th Infantry Brigade.

On the 25th May the Battalion relieved the Fife and Forfar Yeomanry 25th May Battalion in G and H sections of the Centre Divisional outpost line, south of the Abbas Apex. The 74th Division held the sector (north and south of the apex) for nine continuous weeks, the front line running along the top of the Mansura and Abbas Ridges, described by an officer of the Battalion as a "strange freak of nature." It was, indeed, a curious spot, for in rear of the trenches there fell the cliffs of the ridge in which were honeycombed the shelters of the cave dwellers.

"From the rough sides of the ridge through the tumbling, broken ground at its foot there issued the river-beds of many wadis, on which were bestowed the names of the Twelve Tribes of Israel. Tributaries of the Wadi Nukhabir, which joined the big Wadi Ghuzze at Sheik Nebhan, these Tribal wadis and that of Nukhabir too, provided the covered ways of approach to our positions and the homes for supports, Battalion and Brigade Headquarters. . . . To stand on the Mansura Ridge, looking westward, was to look down upon a large amphitheatre of rough, sandy ground, intersected by the numerous deep-cut wadis: to look eastward and north-west was to gaze upon a gently rolling country intersected by the Wadis Sihan, Atawineh, and their tributaries which, except to our immediate front, were indiscernible as they wandered deep between the folds of the ground. It was a fair and comfortable landscape and the presence of the Turk did not intrude itself. A couple of miles formed a No Man's Land and the ocular evidences of an enemy were few, the most noticeable being the Atawineh and the Tank Redoubts; the latter, marked by a derelict British tank perched on the skyline, showed the high-water mark of our advance on April 17th to 18th. Away to the north-west stood Ali el Muntar, the watch tower of Gaza, which was itself hidden from view by its encircling hills, and many a march was in front of us before we came to look upon the town which held us for so long."

With a No Man's Land so broad and wide patrolling was extensive and as a rule without result, but on 28th May, three days after the 12th Somersets had relieved the Fife and Forfar Yeomanry in the line, a patrol taken out by

Lieut. W. R. S. Leversha brought in two Turkish prisoners, one an officer and the other a sergeant. The patrol had visited the Wadi Sihan near Well Farm, and having discovered the two Turks, hid in the banks of the wadi and jumped out on the Turks as they passed by. The next encounter took place on 4th June when at 1.30 a.m. a patrol of Turks about ten in number advanced towards the trenches of the Somersets. They were discovered by No. 1 Standing Patrol of H Section and fired on, and after throwing two bombs the Turks fled back to their own lines. A little later, 5 a.m., the enemy's snipers were busy firing into an O.P. and a patrol, consisting of 2/Lieut. A. V. Hallewell and five other ranks, went out to deal with them. Near Two Tree Farm they found the enemy and after wounding one retired to the

trenches. An exciting patrol encounter took place on the night of 7th/8th June, which reflected great credit on the patrol concerned and the Battalion generally. A patrol of C Company, consisting of Lieut. Leversha (who was in command), 2/Lieut. N. H. Casey and twenty-six other ranks, left "G" Sector at 7.30 p.m. to make a reconnaissance of the enemy's position. They proceeded to Two Tree Farm, where the main body of the patrol was left. Taking with him only six other ranks, Lieut. Leversha then set out to reconnoitre the Aeroplane. On completing his reconnaissance he was returning to the main body of the patrol when suddenly rifle fire was opened on him and his men from front and both flanks at a range of about twenty yards. Leversha and his men returned the fire immediately and drove the Turks, estimated at about twenty-five in number, off about 100 yards. But by this time the enemy had worked round his flanks and opened fire from the rear. Finding himself almost surrounded, the only thing to do was to break through. The gallant little band therefore charged the enemy with the bayonet and after killing one and wounding two of the Turks broke through and reached the main body of the patrol in safety. The whole patrol retired at about 1 a.m. on 8th June. This little affair formed the subject of a Special Order of the Day, issued by the G.O.C. (Major-General E. S. Girdwood) commanding the 74th Division, the preamble of which said: "The G.O.C. desires to bring to the notice of all ranks of the 74th Division the excellent work carried out by a patrol of the 12th Battalion Somerset Light Infantry on the night of June 7th/8th 1917, whereby information of considerable value was obtained and casualties inflicted on the enemy." The Order then details the names of Lieut. Leversha and his gallant comrades. The latter were: 295022 Sergt. A. V. Chapple, 295256 Pte. W. J. Adams, 295378 Pte. W. H. Duke, 295 Pte. S. C. Knight, 20649 Pte. J. Dennett, 295454 L/Cpl. J. Margery.

An amusing little story was in circulation after this affair. It had been discovered that the brilliant moon which shone down on many of the patrols who went out at night, glinted on the bayonets, thereby disclosing their presence to the enemy. It was the practice, therefore, for the patrols to cover their bayonets with strips of sacking. After the affair on the night 7th/8th June one of the men was asked if he had found the sacking over the bayonet any obstruction, and he replied: "Noa, zur, her went in voine." The man of

whom this story was told received the Military Medal. Lieut. Leversha 12th Battalion
was awarded the Military Cross.

On 14th June the Battalion was relieved in the line for twenty-four hours 14th June
and given a great treat: companies were marched down to the sea for a bathe.
This event may seem a small matter to record, but in those days to get a complete
immersion in water was a great thing in Palestine, the usual allowance for a
bath (at rare intervals) being about half a gallon per man.

At last on 2nd July the Battalion's long spell in the Abbas Sector came to
an end, the 229th Brigade being relieved by the 156th Brigade of the 52nd
Division. The Battalion then withdrew to the Wadi Reuben where training
was resumed. Constant practice by companies, battalions and brigades gave
the Somerset men some idea of the part they were destined to play in the next
offensive. It was evidently *not* to be a trench-to-trench attack on the Gaza
side, but long, hot marches, fearfully fatiguing, to the Beersheba flank. This
period of training in the heat of Palestine was very strenuous, though at the
end of it the Battalion was in fine condition.

On the 26th August the 12th Somersets were moved up the coast to 26th August
Regent's Park, just north of the Wadi Ghuzze. Here the Battalion was set
to work to dig a jumping-off trench for the 54th Division to which, for the
time being, the Somerset men were attached. The position allotted to the
Battalion was immediately opposite to, and not a great many yards from,
Bunkers Hill. Covering parties out in front gave the Battalion protection
during the process of digging, the Battalion providing half its strength nightly
for the task. But the best protection from the enemy's rifle and machine-gun
fire (very active and sustained at this period) was to disappear below ground
with all celerity. This new work had hardly been begun before it was detected
by the Turks and after the first night the enemy's guns got to work on the new
trench. Fortunately their aim was not good and casualties were not severe,
one other rank killed and seven wounded being the total losses during these
digging operations. On the night of 3rd/4th September Captain Wheeler
with two other officers and 128 other ranks beat off an enemy attack, the
Turks evidently losing heavily as their stretcher-bearers were seen at work
until dawn.

On the night 5th/6th the Battalion was relieved in the Fusilier Ridge–
Jones Post–Bacon's Boil trench line by the East and West Kent Yeomanry
and marched back to the sandy ridge of Goz el Taire in the neighbourhood
of Belah.

Training was now resumed and every possible feature of the attack was
rehearsed. Night marches and night operations, smoke demonstrations and
the training of specialists brought the troops to a state of great physical fitness.

On the 17th October, to the great regret of all ranks of the Battalion, 17th October
the Commanding Officer—Lieut.-Colonel F. N. Quantock Shuldham—was
sent into hospital.[1] He had brought the 12th Somersets to a fine state of
efficiency and discipline and had had the confidence, devotion and affection

---

[1] Lieut.-Colonel Shuldham never rejoined his Battalion.

12th Battalion

of every officer and man in the Battalion.   Major G. S. Poole assumed command of the Battalion.

October was drawing to a close when on the 25th the 12th Somersets moved to Abu Sitta, and on the 26th to Gamli, bivouacking on the northern bank of the Wadi Ghuzze.   On the 28th the Battalion (in Brigade) marched to El Buggar Camp, the Somersets forming the Advanced Guard of the Brigade.

30th October

At 5.30 p.m. on 30th the Battalion advanced across the Wadi Saba and bivouacked in Dunster Wadi.

The attack of the 74th Division on Beersheba was to be made by the 230th and 231st Brigades, the 229th Brigade remaining in reserve: the 60th Division was on the right of the 74th and the 53rd on the left.

The functions of the 229th Brigade were first to take over the cavalry outpost line and then to form an infantry outpost line both north and south of the Wadi Saba on the front of the 53rd and 74th Divisions.   The 229th Brigade, having taken up its outpost line, the 230th and 231st Brigades were to cross the wadi and form up in their battle positions from which they were to attack the enemy.   These two Brigades, on passing through the outpost line, were to find their own protection on their jumping-off line.   The 230th and 231st Brigades, having formed up in the positions from which they were to attack, the 229th Brigade was to be withdrawn into reserve.

It has already been stated that the capture of Beersheba was the preliminary phase of the Battle and that the attack on the Hareira–Sheria line and Gaza could only be carried out if Beersheba fell into British hands.   Therefore, although there were two other Battalions of the Somerset Light Infantry—

1/5th and 2/4th Battalions

1/5th and 2/4th—engaged in the operations, they were with the 75th Division which, with the 54th and 52nd Divisions, were holding the line in front of Gaza from the coast to (and including) the Mansura and Abbas Ridges.   The part taken by these two Battalions will be described later.

1. The Capture of Beersheba and the Sheria Position

12th Battalion

The night of 30th/31st October was still and fine, one of those entrancing Eastern nights of which the poets sing.   The approach march of the 229th Brigade across the high, level plain was carried out without a hitch and the outpost line taken up successfully and apparently unseen by the Turks.   Later the attacking Brigades passed through the 229th and the rôle of the latter was, as an officer expressed it, "to obliterate ourselves."

31st October

At 8.30 a.m. on 31st October the attack was launched, the first object being to capture Hill 1070.   This was attacked by the 60th Division and as it was strongly defended and heavily wired a vigorous defence was expected. But by 8.45 a.m. the position had been captured by the Londoners.   Beersheba was then assaulted (at 12.15 p.m.), but the capture of the town was not a very difficult matter as the Turks were surprised and had expected the main assault to be delivered on Gaza, the enemy's appreciation of the situation, based on his aerial observation, reading: "An outflanking attack on Beersheba with about one infantry and one cavalry division is indicated, but the main attack

COL. E. F. COOKE-HURLE, D.S.O.
Commanded 1/5th Battalion

LT.-COL. F. D. URWICK, D.S.O., T.D.
Commanded 1/5th Battalion

LT.-COL. F. N. QUANTOCK-SHULDHAM, T.D., D.L.
Commanded 12th Battalion

LT.-COL. G. S. POOLE, D.S.O.
Commanded 12th Battalion

COMMANDING OFFICERS OF THE 1/5TH AND 12TH BATTALIONS

as before must be expected on the Gaza front." Beersheba was captured by 12th Battalion
the Desert Mounted Corps which had a difficult approach march.   Two roads 31st October
were used, both very rough, and although the Corps had to march from 25
to 35 miles during the night, the attack was made up to time.   At first
the Corps met with much opposition, the ground east of the town being
favourable to defence.   Progress was slow until about 6.30 p.m. when the
4th Australian Light Horse, extending, galloped over two lines of Turks
in their trenches and entered Beersheba, a most gallant feat.   Eleven hundred
prisoners and ten guns were taken and the Turks had lost a very strong position.

No demands had been made upon the 74th Division reserve and the 229th
Brigade, though interested spectators of the battle, took no active part in the
capture of Beersheba.   The 12th Somersets bivouacked in their reserve position
and, after a very cold night without blankets or greatcoats, were early astir
on 1st November and marched north-west of Beersheba across the newly
captured Turkish defences.   On the Gaza–Beersheba road the 53rd Division
crossed the line of march, that Division becoming the right Division of the
XX Corps in preparation for the advance on Jerusalem via the Hebron road.
The 2nd November saw the 12th Battalion in the outpost line at Muweileh: 2nd November
the 3rd somewhat hurriedly detached from the 229th Brigade and sent across
the Ain Kohleh road to support the 53rd Division then encountering stiff
resistance as it moved towards Khuweilfeh by way of Abujerwal.

The country through which the troops were advancing was now barren
and water was scarce, and in consequence every one was rationed as well as
the horses and pack animals.   Indeed, orders were issued that neither officers
nor men were to wash or shave until further orders owing to the shortage of
water.

Here for a moment it is necessary to quote from the official despatches
in order that subsequent operations in which the 12th Somersets took part
may be the better understood.

"On November 3rd we advanced north on Ain Kohleh and Tel Khuweilfeh, 3rd November
near which place the mounted troops had engaged considerable enemy forces
on the previous day.   This advance was strongly opposed but was pushed
on through difficult hill country to within a short distance of Ain Kohleh and
Khuweilfeh.   At these places the enemy was found holding a strong position
with considerable and increasing forces.   He was obviously determined not
only to bar any further progress in this direction but, if possible, to drive our
flank guard back on Beersheba.   During the 4th–5th he made several determined attacks on the mounted troops.   These attacks were repulsed.   By the
evening of November 5th the 19th Turkish Division, the remains of the 27th
and certain units of the 16th Division, had been identified in the fighting round
Tel el Khuweilfeh, and it was also fairly clear that the greater part of the hostile
cavalry, supported apparently by some infantry (depôt troops) from Hebron,
were engaged between Khuweilfeh and the Hebron road."

The enemy's action was, however, not allowed to interfere with the

12th Battalion C.-in-C.'s plan for an attack which it had been decided to carry out on 6th November on the Kauwukah and Rushdi systems of the enemy's defences, and an effort made to reach Sheria before nightfall on that date. Tel el Khuweilfeh was to be attacked at dawn on the 6th and the troops were to make every effort to reach the line Tel el Khuweilfeh–Rijm-el-Dhib.

5th November On the afternoon of 5th November all Battalion Commanders of the 229th Brigade were summoned hurriedly to a conference at Brigade Head-quarters. Here the forthcoming operations were explained to the C.O.'s The Kauwukah trenches were to be attacked early on the morning of 6th. No further orders than those given verbally at the conference were issued to the C.O.'s who, in the all too brief hours of daylight left, had still to make a reconnaissance of the position to be attacked. The 229th Brigade had, since the Beersheba operations, been busily engaged on its own front and had there-fore no opportunities of reconnoitring the enemy's position. The C.O.'s, however, hurriedly collected what Company Commanders were available and betook themselves rapidly to the neighbourhood of Muweileh for a glance (it was no more) at the enemy's positions.

The Sheria defences, Kauwukah and the Rushdi and Hareira systems were the objectives of the 10th, 60th and 74th Divisions of the XX Corps, the 53rd Division being strenuously engaged in the attack on Khuweilfeh: the Yeomanry Mounted Division operated between the 74th and 53rd Divisions. The line of the Turkish positions ran roughly north-west and south-east, the southern portions of which were assigned to the 74th Division. The capture of these systems would still further endanger the left of the Turks holding Gaza and would also assure the British possession of the valuable water supply at Sheria.

The attack of the 74th Division was to open the operations, and to the 229th Brigade was assigned the honour of being the spearhead of the attack by the XX Corps. The 12th Somersets and Fife and Forfar Battalions were to lead the 229th Brigade, the 230th Brigade being echeloned on the right rear of the 229th and the 231st to the right rear of the 230th Brigade. As the attack of the 229th Brigade proceeded so would the situation develop on the left, where the 60th and 10th Divisions were to advance in succession.

At 11 p.m. on the night of 5th the 12th Somersets moved to positions of deployment and took up the battle outpost line. The 229th Brigade was then disposed as follows: Somersets on the left, Fife and Forfars on the right and Ayr and Lanarks in support, Devons in reserve. The 12th Somersets were disposed on a two-company front, C (Captain Rattray) and D (Captain Wheeler) Companies leading, with A and B in support.

The first objective was a series of enemy works about 4,000 yards distant over very rough country, and all the information the Battalion had was that the enemy was ahead and well entrenched.

6th November At 5 a.m. on 6th the attack was launched. In spite of the lack of time in which to reconnoitre the position there was no mistake in the direction of advance, neither, as stated by one of the 12th's officers, "was there any lack in the warmth of our reception." From in front and from the right flank the advance was met by heavy machine-gun and rifle fire, the enfilade fire from the right, where the flank of the Battalion was exposed, being specially costly.

The ground over which the attack was going forward was gently rolling and bare of cover. The Turkish trenches were sited on a succession of un- dulations: they were dug deep into the ground and admirably sited, commanding an uninterrupted field of fire over the natural glacis. They were not wired but were literally stiff with machine guns, whilst in close support the Turks had a number of field guns. It was obviously no use attempting to take cover on such ground and the only way of achieving success was to dash at the enemy's trenches and get in with the bayonet as quickly as possible.

An advance over 4,000 yards of ground, absolutely without cover and swept by machine-gun and rifle fire and intermittent shell fire, is no light task, but it was done splendidly, the official despatches speaking of the attack as going forward with great dash. By 7.15 a.m. the Battalion's first objective, the Cactus Garden Ridge, was gained. Besides a number of dead Turks found in the trenches the 12th Somersets had captured 63 prisoners, 6 light field guns, 8 machine guns, a large quantity of ammunition and other trench stores.

But now, before proceeding farther, reorganization was necessary, as the attacking Battalions had become greatly intermingled. While the re- organization was proceeding the left flank of the enemy's position was being attacked by the 60th and 10th Divisions, and then began an exodus of the enemy to the rear from the Hareira and Rushdi systems.

Reorganization complete, the Fife and Forfar Battalion then conformed to the movements of the 12th Somersets, and the advance began on the second objective—the Gaza–Beersheba railway line south of Sheria Station. As the leading line of Somerset men reached the high ground overlooking the railway, the 60th Division on the left front could be seen entering the main defences of Sheria. This furnished the Lewis gunners of the Somersets with splendid targets of Turks, who were retiring on Sheria Station and the high ground north of it. The second objective was reached about 4.30 p.m. So ended a long day, most trying for the troops who, in very great heat, were fighting in their packs. About 7 p.m. the Battalion was withdrawn about 500 yards eastwards and there bivouacked for the night.

Splendidly successful as this attack had been, it had been won only at great expense to the 12th Somersets. Out of a strength of 700 all ranks the Battalion had lost in killed: Captain A. T. L. Richardson, 2/Lieut. N. D. Chadwick and 41 other ranks. In wounded the casualties were Captain A. H. Wheeler, Captain D. P. Thomas, R.A.M.C., T.F. (the Battalion M.O.), 2/Lieuts. S. G. Gallop and R. W. Ryall, and 193 other ranks. Amongst the "other ranks" killed was Corporal W. Burge, who, with Corporal Walrond, had with remarkable gallantry tended and rescued, under heavy fire, a wounded man of the Fife and Forfars. Walrond was awarded the D.C.M. Lance-

12th Battalion

Sergeant Passmore of A Company, after both his officers, the C.S.M. and all sergeants had become casualties, collected the remainder of the Company and led them throughout the day, bringing them out of action when the fighting was over, for which gallant action he also received the D.C.M.

For two days following the Battle the Battalion was kept busily engaged in clearing the battlefield and in the mournful task of burying the dead, bivouacking at night on the line of the objectives of 6th. On the 8th November, when the remainder of the 74th Division turned south, *en route* for Abu Irgeig, Karm and Shellal, the 12th Somersets marched to Sheria, of which place the C.O. became O.C., Troops, and Administrative Commandant. In this pestilential spot (it was nothing else seeing that Sheria was in a state of appalling filth) the Battalion spent over a week until, on 16th, it was relieved by a battalion of the 60th Division and rejoined its Brigade at Shellal, marching

17th November

(in Division) on 17th to St. James's Park, south of Gaza.

11. THE FALL OF GAZA

Meanwhile Gaza had fallen.

1/5th and 2/4th Battalions

The date of the attack at Gaza had been left open till the result of the Beersheba operations was known. It was intended that the former, designed to draw the enemy's reserves towards the Gaza sector, should take place from twenty-four to forty-eight hours previous to the attack on the Sheria position. After the Beersheba operations had proved successful, reports were received at G.H.Q. that an ample water supply would be available in the town and hopes were entertained that it would be possible to attack Sheria on 3rd or 4th November. The attack on Gaza was, therefore, ordered to take place on the morning of 2nd November. Later reports showed that the water situation was less favourable than had been reported, nevertheless it was decided not to postpone the attack. The objectives of the attack were the hostile works from Umbrella Hill (2,000 yards south-west of Gaza) to Sheikh Hasan on the sea (about 2,500 yards north-west of Gaza). The front of the attack was about 6,000 yards and Sheikh Hasan, the farthest objective, was some 3,000 yards from the British front line. A preliminary operation against Umbrella Hill was to be made on the night of 1st November, four hours previous to the main attack on Gaza.

1st November

This preliminary attack was made at 11 p.m. on 1st by a portion of the 52nd Division and was completely successful, though it drew a heavy bombardment, which lasted for two hours, on Umbrella Hill and the British front line. The hostile shell fire ceased, however, before Zero hour for the main attack, i.e. 3 a.m. on 2nd November, and the troops formed up for the attack without interference.

The official despatches show the British troops forming the XXI Corps in front of Gaza at 6 p.m. on 1st November, in the following order: 75th Division on the right, 54th Division in the centre and 52nd Division on the left, with its left resting on the coast-line. The right of the line ran from about

El Mendor north-east to Sheikh Abbas, thence turned sharply round the Abbas 1/5th and 2/4th
Battalions Ridge, north-west to the coast.

The ground over which the attack was to take place was mostly sand dunes, rising in places to a height of 150 feet. The sand was deep and heavy going. Several lines of strongly built trenches and redoubts defended Gaza, the most important of which lay south and south-west of the town. Of these Middlesex Hill, The Maze, Outpost Hill and Umbrella Hill were well garrisoned and protected by thick barbed-wire entanglements.

At 3 a.m. on 2nd the main attack was launched and all objectives were 2nd November reached "except for a section of trench on the left and some of the final objectives in the centre." Sheikh Hasan fell into the hands of the 52nd Division. The enemy apparently suffered very heavily from the preliminary bombardment by the XXI Corps, losing a third of their men in one division, so that a fresh division had to be moved up from their general reserve. This was part of the object of the attack, i.e. to prevent the Turks reinforcing their right where the Beersheba operations were in progress.

From the Diaries of the 75th Division neither the 232nd nor 233rd Brigades were actively involved in this operation and the 2/4th Somerset Light Infantry of the former and the 1/5th Somersets of the latter were therefore not employed in the attack. The 232nd Brigade was in Corps Reserve in the Wadi Simeon area, and the 233rd Brigade held the left sub-sector of the Sheikh Abbas sector. The 2/4th Somersets were at Paisley and the 1/5th Battalion at Queen's Hill and the Slag Heap (south of Burnt Tank).

The 75th Division had been formed of Territorial and Indian units but recently arrived from India, and amongst the Territorials were the 1/5th and 2/4th Somerset Light Infantry. For nearly two and a half years the 1/5th Battalion (Lieut.-Colonel E. F. Cooke-Hurle) had passed an uneventful 1/5th Battalion existence in India. The Battalion had in turn been stationed at Jubblepore, Ambala and Meerut, and in the hill stations of Dagshai and Chakrata. In January 1917 the 1/5th were in training at Rawalpindi and Peshawar when they were told they had been selected for sterner work and were to prepare for active service in one of the theatres of war. On 26th April the Battalion embarked and it was not until the ship was well out to sea that all ranks knew that they were destined to join the Egyptian Expeditionary Force in Palestine. Suez was reached on 6th May and, after a stay at Cairo spent in refitting, the 6th May 1/5th joined the 233rd Brigade of the newly formed 75th Division. Several weeks' training at El Arish and Rafa, where long route-marches through the burning desert fitted the Battalion for the part it was to play in the near future, followed. On 28th August Nos. 1 and 2 Companies of the Battalion went into the trenches in the Sheikh Abbas area, south of Gaza, and were attached to the Argyll and Sutherland Highlanders for preliminary instruction in trench warfare. They were followed later by Nos. 3 and 4 Companies who were also given instruction in trench warfare. The 3rd September is note-worthy, for on this date the Battalion Diary records the first casualties on active service—2 other ranks were killed and 12 wounded by shell fire, all

1/5th Battalion of No. 4 Company. On 12th September the Battalion took over the Apex right sub-sector of the Sheikh Abbas sector, three Companies in the front line and one in reserve. The front taken over was approximately 2,000 yards in length. The remainder of September was uneventful, but the final entry in the Battalion Diary is of interest:—

"The health of the Battalion was not quite so good as previous month. Septic sores were very prevalent and 16 cases of dysentery occurred. The enemy's lines opposite Apex Right are nowhere nearer than 2,000 yards to our front-line trenches and the most important work done is by the night patrols. A considerable amount of work has been done on the trenches, eighteen new dug-outs have been constructed and additional trenches are being dug in our right sub-sector."

The effective strength of the 1/5th Battalion at the end of September 1917 was 24 officers and 884 other ranks and present with unit 20 officers and 814 other ranks.

6th/7th October The first real thrill of excitement the 1/5th had was on the night of 6th/7th October when a well-planned raid was carried out by 8 officers and 160 other ranks of the Battalion under the command of Captain E. S. Goodland.

The section of trenches raided by the Somerset men was known as Old British Trenches which lay about 1,000 yards north-east of Abbas Apex. These trenches consisted of a system of fire lines and were about 700 yards in front of the enemy's line at Tank Redoubt. Repeated reconnaissance had led to the belief that these trenches were held by the Turks every night, probably with a garrison of about thirty men.

The raiders were in two parties, one, the assaulting party, consisting of 6 officers and 100 other ranks including stretcher-bearers, and the other a supporting party of 2 officers and 60 other ranks. Silent patrols to protect the flanks of the raid were to be found by the 3/3rd Gurkha Rifles on the right and the 2/4th Hants on the left.

Brigade Orders to the 1/5th Somersets stated that: "The garrison will be killed or captured, all enemy arms, ammunition or any other material collected or destroyed. Some prisoners for identifications will be obtained, also all papers and telephones."

The raid was carefully rehearsed and practised over a model of Old British Trenches laid out from sketches and aeroplane photographs, until each officer and man knew his job perfectly. Zero hour was fixed for 8.30 p.m. on 6th October.

At 7.35 p.m. on 6th October the raiding party and supporting party, followed by the Gurkha patrol, left the front-line trenches and, halting outside the wire, formed up. A second halt was ordered 100 yards short of Endless Road to allow the signallers to mend a break in the wire. The point of deployment was reached where the assaulting party changed direction and advanced at once. On reaching a point about fifty yards from the Old British Trenches two Turks, who had been lying in the pits on the south-east side of the trenches,

were seen to run back and a few rifle shots were fired at the assaulting party. 1/5th Battalion
The leader of the centre section of the first line (2/Lieut. Elliott), who was 6th October
also directing, at once started to double forward, the whole party following
and making for their objectives.   With frightened cries of "Allah! Allah!"
the Turks began to jump out of the trenches and pits in front of the trenches
and run off in the direction of Tank Redoubt.   They were chased by the
Somerset men and intercepted and, before they could get away, were either
bayoneted or taken prisoner.   Only four or five succeeded in escaping to
the Tank Redoubt, where their cries were taken up by the garrison, the night
air ringing with frantic appeals to "Allah."   At 8.42 p.m. Captain Goodland,
considering that the object of the raid had been achieved, ordered the "G"
to be sounded on the bugle, the prearranged signal for the withdrawal to
begin.   Covered by the supporting party, which now acted as rear-guard,
the raiders successfully reached their starting point.

Captain Goodland estimated that the garrison of the Old British Trenches
consisted of about twenty-three Turks of which twenty were bayoneted or
killed.

The 1/5th lost one N.C.O. (Sergeant Gardiner) killed and one N.C.O.
and one other rank slightly wounded.   Of the former the C.O. of the Somersets
stated: "He was leading one of the sections in the first line and was shot at
close quarters.   He was a gallant soldier and one of my best N.C.O.'s.   I
had recommended him for a commission in the Battalion a few days ago.
His body was brought in on a stretcher."

This successful raid was a feather in the cap of the 1/5th Somersets
who, on the 7th October, received congratulations not only from the G.Os.C.,
Brigade and Division, but from the Corps Commander and the G.O.C., E.E.F.
No further action with the enemy happened during the month.   On the
19th Lieut.-Colonel Cooke-Hurle was admitted to hospital in Cairo and Major
F. D. Urwick took over command of the Battalion.   On the 26th the 1/5th 26th October
Somersets were relieved and moved back to Queen's Hill and the Slag Heap,
which position they held when the assault on Gaza began.

After the 2/4th Somersets (Lieut.-Colonel H. F. Clutterbuck) had arrived 2/4th Battalion
in Dinapore, India, from the Andaman Islands early in January 1916, the
Battalion led the usual life of an Indian garrison.   The "Kitchener Test"
was passed successfully.   About the middle of the year—in July—the 2/4th,
with a number of men of the 1/4th, marched through Bankipore and Patna,
then seething with unrest, but before the column returned to Dinapore cholera
broke out and some deaths occurred.   At Dinapore the men of the 1/4th 1/4th Battalion
who had returned sick from Mesopotamia were formed into a depôt, commanded first by Major Graves-Knyfton and later by Captain T. B. Timmins.
As men became fit they were drafted back to their Battalion in "Mespot," 2/4th Battalion
the 2/4th also providing drafts for its first-line Battalion.   In this way, during
1916, some six officers and more than 800 other ranks were sent to
Mesopotamia as reinforcements.   In May 1917 orders were received by
the 2/4th to proceed to Egypt, but just as the Battalion was ready to move to

Bombay for embarkation, it was ordered to the Lahore District owing to the riots at Amritsar.   Later the Battalion was to have moved to the Waziristan frontier owing to a rising of the Mahsuds, but this order was cancelled.   Next came a move to Poona on the 1st August, and in September the Battalion at last entrained for Bombay and there embarked for Egypt.   Disembarking at Suez the 2/4th Somersets moved up in cattle trucks to Kantara, whence the Battalion began its long trek across the desert to the British line in front of Gaza.   On arrival at Belah in the XXI Corps area the Battalion was allotted to the 232nd Brigade of the 75th Division, and on the 24th October took over trenches from the 2/4th Hants in the Mansura East sub-sector.   When the operations against Gaza opened, however, the 232nd Brigade, as already mentioned, was in Corps Reserve.

Meanwhile the bombardment of Gaza continued and the attack on the town was ordered to take place on the 6th and 7th November.   The objectives on the right—Outpost Hill, Middlesex Hill and the Maze—were to be attacked at 11.30 p.m. on 6th.   At dawn on 7th the line Belah Trench–Turtle Hill was to be assaulted.

The 233rd Brigade (75th Division) order for the attack begins with the following appreciation of the situation: "The situation in the Coastal Sector remains unchanged.   The situation on our right flank is such that as large an enemy force as possible must be held on the Gaza front."   On the right the Sheria–Hareira line was still under attack.

To the 233rd Brigade had been allotted the task of capturing Middlesex Hill and the Maze.   On the right of the Brigade attack the 1/5th Somersets (Major F. D. Urwick, commanding) were to assault and capture Middlesex Hill as far as trench M-M.   The 1/4th Wilts, on the left, were to attack the Maze to points M-N-N, and Outpost Hill, the intermediate objective, was also to be captured by this Battalion and consolidated by special troops detailed for the purpose.

The object of the attack was to seize the objective and induce the enemy to keep troops in the Gaza sector for fear of further attacks, and prevent him sending them elsewhere.   The Outpost Hill Attack was known as Attack No. 1 and that on Middlesex Hill and the Maze Attack No. 2.   The latter was dependent upon the success of the former.

It will be remembered that the 1/5th Somersets had moved up to Queen's Hill and the Slag Heap and the Battalion held these positions when the above orders for the attack were received.   For several days preparations for the attack continued, the dump at the Donga was prepared, ammunition, water receptacles, tools, etc., being collected for the purpose.   The British guns were continually active and kept the Turkish positions under heavy fire. The Turks replied vigorously, but few casualties were suffered by the Brigade, for as the Brigade Diary states, a particularly large proportion of "dud" H.E. shells fell, doing no harm.   No casualties were suffered by the 1/5th Somersets during these days of preparation.

The assembly orders for the attack were as follows: No. 4 Company

was to move independently from the Slag Heap to the Donga east of No. 6 1/5th Battalion
Redoubt, timing its departure from the Slag Heap to be in position in the
Donga at Zero minus two hours (9.30 p.m.); No. 3 and No. 2 Companies
were also to move independently to the Donga at Zero minus two hours and
Zero minus one and a half hours respectively. At Zero minus 19 minutes the
Battalion was to move forward and form up on the line of the New Trenches;
the attack was to be launched at Zero plus 11 minutes, i.e. 11.41 p.m.

It is unnecessary to go further into the details of the attack, for it
so happened that there was very little attacking to be done; the Battalion's
story of the operations is as follows: "The Zero hour was 23.30 (11.30 p.m.)
and at this time the Battalion went forward behind a very heavy barrage and
captured Middlesex (Hill) with complete success. There was little opposition
as the enemy had evacuated the position, leaving only a small covering party
behind. Our casualties were 2/Lieut. C. G. Ames and two other ranks
wounded."

At dawn on 7th the Battalion was ordered to push out patrols into the 7th November
Plantation and Green Hill. The patrols found no trace of the enemy and at
daybreak the Somersets were ordered to move on and occupy Green Hill.
They were shelled by the enemy as they moved forward but no casualties were
suffered. At 7.30 a.m. an officer's patrol (under 2/Lieut. J. G. Turner)
pushed on into Gaza, whilst another patrol commanded by 2/Lieut. W. G.
Bradford, went forward to Ali el Muntar. Gaza was empty, the Turks having
evacuated the town during the night; their rear-guards were still occupying
Beit Hanun and the Atawineh and Tank systems from whence hostile artillery
continued to shell Gaza and El Muntar till dusk, though doing very little
damage.

The whole of the XXI Corps was now on the move. The 1/5th Somersets
at 9.30 a.m. pushed on and soon occupied Fryer Hill, east of Gaza. The
Corps Cavalry advanced to the northern outskirts of the town, whilst other
troops were pushing up to attack west and north-west to the mouth of the
Wadi Hesi, so as to turn the Wadi Hesi line and prevent the enemy making
a stand there.

Both at Green Hill and Fryer Hill the 1/5th Somersets found large
quantities of stores and ammunition, which the Turks had abandoned in their
hurried flight. From the direction of the Atawineh system the Somerset
men came in for a considerable amount of shell fire from the enemy's heavy
guns and sustained casualties, some fourteen other ranks being wounded.
But at nightfall all was quiet, the Battalion bivouacking on the hill.

Thus Gaza had at last fallen and with the network of defences surrounding
the town on the east, south, and west was occupied by troops of the XXI
Corps. North of Gaza the enemy's rear-guard had maintained itself at Beit
Hanun until nightfall and had then retired. By this time also, the force
advancing along the coast had reached the Wadi Hesi and, in spite of considerable opposition, established itself on the north bank, several determined
Turkish counter-attacks having been beaten off with heavy loss to the enemy.

1/5th Battalion
7th November

On the extreme right the situation had remained practically unchanged during the 7th, the enemy maintaining his positions opposite the British right flank guard.   In the centre the Hareira Tepe Redoubt had been captured at dawn. Tel el Sheria had fallen at 4 a.m. to London troops of the 60th Division, who subsequently pushed forward their line about a mile north of Tel el Sheria. On the right mounted troops, moving towards Jemmamah and Huj, met with considerable opposition from hostile rear-guards.

2/4th Battalion

The 2/4th Battalion, Somerset Light Infantry, had taken no active part in the operations.   The Battalion remained at Paisley from 1st to 6th November, but at 12 noon on 7th was sent up to Ali el Muntar, arriving at 6 p.m.   Here

7th November

the Battalion bivouacked.

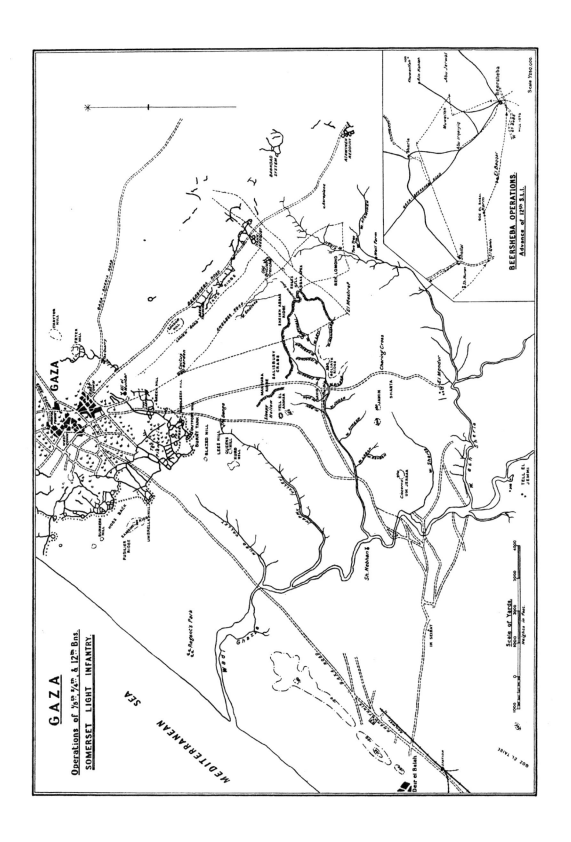

CHAPTER XXVIII

THE ACTION OF EL MUGHAR, 13TH NOVEMBER 1917

ON the morning of 8th November the general advance of the XXI Corps was continued, but interest was chiefly centred in an attempt, if possible, to cut off the Turkish rear-guard which still held the Tank and Atawineh systems. The enemy had, however, retreated during the night 7th/8th, and although considerable captures of prisoners, stores and ammunition were made, no large formed body of the enemy was cut off. Of the Yeomanry charge at Huj, the Somerset men saw nothing. Reports from the Royal Flying Corps stated that the Turks were retiring in considerable disorganization and, if pursued with determination, could offer no very serious resistance.

Throughout the 8th the 1/5th Battalion (233rd Brigade) remained on Fryer Hill spending a quiet day, the Battalion Diary stating that nothing of importance occurred. *1/5th Battalion 8th November*

The 2/4th Battalion at Ali el Muntar had been turned out at 1 a.m. to take up a line of outposts on Middlesex Hill and Outpost Hill at 3 a.m., but at 8 a.m. they returned to El Muntar and similarly spent the remainder of the day in quietude. *2/4th Battalion 8th November*

As a whole, the 75th Division, after occupying the Beer Trenches, Tank Redoubt and Atawineh, evacuated by the enemy during the night 7th/8th, had been able to link up with the left of the 10th Division. The Composite Force, however, relieved the 75th Division during the afternoon, the latter having been ordered to push on to Beit Hanun.

By the 9th the operations had reached the stage of a direct pursuit of the Turks by as many troops as could be supplied so far in front of railhead. Indeed, it was now a question of supply rather than one of manœuvre. Water and forage were the two great difficulties.

Early on 9th the 232nd Brigade received a message from Divisional Headquarters which stated: "You will march to Beit Hanun as early as possible. Every man will take two days' rations." The march began at 11.45 a.m. in great heat. The Brigade set out in the following order—2/5th Hants, 2/3rd Gurkhas, 2/4th Somersets, 1/5th Devons, 229th Machine-Gun Company, and marched via The Quarry and Chaytor Hill. Beit Hanun was reached about 3 p.m., but contrary to expectation the water supply was found inadequate for watering the troops, and it was decided to push on to Dier Sineid, units leaving their water transport behind for refilling. About 5.45 p.m. the Brigade reached its destination, where all units bivouacked for the night. *9th November* *2/4th Battalion*

During the evening of 9th November there were indications that the enemy was organizing a counter-attack from the direction of Hebron towards

Arak el Menshiye, but, as it was obvious that this attack could only be made by troops who were very much disorganized and had lost heavily, the threat was ignored and orders from G.H.Q. gave instructions for the pursuit to continue as early as possible towards Junction Station with the intention of cutting off the Turkish Jerusalem Army: the Imperial Camel Corps was ordered to move to the neighbourhood of Tel el Nejile where it would be on the flank of any counter-stroke from the hills.

It is impossible from the Battalion Diary of the 2/4th Somersets to gather anything of the enormous difficulties which confronted the advance at this stage. Even the Brigade Diary, though it does, here and there (in copies of messages and orders), tear aside the veil and show something of that great effort and wonderful march across the desert, is all too brief in its description of the following up and ultimate defeat of the entire Turkish Army in Palestine.

The first order received from Divisional Headquarters on 10th November by 232nd Brigade Headquarters stated:—

"232nd Brigade will march to Es Suafir el Gharbiyeh, 13 miles north-north-east of Deir Sineid on main road. . . . The object of this march is to give the enemy no chance of recovering, and all ranks must be prepared to undergo considerable hardships and privations. Rations will be got to you this evening and, if possible, on the following evening. Battalions may be thinned out to 500 if you wish men weeded out, leaving their rations with you and being marched to Mansura. . . . Move to be completed by 18.00 (6 p.m.)."

Perhaps it was because of the frank statements in this order (that all ranks must be prepared to suffer privations) that every one responded so splendidly to whatever call was made upon them. No men were sent back, but each British battalion of the 232nd and 233rd Brigades left behind at Gaza a percentage of officers and men, and these details were organized into a column of about 400 men with about 15 officers, which followed up as hard as it could go after the Brigades, and rejoined its various units at Latron on the day the attack on Saris and Enab was made.

At 8 a.m. the Battalion left Deir Sineid and about 5 p.m. arrived about one mile due west of Es Suafir el Gharbiyeh where a line of picquets was put out facing north. Brigade Headquarters then reported to Advanced 75th Divisional Headquarters that it had relieved the 2nd Light Horse Brigade (less one squadron) which remained to cover the right of the 232nd. The Turks were holding Beit Duras and villages about one mile in front of the Brigade, and the 2/3rd Gurkhas were shelled while taking up the position allotted to them. But again the water question was acute, for the Diary reports: "Can water men, but do not think horses or mules. The latter in most cases have had no water for thirty-six horses. Going was very bad." Such was the report sent to Divisional Headquarters. Poor, faithful animals: they, no less than the troops, had responded nobly to the calls made upon them, for the Brigade Diary states: "The animals at this time were beginning to show signs of exhaustion, but had done extremely well, despite being without 2/4th Battalion water for so long. The R.E. materials were quite inadequate to obtain a quick supply of water from the wells." But that was not the fault of the gallant sappers, they could only issue what materials were available and could be brought up. On the morning of 11th information was received at 75th Divisional Headquarters that the enemy was holding the ridge north-east of "S" in Es Suafir el Gharbiyeh and Beit Duras. During the previous evening British Cavalry had captured 1,500 prisoners and 13 guns. The 52nd Division had advanced troops in Esdud but was concentrated at Mejdel. The 232nd Brigade was ordered to hold the line Es Suafir el Gharbiyeh–Beit Duras inclusive: the 233rd Brigade was to move to the neighbourhood of Julis, and the 234th Brigade troops to neighbourhood of Eijeh. These moves were to be completed by 16.00 (4 p.m.).

At 2.30 p.m. on 11th the Somerset piquets were withdrawn and the 11th November Battalion (in Brigade) moved forward according to orders, Brigade Headquarters reporting to Divisional Headquarters: "Beit Duras occupied by our troops, Turks having retired before our mounted troops, who captured two guns. Am advancing my left to Jewish Colony, not marked on map, at D.24a. at 14.00 to-day." The 2/4th Somersets were apparently on the left, for their Diary records that at 15.45 (3.45 p.m.) the Battalion reached Jewish Colony and two picquets were put out facing north-east.

Both on the 10th and 11th the operations had showed that the enemy's resistance was stiffening in the general line of the Wadi Sukereir with centre about El Kustineh, but the threatened counter-attack from the direction of Hebron ended in an ineffective demonstration, and the enemy retired north-east, prolonging the Turkish line towards Beit Jibrin. This increased resistance, taken with the fact that prisoners from almost every Turkish unit had been captured, pointed to the fact that the British advance was no longer opposed only by hostile rear-guards but practically by the remainder of the Turkish Army, which was making a last effort to arrest the pursuit south of the Junction Station—a position of importance.

The 12th November was accordingly spent in preparations for an attack 12th November on the enemy's position covering Junction Station, though the 4th Royal Scots of the 156th Brigade (52nd Division) on the left of the 232nd Brigade (75th Division) made a very gallant, but unsuccessful, attempt to capture Brown Hill. The Hill was finally captured by the 2/3rd Gurkhas and 2/5th Hants of the 232nd Brigade, the 2/4th Somersets covering the right of the Brigade connecting with 233rd Brigade, the 1/5th Devons being in reserve. On this date (12th) the only entry in the Diary of the Somersets is: "12.34 (12.34 a.m.). Put out piquets 200 yards north-east of Jewish Colony. 14.30 (2.30 p.m.). Moved up to support the guns 500 yards to the north and bivouacked there."

By the morning of 13th November the enemy had sprung out his force 13th November on a front of about twenty miles from El Kubeibeh, on the north, to Beit Jibrin to the south. The right half of his line ran approximately parallel with, and only about five miles in front of, the Ramleh–Junction Station Railway, his main line of supply from the north: his right flank was already almost turned.   On this flank he had been forced into this position by the rapid movement along the coast and the maintenance of determined pressure on his rear-guards.

The country over which the attack was to take place was open and rolling, dotted with small villages surrounded by mud walls, beyond which were plantations of trees.   The most prominent feature was the line of heights, upon which were the villages of Katrah and El Mughar.   These two places stood out above the low flat ground which separated them from the rising ground to the west on which was another village, Beshshit, about 2,000 yards distant. The Katrah–El Mughar line was a very strong position and the Turks were expected to put up a stout resistance, seeing that their right flank was threatened.

The first objective of the 232nd Brigade of the 75th Division was the line Yasur–Kustineh,[1] the formation of the attack being: front line—2/4th Somersets on the right, 2/5th Hants on the left; second line—2/3rd Gurkhas on the right, 1/5th Devons on the left.   The 233rd Brigade was on the right of the Somersets.

At 7.45 a.m. the 2/4th Somersets moved to attack, in conjunction with the Hants, the Yasur–El Kustineh line.   The Battalion's frontage was 600 yards.   This objective was carried without opposition, excepting hostile shell fire.   At 13.30 (1.30 p.m.) the advance was continued to the second objective, the ridge beyond the Yasur–El Kustineh line.   During the interval between the occupation of the first objective and the advance to the second, all units, especially the Gurkhas, were heavily shelled, and this shelling continued as the troops advanced.   Hostile rifle and machine-gun fire, at first not heavy, increased in volume rapidly, and the enemy's opposition in front of the Hampshires stiffened considerably.   The Brigadier then withdrew the Gurkhas into Brigade Reserve, intending to break through on the left with his three other Battalions, but the 2/4th Somersets, on the right, were held up by machine-gun fire, and this fact, combined with the existence of a large gap between his right and the left of the 233rd Brigade necessitated the despatch of the Devons to support and prolong the right of the Somersets.   The Devons, working rather wide on the right, charged the enemy with the bayonet, capturing four machine guns.   The attack of the 233rd Brigade developed about this period, with the result that under the attacks of the two Brigades the whole of the Turkish left retired.   Meanwhile the Hants, with the Gurkhas supporting them, had pushed on until held up by machine-gun fire from Cactus Garden.   By this time darkness had fallen and the 232nd Brigade consolidated on the ground won.   The casualties of the 2/4th Somersets up to this period were two other ranks killed and twenty-nine wounded.   "All Battalions," records the Brigade Diary, "behaved very well under most trying conditions." Thus ends the narrative of the action of the 2/4th Somersets of the 232nd Brigade.

[1] Kustineh (exclusive).

El Mughar had been captured by the 52nd Division and mounted troops. 1/5th Battalion

The records of the 1/5th Somersets of the 233rd Brigade (from a regimental point of view) are more interesting, as they are given in greater detail.

From a point north-east of Fryer Hill the 233rd Brigade had set out on 9th November towards the retreating enemy. The Turkish railhead at Beit 9th November Hanun was passed and by late afternoon the Brigade had reached a point between Borbera and Ejje, where all units bivouacked for the night. "It was a long and dusty march," records the Diary of the 1/5th Battalion. At 7.30 a.m. on 10th the Somerset men (in Brigade) were again on the move towards Es Suafu Esh Sherkiye. No Turks were encountered during the day, but everywhere there were signs of the haste with which the enemy had evacuated his positions. On reaching their destination all ranks of the Brigade again bivouacked. The 11th was spent in the same bivouacs, though Captain A. O. Major took forward a party to cover a reconnaissance of the ground between the village and El Kustineh and, on returning, reported having seen large bodies of hostile troops.

On the 12th the Battalion moved forward and occupied a ridge south of 12th November El Kustineh and El Turmus, digging in and remaining in the position during the night 12th/13th. The task allotted to the 233rd Infantry Brigade in the attack to take place on the 13th November was the capture of Tel El Turmus–El Kustineh (both inclusive) with El Mesmiyeh as a further objective.[1]

In phase one the 1/5th Somersets were to attack Tel El Turmus, and the 1/4th Wilts Regt. Kustineh, both Battalions attacking El Mesmiyeh as a further objective. On the capture of Mesmiyeh, phase two was to begin, i.e. the advance of the 2/4th Hants and 3/3rd Gurkhas through the 1/5th Somersets and 1/4th Wilts, to another objective. Phase three consisted of the consolidation of the positions won by the 233rd Brigade and the passing-through of the 234th Brigade, detailed to capture Junction Station.

At dawn on 13th the Brigade was ready formed up for the attack, the 13th November 1/5th Somersets on the right and 1/4th Wilts on the left, with the 3/3rd Gurkhas guarding the left of the Brigade and the 2/4th Hants in Brigade Reserve.

The Somersets disposed No. 1 and No. 4 Companies in the front line with No. 3 in support and No. 2 in reserve.

By 6.50 a.m. patrols of the Somersets and Wilts had reported Turmus and Kustineh clear of the enemy, and at 8 a.m. the leading waves of both Battalions advanced to occupy the two villages and re-form north-east of the latter ready for the attack on El Mesmiyeh. In moving through Turmus the 1/5th came under shell fire, but no casualties resulted and by 9.15 a.m. the Battalion had formed up north-east of the village, as ordered, ready for the next phase of the attack. Kustineh had similarly fallen into the hands of the Wilts Regt., the latter forming up for the next stage of the operations on the left of the Somerset men. Of the latter Battalion No. 3 and Nos. 2

---

[1] It will be remembered that the 232nd Brigade, on the left of the 233rd Brigade, was attacking the line El Kustineh (exclusive)–Yasur (inclusive).

Companies now formed the front line with No. 1 in support and No. 4 in reserve.

At 10.15 a.m. the attack on El Mesmiyeh began. About 1,200 yards from the village the 1/5th Somersets first came under very heavy shell fire and ultimately, as the Battalion approached its objective, violent rifle and machine-gun fire principally from the right flank. But with great steadiness the Somerset men kept on and El Mesmiyeh was stormed and captured "with great dash and gallantry." [1] The village had fallen by 10.55 a.m., but it took another half-hour to clear the cactus hedges and gardens of Turkish snipers who had concealed themselves cleverly. But eventually the last remaining Turk had either been shot down or sent scuttling back to the main body of the enemy, who had taken up position on the ridge running approximately east and west, about 1,000–1,200 yards north of El Mesmiyeh. A counter-attack on the latter was beaten off, but the Turkish guns continued to shell the village heavily while the enemy's rifle and machine-gun bullets tore through the cactus hedges behind which the British troops were lying awaiting further orders. The 3/3rd Gurkhas were now moved up into the village to strengthen the position.

At 3.45 p.m. Brigade Headquarters ordered the 1/5th Somersets and 1/4 Wilts to attack and occupy the ridge north of El Mesmiyeh. For this attack No. 3 and No. 1 Companies of the 1/5th Somersets were lent to the Wilts and came under the orders of Lieut.-Colonel Armstrong, commanding that Battalion.

This attack was again completely successful, the Somerset men and the Wilts attacking the ridge with great determination. They dislodged the enemy who fled in full retreat, the Somerset men capturing three machine guns after killing practically all the crews of the guns. The Wilts took many prisoners. No. 2 and No. 4 Companies of the Somersets guarded the right flank of the attack which was still under heavy machine-gun fire.

At 6.15 p.m. the 233rd Brigade was still moving on the objective of phase 2, but as the 2/4 Hants had not got sufficiently far forward in the initial stages, it was necessary for the Somersets and Wilts to remain the leading Battalions of the Brigade, and they were by now tired with the day's fighting. By dusk the line had still not reached the objective of phase 2, but was some 2,500 yards north-east of Mesmiyeh. In this position the Brigade was ordered to consolidate, the 1/5th Somersets and 1/4th Wilts in the front line, the 2/4th Hants in Mesmiyeh (having reached that place at 6.15 p.m.) guarding the right flank, and the 3/3rd Gurkhas just north of Mesmiyeh supporting the Wilts.

The 1/5th Battalion (with the Wilts) had fought splendidly throughout the day and had most worthily upheld the honour of the Regiment. The Brigadier four days later, in submitting his report to 75th Divisional Head-quarters, said:—

"I should like to bring to your notice the great part played in the day's

---

[1] Battalion Diary, 1/5th Somerset Light Infantry.

fighting by the 1/4th Wilts Regt. and the 1/5th Somerset Light Infantry
who, between them, did practically all the fighting throughout the day and
were from 09.00 (9 a.m.) to dark under shelling which was always very accurate
and at times very heavy, and under continual machine-gun fire from the front
and from the right flank.   I consider that any success that the Brigade achieved
on this day was very greatly due to the able leadership of these two Battalions
by their Commanding Officers, Lieut.-Colonel A Armstrong, 1/4th Wilts
Regt., and Major F. D. Urwick, 1/5th Somerset Light Infantry."

Casualties suffered by the 1/5th Somersets during the fighting on 13th
were one officer (2/Lieut. H. W. Elliott) and five other ranks killed, two
officers (who, however, remained at duty) and 41 other ranks wounded.[1]

The British line on the night 13th halted about a mile west of Junction
Station, which was not occupied owing to the enemy's resistance.   Early on
the morning of the 14th, however, it was found that the enemy had retired
and the Station was occupied by the 234th Brigade.   Later, a heavy Turkish
counter-attack was beaten off.   At 8 p.m. 75th Division orders were received
at 232nd Brigade Headquarters: 234th Brigade was to occupy, and prepare
for defence, the ground round Junction Station, 233rd Brigade was to keep
communication with the right of 234th Brigade at Bridge, and 232nd Brigade
was to furnish outpost lines between the left of 234th Brigade and the 52nd
Division at Mansura.

The Seventh and Eighth Turkish Armies had now been separated,
retiring east and north respectively, and aeroplane reports stated that they
consisted of small scattered groups rather than formed bodies of any size.

The results of the fifteen days' fighting are thus set out in the official
despatches, and are given in full, as from the official diaries it is impossible to
get a collective account of the accumulative effects of the fighting in which
(be it remembered) the Somerset men took an active part:—

"In fifteen days our force had advanced 60 miles on its right and about
forty on its left.   It had driven a Turkish Army of nine infantry divisions and
one cavalry division out of a position in which it had been entrenched for six
months and had pursued it, joining battle wherever it attempted to stand and
inflicting losses on it amounting probably to nearly two-thirds of the enemy's
original effectives.   Over nine thousand prisoners, about eighty guns, more
than one hundred machine guns and very large quantities of ammunition and
other stores had been captured."

[1] For conspicuous gallantry and devotion to duty during the attack on Mesmiyeh Major F. D.
Urwick (C.O. 1/5th Bn.) was awarded the D.S.O.   The citation in the London *Gazette* states that
"Throughout he displayed the utmost indifference to danger and set a magnificent example to his men."
Captains A. S. Timms and G. P. Clarke and 2/Lieut. J. T. Turner were awarded the M.C. also for
conspicuous gallantry and devotion to duty.

CHAPTER XXIX

THE JERUSALEM OPERATIONS

THE BATTLE OF NEBI SAMWIL, 17TH–24TH NOVEMBER 1917

AS already stated, the remnants of the Seventh and Eighth Turkish Armies had now been definitely separated. The former had been driven back on Jerusalem, where it held a north and south line defending the Holy City: the latter defended the River Auja with its left about Mejdel Yaba: Jaffa had been occupied without opposition by British Cavalry on the evening of 16th November.

General Allenby had decided to contain the Eighth Turkish Army and, pivoting on Junction Station, attack the Seventh Army and occupy Jerusalem, though every endeavour was to be made to avoid fighting in, or close to, the Holy City. These operations, therefore, necessitated an advance through the difficult country of Judæa. The western side of the Judæan range of hills consists of a series of spurs which run east and west, separated from one another by narrow valleys. These spurs are steep, bare and stony and, in places, precipitous. Between the foot of the spur of the main range and the coastal plain is a low range known as Shephelah. On the line of the advance there was only one good road, the main Jaffa–Jerusalem Road, and this traversed the hills from east to west. For nearly four miles between Bab el Wad ($2\frac{1}{2}$ miles east of Latron) and Saris this road passed through a narrow defile: the road had been damaged in several places by the Turks. The other roads were mere tracks on the side of the hill or up the stony beds of wadis: without improvement they were impracticable for wheeled transport. Throughout these hills the water supply was scanty without development. Such was the country through which the Somerset men of the 75th Division, with their comrades, were to fight their way to the Holy City—they were the new Crusaders.

General Allenby's plan of attack was briefly as follows: the Yeomanry Mounted Division, supported by infantry of the 52nd Division, was to move through the Judæan Hills by the track 3 to 5 miles north of the main highway and break out on to the main Jerusalem–Nablus high road and so cut off the Turks in Jerusalem. The 75th Division, in the centre, was to seize the Bab el Wad defile, while the 10th Australian Light Horse advanced by the defile farther south through which the railway ran.

On the 14th November the three Brigades of the 75th Division occupied the following positions: 234th—the ground round Junction Station: 233rd Brigade on the right of the 234th; 232nd Brigade in support, but furnishing the outpost line which kept touch between the left of the 234th Brigade and the right of the 52nd Division which held Mansura.

GENERAL VIEW OF JERUSALEM FROM THE MOUNT OF OLIVES

The 1/5th Somersets (233rd Brigade) occupied the ridges west of El *1/5th Battalion* Khesman, but on the 16th moved to Zezazeh, east of Junction Station, and took up a line on a range of low, stony hills. The Battalion remained in this position throughout the 17th, when the operations began. *17th November*

The 2/4th Somersets (232nd Brigade) moved to Abu Shusheh on 16th, *2/4th Battalion* and similarly remained in this place throughout the actions of 17th. On this date Lieut.-Colonel Clutterbuck, commanding the Battalion, was evacuated *17th November* sick to hospital, and Major Dundas of the 2/3rd Gurkhas assumed command.

The Battle began on 17th with an advance by the Yeomanry through the hills direct on Bireh, by Annabeh, Berfilya and Beit ur el Tahta. By the evening of 18th a portion of the mounted troops had reached the latter place, and another Shilta, but beyond Annabeh the route was found impossible for wheels.

On the 19th the infantry advance began. The 75th Division was to *19th November* advance up the main road as far as Kuryet el Enab, with its right flank protected by Australian mounted troops and, in order to avoid fighting in the close neighbourhood of the Holy City, was to strike north towards Bireh by a track leading through Biddu. The 52nd Division was to advance through Berfilya to Beit Likia and Beit Dukka, and thence support the movements of the 75th Division. Orders from Divisional Headquarters, issued during the evening of 18th, stated that the Division was to concentrate about Amwas on 19th as a preliminary move. The situation at this place was then unknown, as the Australians were still attacking it. Units were warned that it might be necessary to attack the Amwas–Latron line (both villages inclusive), in which case the 233rd Brigade was to be on the right with its left on Latron inclusive, and the 232nd Brigade on the left. As soon as these two places were occupied and the Division had concentrated, the 232nd and 233rd Brigades were to march to Kuryet el Enab, the 232nd leading. Strict orders were issued that the tombs from Latron to Enab were to be guarded and all ranks warned that they were on no account to be approached: also "no officers or other ranks will enter Jerusalem or country within a radius of 6 miles of it. Any officer or man found in the town is liable to be shot."

At 7.30 a.m. on 19th the 232nd Brigade left the Abu Shusheh position *2/4th Battalion* and occupied the Latron–Amwas line without opposition. Preparations were *19th November* then made for the advance along the Jerusalem Road. At 11 a.m., covered by Vaughan's Rifles, the 232nd Brigade moved forward in the following order towards Rab el Wad: 1/5th Devons, S.A.F.A., 2/5th Hants and 2/4th Somerset Light Infantry. No opposition was met with, though the Brigade was under long-range artillery fire, causing a few casualties. Just beyond Rab el Wad the Brigade entered the Pass of Bethoron and the heights on both sides of the road were therefore picketed. But now progress became terribly slow. The difficult nature of the ground and the heavy weights of the men's packs prevented anything in the way of a rapid advance. At about 1.30 p.m. the O.C., Vaughan's Rifles, reported that he was in touch with strong enemy forces and two companies of Devons and one company of Gurkhas were sent up the heights on the right and left of the road, respectively, as reinforcements. The enemy was, however, in strength and little or no further progress could be made after 5 p.m. Rain began to fall and a stormy evening followed, darkness setting in early. Under these circumstances the 232nd Brigade bivouacked on the position occupied on, and north and south of, the road. Throughout the night the enemy was active, especially on the left of the road, but he was successfully held off.

Meanwhile the 233rd Brigade had followed in support of the 232nd Brigade. The 1/5th Somersets with the remaining units of the Brigade concentrated on the Jerusalem Road, north of Junction Station and moved forward through Amwas and Latron. Small parties of the enemy were encountered after leaving the latter place, but no serious opposition was met with until the Pass of Bethoron was reached, where the column was held up owing to the difficulty the 232nd Brigade, in front, was experiencing in getting on. The 233rd Brigade was, therefore, withdrawn to the Latron end of the Pass and, in the heavy rain, bivouacked for the night.

At dawn on 20th the advance was again continued, the 232nd Brigade still leading, the 233rd in support and the 234th back at Latron. The 2/5th Hants (less one company) of the 232nd Brigade were pushed out on the right of the road, joining up with 58th Rifles. About 7.30 a.m. the 1/5th Devons were sent up on the left of the road to fill the gap between the Gurkhas' right and the road, and the 2/4th Somersets were brought up from the rear along the road. A general advance then took place. But progress was very slow: the country was extraordinarily difficult and the Turks were in force covering not only Enab, but defending Saris, which would have to be taken before any advance on the former village could take place. On the right especially the Turks held obstinately to their positions, and more than once counter-attacked, but were easily repulsed. About 11 a.m., however, the O.C., 2/4th Somersets, reported that the enemy's resistance in front of Saris showed signs of weakening and the Battalion was therefore ordered to attack the village. Supported by the fire of the L.A.M. Battery the 2/4th Battalion dashed forward and, at the point of the bayonet, captured the village and drove the Turks back on their Enab position: about thirty prisoners were taken by the Somerset men. A Battalion of Gurkhas from the 233rd Brigade (having been lent to the 232nd Brigade) was sent up and, moving forward, occupied the strong ridges about half a mile east of Saris, driving the Turks still farther back and capturing many prisoners. Brigade Headquarters then arrived and began immediately to organize an attack on Enab, the 1/5th Devons and 1/4th Wilts to carry out the assault. By this time (it was late afternoon) the troops of the 232nd Brigade, who had been marching and fighting all day, were dog-tired, but fortunately two more battalions of the 233rd Brigade were placed at the disposal of the Brigadier of the 232nd: these battalions were the 1/5th Somersets and

1/4th Wilts: they replaced the 2/4th Somersets and 1/5th Devons, who were much exhausted.

The attack on Enab was carried out by the 1/5th Somersets in front,

the 1/4th Wilts in echelon in left rear, with 3/3rd Gurkhas on the left of the 1/5th Battalion
20th November
Wiltshires. The formation of the Somersets in this attack was No. 2 and
No. 4 Companies in the front line, No. 3 in support and No. 1 in reserve.
There was a heavy driving rain as the troops moved forward and mist covered
the battlefield, but with great dash the attacking waves advanced and completely drove the Turks from their positions in front of Enab. Getting in
with the bayonet the Somerset men, though met by heavy machine-gun and
rifle fire, were not to be denied and brilliantly carried first the defences in
front of Enab and then the village at a loss of only two other ranks killed and
nine wounded. As a result of this success the whole advancing force was
able to move into the village, though darkness had fallen and heavy rain continued during the time the line was being occupied and consolidated. "All
units under my command," stated the Brigadier of the 232nd Brigade, "both
of my own Brigade and outside it, behaved with great gallantry and endurance
throughout these very trying days and nights."

During the night of 20th/21st November No. 1 Company of the 1/5th
Somersets furnished the necessary outposts.

At 10.15 p.m. orders were issued from 75th Divisional Headquarters 2/4th Battalion
for operations on the following day: the 233rd and 234th Brigades were to
move north of Jerusalem to Bireh whilst the 232nd Brigade carried out a
demonstration east towards the Holy City. The troops detailed for the latter
operations were 2/4th Somersets and 2/5th Hants, supported by the L.A.M.
Battery: the two remaining Battalions of the 232nd Brigade were to act as
baggage guard to the main body of the Division as far as Kutundia. The
orders of the Brigadier of the 232nd Brigade regarding this march are interesting
as well as descriptive. It was expected that the march to Bireh would test
the strength of the troops to the very utmost and he therefore gave orders that
all "crocks will be left here" (Enab).

For two hours during the early morning of 21st the village of Enab was 21st November
shelled heavily by the Turks and, owing to the congested state of the village—
packed with troops and animals—casualties were heavy.

So far as the demonstration towards Jerusalem on 21st is concerned,
there are no details of the operations: the Brigadier of the 232nd Brigade
said of the demonstration that it "calls for no comment," and there it ends,
whilst the Diary of the 2/4th Somersets reads: "Took up a position about
one mile east of Enab. Later moved forward and took up line of outposts
on hills facing E.N.E. at Kustul. About 16.30 (4.30 p.m.) Captain A. C.
Bealey and Captain E. B. Harford were wounded. We bivouacked here."
At nightfall on 21st, Divisional Headquarters ordered those units of the
Division not engaged on the march on Bireh to stand fast. Indeed, from the
21st to the 23rd inclusive the entries in the Diary of the 2/4th Somersets
record nothing more than "still at Kustul." Captain A. C. Bealey died of
his wounds on 21st. On the afternoon of 23rd, however, 75th Divisional 23rd November
Headquarters asked XXI Corps to sanction three Battalions of the 232nd
Brigade, i.e. 2/4th Somersets, 2/5th Hants and 58th Rifles, being sent from

2/4th Battalion

Kustul to rejoin the Division to enable a further effort to be made on Kutundia. These Battalions were relieved on 24th and the Somersets marched to Biddu, arriving at 5 p.m., and bivouacked. But at 10.15 p.m. the Battalion marched back to Enab, arriving in the early hours of 25th.

25th November

1/5th Battalion

Meanwhile the 1/5th Somersets of the 233rd Brigade had again become involved in stiff fighting with the enemy who was posted in strong positions at Nebi Samwil. It will be remembered that the 233rd and 234th Brigades had been ordered to move north of Jerusalem to Bireh, the latter Brigade forming the Advanced Guard and the former the main body.

With Biddu as its objective the 233rd Brigade, in rear of the 234th, left Enab on the morning of 21st, the Battalion Diary of the 1/5th Somersets stating that the march began at 10.30 a.m. along the old Roman road which leaves the Jerusalem Road 400 yards from Enab, thence running north. Over very rocky hills, so rough and steep as to prohibit the use of any transport other than pack mules and camels, the 233rd and 234th Brigades picked their way towards Biddu and, by the afternoon, a point south of the village had been reached. Here, however, the head of the Advanced Guard was held up, the enemy occupying strong positions in force with many guns: the Nebi Samwil line, indeed, formed part of his main defences of Jerusalem. With only mountain guns the 75th Division found it impossible to keep down the volume of hostile artillery fire which came from the hills to the east. It was about 2 p.m. when the Advanced Guard occupied Beit Sarik and the ridge east of it, but the position was overlooked by the Nebi Samwil ridge and it was obviously necessary to occupy the latter before any forward movement could be made towards Kutundia or Bireh. During the evening the ridge on which Nebi Samwil stands was attacked by the 234th Brigade and occupied and the position consolidated, but the 1/5th Somersets do not appear to have taken part in the capture, the Battalion apparently remaining south of Biddu until the following day when, with the 1/4th Wilts, the Somerset men were ordered to attack and capture El Jib and Bir Nebala with a final objective— the village of Kutundia. All these places lay north-east of Nebi Samwil and the top ridge of the latter position, being now in possession of the 234th Brigade, it was essential to clear the enemy out of the two former villages before the advance could continue to Kutundia.

22nd November

At 7 a.m. a combined force (consisting of a squadron of Hyderabad Lancers, the 1/5th Somersets, 1/4th Wilts and a section of the 230th M.G. Company) moved forward to attack and capture the two villages.

The 1/5th Somersets led the advance and supplied two companies, under Captain Major, to form, with the Cavalry, an advanced guard. Progress was necessarily slow, as the country was rocky and precipitous in the extreme. The men, encumbered with full fighting equipment and with their boots cut and torn by the sharp stones, had to scramble down the rough hill-sides into a deep valley and then out again at the far end. Leaving Nebi Samwil on the right, the attacking force advanced in open order in a northerly direction, although El Jib lay to the east. As was proved by subsequent events, the

O.C. the attacking force had mistaken the position of El Jib and was directing 1/5th Battalion
the attack on the more distant village of Beitunia. A compass was the only 22nd November
reliable guide, for it was difficult to distinguish between the villages which
were securely set among the hills to the West of Jerusalem, and were girt
around with rocky terraces presenting an almost impassable front to any
attack.

The advancing troops, themselves unsupported by artillery (which had
been unable to negotiate the hill path to Biddu), now came under regular fire
from the Turks on the hills in front of them.

The O.C. the combined force had himself gone forward with the two
companies of Somersets in the advanced guard, leaving the O.C. 1/5th
Somersets to lead the main body, which was moving painfully forward taking
advantage of any available cover that could be found. The climbing was
arduous and the passage sufficiently difficult as a feat of endurance, without
the unwelcome attentions of the enemy's artillery and machine-gun fire.
Reaching a ridge overlooking a deep valley, which led up to a massive hill
occupied by the Turks, the O.C. 1/5th Somersets was able to engage the
enemy with his Lewis and machine guns, and so help to cover the advance
of the attacking troops who were making slow headway under the difficult
conditions.

The remaining two companies of the Somersets now moved up to support
the attack, and a further attempt was made to continue the advance,
under the direct fire of the enemy. Though the ground was rocky and
broken there was little real cover for the advancing lines, except when passing over dead ground, and the effect of the enemy shell fire and machine-gun
fire was intensified by the rock splinters sent flying by the bullets and bursting
shells.

The casualties began to thin out the ranks, and the Somersets lost three
more officers, wounded, whom they could ill afford to spare (Lieutenants
Bradford, Whitley and Turner). The officer commanding sent back orders
for the 1/4th Wilts to move up in support. But the supporting troops could
make no more headway than their comrades over that rocky country and
under the direct fire of the Turks, who, in the absence of our artillery, were
able to maintain a deliberate and unwavered fire upon the attacking troops.

The attacking lines, however, carried the hill which had held up the
advance earlier in the day and advanced beyond the crest for about 200 yards,
where they were again held up by the enemy who were occupying a further
ridge beyond.

About this time a message from Brigade H.Q., which had now moved
to Beit Izza, intimated that the attack was developing in the wrong direction,
i.e. to the north, instead of on El Jib to the east. It was, however, impossible
at that stage to correct the direction of the attack. Without strong reinforcements no further progress was possible, and even with fresh troops it was
doubtful if much could have been gained without unwarrantable sacrifices of
valuable lives.

But if any further advance was out of the question, it was equally impossible to attempt to withdraw while daylight lasted. Orders therefore came through from Brigade H.Q. for the troops to hold their ground until dusk, and then to withdraw, with their wounded, on Beit Izza, about one and a quarter miles in rear.

So, for the remainder of that long and trying day the tired troops lay out in the open, or behind such cover as they could find, waiting for nightfall.

The stretcher-bearers had worked heroically to try and get the wounded in under cover, but over the steep and uneven country, in full view of the enemy, they had an almost hopeless task.

To ease the position of the attacking force, and also to help to cover the withdrawal when the time came, two companies of the 1/4th Wilts which had been held in reserve were sent to occupy a hill to the right of the main position and on the far side of a valley which ran behind it, approximately north-east and south-west. This was done, and when dusk fell, the withdrawal commenced up this valley, which ran towards Beit Izza. The Somersets, who had been engaged since the early morning, withdrew first, followed by the Wilts, who covered the withdrawal. The greatest difficulty was experienced in getting in the wounded who had been lying out all day without any shelter and whose wounds were aggravated by the delay in being treated, but somehow this was done and the Battalion reached the site allotted to it for the night's bivouac.

The cost of this fruitless day's fighting could now be reckoned, and amongst the casualties was Captain Banes-Walker, who had commanded No. 4 Coy., and who was killed in the earlier stages of the attack. Two of the companies were thus left without any officers at all. Of other ranks, 11 were killed or missing and 23 wounded.

But the fighting was not yet over. After a bitterly cold night (it was the end of November, some 3,000 feet above sea-level and the men wearing khaki-drill shorts and tunics, with no blankets or greatcoats), the troops awoke on 23rd to the knowledge that El Jib was still to be taken. The 1/5th Somersets were detailed for the attack, and at dawn the Commanding Officer went forward with the Brigadier to obtain a view of the objective. Seen from the west, El Jib presented a formidable aspect. A natural stronghold, it stood upon a hill, about a mile to the east, with steep rocky terraces affording natural facilities for defence by enfilading machine-gun fire. The approach to the village was through a valley some 700 yards wide, with Nebi Samwil on the right, and, on the left, high ground and ridges leading forward from Beit Izza. The Mosque on the lofty slopes of Nebi Samwil, which stood out in relief against the surrounding country, was occupied by the 3/3rd Gurkhas, who held on to their position most gallantly after desperate hand-to-hand fighting, in which even boulders were used by the defenders of the Mosque, in almost mediæval fashion.

This, then, was the position which the Somersets were asked to assault, with no other support than the light guns of a mountain battery, with its limited supply of ammunition, and a detachment of the Brigade Machine-Gun Company.

The Battalion was now reduced to an effective strength of about 400 men, and, apart from the C.O., the second-in-command, and the adjutant, there were only four subalterns left to go into action with the companies; No. 3 Company, having no officers at all, was commanded by C.S.M. W. C. Windows.[1]

At 8 a.m. the Battalion left the bivouacs it had occupied overnight and moved up to the place of deployment where the Commanding Officer detailed the plan of attack to his Company Commanders.

The general plan was that the 1/5th Somersets should capture and hold El Jib, after which the 2/3rd Gurkhas were to push on and take Bir Nebala, thus clearing the way for the advance to Bireh.

The enemy were already busy, at this stage, shelling the northern slopes of Nebi Samwil from the direction of the Nablus–Jerusalem road, and as soon as the deployed lines of the Somersets came under observation, the Turks concentrated a heavy fire of shrapnel and high-explosive upon them. As the 75th Divisional Artillery had been unable to reach Biddu, there was no means of keeping down this well-directed and deadly fire.

The attacking lines, however, moved forward with great coolness and precision, in spite of the intense machine-gun fire which opened on them as they came within range. No attack could live long under that fire. As one of the officers with the attack described it, "every other man seemed to be falling . . . it was terrible . . . the lines just melted away."

The machine-gun fire was coming not only from the El Jib position, where it was to be expected, but a particularly galling fire was also raking the attacking lines in enfilade from the northern slopes of Nebi Samwil on the right flank. Nothing daunted, what remained of the attacking lines pressed forward under intense and continuous fire. The fourth company, which had been held in reserve, was now thrown into the attack, together with any of the Battalion Headquarters who could be spared. Captain A. O. Major, who went forward with this company, was first wounded, and then killed outright by a shell.

The leading waves had now reached the foot of the rocky hill on which stood El Jib. Here they were faced by steep and almost unscaleable terraces which they endeavoured to climb. Three Lewis-gun sections managed to scale the terraces with their guns, and small parties of men actually reached the village itself. This was, perhaps, the most gallant feat of arms throughout the whole of the two-days' operation, but, unhappily, it was a forlorn attempt, and none of these brave fellows were seen again. When El Jib was ultimately captured by the 74th Division, identity discs of 27 men of the Somersets were recovered on the position, which seemed to suggest that the men were shot down as they reached the upper terraces.

[1] For conspicuous gallantry and devotion to duty C.S.M. W. C. Windows was awarded the D.C.M.

All the company officers were now out of action, killed or wounded, and the survivors of the attacking lines were finding what cover they could below the lower terraces of the hill. It was humanly impossible to scale and capture the position itself under that murderous fire; there was nothing for it but to take cover, if any could be found and hold on in the hope of reinforcements.

Communication between Battalion H.Q. and the Companies was impossible, as no runner could cross that bullet-swept stretch of ground. The line to Brigade H.Q. was kept connected throughout the day, in spite of the fact that it was cut by shell fire on three or four occasions and only mended by the courage and resource of the Signal Section.

The 1/5th Devons were sent up to the attack on the left of the Somersets, but, in face of the enemy fire, they were unable to make any progress.

It was now evident that a position of such great natural strength, defended by the Turks with all the courage and determination of despair (this was their final stand in defence of Jerusalem after the hurried retreat of the past fortnight), could not be taken by an unorganized and unsupported attack. The order was given to the troops engaged to stand fast and hold their ground, and at nightfall the Somersets received orders to withdraw to the previous night's bivouac area, covered by the 2/3rd Gurkhas.

The enemy fire had continued throughout the day and it had been impossible to collect many of the wounded, who had been lying out all day under fire with their wounds unattended to, or, at best, bound up with a hasty field dressing. These were now collected with great difficulty and brought in, but many of the dead who had been killed in the vicinity of El Jib itself, had to be left behind, as any movement in the advanced positions was at once met by the Turks with rifle fire, and, more effectively, with hand-grenades, which they were able to throw down from the higher terraces on to our men below.

Back in the bivouac area, the Somersets were able to check the rolls and ascertain their casualties. The Commanding Officer (Major F. D. Urwick) and the Adjutant (Capt. E. S. Goodland) were the only two combatant officers left. Of the rest, Captain A. O. Major and 2/Lieutenant W. A. Hannaford had been killed, and Lieutenants Milsom, Clarke and Foster wounded.

The Battalion, which had gone into action on the 22nd November about 450 strong, had suffered 221 casualties in the two days' fighting—3 officers killed and 6 wounded, 51 other ranks killed or missing and 161 wounded.

The next day (24th November) the 52nd (Lowland) Division moved up to renew the attack on El Jib and Bir Nebala in relief of the 75th Division, which was ordered to withdraw to Kuryet el Enab and thence back to Junction Station. But El Jib resisted the further attempts to capture it, and it was not until a much later stage of the operations that this redoubtable hill fortress was finally occupied.

The 75th Division, however, including the two Somerset Battalions, had every reason to be proud of their share in the operations leading up to the capture of Jerusalem. The Division had been marching and fighting for

a fortnight in a difficult country, where water was scarce and commissariat 1/5th Battalion
arrangements highly precarious; it had kept the retreating Turkish army on
the run; it had forced a passage through the Pass to Enab, which had been 25th November
captured at the point of the bayonet after a long and arduous day's work;
it had traversed the Roman hill-road to Biddu with a minimum of transport
and equipment; it had captured the dominating heights of Nebi Samwil,
which was the key to the defences of Jerusalem; and finally, though unsuccess-
fully, it had made repeated and heroic attempts to break through to the Nablus–
Jerusalem road, and so cut off the Turkish garrison. This task was subsequently completed by others, but the 75th Division had done its share.

Lord Allenby in his despatches stated that:—

"The positions reached on the evening of the 21st practically marked
the limit of progress in this first attempt to gain the Nablus–Jerusalem road"
and "it was evident that a period of preparation and organization would be
necessary before an attack could be delivered in sufficient strength to drive
the enemy from his position west of the road." [1]

The 75th Division moved on 26th back to Junction Station, and it was
time for, as one diary states: "many men having no soles to their boots: new
boots had to be obtained before they could march."

THE CAPTURE OF JERUSALEM, 7TH–9TH DECEMBER 1917

From the 27th to 30th November the Turks delivered a series of strong 12th Battalion
counter-attacks from north-east of Jaffa to the Nebi Samwil Ridge: they were
repulsed and, especially at the latter place, the enemy lost heavily. Preparations
for a fresh advance against the Turkish positions west and south of Jerusalem
proceeded rapidly. Roads and tracks were improved, supplies and ammunition
brought up and the water supply developed. The date for the converging
attack on the Holy City was fixed for 8th December. From the south Welsh
troops were pushing up the Hebron–Jerusalem road and by the evening of
6th the head of the column was 10 miles north of Hebron. From the west
the attack was to be made by the 60th (right) and 74th (left) Divisions:
Jerusalem was to be enveloped.

On 23rd November the 74th Division (XX Corps), which had been held
in reserve, was once more on the road northward, the 60th Division was already
on the road when the 74th began its long march. On the night of 23rd the
12th Somerset Light Infantry bivouacked about Gaza and the six days which
followed were days of hard and difficult marching. The time-table of these
marches is as follows: 25th—Gaza to Mejdel, 15 miles; 26th—Mejdel
to Sukereir, 12 miles; 27th—Sukereir to Railway Junction, 12 miles; 28th—
Railway Junction to Latron, 8 miles; 29th—Latron to Beit Sira, 6 miles; 30th
—Beit Sira to Beit Anan, 6 miles.

From Latron the road begins to climb to the lower slopes and foothills

[1] It is interesting to note that in this Battle the 75th Division reached the farthest point of Richard
Cœur de Lion's advance in January 1192.

of the mountains of Judæa and the Somerset men were soon in country which was practically roadless, well suited to goats, "but," as an officer of the Battalion describes it, "for the sweating, burdened foot soldier, absolute hell." As the 12th Battalion approached Beit Sira, the whole of the 229th Brigade marching up a valley between high hills, there looked down upon the moving column a high conical-shaped eminence, with a solitary building perched upon its tip: it was visible through a gap in the nearer hills. This building was the Sh. Abu es Zeitun, which the Battalion, after a terrible climb, captured later, on 27th December.

At early morning on 2nd December the Devons of the 229th Brigade had seized the village of Beit ur el Foka, but in the face of overwhelming numbers and after a splendid resistance had to withdraw. On 3rd December the 12th Somersets, with other units of the 229th Brigade, were in the line north of Ainjufna. The Somersets were put into the outpost line, but on the night of 6th December were relieved and moved south-east on the Ludd–Jerusalem Road, bivouacking for the night in the neighbourhood of Beit Surik. That night was one of profound misery, bitterly cold with a high wind and continuous heavy rain; the Battalion was at an elevation of over 2,000 feet, on very rough and stony ground. When dawn broke on 7th heavy rain was still falling, there was a heavy mist limiting the vision to 200 yards. These conditions continued all day, making reconnaissance impossible. The 12th Somersets were not one of the assaulting Battalions but were to be reserve to the Ayr and Lanarks, who were to attack on the 229th Brigade front: the Fife and Forfar and the Devons were in reserve. The 60th Division was on the right of the 74th, of which the 230th and 231st Brigades were on the left of the 229th. The objectives of the 229th Brigade lay between the village of Beit Iksa and the Wadi Hannina. At dawn on the 8th the attack was launched:—

"To clamber down and to arrive in any sort of formation was difficult enough, to reorganize in the Wadi bed and climb straightforward up a rock-strewn and terraced mountain-side, against trenches known to be held, was a job requiring excellent leading and a very large amount of physical endurance. Such was the task in front of the 230th and our own Brigade (229th) that morning." [1]

The Ayr and Lanarks charged the Turkish trenches and took them, and the 12th Somersets moved across the wadi in the expectation of a further advance, for the operations of the XX Corps for that day were to carry the Corps, facing north, astride the Nablus road, north of Jerusalem. But the Turkish resistance was too strong, Beit Iksa had not been fully captured when darkness fell, neither had the 60th Division made sufficient progress: 4,000 yards advance was all that was made on 8th. The only portion of the 12th Somersets engaged during the day was C Company, who were moved into the

[1] "A Record of the West Somerset Yeomanry," by Captain R. C. Boyle.

line on the left of the Ayr and Lanarks to fill a gap between that Battalion and 12th Battalion
the right of the 230th Brigade.

On the 9th a renewal of the battle was expected and, in anticipation of 9th December
some hard fighting, the reserve Battalions of the 229th Brigade were moved
up in close support during the early morning.   But patrols from the Somersets
and Ayr and Lanarks found the hills in front of them unoccupied and the
74th Division went ahead to the line intended as the final objective on the
previous day. The 12th Somersets first took up a line from Tel el Ful to
Wadi es Dumm, but later advanced farther in support of the Australian Light
Horse, coming under heavy shell fire from the north, during which two men
were killed and 2/Lieut. W. H. Casey and six other ranks were wounded.

All through the 8th and 9th lorries had been observed streaming away
from Jerusalem in a northerly direction, but it was impossible for the British
artillery to shell them as superhuman efforts would have been necessary to
move the guns forward to within range.   The gun positions from which
the artillery had covered the attacks of 8th December were only reached after
the last ounce of strength had been used: it was impossible to move any farther
forward, for the nature of the country prohibited it.

Thus the Turks were able to get all their baggage and impedimenta away
before surrendering Jerusalem.   With British troops holding a line across
the Nablus–Jerusalem road, 4 miles north of the City, and others occupying
a position east across the Jericho road, Jerusalem was isolated and, about noon,
the enemy sent out a Parlementaire and surrendered the Holy City which, for
centuries, had been in the possession of the Turk.

On the 10th the 229th Brigade concentrated and, after bivouacking for 1/5th and 2/4th
the night below Beit Hannina, the Somersets settled down for a few days at Battalions
Beit Iksa.   And here, for a moment, it is necessary to leave the 12th Battalion
and turn to the doings of the 1/5th and 2/4th Battalions during the Capture
of the Holy City.

The 1/5th Somersets, after reaching Enab on 25th November, had marched 1/5th Battalion
(in Brigade) to Junction Station on 26th; to the Jewish Camp at Akir on 27th;
to Ludd on 29th; and to Jimzu on 30th.   On the last day of the month there 30th November
are some interesting figures of the losses of the Battalion during November:
four officers were killed and nine wounded; in other ranks 25 had been killed,
230 wounded and 34 were missing.   The Diary adds:—

"Throughout the month operations which have involved great hardships
and difficulties: the men's spirits have been excellent and the courage and
dash displayed in the actions fought, especially Mesmiyeh and El Jib, has been
remarkable and has earned for the Regiment an enviable reputation in the
E.E.F." [1]

Eight days were spent in Jimzu and on 9th December the Battalion moved
to Ramleh and on the 10th to Surafend, the 232nd Brigade becoming Corps 10th December
Reserve.   Thus the 1/5th saw nothing of the fighting for Jerusalem.

[1] Egyptian Expeditionary Force.

2/4th Battalion

From 27th November to the end of the month the 2/4th Somersets remained at El Mughar, the only incident of importance being the arrival of much-needed reinforcements, i.e. four officers and 171 rank and file. On 1st December the Battalion moved to El Kubeibeh, remaining there until the 7th when a move was made to Ramleh, the 2/4th bivouacking in an orchard some 400 yards south-west of Crusaders' Church. On 9th the Battalion lent an officer and nine other ranks to the 2/3rd Gurkhas for observation purposes. On this day also the Battalion, after leaving A Company to guard the guns, marched to the eastern side of the wadi between Deir Abu Selameh in Brigade Reserve and bivouacked for the night, B Company going out on outpost duty on a hill three-quarters of a mile east of Selameh. On the

10th December   10th C and D Companies were at work on the roads beyond Hadithen.

THE DEFENCE OF JERUSALEM, 26TH–30TH DECEMBER 1917

12th Battalion

Jerusalem was captured, but in order to provide more effectively for the security of the Holy City and of Jaffa it was essential that the line should be advanced. The XX Corps was, therefore, ordered to advance to the line Beitin Nalin, i.e. an advance on a 12-mile front to a depth of 6 miles immediately north of Jerusalem, and the XXI Corps to the line Kibbieh–Rantieh–Mulebris–Sheikh el Ballutah–El Jelil. But before either of these advances could take place a considerable amount of labour was necessary in order to improve the roads and communications. Supplies and ammunition had to be brought up. Heavy rains damaged the railway and turned the roads into seas of mud rendering the use of mechanical transport and camels impossible, and horse transport was slow and difficult. Several days, therefore, elapsed before the advance could be begun.

24th December

The 12th Somersets of the 229th Brigade, up to the evening of 24th December, remained in bivouacs in the neighbourhood of Beit Iksa, the Battalion being engaged in road-making near Biddu. The Turks had planned to attack and recapture Jerusalem, but details of their intentions were known to the Commander-in-Chief who had taken the necessary measures to defeat the enemy's project. As soon as the Turkish assault on the British line north of Jerusalem had developed a counter-attack was to be launched.

On the evening of 24th December the 229th Brigade received orders to march at short notice to the Wadi Selman, north-east of Beit Likia, the 12th Somersets joining the Brigade *en route*. In heavy rain and a howling wind, heavily laden, the troops marched for the greater part of the way along the sides of wadis, with scarce a track of any sort to guide them in the blackness of the night. The distance marched was 8 miles and, although the Brigade

25th December   set out at 6.30 p.m., it was not until 3.30 a.m. on the 25th that units reached their destination. The transport had broken down and the early hours of Christmas Day were rationless and wretched in the extreme. Throughout the 25th and until afternoon of 26th rain fell heavily, but on the latter day the inclement weather gave way to hot sunshine, which dried the clothes of the discomfited troops and generally made things more bearable.

At 11.30 p.m. on the night of 26th the enemy's attack was launched,
the advance posts of the 60th Division east of Jerusalem being driven in:
by 1.30 a.m. on 27th the 60th Division was engaged along its whole front,
the outposts of the Division on the ridge north of Beit Hanninah repulsing
four determined attacks.   The heaviest fighting took place east of the Jerusalem–
Nablus road, but the Turkish gains were negligible.   Various posts held
by the 53rd Division east of Jerusalem were also vigorously attacked by the
enemy without success.   North of Jerusalem after 8 a.m. repeated hostile
attacks, delivered in great strength, and at first successful, were shattered,
counter-attacks at every point restoring the line.   About midday the Turks
had spent their strength.

Meanwhile, at 12 noon, the counter-attacks by the 74th and 10th Divisions,
launched at 6.30 a.m. against the right of the enemy's attack had made themselves felt.   The despatches stated that the 74th Division, climbing the western
slopes of the Zeitun Ridge advanced along it in an easterly direction.   On their
left a brigade of the 10th Division advanced along the neighbouring ridge,
the left of the 10th Division advancing in a northerly direction to form
a defensive flank.

For these operations the 229th Brigade (74th Division) was attached
to, and formed the right Brigade of, the 10th Division.   The Brigade's objective
was the Turkish position on the Sh. Abu Ez Zeitun–Beitunia Ridge.   The
Welsh Horse of the 231st Brigade were in the line about and above Beit ur
el Foka and the attack of the 229th Brigade was to pass through them and
deploy for the assault in the Wadi Imeish.

The Zeitun Ridge, which was to be secured in the first day's operations,
was a tongue of land at whose extreme tip stood a little mosque.   The tongue
ran east and west, the village of Beitunia, the objective of the second day's
attack, being at its eastern extremity.   North and south of the ridge deep
wadis separated the 229th Brigade from the 231st Brigade on the right, and
the 10th Division on the left.

The 229th Brigade was to attack on a two-battalion front, the Ayr and
Lanarks on the right and the 12th Somersets on the left.   A and B Companies
of the Somersets, under the respective commands of Captains Rodd and Keen,
were to lead the attack of the Battalion which was temporarily under the command of Major C. R. Hayward.   The Fife and Forfars were in support and
the Devons in reserve.

The Somersets took up their battle outpost line successfully and were
ready for the signal to advance at 4.30 a.m., but it was 8 a.m. before the word
was given.   In front of the attacking Battalions the hill-side rose like a wall
to a height of over 600 feet from the wadi at its base.   It was a stiff
climb.   Up over very rocky ground, so frequently terraced that it was often
a question of crawling, the Somerset men went.   From the front and right
flank the advance was met by heavy machine-gun fire, but the very nature of
the ground, rocks, terraces and steep sides, protected the attacking troops
from suffering heavy casualties.   Slowly and painfully the attack neared the

summit of the hill, where the Turks were either entrenched or protected by stone sangars, though fortunately there were no wire entanglements to surmount as well.   Under cover of efficient artillery support, the attackers, after a climb lasting an hour and twenty-five minutes, reached the summit and with a cheer charged the Turkish positions and by 9.30 a.m. the first objective was won: "We were in possession of a hill," said Captain R. C. Boyle, "which, for steepness, vies with the cliffs of the Cheddar Gorge"—all Somerset men will appreciate the simile.   The Turks put up a good fight, remaining in their sangars until the attackers were upon them and, even when evicted, they hung on grimly amongst the rocks and boulders of the hill-side.[1]

The two attacking Battalions of the 229th Brigade had made good their first objective at such a speed that they were in advance of the 10th Division on the left.   They had, therefore, to halt until the troops on their flanks came up, and it was not until 12 noon that the advance was continued towards the second objective, the high ground east of Sh. Abu Ez Zeitun.   In the meantime, however, patrols pushed out found the second objective unoccupied by the enemy and two Companies of the Somersets, under Captain Rodd, were then pushed forward and consolidated the position.   At 5.45 p.m. the advance to the third objective was begun by the Ayr and Lanarks on the right and the Fife and Forfars on the left, with the Somersets in support in the line of the second objective, until the remainder of the Brigade had passed through them, when the Battalion marched in Brigade Reserve.   After some brisk fighting, which lasted several hours, the third objective was gained and the 229th Brigade bivouacked for the night on the hill Kh. Biresh Shafat, described in the official diaries as "R.4b."

At 3 p.m. on the 28th the advance was resumed, the Fife and Forfars being on the right and the 12th Somersets on the left.   The former Battalion had been allotted the village of Beitunia as its objective, whilst to the Somerset men was assigned Hill 35, to the north of, and some 2,000 yards from, the village.   In a bare half-hour the Somersets had captured their objective, but the Turks in Beitunia gave the Fife and Forfars some trouble, though the latter eventually captured the village with about seventy Turks, including the complete staff of a Turkish regiment, and seven machine guns: the ridge commanding the village beyond it was also captured.[2]   The enemy then retired northwards to Ram Allah.   Later in the evening the 12th Somersets were relieved on Hill 35 by the Shropshires and advanced to and occupied El Muntar without opposition.   But at this point the Battalion dropped out of the running and the 230th Brigade took over the line held by the 229th.   The 74th Division was now squeezed out of the line by the junction of the inner flanks of the 10th and 60th Divisions, and at the close of the year was in reserve.

The two days' hard fighting (27th and 28th December), in which the 12th Somersets had taken such an active part, cost the Battalion 13 killed

[1] For conspicuous gallantry and devotion to duty Corpl. W. Jones was awarded the D.C.M.
[2] For conspicuous gallantry and devotion to duty L/Cpl. C. Cleal was awarded the D.C.M.

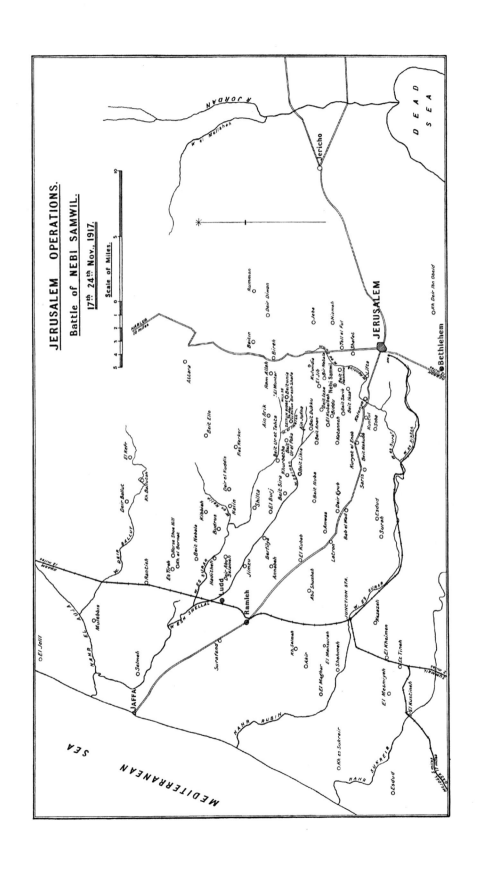

JERUSALEM OPERATIONS.
Battle of NEBI SAMWIL.
17th 24th Nov., 1917.

Scale of Miles.

and 81 wounded other ranks: 2/Lieuts. Cross and Haddon were amongst the wounded.

The final line occupied by the XX Corps at the end of December 1917 ran from Deir Ibn Obeid, south-east of Jerusalem, northwards past Hizmeh and Jeba to Beitin, thence westwards through El Burj, Ras Kerker to Deir el Kuddis.

Meanwhile on 20th and 21st December the XXI Corps, on the left, had effected the passage of the Nahr el Auja, the 52nd Division carrying out this important operation. The 75th Division, on the right of the Corps Line, moved forward automatically, though some stiff fighting in places had to be carried out as the Division advanced. From the standpoint of the Somerset Light Infantry, however, these operations are not of outstanding interest, as both the 1/5th and 2/4th Battalions saw little of the actual fighting.

The 1/5th Somersets moved from Ramleh on 10th December to Surafend, where the 233rd Brigade was placed in Corps Reserve until 18th. On the latter date two Battalions of the 233rd Brigade (of which the 1/5th Somersets was one) were placed at the disposal of the G.O.C., 232nd Brigade, and moved to Haditheh in Divisional Reserve. On 26th the 1/5th moved to Horse Shoe Hill, north of Beit Nebala, and took over part of the front line from the 2/4th Somersets. Here the Battalion remained until the close of the year.

Although continually in reserve or support and occasionally taking over front-line positions from other units of the 232nd Brigade as it advanced, the 2/4th Somersets do not appear to have been involved in any fighting with the enemy during the latter part of December. On 11th, while other units of the Brigade took Midien, Zebdah, Budrus and Sheikh Obeid Rahil, C and D Companies were attached to the 2/3rd Gurkhas, D Company going forward and occupying a hill on a line between Haditheh and a point midway between Sheikh Obeid Rahil and Budrus, the attack passing right and left of (and being covered by) D Company's position. In successive stages the Battalion moved forward to Mukam Iman el Aly, Sheikh Obeid Rahil, Bornat and Horse Shoe Hill. It was at the latter place that the 2/4th were relieved by the 1/5th and moved back to bivouacs at Surafend. The Battalion was now under the command of Lieut.-Colonel E. B. Powell, who had arrived on 18th December and taken over from Major L. K. Bunting.

For the time being any further advance in Palestine was out of the question and in the meantime events had moved apace in France and Flanders.

CHAPTER XXX

FRANCE AND FLANDERS

THE LAST WINTER IN THE TRENCHES, 1917–1918

1st, 6th, 7th and 8th Battalions

THE last winter in the trenches, i.e. 1917–1918, did not vary greatly from those which had gone before, though the front-line trenches were better drained, more substantially built, and the methods adopted in fighting the inclement weather had vastly improved. Bombing, sniping, patrol work and raids, periods of violent shelling by the opposing guns, varied here and there by days and nights of normal conditions which came as a boon and a blessing to all ranks, followed the terrible Battles of Ypres and the sanguinary struggle at Cambrai. For the 1st Somersets December was a quiet month, though the opposing guns made movement uncomfortable in the Monchy sector where the Battalion was located. Bitterly cold weather saw the Old Year out, the last day of which was spent by the Somerset men in hard work, Light and C Companies being out with the R.E., and the remaining Companies at work on the Brown Line.

The 6th Somersets spent the period between the end of August (on 31st the Battalion was in billets at Le Roukloshille) and the close of the year as most infantry battalions did when not engaged in active warfare with the enemy. They had tours in the front line, in support and in reserve. Out of the front line there were always working parties to be provided, training to be carried out, carrying parties to be furnished for the formation of dumps of stores, or to take munitions up to the front lines. Some of these working and carrying parties had a bad time, either through running into a hostile barrage, or the sudden opening of a violent bombardment by the enemy's guns. On the 18th October, for instance (the Battalion was then holding support trenches in Sanctuary Wood), the 6th Somersets had working and carrying parties out when the enemy put down a heavy barrage which resulted in one other rank being killed and two officers (2/Lieuts. Scott and Walker) and eleven other ranks wounded. The 22nd and 23rd October were also bad days for the Somerset men. They had relieved the D.C.L.I. in the front line on the previous night. For some reason or other the enemy was very nervous and frequently put down heavy barrages in front of the front line, behind the support line and Glencorse Wood, Fitzclarence Farm and Inverness Copse. On the 22nd 2/Lieut. B. E. Reader and one other rank were killed and twelve other ranks wounded. On the 23rd casualties were heavier still. Captain D. L. Gough, Lieut. Abbott and 2/Lieut. J. E. Ellis were wounded; 2/Lieut. R. D. W. Maddever died of wounds, 12 other ranks were killed and 30 wounded. Even when out of the front line bad luck pursued the Battalion for, after relief on 24th and during the move back to the Berthen area for training, the 6th Somersets lost 19 other ranks (killed, wounded and missing).

The whole of November was spent out of the line in training, but on 2nd December the Battalion received orders to move to the Wieltje area, and arrived at St. Jean on 3rd.   On the 9th December the 6th Somersets went into front-line trenches east of Ypres, but this tour (and, indeed, the remainder of the year) was uneventful.   The Battalion moved to Moringhem on 26th and here, on 31st, Christmas celebrations took place.

From Sorel-le-Grand, where the Battalion was resting on 3rd December, the 7th Somersets moved successively on 4th to Bouzeaucourt, on 6th to Albert, thence to Embry and on the 12th to La Belle Hautesse (near Hazebrouck), where training was carried out to the last day of December.   No item of abnormal interest happened during this period out of the line.

After the operations early in October the 37th Division was relieved by the 39th Division, and on the 15th of that month the 8th Somersets moved back to Frontier Camp.   The Battalion marched to Moolenacker on 21st and on the 29th moved by bus to a camp east of Ypres for road making and repairing and, on completing their task on 6th November, moved in motor-lorries to the Merris area.   On the 9th the Battalion moved to Pier Barracks, Bailleul, thence to Moated Grange Camp on 10th, where a week was spent in support trenches.   From Toornai Camp, whither the Battalion moved on 17th from Moated Grange Camp, the 8th Somersets took over front-line trenches on 25th, returning to the Camp on the night of 5th/6th December. One more tour was spent in the front line, from 21st to 30th December, after which the Somerset men moved back to Alpha Beta Camp.   During the last tour 2/Lieut. W. L. Ward was killed and 2/Lieut. W. T. Hucke wounded (both on 22nd December), the latter dying of his wounds on 23rd December.

CHAPTER XXXI

THE GERMAN OFFENSIVES, 1918

1st, 6th, 7th and
8th Battalions

FROM the 1st January 1918 to the eve of the Great German Offensive in March 1918, the Battalion Diaries of the 1st, 6th, 7th and 8th Somerset Light Infantry contain nothing of outstanding interest. The second half of the last winter in the trenches differed little from previous periods: rain and snow had once again turned the front-line and communication trenches into filthy ditches, foul with deep, sticky mud, though covered in some sectors, drier than others, with duck-boards. But still the Diaries record that in places the trenches were impassable owing to mud and water. No Man's Land was even worse than in previous years, for the continual shelling had ploughed up the ground, and great gaping shell holes and mine craters, full of water and noisome with the foul stench of decaying human flesh, made patrol work a terrible undertaking. But the spirits of the troops never flagged, their cheerfulness was extraordinary and their optimism might well have shamed the pessimists at home.

In order that the operations in which the 1st, 6th and 7th Somersets were engaged during the German offensive on the Somme may be more easily understood, it is necessary to outline briefly the general situation in France and Flanders up to the time of the enemy's great effort.

The defection of Russia had set free the great bulk of German and Austrian divisions on the Eastern front and already, at the beginning of November 1917, the transfer of German divisions to the Western theatre of the War had begun. It was evident that this would continue until the enemy possessed numerical superiority along the front, from the Swiss frontier to the Belgian coast. Guns and ammunition formerly possessed by the Russian Armies fell into the hands of the enemy and these also were available for use against the Allies. The American Army, though expected eventually to restore numerical superiority to the Allies, was still in training in the United States, and only a very small force (negligible as a fighting force) had as yet arrived in France. In view of these disabilities the Allies therefore adopted a defensive policy, during which preparations were made to meet a strong and sustained hostile offensive. The strenuous efforts of 1917 had left the British forces weak both in numbers and defensive training. Drafts from England to fill the depleted ranks had fallen off considerably and, finally (early in 1918), it was necessary to cut down the numbers of infantry battalions in a division from 13 to 10,[1] whilst several divisions disappeared for the time being from the effective list, having been reduced to cadre strength and their units used to build up other weaker divisions which were in danger of becoming extinct.

[1] Including Pioneer Battalions.

Training had hitherto been directed largely to preparation for offensive opera- 1st, 6th, 7th and
tions, but in view of the expected German offensive, it was essential to give all 8th Battalions
ranks instructions in the defence. But preparations to meet the coming
hostile attack necessitated the construction of new lines of defence and, from
a careful perusal of the Battalion Diaries, it is obvious that whereas units when
not holding front-line trenches should have been in hard training, they were
employed more often in digging new trenches or in strengthening old ones.
Moreover, the British Army had extended its southern line as far as the vicinity
of Barisis, immediately south of the River Oise, an extra front of over 28
miles which had to be manned in spite of the already weakened strength
of the forces under Sir Douglas Haig's command. By the end of January
1918 the British Army held an active front of some 125 miles.

Towards the middle of February, from air reconnaissances and from
various other sources, it had become evident that the enemy's preparations
for his offensive were well forward. He had already transferred some 38
divisions (all practically fresh and rested troops) to the Western Front. His
artillery had also been considerably increased, his rail and road communications
had been greatly improved, and the formation of large dumps of ammunition
and supplies had been observed along the whole front from the Oise to Flanders.
The enemy's preparations were particularly marked opposite the front held by
the Fifth and Third Armies from the Oise to the Scarpe, and as the 21st March
approached it became certain that the Germans were going to launch their
great offensive between the two rivers, with the object of separating the French
and British Armies and capturing Amiens, at this time a vital centre of communication.

On the 19th March Sir Douglas Haig's Intelligence Department reported 19th March
that the final stage of the enemy's preparations on the Arras–St. Quentin
front were approaching completion, and that from information obtained the
actual attack might be expected on the 20th or 21st March. By this date
the British Commander-in-Chief had made whatever dispositions and preparations to meet the attack were possible. His available forces were 31 infantry
and three cavalry divisions, of which 21 infantry divisions[1] were in line.
Against this number the Germans were able to put into the field on the first
day of the operations at least 64 divisions. Little wonder that confidence
reigned at German General Headquarters; indeed, the hostile troops who were
to make the attack had been buoyed up with stories of the approaching end of
the War, as the Allies would most certainly be defeated in this great offensive
and driven back to the coasts of France and Belgium.[2]

Sufficient has been said to give the reader some idea of the general situation
on the eve of the hostile offensive which, without doubt, was the greatest
German effort in France or Flanders during the whole War. Interest in

[1] Counting from the right flank, i.e. 58th Division opposite La Fere to the 4th Division just
north of the Scarpe.

[2] Germans captured after their attack had been launched said openly that they had won and that
the War was practically over.

the coming struggle now centres in three divisions which lay between the Oise and just north of the Scarpe when the storm broke, for these three Divisions—14th, 20th and 4th—contained Battalions of the Somerset Light Infantry.

6th Battalion

The first-named Division, the 14th, which contained the 6th Somersets (Lieut.-Colonel Bellew), held a front-line sector just west of Hamégicourt, Alaincourt and Berthencourt. This Division was one of those moved south early in January for the purpose of taking over the extra 28 miles of front from the French. The right flank of the 43rd Brigade was just north of La Verte Chasseur, just over a mile north of Vendeuil. On 18th March

18th March

the 6th Somersets [1] were holding front-line trenches in the neighbourhood of La Folie, having relieved the 7th K.R.R., and it was in this sub-sector that the Battalion (as will be recorded later) was practically wiped out.

7th Battalion

The 20th (Light) Division was one of the reserve divisions when the Germans launched their attack on the 21st March. The Division had arrived at Nesle (having been relieved by the 37th Division on the night of 18th/19th February) from south of Ypres during the third week of February. It was then placed in general reserve to the Fifth Army and was billeted in the Nesle area. The 7th Somersets (Lieut.-Colonel C. J. Troyte-Bullock) were billeted in Freniches, the 61st Brigade having been allotted the Golancourt area.

11th March

On 11th March the Battalion marched to Curchy and Voyennes, three Companies being billeted in the former village and one in the latter. Work and training now occupied the 7th Somersets until the 20th Division was called upon to help stem the tide of the German onrush.

1st Battalion

On the extreme left of the Third Army the 4th Division held the line east of Arras and here the 1st Somerset Light Infantry (Lieut.-Colonel V. H. B. Majendie) had had a six-weeks' spell out of the line before moving up into the

20th March

front line on 20th March, relieving the 1st Irish Guards in the centre sub-sector north of the Scarpe, and immediately north of the railway, with Battalion Headquarters in Cadiz Trench.

8th Battalion

The 8th Somersets (Lieut.-Colonel H. S. C. Richardson) did not move down from the Ypres area to the Somme until the end of March and therefore the early days of the German offensive concern only the 1st, 6th and 7th

31st March

Battalions of the Regiment.

---

[1] The Battalion Diary for March 1918, signed by the Adjutant, has the following note attached to it: "The War Diary and Operation Orders having been destroyed by shell fire, this copy is copied from memory and any records available."

CHAPTER XXXII

THE GERMAN OFFENSIVES, 1918: THE OFFENSIVE IN PICARDY

THE BATTLE OF ST. QUENTIN, 21ST–23RD MARCH

THREE German Armies, the Seventeenth, Second, and Eighteenth, were to launch the enemy's offensive on 21st March. The Seventeenth Army was to attack the British line from Croisilles to Mœuvres, and the Second and Eighteenth Armies the line from and between Villers Guislain and La Fere. The Flesquieres Salient (called by the Germans the Cambrai re-entrant) was only to be attacked indirectly by the inner flanks of the Seventeenth and Second Armies, the enemy hoping to pinch it off by the weight of his attacks north and south of the Salient.

For some time preceding the 21st March, the enemy had deluged the British front all along the line with a particularly virulent type of gas shell, known as mustard gas. Its effects were deadly. Men who had worn their gas masks for six hours, long after the shelling had ceased, were gassed as soon as they took their masks off, the fumes of the gas having clung to their clothes. The gas clung everywhere, to the ground, to the woods, to anything in fact of an absorbent nature.

Just before dawn on 21st the enemy opened a terrific bombardment with 21st March gas and high-explosive shells, from guns of all calibre, including trench mortars, along practically the whole front of the Fifth (right) and Third (left) Armies. Not only were the front-line and communication trenches swept by a continuous storm of shell, but the road centres and railways as far back as St. Pol were under fire from high-velocity guns. A thick mist hung over the whole battle-field and the S.O.S. signals sent up by the outpost line were hidden from the British O.Ps. and the machine guns of units in the front line.

On the trenches and sub-sector held by the 6th Somersets the enemy's 6th Battalion bombardment appears to have fallen about 4.30 a.m., and the Battalion Diary speaks of the mustard gas as a new kind of shell, the smell of which was not unpleasant, but had the effect of sleeping gas. At 8.30 a.m. the gas shelling ceased though the hostile guns continued to pour high-explosive shell on to the British lines, but long before that hour all telephone wires were cut and visual signalling, owing to the fog, was impossible. The Battalions in the front line were isolated, unable to communicate the situation to Brigade Headquarters or call on their artillery to assist them.

The hour of the enemy's infantry assault varied in different sectors, but shortly before 10 a.m. it had become general along the whole front.

Favoured by the thick fog, in massed formation, shoulder to shoulder, and singing songs to hearten them, the German infantry came on, wave after

281

wave, with the intention of breaking everywhere through the British front and sweeping the remnants back to the coast. The 6th Somersets had posted extra sentries at all points, but the enemy was upon the front line ere ever the gallant troops had an opportunity of repelling them. All detachments holding the outpost positions were overwhelmed or surrounded, in many places before they were able to pass back information concerning the enemy's attack. Behind the front line men had been brought up and battle stations manned, and it was these troops who were able to bring the enemy to a standstill, or hold up his advance after he had overrun the front line. The forward companies of the 6th Somersets held out in their strong points till late in the afternoon. No assistance being sent them these strong points eventually fell one by one, the last falling at about 5 p.m. At about 10.20 a.m. a runner had arrived, breathless almost, with the news that the enemy was in the Battalion's front line. The Support Company of the Somersets and Battalion Headquarters then moved into a strong point named Egypt, but they had scarcely established themselves there when fighting began. Two pigeons, with messages calling for assistance, were then despatched, all papers were burnt and the garrison of the strong point prepared to sell their lives dearly. By 10.30 a.m. the enemy's troops in great numbers were streaming down the St. Quentin road from both flanks: they poured into and overran La Folie Quarry and, five minutes later, were reported pushing towards Benay and Cerizy.

It is probable that by this time the 6th Somersets, as a Battalion, had almost ceased to exist, for now a tiny party consisting of the Adjutant (Captain Frampton), six runners and two signallers began to fight their way back to Brigade Headquarters to warn the Brigadier and all strong points on the way. At 11.10 a.m. the officer reached Brigade Headquarters. He was followed ten minutes later by two of the six runners, and finally one of the signallers succeeded in reaching Brigade Headquarters. They were the sole survivors of 20 officers and 540 other ranks of the 6th Somerset Light Infantry actually in the front line at the time of the attack. They were then attached to another Battalion, the 9th Scottish Rifles, with whom they fell back to Jussy [1] during the early hours of 22nd March. In this village the remnants of the 6th

Battalion spent the night, but on the 23rd with other troops, stiff hand-to-hand fighting took place with the enemy on the embankment before a further retirement was made to the heights of Faillouel and to the Cugny–Uguy le Gay road.

All day long on the 20th the 7th Somersets stood to at Curchy, though the Battalion was not called upon to move. About 3 p.m. on 21st, however, after the German offensive had begun, the 61st Brigade (20th Division) was ordered to occupy battle positions across the angle formed by the Crozat Canal and the Somme, north-east of St. Simon. Lorries carried the Somerset men from Curchy and the Battalion arrived at St. Simon just as it was getting dusk. The Companies were got into position and began to dig themselves in, the lines having previously been wired and spitlocked, but orders were

---

[1] For conspicuous gallantry and devotion to duty at Jussy on 25th March 1918 Sergt. J. Tobin was awarded the D.C.M.

received for the Brigade to withdraw to the western side of the Canal.   The _{7th Battalion}
7th Somersets were then given a sector from the junction of the Canal and _{21st March}
River along the former towards Jussy, where Colonel Troyte-Bullock was told
he would obtain touch with troops on his right.   "As a matter of fact" (said
the C.O. of the Battalion) "the only troops we ever did get in touch with in
that direction were the Huns on the morning of the 23rd."

In pitch darkness, intensified by thick fog, the Battalion managed to
get into position before dawn on 22nd.   Two Companies had dug themselves _{22nd March}
in on the Canal bank, and the other two Companies with Battalion Headquarters
were in support behind the belt of wooded marsh which extended along the
western side of the Canal.   Sappers had prepared the bridges at St. Simon
for demolition and the C.O., 7th Somersets, was ordered to blow them up
as soon as he thought necessary.[1]

The 22nd March was quiet so far as the Somerset men were concerned
and the Battalion, working hard throughout the day to improve its position,
was only subjected to promiscuous hostile shelling.   As to what was happening
east of the Canal the Battalion had no information, but it is practically certain
that there were no British troops in front of the 7th Somersets; they were now
in the front line.

At dawn on 23rd the two Companies on the Canal bank reported the _{23rd March}
presence of German patrols in St. Simon, and that hostile cavalry were advancing
on the Canal.   The charges beneath the bridges were then fired and they
went up with a roar.   As soon as the sun rose the fog became worse and now
it was possible to see only just across the Canal.   About 8 a.m. Battalion
Headquarters were ordered back to Annois in order to be in close touch with
the Brigade.   On reaching the railway Battalion Headquarters came in touch
with some men of the 14th Division, who said that the charges beneath the bridge
at Jussy had failed to explode and that the Germans were across and were
even then coming down the railway.   There was little time to lose and Battalion
Headquarters took up a position astride the railway along a narrow sunken
cart track which had some boggy ground in front.   The only Company of
the Battalion then in touch with Battalion Headquarters was A (Captain
McMurtrie), which was ordered to form a defensive flank from Headquarters
to the three Companies along the Canal bank.   But the marshy ground
effectively prevented this order being carried out, though A Company managed
to keep in touch with Headquarters.

The end came quickly.   Rifle and machine-gun fire had suddenly become
intense and casualties were heavy.   The Acting Adjutant (Lieut. S. G. Berry)
fell dead, Lieut.-Colonel Troyte-Bullock was severely wounded, whereupon
Captain McMurtrie took command of Battalion Headquarters as well as the
survivors of his own Company.   The three Companies on the Canal bank
were completely cut off and surrounded and, fighting all the way, Captain
McMurtrie and his party fell back on to the 7th D.C.L.I., who had taken

---

[1] Capt. J. Scott was awarded a bar to his M.C. and Q.M.S. F. J. Cox and Sergt. W. J. Betty
the D.C.M. for conspicuous gallantry and devotion to duty during these operations.

up a position some 2,000 yards west of Annois, north and south of the railway. From this position, however, it was evident a further retirement would have to be made, for by 6 p.m. the enemy had captured Eaucourt and Brouchy, both in rear of the 7th D.C.L.I. But counter-attacks were organized, and as the 61st Brigade had no reserves left, 100 men of the 284th Army Troops Coy., R.E., were collected by 11 p.m. and lent to the Brigade: they were commanded by Lieut. Jones, 7th S.L.I., Brigade Intelligence Officer. This little party recaptured Eaucourt, though Lieut. Jones was wounded.[1]

THE ACTIONS AT THE SOMME CROSSINGS—HEM TO HAM: 24TH–25TH MARCH

Although in the area of these actions, it is impossible to say what happened to the remnants of the 6th Somerset Light Infantry, who were still under the orders of the 9th Scottish Rifles. The Battalion Diary being lost, the only details mentioned in the substituted copy relate to the fighting on 23rd, the next entry—26th to 30th—stating that the Somersets were at Beaurains Canal, Thiescourt, Elincourt, thence to Estree St. Denis, where the Battalion was re-formed from the 43rd Brigade Pioneers, Transport details, N.C.O.'s and men returned from leave and "D.A.B." and Reinforcements Camp. The 6th Somersets then marched to Breuill, thence to Nogent, whence buses carried the Battalion to Nampty where all ranks billeted. That was on 30th March, and they were still in billets on 31st.

On the morning of 24th March, as soon as the fog lifted, the enemy opened very heavy machine-gun and rifle fire on the 7th D.C.L.I. and the

remnants of the 7th Somerset L.I., who were then about 2,000 yards west of Annois. They had maintained this position all night, but in the morning it was obvious they would soon have to retire. Ammunition began to run out and a retirement was ordered. Captain McMurtrie's party was ordered to form part of the rear-guard and hang on as long as possible to the position. So well did these gallant fellows carry out their orders that when the time came for them to fall back they found themselves completely surrounded and cut off, and Captain McMurtrie and about nine survivors were captured by the enemy. By 1.30 p.m. the remnants of the 61st Brigade were being pressed back on the whole front. First Brouchy, then Villeselve and Golancourt and, a little later, Flavy-le-Meldeux were occupied and fresh endeavours were made by the Brigade to rally on the Stream south-east of Guiscard, to cover Noyon for the night. At 9 p.m. two French battalions were rallied and, with the remnants of the 61st Brigade, formed a defensive line.

On the 25th the exhausted 61st Brigade withdrew to Ecuvilly, arriving about 10 a.m. Here it was reorganized into a Composite Battalion of four

---

[1] The Battalion Diary of the 7th Somersets for 23rd March records the loss of the following officers: 2/Lieut. P. Schambre wounded. Missing, Capts. G. E. L. Willstead, 2/Lieuts. M. H. H. Hayward, E. Palmer, W. J. Major, A. Anderson, H. Cope, H. J. Duncan and T. W. Ellis. Of these Capt. Willstead was afterwards reported killed and 2/Lieut. Hayward died of wounds on 26th March. No details of losses in other ranks are given on this date.

Companies, each Company composed of men of the same Battalion, the fourth 7th Battalion Company of Brigade Headquarters.   The total strength of this force was 25th March 9 Lieutenants and Second-Lieutenants and 440 other ranks.

At 1 p.m. the Brigade was placed at the disposal of the 22nd French Division at Liancourt and moved in motor-lorries from Avricourt.   On the road west of Gruny the Brigade turned out and the 7th D.C.L.I. and 12th King's were sent to Liancourt, 7th Somersets to Cremery and Brigade Headquarters to Gruny.   At 11 p.m. that night the 20th Division and French were ordered to retire, the 61st Brigade to cover the left flank of the Division.

THE BATTLE OF ROSIÈERS, 26TH–27TH MARCH

At 7 a.m. on 26th the 61st Brigade began to withdraw and reached Le 7th Battalion Quesnoy en Santerre at 10 a.m.   The Brigade was now commanded by 26th March Captain Coombes, who had received orders to hold the village at all costs until the 30th Division arrived to hold the old trench system running north and south around Bouchoir.   Le Quesnoy en Santerre stood on high ground commanding a good view of the surrounding country.   Some old trenches and barbed-wire entanglements on the outskirts of the village enabled the Brigade to put up a stout resistance, thereby gaining valuable time.   At 1 p.m. the 30th Division arrived and took up its position north of Bouchoir.   The 61st Brigade was then ordered to cover the retirement of the 20th Division, and Le Quesnoy was garrisoned by about one hundred men and officers under the Brigade-Major, 61st Brigade (Captain Coombes).   Until dusk the garrison held on gallantly to Le Quesnoy, by which time it was almost surrounded by the enemy.   Fighting hard the brave fellows still held on, determined not to retire until orders were received to do so.   At last the order was given, and eleven survivors marched back from the village they had so gallantly defended. Who these men were it is impossible to say, but probably some of them were Somerset men.

By the night of 26th [1] the original 61st Brigade had been reduced to the following: 12th King's—1 officer and 31 other ranks; 7th Somerset L.I.—21 other ranks; 7th D.C.L.I.—1 officer, 40 other ranks; Brigade Headquarters—5 officers, 24 other ranks; C Company, 20th M.G. Battalion— 2 officers, 26 other ranks.

The morning of the 27th was quiet, the enemy showing no disposition 27th March to come on.   The 20th Division held the line Arvillers—Folies—Beaufort, the survivors of the 7th Somersets and 7th D.C.L.I. the eastern end of the latter village.   Excepting considerable shelling of Beaufort during the afternoon and attempts by the enemy to capture Folies, the day was without incident, and at night the 20th Division was ordered to be relieved by a French Division.

[1] On this day Marshal Foch assumed supreme command of the Allied Forces in France and Flanders.

THE FIRST BATTLE OF ARRAS, 28th MARCH

1st Battalion

The northern portion of the line north of the Scarpe, held by the 4th and 56th Divisions, was not attacked by the enemy's infantry until the 28th March, but on this date fighting of the utmost intensity broke out from Puisieux to north-east of Arras, in which both Divisions became involved.

21st March

When the German offensive started farther north on the 21st March, the 1st Somersets held the centre sub-sector of the 4th Division sector north of the Scarpe. On the 21st considerable shelling (including gas shells) during the day and night is recorded in the Diary of the 1st Battalion, two men being killed and three wounded. The 22nd was comparatively quiet, for the enemy's shells fell chiefly on the back areas of the Division. On the 23rd orders came to evacuate the front line, the 1st Somersets apparently withdrawing to a line just west of the Bailleul–Fampoux road. Several attempts by small parties of Germans to advance to the line held by the Somersets were immediately repulsed. On 24th the Battalion was relieved in the front line. Battalion Headquarters and three Companies moved back to Stirling Camp, but B Company went back to Pudding Trench in the Third Trench System. A Company joined B on the 25th in Pudding Trench and at night work was carried out on the Army Line just east of Stirling Camp on both sides of the Scarpe. Dumps were formed and at 5 a.m. on 26th the line was manned, Battalion Headquarters moving into a dug-out in the embankment just north of the river. A Battalion of West Yorkshire Pioneers (the 21st) came under the orders of the O.C., 1st S.L.I., for the purpose of holding the Army Line, and they were put in between Light and C Companies. Heavy hostile shelling

28th March

opened at 3 a.m. on the 28th and the two Companies of Somersets in Stirling Camp were ordered up to the Third System to join the rest of the Battalion. The German barrage was falling north and south of the Scarpe, quantities of gas shells being used.

At 7.30 a.m. the German attack was launched, but a magnificent defence was put up by the 4th Division and the 56th Division on its left. The enemy was held and was only able to occupy the most advanced trenches. The Germans came on in massed formation, providing magnificent targets. About 9.30 a.m., owing to the pressure of the enemy to the south, C Company of the 1st Somersets was sent to form a defensive flank facing south along the Scarpe from the first line Third System to just west of Fampoux to the Army Line and to guard all bridges. At nightfall no change had taken place in the disposition of the Battalion, but Light Company was moved back into the reserve line of the Third System. Throughout the day the casualties of the Battalion were 8 killed, 6 wounded and 1 missing.

According to the Report of the Battles Nomenclature Committee the Battle ended on the night of 28th March, but it is evident from the Diary of the 1st Somersets that the German attacks were continued on the following day,[1] for at 7 a.m., after a heavy hostile barrage, the enemy again advanced

---

[1] Lieut. E. M. Prince was awarded the M.C. and Sergt. W. Wiltshire the D.C.M. for conspicuous gallantry and devotion to duty on 29th March 1918.

and a party of Germans was reported in Stoke Trench, bombing their way down Camel Trench towards the Somerset men. The O.C., A Company, was therefore ordered to send a bombing party up the trench to expel the enemy. The attempt to bomb the enemy back was not successful and a counter-attack with two platoons under Lieut. Prince was made. The men were told they were to attack over the open and retake Stoke, the signal being the firing of a Véry light. The light went up and the attack started and, though progress was slow, the attackers coming under considerable machine-gun fire, the enemy was soon in flight and Stoke was reoccupied, the Somerset men remaining as garrison until relieved by the Rifle Brigade. One officer and 27 other ranks were wounded. A little later, whilst trying to bring in the wounded, Captain A. C. Parsons was killed and Lieut. King-King wounded. In the afternoon Pudding Trench was again shelled and another officer— 2/Lieut. F. W. Perrett—was wounded. The Battalion had now lost 3 officers and about eighty other ranks. With the exception of heavy shelling on 30th and 31st March the Battalion was not attacked by hostile infantry and the close of the month found the 1st Somersets still in the front-line trenches.

THE BATTLE OF THE AVRE, 4TH APRIL

On the 4th April the enemy made a heavy attack between the Somme and the Avre, involving the whole of the British line from the former river to Hangard and the French front, thence to the Avre river. The first attack on the right, delivered at 7 a.m., was repulsed, but on the left the British were obliged to fall back to west of Hamel and Vaire Wood.

On the night of 1st/2nd April the 43rd Brigade had relieved a cavalry brigade in the line in the neighbourhood of Bois Hangard, but, on the following night, French troops took over the line and the Brigade moved to the Bois de Blangy, west of Villers Bretonneux. Here the troops bivouacked until, on the afternoon of the 3rd, the 14th Division having been ordered to relieve the 1st Cavalry and the 16th Divisions from the Somme to the Villers Bretonneux road, the 43rd Brigade moved to reserve positions in Feuilloy and Hamelet: the details of the 6th Somersets to the latter village.

Information of an intended enemy attack had reached the Division and orders were issued to all troops to man their battle positions. At 6.30 a.m. the 6th Somersets, with the 7th K.R.R., were ordered to secure the high ground running north-east from Villers Bretonneux to about 800 yards west of the Bois de Vaire and the Bois de Hamel, from which positions they could support the troops holding the front line. The Battalion Diary of the Somersets states that this position was held for twenty-eight hours before relief came at 10 a.m. on 5th, the remnants of the Battalion being relieved by cavalry. There are no other details of the fighting on 4th April. Six other ranks were wounded. At 6 a.m. on 6th Australians arrived and took over from the 43rd Brigade, which then moved back to Aubigny, thence to St. Fuschien on 8th. Finally, on 14th April, the infantry of the 14th Division reached Reglinghen and here the 6th Somerset Light Infantry, being weak in numbers, were amalgamated with the 5th Oxford and Buckingham Light Infantry and, for the time being, ceased to exist as a separate unit.

THE BATTLE OF THE ANCRE, 1918: 5TH APRIL

On the 5th April the enemy launched a heavy attack on the whole front north of the Somme from Bernancourt to beyond Bucquoy, but excepting some minor readjustments of the line at certain parts, particularly in the neighbourhood of Bucquoy, where he gained the eastern portion of the village, his efforts were entirely without result. Held or driven back at all points he lost heavily, and in the neighbourhood of Rossignol Wood his attack was entirely disorganized by a local attack carried out at a somewhat earlier hour by the 37th Division, the latter not only improving its position but taking 130 prisoners. In this attack the 8th Somerset Light Infantry of the 63rd Brigade (37th Division) were engaged.

This was the first appearance of the 8th Somersets on the Somme in the spring of 1918, the Battalion having passed January, February and March either in the front line south of Ypres or in support or reserve areas at Canada Tunnels or Scottish Wood. The only exciting incident during the period was a raid carried out by B Company on the night of 18th/19th March on General's Dug-out opposite Julia Trench. The dug-out was reached but found unoccupied: no prisoners were captured but a tree, suspected of being used by the enemy as an observation post, was blown up. On the 21st the Battalion moved back to Canada Tunnels in support, having sustained twenty-eight casualties during the tour. On 27th the Somersets moved to Meteren, staying there for two nights. The 37th Division had, however, been ordered south to reinforce the line on the Somme and to replace worn-out troops. The 8th Somersets, therefore (in Brigade), entrained at Caestre on 29th March, reaching Mondicourt on 30th. Here the Battalion detrained and, after spending one night at Grenas, moved to Henu on 31st March.

The 37th Division began to relieve the 62nd Division, west of Bucquoy, on the night of 31st March/1st April. The 8th Somersets, marching from Henu on the 1st, relieved two battalions of the 187th Brigade (62nd Division) from whom the 63rd Brigade (37th Division) took over the Rossignol Wood Sector of the line in front of Gommecourt. The line taken over was, however, considered unsatisfactory and needed straightening out. An attack was, therefore, ordered to take place on 5th April at 5.20 a.m. with the idea of capturing Rossignol Wood, thus flattening out the line held by the 63rd Brigade.

The attack was to be made by the 8th Lincolns on the right, and 8th Somersets (Lieut.-Colonel S. S. Jenkyns temporarily commanding) on the left. Twelve tanks were to co-operate, six being allotted to each Battalion.

Each Battalion was to attack with two Companies in depth, each on a one-platoon front: the remaining Companies to be in close support and reserve.

Both Battalions were to form up in Cod Trench and moved to their assembly positions on the night of 4th/5th April in heavy rain and darkness.

The state of the trenches was terrible, for they had been the scene of much fighting, and were thick in mud and much battered by artillery fire. One of the attacking companies of the Somersets took no less than four hours to move from its trenches to the assembly positions, and had barely reached the latter ere Zero hour arrived.

At 5.30 a.m. (Zero) on the 5th, when the barrage opened on the enemy's trenches, there was some hesitation among the leading companies of Somersets owing to the non-appearance of the six tanks allotted to the Battalion.[1] In waiting for the tanks to appear the leading waves somewhat lost touch with the barrage, and finally had to go over without them, but the first objective was reached and captured with little resistance from the enemy. There was a heavy mist at the time which greatly assisted the attacking troops. Many Germans were found in the first objective, numbers of whom were killed and sixty prisoners taken. The second wave then leap-frogged the first and advanced on the second objective, no serious resistance being encountered until the line of the western edge of Rossignol Wood was reached. Here, however, heavy fighting began. With rifles and machine guns, firing chiefly from the Wood, the enemy met the attacking troops with a devastating fire and the right flank of the 8th Somersets was definitely held up, making practically no further progress during the action. There was no cover for the attacking troops, whereas the enemy was firing from concealed positions. The left Company, however, under Captain C. J. Peard, got into the left of the Wood and forced itself forward capturing more prisoners and machine guns, eventually establishing its left close to the second objective. But owing to the inability of the right Company to get forward, touch between the two Companies was lost, and it was some time before Captain Peard grasped the situation. Immediately he knew that the right Company had been held up, he threw back his right and tried to obtain touch with the right Company, gradually bringing forward his line in the centre. But touch was still not obtained with the right, and the left Company was heavily counter-attacked by hostile bombing parties and machine guns: this attack, however, failed to dislodge Captain Peard and his men. But presently heavy shell fire was opened on them, and now, as casualties became heavy and there were no reinforcements, with a greatly extended line and his supply of bombs running out, Captain Peard realized that his position was becoming untenable. He, therefore, withdrew slowly and in good order to the left flank of the Wood, occupying Hook Trench. Here he reorganized his Company and, having collected a further supply of bombs, forced his way forward again to the edge of the Wood, but was unable to make further progress and at the end of the day was still holding on to Hook Trench.

Meanwhile the right Company had made repeated efforts, all unsuccessful, to get forward, sustaining heavy casualties. A counter-attack launched by the enemy was beaten off, excepting in one part of the line, i.e. on the left of the left Comapny. Here the Germans surrounded the survivors of the left flank of right Company, capturing one officer and about twenty men, the

---

[1] The whole scheme of the attack was based on tank co-operation against a very strong position.

garrison on the first objective taken by the Somersets withholding their fire for fear of shooting their own comrades. The rifles of the captured party had become so clogged with mud that they could put up no resistance. After dark a few survivors regained Roach Trench. Close to the Sunken Road, on the right of the Somersets, the right flank of the right Company advanced in touch with the 8th Lincolns, passed the second objective with its flank in the air and all but reached the final objective. But here, also, the line was forced back under heavy hostile bombing attacks and eventually reached Roach and Cod Trenches. The Somersets' line was reinforced later by some troops of the 4th Middlesex Regiment. The Battalion Diary of the 8th Somersets states that: "The position at the end of the day was much the same as the beginning excepting that we held a greater extent of Roach Trench and had a post in Fish Alley." The 6th April appears to have been spent in the same position. On the 7th the Battalion moved back into reserve in dug-outs.

This attack had cost the 8th Somersets many officers and men. Captain H. G. Baker and 2/Lieuts. H. A. Drakeford, V. L. Plant, J. P. Hewitt and H. G. Stone were killed: 2/Lieuts. G. H. Hearder and F. J. Pickard and 2/Lieuts. P. J. Jones, S. T. Dyte and W. E. Hayes were missing. In other ranks the Battalion lost 151 killed, wounded and missing.[1]

The enemy undoubtedly lost very heavily on 5th April, for he was massing for an attack and the British attack took place when his front-line trenches and support and reserve areas were full of troops, who suffered greatly from the British barrage.

---

[1] For conspicuous gallantry and devotion to duty Capt. C. J. Peard was awarded the D.S.O., Lieut. H. K. Austin the M.C., and Sergts. G. Radford and E. Keith and Corporals W. Haydon and W. J. Durman the D.C.M., during the operations at Gommecourt on 5th April.

CHAPTER XXXIII

THE GERMAN OFFENSIVES, 1918: THE OFFENSIVE IN FLANDERS

THE BATTLE OF HAZEBROUCK, 12TH–15TH APRIL

WHILST the German offensive on the Somme was in progress, the storm clouds in the north were gathering. On the night of 7th April a heavy and prolonged bombardment with gas shell was opened by the enemy along practically the whole front from Lens to Armentières. At 4 a.m. on the 9th the bombardment was renewed with savage fury, gas and explosive shells being poured on to the Allied lines in great quantities. About 7 a.m., in a thick fog which again favoured the enemy, the latter attacked the Portuguese who held the front-line sector west of Aubers, and broke into their trenches. The attack then spread north and south from Bois Grenier to Givenchy. For several days the enemy pressed his attacks, using great numbers of troops, many of his divisions being fresh, while the Allies could only put into the line divisions which had either already been through heavy fighting on the Somme and were much weakened thereby, or else divisions which had been held in reserve to meet the hostile offensive in the north which had been anticipated by the Allied Commanders. From Houthulst Forest, north of Ypres, to Givenchy the line had given way and much ground was lost before the Germans were stayed in their advance and their offensive brought to a complete standstill without their objective (a break through) being obtained.

Certain divisions were, however, brought up hurriedly from the south to reinforce the line, and amongst these was the 4th Division which not only counter-attacked the enemy but regained a small portion of the ground lost, capturing many prisoners and much war material.

On 7th April a Canadian division began the relief of the 4th Division 1st Battalion in front of Arras, and the latter moved back into reserve positions. When the Lys offensive opened on 9th the Division was ordered to be prepared to move at three hours' notice. On the 12th orders to move came to hand and 12th April the 11th Brigade embussed at Duisans and was carried north to Busnes, just north-east of Lillers, where all units were hurried forward into the line, relieving the 78th Brigade along the La Bassee Canal, north of Mt. Bernenchon. This position was the furthermost point west to which the British line had been driven back.

"Our line," said the 11th Brigade Diary, "faces practically due north. The Western Boundary is P.29.c.7.3. (a point where the Robecq road crossed the Canal), the Eastern Boundary is Q.33.c.7.2. (where a road running south from the Bois de Pacaut cuts the Canal above Hinges). This line was held by the 1st Rifle Brigade, on the right, and 1st Somerset Light Infantry, on the left, the dividing line between the two Battalions being a footbridge across the Canal north-west of Les Harisoirs."

Of the Somersets, C and B Companies held from Pont Levis at Douce Creme Farm to Pont Levis at Q.32.c.6.8. (the footbridge north of Les Harisoirs): Light Company was in support in Mt. Bernenchon, and A was in reserve in Bellerive. The only trenches which existed were on the southern bank of the Canal: these had been constructed long before by French troops. They proved, however, of great value.

The 13th was a quiet day. Apparently the German advance was, for the time being, at a standstill, his infantry having got well ahead of his artillery, so that the latter had to be brought up. His forward guns were only moderately active, but during the evening Mt. Bernenchon was shelled and a group of buildings set on fire. Daylight patrols ascertained that the enemy was holding Riez du Vinage, a small wooded village north of the Canal and north-east of Mt. Bernenchon. On one of these patrols Lieutenant J. T. Davies was wounded. During the night of 13th/14th the right Company succeeded in establishing a series of posts from the footbridge to the road just north of it.

At 12 noon on 14th, at a conference of Battalion Commanders with the Brigadier, verbal orders were issued for a local enterprise to take place, having as its object the capture of Riez du Vinage and the establishment of a line of posts from the village to Carvin. The 1st Somerset Light Infantry was selected to carry out the assault on Riez du Vinage and establish a line thence, south to the Canal: the 1st Hampshire Regiment, advancing in rear of the Somersets, was to form a line of posts on the left of the Somerset men, from the village to Carvin.

The Battalion was to attack with three Companies in the front line, i.e. Light on the right, B in the centre, and C on the left: A Company was in reserve. As already stated, the line held by the Battalion ran along the southern bank of the Canal, though a few posts had been pushed out across the latter on the night of 13th/14th along the road to Riez. Owing to the bridges over the Canal being five in number, the attacking Companies would have to assemble in daylight on the northern side—a hazardous operation. In order not to arouse the enemy's suspicions, the men were to dribble across the Canal in ones and twos to their positions of assembly. No movement of forward bodies of troops was to take place before 6 p.m. The barrage was to fall at 6.30 p.m. on the western edge of Riez and would move forward through the village at 6.40 p.m. An artillery and machine-gun barrage was to be put down on the Bois de Pacaut during the attack.

The line of assembly being north of the Canal, it was necessary for the attacking troops to get parallel with the objective, and the Battalion would therefore have to deploy before Zero, facing half-right. The line selected for deployment, and from which to launch the attack at 6.30 p.m., was a north-west–south–east line, through the cross-roads just south-west of Riez, C Company north of the road, B south, each Company on a 300-yards frontage: Light Company held the right on the footbridge and the Canal south-west of Riez: A Company behind C and B, with its centre astride the road. The northern outskirts of the village were allotted to C Company, B was to go through and form a line on the eastern outskirts, and Light was to continue the line from the right of B back to the Canal bank east of Pont Levis.

Battalion orders stated that: "The village will be taken at all costs and every man in the Battalion will be used to attain this object if necessary."

Before 6 p.m. the whole of the 1st Somersets had left their positions south of the Canal and had dribbled across to the northern bank in twos and threes and were concealed in and behind houses. At 6.10 p.m. all Companies began to move forward to their positions of deployment. It was not an easy movement seeing that a half-right direction had to be taken, but it was carried out splendidly. A few heavy shells fell just north of the footbridge, north of Mt. Bernenchon, and several casualties were suffered.

At 6.30 p.m., when the barrage fell, the enemy replied with vigorous machine-gun fire, one gun sweeping the Riez road with deadly precision. Another gun, firing from the Bois de Pacaut, was also very troublesome. Owing to the accuracy of this fire the advance was temporarily held up until Captain L. A. Osborne, in command of A Company, seeing hesitation in front, led two platoons of his own Company through the front Companies. Great credit is due to this Officer[1] who, seeing that if the attack was to be successful, it would have to be pressed at once, gave such an inspiring example to the Battalion by leading his own Company through C and B Companies. The two platoons of A went forward by section rushes and were followed immediately by C and B, advancing similarly. But the two platoons of A were the first to attack the village. On the right Light had also come under heavy machine-gun fire, particularly from the Bois de Pacaut, but here again, inspired by the gallant Commander of A Company, the platoons advanced by section rushes and reached their objective. The hostile machine guns in Pacaut Wood were soon afterwards silenced by the Divisional artillery and machine-gun barrage.

Meanwhile, as A and B Companies approached the village, some Germans ran out and surrendered. But there was much fighting in the village, especially in the southern half, where a good number of Germans were killed. The village was found to be considerably larger than had been shown on the maps and in consequence it took longer to clear than had been anticipated.

As the leading Somerset men approached the eastern exits of Riez, the enemy launched a counter-attack from east of the village and the northern end of the Bois de Pacaut. This counter-attack was at once engaged with Lewis-gun and rifle fire and about 50 per cent of the attacking Germans were shot down. Of the remainder about half ran away and the other half ran towards the Somerset men with their hands in the air crying out "Kamerad!" and were

[1] Subsequently awarded the D.S.O. for conspicuous gallantry and devotion to duty.

1st Battalion
14th April

made prisoners. Six machine guns were captured in Riez and subsequently brought in.

By about 7.15 p.m. the whole objective had been captured and consolidation was begun. The Companies, owing to A having been moved up into the front line, were a good deal intermixed and at this period it was difficult to sort them out. Most of A had been used to fill in gaps in the line, Captain Osborne again rendering valuable services in co-ordinating and consolidating the whole position. During consolidation the enemy heavily shelled the village, but for the most part he did little damage, his shells falling on the western approaches to Riez.

15th April

When dawn broke on the 15th a considerable number of Germans, in full marching order, were seen: they were advancing in twos and threes into shell holes from houses north and north-east of Riez and from the northern end of Bois de Pacaut. Heavy rifle and Lewis-gun fire was opened on them, serious casualties being inflicted, and if a serious counter-attack was intended it was definitely broken up, for no further action was taken by the enemy: his stretcher-bearers were busy for the remainder of the day.

Late in the day orders for another attack were issued. The 1st Somersets were to co-operate with the 10th Brigade in an attack on the Bois de Pacaut, joining up with the left of the Duke of Wellington's Regiment and finally capturing the Riez–le Cornet Malo road. Zero hour was to be 5.40 p.m. (15th). The following orders were issued to Light Company, who had been ordered to co-operate with the Duke of Wellington's Regiment:—

"The right platoon of the Light Company, just north of the Canal, at 'Zero' was to 'left form,' connecting up with the Duke's on the edge of the Wood. As the platoons got level with the left of the next platoon, this platoon was also to 'left form,' and the Company would then advance on a two-platoon front and the other two platoons, when the time came, similarly 'left forming' and following on in support."

But what actually happened was that the Duke's crossed the Canal at Pont Levis (Q.32.a.6.0) and attacked the Wood from the west, coming under hostile artillery fire and suffering heavy casualties. It was impossible to send further orders to the two right platoons of Light Company, and they carried out the orders given to them. At Zero they attacked and entered Pacaut Wood alone. But they were met by serious opposition. Machine-gun and rifle fire played havoc with these gallant fellows and, unable to hold on to the ground won, they were forced to fall back and dug in with the Duke's on their right west of the Wood. These two platoons had lost about half their effectives.

During the night of 15th/16th further reorganization of Companies took place.

16th April

About noon on the 16th the enemy opened a trench-mortar and artillery fire on the line held by the Somerset men: he also shelled the village and the western outskirts of it heavily. A little later he was observed massing immediately north-east of Riez with the obvious intention of wresting the village from the Somersets.   But Captain H. M. Boucher [1] went quickly forward to the front line, rallied the advanced posts who were beginning to fall back, and brought up his supports.   For a few minutes the situation was threatening, but again the Lewis guns did splendid work and the attack was broken up with very heavy losses to the Germans.   The S.O.S. was sent up and the guns answered promptly, placing a heavy barrage on the enemy's positions, which completed his discomfiture: his stretcher-bearers were again busy during the remainder of the day.

About 2 p.m. the Germans were seen retiring in twos and threes: they had given up the struggle, having found the stout opposition put up by the Somersets impossible to break down.

This last incident, the retirement of the enemy, appears to have been the final event in the fighting which had been going on from the 14th to 16th April, and in which the 1st Somersets had added further to their laurels.

The results of this minor enterprise were splendid: (i) The village of Riez du Vinage had been captured; (ii) a battery of British field guns and a battery of 4·5 howitzers, taken by the enemy, had been recaptured; (iii) sixteen light machine guns and four heavy machine guns were taken: a Vickers gun was also recaptured—making a total of 21; (iv) a heavy trench mortar on wheels was taken, but it was not possible to get it away before the Somersets were relieved; (v) at least one German battalion, or the equivalent, was put out of action; 135 prisoners were taken: 60 dead Germans were seen in the village and probably 200 other casualties were inflicted on the enemy.   A statement in the Battalion Diary, however, to the effect that "never before have such targets been presented, or such execution done by the bullet," is hardly correct, for during the War there were many instances of the enemy's troops advancing in massed formation and being shot down in hundreds, if not in thousands. That the Somerset men had taken full advantage of the opportunities presented them, is shown by the fact that one Lewis gunner fired 2,000 rounds from his gun during the period, whilst a rifleman fired in one day from his own rifle 400 rounds.

The casualties of the 1st Battalion between 14th and 16th April were: 2/Lieut. L. B. Johnson died of wounds (15/4/18) and 2/Lieuts. C. S. Lewis, A. G. Rawlence, J. R. Hill and C. S. Dowding wounded: in other ranks the estimated losses were 210 killed, wounded and missing.[2]

On the night of 16th/17th the Battalion was relieved and moved back to billets in Cense La Vallee, the 11th Brigade generally occupying the Beaurepaire area.   The Battle of Hazebrouck was over, but it will be observed from the above narrative that in this (the southern) portion of the front it was the 4th Division, and the Division on its left, which did the attacking and not the

---

[1] Awarded the M.C. for conspicuous gallantry and devotion to duty in this action.

[2] Three N.C.O.'s, Sergts. W. H. Jordan and V. Rogers and Lce./Sergt. J. E. Bancroft, were awarded the D.C.M. for conspicuous gallantry during the fighting at Riez du Vinage.

enemy: it was the British line from just east of Strazeele to north of Ypres which, from 14th to 30th April, was bent back by the enemy's powerful thrusts, for Sir Douglas Haig had not the troops with which to withstand the heavy weight of the German attacks.

THE BATTLE OF BETHUNE, 18th APRIL

In this operation the 1st Somerset Light Infantry, though in the area of the Battle, was not called upon to take an active part in repelling the Germans.

The enemy on the morning of 18th April, after an exceedingly heavy bombardment (more furious, it was said, than even his initial bombardment on 9th April), attacked on nearly the whole line from Givenchy to west of Merville. Only at Givenchy and Festubert did the Germans succeed in entering the British line, but at the end of the day, after much bloody fighting, practically the whole of the lost positions were regained. On the front of the 4th and 61st Divisions the enemy's attack met with no success whatever.

The 11th Brigade in consequence of these attacks was ordered to stand to very early on the morning of 18th, and the 1st Somersets were moved off to positions behind the Mt. Bernenchon–Hinges ridge. But by 10 a m. the enemy had been repulsed and made no further attempt. The 1st Battalion was, therefore, not called upon and, in fact, the whole of the 11th Brigade moved back into billets, the Somerset men marching to Busnettes, having had only one man wounded during the day.

CHAPTER XXXIV

PALESTINE

LOCAL OPERATIONS

ON the 1st January 1918 the British line in Palestine ran approximately from 5 miles east of Jerusalem northwards to Beitin, thence west to Nalin, turning north-west again to the coast near Arsuf, 10 miles north of Jaffa. The XX Corps was on the right, XXI Corps on the left, the Desert Mounted Corps uniting in rear about Mejdul, Esdud and Yebna.

Of the three Battalions of the Somerset Light Infantry, the 12th (in Brigade) was relieved and moved back towards Yalo on the first day of the New Year, and after several days reached their destination. At Yalo there was a composite camp in which two months of refitting, training and road-making were spent before the Battalion again moved up towards the front line. On 5th March the 12th moved up to the neighbourhood of Lake Balua, north of Ram Allah. Here eight days were passed chiefly in repairing the Great North Road and filling in craters caused by exploded mines. On 14th March the 12th Somersets took over a portion of the front line from a battalion of the 159th Brigade, on the Wadi Kola, the left of the Battalion resting on Kefr Malik. Here once again the Somerset men were in touch with the enemy and constantly patrolled the rough and hilly country (by day and by night) in front of the Battalion. The only incident worth recording is a raid carried out by D Company (under Captain A. H. Wheeler) which took place on 27th March. The raiding party consisted of three officers and 100 other ranks. The raiders were observed before reaching the enemy's position and were met by heavy machine-gun fire, but on the raid being pressed the Turks made but feeble resistance and two Turkish officers and seven other ranks were brought back as prisoners; the remaining Turks decamped. The Somersets sustained six other ranks wounded.

On the 9th April the 12th Somersets were relieved and marched back to Dar Jerir. This relief proved to be the last in Palestine, for the 74th Division had been ordered to France, where events were moving fast. On the 10th the Battalion set out to march to Ludd where, on 15th, with other units of the Brigade, the Somerset men entrained for Kattara. After a fortnight in camp at the latter place, the 12th entrained on 29th for Alexandria and embarked on 30th on the "Leasowe Castle" for Marseilles. Disembarkation took place at the latter port on 7th May and on 10th the whole of the 229th Brigade arrived at Noyelles, the 12th Somersets being billeted in Forest Montières: refitting and training began on 11th.

12th Battalion
1st January

9th April

7th May

1/5th Battalion
1st January

In the meantime the 1/5th and 2/4th Somerset Light Infantry of the 75th Division had been involved in the local operations in Palestine.

The 1/5th Somersets, on 1st January, were in the front line west of the village of Rentis, with the 2/4th Hants on the right and 1/4th Wilts on the left. Patrol work was constant, the village of Kulen, the high ground between Beir Aila and Rentis, and both these villages being constantly visited and reconnoitred, but generally there is nothing of outstanding interest in the Battalion Diary for January, and on the 11th February the 1/5th Somersets were relieved and moved to the Corps Reserve area at Ludd where nearly a month was spent.

In the operations in the Jordan Valley and the Occupation of Jericho, which took place in February, the 75th Division was not engaged, but early in March the Division moved forward and the 233rd Brigade, still in Corps Reserve, also advanced. The 1/5th Somersets and 1/4th Wilts moved from

7th March

Ludd to Haditheh on 5th March, and to Kibbiah on 6th. On the 7th, the date on which the advance of the 75th Division took place, all objectives were gained, but still the 1/5th were not required, though the Battalion moved to Rentis on 12th March. Here, on the 16th March (the Battalion supplying a Guard of Honour) H.R.H. the Duke of Connaught presented medal ribbons to officers, N.C.O.'s and men of the Battalion. On 18th March the 1/5th Somersets moved once more into the front line at El Emir, relieving the 1/5th Devons. The night of 27th/28th March saw another advance by the 75th

28th March

Division, and the right sub-sector held by the 233rd Brigade was pushed out across the Wadi Emir. Little opposition was experienced, and by 8 p.m. the new positions were occupied.

2/4th Battalion
1st January

The 2/4th Somersets were in Corps Reserve at Surafend on 1st January, moving to new bivouacs, three-quarters of a mile east of the Ramleh–Ludd road, on 7th, thence on 18th to Haditheh. On 19th the Battalion took over the Dathra sub-sector of the front line. Patrol work began immediately, Rentis being visited frequently. The Battalion Diary of the 2/4th says of February that "little of interest occurred during the month," and it was not

3rd March

until 3rd March that anything of importance is recorded. On this date, however, the Battalion advanced from Dathra to a new position, and on the 12th, when a general advance by the 75th Division was carried out, the 2/4th were allotted Eb Diurah as its objective. This attack was successful, A and C Companies forming the firing line, and D Company being in support. By 8.15 a.m. Ed Diurah was seized with the loss of only two N.C.O.'s wounded. At 12 noon the Battalion was relieved, moving back into Brigade Reserve, and on the 18th into Divisional Reserve at Beir Dakleh for the remainder of the month.

7th April

Early in April (on 7th) the 75th Division again received orders to advance to the general line Berukin–Kh. Fakhakhir–Sheikh Subih–Rafat–Point 839 (V.7.a.). The advance was to be carried out by the 232nd Brigade on the right, and the 233rd Brigade on the left, the 234th Brigade pushing forward its right to north of Wadi Ballut to cover the left of the 233rd Brigade. The attack was to take place in two phases. In the first, the 232nd Brigade was to attack

Berukin and El Kefr, and the 233rd Brigade Rafat: in the second, the 232nd and 233rd Brigades were to secure the line Kh. Fakhakhir–Sheikh Subih– Arara when Berukin and Kefr had been captured.

In phase one of the 232nd Brigade attack the 2/3rd Gurkhas were to capture El Kefr and the 2/4th Somersets Berukin: in phase two the 2/3rd Gurkhas were to advance and occupy the general line S.20.c.5.4.–S.27.a.5.5. and hold the Wadi Lehham; the 1/5th Devons were to advance and occupy the line S.27.a.6.5.–Kh. Fakhakhir; the 2/4th Somersets and 2/5th Hants were to be in Brigade Reserve, but prepared to move as the situation demanded.

In the first phase of the 233rd Brigade attack the 1/5th Somersets were to seize Rafat, whilst the 3/3rd Gurkhas were to take the hill in V.6. central[1]; in the second phase the 1/4th Wilts and 2/4th Hants were to take Sh. Subih and the 1/5th Somersets Arara.

The Battalion Diary of the 1/5th (Lieut.-Colonel E. F. Cooke-Hurle) has the following interesting entry: "Battalion Operation Orders issued: 'I. To-morrow (9th April) Jellalabad Day, the Battalion will advance to the line Rafat–Arara.'"[2]   Even in the far-away desert hills and plains of Palestine the spirit of Jellalabad Day was not forgotten!   Battalion Orders then proceed to allot Companies their tasks.   At 4.15 a.m. Nos. 4 and 2 Companies, with a sub-section of the Machine-gun Company, were to advance to the northern slopes of the Wadi Lehham.   From 5.5 a.m. to 5.10 a.m. the artillery and machine-gun barrage was to fall on Rafat, and No. 4 Company was to rush the village when the guns lifted.   For the second phase, No. 1 Company was to advance forward to the Wadi Lehham and, on reaching the northern slopes, was to change direction half-right and capture the south-eastern peak of Arara: No. 2 Company was to deploy when ordered, ready to advance on the north-western peak of Arara: No. 3 Company was to be in reserve.

Punctually at 5.5 a.m. on 9th the barrage fell and as it lifted, five minutes later, No. 4 Company of the 1/5th Somersets rushed forward to the attack. The Battalion Narrative is brief, but apparently by 5.30 a.m. Rafat had been seized and was in progress of being consolidated when the enemy placed a heavy bombardment on the village and the Wadi south of it.   During the day and following night several counter-attacks were made on the village and on the D.C.L.I., who had seized their objective on the left of the Somersets, but they were all driven off with considerable loss to the enemy.   Owing to the delay in securing Berukin, the second phase of the attack was postponed until 6 a.m. on the morning of 10th, after a preliminary bombardment.

An hour before Zero next morning the enemy heavily bombarded the Wadi south of Rafat, but at 6 a.m. the attack was launched, No. 1 Company of the 1/5th being on the right, No. 3 Company on the left, and No. 2 in reserve.   In spite of heavy machine-gun and rifle fire the ridge between Rafat and Arara was seized by 7.30 a.m., a Turkish machine gun being captured by 2/Lieut. Franks and used later to repel a counter-attack.

---

[1] The positions can only be described in co-ordinates seeing that there were no other landmarks.

[2] The date should be 7th April.

The assaulting companies then attacked Arara. No. 3 Company was held up by three machine guns firing from near the north-west peak of Arara and was unable to advance up the hill. No. 1 Company, though suffering many casualties from a murderous fire, gallantly advanced to within 100 yards of the summit of the south-east peak, but were unable to get to the summit. Throughout the day, though exposed to enfilade fire as well, No. 1 clung with fine tenacity to the upper slopes of Arara, though shelled and machine-gunned mercilessly. No. 3 Company consolidated the ridge between Rafat and Arara, driving off repeated counter-attacks supported by artillery and trench mortars: in repelling these attacks the Divisional Artillery rendered valuable assistance to the hard-pressed Somersets. The latter reported that most of the enemy seen in this quarter of the battlefield were Germans.

At night one company of the 2/3rd Gurkhas was posted on the slope of Wadi Lehham [1] to guard the right flank of No. 1 Company, 1/5th Somersets, and Arara. Two platoons of No. 2 Company were also ordered to reinforce No. 1 Company and, with the latter, rush the summit of Arara; but this, however, proved impossible, for the Turks had been heavily reinforced. No. 1 Company and the Gurkhas were therefore ordered to withdraw before dawn on 11th.

The 1/5th Somersets lost on 10th 2/Lieut. Maloney and three other ranks killed, and three officers and thirty-one other ranks wounded. Three prisoners were taken on this day. On 11th the Battalion's losses were 2/Lieut. Gould and two other ranks killed, three officers and forty-four other ranks wounded and five other ranks missing. [2]

Meanwhile the 232nd had also made splendid progress. It will be remembered that the objective of the 2/4th Somersets (Lieut.-Colonel E. B. Powell) was Berukin. At 4.30 a.m. on 9th the Battalion, less C Company, moved down on to the ridge south of Wadi Ballut. At 5.14 a.m. D and B Companies advanced over the ridge to attack Tin Hat Hill. [3] For the first 250 yards of the advance the enemy mostly withheld his rifle fire, but on reaching the terraced slope of the Hill, heavy rifle and machine-gun fire met the attacking troops. The Lewis guns of A Company (in support) were then brought forward to keep down the hostile fire. By 7.30 a.m. D Company [4] had crossed the Wadi, but B Company, on the left, had been unable to do so.

The descent into the Wadi Ballut, after the first few hundred yards, was most precipitous, necessitating jumps of five or six feet from terrace to terrace which were taped by the Turks' machine guns placed on the lower slopes opposite and on the flank. With the exception of two officers, who were wounded later, the casualty list of eight officers and 50 other ranks occurred during the descent into and crossing this Wadi. Most effective assistance was rendered

---

[1] Given as A.15.d.

[2] Two N.C.O.'s, Sergt. B. Crocker and Corpl. G. T. Knight, were awarded the D.C.M. for their conspicuous gallantry on 10th April 1918.

[3] Given as A.15.a and b.

[4] Sergt. Pinchin of D Company, though wounded seven times, continued to cheer his men on: he subsequently succumbed.

by the Divisional Artillery, and about 8 a.m. the Turks were seen retiring 2/4th Battalion over Tin Hat Hill.   The two attacking Companies—D and B—were therefore 9th April ordered to push on and, by 9.45 a.m., were on the top of the Hill.   The 2/4th Somersets were then told to hang on to the top of Tin Hat Hill, whilst the Devons attacked Berukin.   In the meantime C Company of the Somersets had advanced against Necklace Hill and, though all the while under heavy rifle fire, pushed on down into the Wadi Ballut and up the slopes of the Hill, capturing their objective.   On reaching the summit of Necklace Hill they were able to open fire on the retreating Turks, causing the latter some casualties. During the afternoon the hostile guns heavily bombarded Tin Hat, but their fire was mostly ineffective and at nightfall consolidation was proceeded with.

At dawn on the 10th C Company went forward to take over Berukin, 10th April but the village was in the enemy's hands still, the Turks having regained it in a counter-attack.   However, with the aid of some of the Devons, the Turks were again ejected and the village was consolidated.[1]

During the two days' operations the 2/4th Battalion had lost 2/Lieuts. E. L. B. Fear and G. R. Kitchen and eight other ranks killed, six officers and forty-two other ranks wounded.

From 12th to 18th April the 1/5th Somersets spent a most uncomfortable 1/5th Battalion time at Rafat and on the Rafat Ridge, but were relieved by the D.C.L.I. on that date and moved back into reserve.   On the 20th the C.O. received the 20th April following letter from the G.O.C., 233rd Brigade:—

"Will you please convey to all ranks my admiration of the dash and endurance shown by the unit under your command during the recent most trying operations.   I can best describe the work of the Battalion as *worthy of the finest traditions of the famous 13th Light Infantry.*"

On the 27th April the Battalion again went into the front line, relieving 27th April the 2/3rd Gurkhas and the right company of 2/4th Hants at El Kefr.

The 2/4th Somersets, however, had seen its last fight in Palestine.   From 2/4th Battalion the 11th to 28th the Battalion remained either on Tin Hat Hill or in bivouacs in support, but on the latter date was relieved by the Punjabis.   On the 1st May the 2/4th reached camp at Surafend, entrained at Ludd on the 2nd and arrived at Kantara on 3rd.   Here, until the 23rd, the Battalion remained, training, but on that day moved to Port Said and there embarked on the "Ormonde" for France.   Marseilles was reached on 1st June. 1st June

---

[1] This counter-attack was led with great dash by Lieut. G. A. D. L. Savory and re-established the position.   He was severely wounded and afterwards received the M.C. for his action.   The Battalion Chaplain, the Reverend Eagles, who was particularly prominent in the line during both days in attending the wounded and tracing missing casualties, afterwards received the M.C.

CHAPTER XXXV

THE ADVANCE TO VICTORY, 1918

INTRODUCTION

IN the fact that the Advance to Victory began on the Marne in 1918, many will see the hand of fate. It was across the Marne in 1914 that the French and British Armies hurried the Germans in confusion and almost in rout, back to the Aisne: in 1918 the Germans were again forced back across the River, with the Allies in pursuit, but the advance of the latter was to end finally on the Rhine, in Germany, after the beaten and broken enemy had been forced to sue for peace, and to endure the humiliation of an Army of Occupation entering his dominions.

At the end of April 1918 the situation along the western front in France and Flanders (and especially that portion held by the British) was still critical. The advance of the German Armies had been temporarily stemmed but, although the enemy had failed to break the Allied line, he held strategic points of great importance in front of Amiens and Hazebrouck. It was therefore confidently expected by the Allied High Command that German attacks on a large scale would be renewed as soon as possible on the front Arras—Amiens—Montdidier. The enemy had everything to gain by such an offensive, for he still retained the initiative: his Armies, though they had lost very heavily in the offensives on the Somme and the Lys, were as yet numerically superior to those of the Allies: the Americans had not yet come into the field in sufficient numbers to make their weight felt: the French and British had been terribly weakened in the hard fighting they had just gone through and, so far as the former was concerned, reinforcements mostly consisted of young, partially trained and totally inexperienced recruits whose subordinate commanders had had little or no opportunity of becoming acquainted with their men. Under these conditions, therefore, it was inevitable that the Germans would endeavour to profit by their superior position. But they would have to act quickly.

Upon the British divisions holding the line a policy of active defence was enjoined whereby their front might be preserved unbroken, whilst every opportunity was taken in which to rest, reorganize and train those units which had passed through the fire of the German offensives of March and April. After filling the gaps in the depleted divisions, the next thing was to close the breaches by the construction of extensive defence systems, many of which had been broken into or through by the enemy's heavy attacks. But while intense activity prevailed behind the British front lines, the fighting troops holding the trenches were not idle. Harassing tactics by all arms, especially in the Lys Salient, were continually and successfully adopted, and the enemy's losses in men and material were so enormous that they undoubtedly led to a

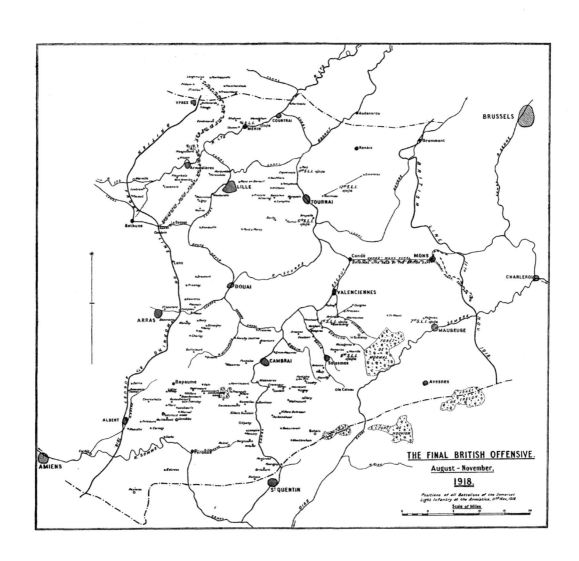

THE FINAL BRITISH OFFENSIVE.

August – November,

1918.

Positions of all Battalions of the Somerset
Light Infantry at the Armistice, 11th Nov. 1918.

Scale of Miles.

postponement of a renewal of the German offensive on this front.   Gradually 2/4th Battalion the strength, both of the British Armies and their defensive positions, increased, so that in May and June minor operations were undertaken.

It was, however, farther south, in Champagne, that the enemy made his final offensive when, from the 27th May to the 6th June, he thrust back the Allied line in the Battle of the Aisne, 1918, creating a huge salient from north of Rheims to Noyon, with its southernmost point resting on the Marne at Chateau Thierry.   Such was the position when, on 18th July, Marshal Foch launched his great counter-offensive, which he had long prepared, on the front between Chateau Thierry and Soissons, supporting this successful stroke by vigorous attacks also on other parts of the German salient.   In this fighting the XXII British Corps speedily became involved, and it was in this operation that the 2/4th Somerset Light Infantry were engaged, having by this time joined the 34th Division as Pioneers.

THE COUNTER-ATTACKS IN CHAMPAGNE
THE BATTLES OF THE SOISSONAIS AND OF THE OURCQ,
25TH JULY–2ND AUGUST 1918

The 2/4th Somersets, on arrival at Marseilles on 1st June, marched to 1st June the Rest Camp at Mont Fouron.   Here three days were spent, the Battalion entraining at Marseilles on 4th for Berguette, reaching that place on 7th. Nearly a fortnight was spent in training for the new kind of warfare before the Battalion, then in stages the Somerset men moved north again to Bourthes (18th), Elnes (28th), Le Paradis (29th) and Wylder (30th).   The 1st July found the Battalion at the latter place, but on the 2nd a move was made to Proven.   Here, on the 5th, the 2/4th were inspected by the G.O.C., 34th Division (Major-General Nicholson), and the Battalion was formed into Pioneers, D Company being disbanded and absorbed by the other three Companies.

During June the 34th Division had been reconstructed and on 1st July 1st July occupied the Bambecque area, but towards the middle of the month received orders to entrain for the French zone and concentrate in the Senlis area by 18th July.

On 17th the Battalion left Proven, marched to Rexpoede and entrained for the French front, detrained at Chantilly on 18th and marched to billets 18th July at Mont l'Evecque.

The 34th Division was one of four Divisions—15th, 34th, 51st and 62nd— which had been sent down to the French front at the request of Marshal Foch: they formed the XXII Corps.   Two (15th and 34th) were attached to the Tenth French Army between the Ourcq and the Aisne Rivers, on the western side of the great salient from Rheims to west of Soissons, and the other two (51st and 62nd) to the Fifth French Army operating against the eastern side of the salient, south-west of Rheims.

On the 18th July (the enemy having counter-attacked east and south-west of Rheims on 15th July, gaining ground as far south as the Marne River)

2/4th Battalion Marshal Foch launched his counter-attack between Chateau Thierry and Soissons, supporting this stroke by vigorous attacks also on other parts of the German salient.   In this fighting which, on the west at least, was immediately successful, the XXII Corps became speedily engaged.   This narrative, however, is confined generally to the operations of the 34th Division and particularly to the part taken in the battle by the 2/4th Somerset Light Infantry.

19th July On 19th the 34th Division moved to Lagny, west of Villers Cotterets, the 2/4th Somersets proceeding by lorry to Vanciennes.   On the night 20th/21st the Division moved again, on this occasion to the Vivieres area north of the Forest de Villers Cotterets: the 2/4th Battalion moved to Vivieres on 21st.   At the latter place the Division was ordered to relieve a French division in the front line about Parcy–Tigny on the night of 22nd/23rd.   The relief duly took place.   The 2/4th Somersets left Vivieres at 10 a.m. on 22nd and marched into position at Min de Villars Helon, moving again at 9 a.m. on 23rd to Caves just south of Montrambœuf Ferme.

The situation on the front of the XX and XXX French Corps (the 34th Division belonging to the latter) was roughly as follows: the enemy held the line Buzancy–Villemontoire–Tigny–Coutremain–western edge of the Bois du Plessier–Le Plessier Huleu.   The 34th Division attacked (with French troops 23rd July on the right and left) on 23rd, with 101st Brigade on the right and 102nd on the left, but the Somersets were not engaged, indeed the Battalion Diary states that from 23rd to 26th inclusive the Battalion remained just south of Montrambœuf Ferme in reserve, moving at 9.30 p.m. on 27th to a position in the Bois de Nadon.   On 28th the 2/4th Somersets were attached to the 102nd Brigade and left the Bois de Nadon at 9 p.m., marching to the Bois de Baillette, where reserve positions were occupied.

The 34th Division again took part in a general attack on 29th, the attacking Brigades being the 101st and 103rd.   The attack began at 4.10 a.m., and at 11 a.m. orders were received to move the Divisional Reserves to occupy the Vers–Soissons railway defence line.   But the move did not take place as the attack had been held up by the enemy, who was strongly posted in Beugneux and woods to the west of that place.   Soon after midday the 2/4th Somersets and 1/7th Cheshires were ordered to attack and capture Beugneux, but the attack was never made and eventually both units were ordered to consolidate the Paris Line, the line from which the attack was to have started.   In this 31st July position the 2/4th Somersets remained until the night 30th/31st July, when the Battalion was relieved by the 1/4th Cheshire Regiment and marched back to the Bois de Baillette.

The position which the Somersets held in the Paris Line was no sinecure.   It was exposed to very heavy shell fire, quantities of gas shell being used by the enemy, and, although the Battalion escaped with light casualties, all ranks had had a hard gruelling.

Captain W. H. Miles and three other ranks were wounded during the night 28th/29th: on the 29th three other ranks were killed, Lieut. M. Date and fifteen other ranks wounded and three other ranks were missing.   On

30th/31st 2/Lieut. A. S. Newton and eight other ranks were killed and fifteen other ranks wounded. 2/4th Battalion

On 31st the 34th Division renewed the attack, the 2/4th Somersets moving to a point of concentration along the Vers–Soissons railway. But, with the exception of having to endure heavy shell fire, of gas and H.E., the Battalion was again not called upon.

On Beugneux being captured the Somersets were moved to that place on 1st August. On the 2nd the Battalion withdrew to the Paris Line once more, north of the Bois de Montceau, remaining there until the following afternoon. Orders had been received at 34th Divisional Headquarters on the 3rd August, withdrawing the Division from the French zone, and during the next few days the Division moved north again to the Second Army area, being established in the Esquelbecq area (in reserve) by the 7th August. The 2/4th Somersets were billeted at Newlands, near Eringhem.

The Diary of the 2/4th Somersets during the Battle of the Soissonais and Ourcq makes dull reading, for it is unrelieved by any incident of importance. The Battalion no doubt felt the change in status, i.e. from that of fighting infantry, as in Palestine, to Pioneers as it was now, in France.

CHAPTER XXXVI

THE ADVANCE IN PICARDY

THE SECOND BATTLES OF THE SOMME, 1918

THE BATTLE OF ALBERT, 1918: 21ST–23RD AUGUST

THE complete success of the Allied counter-offensive south of the Aisne had produced a dramatic change in the whole military situation in France and Flanders. *The German Army had made its effort and had failed.* Plans were then prepared by the Allies for local offensives to be taken in hand as soon as possible with definite objectives of a limited nature. On the British front these objectives were the disengagement of Amiens and the freeing of the Paris–Amiens Railway by an attack on the Albert–Montdidier front, the French and American Armies freeing other strategic railways by operations farther south and east. The situation along the British front also favoured the disengagement of Hazebrouck by the recapture of Kemmel Hill, combined with an operation in the direction of La Bassee. Ultimately it was decided that of the tasks assigned to the British forces the operation east of Amiens was to take precedence.

8th August — The Battle of Amiens began on 8th August and was brilliantly successful and, by the evening of that date, a great wedge had been driven into the German lines between the Avre and the Ancre which, during the following days, was consolidated and held despite violent efforts of the enemy to recapture the lost ground. "August 8th," said General Ludendorff, "was the black day of the German Army in the history of this war." Six or seven German divisions had been completely broken in this attack and, as the Chief of the German Imperial Staff said, "the situation was uncommonly serious."

1st, 2/4th, 6th, 7th, 8th, 11th, 12th Battalions. — But in the first of the great battles of the Advance to Victory fought by the British Armies no battalion of the Somerset Light Infantry was engaged. Yet, from an historical standpoint, it is interesting to note where each of the seven Battalions of the Regiment, then in France and Flanders, was located when the great Advance to Victory began on 8th August 1918. The 1st Battalion was at Censee la Valee, north-west of Bethune, the 2/4th in camp at Newlands, near Eringhem, the 6th at Hubersent, engaged in training after having arrived in France, for the Battalion had been home to England for reorganization purposes. The 7th was in Lorette Camp, Ablain St. Nazaire, the 8th west of Bucquoy, the 11th at Barly, and the 12th holding front-line trenches in the Amusoires line west of Merville.

The first of these six Battalions to be engaged with the enemy in the great drama of the closing months of the War was the 8th, which took part in the Battle of Albert, 1918: 21st–23rd August.[1]

[1] The German withdrawal from the Lys Salient was in progress on this date, as will be seen later.

After the attack on Rossignol Wood on the 5th April the 8th Somersets had moved back to reserve dug-outs on the 7th of that month. On 11th Lieut.-Colonel S. S. Jenkyns (hitherto second-in-command) assumed command of the Battalion. The remainder of April and May were uneventful and early in June the Battalion moved by bus to billets in Picquigny, thence, a few days later, to Prouzel, St. Sauflieu, back to Souastre on the 25th, where the Somersets went again into the front line. On the 5th June Lieut.-Colonel Jenkyns relinquished command of the Battalion, Lieut.-Colonel J. H. M. Hardyman taking over command on 6th. July and the first week of August were, so far as the Somersets were concerned, bare of exciting incidents. But on the night of 10th/11th August the enemy attempted to raid the Battalion's front line which ran just east of the north-eastern end of Bucquoy. Under cover of a creeping barrage and the darkness hostile raiders, about sixty in number, succeeded in capturing several posts, though the garrisons retired to defensive positions. The triumph of the Germans was, however, short-lived, for Private Osborne, who had retired with his comrades to the defensive positions, organized a counter-attack, drove the enemy out of the captured posts and sent him back to his own lines in a hurry. The retreating Germans were caught in the S.O.S. barrage which caused many casualties and threw the survivors into confusion. One of the outstanding features of this raid was the confidence inspired by the personal presence of the C.O. Immediately the S.O.S. signal was sent up Lieut.-Colonel Hardyman rushed off to the scene of action and his presence undoubtedly made all the difference to his men who, as the Battalion Diary has it, "were only boys who had seen little or no previous service."[1] A second raid, attempted by the enemy at about 4 a.m. on 12th August, was repulsed without difficulty.

On the 17th the 8th Battalion marched back to billets in Fonquevillers, moving up into the front line on the night 19th/20th in and west of Bucquoy.

At 4.55 a.m. on 21st August the Battle of Albert, 1918, began. Orders stated that the 37th Division was to capture and consolidate the high ground east of Bucquoy and Ablainzeville. The New Zealand Division would be on the right and the 2nd Division on the left. The 63rd Brigade was to attack with the 4th Middlesex on the right and the 8th Somerset L.I. on the left, both Battalions to attack and consolidate in depth. The 13th Royal Fusiliers on the right and 8th Lincoln Regt. on the left were to support the Middlesex and Somersets respectively. The objective allotted to the 63rd Brigade was the enemy's main line of resistance which ran north-east from south-east of Bucquoy to south of Ablainzeville and, on capturing that line, the Brigade was to push out a line of patrols. The 5th Division was then to pass through the 37th Division to a further objective.

The whole front from which the enemy was attacked on the morning of

---

[1] Lt.-Col. J. H. M. Hardyman was awarded the D.S.O. for his conspicuous gallantry and devotion to duty on this occasion, the award stating that "Thanks to his gallant leadership and endurance, the position which was of great tactical importance was maintained." Second-Lieut. R. T. J. Trent received the M.C., and Pte. T. Osborne the D.C.M., for their gallant conduct.

8th Battalion
21st August

21st August extended from just west of Chaulnes, northwards to and from just west of Bucquoy.

The 8th Somersets, on reaching their assembly position, were reorganized for the attack, two companies in the first line and two in support, the Battalion's objective being the enemy's main line which lay about 300 yards on the reverse side of the high ground east of Bucquoy. Colonel Hardyman had his Battalion Headquarters about 300 yards west of the village, but Battle Headquarters were to be established later in Bucquoy Cemetery, for the latter was held by the enemy before the attack started.

Under an extremely accurate barrage, which greatly assisted the infantry, the attack began at 4.50 a.m. on the 21st. At that hour it was fairly light, but there was a very heavy mist which prevented visibility for more than about forty yards. With great steadiness the 8th Somersets advanced straight on to their objective and captured it with very few casualties, taking sixty prisoners and six machine guns. Touch was quickly gained with flanking units and the Battalion organized in depth, two companies in the front line and two in support. About an hour after the objective had been taken the 5th Division passed through and advanced, capturing Achiet-le-Petit and Log-east Wood.[1]

Until the night of 22nd/23rd the 8th Somersets remained in the line they had captured on the morning of 21st, but on the former date moved to reserve assembly positions east of Ablainzeville. On the following morning (23rd) Achiet-le-Grand and Bihucourt were attacked. In this attack the 8th Somersets provided two companies as mopping-up parties to work with the tanks which were attacking Achiet-le-Grand. These parties captured no less than 200 Germans who were hiding in dug-outs and ruined buildings: also 15 machine guns which the wily enemy no doubt anticipated using on the back of our men as they went forward. At 4 p.m. the Battalion was ordered to take over the line in front of Bihucourt and moved up to do so, but the enemy still held a machine-gun pocket just south of the village. After darkness had fallen one company of the Somersets attacked the pocket and half occupied it, thus practically ensuring the safety of the right flank of the village which previously had been in the air. Thirty more prisoners, as well as three 5·9 howitzers and three machine guns, were captured during the advance on Bihucourt.[2]

24th August

On the morning of the 24th the New Zealanders attacked and captured Grevillers. The 63rd Brigade, being ordered to co-operate in this attack, moved off to form a defensive flank on the left and capture Biefvillers.

The advance began at about 5 a.m. and consisted of section rushes, the enemy's machine-gun fire being very heavy. Eventually, with the assistance of tanks and the New Zealanders, Biefvillers was taken at about 6 a.m.

[1] For conspicuous gallantry and devotion to duty Pte. A. Williams was awarded the D.C.M.
[2] The Battle of Albert, 1918, ends on 23rd August according to the report of the Battles Nomenclature Committee. But it is obvious that heavy fighting continued beyond that date, though no Battle Honours have been granted for it, the next operations on the Somme beginning on 31st August.

But the left flank of the Somersets was in the air and the village under an 8th Battalion
extremely heavy bombardment.   It was therefore decided to evacuate Bief- 24th August
villers and a position was taken up on the high ground immediately west of the
village.

It was during a personal reconnaissance that Lieut.-Colonel J. H. M.
Hardyman, the C.O., was killed by a shell.   With his Battle Headquarters
he had previously moved up to this position in a tank.   The Divisional Commander sent the following message to the 8th Somersets:—

"The Divisional Commander wishes you to congratulate LOGE (8th
Somersets) on the capture of Biefvillers which was of the utmost importance
to the present operations.   He deeply regrets the death of Lieut.-Colonel
Hardyman in the moment of victory.   His splendid leadership and magnificent
gallantry will never be forgotten."

At 5 a.m. on the 26th August the 8th Somersets again advanced, this 26th August
time in support of the Brigade.   But the Battalion captured the Quarry north
of Bihucourt and hung on to it until the remaining units of the Brigade had
established posts in front.   During this operation thirty more prisoners and
four machine guns were captured.   That evening the 63rd Brigade was in
reserve to the successful attack on Favreuil, but about 3 a.m. on 26th the
Somersets were relieved, the relief taking place during a heavy bombardment.
The Battalion (in Brigade) withdrew to the Achiet-le-Petit area where the
remainder of August was spent in resting, reorganizing and salving war material
from the battlefield.

The operations from 21st to 26th August [1] had cost the 8th Battalion
one officer killed (the C.O.), five officers wounded and 164 other ranks killed,
wounded and missing.   But the Battalion had captured 300 Germans, 2
trench mortars, 13 machine guns and 3 5·9 howitzers.

THE SECOND BATTLE OF BAPAUME, 1918: 31ST AUGUST–3RD SEPTEMBER

After the successes which had attended the Battles of Amiens and Albert
the Allied Commanders determined to exploit the advantages gained and
converging attacks were planned

"towards Mezieres by the French and American Armies, while at the same
time the British Armies, attacking towards the line St. Quentin–Cambrai,
would strike directly at the vital lateral communications running through
Maubeuge to Hirson and Mezieres, by which alone the German forces on
the Champagne front could be supplied and maintained."

As Sir Douglas Haig pointed out in his despatches:—

"It was obviously of vital importance to the enemy to maintain intact

[1] For conspicuous gallantry and devotion to duty during the operations from 21st to 26th August
1918, Captains B. Holt and C. H. Madden were awarded the M.C., Capt. G. H. Sims a bar to his
M.C., and C.S.M. R. J. Yew and Pte. E. Pagington the D.C.M.

his front opposite St. Quentin and Cambrai, and for this purpose he depended on the great fortified zone known as the Hindenburg Line."

The next battle to be fought, therefore, was with the object of breaking the St. Quentin–Cambrai front.

It will be remembered that the 63rd Brigade (37th Division) had been in reserve during the successful attack on Favreuil on 25th August, and that on the following day the Brigade was relieved and moved back to the Achiet-le-Grand area. Along the front, however, fighting still went on. Trônes Wood had fallen on 27th August: Hardecourt was captured on 28th: on 27th, 28th and 29th desultory fighting had taken place for the possession of Longueval and Delville Wood. On the latter date the enemy evacuated Bapaume, while on the same day Combles was entered. North of Bapaume the enemy's positions as far as Riencourt-lez-Cagnicourt were reached, a line being established on the western outskirts of Bullecourt and Hendecourt. By the night of 30th August the line of the Fourth and Third British Armies, north of the Somme, ran from Clery-sur-Somme, past the eastern edge of Marrieres Wood to Combles, Les Bœufs, Baucourt, Fremicourt and Vraucourt, and thence to the western outskirts of Ecoust, Bullecourt and Hendecourt.

The Australians stormed Mont St. Quentin on the 30th/31st August, and on 1st September they captured Peronne. The Germans, followed continually by the British who lost no opportunity of occupying the evacuated ground, were now falling back slowly to the high ground about Rocquigny and Beugny, in front of the powerful Hindenburg Line, and it was during this retirement of the enemy that the 8th and 12th Somersets came again into the battlefield.

On 2nd September the 37th Division received orders to relieve the 5th Division in the front line, and instructions were issued to the 112th Brigade to take over the forward positions of the latter Division, the 63rd Brigade to move up in support and the 111th Brigade to reserve. The line of the 5th Division was to be taken over on the night 3rd/4th September.

The 8th Somersets (now commanded by Lieut.-Colonel C. J. de B. Sheringham) marched out of Achiet-le-Petit at 3.20 p.m. on 3rd, and moved forward to the neighbourhood of Favreuil, finally relieving a battalion of K.O.S.Bs., west of Lebuquiere, bivouacking for the night in that area.

In the meantime the 12th Somersets (Lieut.-Colonel C. R. Hayward) were seeing a great deal more of the Battle than the 8th Battalion saw.

After arrival at Marseilles on 11th May from Palestine the 12th Somersets (in Brigade) had moved to the Noyelles area, the Battalion being billeted in Forest Montiers. Here refitting and training were carried out until 20th, when the Brigade moved to the Sus St. Leger area. A further period of training followed until the 26th, when the 12th moved to Lignereuil. It was not, however, until the 23rd July that the Battalion was put into the front line, and in the meantime the 74th Division had moved up north of the La Bassee Canal.

On the night of 23rd July the 229th Brigade relieved the 26th Infantry Brigade in the Robecq (right) sector of the line, one Company (B) of the 12th Somersets going into the Amusoires–Haverskerque sub-sector. On the following night a patrol, consisting of one officer and two other ranks, went out to ascertain the strength of an enemy post and, if possible, deal with it. The patrol found that the post was held by eight Germans with a machine gun, but the officer and his men all became casualties—the first suffered by the 12th Somersets in France. Total casualties during the 24th July were Captain E. F. S. Rodd, 2/Lieut. B. L. Haddon and five other ranks wounded. On 27th July Major C. R. Hayward assumed command of the Battalion *vice* Lieut.-Colonel G. S. Poole. Each night patrol work was carried out until 31st, when the Battalion was relieved and moved back to Brigade Reserve in La Pierriere, from which place (as already related) the Somersets moved up into the Amusoires front and support line on the 7th August.

On 8th August, having completed the relief of the Devons in the front line at 1.30 p.m., the 12th Somersets received orders at 5.30 p.m. to advance their line. The objective of the Battalion was the Courant de Turbeaute. From 5.30 to 6 p.m. the guns heavily bombarded the German line and at the latter hour lifted, when B and D Companies (commanded by Captains Leversha and Wheeler respectively) advanced. The left of the Battalion was already across the Clarence River, while the right faced the village of Calonne. The Turbeaute was a small tributary of the Clarence which flowed southward through Pacaut. B Company had to clear the village of Calonne, but very little opposition was met with and by 8 p.m. the objective was carried and consolidation begun immediately. D Company had, however, lost two officers, the C.S.M. and three sergeants during the attack, but Sergeant E. J. Warfield, quickly grasping the situation, led the Company forward and at once sent back a most valuable report. He was subsequently awarded the D.C.M.[1]

In this small affair (the first in which the 12th Somersets were engaged since arrival in France) eight other ranks were killed, and two officers and twenty-four other ranks wounded. The Battalion was relieved on 10th and moved back to the Amusoires–Haverskerque line: and to billets in Guarbecque on 17th.

The Battalion remained billeted at Guarbecque until 24th August, but on that date, after marching to Robecq, relieved the 24th R. Fusiliers in the front line. But the tour was uneventful excepting for patrol work, and the Battalion Diary for 27th August concludes with these words: "Battalion was relieved by the 11th Battalion Somerset L.I. Relief completed at 1.45 a.m." On the 28th the 12th Somersets billeted at Manqueville. But the 74th Division was under orders for the Somme area and on the 29th the Somerset men (in Brigade) paraded, marched to Burguette Station and entrained for Corbie, and on the 31st of the month reached Maricourt where, having "dumped" packs and greatcoats, the Battalion billeted south of Le Forest.

[1] Second-Lieut. T. S. Price, for conspicuous gallantry and devotion to duty, was awarded the M.C. for his conduct on this date.

At midnight 1st/2nd September the 12th Battalion relieved the 41st and 42nd Australians in the line south-west of Bouchavesnes and some 1,200 yards east of the Bapaume–Peronne road, the 229th Brigade having placed the Somersets on the right, the 14th Royal Highlanders (Fife and Forfar) on the left, and the 16th Devons in support. The 74th Division had the 2nd Australian Division on the right and the 47th Division on the left.

Zero hour for the attack was 5.30 a.m. on 2nd September. The line of advance lay due east between the villages of Haut Allaines, on the right, and Moislains, on the left: Haut Allaines was assigned to the Australians, while the southern end of Moislains abutted on the line of advance of the Fife and Forfar Battalion. To reach their first objective the River Tortille and the Canal du Nord, lying diagonally north-east to south-west across the Battalion front, would have to be crossed. Moreover, the line of advance was across open, though gently undulating, country, where old trenches and shell holes provided the only cover obtainable. Thus the first real battle in which the 12th Somersets were to be engaged since their arrival in France, was going to be fought under considerable difficulties.

At 12.30 a.m. on 2nd September the Battalion moved forward and took up their battle outpost line. A Company (Capt. D. J. B. Taylor), on the right, C Company (Capt. C. Wallis), on the left, with B Company and D Company (commanded by Captains W. A. Keen and F. F. Edbrooke, respectively) in close support.

The forming-up operations were difficult. The enemy had pushed out a line of machine-gun posts during the night and was occupying Broussa Trench. These posts were inside the Barrage Start Line and would have to be cleared before the barrage could be properly followed: it was therefore obvious that before attacking their first objective the Somersets would be involved in fighting in the intermediate ground. This actually occurred.

At 5.30 a.m. the barrage fell on the enemy's front line and immediately the advance began. No sooner were the Somersets on the move than the hostile machine-gun posts, untouched by the barrage, opened heavy fire on the advancing troops. These posts had to be cleared of the enemy, and when that had been accomplished the barrage was too far ahead and the attacking troops were unable to catch it up, for they were moving forward over rough ground, intersected by old trenches and quantities of wire.

Soon after starting, the right of the Somersets (which had jumped off from Scutari Trench) came under a heavy enfilade fire from Haut Allaines. The Battalion instinctively swung towards the opposition and, clearing the village, captured some seventy prisoners, which were taken over by the Australians who had, in the meantime, arrived on the scene.

The Somersets then faced more north towards their proper first objective (the east bank of the Canal du Nord), with the Fife and Forfar on their left, and by 8 a.m. had captured it.

From the east bank of the Canal the Battalion's line of advance lay up gently sloping ground, across country devoid of natural cover   Orders were to push on, and the attack on the second objective—a north and south line some 500 yards east of the Canal—was begun. At this period the line driven into the enemy's position was wedge-shaped and, probably fearing that his flanks would be rolled up, he launched a heavy counter-attack. Then ensued some stiff fighting in which the machine guns of the Somersets, handled skilfully, took heavy toll of the enemy's troops. The Brigade line was, however, forced back to the first objective, but here a stand was made and the enemy finally beaten off. On the right, the Australians, who had been held up, had won through to the line of the first objective, and with the flank secured the Somersets again advanced towards the line of the second objective.

Twice these gallant Somerset men fought their way to the second objective, and twice, having gained it, they had to relinquish it. Eventually, at the close of that hard day of fighting, and in order to conform to the lack of success which had attended the attack northwards, the Battalion was withdrawn, back across the Canal and the Tortille River, to the line of Scutari and Broussa Trenches—a bare 500 yards in advance of their original jumping-off line. The enemy made no further infantry counter-attacks, but his artillery continued to shell the line held by the 12th Somersets with H.E., shrapnel and gas, but the position was maintained.

"We had a heavy toll to pay for our first day with the Fourth Army," said Captain R. C. Boyle, a statement borne out by the following list of casualties: Five officers (Captains T. F. Wallis and D. J. B. Taylor, 2/Lieuts. T. G. F. Wills, J. B. Craike and F. H. Jenkins) and 41 other ranks were killed; Captain W. A. Keen died of wounds. Five officers (Lieuts. C. G. Thomson [1] and J. W. Hartnell, 2/Lieuts. W. E. H. Firman, J. P. O. Vallow and A. W. Piper) and 161 other ranks wounded, and 14 other ranks missing— total 11 officers and 216 other ranks.

For two more days the 12th Somersets remained in the line which, on the night of 3rd September, was advanced about 1,000 yards without opposition. On the night of 4th the 229th Brigade was relieved by the 230th Brigade and the Somersets withdrew to dug-outs west of the Bapaume–Peronne road, in Divisional Reserve.

[1] Awarded the M.C. for conspicuous gallantry and devotion to duty on the 2nd September 1918.

CHAPTER XXXVII

LOCAL GERMAN WITHDRAWALS FROM THE LYS
SALIENT

MEANWHILE during, and as a result of, the great battles east of Amiens and on the Somme events scarcely less important were taking place on the northern portion of the British front. The exhaustion of the enemy's reserves, resulting from the Allied attacks, had made the shortening of the German line imperative and the obvious sector in which to effect this shortening was the Lys front. The enemy's line in the Lys Valley had become a death-trap to his troops. Constantly harassed by the fire of the British guns which caused him severe casualties, robbed of his projected offensive against the Channel Ports, all reasons for remaining in so costly a salient had gone, while the perpetual threat of a British attack was an additional reason why he should withdraw. As early as the 5th August he had begun to effect local withdrawals on the southern flank of the Salient, but it is not until 9th August that the Diary of the 1st Somersets mentions the retirement (the Battalion being then in support in Battle Trench west of Riez du Vinage) in the following words:—

"Battalion relieved 2nd Battalion Seaforth Highlanders and part of 2nd Duke of Wellington's Regt. Brigade system of following the enemy altered. The 1st Rifle Brigade took over the whole of the outposts and the 1st Hants Regt. the right support, 1st Battalion Somerset left support. Enemy retiring very slowly and pursuit continued. We are not pressing the pursuit as it is not considered desirable to engage the enemy in heavy attacks, it being known that they are going back to approximately the Lestrem line. He is being continually harassed, however, and followed very closely."

The very successful small operation carried out by the 1st Somersets on 14th April was followed by a brief spell at Busnettes. On 22nd April the 11th Brigade again attacked the enemy with the object of extending to the south-east the bridge-head already gained, by advancing the line to the Riez-la-Panniere road running through the Bois de Pacaut, a defensive flank being formed from La Pannerie to the Canal at Pont d'Hinges. The 1st Somersets were not involved in this attack, but Captain E. W. Marshall and Lieut. D. L. Moore were killed during the day by hostile shell fire, and twenty-five other ranks became casualties. On the night of 23rd April the Battalion took over the front line from the 1st Hampshire Regt., the relief being carried out under considerable machine-gun fire, during which Captain H. M. Boucher and 2/Lieut. P. Buse were killed.

Following these small operations the 4th Division settled down to stationary warfare for the summer. During this period (and towards the end of July) a popular form of amusement in the Battalion (but not for the Germans) 1st Battalion became common. It was called "winkling." Who originated the name is not known, but the amusement consisted of locating a hostile post, creeping up to it through the corn and across the ditches and returning in broad daylight with the German occupants of the post. The 12th German Reserve Division was holding the enemy's front line at this period, and an officer of the Battalion records that "judging by the way it lent itself to 'winkling' it must have been lamentably lacking in humour and discipline." But no one ever accused the Germans of possessing humour! In these "winkling" operations between the 24th and 30th July the Battalion captured eight Germans and killed one 30th July sergeant-major who showed fight. The story of the death of the latter is interesting.

A German post having been located by the 1st Somersets, Lieut. Gough with Sergeant Winter and another man decided to "winkle" it. They crept out one morning and, working their way along a ditch, approached the post, which was in a short length of trench, from a flank. A German sentry was posted on the near end of this trench and when threatened he behaved in the usual manner and was captured without difficulty. Followed by Sergeant Winter, Lieut. D. L. Gough [1] proceeded down the trench and came to a short traverse, upon the other side of which was a shelter. From the shelter emerged a stalwart sergeant-major, obviously made of sterner stuff than the sentry. The British officer and the German N.C.O. glared at one another for a moment, then emptied their revolvers at each other, but not a single shot took effect. Sergeant Winter was still in rear of Lieut. Gough, whilst a third German was behind the sergeant-major. With empty revolvers in their hands the chief actors in this duel hurriedly withdrew a few paces, but Sergeant Winter now took part in the contest and with a well-directed bomb killed the German N.C.O. and wounded the other man. The latter quickly joined the unwounded prisoner and the little party, augmented by two, returned to the Somersets' trenches. This affair took place on 30th July. The Battalion (in Brigade) was in reserve when, on 5th August, the enemy began to retire. On the 9th 9th August the Battalion was back in the front line.

Very slowly the enemy was followed up, posts being pushed out whenever possible and the main line advanced behind them, and by the 18th of the month the line of the 11th Brigade had reached the Turbeaute, beyond which it had been impossible to advance, orders from the Higher Command being "not to incur more casualties than we can inflict on the enemy and only over-come slight opposition." The 1st Somersets then held the right sub-sector of the Vinage sector, one company in the front line, one in support and two in reserve.

On 18th August British patrols, whose activity all up and down the line had been constant, made considerable advances from west of Merville. On 19th Merville was taken and the British line advanced on the whole front 19th August from the Lawe River to the Plate Becque.

[1] Awarded the M.C. for conspicuous enterprise and gallantry on this occasion.

1st Battalion
20th August

On the 20th August the 1st Somersets relieved the 1st Rifle Brigade in the outpost line and on the 21st, when the Battalion patrols had returned with their report, the line was advanced, in places to a depth of 500 yards. One officer (2/Lieut. W. Crabtree) was killed during the day. At 7 a.m. on 22nd sudden orders were received to co-operate with troops of the 74th Division (on the left of the 4th Division) who were going to advance. The attack by the 74th Division failed, the attacking troops coming under a very heavy machine-gun fire and artillery barrage, with the result that the battalion (of the 74th Division) on the left of the Somersets fell back 700 yards behind their own line. The O.C. C Company, 1st Somersets, then threw back his flank to keep touch with the troops of the 74th Division, helping the latter at dusk to restore the situation on their front. In this operation 2/Lieut. A. P. Mason was killed and Captain L. A. Osborne wounded. That night the Somersets were relieved partly by 74th Division and partly by 19th Division. The 1st Battalion then moved from Chelsea Bridge to Cense la Vallee and on the following day to the Ames training area. From the latter place the Battalion marched to Lillers on 25th and entrained for the St. Pol area, but under sudden orders the 26th saw the Somerset men again on the move to

27th August

St. Lawrence Camp, near Chateau de la Haie, where on 27th the Battalion was accommodated in Nissen huts. The 4th Division was now with the Canadian Corps and, after a few hours' rest, the officers of 1st Somersets went off to Monchy-le-Preux to reconnoitre the ground over which the Canadians had just made a successful attack, as the Battalion was to go into the line on 28th.

11th Battalion

The 11th Battalion Somerset L.I., known first as the "South-Western Brigade Battalion" and formerly the 85th Provisional Battalion, was raised at Yeovil in April 1915. It consisted of home-service and medically unfit men from the 4th and 5th Battalions of the Regiment, and from the 4th Battalion Dorset Regt. and the 4th Battalion Wiltshire Regt. The first C.O. was Colonel W. Helyar, late R. Warwickshire Regt. The Battalion left Yeovil on 29th April 1915, and moved to Sandown, thence to Seaton Delaval on 12th May. While at the latter place Colonel A. V. Kyrke succeeded Colonel Helyar in command of the Battalion. On 23rd March 1916 a move was made to Whitstable and here, on 1st January 1917, the Battalion received its title, "11th Battalion Somerset L.I. (T.F.)." The 11th was sent to Herne Bay on 12th October 1917, and to Wrentham on 12th March

6th May

1918: the Battalion embarked for France on 6th May of the same year under the command of Lieut.-Colonel H. S. Woodhouse. At this period the Battalion consisted of men of "B" category (home service or garrison duty abroad), but they were an extraordinarily staunch crowd. The Battalion was first employed in digging trenches, but the need for men on the Western Front was so urgent that in August the 11th Battalion was called upon to man some front-line trenches south of Arras. About the middle of the month the 11th Somersets, as part of the 177th Brigade, 59th Division, went into

12th Battalion

the line east of St. Venant and Robecq, relieving the 12th Battalion of the

Regiment, as previously stated.   After following the retreating enemy to   11th Battalion
Epinette and Lestrem the 11th Somersets were relieved and returned to bivouacs
at the latter place on 6th September.[1]   6th September

The 2/4th Somersets (Pioneers) of the 34th Division were in camp at   2/4th Battalion
Newlands from 6th to 13th August and then marched to St. Jan Ter Biezen,
via Wormhoudt, where the Battalion remained until 20th.   On the 29th
(the 34th Division again moving up to the line) the 2/4th moved to Scherpenberg, where for some time work on road repairing engaged the attention of
the Battalion.   Lieut.-Colonel E. B. Powell relinquished command of the
Battalion on 10th September.   10th September

---

[1] During this tour in the line Capt. A. Child gained the M.C., and Corpl. W. Stebbing and Pte.
H. J. Evans the D.C.M., for conspicuous gallantry and devotion to duty.

CHAPTER XXXVIII

THE SECOND BATTLES OF ARRAS, 1918

THE BATTLE OF THE SCARPE, 1918, 26TH–30TH AUGUST

1st Battalion

BY the morning of 26th August, when an attack was launched east of Arras, the German line as far south as the Amiens–Roye road (the junction of the French and British Armies) presented a ragged appearance. The Battles of Amiens and Albert had driven deep into the enemy's defences, and here and there the German line presented ugly and awkward salients, difficult to defend—in particular the salient opposite Arras. The general scheme of the operations which began on 26th August (and in which the 1st Somersets were engaged) is thus outlined in the official despatches:—

"By the 25th August our advance had formed a salient of the German positions opposite Arras, and the proper moment had therefore come for the third stage of our operations, in which the First Army should extend the flank of our attack to the north. By driving eastwards from Arras, covered on the left by the Rivers Scarpe and Sensée, the First Army would endeavour to turn the enemy's positions on the Somme battlefield, and cut his system of railway communications which ran southwards across their front."

When the 1st Somersets (Lieut.-Colonel V. H. B. Majendie, commanding) arrived on the battlefield, heavy fighting had been going on for two days. The Battalion on 27th August was at St. Lawrence Camp, Colonel Majendie and his Company Commanders motoring to the forward area (near Monchy) to reconnoitre the ground over which the Somerset men might have to attack. A message was received during the day that on the following morning the 4th Division would move forward and relieve the Canadian Division at night, ready to continue the advance next morning about dawn.

28th August

On the morning of 28th orders came to the 11th Brigade to embus at 2 p.m., the assaulting portions of the Somersets to move off half an hour earlier, i.e. 1.30 p.m. At Blagny the buses stopped and the Battalion marched to the assembly area immediately east of Wilderness Camp which, by the way, had been completely destroyed by shell fire. It was impossible to make any preliminary arrangements for the relief of the Canadians, as it was not known definitely where the line reached by the latter was. Accordingly, each battalion sent a small party ahead to get into touch with the Canadians and, as far as possible, settle details for the relief.

An hour's rest was therefore possible in the assembly area, during which teas were issued. At 7.45 p.m. the Battalion marched off, as ordered, across country in artillery formation as far as the Bois du Vert, keeping Monchy

on the left and the Arras–Cambrai road on the right.   There was considerable
difficulty in keeping direction, the night was very dark and the enemy's H.V.
guns were putting down harassing fire over the area.   At last, after many
difficulties, and the loss of 2/Lieut. R. R. Powell (killed) and about twenty
other ranks (killed and wounded) from shell fire, the Battalion reached the
Bois du Vert, and the line of the railway was found which led to where the
Canadians' guides were waiting to conduct the Battalion to the front line.
The relief was completed shortly before dawn on 29th, the men being very
exhausted after their long and tiring march up.   The Battalion was now
immediately south of Boiry Notre Dame, with two Companies in Lady Lane
and two in support just east of Boiry Lane.

The 1st Battalion was hardly settled in the line ere they were ordered
to push out patrols early on 29th and endeavour to seize the line of the Sensée
River from its junction with the Cojeul River as far as the Moulin du Roi.
A Company was to form a defensive flank by pushing forward patrols to occupy
the line of the railway at O.6.b.o.5. to the north-east corner of Galley Wood,
the 1st Hampshires, on the left of the Somersets, to conform.   Light Company
was to send out patrols to secure a line from the junction of the Sensée and
Cojeul Rivers to P.7.c.6.1., and B Company from Moulin du Roi to P.7.c.6.1.

These patrols came under heavy machine-gun fire and fire from snipers,
but the enemy was forced to retire by a flanking movement.   The Cojeul was
reached but no bridge was found across it, and a tree trunk was improvised
which gave a passage to the troops.   After about three and a half hours the
enemy was driven back to a line south-east of the Sensée, and by 5 p.m. the
line of the Sensée was reported taken.   Light Company had 27 casualties,
including three sergeants: the losses of A and B Companies were about half
that number.

During the night, with a view to attacking and capturing a jumping-off
line, an alteration in the disposition of Companies took place.   The Rifle
Brigade came up into the line, relieving a portion of the Somersets from the
Moulin du Roi to P.7.c.9.4.   A Company was relieved on the defensive
flank near Galley Wood by machine gunners belonging to an independent
Brigade attached to the Corps.   The 1st Somersets then disposed B and
C Companies in the front line, and A and Light in support, just north of the
Cojeul River.   The intention of the operations on 29th August was to secure
a jumping-off line for the forthcoming attack on the Drocourt–Quéant line,
and that this was done reflected considerable credit on the 1st Somersets, for
the Battalion, already tired out, had been hurried into the line, knowing nothing
of the ground to be crossed or of the enemy's dispositions, and there had been
no opportunity of making a preliminary reconnaissance.

On the 30th an attack was made on Eterpigny.   The objective allotted
to the 11th Brigade was Eterpigny and a line running south from the sunken
road north-east of the Chapel, round the eastern outskirts of the village.   The
1st Rifle Brigade was to attack on the right and the 1st Somersets on the left.
The 10th Brigade was attacking on the right of the 11th.

Zero hour was to be 4 p.m. on 30th, the attack to be made under cover of a heavy barrage.

West of Eterpigny Woods, along the line of the Sensée River, the attacking Companies of the Somersets assembled, and just before Zero hour the support Companies dribbled across the Cojeul and took up their positions between the two rivers. The area between the latter was under heavy shell fire and numerous casualties were suffered. "Prospects for the attack," records the Battalion Diary, "not bright, and men tired, the majority wet for twenty-four hours, and most of the senior N.C.O.'s had become casualties." Little or no sleep had been obtained since the night of 27th/28th. But all ranks were cheerful. Indeed, where was the officer or man who was not elated in August 1918? The reports all along the line were enough to hearten the most despondent, but the British soldier had never been that, even in the darkest moments of the tragic happenings of March of that year. At 3.45 p.m. the guns began a destructive shoot on Eterpigny village and wood, and at 4 p.m. the creeping barrage fell 150 yards east of the Sensée River. The attack began.

On the left of the line the barrage was weak and afforded little protection, the assaulting troops, therefore, went forward by section rushes. On the right, however, the barrage was good and the advance swept on more quickly. At various points all along the line the enemy did not wait to meet the advancing troops, but fled, pursued by rifle and machine-gun fire.

Without great difficulty the whole of the objective was gained, though on arrival Companies were very mixed. The whole night was therefore spent in reorganizing, and consolidating the position in depth.

Five officers were wounded in the attack (Captains G. C. V. Greetham and G. C. W. Malet, Lieuts. E. Cockburn and R. W. Ellis and 2/Lieut. N. F. Boyes) and 190 other ranks were killed and wounded.

The 1st Battalion had captured thirty prisoners and several machine guns.[1]

The 31st passed without incident and, after night had fallen, the 1st Somersets were relieved and moved back to the neighbourhood of Monchy. The Battalion had by now been reduced to a strength of 300 rifles, and the men were very exhausted.

BATTLE OF THE DROCOURT–QUÉANT LINE, 2ND–3RD SEPTEMBER 1918

By the end of August the First British Army

"had gained the high ground east of Cherisy and Haucourt, had captured Eterpigny, and cleared the area between the Sensée and Scarpe Rivers, west of the Trinquis Brook. North of the Scarpe, Plouvain was held by us. Our progress brought our troops to within assaulting distance of the powerful trench system running from the Hindenburg Line at Quéant to the Lens

[1] Lieuts. R. D. Strachey and E. Cockburn were awarded the M.C., Sergt. T. Cross and Lce./Cpl. E. E. Hawkins the D.C.M. for conspicuous gallantry and devotion to duty during the operations on Eterpigny.

defences about Drocourt, the taking of which would turn the whole of the ¹ˢᵗ Battalion
enemy's organized positions on a wide front southwards." [1]

The "powerful trench system," named by the British the Drocourt–
Quéant Line, was called by the enemy the Wotan Line. Built in 1917, the
Wotan Line was indeed powerful. From its northern extremity about Dro-
court, it ran through Biache St. Vaast and along the Scarpe to the east of
Monchy in the direction of Bullecourt, where it joined up with the Hindenburg
(or Siegfried) Line.

It was a portion of this line which the 4th Division attacked on the morning
of 2nd September, the 1st Somersets, though terribly weak in numbers and
very much exhausted, again displaying indomitable pluck in endeavouring
to carry to a successful issue the task allotted to the Battalion.

The 1st Battalion had moved back during the night of 31st August to
the neighbourhood of Monchy, where all ranks were given a few hours' rest.
On the 1st September two officers and ten other ranks joined as reinforce- ¹ˢᵗ September
ments, but all told the Battalion could only muster about three hundred.
At noon Colonel Majendie, the C.O., attended a conference at Brigade Headquarters, where plans for the attack on the Drocourt–Quéant Line were
discussed which, briefly, were as follows: The 4th (Canadian) Division, on
the right, and the 4th (British) Division, on the left, were to assault the Drocourt–
Quéant Line from astride the Arras–Cambrai road to the village of Etaing,
and continue the advance to, and beyond, the Canal du Nord. The 11th
Division, on the left of the 4th (British) Division, was to protect the flank of
the latter Division. There were to be four objectives, i.e. the Red, Green,
Blue and Brown Lines. The 4th (British) Division was to assault the Drocourt–
Quéant Line on a frontage of about 1,500 yards avoiding the village of Etaing:
this was the Red Line. After the capture of this objective the advance was
to be continued in a north-easterly direction and the village of Etaing was
to be entered from the south and south-west. The Green Line ran just east
of Recourt Wood and included the German trenches south-west of Lecluse.
The Blue Line included Lecluse and the line of the river to Palluel.

The 12th Brigade of the 4th Division was to capture the Red Line, after
which the 11th Brigade was to pass through the 12th and advance to the
Green and Blue Lines.

During the attack by the 12th Brigade the 11th Brigade was to remain
in position in the area behind the ridge just south-west of Eterpigny.

The 11th Brigade was to attack with the 1st Rifle Brigade on the right,
1st Hampshire Regiment in the centre, and 1st Somerset L.I. on the left.
The Seaforth Highlanders of the 10th Brigade were attached to the 11th
Brigade for the operations. Battalions were to be assembled with two companies in front and two in support, facing east.

The Brigade was to advance to the attack at Zero plus 30 minutes, Zero
hour being fixed for 5 a.m. on 2nd September.

[1] Official Despatches.

At 11.45 p.m. on the night of 1st the Somersets marched off to the position of assembly, described as "P.13 central" in the diaries, i.e. the ridge south-west of Eterpigny. Guides had previously reconnoitred the route and the Battalion arrived about 2.30 a.m. on 2nd and at once proceeded to dig in. But before the men had obtained sufficient cover a heavy burst of shelling took place and at intervals, up to Zero hour, hostile shells fell in the area occupied by the Somerset men. As a result 2/Lieut. A. M. Wright was killed, and Lieut. F. J. Clark wounded: twenty other ranks were also killed and wounded.

At 5.30 a.m., half an hour after Zero, the Battalion, in artillery formation, advanced. Light Company was on the right, B on the left, with A in right and C left, support. The first German trench was reached where (in accordance with orders) a halt for about an hour was made. The advance was then continued to the second German trench where another halt was called. In this position a certain amount of hostile shell fire was encountered. About 7.20 a.m. the advance to the Red Line was continued, the Somersets now facing in a north-easterly direction which should have brought the left of the Battalion on the junction of the Red and Green Lines in the Drocourt–Quéant Line, and just south of Prospect Farm. But as the Somerset men advanced violent machine-gun fire was opened on them from the left flank and from the direction of the Farm. It soon became apparent that the 12th Brigade had kept too far to the south and had neither cleared the Farm, nor the ground to the east of it. However, by moving to the right and taking such cover as the ground afforded, and by advancing in section rushes, Light and B Companies broke into the Drocourt–Quéant Line directly east of Eterpigny. The time was now about 8 a.m. The German trenches at this point were clear of the enemy, but from the left flank machine-gun fire was very persistent. In conjunction with the Hampshires, the 1st Somersets then advanced with the idea of enveloping the enemy in and east of Prospect Farm. But now the enemy's machine-gun fire increased in volume, and from the right front, and left, a withering fire swept the area over which the troops were advancing. It was thus evident that the Red Line had not been captured, and it was impossible to get beyond the Drocourt–Quéant Support Line, the left flank of the Somersets being about 700 yards south of Prospect Farm. Here, elements of the 12th Brigade were found.

The position of the Somersets and Hampshires was now precarious. The left flank was in the air and there was considerable movement of hostile troops behind the hedges and banks of Prospect Farm, foreshadowing an enemy counter-attack. It was then decided to send a mixed party of Somersets and Hampshires up the trench to the north to secure the left flank, while two platoons of the Seaforth Highlanders moved across the open ground in order to clear the area of the enemy. But still the murderous machine-gun fire held up the attacking troops and finally a block was made in the trench running northwards at a point about 500 yards south of the Farm. At 10.30 a.m. a party of the King's Own Regiment arrived and took over the block.

During the attempt to clear the left flank, the 1st Somersets lost their 1st Battalion
Adjutant, Captain E. Paul, who was mortally wounded.[1] He was a very 2nd September
gallant officer and had done splendid work with the Battalion.

The Somerset men now reorganized and set to work to consolidate their
positions in the Drocourt–Quéant front and support lines, south of Prospect
Farm. But the condition of the men was serious, many of them were so
exhausted that they could not be kept awake, and others were so worn out
that it was physically impossible for them to dig. But those gallant souls
who could endure more, stuck to their work with grim and splendid tenacity,
and carried on with that extraordinary spirit of endurance which has always
been the peculiar attribute of the British soldier.

All day long the Battalion, constantly under machine-gun fire from in
front and from both flanks, clung to its positions with dogged determination,
two more officers, Captain C. W. Hall and 2/Lieut. J. Measures, being wounded.

During the night orders were received that another attack was to be made
at 5 a.m. on the 3rd, and the advance continued to the Blue Line.

Preparations for this attack were made, but three minutes before Zero
hour a runner arrived from 11th Brigade Headquarters with a message cancelling the attack. It was only just in time, for the Companies had already
deployed and had moved forward to get parallel with their objective.

At 5.30 a.m., as the enemy seemed suspiciously quiet, a small patrol was 3rd September
collected and a reconnaissance of the enemy's forward positions made by the
C.O. and the Brigade-Major, Captain Lister. No sign of the enemy was
found. The Divisional artillery at the time was shelling the enemy's positions,
but information was at once sent back and the guns ceased firing. Two
strong patrols were then pushed forward immediately to secure the ridge on
each side of a house situated on the sunken road east of Prospect Farm, Captain
Lister accompanying them. Two Companies of the 1st Somersets followed
these patrols, the other two Companies coming on behind in support. By
7 a.m. the ridge was definitely secured. The O.C., 1st Hants Regt., then
placed two of his companies at Colonel Majendie's disposal. These passed
through the Somersets and advanced on Lecluse, whilst the 1st Rifle Brigade
co-operated by moving in the direction of Recourt Wood. Meanwhile,
Captain Lister and Lieut. S. J. Dickinson [2] pushed forward towards Lecluse,
capturing some Germans on the slopes outside the village. These two officers
then pushed on alone into the village, where another party of twenty-five
Germans, who had been left behind as a rear-guard, surrendered. The fact
was then definitely established that the enemy had retired across the Sensée
River. Beyond Lecluse village and wood, however, it was impossible to
establish a line, and posts were accordingly placed, covering with fire the
crossings over the River. Throughout the remainder of the day the Somersets
continued to hold the forward slope of the ridge south-west of Lecluse, and

---

[1] Died of wounds 10th September 1918. He was awarded a bar to his M.C. for conspicuous
gallantry and devotion to duty near Etaing.

[2] Awarded the M.C. for conspicuous gallantry and devotion to duty.

during the night 3rd/4th September the 1st Division took over the front held by the 4th Division, the 1st Somersets, with other units of the 11th Brigade, withdrawing to the neighbourhood of Monchy. The relief was completed just before dawn on 4th.

Thus ended a very strenuous period which had begun on 28th August, since when the 1st Battalion had been continually fighting, having in addition to cover considerable distances. Throughout all that period short snatches of sleep only had been possible. But the Battalion had had the satisfaction of being the first to discover the enemy's retirement, and of having advanced some 1,000 yards before the remainder of the Corps realized the situation.

The casualties during this period amounted to 15 officers (four of whom remained at duty) and some 312 other ranks. In addition to the names of officers already given, that of 2/Lieut. R. R. Powell appears in the list as killed.

After a few hours' rest near Monchy, during which breakfasts were prepared and eaten, the 1st Somersets marched off at 1 p.m. to Tilloy, whence motor-buses carried the Battalion to billets in Camblignuel. Before embussing the 1st Somersets were addressed by the Brigadier-General, who congratulated the Battalion on the fine work it had done when in the line.

A fortnight's rest—well-deserved—was now before the Battalion, when the usual training and refitting were carried out.

The Drocourt–Quéant Line was broken. The maze of trenches and the junction of that line with the Hindenburg (or Siegfried) Line had been stormed and the enemy thrown into precipitate retreat on the whole front of it, for on the right of the First Army, as far south as Peronne, the attacks had been continued by the Third and Fourth British Armies. The enemy was now faced with the task of defending the Hindenburg Line—his great protective belt: if that gave way nothing could save him but a retreat along the whole front, back to his own frontiers.

CHAPTER XXXIX

THE BATTLES OF THE HINDENBURG LINE

THE BATTLE OF HAVRINCOURT, 12TH SEPTEMBER 1918

O F the Battalions of the Somerset Light Infantry engaged in the 8th Battalion Battles of the Hindenburg Line, only one—the 8th—took part in the operations which resulted in the capture of Havrincourt on 12th September.

We left the 8th Somersets in bivouacs, on the night of the 3rd September, just west of Lebucquiere.

The German front on the 3rd September followed the general line of the Canal du Nord from Peronne to Ytres, and thence east to Hermies, Inchy-en-Artois and Ecourt St. Quentin to the Sensée, east of Lecluse. But on the 4th the enemy began to withdraw also from the east bank of the Somme, south of Peronne, and by the night of 8th September was holding the general line Vermand, Epehy, Havrincourt, thence along the east bank of the Canal du Nord.

His withdrawal had, however, been closely followed by the Allies.

On 4th September the 8th Somersets were ordered to send out patrols 4th September at dawn to keep touch with the 112th Brigade (37th Division) and to be ready to move at a moment's notice—D Company on the right, C on the left, B in support and A Company in reserve. The patrols reported that no German troops could be seen, and the Battalion moved to some trenches east of Velu Wood, having on its left the 4th Middlesex Regt. In this position the day passed without incident. On the 5th the 37th Division began the relief of the New Zealand Division, the 8th Somersets (the right Battalion of the 63rd Brigade) moving up to Matheson Road, which lay about half-way between Havrincourt Wood and Ruyaulcourt: the 8th Lincolns were on the left of the Somersets.

The relief, greatly hampered by heavy hostile shelling, was not completed until about 1 a.m. on 6th September. As a result of this shelling Captain W. J. Bennett, Lieut. Woodmansey, 2/Lieut. Matthews, Sergeant Cullender and several others were wounded. During the night an attempt was made by the enemy to cut off C Company, but failed.

On the morning of the 6th, as reports were received that the enemy had 6th September vacated his line west of Metz, patrols were pushed forward to see if he had withdrawn from his posts west of Havrincourt Wood, but these patrols were heavily fired on. At about 5 p.m. the right company, in conjunction with the New Zealanders on their right, advanced their line to the western edge of the Wood. The left company endeavoured to conform, but the left of the company was unable to get so far forward and therefore that flank was thrown back. A line of posts was, however, established in the north-west corner of the Wood.

8th Battalion
7th September

At 3.15 a.m. on the 7th the advance was continued due east. D Company reached the neighbourhood of Place Montmare–Quaff Trench, i.e. almost to the eastern exits of Havrincourt Wood. C Company by 7 a.m. had got as far as Clayton Cross on the left of D Company, but was not in touch on the left with the Lincolns: a defensive flank was therefore formed on the left of C Company. B Company then pushed forward two platoons to support D, and two to support C Companies. The enemy was located in Quadrangle Trench. Hostile shell fire now became severe.

About 1 p.m. a message was received from the New Zealanders that they were trying to get on south-west of Trescault and would be greatly assisted if the Somersets made a further attempt to advance. An effort was, therefore, made by the 8th Battalion to reach Butler Trench, near the Shropshire Spur Road, but the enemy's machine-gun fire was too severe and deadly and the advance was held up. C Company, which had tried to bomb east along Shropshire Reserve Trench, had to desist owing to strong enemy resistance, and casualties were suffered.

On the 8th, 9th and 10th [1] the line was gradually pushed forward and when, on the morning of 11th, the relief of the 63rd Brigade was ordered, the front occupied by the latter ran along the eastern exits of Havrincourt Wood (Tufnell Avenue, west of Trescault), the 37th Divisional front extending from Queer Street, in a north-westerly direction, along the northern exits of the Wood to the Canal du Nord about Yorkshire Bank.

The 63rd Brigade was, therefore, not actually engaged in the Battle of Havrincourt, though all units of the Brigade had done splendid work in helping in the clearing of Havrincourt Wood, making possible the attack on the village, which was carried out subsequently by the 62nd (West Riding) Division. The relief of the 63rd Brigade was carried out during the day, the Brigade moving back into Divisional Reserve, to the Velu–Lebucquiere area, the 8th Somersets being located in the latter village.

Other rank casualties suffered by the Battalion (the officer casualties have already been given) were 105 killed, wounded, missing and gassed.

Back in the reserve area Colonel Sheringham received the following letter from the G.O.C., 63rd Brigade:—

"I wish to thank you, your officers, N.C.O.'s and men, and to place on record my appreciation of the exceptionally good work, great endurance and determination displayed by all ranks in the operations around Havrincourt Wood from 3rd September to 11th September 1918. The duties of clearing up the Wood and establishing a line east and north of it, presented many difficulties owing to the nature of the ground and heavy enemy shelling. That this was done so successfully and with such light casualties reflects the greatest credit on all ranks. Your Battalion has again, therefore, added to

[1] For conspicuous gallantry and able leadership in command of his Battalion on 9th and 10th September 1918 Lt.-Col. C. J. de B. Sheringham was awarded the D.S.O. Second-Lieut. L. N. Ford was awarded the M.C.

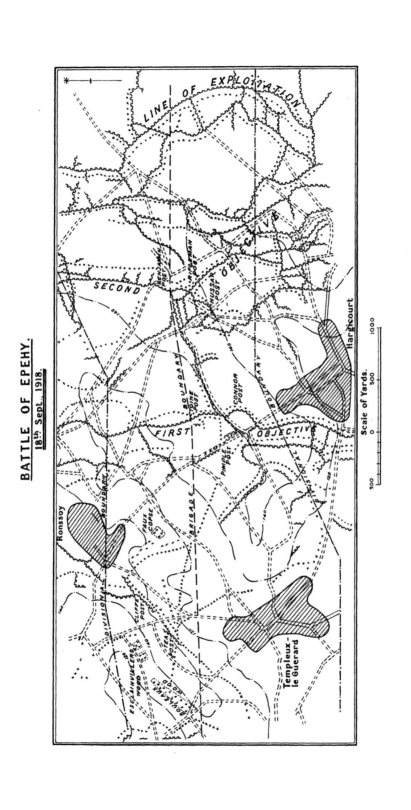

BATTLE OF EPEHY.
18th Sept. 1918.

Scale of Yards.

1000   500   0   500

LINE OF EXPLOITATION

SECOND

OBJECTIVE

FIRST   OBJECTIVE

BOUNDARY

BRIGADE   BOUNDARY

DIVISIONAL BOUNDARY

Ronssoy

Hargicourt

Templeux-
le Guerard

FAUX COPSE

PINE POST

PIMPLE POST

CONNOR POST

HUSSAR POST

FLEEGEMAN POST

its already long list of honours, and I feel sure will continue to do so with its own 8th Battalion
the same gallantry and devotion to the end which is now in sight."

The Brigadier's last phrase "to the end which is now in sight" is interesting, for it does show the feeling which existed all up and down the Allied line in September 1918—that the enemy was beaten and the terrible years of fighting and suffering drawing to a close.

In the attack which took place on 12th September, the 37th Division *12th September* captured Trescault, whilst the 62nd Division (for the second time in its history) once again took Havrincourt village, and positions were secured which were of considerable importance in view of future operations. But the story of the Somerset Light Infantry turns south to the Epéhy front, where, on 18th September, the 12th Battalion of the 74th Division, with other divisions of the *12th Battalion* III Corps (Fourth Army) again penetrated deeply into the enemy's defences.

THE BATTLE OF EPÉHY, 18TH SEPTEMBER 1918

On the morning of 18th September the British line south of Trescault ran just west of Villers, Gouzeaucourt, Epéhy, Le Verguier, crossed the Ormignon brook at Maissemy, thence to the eastern exits of Holnon village which had been captured by the Allies by the evening of 17th September.

At 7 a.m. on 18th the French and Third Armies attacked in heavy rain on a front of about seventeen miles from Holnon to Gouzeaucourt, the French co-operating south of Holnon. In this attack the 74th Division was involved.

From dug-outs west of the Bapaume–Peronne road, whither the 12th Somersets (229th Brigade, 74th Division) had moved on 3rd September, the Battalion marched on the 6th to Aizecourt and on the 7th to Longavesnes. From the latter place the Yeomen again went into the line on 9th, relieving the Cheshire and Shropshire Yeomanry Battalions of the 231st Brigade. The 12th Battalion was in Brigade Reserve, though D Company was attached to the 14th Royal Highlanders (Fife and Forfar) who were holding the left sub-sector of the Brigade front.

At 5.30 a.m. on 10th September the 74th Division attacked the enemy, *10th September* on the left flanking divisions were attacking towards Epéhy. The 12th Somersets, as a whole, were not engaged, only D Company which, under orders of the Highlaners, held the centre of the line of attack. The 229th Brigade attacked the high ground running from St. Emile to Ronnsoy, thence south-west. The greater part of this ground was captured by the 16th Devons, D Company of the 12th Somersets and 14th Royal Highlanders, but it could not be retained as the retention was contingent upon the capture of Epéhy. The latter place, however, resisted capture, and by 9 p.m. the 229th Brigade had returned to its original front line, the 12th Somersets losing Captain F. F. Edbrooke and 24 other ranks missing and 12 other ranks wounded.

The story of the capture of Captain Edbrooke and his 24 men is briefly as follows: D Company, about one hundred strong, not only had to attack in conjunction with the Devons and Fife and Forfar (14th Royal Highlanders) the line of trenches running north and south, 500 yards east of Ronnsoy (the right of the portion allotted to the Somerset men being Tea Post), but Captain Edbrooke had also been ordered to clear Esclainvillers Wood, before Zero hour, which had been fixed at 10 a.m. on 10th. The wood was stubbornly held by German machine gunners, and of the barrage which was to have assisted the attack not a gun was heard. It was late, therefore, when Captain Edbrooke with the remnants of his company—a mere handful—after clearing the wood found themselves upon the line of the objective with no available supports. On the left of the Somersets was a small party of the Fife and Forfar who had also reached the objective, but on the right the Devons were not yet up. Hardly had these gallant fellows reached their objective when the enemy, in large numbers, counter-attacked, enveloped the little garrison on all sides and, as Captain Edbrooke stated later, "jumped into our trenches by hundreds." He, and twenty-four of his men, were cut off, whilst of the Fife and Forfar not more than a quarter of two companies found their way back. As Captain Edbrooke and his men were being led away the Divisional barrage, too long postponed, fell.

On the night of 10th September the 229th Brigade was relieved by the 230th Brigade, and by the 11th the 12th Somersets were bivouacked near Templeux le Fosse. A week was spent in open and shelterless barns and then, on the night of 16th, the Battalion again moved forward to the neighbourhood of Villers Faucon, under the orders of the 230th Brigade.

The Battle of Epéhy was due to begin on the 18th September at 5.20 a.m. and the 74th Division was to attack with the 230th Brigade (plus one battalion of the 229th Brigade) on the right, and the 231st Brigade (plus one battalion of the 229th Brigade) on the left. The 12th Somersets were attached to the 230th Brigade and the Devons to the 231st Brigade. But the Somersets were by now so weak that one company of the Fife and Forfar (14th R.H.) were attached to support the Battalion.

Of the 230th Brigade the Suffolks, on the right, and the Sussex, on the left, were to launch the attack on the first objective, the Green Line which ran just east of the Hargicourt–Ronnsoy road (and east of both villages) and included Connor and Toine Posts: the Buffs, on the right, and 12th Somersets, on the left, were to leap-frog the Suffolks and Sussex respectively and capture the second objective—the Red Line including Rifleman and Benjamin Posts. There was a Blue Line—the line of exploitation—which, on the 74th Divisional front ran east of the Red Line, from Quennemont Farm to Gillemont Farm.

From 1 a.m. to 5.30 a.m. on the 17th September the enemy heavily bombarded the 74th Divisional area with H.E. and Yellow Cross gas. So far as the 12th Somersets were concerned, the results from the H.E. were at first negligible, one casualty only, but with the rising of the sun the gas asserted itself [1] and practically one hundred other ranks were put out of action—a

---

[1] Nearly all the casualties were "blisters" caused by the soaking endured during the night whilst the shelling was going on. The men were nearly all in the open and soaked to the skin with water from the shelled area.

serious loss to an already depleted Battalion: A Company, for instance,
numbered only 29 men.

The attack on the morning of the 18th went splendidly all along the line.
On the 74th Divisional front the Green Line was quickly captured under a
most efficacious barrage. In spite of extremely heavy hostile artillery and
machine-gun fire the Buffs and Somersets crossed the Green Line and dashed
on towards the Red Line, the latter Battalion capturing Benjamin Post and
reaching the second objective with only slight loss; when the Battalion consolidated the position only four other ranks had been killed and Captain
Spittall and 46 other ranks wounded. Against this number the Battalion
captured four German officers and 74 other ranks.

Throughout the remainder of the 18th and the daylight hours of the
19th the Somersets held the position gained. Twice on the 19th, i.e. at
10.15 a.m. and 4.30 p.m., the enemy put down very heavy barrages on the
front line and between the latter and Battalion Headquarters, but only four
casualties—wounded—were suffered. At 11 p.m. the Sussex took over the
line held by the Somersets, the latter marching back to bivouacs near Roisel.
At 4.30 p.m. the Battalion received orders that the 229th Brigade was to
support the 230th and 231st Brigades in an attack on the Blue Line on the
following day. At 9.30 p.m. the Somersets marched forward and occupied
Templeux Quarry in readiness for the attack on 21st.

At 1.30 p.m. on 21st the Somersets moved from Templeux Quarry up
into the Green Line, A and B Companies in Toine Post and C and D in Connor
Post. Late that night the Battalion received a very welcome draft of one
officer and 137 other ranks. The 22nd, 23rd and 24th were also spent in
support, the Battalion moving on 22nd to Hussar road where companies
bivouacked until 11.30 p.m. on 24th, when they were relieved by American
troops. On relief the Battalion marched to the area near Roisel. Casualties
during 22nd and 23rd were: 22nd—Lieut. C. G. Thomson killed and four
other ranks wounded; 23rd—2/Lieut. A. E. Parry and four other ranks
wounded.

On the 25th September the 12th Somersets marched to Tincourt Station
and, with other units of the 229th Brigade, entrained for Corbie. From
the latter place the 229th Brigade moved via Mericourt and Berquette to the
Ham-en-Artois area, the Somersets billeting in Manqueville. On the 26th
(at Corbie) Lieut.-Col. G. S. Poole arrived and once more assumed command
of the Battalion, *vice* Lieut.-Colonel Hayward.

THE BATTLE OF THE CANAL DU NORD, 27TH SEPTEMBER–1ST OCTOBER

Two Battalions of the Somerset Light Infantry—1st and 8th—by reason
of the fact that they were within the battle area during the Battle of the Canal
du Nord, are entitled to this honour. But they took no active part in the
operations, and this chapter is mostly devoted to a brief account of the dramatic
situation which had arisen out of the continued success of the British forces

at Havrincourt and Epéhy—success which made possible the four great converging and simultaneous offensives by the Allies: (i) by the Americans west of the Meuse in the direction of Mezieres; (ii) by the French west of Argonne in close co-operation with the American attack and with the same general objectives; (iii) by the British on the St. Quentin–Cambrai front in the general direction of Maubeuge; (iv) by the Belgians and Allied forces in Flanders in the direction of Ghent.

The results to be obtained from these several attacks depended in a peculiarly large degree upon the British attack in the centre, for here the enemy's defences were most highly organized: the Hindenburg Line had got to be broken, and if that was accomplished the thrust directed on the enemy's vital system of lateral communication would react upon his defences elsewhere. He would again be forced to retreat.

The importance of the British attack in the centre cannot therefore be over-estimated—to the British Army fell the honour of dealing the enemy a final blow which was the means of hurrying him back, at first fighting steadily, but later in headlong retreat, to his own frontier: "I was convinced," said Sir Douglas Haig, "that the British attack was the essential part of the general situation and that the moment was favourable."

For all the details—interesting in the extreme—of the strength of the positions to be assaulted the official despatches should be consulted, but before the Battle of the Canal du Nord the British front ran roughly as follows: On the evening of 26th September the Fourth, Third and First British Armies (in the order given from left to right) between the neighbourhood of St. Quentin and the Scheldt, occupied a line running from Salency (west of St. Quentin) to Gricourt and Pontruet, thence east of Villeret and Lempire to Villers Guislain and Gouzeaucourt, both of which places they held: from Gouzeaucourt the line ran northward to Havrincourt and Mœuvres, thence along the western bank of the Canal du Nord to the floods of the Sensée at Ecourt St. Quentin.

The Third and First Armies were to lead off the British attack at 5.20 a.m. on 27th September, the Fourth Army (which was to deal the enemy the heaviest blow) attacking when the Third and First had broken the enemy's front, and in particular had captured that strong section of the Hindenburg Line north of Gouzeaucourt.

On 26th the French and Americans launched their attacks on both sides of the Argonne between the Meuse and the Suippe rivers. At 5.20 a.m. on 27th the Third and First British Armies attacked the enemy in the direction of Cambrai on a front of 13 miles from Gouzeaucourt to the neighbourhood of Sauchy Lestree: the Fourth Army launched its attack at 5.50 a.m. on 29th September on a front of 12 miles between Holnon and Vendhuille.

In the grey light of early morning on 27th September the attack of the Third and First Armies was launched, and by evening had progressed far beyond the jumping-off line. On the 29th the Fourth Army attack met with similar results. The Hindenburg Line was broken. Thousands of prisoners,

hundreds of guns and vast quantities of stores were captured.   The effect
of this victory upon the subsequent course of the campaign was decisive.

It is not desirable to digress further from the story of the Somerset Light
Infantry in the War, by describing more minutely the great events of this
period, nor would it be possible for any pen to adequately set down the countless
deeds of daring performed by the gallant troops who dealt the enemy such
terrific blows: troops, who for weeks on end had been fighting and marching,
marching and fighting, with very little rest, but in whom the light of victory
burned fiercely.

In common with other units of the 4th Division the 1st Somersets had
returned to the line on 19th September, the Division relieving the 11th Division
east of Monchy.   The Somersets were just east of the village, being in Brigade
Reserve.   On September 29th the 4th Division extended its front to the
right and the Somersets were moved up into the forward trenches on the
right of the 10th Brigade, the right of the Battalion being approximately
1,000 yards south-west of Palluel, its left just clear of l'Ecluse.   The
Battalion had posts on the water's edge, for the Sensée marshes had been
considerably flooded by the enemy and the whole front was completely covered
by water, the opposing lines being some distance apart, separated by this water.
A quiet and pleasant tour was spent in this locality until the 6th October.

The 8th Somersets who, in Brigade, had withdrawn to the Velu-Lebuc-
quiere on 11th September, after another tour in the line from 16th to 20th,
were relieved by troops of the 42nd Division (which had taken over the line
held by the 37th Division) and marched back to Ligny Thilloy where the
Battalion remained until the 30th.

In this village, or rather the ruins of a village that had been, the Battalion
carried out training until the early morning of 30th when, at 7.15 a.m., the
Somersets again moved forward with Bertincourt as their destination.   The
route lay by way of Beaulencourt, Villers au Flos and Haplincourt, villages
broken and blasted by shell fire in the troublous times through which they
had passed.   The utter desolation of the Somme country at this period was
terrible to see.   Gaping shell holes were everywhere, roads had been almost
blotted out and had become mere tracks: villages that had once been the
habitations of men no longer existed as such, tumbled masses of bricks and
stones and rubbish marking the sites upon which cottages and houses had
once stood, with here and there a rough notice-board bearing the words "This
is so-and-so."   The holocausts of 1917 and the Spring of 1918 had passed
over this country and had left it bare and barren, a noisome place, the earth
blood-soaked and stinking with the rotting corpses which lay beneath its
troubled surface.   And on this September morning everywhere traces of
the beaten and defeated enemy were seen from the broken gun carriages,
transport wagons, equipment and other abandoned war material, with the dead
still crying silently for burial.

For the last time the Army was on the march forward over the old Somme
battlefields, for the last time the Hindenburg Line had been assaulted, no

more a life of seemingly endless days and nights in water-logged trenches, listening to the howling and screeching of the shells as they passed overhead to the back areas, or the hurtle of trench-mortar bombs as they came "plomp-plomp" towards the front and support lines in which men crouched wondering whether the infernal things were going to fall and explode in their trench and make a terrible mess of themselves or their comrades: static warfare had gone—the enemy was on the move, all up and down the line from the fields of Flanders to the Swiss Frontier every one knew that the enemy was fighting with his back against the wall in a vain effort to stave off final and ignominious defeat.

So the Somerset men were in great fettle as they moved forward on 30th September as part of the 37th Division, which had been ordered to relieve the 5th Division in the front line between Ribecourt and Beaucamp. The 8th Somersets reached Bertincourt at about 11 a.m. on 30th and, after the 37th Division had relieved the 5th Division, the Battalion moved to the south-eastern corner of Havrincourt Wood. Here the Somersets remained until the 5th October, when the 63rd Brigade moved to the valley north of Gouzeau-court, still in reserve.

THE BATTLE OF CAMBRAI, 1918, 8TH–9TH OCTOBER
AND THE PURSUIT TO THE SELLE

On the evening of the 7th October the British line, from its junction with the First French Army at about Thorigny (just north of St. Quentin), ran northwards to Montbrehain through Beaurevoir, thence between the villages of Villers Outreaux and Aubencheul to Crevecœur: from the latter village, just west of Cambrai to Blecourt, thence in a north-westerly direction to Pressies, on the southern banks of the Sensée.

The Battle of Cambrai [1] was, in effect, the development, exploitation and continuation of the Battles of the Hindenburg Line, and Sir Douglas Haig stated that the fighting which took place at this period "falls into three stages, the break between the different battles being due chiefly to the depth of our advance and the difficulty of re-establishing communication. In the first of these stages (the Battle of Le Cateau [2]) certain incomplete defences still held by the enemy were captured, and his troops, compelled to evacuate Cambrai, fell back behind the line of the Selle River. In the second stage the Selle River was forced, and by the development of this operation our front pushed forward to the general line, Sambre Canal—western edge of the Mormal Forest—Valenciennes, where we were in position for the final assault upon Maubeuge."

Only one battalion of the Somerset Light Infantry—the 8th of the 37th Division—was engaged in the Battle of Cambrai, the 1st Battalion being billeted in Berneville from 7th to 11th, moving on the latter date to Fontaine Notre Dame after Cambrai had been captured.

[1] The official despatches name this Battle "The Battle of Le Cateau (8th–12th October)."
[2] See above note.

The story of the 8th Somersets (Lieut.-Colonel Sheringham) in the 8th Battalion Battle is worthy of a place amongst the proudest records of the Regiment: it is one of splendid tenacity and courage in the face, not so much of strong opposition from the enemy (though at times the Battalion encountered very stiff fighting), as dogged perseverance in a form of fighting new to the Somerset men, i.e. fighting in open country. Long marches, little sleep, constant vigilance, harassed by machine-gun fire, and constantly shelled heavily, these men of the West Country for four continuous days went on from objective to objective, following up the retreating enemy, fighting him, bombing him, forcing him still farther back, and though dead-beat often, carried on with a magnificent disregard for their own poor worn bodies and jaded nerves. Fine indeed were these men who harried and hurried the beaten enemy back upon his last strongholds.

On the 8th October the Third Army (at 4.30 a.m.) and the Fourth Army (at 5.10 a.m.) again attacked the enemy on a 17-mile front from Seque-hart to south of Cambrai. South of the Fourth Army, French troops attacked as far south as St. Quentin. East of the Meuse and in Champagne French and American troops also fell upon the enemy and made important progress.

But it is only possible to deal with that part of the front attacked by the 37th Division, which had on its right the 21st Division,[1] and on its left the New Zealanders.

At 5.30 p.m. on 7th October the 8th Somersets moved to a sunken road 7th October running north-east from Gouzeaucourt, the 63rd Brigade being then in Divisional Reserve.

The 37th Division had three objectives: (i) Red Line—the Masnières–Beaurevoir Line and the sunken roads south of Lesbain; (ii) Green Line—the high ground between Hurtebise Farm (inclusive) and Le Grand Pont; (iii) to exploit success to the east of Briseaux Wood. To the 111th Brigade had been allotted the Red Line, the 112th Brigade was to capture Green Line and the 63rd Brigade was in reserve to be called upon at any moment.

At Zero hour (5.30 a.m.) on 8th October, after the attacking Brigades 8th October had advanced, the 8th Somersets began to march eastwards. The Battalion had been ordered to the Hindenburg Support Line north-west of the Bois de Vaucelles and on the eastern side of the Canal de l'Escaut. The Battalion had, therefore, a 4- or 5- mile march, but by 7.15 a.m. the Somersets, having crossed the Canal near the Factory north of Banteaux, reached their destination: the Lincolns were on the left of the Somersets, but the Middlesex had been detached and were under the orders of the 112th Brigade. At 3 p.m. further orders were received: the Somersets and Lincolns were to move forward to assembly positions south of Pelu Wood. But fifteen minutes later these orders were changed and both units were told to go straight through to the line Bout du Pre–Cross Roads, north of Chateau Briseux. An attack was to take place at 6 p.m. in a south-easterly direction with the object of securing the high ground east of the Esnes–Walincourt Road.

[1] It will be remembered that the 21st Division was the 8th Battalion's old Division.

After a march of over 7 miles across country the 8th Somersets arrived in position, but on the way up the attack had been postponed until 8.30, and the formations of the Battalion changed, so that the Lincolns were on the right and the Somersets on the left. The Middlesex were then on the western edges of the Wood, south of the Chateau Briseux. It was dusk when the Battalions reached their assembly positions and there were no opportunities of making a reconnaissance of the ground over which the attack was to be made.

At Zero both the Lincolns and Somersets advanced gallantly to the attack. But some of the Divisional gunners were short shooting and for a while the barrage could not be followed until these guns lengthened their range. As soon as the guns permitted, the advance was continued and a line taken up on the high ground east of the Esnes–Guillemin road. A farm on the Battalion front, from which machine-gun fire spitted viciously as the Somerset men were advancing, was mopped up at about 1 a.m. on 9th.

At 11.30 p.m. the Battalion was ordered to continue the advance at 5.30 a.m. on 9th October under a barrage. The objective was Haucourt and the high ground south of the village. These orders necessitated the immediate assembly of all Companies along the line of a sunken road east of the Esnes–Guillemin road. Almost dead-beat after the miles they had advanced during the day, the men had to be shaken out of their slumbers, and it was 5 a.m. before all Companies, B on the right, A in the centre, and D on the left with C in close support, were assembled ready to move off twenty minutes later at Zero hour.

Under cover of the barrage the advance started punctually, a company of Middlesex coming up on the right of the Somersets and the New Zealanders advancing on the left of the 8th Battalion.

There was no opposition and Haucourt was entered and captured, though the Somersets were delayed for half an hour 150 yards from the eastern outskirts of the village on account of short shooting by the Divisional guns. With positions changing so rapidly, when the guns like the infantry were continually on the move forward, short shooting was practically unavoidable. The Battalion line was then established in a sunken road east of Haucourt, and shortly afterwards the 112th Brigade passed through the 63rd Brigade to exploit the success as far as Caudry.

Haucourt, Caudry! Strange indeed that Somerset men should come to these places again after four years of the most terrible and bloody warfare the world had ever known. From their sunken road east of Haucourt the 8th Somersets had Ligny on their right front and Fontaine au Pire on their left: Caudry was in front. All these places were known to the 1st Somerset Light Infantry in August 1914. It was at the Carrieres, a bare thousand yards away on the left from where the 8th Somersets were now, that the 1st Battalion in the Battle of Le Cateau, 26th August 1914, first exchanged rifle shots with the enemy. Then the Bosche, in the first flush of victory, was sweeping on, driving all before him back upon Paris. Now he, in turn, was

in dire peril, clinging desperately wherever he could to whatever positions
offered, in the vain hope of stemming the tide which threatened to overwhelm
him as it swept him back the way he had come. Not one of those gallant
fellows of the old 1st Battalion in 1914 retired beaten and demoralized as did
the Germans before the 8th Battalion, and all along the line in front of the
Allied Armies in October 1918. It was through Ligny that the 1st Somersets
in 1914 set out on the retreat to the Marne.

        After Haucourt had been occupied by the 8th Somersets, Colonel Shering-
ham moved his Battalion Headquarters into the village, and there the cookers
were brought up and a hot meal served out to the men at about 4.30 p.m.

        At 6.30 the next morning (10th) Companies assembled in the road
running north-west from Ligny, and at about 8.15 a.m. moved forward north
of the village but directly east until they reached the railway south-east of
Caudry, which they crossed and then halted. The retiring enemy had blown
great holes in, and otherwise rendered impassable, all roads, and the track
had to be reconstructed before the Battalion transport could be brought up.

        At 10 a.m. the Battalion again advanced and occupied some German
practice trenches just east of Caudry. At 12.15 A Company was sent on as
advanced guard, the remaining Companies following at 1 p.m. to Petit Caudry,
where the Battalion was concentrated. A Company, however, still advanced
and, passing Clermont Chateau, reached the road junction immediately south
of Viesly. During a conference of Company Commanders, held at Petit
Caudry at 2 p.m., orders were received for the Somersets to pass through
the 112th Brigade and attack the ridge running south from Briastre, the
Lincolns on the right and the Somersets on the left.

        The attack began at about 5 p.m. B Company of the Somersets was on
the right, D in the centre, A on the left, and C was in reserve.

        In spite of heavy machine-gun and artillery fire the advance went on
towards the high ground whence the Bosche machine gunners, in posts, raked
the line of the Somerset men. In the latter stages of the War the enemy's
machine gunners were the bravest troops in the German Army. With extraordinary tenacity they clung to every position, and when they were forced to
retire, fell back, only to take up defensive positions from which they again
opened fire on the advancing British troops. They were brave fellows those
German machine gunners: they fought with their backs against the wall,
often long after their artillery had deserted them and their infantry had fled.

        The Somerset men reached the ridge and by individual section enterprise
and initiative the hostile machine-gun posts were rushed and the garrisons
either killed, taken prisoner or forced to retire. Having cleared the crest
the leading wave was ordered to dig in at once on the reverse slope and put
out observation posts on the forward slope.

        The light was now waning, and the falling darkness mercifully hid the
Somerset men from the enemy's guns: as a consequence serious casualties
were avoided. On the left flank A Company was somewhat in the air, the
New Zealanders not having advanced as far as the Somerset men. A platoon

of C Company, from reserve, was therefore sent out to the left to form a defensive flank as a temporary measure until the leading companies were reorganized in depth. This was done by about 8 p.m. and the platoon of C Company withdrawn. All three Companies of the Battalion were now in line, i.e. B, D and A, the left of the latter thrown back to join up with the New Zealanders.

When darkness had fallen all Companies sent out patrols to report any available crossings over the River Selle. They returned with the information that no crossings could be found, that the Selle was from twenty to thirty feet wide, and that there were no trees which could be felled for the construction of temporary bridges. But about 3 a.m. on 11th an officer of the 153rd Company, R.E., said that he would endeavour to erect some sort of bridge. B and C Companies of the 8th Somersets and one company of the Lincolns were then instructed to hold three platoons in readiness to cross the river if ordered to do so.

In the meantime a platoon of A Company, under 2/Lieut. H. Brooks, pushed on to reconnoitre Briastre, on the western banks of the Selle: the platoon met with no opposition and reached the middle of the village,[1] where they fell in with the New Zealanders. Soon after daylight several Germans were captured in the village; they had concealed themselves all night. This platoon of A Company, finding that another R.E. officer had just completed a bridge over the Selle, pushed across the river whilst Lieut. Brooks went back to bring up the remainder of his Company into the village. He also sent back a message to the Os.C., B and D Companies, and to the Lincolns, to send their platoons down the sunken road. Soon the Battalion had established its front on the eastern banks of the Selle, with the Lincolns on the right and the New Zealanders on the left.[2]

Finally on the night of 12th the line of the railway east of the Selle from Belle Vue southwards to about 700 yards north-west of Neuvilly, was held by the Somersets and Middlesex. During the night the 8th Battalion was relieved and moved back to Caudry in billets, where at last several days of rest and training were given the tired-out Somerset men. The 37th Division thus reached and occupied the line of the Selle River ready for the next advance.

[1] The Divisional boundary between the 37th Division and the New Zealand Division ran through the centre of Briastre.

[2] For conspicuous gallantry and devotion to duty during the operations between 9th–12th October Capt. C. H. Madden was awarded a bar to his M.C., 2/Lieut. H. Brooks the M.C., and Corp. G. F. Tucker and Pte. H. G. Muddle the D.C.M.

CHAPTER XL

THE WITHDRAWAL FROM LENS AND ARMENTIÈRES

THE enemy had withdrawn from his outpost positions astride the La Bassee Canal at the beginning of September, the activity of the British patrols leading to some stiff fighting. But the situation on the Lys front remained thereafter practically unchanged until the 30th September when divisions of the Fifth British Army made certain small advances south of the Lys. On the 2nd October, however, the enemy once more began an extensive withdrawal, falling back on the whole front from south of Lens to Armentières. In the sector south of Lens patrols of the 20th Division on this day met with considerable resistance about Acheville and Mericourt, but progress was made.

This mention of the 20th Division is the first in the official despatches for several months, for the Division, after the hard fighting through which it had passed during the Great German Offensive on the Somme in March, had been withdrawn from the line on 20th April to the Quevauvillers area, 10 miles south-west of Amiens. A few days later the Division moved north into the Arras area, the 7th Somersets finding billets in Averdoignt.[1]

Between the 1st and 3rd May the 20th Division relieved the 3rd Canadian *7th Battalion* Division in the Avion and Lens sectors, the 61st Brigade taking over the latter. The 7th Somersets moved from Averdoignt by motor-bus to Souchez on 30th April, but did not go into the front line until 7th May, when the Battalion took over the left sub-sector from 7th D.C.L.I. in front of Lievin, but with the exception of occasional heavy bombardments there is little to report during May and June, and it is not until July that the Diaries contain any incident of importance.

By the middle of July, however, conditions had changed considerably. The 20th Division, reinforced, had been through a period of hard training and the new drafts fresh out from England had been absorbed and inculcated with the fine fighting spirit of the Division, so that in July a series of raids on the enemy's trenches were planned for the purpose of obtaining identifications. The first of these raids took place on the night 22nd/23rd July, each battalion *22nd/23rd July* of the 61st Brigade—12th King's, 7th D.C.L.I. and 7th Somersets (holding the left sub-sector)—sending out a party. The 61st Brigade at this period held the Lens sector.

The King's party was formed of one company, the Cornwalls two platoons, and the Somersets one platoon made up of 2/Lieut. Hingston and one section,

---

[1] Whilst at Averdoignt Major K. Hunneyburn, who had taken over command of the 7th Somersets on 8th April, was succeeded by Lieut.-Col. H. A. Fulton, who commanded the Battalion until 18th May, when Lieut.-Col. R. P. Preston-Whyte rejoined.

and 2/Lieut. Jarvis and three sections, all of B Company. The three raids began at 11.30 p.m. under a creeping barrage. The enemy's trenches in the Lens sector were not easy to raid, in many places extremely difficult. No Man's Land was literally pock-marked with shell holes and littered with masses of debris. Ruined houses constituted formidable obstacles, whilst the gaps between the ruins, and the spaces inside the houses, were filled with barbed wire. The enemy had numerous machine guns mounted in strong concrete emplacements and these were difficult to silence, trench-mortar bombs having no effect on them.

The Somersets advanced in two platoons and succeeded in penetrating the enemy's defences but were unable to secure an identification. Eventually the platoons returned, having suffered three casualties.

Another raid, with the same objectives, was carried out on the night

of 30th/31st July by C Company. One party consisted of two rifle sections under 2/Lieut. Moorhouse, and the other two rifle sections under 2/Lieut. Shillson, the whole raid being commanded by Lieut. McCracken. The enemy's trenches were again entered and a German was captured. 2/Lieut. A. R. Shillson [1] personally captured the man who was running away, and brought back his party within fifteen minutes of starting, without loss. Sergeant H. Smith showed great initiative and gallantry. An enemy post was in his line of advance, but nothing daunted Smith rushed the post, killing or wounding three of the occupants with his revolver, a fourth German running away. Two other ranks were slightly wounded in this raid.

August was a quiet month, the enemy being closely engaged on other

parts of the front. On the 27th the 20th Division relieved the 8th Division in the Acheville sector,[2] the 61st Brigade taking over the front line. Early in September the enemy began to show greater activity and Somersets' patrols frequently encountered German patrols in No Man's Land. By the end of the month the development of the general situation began to affect directly the position of the enemy along the front of the 20th Division, though up to the 6th October he clung obstinately to his trenches opposite the Division. Although pressed by fighting patrols from each brigade he gave up little ground, excepting immediately south of Lens.

But in the first week of October all three Brigades of the Division advanced.

On the 5th October the 7th Somersets had moved up and occupied trenches in front of the village of Fresnoy. The next morning battle patrols of the Battalion attacked Fresnoy and captured it. There are, however, but few details of this small action, but such as exist are given in full as this was the last time the 7th Somerset Light Infantry were in action in France before the Armistice:—

"Battalion holding the line at Fresnoy. Battle patrols were pushed forward at dawn by B and D Companies. These patrols were engaged all

---

[1] Awarded the M.C. for conspicuous courageous determination.
[2] Pte. L. N. Wilcox was awarded the D.C.M. for conspicuous gallantry during an enemy raid on 28th August.

day with the enemy rear-guards.   Our line was advanced about 400 yards 7th Battalion
in front (east) of Fresnoy.   Casualties—4 killed, 7 wounded.   Battalion
was relieved by 1/1st Cambs R. and moved by motor-lorries to billets in
Averdoingt.   On the 8th October the 20th Division was relieved by the 8th October
12th Division and marched back to the Averdoingt area for a rest.   On the
30th October the 20th Division moved at short notice to Cambrai, thence
following up the leading divisions in the general advance, but taking no part
in the fighting until the 11th November, by which date the 61st Brigade had
reached Feignies, near Maubeuge.   In Feignies the 7th Somersets passed
the remainder of Armistice Day, the Battalion having marched early that 11th November
morning from St. Waast."

CHAPTER XLI

THE FINAL ADVANCE

I

FLANDERS: 28TH SEPTEMBER–11TH NOVEMBER 1918

THE BATTLES OF YPRES, 1918: 28TH SEPTEMBER–2ND OCTOBER

IN the meantime the Allied Forces—Belgians, French and British—under the command of the King of the Belgians, had made splendid progress in Flanders. At 5.30 a.m. on 28th September two Corps of the Second British Army (in conjunction with attacks by French and Belgian troops) attacked the enemy without preliminary bombardment on a front of about four and a half miles, south of the Ypres–Zonnebeke road, and the Germans were driven rapidly from the high ground east of Ypres which they had so fiercely contested during the Battles of 1917. By the evening General Plumer's Second Army had reached and captured Kortewilde, Zandvoorde, Kruiseecke and Becelaere, whilst on the left the Belgians had taken Zonnebeke, Poelcapelle and Schaap Baillie, and had cleared the enemy from Houthulst Forest. South of this (the main) attack, successful enterprises had been carried out by the 31st, 30th and 34th British Divisions and the line pushed forward to St. Yves and the outskirts of Messines. Wytschaete was captured and on the line of the ridge between that village and the canal north of Hollebeke the attacking troops had established themselves.

The task set the 34th Division was to establish itself on the Ypres–Comines Canal south of the bend at Hollebeke: this involved the capture of the Wytschaete Ridge. The Division pushed off at 5.30 a.m. on 28th September for the Vierstraat Line, with the 30th Division on the right and the 41st Division on the left. The objectives (including Wytschaete) were captured, but by nightfall the 34th Division (owing to the converging attacks of the 30th and 41st Divisions) was squeezed out of the line and assembled on the Wytschaete Ridge.

2/4th Battalion

29th September

The 2/4th Somersets, the Pioneers of the 34th Division, were engaged in repairing the roads and communication trenches in the forward areas east of Kemmel, Battalion Headquarters moving to Scherpenberg on 29th September. Here and there the official despatches make brief reference to the Pioneers, but generally their praises are unsung, though in the Final Advance to Victory their work was of the utmost importance. At all hours of the day and night they laboured to put the roads and communications into a state of repair. The infantry advanced so rapidly that it was almost impossible for the guns, regimental transport, ambulances, supply wagons and all the impedimenta of a moving army to go forward unless the roads were made passable, for the retreating enemy had damaged them and had blown them up.

340

On the 10th September Lieut.-Colonel E. B. Powell relinquished com- 2/4th Battalion
mand of the Battalion and on 25th Lieut.-Colonel A. W. Reid arrived and
assumed command.   The Battalion moved to St. Eloi on 1st of October and 1st October
until the 16th of the month the Pioneers were engaged on the upkeep of roads.

The Battle of Courtrai, 14th–19th October 1918

Meanwhile the 34th Division had pushed on and by the night of
13th October held a line just west of Gheluwe, which place was to be attacked
on the following day and the line advanced to Menin.   The 2/4th Somersets
moved to Zandvoorde on 13th and for the operations of 14th B Company
was split up, one half being attached to each of the two attacking infantry
brigades of the division.

Zero hour was 5.35 a.m., and again the attack was successful, the Pioneers 14th October
following up the victorious infantry, consolidating the gains as won, and
digging a support defence line.   On the night of 14th the Division had gained
the Brown Line which ran roughly from just west of Coucou and west of Menin
to Snooker Farm, about 1,500 yards north of Menin.   In the attack on, and
capture of, Menin on 15th October the Pioneers were again hard at work
on the defences and communications.   Battalion Headquarters moved to
Gheluwe on 16th, on which date half of A Company was placed at the disposal
of the 101st Brigade.

Troops of the 34th Division crossed the Lys on the 17th, having fought
their way to the River.   By this date the British front east of Ypres ran from
the northern bank of the Lys at Frelinghien to opposite Harlebeke.   On
19th the Division as a whole crossed the river, A Company of the 2/4th
Somersets accompanying the 101st Brigade, the Advanced Guard, C Company
being attached to the 102nd Brigade in support and B Company to the 103rd
Brigade in reserve.   Battalion Headquarters were then established at Lauwe.
On 20th the Division became Corps Reserve.

The concluding story of the 2/4th Somersets, however, is now summed
up in a series of moves.   On 24th the Battalion moved to Belleghem, and
three days later back to Lauwe.   The 34th Division was transferred to the
II Corps on 28th October and moved to the Harlebeke area, north of Courtrai,
the 2/4th Somersets billeting in Deerlyck.   On the 1st November the 34th
Division was again squeezed out of the line by the 41st (French) and 31st
British Divisions which joined hands across the 34th Divisional front at
Elseghem, and on the 3rd the Division marched back to west of Courtrai,
the 2/4th Somersets to Wevelghem.   Here the Somerset men were in training
until 14th November and the Battalion was thus engaged when the Armistice was
concluded at 11 o'clock on the morning of 11th November.   For the gallant 11th November
Pioneers—the 2/4th Battalion, Somerset Light Infantry—the War was over.[1]

[1] The 2/4th formed part of the Army of Occupation in Germany prior to being disbanded, and
were presented with the King's Colour by General Plumer.   It hangs in Bath Abbey near the
Battalion War Memorial.

CHAPTER XLII

THE FINAL ADVANCE

II

ARTOIS: 2ND OCTOBER–11TH NOVEMBER 1918

THE advance north of the Lys, which had begun on 28th September, and the Pursuit to the Selle had, by the middle of October, brought the British line far to the east of the Lille defences on the northern side, whilst south of Lille the defence of the town had been turned owing to the victorious progress on the Le Cateau front. It now became imperative for the enemy, between the Sensèe and Lys Rivers, either to withdraw his forces still farther or stand and give battle to troops, flushed with victory, and of whom not an officer or man was ignorant that final and complete success was only a matter of hard fighting and "sticking it" for a little while longer. The enemy chose to withdraw.

The movement began on 15th October, the enemy employing his machine guns and trench mortars to delay the advance of the Allies, whilst he withdrew his vast masses of troops and stores, and to cover the demolition of roads, by which he hoped still further to arrest the progress of the pursuing British divisions. In this great movement eastwards three battalions of the Somerset *6th, 12th and* Light Infantry—6th, 12th and 11th—in that order from right to left, took *11th Battalions* part, one of them, the 11th Battalion, entering Lille.

6th Battalion Since the 14th April (after the 14th Division had passed through the fire of the Great German Offensive on the Somme) when, being so weak the Battalion was temporarily amalgamated with the 5th Oxford and Bucks L.I. at Laires, the 6th Somersets had passed through varied experiences. From Laires, the Battalion, on 15th April, (as 5th Oxford and Bucks L.I.) marched off to Isberques, then on 19th to Wambelourt. But on 29th the Composite Battalion was broken up and the Somersets proceeded to Saint les Fressins and there billeted. In May the 14th Division was reduced to training cadre and the 6th Somersets were transferred to the 16th Division. The latter returned to England in June and reached Aldershot on 18th.

1st August On 1st August the 6th Somersets, with other units of the 49th Brigade (16th Division) embarked at Folkestone for France, and on the 2nd reached Hubersent where, until 20th August, training was carried out. On the latter date the move forward to the front line began, and on 22nd the Battalion was in the trenches in the Cambrin sector, just south of the La Bassee Canal. September saw two small attacks [1] made by the Somersets and 18th Glou-

---

[1] In the first attack the Brickstacks and the Railway Triangle were captured, and in the second attack La Brique and Auchy-les-La Bassee.

cesters, and the line was pushed forward a short distance. In this attack, 6th Battalion
which took place on 11th, Captain C. H. C. Cook [1] and 2/Lieuts. F. W. 11th September
Parsons and R. G. Benham were wounded, the latter dying of his wounds.
On 1st October the Battalion was out of the line at Drouvin, on 3rd at Sailly-
Labourse and on 8th marched to Nœux les Mines where a further period of 8th October
training was begun.

The 12th Somersets on 28th September were at Manqueville, in the 12th Battalion
Ham-en-Artois area, where much-needed reinforcements joined the Battalion,
bringing it almost up to war strength again, for of the gallant fellows who had
arrived on the Somme some months earlier, close on six hundred had been
killed, wounded and missing, and it was but a remnant which had reached
Manqueville.

On 10th October the 229th Brigade of the 74th Division once more went 10th October
into the front line. The 12th Somersets had moved from Manqueville to
Essars, thence to Herlies, and on the night of 10th/11th October relieved
portions of the 231st Brigade along the road leading north-north-west from
Ligny, with the village of Beaucamps at about the centre of the Battalion
front. Parallel with this line, and about a kilometre away, the enemy was
holding the line of the Armentières–Wavrin light railway in considerable
strength. As all indications pointed to a quick withdrawal of the enemy,
close touch with him had to be maintained by means of patrols, but by the 14th
the Battalion was back in Petit Harbourdin, in support, and the Somerset men
were thus out of the line when the enemy's withdrawal began on 15th.

The Fife and Forfar had relieved the 12th Somersets on 14th, the former
Battalion having to maintain close touch with the enemy, whilst the latter
Battalion remained in a state of constant preparedness in Petit Harbourdin.

On the 17th the enemy, no longer able to maintain his position, was off
as fast as he could back towards Lille, with the British close upon his heels.
But Lille was not entered by the 74th Division, which pushed forward due
east, south of the city, whilst the flanking division on the left circled round
the north of it. The 229th Brigade pressed on via Harbourdin, Thumesnil
and Lezennes. During the night 18th/19th October the enemy withdrew
his line still farther east and the 16th Devons crossed the Marcq at Pont à
Tressin, taking up an outpost line through Chering. Orders had been issued
that no farther advance was to be made on 19th, but the enemy was still retiring
and the Division on the left of the 74th had advanced, so that the latter was
ordered to continue its movement eastwards.

The 12th Somersets therefore passed through the Devons as Advanced
Battalion, with the Fife and Forfar in support, the Devons in reserve. The
advance continued to a north and south line through Baissieux, where billets
for the night were found.

At 8 a.m. the next morning (20th) the troops were off again, closely 20th October
following up the enemy, but the enemy's resistance was hardening and just
west of Marquain the Somersets were held up for a while until the village

---

[1] Awarded the M.C. for conspicuous gallantry and devotion to duty.

was cleared. Once through Marquain, however, hostile machine-gun fire became heavy and orders were received to dig in on a line about 400 yards east of the village. Here the leading Company of the Somersets spent an uncomfortable night in heavy rain whilst endeavouring to gain touch with the division on their right. On this day 2/Lieuts. Williams and McLaghlan and six other ranks were wounded.

The country over which the 12th Battalion was advancing was almost wholly devoid of cover—bare and gently undulating: good country in which to operate with machine guns, but costly to attacking troops. And the enemy took full advantage of it, sweeping the line of advance with very heavy machine-gun and trench-mortar fire, so that on the 21st the Somersets could not get on until the evening. At 9.10 p.m., after a strong artillery bombardment, the Battalion attacked Orcq and, having cleared the village, largely owing to the gallant conduct of 2/Lieut. H. Wilde,[1] who had reconnoitred the village under great danger previous to the attack, established a north and south line running through the eastern outskirts. During the day's operations four other ranks had been killed and 2/Lieut. H. Wilde and twenty-three other ranks wounded.

No advance was made by the Somersets during the 22nd October, though patrols were pushed out in order to obtain information as to the strength of the enemy's position. His front was found protected by strong belts of wire, behind which were many machine guns and trench mortars. The 22nd October is of particular interest to the 12th Somerset Light Infantry, for on this day the Battalion incurred its last casualties in action during the War, losing two other ranks killed and twenty wounded. Two Military Medals were also won on this day—by an N.C.O. (L/Cpl. W. A. Bide) and a private (Private A. Hippersley), who (though they were unaware of the fact) celebrated what was to be their last day's campaigning by signal acts of great courage and endurance.

These two men were occupying positions swept by heavy machine-gun fire from hostile guns some 300 yards away. Having first armed themselves with all the available rifle grenades they could lay hands on, they crawled out together to within eighty yards of the hostile machine-gun post and set to work to knock out the gun. This they did and then returned for more grenades. Again they crawled out and having located a gun in another post, knocked that out also. With the silencing of these two guns, the heavy machine-gun fire to which they and their comrades had been subjected ceased altogether and, after an outing which lasted about three hours, they regained their front in safety. That night the 12th Somersets were relieved in action for the last time by the Fife and Forfar, and on the 24th the 229th Brigade marched back to Camphin. Here the Battalion remained, engaged in the familiar task of reorganizing, re-equipping and training until 10th November, when at 8 a.m. the Somerset men marched eastwards again to Havinnes via Tournai, where billets were found.

[1] Awarded the M.C. for conspicuous gallantry and devotion to duty.

Early astir on 11th the Battalion marched out of Havinnes *en route* for 　12th Battalion
Escalette, still eastwards, and while on the march news that the beaten enemy 　11th November
had signed an Armistice was received, and that hostilities were to cease at
11 a.m.　That great historic event is thus described in the Battalion Diary :

"Marched at 08.00 (8 a.m.), *en route* for Escalette.　At 10.45 a.m. when on
the road—news was received that an Armistice had been signed by the enemy
and that hostilities would cease at 11.00, whereupon a halt was made.　The
march was resumed at 14.30 (2.30 p.m.), reaching Escalette at 17.00 (5 p.m.)
and billeting."

At home, throughout the United Kingdom, the news was received with
uproarious and mad manifestations of joy, but along that road to Escalette on
the morning of 11th November (and indeed along the whole of the Western
Front), when the Great Silence fell at 11 a.m. there were no shouts or exul-
tations.　In the hearts of officers and men, those who had come through,
there was a most profound feeling of relief and deep gratitude to the Almighty.
It was the Army's way of signalling a great victory, for no one forgot the gallant
and noble souls who had given their lives, had made the great sacrifice, that
they (the living) might come to where they then stood.

The 16th Division appears to have been in reserve when the enemy began
to withdraw from the eastern banks of the Hautedeule Canal on 15th October,
the 6th Somersets being then in billets in Nœux les Mines.

On 17th October the 49th Brigade (of the 16th Division, to which the 　6th Battalion
6th Somersets belonged) was ordered forward, the Somersets marching to
Cambrin, to Bervlau and Annoeulin on 18th, Pont Amarcq on 19th, to Les
Ascoeuils and Bachy on 20th, and to Rumes on 21st.　In the Rumes area the
49th Brigade spent the 22nd, 23rd and 24th October.　On the 25th they
relieved the 47th Brigade in the line east of the village.

The 6th Somersets took over the front line, the relief being completed
at 3 a.m. on 26th October.　The enemy's artillery and machine guns were 　26th October
active all night, but the day passed quietly.　On 27th, however, there occurred
an incident which is worth recording, as it was the last of any importance in
the history of the 6th Somersets during the War.

At 3 a.m. a German raiding party, consisting of three officers and fourteen
other ranks, attempted to raid a post garrisoned by a section (six men) of the
Battalion.　The raiding party reached a point within fifty yards of the post
and shouted "Hands up."　They then attempted to rush the post, but were
driven off by rifle fire.　With great determination the Germans again attacked
the post, but were similarly repulsed, two of the officers being killed and the
third wounded and taken prisoner, though he died later.　The only casualty
amongst the Somerset men was one man, the N.C.O. in charge of the post,
slightly wounded.　At nightfall on 29th October the 6th Battalion marched
back, on relief, to Taintignies where, until 6th November, the Somerset men
supplied working parties for the forward area.　On the 7th the Battalion 　7th November
moved back to Rumes and on the 10th forward again to Bruyelle, on the

western bank of the Escaut River. This was the most easterly point reached by the Battalion during hostilities, the 6th being still in the village when the Armistice was signed at 11 a.m. the next morning. Thus ended the war service of yet another Battalion of the Somerset Light Infantry—a fine Battalion whose hard fighting, especially in March 1918 during the Great German Offensive when the 14th Division had been practically wiped out, had won for the Regiment great renown.

There was yet one other Battalion of the Regiment in Artois—the 11th —while the enemy was being driven back eastwards.

The 11th Somersets (177th Brigade, 59th Division) were, on 6th September, in Epinette, the 177th Brigade then occupying the Epinette–Paradis area, but it was not until 13th that the Battalion moved up into the front-line trenches north-east of Laventie. The general advance had not then begun and inter-battalion reliefs took place until the night of 22nd, when the Somerset men were relieved and moved to billets at Bout Deville. Here training was continued until the end of the month. On the 16th the 11th Battalion had a new C.O., Lieut.-Colonel W. A. Gilliat arriving and taking over command *vice* Lieut.-Colonel H. R. S. Woodhouse.

It should not be forgotten that the 11th Somersets were originally formed as a garrison guard battalion, consisting of elderly men whose health was not of the best, unfitted for the heavy strain in the battle areas imposed upon younger and physically fit soldiers. All the more credit, therefore, is due to the Battalion whose officers and men, seeing the urgent need of troops, trained hard, and by sheer grit fitted themselves for the front line, so that finally the words "Garrison Guard" were dropped and they became a fighting Battalion.

On 3rd October the 11th Somersets again went into the front-line trenches in the Bois Grenier sector, the Battalion taking over the left sub-sector with the 2/6th D.L.I. on their right, but the relief was hampered by the fact that the British front line was on the move forward, and it was not until 6.30 a.m. on 4th that the Somersets and Durhams were finally settled in the line: A and D Companies of the Somersets in front and B and C in support.

Orders were issued that a further advance was to take place on 5th, and during the night 4th/5th patrols were sent out by both front-line battalions. Considerable progress was made until the enemy, strongly entrenched, was met with. The Durhams, however, succeeded in establishing themselves on the Armentières–Wavrin railway, and the Somersets at Grand Marais and in the Distillery. Again on 5th patrols were pushed out by both Battalions, but soon met with strong resistance, nevertheless when darkness had fallen the Somersets had succeeded in advancing to Large Farm and the Brewery, whilst the Durhams gained 300 yards of ground east of the railway.

Assisted by Stokes mortars and the guns, the Durhams made further progress on 6th, but the Somersets who attempted to clear a wood on their front were driven back.[1] B and C Companies of the latter Battalion now

6th Battalion (margin)
11th November (margin)
11th Battalion (margin)
16th September (margin)
5th October (margin)

---

[1] There is a note in the Battalion Diary which states that: "2/Lt. Howie and No. 2 Platoon of A Company on this occasion did splendid work."

relieved A and D, but nothing of interest occurred until the 10th, when the 177th Brigade was relieved by the 178th and moved back to an area north-west of Fleurbaix, the 11th Somersets to Croix de Rome, where for six days the usual programme of training was carried out.

On the 16th October there began a series of moves and marches which eventually brought the 11th Somersets to the River Escaut, where they gained possession of the crossings in the face of much opposition from the enemy.

The first of these moves took place on 17th October, when the Battalion marched to Perenchies and billeted for the night in the village. The next morning the march was continued to Marquette, which place was reached at about 4 p.m. Billets were obtained, but later, orders were received to move on to Mons-en-Bareuil, east of Lille. At 8.15 p.m. the Somersets moved off with a three-hours' march before them. No mention is made in the Diaries that the Battalion passed through the northern suburbs of Lille, but such was the case—the 11th Somersets were probably the first British soldiers to enter the city after its evacuation by the enemy.[1] At noon on 19th the Somersets set out to march to l'Hempon Pont, arriving at 4 p.m. The march ended at Willems on 20th, where until 22nd the Battalion "stood by" awaiting further orders. On the 22nd the 11th Somersets were ordered to take over the front line from the 17th Royal Sussex Regt. The Battalion left Willems for Esinette at 11 a.m. At 1 p.m. dinners were served at Templeuve, and at 2 p.m. the advance began to the line held by the Sussex. That night, after relieving the Sussex, the Somerset men with great daring floated a raft and their patrols succeeded in crossing the river and gaining valuable information.

The enemy was in force on the eastern banks of the Escaut, which apparently he had decided to hold, at least temporarily. On the 23rd his guns were very active and a barn, in which C Company (one of the support Companies) had taken shelter, received a direct hit, with the result that nine other ranks were killed and nine wounded.

On the 24th the hostile artillery was again active, though the Battalion escaped casualties. After darkness had fallen a patrol, consisting of one officer (2/Lieut. J. A. Proctor) and nine N.C.O.'s and men of C Company, crossed the river and, after obtaining information concerning the enemy's position, took a machine gun from him and retired without sustaining a single casualty. The Brigadier visited Battalion Headquarters and congratulated Lieutenant Proctor and his gallant comrades.

During the early morning of 25th C Company was relieved by B Company in the front line. Again the enemy's guns were active, and again a patrol, this time from A Company under the direction of O.C., Company (Captain R. H. Ridler), crossed the Escaut after dark. The patrol was led by 2/Lieut. A. W. Jenkins,[2] who had with him twelve N.C.O.'s and men. This party not only carried out their patrol work, but also captured a machine gun and

---

[1] By 5.50 a.m. on 18th Lille had been encircled by British troops, the enemy having retired precipitately from the city.

[2] Awarded the M.C. for his "marked courage and skill" during the patrol.

four Germans. The same evening a party of ten N.C.O.'s and men, under Sergt. A. Bainfield, went out to cover a party of sappers who were to build a footbridge across the river. The party occupied the captured German machine-gun post, but after two hours was compelled to withdraw owing to hostile trench-mortar and machine-gun fire.

The morning of 26th brought a letter of congratulation from the Brigade-Major: "The Brigadier wishes me to convey to you his congratulations on the very successful patrol enterprise carried out last night which resulted in the capture of four prisoners and a machine gun. The identification obtained was most valuable. He considers that the whole affair reflects great credit on the 11th Somerset L.I. and in particular on 2/Lieut. Jenkins and 12 other ranks who carried out the operation."

A fine "stunt" indeed for Category "B" men, but they had "A1" spirits.

On this day the Somersets were relieved and moved back to billets in Hulans until 30th, when they again moved up to the front line. On 31st 2/Lieut. le Brunn was shot dead by a sniper.

The Battalion now held Esquelmes. Across the river was the Cabaret Lietard—used by the enemy as a machine-gun post. At 10 p.m. on the night of 1st November A Company raided this place and took one light machine gun and six more prisoners, killing the remainder of the garrison. The raiders then returned. On the 5th a fighting patrol from B Company was sent across the river at 3 a.m. after a five-minute barrage, to reconnoitre the Cabaret Lietard. The village was searched but no signs of the enemy were found. Another patrol, under Captain Moseley, then went out and advanced beyond the railway without encountering the enemy. Subsequently, on passing this information back to Brigade Headquarters, the Somersets were ordered to occupy the village and A Company advanced to do so. But the enemy had returned and a heavy machine-gun fire met the advance, the Company being forced to retire to the banks of the river. B Company relieved A at 3 a.m. on 6th November. A Company had suffered heavy casualties.[1] That night the Battalion was relieved and marched back to Hulans.

The 11th Somersets had served their last tour in the front line, for on 9th they moved back to Toufflers and were still in billets when the Armistice came into force, though on 10th they again moved forward to the neighbourhood

of Pecq and Trieu de Wasmes. But they had done splendidly. Their grit, tenacity and perseverance were an example to younger men: their fighting qualities were first class, though they were graded as men "unfit for general service."

Thus ends the story of those Battalions of the Somerset Light Infantry engaged in the Final Advance in Artois.

[1] No casualties are given in the Battalion Diary

CHAPTER XLIII

THE FINAL ADVANCE

III

PICARDY: 17TH OCTOBER–11TH NOVEMBER
THE BATTLE OF THE SELLE, 17TH–25TH OCTOBER

IN Picardy the second stage of the concluding phase of the British offensive opened with the forcing of the Selle River. In the first stage (the Battle of Cambrai, already described) the enemy had been forced to evacuate Cambrai and fall back behind the line of the Selle. By the 13th October the western bank of the river south of Haspres had been reached and bridge-heads established at a number of places. But by this time the British lines of communication, owing to the rapidity of the advance, were greatly in need of improvement and it was the 17th before it was possible to recommence operations of a more than local character. The operations were designed for the purpose of attaining the general line—Sambre and Oise Canal–western exits of the Forêt de Mormal–Valenciennes. The attack was to take place in two phases—(i) by the Fourth Army from Le Cateau southwards in conjunction with the First French Army operating west of the Sambre and Oise Canal, and (ii) by the Third and First Armies north of Le Cateau along the line of the Selle River.

The 1st and 8th Battalions of the Somerset Light Infantry (of the 4th and 37th Divisions respectively) were in the area of the Battle, though only the 1st was actually engaged with the enemy. The 1st Battalion moved from Berneville on 11th October to Fontaine Notre Dame, and on 13th to Escaud-œuvres, on the outskirts of Cambrai. 1st and 8th Battalions

On the 17th October the 4th Division relieved the 49th Division in the front line which, at this date, was situated on the forward slopes of the high ground leading down to the Selle River, and facing Haspres and Saulzoir. The 1st Somersets, however, did not go at once into the front line but, as right support Battalion, dug in on the open ground (there being no other cover) south of Avesnes le Sec. The night was quiet and no casualties were suffered from hostile shell fire. On the 18th the Battalion found working parties. The enemy's guns were more active and two other ranks were wounded. Working parties were again furnished until dusk, when the Battalion moved north-east to just south of Avesnes. An attack on Haspres had been ordered for the 20th: the Somersets were to supply 2 officers and 152 other ranks to carry bridges, machine-gun and trench-mortar ammunition for the assaulting troops. This attack was cancelled, as the enemy had withdrawn his advanced posts. 1st Battalion 18th October

On the 20th the Battalion received orders to capture the village of Haspres from the south-east, i.e. on a north and south line running from the north-eastern exits of Saulzoir which had already been captured by troops of the 10th Brigade. These orders came to hand at 9.48 a.m. after which the Battalion, under very heavy shell fire, had to march over 5 miles to the assembly area through Saulzoir. No casualties were suffered and five minutes before Zero hour—12.30 p.m.—the Somersets were in position with B Company on the right, C on the left, A right support and Light left support. The railway from Saulzoir to Haspres was the dividing line between Companies. The two leading Companies were ordered to go straight through to the objective, Light Company being detailed to mop up the village. As the advance proceeded A Company was to right form in succession and take up a position with its left flank on the Haspres–Monchaux road and its right about midway between Haspres and Verchain, joining up with the left of the 10th Brigade.

Little was known of the exact situation in Haspres or whether the Germans were holding it in strength. If the Hampshires, who were on the left of the Somersets, had been able to send patrols across the Selle into the village, the attack would be cancelled, though it would be impossible to inform the latter of this before Zero hour. No definite orders had been issued on the subject, but in order to be prepared for such a contingency Companies were ordered to push forward strong patrols at once into the village and endeavour to secure the objectives.

Owing to faulty information Battalion Headquarters of the Hampshires reported to Brigade Headquarters that their patrols were in the village and the attack was cancelled. When, therefore, the mistake was discovered the attack, as originally planned, was ordered to take place at 3.30 p.m. But, as already explained, it was impossible to get information to the 1st Somersets and that Battalion was well inside Haspres when the second attack was ordered and in danger of being caught under the barrage of their own guns. A mounted orderly galloped back to Brigade Headquarters and the barrage was cancelled almost as the guns were being loaded.

Without serious opposition Haspres was captured and a line established east, north-east and north of the village—A and B Companies holding the front line with C and Light in support. During the night patrols searched the ground out in front of the Battalion and at about 4 a.m. on 21st a German machine-gun post was surprised, the gun was captured and its crew of four men killed. A little later it was discovered that the enemy was continuing his retirement.

At dawn on 21st the advance was continued in close pursuit of the enemy. No organized resistance met the Battalion, but machine-gun and rifle fire from the enemy's rear-guards and posts hampered the forward movement of the troops. Due credit must be given to the enemy's machine gunners: they fought well and at times heroically, dying at their posts after delaying as long as possible the advance of their opponents. Often deserted by their own artillery they yet remained behind, faithful to their duty.

The high ground which looked down on to the River Ecaillon was reached without serious casualties and here the Somersets dug in, for it was obvious that the river crossings were held in strength and even west of the river hostile posts had been established to dispute and hold up, if possible, the British advance.

The ground in front of the Battalion sloped steeply down to the river and was very exposed. During the afternoon the enemy shelled the high ground though, fortunately, most of his shells fell in rear of the Somersets. Again at dusk patrols were pushed forward and one (on the right) after the third attempt drove the enemy from the Ferme de Bouveneule: thus the line of the sunken road, west of the Ecaillon River, was reached and held as Companies followed in the wake of the patrols.

During the night of 21st/22nd the 1st Rifle Brigade relieved the 1st Somersets and the latter moved back to Haspres, where officers and men were accommodated in cellars. The operations so far had only cost the Battalion six other ranks killed and 21 wounded: extraordinarily light losses in view of the extent of the advance.

The 22nd and 23rd were rest days, though Haspres was still under hostile shell fire and 5·9's were continually arriving in the village. No further casualties were, however, suffered.

At 11.45 p.m. on 23rd the 1st Somersets again moved forward to take part in an attack which had for its object the capture of the river crossings and the village of Monchaux. Zero hour was to be 4 a.m. on 24th.

In this attack the 1st Battalion was to be on the right and the Hampshires on the left: the 11th Brigade was to assault from the sunken road west of the river, this line having been captured by the former Somersets on 21st October.

There were three objectives—the Blue, Yellow and Green Lines. The first followed the line of the road running south-east from Monchaux and east of the Ecaillon. The second was a line about 1,000 yards east of the first, and the third a portion of the line of a road running almost due south from Maing: there are no other means of describing these objectives [1] for the country was open and bare of outstanding points. The Brigade front, however, decreased as the advance proceeded and, in consequence, the Hampshires were allotted the capture of Monchaux and were not ordered to attack farther, while the Somersets were given the task of capturing the Yellow and Green Lines on the whole of the Brigade front.

Light and C Companies (right and left respectively) were to lead the attack of the 1st Battalion, with B supporting Light and A supporting C. B and A were to leap-frog Light and C on the line of the first objective and push home the attack to the third objective, i.e. the Green Line. In order to cross the river wooden bridges were constructed and these were to be carried

---

[1] In co-ordinates the objectives are expressed as: 1st, the road from Monchaux through P.5 Central; 2nd, J.29d.2.4.–J.36c.3.3.–Q.1a.5.o.; the 3rd, the road from cross-roads at J.30d.7.8. through K.31a and c.

forward by carrying parties supplied by the 1st Rifle Brigade. Two of the bridges were allotted to Light Company and two to C.

By 2 a.m. on 24th October Companies were assembled along the road running through Ferme de Bouveneule, the Battalion's jumping-off place extending for about 500 yards north and south of the Farm. At 4 a.m. a heavy creeping barrage was placed on the enemy's positions and behind it the troops went forward rapidly. West of the Ecaillon no opposition was encountered, though about twenty Germans were discovered in Ferme de Pluvinage by a mopping-up party: one man was shot and the remainder surrendered immediately. At one place the troops were so anxious to get across the river that they ran into their own barrage and several casualties resulted. Without much difficulty the left bridge was thrown across the river, but considerable trouble was experienced in getting the other three across. Delay ensued, during which the enemy, taking full advantage of the temporary hold-up of the attackers, raked the line with machine-gun and rifle fire, while his posts on the exposed slopes of the ridge east of the river had good targets of which they made full use. But the dour spirit of the West Countrymen was equal to the occasion: plunging into the water some swam the river, others helped in fixing the three bridges, after which the troops poured across rapidly. The western banks of the Ecaillon had been wired and at one place at least there was wire in the middle of the stream. During the hold-up, before the bridges were placed in position, Companies had become very much compressed, but once across the river they opened out and advanced quickly on the first objective.

In front of the Blue Line (1st objective) was part of the Hermann Line, practically the enemy's last line of organized defence. The centre portion of it ran from just east of Bohain, thence through Le Cateau, Solesmes, Valenciennes, Conde and Tournai, but the southern portion of it, along the British front, had already given way: Le Cateau and Solesmes had fallen.

Those parts of the Hermann Line still held by the enemy were held in force, and along the front of the 11th Brigade on the morning of 24th October they consisted not of a continuous trench system, but of a series of isolated posts and short lengths of trench strongly held by riflemen and numbers of machine guns.

The attack took the form of advances by "Section Worms": the name indicates the method of going forward. A series of detached fights was the outcome, each section working on its own. It was, indeed, a curious sight to see these sections "worming" themselves forward, each section, where it encountered a hostile post, extending and attacking it, making full use of their rifles and Lewis guns, whilst other parties worked round the flanks. Attacked in front and flank the Germans, though fighting stubbornly, in almost every instance surrendered.

The Hermann Line having been captured, the leading Companies passed on quickly to the Blue Line without meeting serious opposition. The troops attacked this line with the bayonet and their cheers and yells as they

rushed forward must have put terror into those of the enemy's troops who
intended putting up a further fight.   On reaching the Blue Line Light and
C Companies at once manned it and opened heavy fire up the slopes of the
ridge beyond, whilst the Support Companies, B and A, passed through to
assault the Yellow and Green Lines.

Various machine-gun posts were met with, but the Support Companies
dealt with these as the other posts had been dealt with, viz.: by Lewis-gun
and rifle fire and outflanking movements.   In a sunken road about half-way
between the Blue and Yellow Lines the Companies surprised a large number
of the enemy and compelled them to surrender.

The Yellow Line was captured and Light and C set to work to consolidate
it, while B and A prepared for the advance to the Green Line.   But now a
serious difficulty arose.   The 10th Brigade, on the right of the 11th, had been
unable to reach the Yellow Line so that B and A came under very heavy enfilade
rifle and machine-gun fire from the right.   Nevertheless, with great gallantry
the two Companies persisted in their efforts to secure the Green Line.   Movement in the open was extremely hazardous, yet the Somerset men gradually
worked their way forward and eventually a mixed party from the two Companies,
numbering about eighty men with Lieut. J. A. Radford [1] in command, reached
the Green Line.   Here another serious obstacle presented itself: the line
was strongly wired and could not be surmounted.   Further progress was
impossible and the gallant little party dug in about forty yards from the German
wire.   Although their right flank was in the air, they hung on all day.   On
the left touch was established with elements of the 51st Division who had
also reached the Green Line.

The left of B and A Companies rested on a communication trench running
from the Green Line towards the Yellow Line.   As soon as it was dark the
enemy launched a strong bombing attack down this trench, but he was beaten
off.   Low-flying enemy aeroplanes had all day hovered about the Green
Line machine-gunning the Somersets, who suffered a number of casualties.

At dusk a company of the Rifle Brigade was sent forward to form a
defensive flank by establishing posts between the right of B and A Companies
and the left of the 10th Brigade.

During the evening, under orders, the advanced troops fell back to a
position 300 yards from, and parallel with, the Green Line, preparatory
to a further attack by the 12th Brigade on the following day.

During the night 24th/25th October the 1st Somersets were relieved
and moved back to Haspres.   They had had a very successful day's fighting
and their spirits and morale were excellent.   At least 150 prisoners must
have been taken, as well as a large number of trench mortars and machine guns
which it was not possible to count accurately.   A great many Germans had
been killed and the records state that the number of enemy dead to be seen on
the battlefield was far above the average.   But the Battalion had also suffered
heavily.   Three officers (2/Lieuts. P. E. Austin, A. J. Gardiner and L. A. Young)

[1] Awarded the M.C. for conspicuous gallantry and devotion to duty.

1st Battalion

died of their wounds: five more officers (Lieut. E. Cockburn and 2/Lieuts. R. P. C. Smith, M. Hetherington, H. T. Trew and T. C. Hackwell) were wounded, and the losses in other ranks were 149 killed, wounded and missing.[1]

28th October

On the 28th the 1st Battalion again moved forward, relieving the 2nd Essex Regiment in Brigade Support.[2] Light and B Companies held the railway embankment between Querenaing and Artres (for since the 24th the latter had been captured and the front line ran along the banks of the River Rhonelle), while A and C were just west of the former village.

An attack planned for the 30th October was eventually postponed until 1st November: this was the Battle of Valenciennes.

The Battle of Valenciennes, 1st–2nd November [3]

"At 5.15 a.m. on the 1st November the XVII Corps of the Third Army and the XXII and Canadian Corps of the First Army attacked on a front of about 6 miles south of Valenciennes, and in the course of two days' fighting inflicted a severe defeat on the enemy. During these two days the 61st, 49th and 4th Divisions crossed the Rhonelle River, capturing Maresches and Preseau after a stubborn struggle and established themselves on the high ground 2 miles to the east of it. On their left the 4th Canadian Division captured Valenciennes and made progress beyond the town."—*Official Despatches.*

1st Battalion

"Preseau"—it was here that the 1st Somerset Light Infantry ended its glorious record of fighting in the Great War, for the 4th Division was withdrawn after the Battle of Valenciennes and was not engaged during the Battle of the Sambre, the final act in the great drama of victory.

It was, perhaps, a matter for regret that the 1st Battalion in this last action, though fighting with all its old spirit and splendid tenacity, fought not as a Battalion but was split up and attached to other units. For, briefly, the scheme of attack was as follows: the 4th Division was to attack Preseau and the high ground to the north of the village, in conjunction with the 61st Division on the right and 49th Division on the left. The Rifle Brigade, plus B Company [4] of the Somersets, was to attack on the right, and the Hampshire Regiment, with Light and A Companies, was to be on the left. The Battalion, reduced to Battalion Headquarters and C Company, with two companies of the 1st King's Own of the 12th Brigade attached, was in support. B, Light and A Companies assembled with the Battalions to which they were attached, and Battalion Headquarters and C Company along the railway embankment between Querenaing and Artres.

Four footbridges had already been thrown across the Rhonelle and four

---

[1] For conspicuous gallantry and devotion to duty during the operations at Verchain, Capt. P. J. K. Harris and 2/Lieut. R. P. Cecil-Smith were awarded the M.C., and C.S.M. R. Johnston, Sergt. M. Webb, Corpls. P. Gregory and C. W. T. Bozzard and L/Cpl. A. W. Simpson the D.C.M.

[2] On this date (28th) Lieut.-Colonel V. H. B. Majendie, after much gallant service with the 1st Somerset L.I., was invalided to England for three months, and Major A. J. Harington assumed command of the Battalion.

[3] The official despatches refer to the whole operation between the 1st and 11th November 1918 as the Battle of the Sambre.

[4] The Diary of the 1st Somerset L.I. states that B Company was attached to the Hampshire Regt., but in Battalion Orders the Company is attached to the Rifle Brigade.

more were allotted to the Hampshire Regiment: A Company of the 1st 1st Battalion
Somersets (attached to the Hampshires) was to carry forward these bridges
and place them in position for the leading Companies to pass over.   Light
Company was to follow in close support of the Hampshires as far as the centre
road of the three roads between Preseau and Aulnoy, where the Company
was to leap-frog the Hampshires and capture the final objective.   B Company,
supporting the Rifle Brigade, was to push home the attack if and when required,
and after the village was captured was to consolidate a line from the Old Mill
to the Church on the south-western outskirts of Preseau.   The Battalion was
to move forward as soon as the objective had been captured and consolidate
a north and south line east of the Rhonelle—in the angle formed by the Sameon
ravine and the river.

By 3 a.m. on the morning of 1st November all troops were assembled 1st November
in their positions.   From midnight onwards the enemy's artillery had carried
out active harassing fire, but it in no way affected the forming-up operations.

At 5.15 a.m., behind an excellent barrage, the advance began.   On
the right little opposition was met with as the troops moved off, but about
1,000 yards from Preseau a strong point was encountered and had to be
captured before the advance continued.   B Company, pushing forward into the
front line, had overcome the momentary hostile resistance, but in doing so
the Company Commander, Captain L. A. Osborne, fell seriously wounded.

After this strong point had been dealt with, B pushed on and were the
first to enter Preseau, where the Germans were holding the houses in strength.
The Company dug in on the line from the Old Mill to the Church as ordered,
while the Rifle Brigade went on through the village to the final objective, just
east of Preseau.

On the left the advance went well and Light Company, leap-frogging
the Hampshires, consolidated along the sunken road running north-west from
the northern outskirts of the village: this was just short of the final objective.

About 9.30 a.m., however, the enemy put down a heavy barrage and
counter-attacked the right flank of the 11th Brigade.   The 61st Division was
forced back, which uncovered the right of the Rifle Brigade, and the latter
was forced to conform by giving up the village—a bitter disappointment.
The Riflemen retired through B Company of the Somersets (then dug in from
the Old Mill to the Church) and took up a position 300 yards west of the Old
Mill.   Later B Company was also forced to conform and moved back into
position on the right of the Rifle Brigade.   Touch with the 61st Division
was not secured until later in the day.

About 4 p.m. the enemy launched another counter-attack in force, on
this occasion against the left flank.   The 49th Division gave ground and
part of Light Company of the Somersets was driven back some 200 yards.
But this was too much for Light Company.   Assisted by Company Sergeant-
Major R. Johnson, Captain P. G. K. Harris [1] rallied his men and ordered

---

[1] For conspicuous gallantry and devotion to duty Capt. P. G. K. Harris was awarded a bar to
his M.C. and C.S.M. A. H. Cook the D.C.M.

them to charge. The whole line sprang forward with a cheer and, with the bayonet, flung the Germans back and reoccupied their original position. Some prisoners and a machine gun were captured and many Germans killed, while the barrage which fell in response to the S.O.S. accounted for many more of the enemy. Unfortunately the line had again to be withdrawn to conform to the situation on the right.

When darkness had fallen the 1st King's Own relieved the Hampshires, and the 2nd Seaforth Highlanders the Rifle Brigade. The two relieved Battalions moved back to Artres, while the Somersets were ordered to concentrate about 2,000 yards due west of Preseau.

At 10 p.m. orders stated that the Somersets would support the Seaforths who, in conjunction with the King's Own, were to attack Preseau again on the morning of 2nd November at 5.30 a.m. Instructions were sent out immediately to all four Companies to move at once south-east to the southern side of the Artres–Preseau road, 300 to 400 yards in rear of the Seaforths, who were assembling along the road running from the Old Mill to Maresches. But when these orders were received the exact positions of Light, A and B Companies were not known as they were even then being relieved in the front line. Only C Company, therefore, received orders in time to dig-in in the assembly area before Zero hour. Light and A Companies only reached their assembly positions as the attack began, but B Company did not receive orders until after the attack had started.

The operations were the same as on the 1st November, and the task allotted to the Somersets was to move close behind the Seaforths and mop up Preseau. This was no easy matter, for failure to do the mopping-up business properly was mainly responsible for the inability to hold the village in the previous attack. In addition to clearing Preseau, the Battalion was to drive home the attack if held up and, after clearing the village, consolidate a line on the eastern outskirts.

At 5.30 a.m. a heavy 18-pounder barrage fell on the German positions and the attack began, the troops moving quickly behind the screen of fire. The Seaforths swept on through the village, leaving the latter to the Somersets, who then began to mop up the place. This was no easy task. Large numbers of German snipers were still active in the village and nearly all the cellars contained Germans who readily surrendered when called upon to do so. The snipers were more difficult to deal with and caused considerable casualties before they were finally mopped up—a long job not completed for some hours.

Colonel Majendie describes an amusing incident which took place during the mopping-up operations in Preseau:—

"Captain P. G. K. Harris, M.C., was the chief performer in an incident which gave rise to some merriment. He was standing at the top of some cellar steps collecting prisoners when a German came up from below 'Kamerad-ing' with such enthusiasm that he collided with Captain Harris and knocked him down. Captain Harris sat down violently on top of a dead German

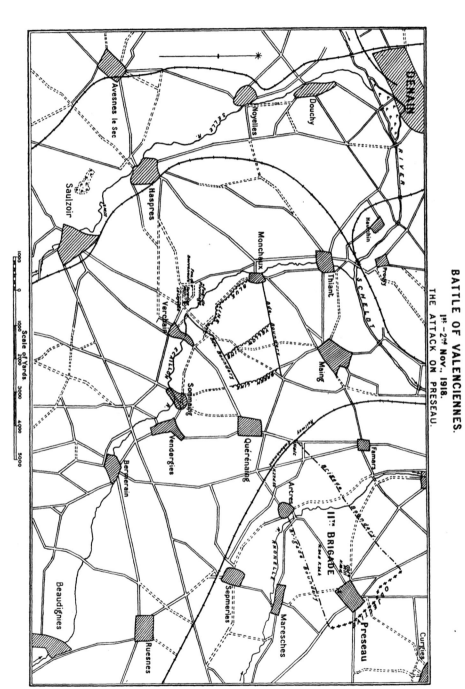

BATTLE OF VALENCIENNES.
1ˢᵗ – 2ⁿᵈ Nov., 1918.
THE ATTACK ON PRESEAU.

and in his efforts to rise put his hand on the dead man's face.   This was too 1st Battalion
much for Light Company's Commander: he leapt at the offender and, mindful
of his Oxford days, caught him such a left under the jaw that the unhappy
German did not recover consciousness for a long time." [1]

At 9 a.m. B Company joined the other Companies and finally the whole
Battalion dug in east of the village: Preseau had been finally captured.

The Battalion withdrew west of the village at 9.45 and dug a line there
where, after dark, it was relieved by a company of the 9th West Yorkshires
of the 11th Division and marched back to Haspres.

The Diary of 11th Brigade Headquarters records the attacks of 1st and
2nd November as "one of the finest performances the Brigade has ever done,"
but on looking back over the numerous actions in which, during the preceding
four years, the Brigade was engaged it is hardly possible to agree: of the many
fine attacks made and desperate counter-attacks repulsed, it is doubtful if
the term finest can be applied to any one in particular.   Most worthily the
11th Brigade upheld the splendid fighting traditions of the Army and the
fine Division (4th) of which it formed part.

In Haspres, on the night of 10th November, news was received of the
acceptance by Germany of the Armistice terms and unconditional surrender.

On the 11th the 11th Brigade group moved forward from Haspres to 11th November
Curgies.   The 1st Somersets set out at 9.30 a.m. and the Battalion was *en route*
at 11 a.m. when the Armistice came into force, for billets in Curgies were not
reached until 2.30 p.m.

THE BATTLE OF THE SAMBRE, 4TH NOVEMBER

Only one Battalion of the Regiment—the 8th—was in the last Battle 8th Battalion
of the Great War, the final stroke which completed the defeat of the enemy
and forced him to an unconditional armistice—the Battle of the Sambre.

From the 12th to the 21st October the 8th Somersets occupied billets
in Caudry, just south of Solesmes, where training was carried out and preparations made for the next attack.   On the 23rd the Battalion moved to Viesly 23rd October
and to Briastre later in the day: both these places are of unforgettable interest
to the 1st Battalion who passed through them in August 1914.   The following
morning, at 9.30 a.m., the 63rd Brigade moved forward to the Beaurain area,
the 8th Lincolns being sent off to just west of Neuville, the 4th Middlesex
and Somersets receiving orders to be ready to move at any time after 12 noon.
Between 1 and 2 p.m. movement orders were received from Divisional Headquarters and the Brigade relieved the 111th Brigade in support, the two
Battalions taking over the following positions: 8th Lincolns—one company
along the railway about half-way between Viterlan and Ghissignies, two companies in Salesches, one company just west of the company on the railway;
8th Somersets—one company supporting the Lincolns, one company in

---

[1] "History of the 1st Battalion, Somerset L.I., 1916–1918.'

Viterlan, one company on the railway south-east of Viterlan, one company round the Chapel in the south-east end of the village; 4th Middlesex—in Brigade Reserve. The 63rd Brigade had been so disposed in order to form a defensive flank on the right of the 37th Divisional front, and during the 24th and 25th patrols kept close touch with the flanking Division on the right, i.e. the 21st Division.

On the 27th a warning order was received that the Brigade would have to relieve the 112th Brigade in the front line on the night 27th/28th October. The relief took place and was completed by 10.40 p.m., the 8th Lincolns, on the right, holding a line from and including some orchards just north of Ghissignies to the Halt on the railway at the south-eastern end of the village: the 8th Somersets on the left, holding the line of the Sunken Road from the sunken cross-roads north of Ghissignies to immediately south-west of the grounds surrounding the Fme. de Beart.

In these positions the 28th, 29th and 30th passed without incident, although active patrol work was carried out, resulting in the gain of much useful information concerning the enemy's method of holding the railway along the Brigade front.

On the night of 30th/31st, however, a successful raid (the last by the Battalion) was carried out by two platoons of the Somersets in conjunction with two platoons of the 1st New Zealand Rifle Brigade on the left. The positions raided were along the railway at a point just south of the south-west corner of the Drill Ground, south of Le Quesnoy.

The two platoons, under 2/Lieut. E. L. Carter [1] and 2/Lieut. D. A. Hill, formed up just clear of the orchards and advanced under an excellent barrage. The leading platoon, on reaching the railway, was to work north and south whilst the other platoon mopped up and reconnoitred the ground east of the railway.

It is not possible to give full details of this raid, but besides the two officers in command of the raid, the names of Corporals Head, Atherton, Cotton, Boskill, Calvert and Rudge are mentioned as having done good work. The result of this raid was that one prisoner was taken who provided the necessary identification, thirty to forty of the enemy were killed and several machine guns were destroyed, all at the surprisingly small loss of one officer and one other rank slightly wounded.

The 31st October passed quietly, though occasionally the enemy shelled the front line and Ghissignies. On the 1st November the 8th Somersets were withdrawn to Salesches in Brigade Reserve, where the Battalion remained until the morning of 4th.

Orders to continue the advance due east on the morning of 4th November were issued from 63rd Brigade Headquarters on the 2nd, but the attack was to be carried out by the 111th Brigade (37th Division) which was to capture the first two objectives: the 112th Brigade was then to pass through the 111th

---

[1] Subsequently awarded the M.C. for conspicuous gallantry and good leadership. L/Cpl. W. J. R. Atherton received the D.C.M. for similar conduct during the raid.

and capture the remaining objectives.   The 8th Battalion was, however, to
be attached to the 112th Brigade for the operation.

At 5.30 a.m. on 4th the attack began and apparently made good progress,
for the Somersets were early on the move.   At 6.30 a.m. the Battalion marched
off from Ferme Bernier, Salesches, across country to the Louvignies–Futoy
road, thence through an orchard to Haute Rive Farm, where Battalion Headquarters were established.   A and B Companies then went forward to just
west of Byau de Pont à Vache, D Company to an orchard west of A and B,
and C Company to the neighbourhood of Fme. Croix Rouge.

Shortly after 9 a.m. Colonel Sheringham sent out an advanced party
to see if it was possible to establish Battalion Headquarters at Pont à Vache.
For nearly an hour he waited, but as no information came to hand he went
forward himself.   Passing C Company on the way at Croix Rouge he gave
the O.C., Company, orders to go forward.   He then found D Company and
gave them orders to push forward patrols, keeping touch on the flanks with
the 13th Royal Fusiliers.   In the valley near Pont à Vache he found A and
B Companies and there learned that the O.C., A Company (2/Lieut. H. W.
Brooks), had been killed.   From an orchard south-west of Jolimetz hostile
machine-gun fire was intense and enemy snipers were very active restricting
movement down into the valley.   The O.C., B Company (Capt. O. Briggs),
could not be found, but soon afterwards information came to hand that he
also had been killed.   Both Company Commanders had lost their lives whilst
gallantly reconnoitring the country forward with a view to merging with the
1/1st Herts Regiment in a further attack.

No further advance was made until 1 p.m., when the C.O. ordered Companies to push out patrols in order to keep touch with the enemy.   And at
2 p.m. the two leading Companies—A and B—were ordered to push forward
in conjunction with the 1/1st Herts as soon as possible.

The Somersets, and the troops of the 112th Brigade to whom they were
attached, were now almost at the extreme western edge of the Forêt de Mormal,
the direction of the attack being due east on Pont sur Sambre, a small village
east of the Forest.   A report then came to hand (at 2.20 p.m.) that the enemy
was retiring, and immediately Companies were told to push right on to Jolimetz
and beyond.   For over an hour no information reached Col. Sheringham of
the situation of his Battalion until, at 3.40, the Supporting Company reported
being in touch with B, the right attacking Company.   Going up again to
the front line, the C.O. found the larger portion of his leading Companies on
the main road just west of the Forest, took them forward and started them
through the wood.   At 5 p.m. he received reports from A Company that
they were well into the Forest, but were meeting heavy machine-gun fire on
the right flank, having lost touch with B Company.   .

The Somersets were now engaged in fighting entirely novel to them.
They had, of course, fought in woods along the old front lines, but they were
woods only in name.   Mormal, however, was a thick forest, and about 7.40
A reported that progress was difficult owing to the thickness of the under-

growth. This Company, a little while before this report was sent, had encountered three hostile machine guns and a sniper. Fire with rifles and Lewis guns was opened on the enemy, who were seen to withdraw carrying a wounded man. An attempt made to follow up the Germans failed owing to the thickness of the Wood. B Company, farther south, had a similar experience, the hostile machine-gun crew withdrawing as the Somerset men advanced, the enemy escaping into the darkness.

The Support and Reserve Companies of the 8th Battalion, led by strong platoon patrols supported by a second platoon, were then pushed along the main rides of the Forest on the Battalion front. They worked their way gradually eastwards and eventually found themselves on the eastern exits of the Forest. Three officer patrols then went forward to a point on the railway about fifty to one hundred yards from the eastern edges of the wood where, in the near distance, small parties of the enemy were observed round camp fires.

Very early next morning Colonel Sheringham was informed that the 5th Division was going to pass through the 37th Division and would use the main drives and railways through the Forest. He therefore ordered all Companies to establish posts at the eastern exits of the Forest and along the Battalion front in order to draw the enemy's observation away from the drives and railway. Between 3.20 and 4.20 a.m. on 5th November leading Battalions

of the 5th Division reached Battalion Headquarters, 8th Somersets, with the intention of forming up along the western edge of the Forest and attacking through it, being unaware that the Somersets and troops of the 112th Brigade had already reached the eastern edge. Colonel Sheringham urged them to push on down the drives.

Between 6.30 and 6.40 a.m. the 5th Division troops passed through the Somersets and flanking units, crossing the eastern edge of the Forêt de Mormal. Shortly afterwards a report was received that they had reached their objective.

During the morning the 8th Somersets were withdrawn to Pont à Vache where the Battalion cookers were found, and all ranks enjoyed a well-earned breakfast.

Throughout the operations the Battalion Signallers had done splendid work: they maintained unbroken communication between Div. H.Q. and Bn. H.Q., no easy task where the situation was changing continually.

The last page of the final "Narrative of Operations" in the Battalion Diary records: "The Battalion then marched by companies via Louvignies and Salesches to billets in Neuville, reaching Neuville between 15.30 and 16.00 hours (3.30 and 4 p.m.)."

In this final and very creditable fighting the 8th Somersets lost Captain O. Briggs and 2/Lieut. H. W. Brooks killed, and 2/Lieut. S. A. Palmer wounded. The losses in other ranks were: killed—8, wounded—22, "missing, believed wounded"—3. The Battalion captured 20 machine guns and one 5.9 howitzer.

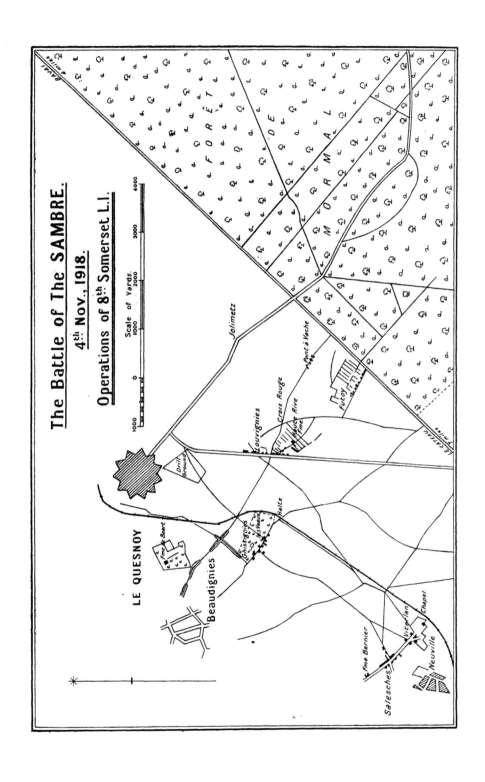

The Battle of The SAMBRE.
4th Nov., 1918.

Operations of 8th Somerset L.I.

Scale of Yards.
1000   0   1000   2000   3000   4000

There is a letter of congratulation [1] with the Battalion Diary for November 8th Battalion in which the writer says: "It was splendid the way your fellows pushed through in the afternoon and got to their objective."

In Neuville the 8th stayed until the morning of 11th November, cleaning up and training.   On the 11th the Battalion marched to billets in Caudry— 11th November its fighting days were over.

[1] From the Brigadier-General, commanding 112th Infantry Brigade, to which the 8th Somersets were attached.

CHAPTER XLIV

THE INVASION OF PALESTINE

THE FINAL OFFENSIVE: 18TH SEPTEMBER–31ST OCTOBER 1918

THE BATTLE OF SHARON, 19TH–25TH SEPTEMBER

1/5th Battalion

IN Palestine the Final Offensive opened with the Battles of Megiddo, i.e. the Battles of Sharon and of Nablus, both taking place from 19th to 25th September.

But only with the first (Sharon) is this narrative concerned, one Battalion of the Somerset Light Infantry—the 1/5th of the 233rd Brigade, 75th Division—taking part in the operations.

27th April

We left the 1/5th Battalion at El Kefr on 27th April, having just taken over the front line from the Gurkhas and a company of the Hampshires.

The centre of the Battalion sector was El Kefr, the trenches being from 400 to 500 yards north of the village. East of El Kefr and within the British lines, was a hill called the Necklace, and north-east another, Toogood Hill. West of Kefr was Cornwall Hill and, nearly 1,000 yards behind and below the hill on which the village stood, ran the Wady Deir Ballut. Out in front of the trenches, north-west of those held by the Somersets, was Gurkha Hill, north-east of which was Somerset Wady, the Turkish trenches lying just beyond. Nearly 6,000 yards north-east of El Kefr was Bidieh, a fair-sized village well within the Turkish lines.

The Hampshires were on the right of the Somersets and the 3/3rd Gurkhas on the left. On the evening of 20th April at about 6.15 the enemy opened a heavy bombardment of the line which continued until darkness had fallen. The bombardment was followed by a barrage placed on the western approaches to Kefr Hill. Under cover of the barrage the Turks at about 11 p.m. attacked Toogood Hill held by the Hampshires, but were successfully repulsed. The 1/5th were not called upon but lost three other ranks killed and three wounded as the result of the bombardment.

5th May

On the 5th May a patrol of one officer and four other ranks went out to Somerset Wady. None of the enemy was encountered, but the interesting point is that the Battalion Diary records the fact that "propaganda literature" was left in the Wady and when, on 11th, a patrol again visited the Wady the papers left there had been removed: a further supply was left for the enemy. On this occasion 8 dead Turks were found in the Wady, the bodies not being there on 5th. Later on in the month when more propaganda literature was left in the same Wady some German papers were found.

The enemy complained much of our propaganda work and on the Western Front especially General Ludendorff frequently inveighed against the success attained in sowing the seeds of discontent amongst his troops. From an historical point of view it is interesting to note that the method was in force 1/5th Battalion in Palestine as well: coming generations may know that war in the front line was not only waged with bullet and shell.

About the end of May the 1/5th were relieved for the first time and went back to Rentis for resting and training. Then followed a tour in the Wady Zerka (in the second line of defence) during which working parties were supplied, after which the Battalion once again went into the front line, on this occasion taking over the centre sub-sector of the left section of the 75th Divisional front, i.e. Deir Ballut. A portion of the line ran along the Sanger Ridge, the village of Rafat being on the Battalion's right. Patrol work, during which on several occasions shots were exchanged with the enemy, completes the story for June. July 13th witnessed a mild attack on Rafat 13th July by the Turks, but it was broken up by artillery fire before the enemy reached our wire.[1] Apart from the usual hostile shelling of Ballut Ridge and patrol work out in the Fig Grove and towards Three Bushes, the month of July passed quietly and on the 30th the Somersets were relieved by Outram's Rifles and moved back to the bivouac area adjoining the Ain Zerka. The Brigade was now in Divisional Reserve, and working parties were supplied by the 1/5th until, in the second week in August, the 233rd Brigade received orders to move to the plains for training. On 10th the 1/5th Battalion moved to Rentis and on the following night (in Brigade) to an area near Deir Tureif for training in open warfare. Towards the end of the month the Brigade moved back into the front line, the Somersets relieving the 1/4th Wilts Regt. on the night of 23rd/24th on Tin Hat, Berukin and Toogood Hill. The right of the Battalion joined up with the 10th Division, holding Kefr Ain Hill.

But in this position the Somersets were not to stay long, preparations were in force for operations to begin on 19th September, and on 13th September 13th September the 75th Division was relieved by the French Palestine Detachment and the 10th Division and moved back to Beit Nabala for final training before being transferred to the north-western portion of the line nearer the coast and opposite the Tabsor Defences. On the night of 16th/17th September the 233rd Brigade (in Division) marched to the Mulebbis area, and on the night of 17th/18th relieved troops of the 3rd and 7th Divisions holding that portion of the line which ran from the Hadrah Road (inclusive to 75th Division) in a north-westerly direction for about 2,500 yards. This line (the whole of the 75th Divisional front) was taken over by the 1/5th Somerset L.I. who held Posts E.12, E.13, E.14, E.15, E.15a and E.16.[2]

On taking over this line patrols were immediately pushed forward into No Man's Land to cover preparations for the attack then being made out in front of the wire.

On the 18th orders for the attack were received which, summarized

---

[1] One officer (2/Lieut. Avelans) and three other ranks of the 1/5th were wounded during this affair.

[2] This front in co-ordinates is expressed as from C.4a. to A.33d. Positions of posts are not marked on the maps available.

briefly, were as follows: The 19th was "Z" (Zero) day when the XXI Corps would attack the enemy along the whole of the front from Three Bushes Hill to the sea.   The 3rd Division was attacking on the right of 75th and the 7th Division on the left.

The 75th Division was to attack the Tabsor Defences and push through to and beyond Et Tireh and the Tireh Defences.   The 232nd Brigade was to be on the right and the 234th on the left: the 233rd Brigade (less 1/5th Somersets) was to be in Divisional Reserve, assembled some 3,000 yards in rear of the right attacking Brigade, but advancing at Zero hour by bounds, first to No Man's Land and then to the Wady Moab.

Two Companies of the 1/5th Somersets were to be attached to the 234th Brigade for the special purpose of capturing the most advanced Turkish outpost, F.13.   On completing the capture and mopping up of F.13 these two Companies were to remain as much under cover as possible in the neighbourhood of the post until the arrival of the 233rd Brigade on the line of its first bound, i.e. No Man's Land.   The other two Companies of Somersets were to remain in their present positions (i.e. the front line) until the arrival of the main body of the 233rd Brigade, when the whole of the Battalion was to form the Brigade Reserve Battalion.

Nos. 2 and 3 Companies (under Major Watson) were the two attached to the 234th Brigade, Nos. 1 and 4 patrolling No Man's Land in order to cover the deployment of the attacking troops in front of the wire.

Under cover of an intense artillery bombardment the attack began at 4.30 a.m. on 19th September all along the line from Three Bushes to the sea. The XX Corps, on the right of the XXI, was not to attack until the evening of Zero day, by which time the C.-in-C. had hoped to roll up the right of the Turkish forces on the coast.[1]

The intense bombardment lasted fifteen minutes, under cover of which the infantry left their positions of deployment and advanced on the enemy.

With the 1/152nd Infantry on their right and 58th Rifles on their left, No. 2 and No. 3 Companies of the 1/5th Somerset L.I., under Major Watson, went forward to the attack.   This attack (of short duration) was completely successful and in the surprisingly short period of fifteen minutes the Turkish advanced outpost, F.13, was captured with two prisoners and a machine gun. No casualties were suffered by the 1/5th in this action, though subsequently two other ranks were killed and five wounded during the work of consolidation.

Ultimately the 233rd Brigade assembled in No Man's Land as originally ordered and No. 1 and No. 4 Companies of the Somersets came into position behind the 3/3rd Gurkhas.   As the Brigade advanced towards the Wady Moab, No. 2 and No. 3 Companies rejoined the Battalion.   With great rapidity the general advance continued successfully and by midday Tireh had been captured by the 232nd and 234th Brigades.   The 233rd Brigade

---

[1] The official despatches should be read in conjunction with this Chapter, as it is impossible to give all the details of Lord Allenby's plan of campaign.

was then halted some 2,500 yards from Tireh and the Somersets rested close 1/5th Battalion to Miskeh, moving later in the day to a bivouac area east of the village.

At Et Tireh the 75th Division was ordered to remain in Corps Reserve: the Division had splendidly performed the task allotted to it, and to other Divisions and the Cavalry were left the task of completing the discomfiture of the Turks. For between 4.30 a.m. on 19th September and 5 p.m. on 20th the greater part of the Eighth Turkish Army had been overwhelmed and the Seventh Turkish Army was in full retreat through the hills of Samaria, the exits from which were already in possession of the British Cavalry, so that there was no escape. Practically the whole of the two Turkish Armies, with their guns and transport, were captured, while the Fourth Army, east of the Jordan, was in retreat, the remnants of which were captured finally by the Desert Mounted Corps.

But the 1/5th Somersets had seen their last fight on 19th September. Thereafter the Battalion remained in the Miskeh area for several days, marching to Bir Adas for bathing and fumigation. On 26th September another move was made to the Kalkilieh area and here, in road-making and training, the remainder of September and the whole of October were spent.

The last entry in the Battalion Diary for October, i.e. on 31st, reads thus: 31st October "Received the following wire: 'An Armistice has been concluded with Turkey by terms of which hostilities between the Allies and Turkey cease at 12.00 (12 noon) to-day.'" It is signed by the C.O., Lieut.-Colonel E. F. Cooke-Hurle.

Thus Turkey was out of the War, beaten with a thoroughness which Lord Allenby described in the following words: "Such a complete victory has seldom been known in all the history of war."

CHAPTER XLV

MESOPOTAMIA

UNTIL July 1916 the 1/4th Somersets remained encamped at Makina Masus, but at 3 a.m. on 12th of that month C Company left for Shaiba: B Company with the machine-gun section and signallers followed on 13th, and D and A Companies on the 14th and 15th respectively. Companies were moved in this way in order that as each arrived the men could have breakfasts immediately in their tents, which had already been pitched.

But at Shaiba sickness attacked the Battalion. The brackish water was responsible. The transport animals also suffered; one of the machine-gun mules died of colic. This sickness in the Battalion prevented the 1/4th Somersets returning to Kut, taking part in its capture, and in the subsequent march to Baghdad. By the end of the month, however, the health of the men improved—the well water becoming sweeter through frequent use. During August the first of a series of bombing courses was started, the bombers of each Company undergoing training in turn.

About the middle of September a very noticeable change in the weather took place. Although during the day the temperature was still above 100° the nights became distinctly cold—a very welcome change. At this period also the Battalion was somewhat split up, parties of officers and men being detached to Ashar, Margil and Makina for various duties: Battalion Head- quarters, however, remained at Shaiba. On 19th October the Shaiba Mobile Column was formed, the 1/4th Somersets being ordered to furnish 150 men. This Column was to be ready to reinforce posts on the Nasiriyeh line as required. Lewis guns (four) were first issued to the Battalion on 21st November. By the 11th December Beri-beri (the Battalion Diary records) had increased considerably in the Battalion, several new cases being discovered, while about 150 men were put on light duty as "suspects." But towards the end of the month, after strenuous efforts had been made to stamp out this distressing disease, the records stated that it "seemed to be stopping altogether."

After several months of inactivity (of which, however, much might be written were this a history of one Battalion of the Regiment only), the 1/4th Somersets on 16th April 1917 left Shaiba for Nasiriyeh, having been relieved by the 1/6th Devon Regt. which had arrived on the previous day. The Somerset men left Shaiba with a strength of 18 officers and 639 other ranks. Lieut.-Colonel W. C. Cox was still in command of the Battalion. Nasiriyeh was reached on 17th, the Battalion at once proceeding to camp on the banks of the Euphrates, where training was carried on. On the 23rd July the Battalion suffered a serious loss, Lieut.-Colonel E. H. Openshaw, Second-in-Command, dying from heart failure following a heat stroke.

In November there occurred an incident which, as casualties are recorded 1/4th Battalion in the Battalion Diary, is worthy of mention:—

On 22nd orders were received at Battalion Headquarters, 1/4th Somersets, 22nd November to hold in readiness two officers and 108 men to proceed to Samawa on a reconnaissance. In pursuance of these orders Captain Harris, 2/Lieut. Vallis and 100 N.C.O.'s and men with ten days' rations and 500 rounds of ammunition per rifle, embarked in the River Boat "T.1." Four men were also sent to H.M.S. "Firefly" and four to H.M.S. "Greenfly" to work the machine guns on those boats. The three boats left for Samawa at 9.30 a.m. on 23rd.

But misfortune soon overtook the "T.1." What with the party of 100 men and officers aboard, as well as her armour plates, the little boat was heavily loaded and drew six feet of water. This was disastrous for, between Nasiriyeh and Samawa, there were several bars across the Euphrates, with the result that on the 24th the "T.1" ran aground. She was, however, after about two and a half hours' strenuous labour started again and reached Durraji (about half-way and the limit of the Arab Police posts) on 25th. The next day, having left Durraji, the "T.1" again ran aground. Captain Harris and fifty other ranks were therefore transferred to the two gun-boats and 2/Lieut. Vallis and the remainder of the men escorted the "T.1" back to Durraji, reaching Nasiriyeh on the 29th.

Thus only Captain Harris and his men were participants in the small affair under narration. A Political Officer (Captain Dickson) from Nasiriyeh was aboard one of the gun-boats and he had received information that the Political Officer at Samawa (Capt. Goldsmith) was having trouble with the natives. An Arab was sent up to find out what was happening, but the unfortunate man was caught, stripped, beaten and then sent back. In the meantime Captain Goldsmith arrived from Samawa: he had been fired on by a large body of Arabs, had had to swim his horse across the river and continue his journey on the farther bank. On the 27th the gun-boats passed Al Khidr. Information now came to hand concerning a pirate village farther up the river, at which all river-boats were stopped and robbed. This village soon came into sight. A few 4-in. shells blew the place to pieces and a landing party was sent ashore. Three tons of wheat and other stores were taken, which were distributed amongst the friendly Arabs. Samawa was reached the same day. Here all was commotion, the population lining the banks of the river and welcoming the arrival of the gun-boats with loud hand-clappings and frenzied yells. Dissension had been rife in the village since the departure of the Turks, and only two hours before the arrival of the gun-boats there had been fighting between the rival parties. The leader of one party, on the arrival of Captain Goldsmith, fled to his house some 3 miles north of Samawa. It was this man who had occasioned the last fight in the village. He was sent an order to "come in" by the 29th but as, on that day, he had not complied with the order, H.M.S. "Greenfly" steamed up the river to opposite the house and blew it up. The house was full of loot, but it was dark and as there were no troops the crew were unable to land.

The two gun-boats, with Captain Harris and his party aboard, left Samawa at 7 a.m. on 30th and reached Nasiriyeh at 11 p.m.

The Battalion Diary of the 1/4th Somersets records that: "There were not many casualties" in this affair—"10 killed and 17 wounded," but does not state whether they were all Somerset men.

In December Beri-beri again made its appearance and numerous cases were diagnosed and the men sent to hospital. Twice a week the Battalion paraded by Companies, when the men were dosed with Marmite.

On 5th March the 1/4th Somersets left Nasiriyeh for Basra *en route* for Baghdad. After an interesting trip up the river the Battalion arrived at Khirr Camp, below Baghdad, on 13th. On 16th A and B Companies left for Hillah, the march being carried out in four stages. The Camp was reached on 19th March. Battalion Headquarters with C and D Companies, instead of joining up with A and B at Hillah, were ordered on 25th March to prepare to move on "operation scale," and on the 26th (less two platoons which had been detached as escort to 159th Siege Battery) moved by route-march to Kufa, arriving at 10.15 a.m. on 1st April. From Kufa, Battalion Headquarters and C and D Companies marched to Nedjf Blockade Camp, 5 miles away, and dug in during the evening. The next morning two strong platoons of D Company of the Somersets relieved a company of the 1/9th Middlesex at Attiyah's Khan, the latter being 200 yards from the city walls: B.1 and A.5 Posts were also taken over by the Somerset men. Thus, at the beginning of April 1918, A and B Companies of the 1/4th Somersets were at Hillah and Battalion Headquarters with C and D Companies astride the walls of Nedjf. The Battalion now formed part of the 56th Brigade.

Nedjf, the Holy City of the Shiite Mohammedans, was some 30 miles from Hillah Camp. It was a walled city of the desert, held in great reverence by the Arabs. But in Nedjf on 21st March Captain W. M. Marshall, the Political Officer, was murdered by reactionaries, calling themselves the "Committee of Rebellion" who, though in the minority, terrorized the remaining inhabitants. A blockade of the city was ordered until all those implicated in the murder were given up, and it was for this purpose that Battalion Headquarters with C and D Companies of the 1/4th Somersets (with other troops) formed a cordon of military posts, joined up by barbed wire, round the place. Owing to the holy shrine within Nedjf, which was surrounded by a very high wall, it was deemed inadvisable to shell the city, or even to attempt to take it by direct assault. Blockade methods were therefore adopted.

The city was irregular in shape—six-sided, the principal post, Kufa Gate, being on the south-eastern side. Outside the gates there were a number of buildings through which the tram-lines ran to Blockade Camp some 2,000 yards away. Immediately east of the Tram Shed was Attiyah's Khan (or Marshall's Serai). North of this place was a little house called Somerset House, and north again of the latter was the large Arab graveyard. B.1 and

A.5 Posts were east of the Graveyard.   In the south-eastern corner of the 1/4th Battalion city walls was the Hawaish Gate, and outside the gate the Hawaish Mound. North of Kufa Gate were the Turkish Barracks and Misraq Bastion, for the walls of the city were bastioned.

When the Somersets arrived the barbed wire ran from Bullock's Mound south-east of the Tram Shed, thence east and north-east round the eastern side of the Graveyard.

On the 3rd April the two platoons of C, which had escorted the Siege 3rd April Battery, arrived and camped 1,500 yards south of Blockade Camp.   On this date all posts were improved and sand-bag protections thickened, as the defences at Attiyah's Khan and B.1 Post were not bullet-proof.   All day long there was a good deal of sniping, the truculent Arabs finding excellent cover on the high walls of the city and in the bastions.   A platoon of D relieved a platoon of Punjabis at Bullock's Post on 4th April.

On the 5th at midday two holy men (Ulemas) came out of the city. They stated that there was no barley, the staple food of the poor in Nedjf: bread and fowls were expensive but dates were cheap.   On the 6th there was a great deal more sniping than usual and at 6 p.m. Captain Morse, with one platoon of D Company, moved off to a position 200 yards south of Bullock's Post as reserve to a party of 5th Gurkhas who were to raid the two mounds near the Hawaish Gate early on the 7th.

At 6 a.m. on the latter date the siege guns shelled the mounds for eighteen minutes, dropping forty-five shells on them.   The mounds were then rushed by the Gurkhas, who suffered only one casualty.   The Gurkhas subsequently established a position on the city walls.   During this operation all posts were ordered to make a demonstration by firing into the city.   The moral effect on the Arabs of this successful little affair was considerable, for after the bombardment there was very little sniping.

Valhalla, another post south of B.1, was occupied on the night of 7th/8th by two sections of Somersets.   This was the first step in the advance of the whole line which now gradually began to close round the city.   Somerset House (100 yards north of Attiyah's Khan) was next occupied (on 8th) by a platoon of D Company, the new front being wired and new sentry posts dug during the night.   The line now ran from Bullock's Post through Attiyah's Khan, Somerset House and Valhalla to B.1.

After dark on the 9th the heavy guns moved into position north of Blockade Camp.   The right of the line was also advanced about 400 yards, B.1 Post being moved forward to the edge of the tombs which surround Nedjf. B.2 was then taken over by the Somersets.

On 10th the heavy guns shelled White House, outside and on the western 10th April side of the city.   A party of Middlesex then rushed the mounds close to the walls on the northern side of the city and occupied them, having only one casualty.

During the night 10th/11th the right of the Somersets advanced again, extending along Durdham Downs, within eighty yards of Turkish Bastion

1/4th Battalion and Misraq Bastion and of the city walls, but the old line was also maintained as the ground was honeycombed by subterranean passages leading from the city to the tombs in the Graveyard—a means of escape.

On the 11th a hole was discovered in the city wall at the foot of Turkish Barracks Bastion opposite Durdham Downs and, after a reconnaissance, a platoon of Somersets went forward and, after occupying the bastion, wired it. Beyond slight sniping there was no opposition.

That night orders were received to take the Kufa and Tramway Gates and the Misraq Bastion.

12th April At 5.30 a.m. on 12th one platoon of D Company moved off in two parties to seize the Tramway and Kufa Gates, a platoon of C Company moving off to take the Misraq Bastion. Each platoon was divided into two parties, a bombing party with orders to move along the top of the wall or inside the city, and a battering party to move astride the wall and force an entrance under cover of the bombers. By 5.40 a.m. all positions were occupied without opposition, but it was some time before an entrance was effected by battering parties as tons of loose masonry had been piled against the two gates on the city side. All positions were now strongly consolidated, only a few shots being fired by hostile Arabs. Patrols then moved into the city and found everything extremely quiet. Near the Misraq Bastion several houses had to be blown up to provide a clear field of fire in case of counter-attacks.

But by now the inhabitants of Nedjf were completely subdued and on the morning of 13th three prisoners—some of the reactionaries—were brought in by loyal Arabs, who had at last bestirred themselves and had gained the upper hand over the malcontents.

The situation in and around Nedjf was now peaceful. The city walls were all searched and on the 19th six more prisoners were handed over by the loyal Arabs, who again on the 20th and 21st brought in three more. From 22nd to 25th a further batch of eleven prisoners was brought in. The blockade of Nedjf was raised at 12 noon on 4th May. Finally eleven Arabs, who had been tried and condemned to death for the murder of the Political Officer, were hanged on 30th May.

Thus ends the interesting story of Battalion Headquarters and C and D Companies of the 1/4th Somersets at Nedjf: A and B Companies remained all the while at Hillah Camp, but moved to Kufa at the end of May, the whole **31st October** Battalion being reunited at Nedjf on 31st.

This incident has been dealt with fully because it is the last of outstanding interest recorded in the Diaries of the 1/4th Somersets. The Battalion was not in the final round up of the Turks, but left Nedjf in October and moved by train from Baghdad to Tekrit, and when the Armistice came into force the Somerset men were employed in extending the railway line.

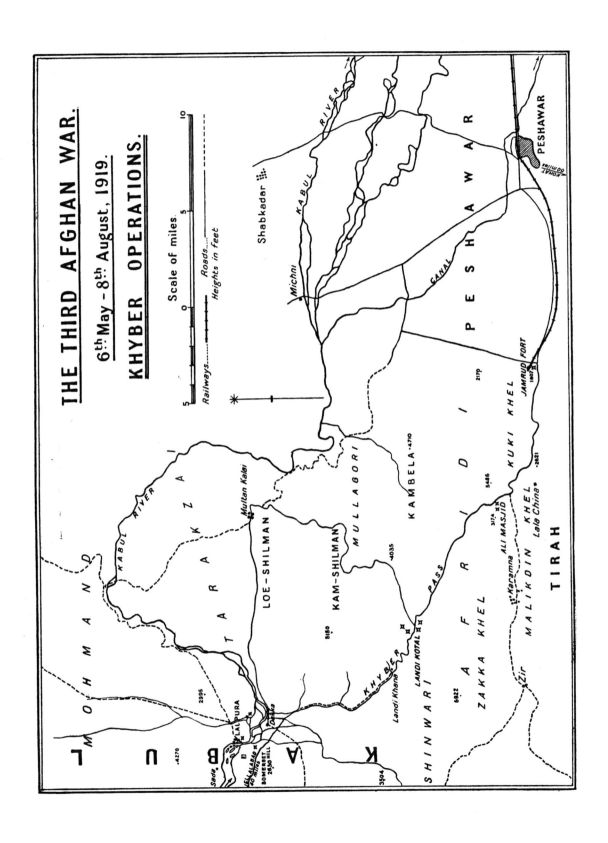

THE THIRD AFGHAN WAR.

6th May – 8th August, 1919.

KHYBER OPERATIONS.

Scale of miles.

Railways........
Roads........
Heights in feet

PESHAWAR

KOHAT 00 miles.

Shabkadar

Michni

KABUL RIVER

CANAL

PESHAWAR

2170

JAMRUD FORT
1607

KUKI KHEL

2621

KAMBELA 4470

MULLAGORI

5486

3174

ALI MASJID

Karamna

MALIKDIN KHEL

Lala China

KAM-SHILMAN

4035

Multan Kalai

LOE-SHILMAN

5150

KHYBER PASS

Landi Kotal

Landi Khana

Zir

ZAKKA KHEL

6922

TIRAH

AFRIDI

SHINWARI

KABUL RIVER

T A R A K Z A I

M O H M A N D

B U L

2295

LALPURA

Dakka

Seda

GIRDI
KALAK
40

SOMERSET
HILL 2650

3504

4270

KABUL

AFRIDI

CHAPTER XLVI

INDIA

THE NORTH-WEST FRONTIER CAMPAIGN

IN India the outbreak of war occurred at an inconvenient juncture for 2nd Battalion mobilization purposes and the despatch of forces overseas. A large number of British troops were in summer quarters in the hills, and others were located long distances from the railway: the Indian troops were largely on leave and many British officers were in England on furlough, several hundreds of whom were detained for duty under the War Office. But in spite of these difficulties no time was lost in mobilizing the necessary forces, and the first contingent of troops (British and Indian Regulars) for France from India sailed on the 25th August 1914.

It was, however, undesirable to denude the country of regular troops and, although those regiments which were sent first to France and then to Mesopotamia were to a large extent replaced by Territorial and Garrison troops from England, yet the Government was forced to retain in India during the whole course of the war British and Indian Regulars. Amongst the eight infantry battalions[1] of British troops thus retained was the 2nd Battalion Somerset Light Infantry.

For the 2nd Somersets this was a bitter disappointment. The Battalion when war broke out was stationed at Quetta, under the command of Lieut.-Colonel E. H. R. C. R. Platt, and was in splendid fettle. But the Somerset men were perforce bound to content themselves with the decree of the higher authorities, keeping fit in training, though called upon to do little more than garrison duty while their comrades of the 1st Battalion were fighting hard in Europe.

The "Digest of Service" of the 2nd Battalion for the whole course of the war, 1914–1918, shows but little variation from the ordinary round of duty carried out in peace time. There are no entries in the digest between 1st August and 30th October 1914. On the latter date three companies (Nos. 30th October 1, 2 and 3) left Quetta for Nagpur, Jubblepore and Indore respectively, there to await the arrival of Territorial troops from England. By the early days of December that year these companies had returned to Quetta.

---

[1] These eight battalions were: 2nd King's Regt. (Liverpool), 2nd Somerset Light Infantry, 1st Yorkshire Regt., 1st Duke of Wellington's Regt., 1st Royal Sussex Regt., 1st South Lancs Regt., 2nd North Staffordshire Regt., and 1st Durham Light Infantry. Of these troops the C.-in-C. in India said: "The backbone of the Army in India at this period was the small contingent of British and Indian regular troops who, though precluded from sharing in the honours won by their comrades overseas, played a no less efficient and important part in the attainment of the common end by guarding the frontiers of India with a vigilance and devotion to duty which enabled the training of the Territorial units to proceed without interruption and the Indian Army to expand in a measure never before contemplated." Artillery units and one regiment of cavalry were also among the British troops retained.

2nd Battalion

The infantry battalions kept in India during the war, however, served other purposes than garrison duty. Being highly trained troops they were called upon to furnish promising N.C.O.'s for commissions, signallers, etc., for other units.

January, 1915

In January 1915 No. 4 Company left Quetta for a tour of duty in Hyderabad, Sind. They returned in July, having been relieved by A Company.[1] The latter reached Quetta again on 21st October.

The death of Lieut. C. W. H. Swayne is announced on 25th May 1917 at the Station Hospital, Quetta. On 26th July Lewis guns were first issued to the Battalion.

14th December, 1917

On 14th December 1917 the 2nd Battalion left Quetta for Peshawar. The Somersets reached their destination three days later, the strength of the Battalion being then 23 officers and 884 other ranks.

From this date onwards until the end of the war there are only one or two items of interest in the digest which need be recorded. On 9th October 1918 Lieut.-Colonel Platt relinquished command of the 2nd Somersets and Major E. W. Worrall assumed temporary command.

11th November, 1918

The Armistice is referred to in the following manner: "11–11–18. Cessation of hostilities."

The Great War was over without the 2nd Somersets having had an opportunity of showing their fighting qualities, but across the North-West Frontier a storm was brewing and in 1919 the Battalion at last found itself ranged in battle against a hoary enemy—the wily Afghan.

1919

The sequence of events which led up to the outbreak of war between Great Britain and Afghanistan (Third Afghan War, 6th May–8th August 1919) are briefly as follows: Towards the end of April 1919 the Afghan Commander-in-Chief arrived at Dakka with an escort of two companies of infantry and two guns, for the ostensible purpose of inspecting the Afghan frontier. On 3rd May a caravan, accompanied by the usual military escort, proceeding through the Khaiber Pass, was confronted by piquets of armed Afghans on the disputed zone between Tor Kham and Landi Khana. That night five coolies, employed at the waterworks, were killed by tribesmen. On 4th May large numbers of an order (*farman*), signed by the Amir, and concluding with exhortations to make war (*jehad*) were distributed in Peshawar City through the agency of the Afghan Post Office there, and on the same day the Afghan fabrication arrived from Jalalabad with a motor-car laden with leaflets, printed at Kabul, announcing that the Germans had resumed war and that India and Egypt had risen against the British.

3rd May

5th May

On 5th May the Field Army of India received orders for mobilization and on the same day the Peshawar Flying Column[2] (held in readiness always for the purpose of moving instantly to reinforce outlying posts and repel raids)

---

[1] Apparently the designation of companies was changed early in 1915, Nos. 1, 2, 3 and 4 Companies becoming A, B, C and D respectively.

[2] Consisting of one section (2 guns) mountain artillery, one company British infantry, two companies of Indian infantry, with Medical Supply units.

moved to Landi Kotal. With this Column went one officer (Lieut. Lias) 2nd Battalion and 6 signallers of the 2nd Battalion Somerset Light Infantry. On the 6th orders came for the whole Battalion to move to Landi Kotal with the 1st Infantry Brigade. But this order was afterwards countermanded and the Somersets were ordered to move by motor-lorry the following day.

The Somersets received orders to mobilize on 5th May. Mobilization 5th May came at an awkward moment, for demobilization had already commenced, the hot weather was approaching and everything had been made ready for the movement of details to the hills. In spite of these disadvantages, however, equipment and ammunition were drawn and establishments were detailed, fitted and clothed. At 7.45 a.m. the 2nd Somersets [1] (Lieut.-Colonel E. W. Worrall, commanding) left Peshawar in 37 motor-lorries for Landi Kotal. On arrival at the latter place Lieut.-Colonel Worrall assumed command of the Force, the Somersets forming a Perimeter Camp under the walls of Landi Kotal Fort.

The enemy had evidently based his plan of campaign on the co-operation of the frontier tribes, who were expert in all forms of guerrilla warfare, armed with modern rifle and numbering somewhere in the region of 120,000 men. The Afghan plan apparently contemplated operations on three fronts, viz. from Jalalabad on the Khaiber and Mohmand sector, from Gardez on the Kurram and Waziristan border, and from Kandahar on the Chaman border.

In order to counter these operations the British plan was an offensive towards Jalalabad with the main striking force, with the idea of dividing the Mohmands and Afridis (two of the most influential tribes on the North-West Frontier) and cut them off from Afghan influence and support: to strike also at any Afghan concentration within reach and to induce the withdrawal of Afghan forces from the tribal borders elsewhere, for the purpose of covering Kabul. On other portions of the British front an active defence was prepared. The main effort was on the Khaiber front, with Dakka as the first objective.

On arrival at Landi Kotal the troops quickly realized they were on active service, for that night the occasional sharp bark of a rifle at fairly close quarters warned all ranks that Afghan snipers were busy. No casualties were, however, suffered, but the lesson was never forgotten.

At 7 a.m. on 8th Headquarters, B Company and one section mountain battery carried out a reconnaissance to Piquet 4579 and Pizgah. Brigadier-General G. D. Crocker and the 1st Infantry Brigade reached Landi Kotal that day by march from Jamrud. In the evening A Company of the Somersets with 100 rifles piqueted the hill south of the Fort.

A heavy storm broke over Landi Kotal on the night of 8th/9th during which the camp and piquets were again sniped by the Afghans.

At 4.45 a.m. on 9th the Force attacked Afghan regular and irregular troops, 9th May who were holding positions guarding the water supply near Bagh Springs. The 2nd Somersets were in reserve on Suffolk Hill during the engagement, which ended in the defeat of the enemy. At night the Battalion returned to

---

[1] Strength 12 officers, 129 N.C.O.'s, 9 Buglers, and 416 privates, total 566 all ranks.

camp.   A hostile gun fired several rounds into the camp but no casualties were suffered.

On the 10th Suffolk Hill was again piqueted by the Somersets.

On the 11th the 1st and 2nd Brigades attacked the hills round Bagh. In this attack A Company, with details of B, C and D Companies and Headquarters (strength about 300 rifles), with one section No. 263 Company, M.G.C., under Lieut.-Colonel Worrall, took part, C, B, and D Companies, under Major Williams, remaining on piquet. Colonel Worrall's party did not take part in the main attack but, moving out before dawn, piqueted on the left flank of the attack and was engaged all day in beating off snipers and flank attacks by the Afghans. Three men of D Company were killed and Lieut.-Colonel Worrall, with seven other ranks of A and B Companies, wounded. In the evening the Force withdrew to camp, Major Williams assuming temporary command of the Battalion. B, C and D Companies were relieved from piquet and returned to camp.

The 12th May was spent by the Battalion in resting and washing.

On the 13th Dakka was occupied by the 10th Cavalry Brigade and other troops without firing a shot, but the 2nd Somersets did not move from Landi Kotal. The Battalion was ordered to hold itself in readiness to move to Dakka on 14th, but late at night the order was cancelled. Indeed, the Battalion on that date took over another portion of the perimeter and shifted camp. The strength of the 2nd Battalion was now 18 officers and 503 other ranks.

Throughout the 15th May also the Somersets stood fast, but at 6.30 a.m. on 16th set out with other troops on the march to Dakka. For four or five hours in great heat the Battalion was on the road, reaching the village just before noon. The Afghans were already being attacked when the Somersets arrived, but the Battalion was in reserve all day and made no direct assault on the enemy. On reaching Dakka B Company was sent off to piquet the far side of the village and C Company to a sangar on the extreme edge of the perimeter towards the Khaiber Pass. The remainder of the Battalion sangared in the perimeter. All day long the camp was shelled by the enemy and his snipers were extremely active. The Somersets had one man killed and seven others wounded.

The next morning (17th May) at 5.30 a.m. the 1st Brigade attacked the Stonehenge Ridge, west of Dakka, which the Afghans were holding in force with artillery and machine guns.

The initial attack was made by the 15th Sikhs, 35th Sikhs and 1/9th Gurkhas, but was held up. About 1 p.m. the 2/1st Gurkhas, the 1st Yorks and the Howitzers arrived from Landi Kotal and at 2 p.m. the 2nd Somersets were ordered to attack Stonehenge, carrying with them any parties of any units found on the hill.

Covered by the guns and machine-gun fire this attack was launched by A, C and D Companies, B remaining behind in Dakka.

The attack was successful, the Afghans began to evacuate the hill and by 3.45 p.m. the victorious Somersets had reached the crest of the hill: the enemy

had fled.   All three companies then sangared on the hill with four sangars 2nd Battalion
and remained in occupation.   During the night 17th/18th large stores of
material were located by patrols and some abandoned guns were found and
their positions reported to Force Headquarters.

Only six wounded were suffered by the Somersets during the action,
but the heat was intense and several cases of heat exhaustion were reported.
Early next morning the 2nd Battalion was relieved and withdrew to camp at
Dakka.   At 1 p.m. B Company was relieved from piquet duty in Dakka
village and just before 6 p.m. the whole Battalion moved to Camp Robat, where
a perimeter was dug.

The Somersets now became part of the "Infantry Striking Force" of the
Dakka Force.   The name of the hill they had captured was changed from
Stonehenge Hill to Somerset Hill and formed part of the outer line of piquet
defences.   One of the Afghan captured guns was allotted by the G.O.C. to
the 2nd Somersets who made an official claim for it as a trophy of war.

Following the successful action of 17th May the main Afghan Army
dispersed and for the time being practically ceased to exist as an organized
force.

After the operations, terminating on 17th May, and up to the evacuation
of Afghan territory and the return to Peshawar on 13th September, there was
very little fighting of any sort on the Dakka front.   The Force (of which the
2nd Somersets continued to form part) was situated in a standing camp protected by piquet positions on the surrounding hills.   These positions were
held by units in turn.   Occasionally the Battalion was employed on foraging
expeditions, but these ceased in July.   The camp was subjected to sniping
fire from tribesmen on the left bank of the river and this was never frustrated:
it is part of life on the frontier.   Very few casualties were, however, inflicted
by snipers.   From time to time weak attacks were made on the outer line of
piquet positions, but they were easily beaten off and the tribesmen dispersed as
quickly as they had assembled.

The heat throughout the summer was intense but the nights were fortunately cool.   Dust storms were frequent.   Considering the severe climatic
conditions through which the Battalion passed, the health of all ranks was
good.   When not occupying piquet positions the Somersets were employed
in various camp fatigues and in training, but no work was carried out between
the hours of 10 a.m. and 6 p.m. on account of the heat.

Changes in the command of the Battalion took place during the time at
Dakka.   On 31st May Lieut.-Colonel W. N. S. Alexander, Connaught 31st May
Rangers, arrived and assumed command vice Lieut.-Colonel E. W. Worrall,
wounded.   On 18th August Lieut.-Colonel C. A. Williams took over command
from Lieut.-Colonel Alexander.

The 2nd Somersets marched out of Dakka to Landi Kotal on 8th September
1919, *en route* for Peshawar.   On the 10th they moved to Ali Musjia, on the 8th September
11th to Jamrud and on 13th reached Peshawar.

CONCLUSION

THE pages of this History show well how splendidly the Somerset Light Infantry served their King and Country throughout the long years of the Great War. Their dogged perseverance (ever a dominant feature in the character of the West Countryman from the days of Francis Drake), their tenacity and fine courage, were clearly demonstrated in the truly titanic struggles through which they passed. In the long line of trenches, in fair weather or foul, in France and Flanders, on the sandy plains and in the rocky hills of Palestine, in the torrid heat or Mesopotamia, amidst the snowy wastes of Northern Russia, and lastly in the wild and lawless country which bounds the north-west frontier of India, Somerset men gave their lives most nobly not only as a sacrifice to their country but that Right might triumph over Wrong. They fought Germans and Turks and Bolsheviks, Arabs and Afghans, and had beaten them not once, nor twice, but again and again. They gave hard knocks and took them too, as all good soldiers should.

In his final despatch from France and Flanders, Sir Douglas Haig pays the following fine tribute to the troops under his command: "In our admiration for this outstanding achievement, the long years of patient and heroic struggle, by which the strength and spirit of the enemy were gradually broken down, cannot be forgotten. The strain of those years was never ceasing, the demands they made upon the best of the Empire's manhood are now known. Yet throughout all these years, and amid the hopes and disappointments they brought with them, the confidence of our troops in final victory never wavered. Their courage and resolution rose superior to every test, their cheerfulness never failing however terrible the conditions in which they lived and fought. By the long road they trod with so much faith and with such devoted and self-sacrificing bravery we have arrived at victory." These things were true not only of the soldiers of the Empire in France and Flanders, but in all the theatres of war where British soldiers met the enemy.

There remains little more to be said. The 1st Somersets did not form part of the Army of Occupation in Germany, but remained in France and Belgium. The Battalion, after the Armistice, was billeted in Curgies, a few miles from Valenciennes, and later at Haine St. Pierre and Binche in Belgium, returning to England as a cadre about the middle of June 1919.

The 1/4th Somersets, shortly after the Armistice, moved down to Baghdad from Tekrit, thence to Mirjanna. Here demobilization began, and when reduced to cadre strength the Battalion proceeded to Basra, arriving there on 15th March 1919. The cadre arrived at Plymouth on 2nd May and, proceeding immediately to Bath, received a great welcome from that City.

The 2/4th Somersets was the only battalion of the Regiment to join the Army of Occupation in Germany. When the Armistice came into Force the Battalion was at Wevelghem in Belgium. In January 1919 the 2/4th pro-

A PRIVATE SOLDIER IN MARCHING ORDER—
GREAT WAR PERIOD

ceeded to join the Army of Occupation and were stationed first at Bonn and then at Troisdorf. Eventually the time came for demobilization and all men who could not be demobilized were transferred to the 15th Hants and the cadre left for England, disembarking at Tilbury on 27th May 1919. The cadre arrived in Bath on 2nd June and were accorded a welcome no less enthusiastic than that accorded the 1/4th.

The 1/5th Somersets after the Armistice moved back to the Suez Canal and for several weeks were engaged in quelling Nationalist riots which had broken out in Egypt. On 28th March 1919 the Battalion left Cairo for Wastra, where work on the railway was begun. Trouble with the natives at Shobak el Gaffara, which ended in five of the latter being shot, kept the 1/5th on garrison duty in the disturbed area during April, but at the end of that month, the riots having subsided, the Battalion moved back to Cairo and thence to Suez. On 25th December the cadre of the Battalion sailed from Alexandria, reaching Plymouth on 6th January 1920. Late that night the cadre reached Taunton after an absence of five years overseas.

The 2/5th Somersets, who were stationed in India throughout the War, had led a disturbed existence from 1917, quelling riots in the Arrah and Gaya districts round Dinapore. In 1918 the forces of the Barrackpore detachment prevented some minor disturbances in Calcutta from developing into serious riots. After the Armistice Battalion Headquarters moved from Dinapore to Calcutta, and towards the end of 1919 the cadre returned to England: on 25th February 1920 the 2/5th were officially disbanded.

The 6th Somersets, which at the Armistice were at Broyelles, moved to Rumes on 15th November, and to Bersee where the remainder of November and the whole of December were spent. The Battalion returned to England in 1919 for disbandment.

The 7th Battalion, who had reached Feignes near Maubeuge on 11th November 1918, concentrated with 20th Divisional troops in the district round Marieux on 2nd December. Demobilization began in January 1919 and the 20th Division ceased to exist as a fighting force. In March the Division was at cadre strength, the cadre of the 7th Somersets returning to Taunton for final disbandment on 9th June 1919.

The 8th Battalion, which had reached Caudry on 11th November, billeted there until the morning of 1st December and then moved to Haussy and Orsinval, remaining at the latter place until 13th. From Orsinval the Battalion moved to several places—Sous les Bois, Grand Reng, Binche, Courcelles and Frasnes-lez-Grosselies, where Christmas Day was spent. Demobilization had already begun and early in 1919 the cadre returned to England for disbandment.

In the neighbourhood of Pecq and Trieu de Wasmes the 11th Somersets were billeted until 16th November. On the latter date a move was made to Seclin, south of Lille. Several more moves followed, the final billeting place of the Battalion being Les Attagues, near Calais. The 11th returned to England and were disbanded about the middle of 1919.

The 12th Somersets, who on the 11th November were on the road to Escalette when the Armistice was announced, marched on to Ollignies and took part in a peace celebration, the Burgomaster presenting the Battalion with a Belgian flag, which now rests in St. Mary's Church, Taunton.   It was not, however, until the middle of June 1919 that the Somerset Yeomen were reduced to cadre strength and returned to England.   The cadre reached Taunton on 21st June and received a great welcome from the townspeople as it marched through the streets behind the cadre of the 1st Battalion of the Regiment—a fitting close to a most wonderful period in the history of the Regiment.[1]

A number of officers and men of the Somerset Light Infantry served in North Russia in 1919, with the Relief Force.   The original intention was to send out a Company of Somersets, but this was abandoned and those of the Regiment who went to Russia were merged in the 2nd Bn. Hampshire Regt.—a Composite Battalion formed of officers and men from many Regiments.

LT.-GEN. SIR WALTER P. BRAITHWAITE, K.C.B.

APPENDIX A (1)

MENTION IN DESPATCHES

The rank is given as stated in the *Gazette*; in the case of more than one Mention the highest rank is given and the number of Mentions is inserted in brackets.

ALL RANKS

Allfrey, Major H. I. R., D.S.O., M.C. (6)
Andrews, Sergt. H., attached Signal Service.
Anglin, Sergt. J.
Archer, Sergt. W. E.
Armstrong, 2nd Lieut. H. L.
Atwell, Lce. Corpl. A. G.

Baily, Major E. M.
Baker, Sergt. A.
Baker, 2nd Lieut. J.
Baker, Pte. W. B.
Bally, Major E. D.
Barrett, 2nd Lieut. J. W.
Barrington, Co-Sergt-Major E.
Barnes, Lce. Corpl. F.
Barnes, Sergt. L., D.C.M.
Barry, Major A. P. (2)
Beard, Sergt. E.
Beaver, Sergt. G. H.
Bellew, Major F. D., D.S.O., M.C. (4)
Bennett, Pte. F.
Bennett, Lieut. R. H. E., M.C. (2)
Birkett, 2nd Lieut. C. E. W., attached King's Royal Rifle Corps.
Bishop, Lieut. G. W. R., attached Dorset Regiment.
Black, Captain J. N.
Blake, Captain A. L.
Blood, Pte. E. A., attached Royal Army Ordnance Corps.
Boldero, Major A. G.
Bond, Co-Sergt-Major A. H. (3)

Bond, Co-Sergt-Major J.
Bond, 2nd Lieut. W. H. (2)
Boucher, 2nd Lieut. H. M.
Bowker, Major W. J., D.S.O.
Bradford, Lieut. W. G.
Braithwaite, 2nd Lieut. V. A. (2)
Braithwaite, Major-General Sir W. P., K.C.B. (9)
Bridge, Pte. S.
Broadmead, Lieut. H. H.
Brodie-Innes, 2nd Lieut. I. S.
Brown, 2nd Lieut. A. E.
Brown, Sergt. F., attached Local Resources.
Browne, Major H. H. G. (2)
Bull, Sergt. F. T.
Bullen, Major T., attached Royal Flying Corps and Royal Air Force.
Bullen, 2nd Lieut. T. F., attached Royal Flying Corps and Royal Air Force.
Bullock, 2nd Lieut. J., attached Royal Flying Corps and Royal Air Force.
Burges-Short, Major H. G. R.
Burgess, Corpl. H., attached Local Resources.
Butler, Captain P. F.

Caillard, Lieut. F. C. V. D.
Calver, Sergt. B. J.
Capel, Lieut. A. J. attached Royal Flying Corps. (2)
Cavill, Pte. C. J.

Chamberlain, Sergt. E.
Champion, Pte. W. B.
Chanell, Lce. Corpl. S.
Chappell, Corpl. H. J.
Chappell, Lieut. P. E. E., D.C.M.
Chislett, Corpl. G.
Clarke, Sergt. E. C.
Cleall, Pte. J.
Cleator, Sergt. A. W.
Coleman, Pte. W.
Compton, Lieut-Colonel C. W., C.M.G. (5)
Conduit, Pte. J. G.
Cook, Sergt. J. W.
Cooke-Hurle, Lieut-Colonel E. F.
Cooley, Lce. Corpl. J. J.
Cooper, Lce. Corpl. A.
Coradine, Lieut. A. J. B.
Cornish, Pte. A. V.
Couchman, Colonel G. H. H., D.S.O.
Cousins, Qr. Mr. and Hon. Captain G.
Cox, Pte. C. R.
Cox, Lce. Sergt. F. J.
Cox, Lieut.-Colonel W. C.
Cridge, Corpl. W. E.
Croker, Pte. W.
Currie, Bt. Lieut-Colonel R. A. M., D.S.O. (8)
Curtis, Co-Qr-Mr-Sergt. H. P.

Daly, Corpl. E.
Day, Co-Qr-Mr-Sergt. F. E.
Delamere, Sergt. H.
Deverell, Pte. T. H.
Dillon, Sergt. R.
Doel, Co-Sergt-Major H. H.
Doran, Pte. J.
Dudley, 2nd Lieut. H. E.
Dulborough, Sergt. J.
Durrant, Pte. H.
Dyer, Sergt. R.

Eatwell, Pte. A. G.
Eatwell, Sergt. F. E.
Elger, Major E. G., D.S.O. (2)
Elgey, Sergt. P. T.

Elliott, Lce. Sergt. W. H.
England, Pte. B.
England, Lce. Corpl. G.
Eno, Sergt. H., attached Dorset Regiment.
Erskine, 2nd Lieut. R.
Evans, Co-Qr-Mr-Sergt. D. W.
Everett, Colonel Sir H. J., K.C.M.G., C.B. (6)

Fear, Sergt. W. F.
Field, Lieut. R. E.
Flay, Co-Sergt-Major W. J.
Fleming, Bt. Lieut-Colonel G., D.S.O. (4)
Ford, Lieut. H. A. de F., attached Royal Warwickshire Regiment.
Fox, Captain F. E.
Frampton, Captain H.
Freestun, Bt. Lieut-Colonel W. H. M., D.S.O. (6)
Frith, Colonel H. C. (2)
Frost, Corpl. L.

Gibbons, Sergt. W. F.
Gilbertson, Captain H. M., Royal Army Medical Corps, attached.
Gilham, Lce. Sergt. T.
Goodland, Captain E. S., M.C. (2)
Goodland, Sergt. H. B.
Gould, Lieut. C. A.
Gratten, Lce. Corpl. F. W.
Greenwood, Pte. J.
Greswell, Lieut. W. T.
Griffiths, Sergt. F.
Gunner, Pte. P.
Guy, Pte. D., attached Royal Army Medical Corps. (2)

Haddon, Lieut. B. L.
Hale, Qr. Mr. and Hon. Lieut. A. J.
Hammond, Sergt. V. E. (2)
Harding, Lieut. A. F.
Hardyman, Lieut-Colonel J. H. M., D.S.O., M.C. (2)

Harford, Captain E. B.
Harington, Lieut. A. J.
Harris, Captain F. J.
Harris, Lieut. P. G. K.
Harrison, Major J. S. N., D.S.O. (3)
Hartnell, Sergt-Major W. G.
Harvey, Pte. G.
Hatt, Captain A. B. (2)
Hawkins, Pte. R.
Hayes, Bugler R. S.
Hayward, Captain C. R.
Hayward, Lieut. K. J., attached Royal Engineers.
Heard, Regtl-Qr-Mr-Sergt. F. W. (2)
Hibbert, Corpl. J.
Hickman, Pte. H. C.
Hiscock, Pte. W. W.
Hobhouse, Captain P. E. (2)
Holme, Captain R. C. L.
Hopkins, Lce. Corpl. J.
Horler, Pte. H. B.
House, Pte. A. G., attached Works.
Howard, Lieut-Colonel L. C. (2)
Howe, Captain W. T. (3)
Hudson, Pte. R. H.
Hughes, Lieut. C. E., attached Royal Air Force.
Hunt, Lieut. W. E., attached Local Resources.
Hunter, Pte. E. W.
Huntingdon, Major R. H.
Hyatt, 2nd Lieut. P. T., attached Labour and Porter Corps. (2)

Jakeman, Sergt. J.
Jennings, Corpl. A. R.
Johnson, Co-Sergt-Major R.
Jones, Corpl. A.
Jones, Lieut. E. P. (2)
Jones, 2nd Lieut. S. W. F.
Jones, Pte. W. F.
Jones-Mortimer, Captain L. A. (2)

Kellett, 2nd Lieut. W.
Kerrison, Pte. W. S. H.
King, Pte. C. W. A.

Lance, 2nd Lieut. E. C. (2)
Lane, 2nd Lieut. H. (2)
Lee, Sergt. G. W.
Lewis, Captain W.
Little, Major C. H., D.S.O. (2)
Long, Pte. F.
Longley, Sergt. W. N.
Lyon, Major E. L., 13th Hussars, attached 7th Bn.

Macey, Regtl-Sergt-Major A.
Mackie, Captain J. B., Political Department.
Mackie, Captain J. R.
Majendie, Captain V. H. B., D.S.O. (4)
Major, Lce. Corpl. T.
Manson, Captain G. P.
Masters, Corpl. W. H.
Millard, Sergt. F. J.
Miles, Captain Sir C. W., Bart., O.B.E.
Miles, Captain W. H.
Milln, Captain K. J.
Minns, Lieut. A.
Mitchell, 2nd Lieut. B. E. F.
Molesworth, Captain G. N.
Montgomery, Captain R. V., M.C. (2)
Moore, Pte. A. W.
Moore, Captain T.
Moore, Lieut. R. L.
Mordaunt, Captain J. F. C., M.C., attached Hampshire Regiment.
Mordaunt, Bt. Lieut-Colonel O. C., D.S.O. (5)
Morgan, 2nd Lieut. A. P.
Moses, Corpl. C. S.
Moss, Co-Sergt-Major W. H.

Neate, Qr. Mr. and Hon. Captain A. (2)
Needham, Corpl. F. J.
Neville, 2nd Lieut. G. H. (2)
Newton, Pte. J.
Newman, Corpl. A. E.

Newman, Corpl. B.
Norman, Co-Qr-Mr-Sergt. E. J.
Norris, Co-Sergt-Major W.

Oliff, Sergt. W.
Osborne, Lieut. L. A., D.S.O., M.C.

Paterson, Major A. W. A.
Paul, 2nd Lieut. E. (2)
Paull, Lieut-Colonel J. R., O.B.E., T.D.
Parsons, Corpl. F.
Pavey, Sergt. S. C.
Peard, Lieut. C. J.
Peard, Lieut. J. C. N.
Peart, Lieut. J. B.
Penny, Lce. Corpl. A.
Perry, Pte. A.
Phillips, Captain A. W.
Phillips, Captain W. E.
Pike, Lieut. H. (2)
Pike, Lce. Corpl. H.
Pointing, Pte. R. H.
Pollock, Lieut-Colonel A. W. A.
Powell, Major E. B., Rifle Brigade, attached.
Pratt, Lieut. G. H.
Precious, Lce. Corpl. D.
Preston, Sergt. J. E.
Preston-Whyte, Major R. P. (4)
Pretyman, Lieut. E. R. (2)
Pretyman, Captain G. F., D.S.O., attached Royal Flying Corps and Royal Air Force (3)
Price, 2nd Lieut. W. A. W.
Prideaux, Lieut. G. A., M.C.
Pring, Lieut. H. O.
Pritchard, Sergt. A.
Proctor, Major J., King's Royal Rifle Corps, attached 4th Bn.
Proctor, 2nd Lieut. J. A.
Prowse, Bt. Lieut-Colonel C. B. (5)

Radford, Lieut. J. A.
Rattray, Captain T. A.
Rawling, Bt. Lieut-Colonel C. G., C.M.G., C.I.E. (5)

Rawlings, Captain G. N.
Ridler, Captain R. H., London Regiment, attached 11th Bn.
Ritchie, Major T. F., D.S.O. (3)
Roche, Captain V. W.
Rockey, Co-Sergt-Major F.
Rodd, Captain E. F. S.
Rogers, 2nd Lieut. S. E.
Romilly, Lieut. H. A.
Rumbold, 2nd Lieut. R. S., attached Royal Flying Corps.
Ryall, Lieut. R. W.

Salisbury, Lce. Sergt. J. S.
Salmon, Co-Sergt-Major J.
Schooling, Qr. Mr. and Hon. Lieut. J. J.
Scott, Lieut-Colonel J. W., D.S.O., Oxfordshire Yeomanry, attached 8th Bn.
Sculthorp, Sergt. A.
Seabright, Corpl. W. (2)
Sheringham, Captain C. J. de B., D.S.O., M.C.
Shortman, Lce. Corpl. R. T., attached Local Resources.
Shufflebotham, Lieut. B. M.
Silcox, Corpl. F.
Smith, Sergt. G. C.
Smith, Major I. M., D.S.O., M.C. (5)
Smith, Sergt. S. W.
Snook, Pte. H.
Snook, Corpl. W. C.
Snow, Major-General Sir T. D'O., K.C.B., K.C.M.G. (6)
Somers-Cocks, Lieut. R.
Sommerville, Captain R. A.
Sorrell, Sergt. A. W.
Squire, Pte. F. F. (2)
Stileman, Lieut. R. F.
Stone, Major N. H.
Street, Lieut. A. R.
Stuart, 2nd Lieut. J.
Sugg, Sergt. E.
Sutton, Bt. Major W. M., M.C. (5)

Tapscott, Corpl. F. W. (2)
Taylor, Pte. J.
Thatcher, 2nd Lieut. C.
Thatcher, Captain R. S., M.C.
Thicknesse, Major J. A. (2)
Thorne, Co-Sergt-Major G.
Thurlow, Bt. Lieut-Colonel E. G. L., D.S.O. (6)
Townsend, Lce. Corpl. W. E.
Tritton, Lieut. L. J.
Troyte-Bullock, Major C.J., D.S.O.(4)
Trump, Sergt. W. A.
Tubbs, Lieut. C. B., M.C.

Urwick, Major F. D., D.S.O.

Vagg, 2nd Lieut. H. R., attached Royal Flying Corps.
Vallis, Lieut. R. W. H.
Vearncombe, Co-Sergt-Major F. J.
Venning, Pte. W. E.
Vernon, Pte. C. H.
Viner, Sergt. H. C.
Vranch, Sergt. E. J.

Waddy, Captain R. H.
Waldron, Pte. S. A.
Wallace, Qr. Mr. and Hon. Lieut. A. D., Royal Scots Fusrs., attached.
Walsh, Major T. A., D.S.O. (2)

Watts, Pte. F. H.
Watts, Captain R. A. B. P.
Watson, Major D. S., T.D.
Watson, Captain W. (2)
Way, Pte. W.
West-Skin, Pte. J.
Weston, Pte. G. T. attached Signal Service.
Whetstone, Lce. Corpl. P.
White, Sergt. G. H.
White, Corpl. S.
Whittle, Pte. C.
Whittuck, Captain G. E. M., M.C.
Wilcox, Corpl. F. (2)
Wilcox, 2nd Lieut. J. J. (2)
Willcox, Sergt. C. (2)
Wild, Lieut. L. T.
Wilkins, Colour-Sergt. L.
Williams, Sergt. E.
Williams, Sergt. T.
Wilson, Major A. E. J., D.S.O. (3)
Wilson, Co-Sergt-Major J. A.
Worthington-Wilmer, Major L. E. C. (3)
Wride, Sergt. F. E.
Wright, Lce. Cpl. F. J.

Yatman, Captain A. H. (4)
Yaw, Co-Sergt-Major R. J.

APPENDIX A (2)

MENTION " B " (FOR RECORD)

Brought to the notice of the Secretary of State for War for valuable services rendered in connection with the War.

Addis, Captain P. E. D., attached Royal Air Force.
Chainey, Sergt. S. W.
Chambers, Sergt-Major G. D.
Copp, Co-Qr-Mr-Sergt. W. J.
Couchman, Colonel G. H. H., D.S.O.
Denning, Sergt-Major T.
Denny, Captain R. B.
Earle, Major F. A., Royal Warwickshire Regiment, attached.
Fox, Major A. B.
Frith, Colonel H. C., C.B.
Garrad, Captain A., attached Royal Air Force.
Hardman, Major H. Fitz W.
Hartnell, Qr-Mr-Sergt., W. G.
Heathcoat-Amory, Lieut-Colonel H. W. L. H.
Hicks, Lieut-Colonel and Hon. Colonel H. E.
Hillman, Captain F., Royal Flying Corps and Somerset Light Infantry.
Husbands, Captain R. G. W.
Jerrard, Major, A. G. A.
Johnstone, Major H. C.
Jones-Mortimer, Major L. A.
Keevil, Sergt. J. J.
Kite, Major H. T.
Llewellyn, Lieut-Colonel A.
Maud, Major W. H., C.M.G.
Milln, Captain K. J.
Milnes, Captain R.
Morgan, Quarter Master and Hon. Captain W. E.
Napier-Clavering, Bt. Colonel C. W.
Power, Lieut. P. D., Special List, attached.
Powis, Quarter Master and Hon. Captain H.
Pulman, 2nd Lieut. W. P.
Sturt, Quarter Master and Hon. Major F.
Swayne, Lieut-Colonel E. H.
Thurlow, Major E. G. L.
Uphill, Qr-Mr-Sergt. A. A.

Vickery, Sergt-Major T.
Walsh, Colonel H. A., C.B.
Williams, Brig-Gen. R. B., C.B.

Brought to the notice of the Government of India for valuable services rendered in India in connection with the War up to 31st December 1918.

Goodland, Captain C. H.
Hood, Quarter Master and Captain T.

APPENDIX B (1)

REWARDS

ALL RANKS

(The ranks shown are those held at the time of award.)

V.C.

Sage, Pte. T. H.

K.C.B.

Braithwaite, Major-General W. P., C.B.

Snow, Major-General T. D'O., C.B.

C.B.

Compton, Lieut-Colonel C. W., C.M.G.

Everett, Colonel H. J.

Frith, Colonel H. C.

Kennedy, Major F. M. E.

K.C.M.G.

Everett, Colonel H. J., C.B.

Snow, Major-General Sir T. D'O., K.C.B.

C.M.G.

Bowker, Major W. J., D.S.O.

Compton, Lieut-Colonel C. W.

Currie, Major and Bt. Colonel R. A. M., D.S.O.

Everett, Colonel H. J., C.B.

Freestun, Bt. Lieut-Colonel W. H. M., D.S.O.

Little, Colonel C. B.

Rawling, Major C. J., C.I.E.

C.B.E.

Jerrard, Lieut-Colonel A. G. A.

O.B.E.

Bally, Major E. D.

Blake, Captain A. L.

Field, Lieut. R. E.

Howe, Captain W. T.

Hyatt, Lieut. P. T.

Miles, Captain Sir C. W., Bart.

Neate, Qr. Mr. and Hon. Captain A.

Paull, Lieut-Colonel J. R.

Pretyman, Major G. F., D.S.O.

Swayne, Lieut-Colonel E. H.

Thatcher, Captain R. S., M.C.

M.B.E.

Campbell, Qr. Mr. and Hon. Lieut. D. G.

Goode, Captain T. C.

Hartnell, Qr. Mr. Sergt. W. G.

Knapp, Lieut. E. C.

Minns, Lieut. A.

Pavey, Lieut. G. P.

Porter, Lieut. E. E., D.C.M.

Romilly, Lieut. H. A., attached Signals.

Stoodley, 2nd Lieut. F.

D.S.O.

Allfrey, Major H. I. R., M.C.

Bellew, Major F. D., M.C.

Browne, Major H. H. G.

Burges-Short, Major H. G. R.

Cooke-Hurle, Lieut-Colonel E. F.

Currie, Major R. A. M.

Fleming, Captain G.

Freestun, Major W. H. M.

Hardyman, Lieut-Colonel J. H. M., M.C.

Harrison, Major J. S. N.

Hayward, Captain C. R.

MAJOR-GEN. SIR HENRY J. EVERETT, K.C.M.G., C.B.

BRIG.-GEN. R. B. WILLIAMS, C.B.

BRIG.-GEN. H. C. FRITH, C.B.

BRIG.-GEN. W. J. BOWKER, C.M.G., D.S.O.

FORMER OFFICERS WHO SERVED AS GENERAL OFFICERS DURING THE GREAT WAR

Howard, Lieut-Colonel L. C.

Hunnybun, Major K., Army Cyclist Corps, attached 7th Bn.

Huntingdon, Captain R. H.

Lance, 2nd Lieut. E. C.

Little, Major C. H., attached Egyptian Army.

Majendie, Captain V. H. B.

Mordaunt, Major O. C.

Osborne, 2nd Lieut. L. A., M.C.

Paterson, Major A. W., attached Royal Irish Fusiliers.

Peard, Captain C. J.

Poole, Major G. S.

Preston-Whyte, Major R. P.

Pretyman, Lieut. G. F.

Prowse, Bt. Lt-Colonel C. B.

Rawling, Major and Bt. Lt-Colonel C. G., C.M.G., C.I.E.

Ridler, Captain R. H., London Regiment, attached 11th Bn.

Ritchie, Major T. F.

Sheringham, Captain C. J. de B., M.C.

Skrine, 2nd Lieut. S. H.

Smith, Major I. M., M.C.

Sutton, Captain and Bt. Major W. M., M.C.

Thurlow, Captain E. G. L.

Troyte-Bullock, Major C. J.

Urwick, Major F. D.

Waddy, Captain R. H.

Walsh, Major T. A., attached Yorkshire Light Infantry.

Watson, Major D. S.

Watts, Captain R. A. P. B.

Wilson, Major A. E. J.

Withers, 2nd Lieut. F. D.

Yatman, Major and Bt. Lt-Colonel A. H.

Bar to D.S.O.

Walsh, Major T. A., D.S.O., attached Yorkshire Light Infantry.

D.F.C.

Munden, Lieut. H. W., attached Royal Air Force.

A.F.C.

Pretyman, Major E. R., attached Royal Air Force.

M.C.

Akerman, 2nd Lieut. J. P.

Allfrey, Captain H. I. R.

Austin, Lieut. H. K.

Baker, 2nd Lieut. F. H.

Baker, Lieut. H. G.

Baker, 2nd Lieut. J., attached Manchester Regiment.

Baker, 2nd Lieut. W. G.

Barlow, 2nd Lieut. F. C.

Bellew, Captain F. D.

Bennett, Lieut. R. H. E.

Betteley, 2nd Lieut. W. L.

Birkett, 2nd Lieut. C. E. W.

Blaine, Captain G.

Blenkiron, 2nd Lieut. A. V., attached Royal Flying Corps.

Bond, Lieut. W. H.

Boucher, Lieut. H. M.

Braithwaite, 2nd Lieut. V. A.

Brooks, 2nd Lieut. H.

Brown, 2nd Lieut. A. E.

Brown, 2nd Lieut. W. R. H.

Caillard, Lieut. F. C. V. D.

Carter, 2nd Lieut. E. L.

Cartwright, Lieut. E. C.

Cecil-Smith, 2nd Lieut. R. P.

Chichester, Lieut. R. A. A.

Child, Captain A., London Regiment, attached.

Church, Co-Sergt-Major E.

Clarke, Lieut. G. P.

Clive, Lieut. R.

Cockburn, Lieut. E., Liverpool Regt., attached.

Cook, 2nd Lieut. H. C.

Cooksley, 2nd Lieut. F. R.
Corballis, 2nd Lieut. B. J.
Cridland, 2nd Lieut. B. E.
Curtis, 2nd Lieut. W. S. C., attached
Royal Fusiliers.

Dickinson, Lieut. S. J.
Dommett, 2nd Lieut. J. A.
Drake, 2nd Lieut. R. G. C.

Edbrook, Lieut. E. F.
Edwards, Captain D. C. H.

Fellowes, Lieut. H. G. A., 11th King
Edward's Own Lancers, attached
1st Bn.
Foley, Lieut. H. A.
Ford, 2nd Lieut. L. N.
Frampton, Captain H.
Franks, 2nd Lieut. H., Yorks &
Lancs Regt., attached.

Gegg, 2nd Lieut. J. H. B.
Giles, Co-Sergt-Major W.
Goode, 2nd Lieut. J. H.
Goodland, Lieut. E. S.
Gough, Lieut. D. L.
Gould, Lieut. C. A.
Greetham, Lieut. G. C. V.

Hall, 2nd Lieut. A. H.
Harding, Lieut. A. F.
Hardyman, Lieut. J. H. M.
Harington, Lieut. A. J.
Harris, Lieut. P. G. K.
Hatt, Lieut. A. B.
Hawkins, Lieut. W.
Hill, 2nd Lieut. J. H.
Hinton, Lieut. F. G.
Holme, Lieut. R. C. L.
Holt, Captain B., Army Service Corps,
attached.
Humphreys, Lieut. F. C.
Hunt, 2nd Lieut. H. J.
Hunt, Lieut. L. W., attached Lan-
cashire Fusiliers.

Jenkins, 2nd Lieut. O. W.
Jenne, 2nd Lieut. T. G.
Johnson, Co-Sergt-Major T. J.
Jocelyne, 2nd Lieut. L. A.

Knight, 2nd Lieut. S. H.

Lane, Lieut. H.
Leacroft, Captain G. C. R.
Leversha, Lieut. R. J.
Lewin, 2nd Lieut. C. J.

Madden, 2nd Lieut. C. H.
Male, Sergt-Major W.
Mann, 2nd Lieut. D., attached Ma-
chine Gun Corps.
Mann, 2nd Lieut. D. B. U.
Manson, Captain G. P.
Marshall, Lieut. E. W.
Millar, Lieut. R. M., attached Sig-
nals.
Mitchell, 2nd Lieut. B. E. F.
Montgomery, Captain R. V.
Mordaunt, Captain J. F. C.

Neville, 2nd Lieut. G. H.

Osborne, 2nd Lieut. L. A.
Owen, 2nd Lieut. A. C.

Paul, Regtl-Sergt-Major E.
Peard, Lieut. J. C. N.
Peppin, Co-Sergt-Major T.
Pople, 2nd Lieut. H. A.
Price, 2nd Lieut. H. A., attached
Machine Gun Corps.
Price, 2nd Lieut. T. S., South Wales
Borderers, attached.
Price, Sergt-Major W.
Prideaux, Lieut. G. A.
Prince, Lieut. E. M.
Pring, Lieut. H. O.

Radford, Lieut. J. A.
Rattray, Captain T. A.
Ridge, Lieut. G. T.

Saunders, Captain M. K. F.
Savory, 2nd Lieut. G. A. D. L.

Schooling, Qr. Mr. and Hon. Lieut. J. J.
Scott, Lieut. J.
Sheringham, Captain C. J. de B.
Shillson, 2nd Lieut. A. R.
Shore, 2nd Lieut. M. F., attached Machine Gun Corps.
Sims, 2nd Lieut. G. H.
Skrine, 2nd Lieut. H. S., attached Trench Mortar Battery.
Smith, Captain I. M.
Smith, Captain J. E. G.
Somers-Cocks, Lieut. R.
Sommerville, Captain R. A.
Spark, Lieut. D. S.
Strachey, Lieut. R. C.
Sutton, Captain W. M.
Sylvester, Lieut. P. J.

Tarbit, Lieut. J., King's Royal Rifle Corps, attached.
Tawney, 2nd Lieut. R. L.
Taylor, 2nd Lieut. L. B.
Thatcher, Captain R. S.
Thomson, Lieut. C. G., West Somerset Yeomanry, attached.
Timms, Captain A. S.
Trent, 2nd Lieut. R. T. J., attached Welsh Regiment.
Tubbs, 2nd Lieut. C. B.
Turner, 2nd Lieut. J. T.

Whall, Captain W. E.
Wheeler, Captain A. H.
Whittuck, Captain G. E. M.
Wilcox, 2nd Lieut. J. J.
Wilde, 2nd Lieut. H., South Lancashire Regiment, attached.
Willis, 2nd Lieut. H. B., attached Hampshire Regiment.
Wilson, Co-Sergt-Major J. A.
Withers, 2nd Lieut. F. D.
Wood, 2nd Lieut. G. H., attached Norfolk Regiment.
Wright, Lieut. C. W. G.
Wright, Captain E. G. E.

Bar to M.C.

Brooks, 2nd Lieut. H., M.C.
Boyes, 2nd Lieut. N. F., M.C.

Caillard, Lieut. F. C. V. D., M.C.
Chichester, Lieut. R. A. A., M.C.

Harington, Lieut. A. J., M.C.
Harris, Captain P. G. K., M.C.
Hill, 2nd Lieut. J. H., M.C.

Lane, Captain H., M.C., attached Tank Corps.

Leversha, Lieut. R. J., M.C.

Madden, 2nd Lieut. C. H., M.C.

Paul, Lieut. E., D.C.M., M.C.

Scott, Captain J., M.C.
Sims, Lieut. G. H., M.C.

Whittuck, Captain G. E. M., M.C.

D.C.M.

Allsopp, Lce. Corpl. A., attached Royal Engineers.
Archer, Sergt. W.
Atherton, Lce. Corpl. W. J. R.

Baker, Co-Sergt-Major E.
Baker, Pte. R. G. K.
Bamford, Lce. Corpl. H. J.
Bancroft, Lce. Sergt. J. E.
Barnes, Sergt. L.
Barrett, Bandsman W.
Bartlett, Sergt. T.
Bawden, Sergt. H. G.
Beale, Pte. A. G.
Betty, Sergt. W. J.
Black, Lce. Sergt. J.
Bowdidge, Lce. Corpl. J. S.
Bozzard, Lce. Corpl. G. W. T.
Brake, Co-Sergt-Major E.
Bryant, Sergt. W. G.
Bulson, Sergt. H. S.
Burge, Sergt. B.
Buss, Sergt-Major C. H.

Chappell, Co-Sergt-Major P. E. E.
Cleal, Lce. Corpl. C.
Coles, Sergt. A. J.
Cook, Co-Sergt-Major A. H.
Cooper, Regtl-Qr. Mr. Sergt. A. G.
Cornwell, Sergt. H.
Cox, Corpl. E. A. E.
Cox, Corpl. F. J., M.M.
Coxon, Sergt. J. W.
Crocker, Sergt. B.
Cross, Sergt. T.

Dare, Pte. D. H.
Davis, Co-Sergt-Major F.
Davis, Sergt. W.
Dolling, Pte. F.
Durman, Corpl. W. J.
Dyer, Sergt. E.

Eno, Sergt. H., attached Dorset Regiment.
Evans, Pte. H. J.

Fenwick, Corpl. A. L.
Field, Sergt. T.
Frampton, Lce. Corpl. A. T.
Francis, Lce. Corpl. H. J.

Gane, Corpl. G. C.
Gay, Corpl. S. E.
Gibbs, Lce. Corpl. A. J. H.
Goloska, Qr. Mr. Sergt. J.
Gregory, Corpl. F.
Gunner, Lce. Corpl. P.

Hawkins, Pte. E. E.
Hayden, Corpl. W.
Hedley, Lce. Sergt. W.
Henman, Co-Sergt-Major W.
Hillier, Lce. Corpl. A. J.
Hobbs, Lce. Corpl. G. W. A.
Horler, Qr. Mr. Sergt. T.
Howse, Corpl. F. W. F.
Hughes, Pte. R. J.

Isaacs, Sergt. A.

James, Sergt. H. W. P.
Jefferies, Pte. A. F.
Jenkins, Pte. G.
Jenner, Sergt. T.
Johnston, Co-Sergt-Major R.
Jones, Corpl. W.
Jordan, Sergt. W. H., M.M.
Joyce, Sergt. F.

Keith, Sergt. E.
Kell, Pte. J., attached Royal Engineers.
Killen, Pte. T.
King, Sergt. C. L.
Knight, Corpl. G. T.

Mildon, Co-Sergt-Major J. E.
Miller, Pte. J.
Miller, Pte. J. J.
Mounty, Sergt. J. E.
Muddle, Pte. H. G.

Newbery, Lce. Corpl. F.
Newman, Sergt. B.

Osborne, Pte. T.

Pagington, Pte. E.
Passmore, Lce. Sergt. W.
Paul, Regtl-Sergt-Major E.
Perry, Sergt. R. A.
Phippen, Co-Sergt-Major F. H.
Prince, Pte. R. L.

Radford, Sergt. G.
Rawlings, Sergt. S. G.
Rogers, Sergt. V.
Rousey, Corpl.
Rumley, Pte. N. E.

Salter, Pte. F.
Saunders, Pte. W.
Shortman, Sergt. J.
Simpson, Lce. Corpl. H. W.
Spratt, Lce. Corpl. C.
Stebbing, Corpl. W.

Taylor, Pte. B. A.
Tobin, Sergt. W. J.

Towler, Lce. Sergt. S. J. W.
Trenchard, Sergt. S.
Trott, Sergt. A. J.
Tucker, Corpl. G. F.

Venn, Corpl. W. J. D.
Viner, Sergt. H. C.

Walrond, Corpl. G.
Ward, Lce. Corpl. C.
Warfield, Corpl. E. J.
Watkins, Lce. Corpl. W. V.
Webb, Corpl. H. W.
Webb, Sergt. M.
Wells, Sergt. F.
Wilcox, Corpl. F.
Wilcox, Pte. L. N.
Willcox, Sergt. C.
Williams, Pte. A.
Williams, Sergt. E.
Willson, Sergt. J. H.
Wiltshire, Sergt. W.
Windows, Co-Sergt-Major W. C.

Yaw, Co-Sergt-Major R. J.

Bar to D.C.M.
Killen, Pte. T., D.C.M.

M.M.
Adams, Pte. A.
Adams, Pte. W. J.
Amery, Sergt. T.
Anderson, Sergt. J. A.
Arnold, Pte. T.
Arnold, Sergt. W. E.
Arscott, Co-Qr. Mr. Sergt. H.
Arthurs, Pte. G.

Bagwell, Sergt. H. J.
Baker, Sergt. A.
Baker, Pte. A.
Baker, Pte. F.
Baker, Pte. G.
Baker, Pte. H.
Ballantyne, Lce. Corpl. J. T.
Barrow, Pte. C.

Bawden, Pte. V. H.
Beare, Pte. F. C.
Beaver, Sergt. G. H.
Beer, Pte. E. K.
Bemand, Lce. Corpl. H.
Bethel, Pte. C.
Biddicombe, Corpl. A.
Bide, Corpl. W. A.
Biggs, Pte. J. J.
Bird, Corpl. W. E.
Biss, Co-Sergt-Major H. C.
Blake, Pte. W. T.
Bolwell, Sergt. A.
Bond, Lce. Sergt. E. G. S.
Bough, Pte. H.
Bradbury, Pte. W. G.
Braddick, Pte. H. C.
Bradfield, Pte. E. E.
Bridge, Pte. F. W.
Bridges, Pte. T.
Brimble, Pte. W. G.
Bristow, Sergt. J.
Britton, Lce. Corpl. R. S.
Broman, Pte. A. J.
Brown, Pte. P.
Buckley, Co-Sergt-Major D. C.
Burridge, Pte. J.
Burroughs, Pte. J.
Butler, Sergt. S. R.
Buttle, Pte. T.
Bryan, Lce. Corpl. R. H.

Cainey, Lce. Sergt. H.
Callan, Pte. P.
Carruthers, Pte. W.
Carter, Pte. A.
Carter, Corpl. C.
Channing, Sergt. E.
Chapman, Corpl. A. H.
Chislett, Corpl. F.
Clarke, Lce. Corpl. A. E.
Clennen, Corpl. O. T.
Clifford, Corpl. W.
Coggins, Lce. Corpl. C.
Collard, Sergt. G.

Collins, Sergt. G. J.
Cook, Co-Sergt-Major A. H.
Coombes, Pte. W.
Coombs, Sergt. H. G.
Coran, Pte. W. J.
Cornelius, Pte. H. P.
Cornwell, Sergt. H.
Cope, Sergt. B.
Councill, Pte. A.
Cousins, Lce. Corpl. F.
Cox, Corpl. C. H.
Cox, Corpl. F. J.
Coxswell, Sergt. R. S.
Creech, Pte. B.
Crew, Sergt. A. E.
Cridland, Pte. W.
Crockford, Lce. Corpl. J.
Cullen, Lce. Corpl. P.
Curley, Pte. W. H.

Damarell, Pte. G.
Dane, Lce. Corpl. G.
Davis, Lce. Corpl. F.
Davis, Pte. G.
Day, Co-Qr-Mr-Sergt. F. E.
Deadman, Pte. W.
Denman, Pte. G.
Denney, Sergt. W. E.
Derrick, Pte. H. A.
Dillon, Sergt. T.
Dixon, Lce. Corpl. J.
Doe, Qr. Mr. Sergt. P.
Dolman, Sergt. R.
Donovan, Pte. A. G.
Duley, Lce. Corpl. A.
Durston, Sergt. F.
Durston, Pte. G.
Dutch, Pte. J. H.
Dyer, Pte. D. S.

Edmonds, Sergt. J.
Edwards, Pte. V. M.
Elliott, Lce. Corpl. W. H.
Elworthy, Pte. E.
English, Lce. Sergt. W. J.
Eno, Pte. H.

Evans, Pte. T. R.
Evis, Lce. Corpl. B.

Feltham, Pte. F.
Ferguson, Pte. A.
Ffitch, Pte. M.
Fleming, Pte. H. O.
Flower, Lce. Corpl. W.
Ford, Pte. E. B.
Ford, Pte. P.
Fowler, Corpl. F.
Frankcom, Sergt. S.
Friday, Corpl. C. St. C.
Fry, Pte. A. W.
Fryer, Pte. A. H.
Fussell, Pte. C. H.

Gardner, Pte. C. W. E.
Garland, Pte. H.
Garland, Lce. Corpl. W.
Geach, Corpl. W. A.
George, Lce. Corpl. E.
Gibbings, Pte. J. W. C.
Gibson, Pte. L. A. G.
Giles, Pte. G. S.
Gillard, Pte. E. E.
Gillett, Corpl. W.
Goodall, Sergt. F. E. J.
Goodhind, Sergt. W.
Gooding, Pte. A.
Greedy, Pte. B.
Gregory, Pte. S.
Green, Lce. Corpl. H. G.
Greenway, Pte. J. A.
Grice, Sergt. A. L.
Griffin, Lce. Corpl. A. E. C.

Hames, Pte. C. B.
Handy, Corpl. W. J.
Hansford, Sergt. S.
Harcombe, Sergt. J. D.
Harman, Pte. W. G.
Harrison, Lce. Corpl. G.
Hawkes, Lce. Corpl. R.
Hawkins, Pte. E. E.
Hawkins, Pte. J.

Haysham, Pte. E.
Hayward, Corpl. W. J.
Heal, Pte. F. C.
Heal, Pte. F. S. G.
Heard, Pte. J.
Hedges, Pte. B.
Hedley, Sergt. W.
Henderson, Sergt. R.
Hendy, Pte. E.
Hennessy, Sergt. P.
Herbert, Pte. E. W.
Hext, Pte. S.
Hibbard, Pte. B.
Hill, Lce. Corpl. A. A.
Hill, Pte. H. J.
Hill, Pte. G.
Hill, Pte. M.
Hill, Pte. R. V. E.
Hillier, Sergt. W. H.
Hippesley, Pte. A.
Hodges, Pte. W. J.
Hogg, Lce. Corpl. S.
Holder, Pte. C. T.
Holder, Sergt. W.
Holley, Lce. Sergt. E.
Holmes, Pte. W.
Hood, Sergt. J.
Hookings, Lce. Corpl. E.
Hooper, Pte. J.
Hooper, Pte. J. C.
Hopkins, Pte. C. J.
Horn, Corpl. R. H. W.
Horsey, Lce. Corpl. R. G.
Horwood, Sergt. F.
Hucker, Lce. Corpl. W. T.
Hughes, Pte. P.
Hurley, Lce. Sergt. A.
Hussey, Pte. W.

Imber, Sergt. S.

Jackson, Corpl. W.
James, Pte. A.
Jennings, Corpl. A. R.
Johnson, Pte. F. C.
Jones, Corpl. F. G.

Jones, Pte. J. E.
Jones, Corpl. J. R.
Jones, Pte. W.
Jordan, Corpl. W. H.
Jouxson, Lce. Corpl. E. W.
Jupp, Pte. J. R.

Kerr, Pte. J. W.
King, Pte. F. J.

Lacey, Corpl. E. H.
Lack, Pte. F.
Lambert, Sergt. G. H. G.
Lambley, Sergt. T.
Lancaster, Pte. F.
Langley, Pte. F. E.
Laverack, Pte. G.
Laws, Pte. J.
Leach, Corpl. W. A.
Lee, Sergt. G. W.
Lee, Lce. Corpl. W.
Lewins, Lce. Corpl. T.
Lewis, Pte. T.
Leydon, Sergt. G. J.
Lindsay, Pte. I. W.
Lippett, Pte. E.
Lockyer, Pte. H. J.
Long, Pte. A. G.
Long, Pte. J.
Loveridge, Pte. T. G.
Luton, Lce. Corpl. W. A.

Marley, Corpl. J. G.
Marshall, Sergt. A. H.
Martin, Pte. A. H.
Martin, Sergt. S. J.
Marvin, Sergt. A. F.
Maskell, Pte. A.
Maunder, Sergt. J.
Maunder, Lce. Corpl. W. R.
May, Corpl. R.
Measures, Sergt. J.
Meddick, Pte. W. H.
Miles, Pte. G. A.
Millard, Pte. E.
Mitchell, Pte. H.

Moir, Sergt. R.
Moore, Pte. A. S.
Moore, Corpl. E.
Moore, Corpl. G. M.
Moore, Pte. L.
Moreman, 2nd Class Air Mechanic S.,
    R.F.C., late Som. L.I.
Morris, Pte. A. J.
Morris, Sergt. W.
Moss, Co-Sergt-Major W. H.
Mulliss, Lce. Corpl. H. R.

Nelson, Lce. Sergt. J. E.
North, Pte. M. W. W.
Norris, Co-Sergt-Major W.
Norman, Lce. Sergt. H. G.
Nutt, Lce. Sergt. W.

Oakham, Pte. E.
Overd, Pte. H.

Paine, Pte. R.
Parker, Pte. W.
Parker, Sergt. W. E.
Parrish, Pte. T. W.
Parsons, Pte. W. G.
Pascoe, Pte. R.
Pavey, Pte. J. H.
Peppin, Sergt. J. B.
Percival, Corpl. F. E.
Perkins, Sergt. A. J.
Petvin, Pte. E. V.
Phillips, Pte. W. H.
Phippen, Sergt. L.
Pickford, Pte. J. J.
Pike, Lce. Corpl. H. J.
Pitman, Sergt. J.
Pocock, Sergt. H.
Powell, Sergt. J.
Powell, Pte. W. H.
Prior, Lce. Corpl. T. B.
Proll, Lce. Corpl. J.
Protheroe, Pte. J.
Prout, Pte. A.
Prout, Lce. Corpl. G.
Prowse, Pte. H. W.

Pugh, Pte. G.
Pyrmont, Sergt. H.

Raffill, Pte. J. W.
Rawles, Pte. S.
Rawlings, Sergt. S. G.
Reavley, Sergt. W.
Redford, Corpl. F.
Reed, Pte. W. J.
Ridout, Pte. E.
Roberts, Pte. T. J.
Robey, Pte. A. H.
Rogers, Pte. A. G.
Rogers, Sergt. B.
Rose, Corpl. J. A.
Rouse, Pte. V.
Rowland, Pte. P.
Rowles, Pte. J. E.
Rowley, Pte. A.
Rowley, Pte. W.
Rowsell, Pte. H. J.
Russell, Lce. Sergt. H. H.

Salisbury, Sergt. J. S.
Saunders, Pte. E.
Scott, Sergt. W.
Sculthorp, Sergt. A.
Seabrook, Corpl. E. A.
Sellick, Pte. G.
Sellick, Pte. W.
Shore, Pte. J.
Sibley, Lce. Corpl. T.
Simmons, Pte. F. W.
Slack, Pte. F. E.
Slade, Pte. S. W.
Smart, Pte. G.
Smith, Sergt. C. F.
Smith, Pte. G. H.
Smith, Corpl. H.
Smith, Pte. J.
Smith, Pte. J. P.
Smith, Pte. R. F.
Smith, Pte. W. J.
Snook, Pte. E. E.
Sparkes, Pte. G. A.
Stagg, Pte. G. P.

Strang, Pte. A. J.
Stebbings, Pte. A. W.
Steele, Pte. F. W.
Stoker, Lce. Sergt. N.
Storey, Corpl. G.
Strawbridge, Corpl. J.
Summerhayes, Sergt. T. R.
Symington, Corpl. H. G.

Tarbox, Sergt. A. F.
Tavener, Lce. Corpl. H. G.
Taylor, Pte. G.
Taylor, Lce. Corpl. G. H.
Taylor, Sergt. J.
Thomas, Pioneer-Sergt. E.
Timms, Pte. S.
Tizzard, Lce. Corpl. L.
Toghill, Pte. N. F.
Tooke, Pte. W. E.
Tucker, Lce. Corpl. A.
Tucker, Sergt. A. W.

Varndell, Pte. F. J.
Vaughan, Sergt. J.
Vearncombe, Sergt. F. J.
Venning, Pte. W. E.
Vickery, Pte. W.
Villis, Lce. Corpl. C.

Walker, Lce. Sergt. H.
Walker, Pte. J.
Walker, Pte. W. H.
Walker, Corpl. W. H.
Wallington, Lce. Corpl. A. J.
Waters, Corpl. J
Watts, Sergt. G.
Webber, Pte. A. C.
Welch, Lce. Corpl. J.
Weston, Pte. G. E.
Whiston, Sergt. C. B. W.
White, Pte. W. H.
Whitehead, Pte. R.
Whitlock, Lce. Corpl. R.
Whitmore, Pte. A.
Wilkinson, Pte. C.
Willets, Sergt. E.

Willey, Corpl. G.
Williams, Corpl. A.
Williams, Sergt. R.
Williams, Pte. P.
Willis, Pte. G.
Wilmhurst, Sergt. J.
Wilmott, Pte. A. G.
Wilson, Pte. L. J.
Wilson, Sergt. W. G.
Winter, Sergt. A.
Winter, Pte. T.
Woodland, Pte. R. J.
Worrell, Pte. H.
Wren, Pte. T. J. F.
Wright, Lce. Corpl. F. J.

Yeandole, Pte. W. A.
Youdle, Pte. W.

Bar to M.M.

Ballantyne, Sergt. J. T., M.M.
Burroughs, Pte. J., M.M.

Chapman, Sergt. A. H., M.M.
Clarke, Pte. A. E., M.M.
Collard, Sergt. G., M.M.
Cornelius, Corpl. H. P., M.M.

Heal, Pte. F. C., M.M.
Hill, Pte. M., M.M.
Hillier, Sergt. W. H., M.M.

Jennings, Sergt. A. R., M.M.

Lewins, Sergt. T., M.M.

Norman, Sergt. H. G., M.M.

Prior, Corpl. T. B., M.M.

Smith, Sergt. H., M.M.

Thomas, Sergt. E., M.M.

Winter, Sergt. A., M.M.

M.S.M.

Andrews, Sergt. H.

Baker, Corpl. H. W. V.
Barnes, Lce. Corpl. F.

Beard, Staff-Sergt. E. J.
Bellamy, Co-Sergt-Major J. H.
Biffen, Co-Qr-Mr-Sergt. A. G.
Blackmore, Sergt. C.
Burnell, Pte. A.

Carter, Sergt. E. P.
Chard, Co-Sergt-Major T.
Charlesworth, Corpl. A. H.
Chanell, Lce. Corpl. S.
Constance, Co-Sergt-Major F.
Cooper, Pte. C.
Cox, Pte. G. R.
Crees, Co-Sergt-Major J.
Culverhouse, Pte. C. E.
Cundick, Corpl. T. F.

Davis, Co-Sergt-Major C. R.
Doe, Co-Sergt-Major P.
Drew, Co-Sergt-Major O. W.
Durnell, Co-Qr-Mr-Sergt. W.
Dyer, Co-Qr-Mr-Sergt. R.

Ferris, Clr-Sergt. (O.R.S.) G.
Fortescue, Regtl-Qr-Mr-Sergt. T. H.
Fry, Regtl-Sergt-Major W.

Gange, Regtl-Sergt-Major E. W.
Grace, Pte. E. A.

Hall, Sergt. A.
Hartnell, Sergt-Major W. G.
Harvey, Sergt. G.
Heard, Regtl-Qr-Mr-Sergt. F. W.
Hickman, Pte. H. C.
Hiscocks, Qr-Mr-Sergt. P. C.
Hoddinott, Sergt. C. T. W.
Hutton, Pte. R.

Jones, Co-Sergt-Major S.

Lang, Sergt. F.

MacDonald, Co-Qr-Mr-Sergt. R.
Masters, Lce. Sergt. W. H.

Millar, Clr-Sergt. (O.R.S.) J. W.
Moss, Co-Sergt-Major W. H.
Muckelt, Sergt. J. W.

Newman, Pte. A. E.
Norman, Pte. H. M.

Oliver, Sergt. J.

Padfield, Sergt. G.
Paine, Sergt. H. W.
Payne, Co-Sergt-Major A. G. E.
Pells, Sergt. J.
Perry, Sergt. W. S.
Poole, Pte. A. S.

Read, Sergt. F.
Robins, Pte. G. A.
Routledge, Regtl-Qr-Mr-Sergt. J.
Rudge, Co-Qr-Mr-Sergt. F. M.

Salmon, Co-Sergt-Major J.
Sheperd, Sergt. J. B.
Shepherd, Qr-Mr-Sergt. F. H.
Smith, Sergt. A. W.
Snook, Lce. Sergt. W. C.
Somerton, Sergt. R. C.
Sorrell, Sergt. A. W.
Souch, Pte. H. G.
Stanley, Pte. G. R. D.
Steele, Co-Sergt-Major J.
Stone, Sergt. W.

Venner, Regtl-Qr-Mr-Sergt. A. B.
Vickery, Sergt-Major T.

Walters, Sergt. E.
Warr, Sergt-Major E.
West-Skin, Pte. J.
Wheadon, Sergt. G.
Williams, Sergt. A.
Williams, Sergt. T.

Yendole, Sergt. G. H.

APPENDIX B (2)

PROMOTIONS FOR SERVICE IN THE FIELD

To be Lieutenant-Generals :—

Braithwaite, Major-General Sir W. P., K.C.B.
Snow, Major-General Sir T. D'O., K.C.B., K.C.M.G.

To be Major-General :—

Braithwaite, Colonel W. P., C.B.

To be Brevet Colonel :—

Currie, Major and Bt. Lieut-Colonel R. A. M., D.S.O.

To be Brevet Lieut-Colonels :—

Allfrey, Major H. I. R., D.S.O., M.C.
Channer, Major O. R. M.
Currie, Major R. A. M., D.S.O.
Fleming, Major G., D.S.O.
Freestun, Major W. H. M., D.S.O.
Little, Major C. H., D.S.O.
Maud, Major W. H., C.M.G.
Mordaunt, Major O. C., D.S.O.
Preston-Whyte, Major R. P.
Proctor, Major J., King's Royal Rifle Corps, attached 4th Bn.
Prowse, Major C. B.
Rawling, Major C. G., C.M.G., C.I.E.
Thurlow, Major E. G. L., D.S.O.
Troyte-Bullock, Major C. J., D.S.O.
Wilson, Major A. E. J., D.S.O.
Worthington-Wilmer, Major L. E. C.
Yatman, Major A. H.

To be Brevet Majors :—

Bennett, Captain R. H. E., M.C.
Boldero, Captain A. G.
Currie, Captain R. A. M.
Denny, Captain R. B.
Freestun, Captain W. H. M.
Jones-Mortimer, Captain L. A.
Majendie, Captain V. H. B., D.S.O.
Pretyman, Captain G. F., D.S.O.
Sutton, Captain W. M., M.C.
Watson, Captain W.

To be Major :—

Quarter-Master and Hon. Captain H. French, D.C.M.

To be granted the next higher rate of pay under the provisions of the Royal Warrant :—

Quarter-Master and Hon. Major D. J. Owens.

To be Second Lieutenants for Service in the Field :—

Bullen, Sergeant-Major T., from Royal Flying Corps.
Bullock, Sergeant-Major J., from Royal Flying Corps.
Chappell, Company-Sergeant-Major P. E. E.
Deeming, Corporal W., from Royal Warwickshire Regiment.
Lance, Lance-Corporal E. C., from West Yorkshire Regiment.
Neville, Company-Sergeant-Major G. H.
Paul, Regimental-Sergeant-Major E.
Porter, Sergeant E., from Royal Flying Corps.
Rumbold, Sergeant-Major R. S., from Royal Flying Corps.
Stanley, Sergeant R. B.
Vagg, Sergeant-Major H. R., from Royal Flying Corps.
Webber, Sergeant H. V.
Wills, Company-Sergeant-Major J. C., from Coldstream Guards.

APPENDIX B (3)

FOREIGN DECORATIONS

ALL RANKS

(The ranks are those shown at the time of award.)

BELGIUM

Ordre de Leopold (Grand Officier)

Snow, Lieut-General Sir T. D'O., K.C.B., K.C.M.G.

Ordre de Leopold (Commandeur)

Compton, Lieut-Colonel C. W.

Ordre de la Couronne (Grand Officier)

Braithwaite, Major-General Sir W. P., K.C.B.

Ordre de la Couronne Avec Croix de Guerre (Chevalier)

Kent, 2nd Lieutenant W. B.

Croix de Guerre

Bevan, Pte. R. J.
Braithwaite, Major-General Sir W. P., K.C.B.
Cockram, Pte. G.
Currie, Major and Bt. Colonel R. A. M., C.M.G., D.S.O.
Farwell, Captain E. W.
Gamblin, Pte. J.
Lancaster, Pte. F.
Lang, Sergt. F.
Mackie, Captain J. R.
Snow, Lieut-General Sir T. D'O., K.C.B., K.C.M.G.

Decoration Militaire Avec Croix de Guerre

Hollier, Pte. H.

Decoration Militaire

Campbell, Pte. P. H.
Elliott, Sergt. W. H.

EGYPT

Order of the Nile, 4th Class

Calway, Captain F. H. F.
Duke, Captain J.

FRANCE

Legion d'Honneur (Croix de Commandeur)

Braithwaite, Major-General W. P., C.B.
Snow, Major-General Sir T. D'O., K.C.B., K.C.M.G.

Legion d'Honneur (Croix de Chevalier)

Currie, Bt. Lieut-Colonel R. A. M., D.S.O.
Freestun, Major and Bt. Lieut-Colonel W. H. M., C.M.G., D.S.O.
Jones-Mortimer, Captain L. A.
Powell, Major E. B., Rifle Brigade, attached.

Medaille Militaire

Archer, Sergt. W. E., D.C.M.
Gay, Sergt. S. E.
Hedley, Lce. Sergt. W.
Hiscocks, Regtl-Qr-Mr-Sergt. P. C.
Mildon, Co-Sergt-Major E. J.
Smith, Sergt-Major G. F.
Wilson, Co-Sergt-Major J. A.

Croix de Guerre

Akerman, Major E. J. B., M.C.
Bancroft, Sergt. J. E., D.C.M.
Beale, Pte. A. G., D.C.M.
Bennett, Captain R. H. E., M.C.
Braithwaite, Major-General Sir W. P., K.C.B.
Chambers, Captain C. S., Loyal N. Lancs Regt., late Somerset L.I.
Chinnock, Co-Sergt-Major H.
Davis, Co-Qr-Mr-Sergt. R.
Everett, Colonel Sir H. J., K.C.M.G., C.B.
Freestun, Bt. Lieut-Colonel W. H. M., C.M.G., D.S.O.
Goodland, Captain E. S., M.C.
Jones, Pte. F. W.
Lewis, Captain W.
Llewellyn, Lieut. A. H.
Montgomery, Captain R. V., M.C., attached Royal Engineers.
Mordaunt, Major O. C., D.S.O.
Owen, Pte. W. S.
Paul, 2nd Lieut. E.
Taylor, Lce. Corpl. R.
Thatcher, Captain R. S., O.B.E., M.C.
Thomas, Lieut. G. A.
Waddy, Captain R. H., D.S.O., attached West Yorkshire Regiment.
Walton, Pte. G. A.
Weeks, Pte. A. M.
Whitmarsh, Sergt. A. H.

Croix de Guerre avec Palme
Braithwaite, Lieut-General Sir W. P., K.C.B.
Mordaunt, Bt. Lieut-Colonel O. C., D.S.O.

Medaille d'Honneur avec Glaives " en Vermeil "
Burrows, Regtl-Sergt-Major J.

Medaille d'Honneur avec Glaives " en Argent "
Anderson, Regtl-Sergt-Major A. D.
Hunt, Lce. Sergt. W.

Medaille d'Honneur avec Glaives " en Bronze "
Sorrell, Actg. Coy-Sergt-Major A. W.

Ordre de Merite Agricole
Officier—
Sutton, Captain and Bt. Major W. M., M.C.

Chevalier
Wilson, Lieut. H. S.

GREECE

Order of the Redeemer, 2nd Class (Grand Commander)
Everett, Colonel H. J., C.B., C.M.G.

Greek Military Cross
Yatman, Bt. Lieut-Colonel A. H., D.S.O.

ITALY

Order of the Crown of Italy (Cavalier)
Duke, Captain J.
Thatcher, Captain R. S., M.C.

Croce di' Guerra
Mordaunt, Bt. Lieut-Colonel O. C., D.S.O.

Silver Medal for Military Valour
Brown, 2nd Lieut. A. E., M.C.

Bronze Medal for Military Valour
Coleman, Pte. W.

JAPAN
Order of the Rising Sun (5th Class)
Denny, Captain R. B.

PORTUGAL
Military Order of Avis (Commander)
Allfrey, Major and Bt. Lieut-Colonel H. I. R., D.S.O., M.C.

Military Order of Avis (Officier)
Hargreaves, Major A. J. G.

ROUMANIA
Order of the Star of Roumania (with swords)
Officer
Thurlow, Major and Bt. Lieut-Colonel E. G. L., D.S.O.

Chevalier
Baker, Lieut. J., M.C.

Order of the Crown of Roumania
Officer
Cooke-Hurle, Lieut-Colonel E. F.

Chevalier
Pring, Lieut. H. O.

Croix de Virtute Militara
1st Class
King, Pte. F. J.

2nd Class
Jones, Co-Sergt-Major S.
Moses, Corpl. C. S.

Medaille Barbatie si Credinta (3rd Class)
Cobb, Pte. C. E.

RUSSIA
Order of St. Stanislas
2nd Class (with swords)
Everett, Colonel H. J., C.B.
Frith, Colonel H. C., C.B.

3rd Class (with swords)
Chichester, Lieut. R. A. A.
Fleming, Major G., D.S.O.

Order of St. Anne, 3rd Class (with swords)
Cox, Lieut-Colonel W. C.

Order of St. George, 3rd Class
Packer, Co-Qr-Mr-Sergt. F. C.

Order of St. George, 4th Class
Bryant, Sergt. W. G.
Cullen, Sergt. H. J.
Day, Co-Qr-Mr-Sergt. F. E.
Harris, Sergt. F.
Newbery, Lce. Corpl. F.
Willcox, Sergt. C.

Medal of St. George, 1st Class
Vranch, Sergt. E. J.

Medal of St. George, 2nd Class
Snell, Actg. Regtl-Sergt-Major F.

Medal of St. George, 3rd Class
Prince, Pte. R. L.

Medal of St. George, 4th Class
Bowdidge, Lce. Corpl. J. S.
Delamere, Lce. Corpl. H.
Gunner, Pte. P.
Lagdon, Pte. W. H.
Oliver, Pte. J.

SERBIA

Order of the White Eagle, 4th Class
Maud, Major W. H., C.M.G.
Smith, Major I. M., D.S.O., M.C. (with swords).

Order of the White Eagle, 5th Class
Pretyman, Lieut. E. R., attached Royal Air Force.

Order of Karageorge Star (with swords)
Barry, Major A. P.

Cross of Karageorge, 1st Class (with swords)
Bale, Co-Sergt-Major R.
Horwood, Sergt. G. E.
Maggs, Sergt. G. H.

Gold Medal

Anstey, Pte. H. S.
Burfitt, Pte. W. G.
Dill, Pte. G. R.
Elcock, Pte. G. S., Royal Army Medical Corps, attached.
Kidley, Pte. W.
Shortman, Bugler T.

Silver Medal

Gay, Pte. J.

APPENDIX C

Brief record of services of General and other Officers formerly of The Somerset Light Infantry; Regular Officers employed elsewhere than with a Regular Battalion of the Regiment; and Retired Regular Officers re-employed; during the Great War, 1914–19.

Note.—The rank shown is the highest substantive (or brevet) rank attained during the War.

The following abbreviations have been used to indicate theatres of war or service at Home:—

(D)	Darfur.		the Islands of the Ægean Sea.
(E)	Egypt.		
(EA)	British, German, and Portuguese East Africa, Nyassaland, and Northern Rhodesia.	(HM)	Home.
		(I)	Italy.
		(M)	Mesopotamia.
(F)	France.	(MS)	Operations against Mohmands and Swatis.
(G)	Gallipoli.		
(GM)	Greek Macedonia, Serbia, Bulgaria, European Turkey and	(P)	Persia.
		(R)	Russia.
		(TC)	Transcaspia.

AKERMAN, Lt. J. P., M.C.
With 8 Bn. Som. L.I. (F) 1915–19.

ALLFREY, Bt. Lt-Colonel H. I. R., D.S.O., M.C.
Staff (F) 1914–18.

ATKINSON, Captain G. N.
With 7 Bn. Som. L.I. and 21 Bn. Midd'x. Regt. (F) 1917. Staff (HM) 1917–18. Spec. Appt. (HM) 1918–19.

BALLY, Major E. D., O.B.E.
With Egyptian Army 1914–19; (D) 1916; (E) 1917.

BARRY, Lt-Colonel A. P.
Staff (G) (E) 1915–16. With 12 Bn. Hamps. Regt. 1917; Bn. Comdr. 2 Garr. Bn. R. Ir. Fus. and 8 Bn. Oxf. & Bucks. L.I. 1918.

BELLEW, Captain F. D., D.S.O., M.C.
With 6 Bn. Som. L.I. (HM) (F) 1914–18. Bn. Comdr. 6 Bn. Som. L.I. (F) 1918.

BENNETT, Bt. Major R. H. E., M.C.
Staff (HM) 1916–17, (F) 1917–19.

405

BOWKER, Lt-Colonel W. J., C.M.G., D.S.O.
Bn. Comdr. Serv. Bn. Suff. Regt. (G) 1915; 6 Bn. Essex Regt. (E) 1916–17. Bde. Comdr. (E) 1917–18.

BRADNEY, Captain P. E.
With 6 Bn. Som. L.I. (HM) (F) 1914–15. Killed (F) 31.7.15.

BRAITHWAITE, Lt. V. A.
Staff (G) 1915. Killed (F) 2.7.16.

BRAITHWAITE, Lt-General Sir W. P., K.C.B.
Staff (HM) 1914–15. Chf. of Gen. Staff (G) 1915. Div. Comdr. (HM) (F) 1915–18. Corps Comdr. (F) 1918–19; Rhine Army 1919.

BURGES-SHORT, Major H. G., D.S.O.
Bn. Comdr. 7 Bn. D.C.L.I. (F) 1916–19.

BROCKLEHURST, Major R.
Staff (HM) 1914–15. With 3 Bn. Som. L.I. (HM) 1915–17. With 7 Bn. Som. L.I. (F) 1917.

CAILLARD, Lt. F. C. V. D., M.C.
With 6 Bn. Som. L.I. (F) 1915–18. Staff (F) (E) 1918–19.

CAMPBELL, Major N. A. H.
Staff (HM) 1914. With 8 Bn. Som. L.I. (F) 1916. Staff (HM) 1917.

CHAPPELL, Lt. P. E. E., D.C.M.
Adjt. 18 Bn. Welch Regt. and 7 Bn. Som. L.I. (F) 1917.

CHICHESTER, Lt. R. A. A., M.C.
With 4 Bn. K.R.R.C. (F) 1915. Adjt. N. Russia 1919.

COCKAYNE-CUST, Major A. O.
With Depôt Som. L.I. (HM) 1914. Staff (F) 1915–17.

COMPTON, Colonel C. W., C.B., C.M.G.
Bde. Comdr. (F) 1915–17; (HM) 1918; (F) 1918–19.

CORBALLIS, Lt. B. J., M.C.
With Machine Gun Corps (F) 1915–19.

COUCHMAN, Colonel G. H. H., D.S.O.
Bde. Comdr. (HM) (F) 1914–15; Staff (F) 1918–19.

Cox, Lt-Colonel W. C.
Bn. Comdr. 1/4 Bn. Som. L.I. (HM) 1914; (MS) 1915; (M) 1916–18. Died 21.4.19.

CURRIE, Bt. Colonel R. A. M., C.M.G., D.S.O.
Staff (F) 1914–17. Bde. Comdr. (F) 1917; (HM) 1917–18; (F) 1918–19.

CURTIS, Lt. W. S. C., M.C.
With 1 Bn. Dorset Regt. (F) 1918. With 46 Bn. R. Fus. (N. Russia) 1919.

DENNY, Bt. Major R. B.
Staff (HM) 1915–17. Asst. Mil. Attaché, Pekin, 1917.

DENNYS, Lt. K. G. G.
With W. Afr. Regt. 1918–19. Employed British Guiana, 1919.

DICKINSON, Captain H. C.
With King's Afr. Rif. (EA) 1914–18. Died (EA) 18.12.18.

ELGER, Major E. G., D.S.O.
Staff (F) 1915–18.

ELLIS, Lt. R. W.
With 45 Training Res. Bn. (HM) 1917–19.

EVERETT, Colonel Sir H. J., K.C.M.G., C.B.
Staff (HM) (F) 1914–16; (GM) 1916–19.

FIELD, Lt. R. E., O.B.E.
Staff (HM) 1915; (F) 1915–16; (HM) 1916–19.

FLEMING, Bt. Lt-Colonel G., D.S.O.
Staff (E) 1916. Bn. Comdr. 7 Bn. Gloster Regt. (M) 1916–17; 7 Bn.
N. Staff. Regt. (M) 1917; 9 Bn. R. War. Regt. (P) (TC) 1917–19.

FOORD, Major A. R.
With 7 Bn. Som. L.I. (HM) 1914–15; 9 Bn. Som. L.I. (HM) 1916;
45 Training Res. Bn. (HM) 1916–17; 13 Bn. Som. L.I. (HM) 1918.

FOSTER, Major M. A., D.S.O.
Embarkation Staff (HM) 1914–15. Employed as Area Comdt. (HM)
1915–17; Comdt. Prisoners of War Camp (HM) 1917–19.

Fox, Major A. B.
R.T.O. (F) 1914–19.

FREESTUN, Bt. Lt-Colonel W. H. M., C.M.G., D.S.O.
Staff (F) (E) (F) 1914–18.

FRITH, Colonel H. C., C.B.
Bde. Comdr. (E) (G) (F) (HM) 1914–18.

GALLWEY, Colonel E. J., C.B.
Officer i/c Records and Comdg. No. 11 District (HM) 1915–17.

HARDING, Lt. A. F., M.C.
With Machine Gun Corps (E) 1915–18. Staff (G) 1915; (E) 1916.

HARDMAN, Major FitzW.
Bn. Comdr. 11 Bn. E. York Regt. (F) 1916.

HARGREAVES, Major A. J. G.
Spec. Employed War Office (HM) 1918–19.

HARPER, Lt. J. W.
Served in N. Russia 1919.

HARRISON, Major J. S. N., D.S.O.
 Staff (India) 1916–17. Bn. Comdr. 6 Bn. L.N. Lan. Regt. (M) 1917–19.

HOWE, Captain W. T., O.B.E.
 Attached Army Signal Service (M) 1916–18; (F) 1919.

JOHNSTONE, Major H. C.
 Staff (HM) 1915–17.

KENNEDY, Major F. M. E., C.B.
 Employed as Sec. Somerset Terr. Force Assn. (HM) 1914–19.

KENNEDY, 2nd Lt. J. H.
 Attached Sco. Rif. Killed 10.1.15.

KING, Lt. K. E. K.
 Served in N. Russia 1919.

LANCE, Captain C. E., D.S.O.
 With 6 Bn. Som. L.I. (F) 1916–19.

LANE, Lt. H., M.C.
 With Army Cyc. Corps (F) (HM) 1914–17. Machine Gun Corps (F) 1917. Tank Corps (F) 1917–19. Spec. Employed War Office (HM) 1916.

LAWSON, Captain G. W.
 With 7 Bn. W. York. Regt. (F) 1917–18. Staff (HM) 1918–19.

LITTLE, Colonel C. B., C.M.G.
 Staff (E) 1914–15.

LITTLE, Bt. Lt-Colonel C. H., D.S.O.
 Employed with Egyptian Army, and Staff (E) (D) 1914–16. Bn. Comdr. 23 Bn. Lond. Regt. (E) 1918; S. Lan. Regt. (F) 1918.

LLEWELLYN, Major W. W.
 With 1 Bn. K.R.R.C. (F) 1914–15. Employed with Offr. Cadet Bn. (HM) 1916–17. With 3 Bn. Som. L.I. 1917–18.

LOVETT, Major H. W.
 Adjt. Depôt Som. L.I. (HM) 1914. Comdt. Q. Mary's Hosp. Roehampton (HM) 1915. Att. No. 4 Dist. (HM) 1916.

LUMB, Major A.
 With 16 (Res.) Bn. King's L'pool Regt. (HM) 1915–16.

MACBRYAN, Captain J. C. W.
 With 1 Bn. Som. L.I. (F) 1914.

McMURTRIE, Lt. G. D. J.
 With 7 Bn. Som. L.I. (F) 1917–19.

MAHONEY, Lt. N. E. C. B.
 With Machine Gun Corps (India) 1918–19.

MAJENDIE, Bt. Major V. H. B., D.S.O.
 Comdr. Sub-Area (F) 1919.

MAUD, Bt. Lt-Colonel W. H., C.M.G.
Staff (HM) 1914–19.

MIERS, Lt. M. C. C.
5 Bn. Midd'x. Regt., with Motor Machine Gun Service (F) 1915–17.
Attd. 8 Bn. Som. L.I. (F) 1917. Died of wounds 9.8.17.

MILES, Captain Sir C. W., Bart., O.B.E.
Adjt. 1/4 Bn. Som. L.I. (MS) 1915, (M) 1916. Staff (India) 1916–18.

MILLAR, Lt. R. MacG., M.C.
With E.E.F. 1916. Army Signal Service (F) 1918.

MILLS, Captain F. S.
With 7 Bn. Som. L.I. (HM) (F) 1914–17. Killed (F) 5.8.17.

MONTGOMERY, Captain R. V., M.C.
With Army Signal Service (F) 1915–19.

MORAN, Hon. Major P.
With A.S.C. (HM) 1914–19.

MORDAUNT, Bt. Lt-Colonel O. C., D.S.O.
With Army Signal Service (G) 1915; (F) 1916–17; (I) 1917–19.
Comdg. School of Signals (HM) 1919.

MUNDEN, Lt. H., D.F.C.
With R.F.C. (F) (M) 1916–18. Employed under Air Ministry (M)
(P) 1918–19.

NAPIER-CLAVERING, Colonel C. W.
Comdg. Depôt Som. L.I. (HM) 1914–16.

OLIVER, Lt. J. L.
With Machine Gun Corps 1915–19.

PATERSON, Major A. W. S., D.S.O.
Offr. Co. of Gent. Cadets and Staff (HM) 1914–15. Bn. Comdr.
6 Bn. R. Ir. Fus. (GM) 1916; 5 Bn. R. Innis. Fus. (E) (F) 1917–18;
11 Bn. Som. L.I. (F) 1919.

PAYNE, Major General R. L., C.B., D.S.O.
Div. Comdr. (India) 1914–16.

PEREIRA, Lt. G. W. T.
With K.R.R.C. 1915. With R.F.C. 1918–19.

PHILBY, Captain O. G. B.
Staff (HM) 1919.

POLLOCK, Lt-Colonel A. W. A.
Bn. Comdr. 10 Bn. Yorks L.I. (HM) (F) 1914–16. Staff 1917–19.

POWIS, Hon. Major H.
Qr. Mr. Depôt Som. L.I. (HM) 1914–17.

PRETYMAN, Lt. E. R., A.F.C.
    With R.F.C. (HM) (E) 1915–16; (GM) 1916; (HM) 1916–18; (F) 1918–19.

PRETYMAN, Bt. Major G. F., D.S.O., O.B.E.
    With R.F.C. (F) 1914–15; (HM) 1915; (F) 1915–17; Employed under Air Ministry (HM) 1918–19.

PRIDEAUX, Captain G. A., M.C.
    Staff (F) 1916–17. Killed (F) 19.1.17.

PROWSE, Bt. Lt-Colonel C. B., D.S.O.
    Bde. Comdr. (F) 1915–16. Died of wounds (F) 1.7.16.

RAWLING, Bt. Lt-Colonel C. G., C.I.E., C.M.G., D.S.O.
    Bn. Comdr. 6 Bn. Som. L.I. (HM) (F) 1914–16. Bde. Comdr. (F) 1916–17. Killed (F) 28.10.17.

RITCHIE, Major T. F., D.S.O.
    With 6 Bn. Som. L.I. (HM) (F) 1914–16. Bn. Comdr. 6 Bn. Som. L.I. (F) 1916–18.

ROMILLY, Lt. H. A., M.B.E.
    Attached Indian Signal Service (M) 1917–18.

RONEY-DOUGAL, Major G. B.
    Staff (F) (G) 1914–15; (GM) 1916–17. Remount Service 1918–19.

SAMUDA, Major C. M. A.
    With 6 Bn. S. Wales Bord. (GM) 1916–17. Died of wounds 2.7.17.

SKRINE, Lt. H. L.
    With 6 Bn. Som. L.I. (HM) (F) 1914–15. Killed (F) 25.9.15.

SMITH, Major I. M., D.S.O., M.C.
    Staff (G) 1915; (E) (GM) 1915–19.

SNOW, Lt-General Sir T. D'O., K.C.B., K.C.M.G.
    Div. Comdr. (F) (HM) (F) 1914–15. Corps Comdr. (F) (HM) 1915–18. G.O.C.-in-C. (HM) 1918–19.

STEER, Captain G. P.
    Attached 2 Bn. Wilts Regt. (F) 1914–15. Died of wounds 26.12.15.

STEPHENS, Lt. R. W.
    Special Appt. (F) 1918–19.

STILEMAN, Lt. R. F.
    Staff (M) 1916–18.

STONE, Major N. H.
    Bn. Comdr. 1/4 Bn. Som. L.I. (M) 1918–19. Served in N. Russia 1919.

STRACHEY, Lt. R., M.C.
    With K.R.R.C. (F) 1915–17.

STURT, Hon. Major F.
    Qr. Mr. Depot K.O. Sco. Bord. (HM) 1914–15.

SUTTON, Bt. Major W. M., D.S.O., M.C.
Staff (F) 1915–19.

SWAYNE, Lt-Colonel E. H., O.B.E.
Bn. Comdr. 9 Bn. Som. L.I. (HM) 1914–16; 45 Training Res. Bn.
(HM) 1916–18; 13 Bn. Som. L.I. (HM) 1918–19.

SWAYNE, Captain J. G. des R.
With Army Signal Service (F) 1914.

TAYLOR, Captain J. B.
Staff (R) 1919.

THICKNESSE, Major J. A.
Staff (HM) 1914–15. Killed (F) 1.7.16.

THURLOW, Bt. Lt-Colonel E. G. L., D.S.O.
Staff (F) 1914–16; (GM) 1916–18; (HM) 1918–19.

TROYTE-BULLOCK, Bt. Lt-Colonel C. J., D.S.O.
Bn. Comdr. 7 Bn. Som. L.I. (HM) (F) 1914–18. With Machine Gun
Corps (HM) 1918–19.

TURNER, Lt. F. M.
With W. Kent Yeo. (F) 1918–19.

WADDY, Lt-Colonel J. M. E.
With 2/4 Bn. Som. L.I. (HM) (India) 1914–16. Bn. Comdr. 2/4 Bn.
Som.L.I. (India) 1915–16. Specially employed (India) 1916–19.

WADDY, Captain R. H., D.S.O.
Bn. Comdr. 2/5 Bn. W. York. Regt. (F) 1917–18; 9 Bn. W. York.
Regt. (F) 1918–19.

WALSH, Colonel H. A., C.B.
Comdg. No. 8 District (HM) 1914–16. Died 25.11.18.

WALSH, Major T. A., D.S.O.
Adjt. H. A. C. (F) 1914–15. Staff (F) 1915–16. Bn. Comdr. 13 Bn.
North'd. Fus. (F) 1916–17.

WATSON, Major W.
Bn. Comdr. 5 Bn. Yorks L.I. (F) 1916–17. Killed (F) 3.5.17.

WATTS, Captain R. A. P. B., D.S.O.
Staff (HM) 1915. With Serv. Bn. Som. L.I. (F) 1916. With Serv.
Bn. York. and Lanc. Regt. 1917 (R) 1919.

WHITTUCK, Captain G. E. M., M.C.
Staff (F) 1914–15. With 3 Bn. Som. L.I. (HM) 1915–16. Staff (F)
1916–19; Rhine Army 1919.

WILLIAMS, Colonel R. B., C.B.
Bde. Comdr. (HM) (F) 1914–15. Group Comdr. (HM) 1916. Bn.
Comdr. 2 Garr. Bn. Oxf. & Bucks L.I. (F) 1916; 2 H.S. Garr. Bn.
N. Staff. Regt. and 17 Bn. R. Def. Corps (HM) 1916–18.

WILSON, Bt. Lt-Colonel A. E. J., D.S.O.
    Staff (F) 1916–19; (HM) 1919.
WORRALL, Major E. W.
    Staff (India) 1916–18.
WORTHINGTON-WILMER, Bt. Lt-Colonel L. E. C.
    With 6 Bn. Som. L.I. (HM) (F) 1914–16.   Staff (F) 1916–18.
YATMAN, Bt. Lt-Colonel A. H., D.S.O.
    Bn. Comdr. 11 Bn. R.W. Fus. (GM) 1916–19; 7 Bn. S. Wales Bord.
    (GM) 1919.

APPENDIX D

CASUALTIES

The History Committee have fully considered the question of publishing some comprehensive list of the casualties which the Regiment incurred during the Great War.

As might be expected, the list of casualties is an enormous one, and if the list of those killed, died, wounded and missing were published it would make this volume far too long.

It may be mentioned, however, that the death casualties have been published by Authority under two headings:—

(1) Soldiers died in the Great War, 1914–19. Part 18. Prince Albert's (Somerset Light Infantry). Printed by His Majesty's Stationery Office, price 2s. 6d.

(2) Officers died in the Great War, 1914–19. Printed by His Majesty's Stationery Office, price 7s. 6d.

In addition, the names of those of the Regiment who died for their Country are included in the Somerset Book of Honour deposited in Wells Cathedral on November 30th, 1922.

The title-page of this book contains the following inscription:—

"ALL WHOSE NAMES ARE INSCRIBED IN THE PAGES OF THIS BOOK OF HONOUR WERE NUMBERED AMONGST THOSE WHO AT THE CALL OF KING AND COUNTRY LEFT ALL THAT WAS DEAR TO THEM, ENDURED HARDSHIP, FACED DANGER, AND FINALLY PASSED OUT OF THE SIGHT OF MEN BY THE PATH OF DUTY AND SELF-SACRIFICE, GIVING UP THEIR OWN LIVES THAT OTHERS MIGHT LIVE IN FREEDOM.

"LET THOSE WHO COME AFTER SEE TO IT THAT THEIR NAMES BE NOT FORGOTTEN."

The following is a Summary of the War Office Publication:—

OTHER RANKS

Unit.	Killed in Action.	Died of Wounds.	Died.	Total.
Depôt	—	—	11	11
1st Battalion	1,005	256	54	1,315
2nd ,,	2	—	41	43
3rd ,,	—	1	29	30
6th ,,	619	167	63	849
7th ,,	465	147	51	663
8th ,,	681	121	19	821
9th ,,	—	—	13	13
10th ,,	—	—	4	4
1st Garrison Battalion	—	—	43	43

	Killed in Action.	Died of Wounds.	Died.	Total.
11th Battalion	35	14	12	61
12th ,, ...	147	53	12	212
13th ,, ...	—	—	3	3
4th Reserve Battalion . . .	2	—	7	9
1/4th Battalion	28	12	78	118
2/4th ,, ...	26	12	34	72
5th ,, ...	—	—	10	10
1/5th ,, ...	91	26	57	174
2/5th ,, ...	4	3	29	36
Total	3,105	812	570	4,487
OFFICERS	197	45	27	269
Grand Total . . .	3,302	857	597	4,756

Note.—Unfortunately it has not been found possible to make out the Officers' List by battalions owing to the fact that many of the Officers had not been at the time of their death posted officially to the battalions they were serving with, or were employed on the staff or with other units.

APPENDIX E

THE SOMERSET LIGHT INFANTRY (PRINCE ALBERT'S)
Allocation of Battalions to Brigades and Divisions 1914-1918, showing changes

1st Battalion. Went out to FRANCE with the 11th Brigade, 4th Division, in August 1914, and continued in these formations till the end of the War.

2nd Battalion. In INDIA at Quetta, subsequently in 1st Indian (Peshawar) Division.

3rd Battalion (Reserve). HOME. Devonport, 1914–17. Londonderry and Belfast, November 1917 to September 1919, when relieved by 1st Battalion.

4th Battalion (Reserve) T.F. HOME. Formed in 1917 by the amalgamation of the 3/4th and 3/5th Battalions, who were formed early in 1915.

1/4th Battalion (T.F.). Went out to INDIA with 43rd Division, October 1914. Went to MESOPOTAMIA in February 1916 with 37th Indian Brigade; transferred to 41st Brigade (L. of C. Troops) April 1916: to 56th Indian Brigade (attached 15th Indian Division) May 1918.

2/4th Battalion (T.F.). Went out to INDIA with 45th Division, December 1914; went to EGYPT in September 1917, posted to 232nd Brigade, 75th Division: moved to FRANCE, May 1918; posted to 34th Division as Pioneers, 17th June 1918.

1/5th Battalion (T.F.). Went out to INDIA with 43rd Division: went to EGYPT in May 1917; posted to 233rd Brigade, 75th Division.

2/5th Battalion (T.F.). Went out to INDIA with 45th Division: in 8th Indian (Lucknow) Division.

6th (Service) Battalion. Went out to FRANCE with 43rd Brigade, 14th Division, in May 1915; reduced to Training Cadre, May 1918, and transferred to 16th Division with which it returned to ENGLAND in June 1918; reformed and went out again to FRANCE in 49th Brigade, July 1918.

7th (Service) Battalion. Went out to FRANCE with 61st Brigade, 20th Division, in July 1915, and continued in that formation till the end of the War.

8th (Service) Battalion. Went out to FRANCE with 63rd Brigade, 21st Division, in September 1915: transferred with Brigade to 37th Division, July 1917.

9th (Service) Battalion. Raised autumn, 1914, for HOME Service; became 45th Territorial Reserve Battalion, May 1915, and early in 1916 they ceased to wear the Regimental Badge.

11th Battalion (T.F.). Formed from the 85th Provisional Battalion on 1st January 1917; went to FRANCE, May 1918, and posted to 177th Brigade, 59th Division, as a Garrison Battalion till 16th July 1918, when the title Garrison was dropped.

12th Battalion (T.F.). Formed in EGYPT in February 1917 out of West Somerset Yeomanry and posted to 229th Brigade on formation of 74th Division in March 1917. This Division moved to FRANCE, April 1918.

13th Battalion. Raised for HOME Service from 11th Battalion when the latter went to France in May 1918.

1st Garrison Battalion. HOME.

The 1st, 2nd and 3rd Battalions Somerset Volunteer Training Corps were designated the 1st, 2nd and 3rd Volunteer Battalions of the Regiment in 1918.

INDEX

Printed in the United Kingdom
by Lightning Source UK Ltd.
135650UK00001BA/23/A

9 781843 422167

THE CHANGING F

Marston

BOOK TWO

Carole Newbigging
and
Angela Wood

Robert Boyd
PUBLICATIONS

Published by
Robert Boyd Publications
260 Colwell Drive
Witney, Oxfordshire OX8 7LW

First published 1997

Copyright © Carole Newbigging, Angela Wood and
Robert Boyd Publications

ISBN: 1 899536 12 4

Anyone can publish a book — why not you!

Have you ever wanted to publish a book? It is not as difficult as you might think. The publisher of this book provides a service to individuals and organisations large and small.

Advice can be given on all facets of production: typesetting, layout and design, paper stocks, styles of binding including wired, perfect, sewn, limp and cased binding, the options are almost endless. If you have a project you would like to discuss why not contact:

Robert Boyd
PRINTING & PUBLISHING SERVICES
260 Colwell Drive
Witney, Oxfordshire OX8 7LW

Printed and bound in Great Britain at The Alden Press, Oxford

Contents

Cover illustrations

Front: Outing from The Red Lion c1950

Back: Romany gipsies in The Copse

Acknowledgements

The compilers gratefully acknowledge the help and assistance given so willingly by so many people. In particular they thank the following for permission to use personal photographs, and for assistance given in identifying those photographs: Mrs V Andrews, Mr C Barnes, Mrs G Batts, Mr I Blackford, Mr and Mrs H Bridges, Mrs B Brown, Mr B Carpenter, Miss H Clifford, Mr T Cox, Mr and Mrs Davis, Mr H Elmey, Mrs Gills, Mr W Greenough, Mr D Grimsley, Mrs L Harley, Mr B Haynes, Mrs E Hewlett, Mr D Holt, Mrs L Hughes, Mr T James, Miss H Jones, Mrs B King, Mr J Kirby, Mrs Merryman, Mr H Messenger, Mrs M Nuttall-Smith, Rev T Price, Mr A Rhymes, Mr and Mrs Rickets, Mrs N Saunders, Miss D Shaw, Mr G Ward, St Nicholas, St Michaels, Marston Middle and Milham Ford Schools. In addition we acknowledge assistance given by the Photographic Archives of the Centre for Oxfordshire Studies and Reed Information Services for permission to use extracts from Kellys Directory.

Special thanks to Chris Fenn for the maps, and to Mrs Bettina Brown (nee Barnes) for permission to quote from her manuscript book *Child's Eye View of World War Two,* and to Mr Derek Holt for permission to quote from his letters, both of which we believe enhance the readers enjoyment and appreciation of the area.

Area map of Old and New Marston, 1922.

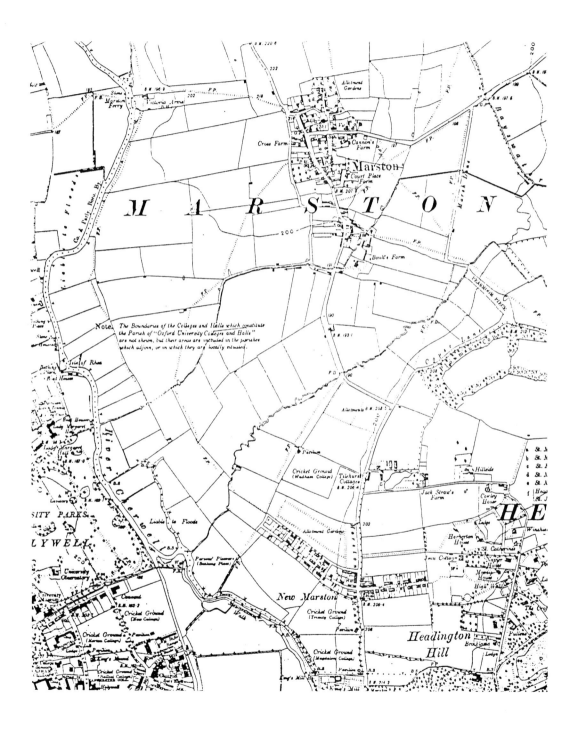

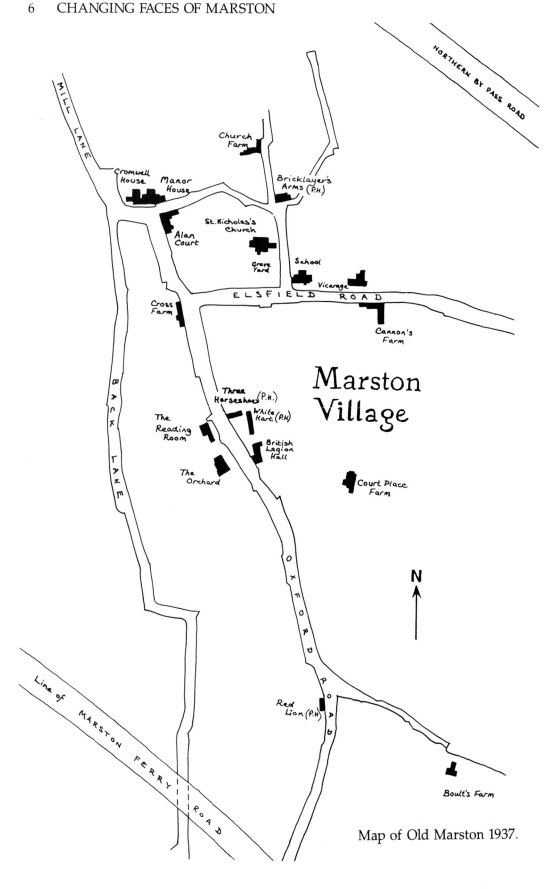

Map of Old Marston 1937.

This Declaration of Trust

is made the *eighth* day of *May* One thousand
nine hundred and forty three B E T W E E N JOHN
HAMILTON MORTIMER of Marston Vicarage Marston in the
County of Oxford Clerk in Holy Orders (hereinafter called
"the Donor") of the one part THE OXFORD DIOCESAN BOARD OF
FINANCE an Association incorporated under the Companies
Act not for profit whose registered office is at Number 88
St. Aldates in the City of Oxford (hereinafter called "the
Board") of the other part ——————————

W H E R E A S the Donor recently handed to the
Board the sum of Fifteen thousand pounds which by arrange-
ment has been invested in the purchase of Fourteen
thousand one hundred and ninety one pounds eighteen
shillings and eightpence three and one half per cent War
Stock to be held by the Board for the Ecclesiastical
purposes upon the trusts and with and subject to the power
and provisions hereinafter declared of and concerning the
same ——————————

N O W   THIS DEED WITNESSETH AND IT IS HEREBY AGREED
AND DECLARED as follows that is to say:- ——————————

1. THE Board shall stand possessed of the said sum of
Fourteen thousand one hundred and ninety one pounds
eighteen shillings and eightpence three and one half per
cent War Stock and the investments and moneys from time
to time representing the same (all of which are hereinafter included in the expression "the Trust Fund") Upon
trust to pay or apply the income thereof in the manner
hereinafter provided ——————————

2. THE purposes for which the income of the Trust Fund
shall be paid or applied shall be for or towards the
payment of the salaries of ——————————

(1) A Priest-in-Charge of the existing district of New
Marston and ——————————

(2) A Lay worker for the Parish of Marston (who shall if
the Board sees fit be a woman) such salaries to be at the
rate of not less than Two hundred and fifty pounds and
One hundred and eighty pounds per annum respectively)
until a new Parish shall be formed out of or including
such district ——————————

(3) From and after the formation of any such new Parish

Copy of a Declaration of Trust dated 8 May 1943, by which John Hamilton Mortimer,
Vicar of Marston (1904-1952), donated the sum of £15,000 to the Oxford Diocesan Board
of Finance. The purpose of this donation was to provide towards the payment of
salaries of a Priest in Charge 'of the existing district of New Marston' and a Lay worker
for the Parish of Marston 'until a new Parish shall be formed out of or including such
district'.

Old Marston

The church of St Nicholas, dedicated to the patron saint of sea-farers, pawn-brokers, children, and all people in trouble, is first mentioned in 1122, when Henry I granted the chapel of Marston to the canons of St Frideswide's.

I sang in the choir twice every Sunday, with choir practise in the week. It was quite a good choir with a man named George Gunn in the basses, booming it out, and Bill Brain singing tenor, and lots of my friends at school were in it. The vicar would accompany the choir on his tinkly little dulcimer which he kept by his elbow so that he could reach it from his seat without moving. Whilst on the organ was a marvellous old lady called Mrs Woolgrove. She dressed all in black with a little bonnet on her head, and she chewed garlic, which one found a bit off putting to say the least. She was related to the Frank Cooper marmalade family and she lived in a flat at the top of a lovely house in the village, owned by a Mrs Honour. (Brown)

Mary Garvey organist at St Nicholas Church.

Church choir early 1930s. Left to right back row: William Plumley, Percy Parsons, R Harris, Bill Robinson, N Bennet (verger), Harold Messenger, Reginald Gorge. Front row: Harry Parsons, Bernard Plumley, Arthur Hayle, Clement Gibson, Gerald Haynes, William Gorge, Frederick Gorge.

c1956 including Mr Gwyn Davies, Mr W Brain, Mrs Eva Savage, Mrs Nancy Vernede.

Miss Hilda Jones outside Primrose Cottage, before it was rethatched. Originally two cottages, numbers 63 and 65 Oxford Road, the cottage on the left, number 63, was a one-up and one-down with outside wash house at the rear comprising a 'kitchen' and WC. It was inhabited until c1969 by Mr and Mrs Bert Ward.

Colthorne Farm now called The Farmhouse in Oxford Road, Old Marston.

Graham Ward in the paddock of Canons Farm with Little Acreage house in the background.

May Day parade through the streets of Old Marston.

Church Farm in the 1930s

Butlins holiday camp in the 1940s. Mrs Florence Haynes, Dot and Herbert Cummings, Pam Haynes. Florence and Dot were sisters, daughters of William Kimber, the legendary Oxfordshire folk dance figure. Bert's father was a rose grower in Marston.

Photo of Kimber family c1910, Maud and Dot at the back, with Fred and Mary in front. The Kimber family lived at Church Farm.

Haymaking in the mid 1950s, the field is now the site of Horseman's Close. The house in the background is Boults Farmhouse. Left to right: Bryan Haynes, Annie Haynes, Gerald Haynes, Flo Haynes, Charlie Haynes jnr, Rosemary Haynes, Charlie Haynes snr driving tractor.

Haymaking in the summer of 1942, Clifford and Alice Messenger.

Mr Lamburn was the village carpenter and undertaker and is seen here in the late 1920s with apprentices Reg Cox and Harold Hemmings, with newly completed portable building outside the workshops opposite 38 Oxford Road. Evelyn and Doris Lamburn are on the balcony.

Charlie Gurden in the Elsfield Road 1939, demonstrating how to sow runner beans. As the holes were made a small boy would follow behind and sow the beans.

Mr Denton c1954 outside Elm View in Mill Lane.

Betty Barnes, Mrs Barnes and Chris Barnes mid 1940s at 34 Mill Lane. *We moved during the October of 1941. I suppose to someone born and bred in London like my mother was, it must have seemed like the last outpost of the outback. The council house at Old Marston was like Buckingham Palace after our derelict cottage at Towersey. It was only about eight years old, and had a nice little kitchen, with a deep sink and running water. An upstairs toilet — what luxury — and for the first time in our lives we had a proper bathroom, complete with a gas copper over which there was another tap. No more lifting of heavy buckets out of the well, no more emptying baths of water — it seemed like paradise. We had long gardens front and back, which my father soon had planted with vegetables, three apple trees, various fruit bushes and lots of flowers. But not everyone was as pleased with our move as we were — we had a brick through the front window the first night we were there! The local people obviously took umbrage over a family of outsiders coming in and taking over one of their council houses, it was understandable looking back. (Brown)*

Mid 1940s Mill Lane looking towards Cromwell House. On the left hand side, the site of Pond Cottage, were allotments for fruit and vegetables.

Mid 1940s Mill Lane looking north. Minutes of the Parish meeting records, 23 March 1944, residents of Mill Lane complained of pits and high refuse dumps operated by Mr Dennis. (*Notes of Parsh Meeting*)

Mrs Alice Haynes, affectionately known as 'Johnny', seen here in the farmyard at Hill Farm mid 1920s. Hill Farm was worked by Hubert Haynes from the early 1900s to 1949.

Haymaking at Hill Farm, showing hay elevator on left hand side.

Hubert Haynes holding horse. Note the lettering on the waggon, which was typical of those used in Oxfordshire and usually painted yellow.

The rick yard at Hill Farm, showing steam engine driving the threshing machine.

Hubert Haynes with hay rake.

Mid 1940s the corner of Boults Lane — May Queen celebrations. *The Garland, The Garland, The very prettiest Garland, that ever you did see. 'Tis fit for Queen Victoria, So please to remember me.* Early May Day rhyme sang by the children of Marston.

Tom Ward and granddaughter Lisa Blackburn at Burnt Mill Farm which was a riding school in the 1970s. It was situated at the end of Mill Lane and so called because the Old Mill had burnt down.

Church trip from St Nicholas 1950s.

Believed to be a church fete, possibly on the Recreation Ground.

Mr and Mrs R E Tackley extending their weaving plant in Church Lane to employ up to 50 people. Extract from parish council minutes July 1947.

Newly out of the Royal Air Force in 1948, John Davis, a Londoner, joined a wartime comrade in a small textile mill at Old Marston, to run the office. Soon afterwards he found himself running the whole operation and had to learn the work of the looms and other machines to keep things going. News report in 1968, at which time Vardoc Fabrics employed four full-timers — two machinists, a weaver and Mrs Eve Duthie, Mr Davis's *indispensable general factotum on whom he relied completely to supervise the day to day operations.*

Founded in a wooden hut and Nissen building in Church Lane, behind the Bricklayers Arms, the business eventually became Vardoc Fabrics, which operated until 1987. Vardocs were very successful, exporting thousands of woollen ties abroad.

Hand Machine at Vardoc Fabrics.

Walter Kemp and John in the Weaving Shed.

Beryl Agent

A selection of ties from the factory.

New Marston

Although my paternal grandparents lived in Old Marston, New Marston was the place I knew best. In the days when we first lived there, New Marston was little more than three roads leading off the Marston Road, known as Main Road. Of the three, William Street was the best established, with houses along the greater part of its length and, as far as I can remember, having a decent road surface. William Street finished as virtually a dead end, the only exit being at the top, through large gates which gave access to High Wall House. (Holt)

The Weller family in 1954 at the Golden Wedding celebrations of Mr and Mrs Fred Weller, in the garden of 9 William Street. Left to right: Malcolm Weller, Pat Palfrey (nee Weller), Molly Morgan (nee Weller), George Weller, Fred Weller, Joan Rodaway (nee Weller), Mrs Weller, Fred Weller jnr, Bet Weller, Rose Hudson (nee Weller), Harry Weller, Jim Weller.

The Phipps Family of 3 William Street. Back row: Elsie, Hilda, Sydney, Beatrice. Front row: Reginald, Florence, Laura, Winifred. Taken in the 1940s in the scout hall in William Street.

Cast of a concert, outside the Congregational Hall in New Marston, including Win Daniels, Winifred Phipps, Francis Buckingham. *The Congregational Hall played an important part in our lives, not only for church meetings, but for various social events. We were a very close knit community in our part of Marston* . (Jones)

Sunday School group of late 1920s outside the Congregational Church (later the United Reform Church) Hall. The original building was next to the scout hall at the bottom of William Street, but the church later moved to the top of Croft Road. The original hall is still in use.

Outside the New Marston Congregational Church Hall c1925, including Winifred Phipps, Minnie Edle, Win Daniels.

Ferry Road c1933 looking towards Marston Road *When we arrived in Ferry Road in 1927 the street was unmade — although we did have gas, water and a sewage system connected to a collecting and pumping station further down the road, but no electricity or street lights.* (*Holt*)

Ray Holt 1945 in the field behind 69 Ferry Road. *Digging in the garden of number 69 I discovered a well, and wondered whether this land had originally been connected to number 73, which I understood to be the oldest house in the road. Later the old orchard on the opposite side of the road, where Scarrot kept his donkey, was developed.* (*Holt*)

Edgeway Road (or the Back Lane to us) was a muddy track with a number of houses on the south side only. Along that lane was a gipsy caravan site occupied by the Rawlings. On the north side were allotments which were divided from the road by a ditch and a hedge which contained a number of large elm trees. Also on the north side, although not in Edgeway Road itself, was a wooden bungalow farmhouse of Park Farm, located in the corner of the farm field closest to Edgeway Road. The Browns came to Marston from Somerset to run this dairy with its TT tested grade A herd. I spent many happy hours on Park Farm, helping out in the dairy, doing the haymaking or getting in the way. (*Holt*)

Marston Road looking south to New Marston, May 1937, during widening of the road. (*OPA*)

Even though the road from Oxford was referred to as the Main Road, it was just as often called the Mason Road (sic). Prior to this road being widened it was a pleasant country lane with grassy banks and large Elms along its length, the only problem was a tendency to flooding. (*Holt*)

Widening of the Marston Road June 1937, looking south to New Marston. (*OPA*)

Looking north in May 1937, Jack Straws Lane on the right. *Carter's brickworks in Jack Straw Lane had long since stopped producing bricks when I was young, with the pit now being used as a waste tip (one unfortunate horse being dragged into the pit by its cart and drowned). Nelson Eadle, from William Street, sold vegetables, milk and coal from the old kilns, while my great uncle Bert Ward delivered coal by horse and cart. In the summer I often met my great uncle and Nelson haymaking on the old sand field quarry. This field was originally rented by Mark Carter from Headington Manor to extract the sand for intermixing with the Oxford brick clay. Nelson seemed to be a permanent fixture in Marston and I always expected to find him on his regular route pushing his bicycle, loaded with milk, up Jack Straws Lane.* (*Holt*)

Early 1950s photograph taken in the field behind Jack Straws Lane, George Mathews and Bryan Haynes attending to farm machinery.

August 1937 laying the cycle track on Marston Road. Edgeway Road is on the left, but Nicholson Road is not yet built.

That section of the road from St Clements to the end of the University Grounds was known as Marston Road and was considered to be in the parish of St Clements. The Marston Road was known as Main Road, and eventually the whole road became Marston Road. To the south of New Marston, towards St Clements, was the Kings Mill, being the southern boundary of Marston, seen here in the 1960s, much as it was for the past several hundred years.

A brick extension was added just before the war, which housed the kitchen and bathroom. This was demolished in 1983 by the current owner, an architect, during repairs and renovation, for which she received an award from the Oxford Preservation Trust. Photograph shows the 1983 extensions.

On the opposite side of Marston Road lay the Government Buildings. This photograph of 1943 was taken to celebrate Mr and Mrs Crawford taking over the running of the canteen. Left to right back row: Mr H Crawford, Mrs R Crawford, Mr Savage, Mr Hook, Mr De'Luc. Front row: –, –, –, –, Nora –, –, –, –, Edith Spinks, June –, Annie Wood, –.

1954 Government Buildings demonstration of emergency feeding methods. (*OPA*)

The main period of development, to the west of the Marston Road, was between 1934 and 1938, when many municipal housing schemes were implemented, and new roads were named. Several streets were named after musicians, such as Weldon Road, Purcell Road, Crotch Crescent after Sir William Crotch, and Nicholson Road after Richard Nicholson organist at Magdalen College. Hugh Allen Crescent was named in 1937 after Sir Hugh Allen, who studied at Oxford in 1901.

Croft Road was named in 1936 after Croft School, which became part of Rye St Anthony School in 1944. Heather Place was named in 1935 and Farmer Place in 1938. Ouseley Close, first known as Upland Estate, was named in 1935.

Streets within the Estate now known as Northway, were named after English Lakes, and the area was known as 'The Lake District'. These include Ambleside Drive named in 1936, Derwent Avenue 1938, Coniston Avenue 1935, and Bowness Avenue 1934. Copse Lane was developed in 1936 and was originally known as Hillside Estate. Headley Way was first known as Town Planning Road in the Great Headley Estate of 1937.

Other streets commemorate the connection with Cromwell and the Civil War, such as Cromwell Close names after Sir Oliver Cromwell, and Fairfax Avenue after Thomas Fairfax the leader of the Parliamentary Army.

Other areas remember well known characters and families of Marston, such as Rippington Drive, Mortimer Drive after the Reverend John Mortimer, Rimmer Close after Reverend Paul Rimmer, Gordon Close after Reverend Gordon the vicar of Elsfield who, in 1849, became vicar of Marston. Carters Estate was developed on allotments in 1947 and the parish council minutes of March 1947 tell us that the *allottees were to be allowed to cultivate allotments until 25 March 1948*. Haynes Road is one of the roads within this estate named after the well known local family.

A contingent of gipsies – all Bucklands – always established themselves for the winter in one of the fields just over the little brook at the entrance to the village on the right hand side going towards Oxford, now of course built over. They were very decent people and no trouble to anyone. We used to hear them talking to each other in Romany when we met them and their strings of horses on the roads.

There was a very old half gipsy woman in the village, whose granddaughter was one of the numerous 'tweenies' that passed through my mother's hands. Her name was Cinderella Sarah Hornsby and she was reputed to be over 90 when she died. She and her old husband lived under filthy conditions. She used to talk of how her grandmother used to tell her about 'battles' fought between Marston and Islip. (WI scrapbook)

Could this be a long distant folk memory of the Civil War and the Battle of Islip Bridge?

In the area of open ground between Old Marston and New Marston groups of Romany gipsies would set up camp annually to clear the Copse and make pegs and bean sticks. This area became the site of The Friar and the present Copse Lane.

11 July 1968 floods in Oxford Road, Old Marston, with Beechey Avenue in the foreground.

Development of the Wimpey Estate in Marsh Lane 1967 (*OPA*)

St Michael and All Angel

Built by Kingerlee & Sons, builders, from a design by the architect Lawrence T Dale.
Founded in 1954 and consecrated in 1955.

St Michael and All Angel

In 1888 the Reverend Charles Morris of Marston and the Reverend Edmund F G Tyndale of Headington, among others, were instrumental in securing a site for a new church to accommodate the population of the District of New Marston, which, at that time, was about 400. The cost of the site and the new building was estimated at £900.

The Mission Room was originally built to become two cottages, but, being considered unsafe, was used as a Mission Church from 1889 to 1911, when the present church was built. The room then had a varied career, being at one time an old furniture shop. It was bought back in 1936 by the vicar, and on occasions, has had services held in it, but was used as a vestry by 1942. The Mission Church in Ferry Road was erected by Mr Bray, September 1911, at a total cost of £252. 12. 0.

The Church was re-opened after extensions and alterations, costing £355. 0. 0. and a Service of Dedication was held 21 April 1937. The service also included the Blessing of the New Chancel, the Children's Corner, the Dedication of the adjacent Mission Room, the tower and bell, and the pulpit and Altar rails.

My dear Hope, I have been asked by the Diocesan to inquire whether you would like to be considered by him for appointment as priest in charge of the new conventional district which is to be formed in New Marston. It is a new-building area, at the moment attached to an old village, but about to be detached from it and to have a priest of its own. There is a nice district church (St Michael's) accommodating about 100, and there are plans, a site and a considerable amount of money for a magnificent basilica, as soon as permission to build can be obtained. Letter of 15 April 1948 to Rev Hope from Gerald Dorchester (Bishop). The site here mentioned was the piece of ground of the Old Mission Room and around it, in Ferry Road. This was seen to be unsuitable because of its situation in a side road and because it was at the extreme end of the district.

The Foundation Stone of the present building was laid 3 July 1954 by Lord Bicester, Lord-Lieutenant of Oxfordshire. *A wonderful procession from the present Church to the site of the New Church along Marston Road began the Ceremony*. The parish priest at this time was the Reverend Dr Constantin Ludwig Adolph Rudolph Hope. Mrs Hope played an important part in the parish, helping to design the pews, the layout of the paths, and organising fund-raising.

A life size statue of St Michael, sculpted in Bath stone by Mr Michael Groser of Kirtlington, and dedicated in memory of the Right Rev Kenneth E Kirk, Bishop of Oxford from 1937 until his death in 1954, is within the church, which also contains a replica of the Ancient Old Marston Chalice, also an 18th century chalice. The original organ was a gift by Miss Lucy Mortimer and the late Reverend J Mortimer and was Dedicated on 20 December 1959. (Check current organ)

The consecrated piece of garden on the south-side of the church, unique and the first in the parish history of English churches, is for the interment of ashes in consecrated ground. The parsonage in 1948 was at 88 Staunton Road. The New Vicarage ground in Jack Straw's Lane was purchased by Reverend Hope and the New Marston PCC in 1952. The building was started in March 1966 and was completed by the summer of 1967.

Dr Hope died 13 January 1970, and Rev N J C Greenfield was inducted as vicar on 9 March.

Dr Hope second from right with Dr H J Carter, Bishop of Oxford at the top of church spire — Milham Ford School in background.

East Window from a postcard of 1937. The East Window and Reredos is in memory of Ada Louisa Jackson.

Church choir in 1936 outside the old church in Ferry Road, New Marston *I was recruited into the choir at the church in Ferry Road by Welshman, the Rev C Beverley Davis. The Church was smartened up, extended and had a new tower added during this period. The hall next door was connected by a passage so that we could use it as the vestry and for choir practice. My maternal grandmother, being a business woman, was, in common with a great many business people at that time, Liberal and non-conformist, which meant that for Sunday school I was sent to the Congregational chapel next door to the scout hall. The outcome of this was that I had two summer outings and two Christmas parties each year. At some date before the war the hall was, with the help of the Rev Mortimer, converted into a Billiard hall and sweet shop with ex-Wall's ice cream salesman, Jack Shrimpton, in charge. (Holt)*

On 19 May 1973 a young choir from the church took part in the 20th Tilehurst Eisteddfod where they were successful in the choral class for hymn singing, for 12 years old and over.

SECTION FOUR

Old Marston Schools

St Nicholas School, original building at Old Marston, opened in 1851 by the Bishop of Oxford, and now used as a village hall. *Three village boys broke into the school and stole a quantity of cotton and pencils and threw a quantity of magnesium peroxide over the needlework and broke thirty five panes of glass. Hauled before the magistrate of County Hall, Oxford. One lad sent to reformatory for three years, another bound over to keep the peace and another, John Drewitt, was birched and sent to reformatory for five years. (School Log Book 1904)*

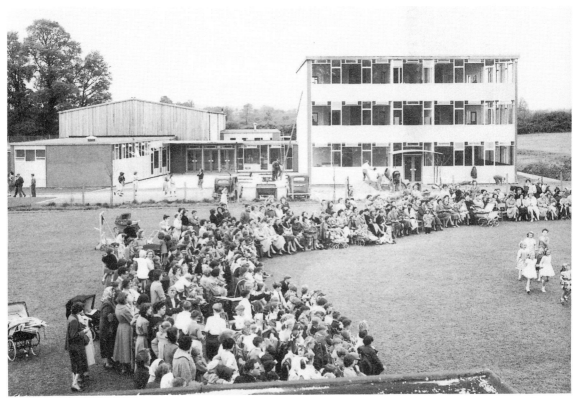

Opening of new school classrooms, January 1959. Reverend Gordon Savage in the middle.

Celebrations possibly at above opening 1959.

St Nicholas group of teachers: Cyril 'Pop' Jennings seated third from left. Mrs Hilditch, secretary, and Mr Lewis, caretaker, are standing on the right.

School dinners at St Nicholas's school.

Canteen ladies, St Nicholas's school.

Christmas 1962 Class 4 of 5 to 6 year olds performing 'The Rainbow Glade', at Eynsham for an Old Folks afternoon.

May Queen celebrations.

May Queen and attendants and parents.

Dance Group performing at the Old Fire Station c1962, and including, Katherine Bleay, Christine Merryman, Sheila Robinson, Melinda Holland, Maxine Shaw.

Football team 1961-62, left to right, back row: Geoffrey Legg, Roger Parker, Clifford Price, Mr C H Webley, Ian Ray, David Hagar, Derrick James, Terry Jones. Front row: Paul Harris, Peter Dodgson, Barry Smith, Patrick Brennan, Graham Bowen.

St Nicholas Football team 1965. Left to right, back row: Phillip Wallen, Michael Howard, Paul Beilie, Mr Mike Dunhill, Paul East, Ian Handley, Trevor Loveless. Front row: Peter Washington, Trevor James, Mark Drewitt, Stephen Simmonds, Kevin Jones.

Netball team c1965. Left to right back row: Linda Whiterod, Mary Bridges, Miss Richards, Barbara Webster. Front row: Angela North, Jacki Gardener, Rita Rutt, Gay Locket, Louise Holt.

St Nicholas School viewed from The Old Barn, subsequently cleared for the new secondary school.

The Old Barn.

John Swain and camera, just before the site was developed.

Old Marston County Secondary School opening by Her Grace The Duchess of Marlborough and Dedication by the Archdeacon of Buckingham, Thursday 22 May 1958. Governors at that time: Professor V T Harlow, Mr R V Vernede, Miss H C Deneke, Professor E R Dodds, Mr W H Dunkley, Mr H L Francis, Mrs E Harley, Mrs F Rowlands, Mr A R Woolley, Mr A R Chorlton. Staff: Mr D E Smith (headmaster), Miss E A Jones (senior mistress), Mr D Burden, Mr R C Franklin, Miss M M Guiry, Mr N Jewels, Mrs E E Leask, Mrs J M MacPherson, Mr L W Taylor, Mrs C E Wheeler (school secretary), Mr E Weaver (caretaker), Mrs K Tucker (cook caterer), Mr C O'Connor (gardener groundsman).

Aerial view of the school.

PROGRAMME

ARRIVAL of Her Grace the Duchess of Marlborough at 2.55 p.m. (The car door will be opened by the Head Boy—Frost, G.)

The Chairman of the Governors and the Headmaster will escort Her Grace to the MAIN HALL.

THE DEDICATION SERVICE will be conducted by the Archdeacon of Buckingham and the Reverend G. E. Beck.

WELCOME by the Chairman of the Governors, Professor V. T. Harlow, who will invite the Duchess to declare the School open.

SPEECH by Her Grace.

Presentation of BOUQUET by the Head Girl (Kathleen Mason).

The Headmaster will thank Her Grace.

The Audience will then be arranged outside the Main Doors (weather permitting), while the Chairman introduces Governors and Official Guests to the Duchess.

Her Grace will complete the planting of an OAK TREE symbolic of the site having been part of a Royal Forest and of its consequent inclusion in the School Badge.

" Three Cheers for Her Grace the Duchess of Marlborough."

TEA will then be served in the Dining Hall for Parents and Friends, and in the Library for Governors and Official Guests.

After tea the Chairman and the Headmaster will take the Duchess on a tour of the building.

All Visitors are invited to look over the building; the Prefects will be available as Guides.

A page from the programme.

Old Marston Secondary School during construction 1958.

Planting of a tree by the Duchess of Marlborough attended by head boy Geoff Frost, 1958.

Duchess of Marlborough at the opening of the school

Audience at school opening, 1958.

Tea being served at the school opening.

The canteen obviously doubled as a gym, note the nets and boards at the far end.

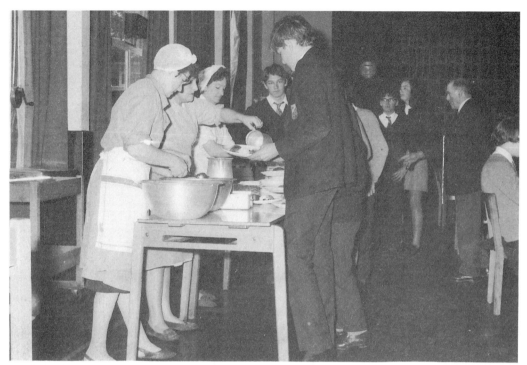

Lunch being served in the canteen.

Ballroom dancing for boys and girls.

Woodworking

Music

Typing

A studious class.

May dancing, c1971.

Morris dancing, c1971.

Pantomime, 1974.

The river has always played an important part in Marston's history. This photograph shows Duke of Edinburgh candidates taking canoeing instruction. Mrs Harley, school governor, looks on.

Was fishing part of the school curriculum, or is this a competition?

New Marston Schools

Shortly after our arrival in Ferry Road the school was opened, which meant that I was taken there as one of the first pupils. Even so, we were still taught in the dirty, dusty Scout Hall by Miss Carter. Eventually we moved on to Miss Chandler (surely one of the worst teachers ever to be entrusted with children!). (Holt)

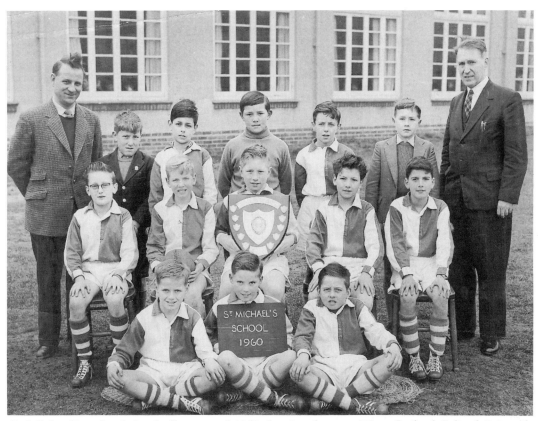

St Michael's school football team of 1960, having beaten West Oxford School 2-1 and winning the Oxford City FC Supporter's Club Shield, put up for competitions for the first time. Left to right back row: B N Foster (sportsmaster), Raymond Mansell (reserve), Roy? Slatter, John Roberts, Robert Small, Robert Turley (reserve), W J Willis (headmaster). Middle row: A Gerald Watson, Raymond Long, Philip? Young (capt), Anthony Baldwin, Nigel Wates. Front row: Colin Harris, Melvin Moss, Anthony Tucker.

St Michael's football team of 1961, beating New Hinksey 1-0 for the second year in succession. Left to right back row: Robert Cross, John Roberts, Melvin Moss, B N Foster (sportsmaster). Middle row: Robert Small, Anthony Tucker, Colin Harris (capt), Lister Evans, Robert Turley. Front row: David Shipperley, Robert Godfrey, Geoff Bramell.

St Michael's Class 4 of 1969.

St Michael's Athletics and Swimming team 1971

St Michael's School Fete 1950. Lady Tweedsmuir presenting prize for Fancy Dress to Michael Webb. Reverend Hope is on the left.

Lady Tweedsmuir lived in the nearby village of Elsfield. Her husband John Buchan, Lord Tweedsmuir, had died in 1940. He was a novelist, historian, barrister, politician, soldier and one-time Governor General of Canada.

Admission No.	Date of Admission (or Re-Admission) Day.	Mon.	Year.	FULL NAME OF CHILD.	NAME OF PARENT OR GUARDIAN.	ADDRESS.
70	9	1	28	Hansford Sybil Gertrude	Mr William Hansford	39 William Street ✓
71	9	1	28	Young Thomas William	Mr Harold Young	3 Edgeway Road ✓
72	16	4	28	Haynes George Richard	" Richard Haynes	Main Road ✓
73	16	4	28	Giles Florence May	" Walter Giles	Ferry Road
74	16	4	28	Whitman Wallace	–	Main Road ✓
75	16	4	28	Brown Audrey	" William Brown	New Bungalow, Ferry Rd ✓
76	16	4	28	Adams Albert George	" Henry Adams	2 Edgeway Road ✓
77	25	4	28	Gray Frederick	" Alfred Gray	4 Edgeway Road ✓
78	5	6	28	Goodchild June Alwyn	" William Goodchild	2 Daphne Cottages, Ferry Rd ✓
79	5	6	28	Harris Eileen	" Reginald Harris	49 William Street ✓
80	5	6	28	Mackenzie Ernest James	" Richard Mackenzie	7 Ferry Road
81	11	6	28	Green Mavis Gertrude	" Cyril Fred. Green	Main Rd ✓
82	10	9	28	Collett Brenda Gwendolin	" Frank Collett	Chapel House, Ferry Road
83	10	9	28	Collett Ida Isabel	" "	" "
84	10	9	28	Frun Elizabeth Joan	" John Frun	2c William Street ✓

A page from St Michael's School Log Book 1928.

The clear division between Old and New Marston which was created by fields, allotments and playing fields, was given up to unattractive suburbia, although saved to a small degree by the construction of Milham Ford School. (Holt)

Begun as a nursery school in the Iffley Road around 1895 by two sisters, Emma and Jane Moody, the school had moved to a small house in Cowley Place by 1900, and took its name from the nearby ford across the River Cherwell below Magdalen Bridge. Miss Catherine Dodd became its Headmistress. By 1906 the school was housed in purpose-built premises in Cowley Place (now part of St Hilda's College), but it was soon too small for the growing number of pupils and extra temporary buildings, known as 'the huts', sprang up around it.

In 1938, after years of planning, the school moved to buildings designed for it by the City Architect, Douglas Murray, on a spacious, sloping 16-acre site bounded by Jack Straws Lane, Marston Road and Harberton Mead. It also then ceased to take boarding pupils. During World War II the premises were shared until 1943 with Burlington School pupils and teachers who had been evacuated from London. With the 1944 Education Act, Milham Ford, having shed its boarders and its primary department, became a state grammar school, providing free secondary education for girls. In 1974 it became a single-sex girls comprehensive.

Milham Ford School was opened on 8 March 1939 by HRH Princess Alice, Countess of Athlone. The youngest girl in Form II presented to Princess Alice a bouquet of blue irises, white lilac and white carnations tied with the school colours. Afterwards the entire school marched from the back of the building and lined the drive to the front gate for the royal car. *September 29, 1939: first day in new school and war imminent - perhaps within 24 hours . (School Log Book)*

Milham Ford School Choir c1946 leading morning prays, including Jean Smith, Ann Clovey, Daphne Cole, Marion Lewis, Jackie Gorbould, Christine Rogers, Peggy Harris, Maureen Juggins.

1st Cricket Eleven 1948. Left to right back row: Betty Fathers, W Barber, O Bloice, M Poole, I Gardener. Front row: Eva Taunton, J Kerry (Vice-Captain), B Dell (Captain), Elizabeth Stevens, A Tyers. In front: J Tyers.

Hockey 1948-9. Left to right back row: Betty Fathers, J Dickson, Sheila Prickett, Eva Taunton, Diane Coates, A Bown. Front row: R Turner, P Barnes (Vice Capt), J Goldsmith (Capt), A Collett, Elizabeth Stevens.

The School Dramatic Society cast of 'She Stoops to Conquer' 11 and 12 May 1950. Marlow was played by Jean Lewis, Pat Spargo played opposite 'him', taking the part of Miss Hardcastle. Hastings was played with graceful affectation and skill by Joan Bell, and opposite her Anne Collett made a demure Miss Neville. (Milham Ford School Magazine, 1950)

Action shot of hockey on school playing fields c1950, showing the line of poplar trees that remained a landmark along the Marston Road until recently.

Old Girls' Hockey Team 1949. Left to right, back row: Anne Tyers, Audrey Smith, –, Margot Kozlow, Mary Pippington, Jane Tyers. Front row: –, Sylvia Coleman, –, Wendy Harrington, Beryl Cook.

The Milham March, seen here in 1952, was held annually on Sports Day. All the girls, in height order, marched onto the playing fields to the tune of 'Colonel Bogie'. It was an impressive sight, and was practised for three days prior to Sports Day. This tradition ended in 1955.

Cricket team 1959. Left to right back row: Fred Pitter groundsman, Margaret Palmer, Barbara Green, Monica Mendelssohn, Mr Hunt. Middle row: Christine Job, Primrose Salt, Christine Sibbit, Roseanne Salt, Josephine Peddie. Front row: Linda Hickman, Anne Chalton. Mr Pitter was groundsman at the school for forty years.

Miss Price and the Prefects 1959: Senior Prefect J Campbell, Deputy Senior Prefect A Wolfe, P Andrew, L Brooks, D Burton, M Coggins, H Drake, S Gilbert, V Greggain, C Hammond, J Hutton, D Hurn, C Job, F Jones, J Jones, U Mendelssohn, G Offen, J Poole, C Sibbit, C Smith, J Tanner, D Whatley, S Wheal, M Willetts.

Miss Price was welcomed to the school on 8 June 1949. The School and Higher Certificate Examinations were held for the last time in 1950. In 1951 the General Certificate of Education came into being. At this time trophies were awarded to form classes for Swimming, Cricket, Tennis, Rounders, Verse Speaking, Singing, Hockey, Netball, and Deportment. *'Every form in the school is graded for deportment, and everyone who reaches a sufficiently high standard is given a badge, which may, however, be taken from her at any time'*. Clubs were popular, and included The Senior and Junior Debating Societies, Handwork Club, Needlework and Dressmaking, Field Club, Explorers' Club, Architecture Club, Art Club, Sketching Club, Music Club, Country Dancing and Dramatic Society.

Miss Haywood's Class, Lower 5J in 1960, gathered on the playing fields facing Jack Straws Lane.

These girls seen here c1960 in the School Quad are continuing the tradition of wearing straw hats, known as 'bashers'. The girls can be identified as Prefects by the wearing of the striped hat band. School sixth formers boasted their own room, named Valhalla, as it was 'up in the Gods'.

The school celebrated the official opening of its long awaited swimming pool 1 July 1964, by Mr Garne, Chief Education Officer.

Milham Ford School Staff, 1966: Left to right, back row: Joan Shiels, Marjorie Scaife, Francis Simpson, Gill Slack, Margaret Smith, Mrs Teng, Judy Walls, Pat Woods. Fourth row: Mrs Helsby, Mrs Sillery, –, Pam Jordon, –, –, Mrs Patrick (School Secretary), Di Shaw. Third row: Muriel Copson, Pam Hampton, Di Clarke, Margaret Hamer, Josie Howe, Audrey Hayes, Ida Jackson, Brenda Jillard, Dorothy Pane. Second row: Cicily Osmond-Smith, Janet Mathews, Brenda Blakeley, Elizabeth Burra, Celia Adams, Judy Billen, Dorothy Heelas, Ursula Maddy. Front row: Mary Williams, Elizabeth Gill, Evelyn Maddock, Jean Sloan, Mary R Price (Headmistress), Jo Kenworthy, Renee George, Miss Gladman (Office), Margaret Cross.

Miss Shiels class of 1966. Each class was photographed to commemorate the retirement of Miss Mary Price, headmistress since 1949. Left to right back row: Janice Gibbons, Angela Clarke. Third row: Erica Willets, Paula Greenwood, Judy Turner, Rosemary Beesley, Beverly Roger, Hazel Cusack, Susan Morris, Judith Parker, Jane Shorter. Second row: Sharron Delcoy, Pauline Shepheard, Rosamund Tricker, Sally Brunt, Jane Laurie, Annette Brown, Sally Etheridge, Valerie Gane, Carole Young, Joanna McFarlane. Front row: Barbara Booker, Sheila Simms, Vicky Alwinger, Sheila Post, Miss Shiels, Gloria Woodward, Julie Howells, Valerie Spackman, Janet Bull.

The school centenary was celebrated on 26 June 1993 and brought together past Headmistresses: Alice Wakefield (1979-86), Janet Edwards (1986-87), Eliza Higgins (1987-96), Winifred Laws (1966-79). Seated: Mary Price (1949 to 1966).

Recreation, Sport and Scouts

Our musical circle took off at Old Marston. We lived next door to the Police House, and the policeman and his wife, Mr and Mrs Brooks, became good friends. Fred Brooks sang with a bass voice and played the flute, and Mrs Brooks had a highly trained soprano voice, she could sing beautifully, and with my father on the violin and my mother on the piano, they became known locally as 'The Four Bs', i.e. Barnes and Brooks....

We would support the local cricket team, and cheer them on whenever they turned out to play. We had the choir of course, and a club was formed in the village which they called 'The Optimists'. Cyril Jennings, the headmaster, was a founder member. Lots of interesting things went on there. Once a month it was held and people came to talk and entertain, and of course The Four Bs' did their share. (Brown)

A Concert during the 1950s

The audience included, front row Martin Barnsley, Mrs Barnsley, second row Mrs Wren, Jenny Wren, Mr Wren, Mrs Gunn, Mr Gunn.

Front row includes Bob Hayes, Richard Herley, Rosemary Hayes, Gwen Oliver. Second row includes Mrs Wren, Jenny Wren, Mr Wren, Mrs Gunn, Mr Gunn, Peter Hayes, Joan Hayes, Lindsay Harley, Jimmy Hayes, Raymund Haynes, Lucy Haynes, Mary Grimwood.

A Christmas tableau presented by young members of the Congregational Chapel New Marston c1936.

The Audrey Shave Dancers during the 1940s.

'The Roundheads', a popular local skiffle band in the mid 1950s. Left to right: Tony Carpenter, Brian Carpenter, Dave Woodward, Maurice 'Tiny' Tanner. The band's name reflected Old Marston's historic connection with Oliver Cromwell, *for it was at the Manor House behind the church, at which Sir Thomas Glenalm signed the surrender of the Royalist Troops to Lord Fairfax, after the siege of Oxford in 1645. Cromwell and Fairfax discussed operations in the Manor House, and from the Tower of the Church Fairfax was able to study the movements of Royalist forces. (Extract from booklet of St Nicholas's Church, Old Marston).*

The Reading Room in Old Marston was the hub of social activities, including the meeting room for The Optimists and the local Youth Club. Left is Christine Carpenter with Monica Case on the right.

There were often garden parties held in the garden of the Old Vicarage at Old Marston. This photograph was taken during the 1960s when attendees dressed in Victorian costume. Margaret Baker on the left with Hilda Jones on the right.

Marston Girls Club in outfits worn in competition at Wembley 1938. Taken in Mrs Brierley's garden in Harberton Mead. Left to right, back row: Eileen Harris, − (Club Leader), − (Keep Fit Leader), Beryl Allington, Helen Gardener, Dory Neale. Front row: −, −, Betty Smith, Beryl Bestley, Doreen Deacon, Jean Webster, Mary Deacon.

Marston Girls Club 1938 in Tap Dancing Dresses, also in Mrs Brierley's garden in Harberton Mead. Back row standing: Club Leader, Jean Webster, Mary Deacon, Keep Fit Leader. Middle row: Margaret Coley, Eileen Harris, Helen Gardener, Dory Neale. Front row: Beryl Bestley, Betty Smith, −, −, Doreen Deacon, Beryl Allington.

Marston Girls Club dance team, in outfits worn in competition at Wembley in 1938. Left to right back row: Hazel Bates, –, Margaret Coley, four leaders unknown, Mrs Lowe, –, –, –. Middle row: –, Eileen Harris, –, –, –, Helen Gardener, Dory Neale. Front row: –, Beryl Bestley, Betty Smith, Jean Webster, Mary Deacon, Doreen Deacon, Beryl Allington.

Members of the Girls Friendly Society, entrants in a singing competition in 1932, photograph taken at East Oxford School. Back row: Mrs Hine, Bubbles Hine, Eileen Harris, Helen Gardener, Betty Fruin, Jean Webster, Mrs Ward. Middle row: Audrey Brown, Maureen Webster, Marjorie Gurden, Eda Rhymes, Doreen Deacon. Front row: Sheila Hunt, Audrey Rogers.

Sunday school outing to Bournemouth in 1938. Group includes Harold Elmey, Raymond Harris, Vernon Clements, Dorothy Reason.

Hellenic League Cup Winners 1965-66, Division 1 Winners and promoted to Premiere Division. Left to right, back row: Bill Greenough, Len Moss, Brian Smith, Bob Foster, Mick Allday, Maurice Winstone, Colin Harris, Nick Wilkins, Fred Smith. Front row: Les Smith, Keith Wickson, Peter Fergason, Paul Holdon, Doug Foreman, Bobby Spokes.

Cricket match 1940s taken on the Recreation Ground.

Fete during the 1940s on the Recreation Ground. The house on the right hand side is
Walnut Tree House.

The Marston Midgets, the younger side of the Marston Saints, at Mortimer Hall in 1973. Left to right, back row: Dick Lucas of Oxford United, Ray Timms, manager, Brian Beesley, Mrs Lucas, −, Middle row: Clive Woodhouse, Barry King, Paul Goodchild, Paul Rodgers, Michael Beesley, Peter Collins, Mark Allington, Philip Breach. Front row: Andrew Baker, Nicky Webb, Mark Gee, Darren Timms, David Cox, Neil Russell.

Marston Midgets at the Manor Ground Headington in 1974 having reached the final of the Oxford Boys Sunday League. Brian Beesley and Ray Timms manager at the back. Left to right, back row: Shamus Collins, Paul McKay, Barry Parsons, John Ryder, Alex Wharton, John Havard, Spencer Watts. Front row: Michael Beesley, Richard Moore, Darren Timms, Mark Gee, Nicky Webb.

9th Oxford (Marston) Cub Pack 1949. Leaders: Bill Greenough, Noel Minett, Ken Anderson, Dixie Dike, Denis Morris, Liz Dike.

St Michael's Cub Pack, 34th Oxford, c1958-59, in Jackstraws Lane. Scoutmaster, Mr Leatch, at the back, with Mrs Leatch on left and Carol Matthews on right. Back row: –, Stanley Long, –, Ron Cross, –, Colin Chipperfield, Raymond Long, Brian Matthews, –. Middle row: –, Paul Young, Anthony Baldwin, –, –, –, Nigel Waters. Front row: –, –, Ralph Collins, Gerald Walton, –, –.

The first boys awarded Cycling Proficiency Certificates in Oxfordshire, c1957. Left to right: −, −, Chris Payne, Dave Shephard, Rodney Hannah, −, Trevor Cox, Geoff Frost, −, Robert Davidson, Michael Masters, John Wheeler.

c1956 back row: Denis Morris, Derick Colverson, Bill Greenough. Middle row: Mike Masters, Geoff Frost, Barry Brackley. Front row: Chris Payne, Rodney Hannah, David Jarrott.

Group photograph of 9th Marston Boy Scouts celebrating their Golden Jubilee in Marston Scout Hall, Friday 11 December 1959.

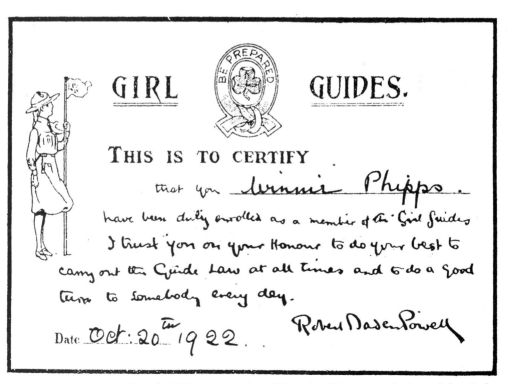

Girl Guide certificate dated 1922 awarded to Winnie Phipps and signed by Robert Baden Powell.

New Marston Girl Guides 1929 on a trip to the Cotswold Downs. Second from the right is Phyllis Brooks.

New Marston Girls' Friendly Society c1928.

Marston Brownies at Fox Lease, New Forest in 1973.

SECTION SEVEN

Pubs and Parties

The Friar in Marston Road, c1945. (OPA)

Mr Horace Blackford was landlord of The Friar from April 1937, when it was first built, until he died. His wife took over as landlady until September 1970. During the Second World War part of the cellar was the ARP Post and was manned 24 hours a day, with bunk beds and its own emergency food. The air-raid siren was positioned outside by the pub sign.

Horace Blackford, landlord of The Friar, c1946.

Mr and Mrs Blackford's silver wedding anniversary, being presented with a rose bowl by the Ladies Darts Team, 1954.   Back row: Jean Roberts, Mary Blackford, Min Blackford (holding bowl), Horace Blackford, Mrs Austin, −, Mrs Wallin, Mrs Stone. Middle row: Mrs Allsworth, Mary Wilson, Barbara Juggins, −, −, −, Mrs Wickson, Mrs Smart. Seated: Rose Newman, Jean Short, Sylvia Newman. In front: Annie Wood, Mrs Walton.

New Marston outing to celebrate coronation of George VI 1936, possibly from The Friar. Back row: −, Mrs Rose Ward, − Saunders, − Saunders, Mrs Ash, − Saunders. Front row: Mrs Millicent Denton, Mrs Annie Wood.

The Friars outing early 1950s. Back −, −, −, −, Mr Walton, Max Smith, −, Mr Harris snr, Mr Axtell, Oliver King, −, −, Front: Jack Pennycar, Mr Irvine, Victor Wilson, Francis King, −, Fred Wood, Horace Blackford, −.

Outing from The Somerset possibly darts or Aunt Sally team.

The Jack Russell in Old Marston was built by Morland Brewery in the 1960s. It took its name from The Reverend John (Jack) Russell who attended Exeter College in Oxford from 1814 for four or five years. It was during his time at Oxford University that he acquired a milkman's dog called Trump, which was the forerunner of the Jack Russell terrier, named after him. The Reverend moved to Swimbridge in Devon where he stayed for forty seven years. The public house opposite the church in Swimbridge is also called 'The Jack Russell'.

The White Hart early this century with Harry Gilbert and family.

The Gurden family. Back row: Edwin, Alfred, Charles. Front row: James Henry, James snr, Richard. James senior was publican at The Bricklayers Arms in Church Lane in 1881. Richard was landlord of The Three Horseshoes in 1891.

Arthur and Ruth Hayle seated with their children, left to right: Ivy known as John, Rene, Arthur known as Bun, Lowden known as Bob with William in front, Rudolf known as George, Dine, Olive known as Cook. Arthur and Ruth Hayle moved from Kidlington to the White Hart in November 1926; Ruth died in 1938. The following year the second youngest son, Lowden, took over the tenancy. He had married Dorothy Belson from New Marston in 1932, and they began to expand the trade. As well as beer you could buy parafin, eggs, chicken, vegetables and fruit grown in the orchard at the back of the property. In the 1950s the room known as the bottom room, now the lounge, was used as a temporary school dentist and the Summer House was used as a classroom. By tradition the White Hart always gave the communion wine to St Nicholas's Church. The Hayle family left the White Hart in November 1971.

Coach outing from The Red Lion c1950. Standing left to right: –, –, Alice Mathews, –, Albert Saunders with baby Janet Saunders, –, Mr Quinn with baby, –, Mrs Quinn, Joe Ward, Rose Ward, Nell Coley (landlady), Alice Jones, Wynn James, Walter Mathews, –, –, –, –. Front row: Anne Harper, Brenda Saunders, Margaret Harper, –, Monica Mathews, Nora Saunders, Jean Westall, Rose Westall, Philip and Patricia Harper with Ronald Harper, Stanley Mathews, Wally Ward with young Tony Harper, George Roberts.

1950s Fancy Dress Party in Stainer Place.

1977 Crotch Crescent residents watching the Silver Jubilee street party 1977. Mrs Hulcup, Mrs Hawkes, Mrs Watkins, Mrs Panks, Joan –.

The first thing to be arranged after deciding to have a street party to celebrate the Queen's Silver Jubilee, was to form a committee, seven of us volunteered, and were known as The Magnificent Seven. We raised money by having jumble sales, raffles and house to house collections.

On the morning of the big day, most of the dads could be seen hanging red white and blue bunting from lamp post to lamp post, accompanied with balloons and flags. Various individuals also decorated their own homes, we were very lucky the weather was nice. All was ready for the afternoon, the tables were put out in the middle of the road and food was supplied by the residents of the Crescent. We had arranged to have the road closed to traffic to make it safe for everyone. While the children were eating, the mayoress paid us a visit, the children were very excited to see her.

The Silver Jubilee party in Crotch Crescent 1977. Back row: Graham —, Les Clements. Middle row: Alex Firkin, Anthony Flanagan, Kenneth Fogden, Kevin Warland, Dawn Warland, Marnie Rowles, Karen Warland, Louise Flanagan, Sarah Firkin, Nicky Dale, Craig Bowers, Louise Pill, Susan Nutt, Hazel Thomas, Paul Stallard, Scott Bowers. Front row: Ian Dale, Tracey Spicer, —, John Flanagan, —, —, Kevin Dale, —, —, —, Rebecca Nutt, Mark Walton, — Clements, —.

When everyone had finished, the tables were cleared away and the fun started. We had a fancy dress parade and a 'best decorated bicycle' competition. After the judging, the children, with one of their parents, joined in a 'relay wheelbarrow race', we played other games and sang to the music, finishing with a treasure hunt.

All the children were given a celebration jubilee coin to keep as a souvenir, plus a present out of the 'lucky dip' barrel. In the evening the adults had their little fling, singing and dancing and doing the conga up and down the Crescent. Our favourite song was 'I'm forever blowing bubbles'. The whole day was a great success.

Party in the Scout Hall, New Marston to celebrate the Silver Jubilee of George V, May 1935. (*OPA*)

STREET DIRECTORY.   FER 65

13 Yates Geo. Fredk. contracting gardener
14 Hombersley Miss
15 Thorpe John Parkin
16 Lambert   Archibald
.   George Henry
17 Godfrey William Fredk
18 Cossar Mrs
19 Drew Miss
20 Sweet Mrs. Henry
21 Buxton Rev. J. Frank M.A
22 Dolley Mrs
23 Hurst Miss G. E
24 Plant Sydney Glenn Preston M.A., B.SC., D.Phil. (University demonstrator in chemistry)
25 Lawley Hugh
26 Hughes Leonard George
27 Cleaver W. E. I. garage

Farrows yard.

See ABBEY PLACE.

FERRY   LANE, from Jack Daw lane.

Brunsdon Thos. hardware mer

FERRY ROAD (Jericho), from 14 Canal street.
SOUTH SIDE.
1 Rose Thomas
3 Harris Albert Edward
5 Collett Vernon Victor
7 Paddon Archbld. Andrew
9 Carter William George
Gilks Wm. P. (Ferry ho)
NORTH SIDE.
2 Wall Thomas
4 Smith Miss
6 Woodward Francis
8 Rayson Thomas
10 Mayes Henry John

FERRY   ROAD   (New Marston), from Main road.
NORTH SIDE.
Clifford Harry (Frenchay)
1 Galloway Chas
2 Fletcher Harry Jas
3 Carter Jn. coal mer
4 Jennings Mrs
OXF.

Weller Harold (Belmont)
Weller Fred, road transport contractor (The Garage). See advert
Madden Alex. Jas. (Vine cott)
Oxford Joshua (St. Helens)
Stone Geo. (Valetta)
Smith Wm. (Cherwell cotts)
Morris Fredk. (Cherwell cotts)
12 Young Fredk
Scarrott Mrs. Rose, genl. stores
CHAPEL OF ST. NICHOLAS
Rogers Chas. Fredk. (Pendennis)
Hopcraft Chas. Hazlewood (Hazledene)
Walters Regnld. Jas. (Glenville)
Giles Wltr. Jn
Hansford Alfd. Wm. M. (Cornwall ho)

GORDON COTTAGES:
1 Grange Mrs
2 Blagrove Rt
3 Beyer Carl
4 Newport Albt

___

Gardner Jas. (Dunholm)
Smith Chas. Fredk
Howe Wm. Ernest
Cooper Edwd. Percvl. (Park View cott)
Adams Mrs. (Tower view)
Titcomb Mrs. (Rose Tree cott)
Peach Edwd
Peach Ernest, painter
Dobson Edgar (The Laurels)
Keogh Alfd. L. (Park view)
SOUTH SIDE.
Durham Mrs. (Rookley)
Carter Harold (Roseville)
Stevens Wm. A. (Seaton)
Hunt Regnld. (St. Boniface)
Gilks Basil (Grant cott)
Carter Miss (Daphne cotts)

Goodchild Wm. Rt. (Daphne cotts)
Evans Mrs
Akers Wm
West Jn
Young Wm
Turner Thos
Walker Edwd. Thos. (Miltonville)
Topp Geoffrey T. motor engnr. (Willsfield)
Clark Miss (Woodville)
Webster Thos. (East vw)
Inwood Jesse
Webb Wm. (Ivydene)
Jones Mrs
7 MacKenzie Rd. Jas
Edwards Wm
Akers Jn. E (Ken Goed)
Holt Lewis (Mendip)
Gurden Monty (Rosedene)
18 Millin Wm
Angel Vivian S. (Harrow dene)
Poole Bryan Edgar (Lyttleholme)
Forrest Chas. Wilfred (The Ferns)
Collett Chas. (York ho)
Winslow Miss (The Cottage)
Worthington Thos. (Eventide)
New Marston Pumping Station (Ernest Allan, in charge)
Norridge Arth. E. & Son, bldrs. (The Bungalow)

FERRY HINKSEY ROAD, from 25 Botley rd.
WEST SIDE.
1 Archer Albert William
2 Pritchard Mrs
3 Howkins Henry Thomas
4 Griffett Mrs
5 Phillips Alfd. Hy
6 Launchbury Arthur
EAST SIDE.
101 Coleman Albert George
102 Faulkner Herbert
103 Tooby Albert Edward
104 Martin George
105 Carter Vincent Alfred
106 Allday Harry

3

War Years

We had seen no sign of World War Two at Towersey, apart from the Home Guard parades outside the village hall every Sunday morning. But Old Marston had a large army camp situated either side of the main northern bypass. It was a big camp, as I recall, masses of tents and army vehicles all over the place, and lots of soldiers, or 'Poor Boys' as my mother used to call them. 'Miles away from their families and homes'. Some of the 'Poor Boys' looked mighty old to me, I was still only eleven years of age. (Brown)

Area L Post 112 October 1940 outside The Friar. Back row: G Morris, G A Harrison, A H J Pennicard, H L Blackford, F Crawte, L T Jones, H Long, H J Fouracre, L G Lowe. Middle row: H Moore, F E Mills, D N Plant, P Kilbee, J Bilton, Miss M E Jones, W Carter, S F Watson, H Webb, R H Reason, L F A Marlow. Front row: Mrs N B Kilbee, J N Dunstan, A W Jackson, F S Keen, A E Wallis, D G Perry, A Everitt, J E Mott, Mrs S M Blackford.

6th Oxford Home Guard, Marston Platoon, taken outside the Bricklayers Arms. Officers and NCOs October 1944. Middle row left to right: Ted Barnes, −, Gerald Haynes, −, −, −, Bill Bleay (landlord of the Bricklayers Arms), −. Front row Bill Lambourne second from right. *My father would dress up in his uniform every Sunday morning, and evening as well, and go to the Home Guard Headquarters which were at the rear of the Bricklayers Arms, round the back of the church. I remember he was issued with a revolver and some ammunition. The revolver was taken out and cleaned meticulously after each Home Guard meeting. Rows of cleaning rods and lots of rag, and oil. Even the pouch it went in was waxed. One day the Home Guard held an exercise with the soldiers from the camp down the by-pass. We were all told to keep indoors and away from the windows, everyone had to clear the streets. Nothing happened for a bit, then we heard gun fire, and men in uniform came tanking down the back garden and out of the front gate. Presently some more came belting down the road and crouched inside the garden gate. Now my father had got hold of a spare forage cap from somewhere (one of those small pointed caps that sat along the top of the head) and my brother thought this was a good day to wear it, being the day of the military exercises. So he put it on. Unfortunately, one of the soldiers spotted it through the window and thought we were harbouring one of the 'enemy'. We were ordered to 'open up the house' and the army searched us, even though they could see my brother standing in the room with this cap on his head. (Brown)*